Compiler Construction
Principles and Practice

Kenneth C. Louden
San Jose State University

PWS Publishing Company

I(T)P

An International Thomson Publishing Company

Boston • Albany • Bonn • Cincinnati • Detroit • London • Madrid • Melbourne • Mexico City • New York

Pacific Grove • Paris • San Francisco • Singapore • Tokyo • Toronto • Washington

PWS PUBLISHING COMPANY
20 Park Plaza, Boston, MA 02116-4324

I(T)P™
International Thomson Publishing
The trademark ITP is used under license.

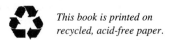

*This book is printed on
recycled, acid-free paper.*

For more information, contact:

PWS Publishing Company
20 Park Plaza
Boston, MA 02116

International Thomson Publishing Europe
Berkshire House I68-I73
High Holborn
London WC1V 7AA
England

Thomas Nelson Australia
102 Dodds Street
South Melbourne, 3205
Victoria, Australia

Nelson Canada
1120 Birchmont Road
Scarborough, Ontario
Canada M1K 5G4

International Thomson Editores
Campos Eliseos 385, Piso 7
Col. Polanco
11560 Mexico D.F., Mexico

International Thomson Publishing GmbH
Königswinterer Strasse 418
53227 Bonn, Germany

International Thomson Publishing Asia
221 Henderson Road
#05-10 Henderson Building
Singapore 0315

International Thomson Publishing Japan
Hirakawacho Kyowa Building, 31
2-2-1 Hirakawacho
Chiyoda-ku, Tokyo 102
Japan

Library of Congress Cataloging-in-Publication Data

Louden, Kenneth C.
    Compiler construction : principles and practice / Kenneth C.
Louden.
        p.   cm.
    Includes bibliographical references and index.
    ISBN 0-534-93972-4
    1. Compilers (Computer programs)   I. Title.
QA76.76.C65L68   1997
005.4′53—dc21   96–49664
                                            CIP

Sponsoring Editor: *David Dietz*
Marketing Manager: *Nathan Wilbur*
Editorial Assistant: *Susan Garland*
Production Coordinator: *Pamela Rockwell*
Manufacturing Coordinator: *Andrew Christensen*

Compositor: *Better Graphics*
Cover/Text Designer: *Pamela Rockwell*
Cover Printer: *Coral Graphics*
Text Printer and Binder: *Quebecor/Fairfield*

Printed and bound in the United States of America.
97 98 99 00 — 10 9 8 7 6 5 4 3 2 1

For Andrew

Contents

8 CODE GENERATION 397

Appendix A: A COMPILER PROJECT 491

Appendix B: TINY COMPILER LISTING 502

Appendix C: TINY MACHINE SIMULATOR LISTING 545

Bibliography 558

Index 562

Preface

This book is an introduction to the field of compiler construction. It combines a detailed study of the theory underlying the modern approach to compiler design, together with many practical examples, and a complete description, with source code, of a compiler for a small language. It is specifically designed for use in an introductory course on compiler design or compiler construction at the advanced undergraduate level. However, it will also be of use to professionals joining or beginning a compiler writing project, as it aims to give the reader all the necessary tools and practical experience to design and program an actual compiler.

A great many texts already exist for this field. Why another one? Because virtually all current texts confine themselves to the study of only one of the two important aspects of compiler construction. The first variety of text confines itself to a study of the theory and principles of compiler design, with only brief examples of the application of the theory. The second variety of text concentrates on the practical goal of producing an actual compiler, either for a real programming language or a pared-down version of one, with only small forays into the theory underlying the code to explain its origin and behavior. I have found both approaches lacking. To really understand the practical aspects of compiler design, one needs to have a good understanding of the theory, and to really appreciate the theory, one needs to see it in action in a real or near-real practical setting.

This text undertakes to provide the proper balance between theory and practice, and to provide enough actual implementation detail to give a real flavor for the techniques without overwhelming the reader. In this text, I provide a complete compiler for a small language written in C and developed using the different techniques studied in each chapter. In addition, detailed descriptions of coding techniques for additional language examples are given as the associated topics are studied. Finally, each chapter concludes with an extensive set of exercises, which are divided into two sections. The first contains those of the more pencil-and-paper variety involving little programming. The second contains those involving a significant amount of programming.

In writing such a text one must also take into account the different places that a compiler course occupies in different computer science curricula. In some programs, a course on automata theory is a prerequisite; in others, a course on programming languages is a prerequisite; while in yet others no prerequisites (other than data structures) are assumed. This text makes no assumptions about prerequisites beyond the usual data structures course and a familiarity with the C language, yet is arranged so that a prerequisite such as an automata theory course can be taken into account. Thus, it should be usable in a wide variety of programs.

A final problem in writing a compiler text is that instructors use many different classroom approaches to the practical application of theory. Some prefer to study the techniques using only a series of separate small examples, each targeting a specific concept. Some give an extensive compiler project, but make it more manageable with the use of Lex and Yacc as tools. Others ask their students to write all the code by hand (using, say, recursive descent for parsing) but may lighten the task by giving students the basic data structures and some sample code. This book should lend itself to all of these scenarios.

Overview and Organization

In most cases each chapter is largely independent of the others, without artificially restricting the material in each. Cross-references in the text allow the reader or instructor to fill in any gaps that might arise even if a particular chapter or section is skipped.

Chapter 1 is a survey of the basic structure of a compiler and the techniques studied in later chapters. It also includes a section on porting and bootstrapping.

Chapter 2 studies the theory of finite automata and regular expressions, and then applies this theory to the construction of a scanner both by hand coding and using the scanner generation tool Lex.

Chapter 3 studies the theory of context-free grammars as it pertains to parsing, with particular emphasis on resolving ambiguity. It gives a detailed description of three common notations for such grammars, BNF, EBNF, and syntax diagrams. It also discusses the Chomsky hierarchy and the limits of the power of context-free grammars, and mentions some of the important computation-theoretic results concerning such grammars. A grammar for the sample language of the text is also provided.

Chapter 4 studies top-down parsing algorithms, in particular the methods of recursive-descent and LL(1) parsing. A recursive-descent parser for the sample language is also presented.

Chapter 5 continues the study of parsing algorithms, studying bottom-up parsing in detail, culminating in LALR(1) parsing tables and the use of the Yacc parser generator tool. A Yacc specification for the sample language is provided.

Chapter 6 is a comprehensive account of static semantic analysis, focusing on attribute grammars and syntax tree traversals. It gives extensive coverage to the construction of symbol tables and static type checking, the two primary examples of semantic analysis. A hash table implementation for a symbol table is also given and is used to implement a semantic analyzer for the sample language.

Chapter 7 discusses the common forms of runtime environments, from the fully static environment of Fortran through the many varieties of stack-based environments to the fully dynamic environments of Lisp-like languages. It also provides an implementation for a heap of dynamically allocated storage.

Chapter 8 discusses code generation both for intermediate code such as three-address code and P-code and for executable object code for a simple von Neumann architecture, for which a simulator is given. A complete code generator for the sample language is given. The chapter concludes with an introduction to code optimization techniques.

Three appendices augment the text. The first contains a detailed description of a language suitable for a class project, together with a list of partial projects that can be used as assignments. The remaining appendices give line-numbered listings of the source code for the sample compiler and the machine simulator, respectively.

Use as a Text

This text can be used in a one-semester or two-semester introductory compiler course, either with or without the use of Lex and Yacc compiler construction tools. If an automata theory course is a prerequisite, then Sections 2.2., 2.3, and 2.4 in Chapter 2 and Sections 3.2 and 3.6 in Chapter 3 can be skipped or quickly reviewed. In a one-semester course this still makes for an extremely fast-paced course, if scanning, parsing, semantic analysis, and code generation are all to be covered.

One reasonable alternative is, after an overview of scanning, to simply provide a scanner and move quickly to parsing. (Even with standard techniques and the use of C, input routines can be subtly different for different operating systems and platforms.) Another alternative is to use Lex and Yacc to automate the construction of a scanner and a parser (I do find, however, that in doing this there is a risk that, in a first course, students may fail to understand the actual algorithms being used). If an instructor wishes to use only Lex and Yacc, then further material may be skipped: all sections of Chapter 4 except 4.4, and Section 2.5 of Chapter 2.

If an instructor wishes to concentrate on hand coding, then the sections on Lex and Yacc may be skipped (2.6, 5.5, 5.6, and 5.7). Indeed, it would be possible to skip all of Chapter 5 if bottom-up parsing is ignored.

Similar shortcuts may be taken with the later chapters, if necessary, in either a tools-based course or a hand-coding style course. For instance, not all the different styles of attribute analysis need to be studied (Section 6.2). Also, it is not essential to study in detail all the different runtime environments cataloged in Chapter 7. If the students are to take a further course that will cover code generation in detail, then Chapter 8 may be skipped.

In a two-quarter or two-semester course it should be possible to cover the entire book.

Internet Availability of Resources

All the code in Appendices B and C is available on the Web at locations pointed to from my home page (http://www.mathcs.sjsu.edu/faculty/louden/). Additional resources, such as errata lists and solutions to some of the exercises, may also be available from me. Please check my home page or contact me by e-mail at louden@cs.sjsu.edu.

Acknowledgments

My interest in compilers began in 1984 with a summer course taught by Alan Demers. His insight and approach to the field have significantly influenced my own views.

Indeed, the basic organization of the sample compiler in this text was suggested by that course, and the machine simulator of Appendix C is a descendant of the one he provided.

More directly, I would like to thank my colleagues Bill Giles and Sam Khuri at San Jose State for encouraging me in this project, reading and commenting on most of the text, and for using preliminary drafts in their classes. I would also like to thank the students at San Jose State University in both my own and other classes who provided useful input. Further, I would like to thank Mary T. Stone of PWS for gathering a great deal of information on compiler tools and for coordinating the very useful review process.

The following reviewers contributed many excellent suggestions, for which I am grateful:

Jeff Jenness
Arkansas State University

Jerry Potter
Kent State University

Joe Lambert
Penn State University

Samuel A. Rebelsky
Dartmouth College

Joan Lukas
University of Masschusetts, Boston

Of course I alone am responsible for any shortcomings of the text. I have tried to make this book as error-free as possible. Undoubtedly errors remain, and I would be happy to hear from any readers willing to point them out to me.

Finally, I would like to thank my wife Margreth for her understanding, patience, and support, and our son Andrew for encouraging me to finish this book.

K.C.L.

Chapter 1

Introduction

Compilers are computer programs that translate one language to another. A compiler takes as its input a program written in its **source language** and produces an equivalent program written in its **target language**. Usually, the source language is a **high-level language**, such as C or C++, and the target language is **object code** (sometimes also called **machine code**) for the target machine, that is, code written in the machine instructions of the computer on which it is to be executed. We can view this process schematically as follows:

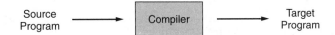

A compiler is a fairly complex program that can be anywhere from 10,000 to 1,000,000 lines of code. Writing such a program, or even understanding it, is not a simple task, and most computer scientists and professionals will never write a complete compiler. Nevertheless, compilers are used in almost all forms of computing, and anyone professionally involved with computers should know the basic organization and operation of a compiler. In addition, a frequent task in computer applications is the development of command interpreters and interface programs, which are smaller than compilers but which use the same techniques. A knowledge of these techniques is, therefore, of significant practical use.

It is the purpose of this text not only to provide such basic knowledge but also to give the reader all the necessary tools and practical experience to design and pro-

1

gram an actual compiler. To accomplish this, it is necessary to study the theoretical techniques, mainly from automata theory, that make compiler construction a manageable task. In covering this theory, we do not assume that the reader has previous knowledge of automata theory. Indeed, the viewpoint taken here is different from that in a standard automata theory text, in that it is aimed specifically at the compilation process. Nevertheless, a reader who has studied automata theory will find the theoretical material more familiar and will be able to proceed more quickly through those sections. In particular, Sections 2.2, 2.3, 2.4, and 3.2 may be skipped or skimmed by a reader with a good background in automata theory. In any case, the reader should be familiar with basic data structures and discrete mathematics. Some knowledge of machine architecture and assembly language is also essential, particularly for the chapter on code generation.

The study of the practical coding techniques themselves requires careful planning, since even with a good theoretical foundation the details of the code can be complex and overwhelming. This text contains a series of simple examples of programming language constructs that are used to elaborate the discussion of the techniques. The language we use for this discussion is called TINY. We also provide (in Appendix A) a more extensive example, consisting of a small but sufficiently complex subset of C, which we call C-Minus, which is suitable for a class project. In addition there are numerous exercises; these include simple paper-and-pencil exercises, extensions of code in the text, and more involved coding exercises.

In general, there is significant interaction between the structure of a compiler and the design of the programming language being compiled. In this text we will only incidentally study language design issues. Other texts are available that more fully treat programming language concepts and design issues. (See the Notes and References section at the end of this chapter.)

We begin with a brief look at the history and the raison d'être of compilers, together with a description of programs related to compilers. Then, we examine the structure of a compiler and the various translation processes and associated data structures and tour this structure using a simple concrete example. Finally, we give an overview of other issues of compiler structure, including bootstrapping and porting, concluding with a description of the principal language examples used in the remainder of the book.

1.1 WHY COMPILERS? A BRIEF HISTORY

With the advent of the stored-program computer pioneered by John von Neumann in the late 1940s, it became necessary to write sequences of codes, or programs, that would cause these computers to perform the desired computations. Initially, these programs were written in **machine language**—numeric codes that represented the actual machine operations to be performed. For example,

    C7 06 0000 0002

represents the instruction to move the number 2 to the location 0000 (in hexadecimal) on the Intel 8x86 processors used in IBM PCs. Of course, writing such codes is extremely time consuming and tedious, and this form of coding was soon replaced by

assembly language, in which instructions and memory locations are given symbolic forms. For example, the assembly language instruction

```
MOV X , 2
```

is equivalent to the previous machine instruction (assuming the symbolic memory location X is 0000). An **assembler** translates the symbolic codes and memory locations of assembly language into the corresponding numeric codes of machine language.

Assembly language greatly improved the speed and accuracy with which programs could be written, and it is still in use today, especially when extreme speed or conciseness of code is needed. However, assembly language has a number of defects: it is still not easy to write and it is difficult to read and understand. Moreover, assembly language is extremely dependent on the particular machine for which it was written, so code written for one computer must be completely rewritten for another machine. Clearly, the next major step in programming technology was to write the operations of a program in a concise form more nearly resembling mathematical notation or natural language, in a way that was independent of any one particular machine and yet capable of itself being translated by a program into executable code. For example, the previous assembly language code can be written in a concise, machine-independent form as

```
X = 2
```

At first, it was feared that this might not be possible, or if it was, then the object code would be so inefficient as to be useless.

The development of the FORTRAN language and its compiler by a team at IBM led by John Backus between 1954 and 1957 showed that both these fears were unfounded. Nevertheless, the success of this project came about only with a great deal of effort, since most of the processes involved in translating programming languages were not well understood at the time.

At about the same time that the first compiler was under development, Noam Chomsky began his study of the structure of natural language. His findings eventually made the construction of compilers considerably easier and even capable of partial automation. Chomsky's study led to the classification of languages according to the complexity of their **grammars** (the rules specifying their structure) and the power of the algorithms needed to recognize them. The **Chomsky hierarchy**, as it is now called, consists of four levels of grammars, called the type 0, type 1, type 2, and type 3 grammars, each of which is a specialization of its predecessor. The type 2, or **context-free, grammars** proved to be the most useful for programming languages, and today they are the standard way to represent the structure of programming languages. The study of the **parsing problem** (the determination of efficient algorithms for the recognition of context-free languages) was pursued in the 1960s and 1970s and led to a fairly complete solution of this problem, which today has become a standard part of compiler theory. Context-free languages and parsing algorithms are studied in Chapters 3, 4, and 5.

Closely related to context-free grammars are **finite automata** and **regular expressions**, which correspond to Chomsky's type 3 grammars. Begun at about the same time as Chomsky's work, their study led to symbolic methods for expressing the structure of the words, or tokens, of a programming language. Chapter 2 discusses finite automata and regular expressions.

Much more complex has been the development of methods for generating efficient object code, which began with the first compilers and continues to this day. These techniques are usually misnamed **optimization techniques**, but they really should be called **code improvement techniques**, since they almost never result in truly optimal object code but only improve its efficiency. Chapter 8 describes the basics of these techniques.

As the parsing problem became well understood, a great deal of work was devoted to developing programs that would automate this part of compiler development. These programs were originally called compiler-compilers, but are more aptly referred to as **parser generators**, since they automate only one part of the compilation process. The best-known of these programs is Yacc (yet another compiler-compiler) written by Steve Johnson in 1975 for the Unix system studied in Chapter 5. Similarly, the study of finite automata led to the development of another tool called a **scanner generator**, of which Lex (developed for the Unix system by Mike Lesk about the same time as Yacc) is the best known. Lex is studied in Chapter 2.

During the late 1970s and early 1980s, a number of projects focused on automating the generation of other parts of a compiler, including code generation. These attempts have been less successful, possibly because of the complex nature of the operations and our less than perfect understanding of them. We do not study them in detail in this text.

More recent advances in compiler design have included the following. First, compilers have included the application of more sophisticated algorithms for inferring and/or simplifying the information contained in a program, and these have gone hand in hand with the development of more sophisticated programming languages that allow this kind of analysis. Typical of these is the unification algorithm of Hindley-Milner type checking, used in the compilation of functional languages. Second, compilers have become more and more a part of a window-based **interactive development environment**, or IDE, that includes editors, linkers, debuggers, and project managers. So far there has been little standardization of such IDEs, but the development of standard windowing environments is leading in that direction. The study of such topics is beyond the scope of this text (but see the next section for a brief description of some of the components of an IDE). For pointers to the literature, see the Notes and References section at the end of the chapter. Despite the amount of research activity in recent years, however, the basics of compiler design have not changed much in the last 20 years, and they have increasingly become a part of the standard core of the computer science curriculum.

1.2 PROGRAMS RELATED TO COMPILERS

In this section, we briefly describe other programs that are related to or used together with compilers and that often come together with compilers in a complete language development environment. (We have already mentioned some of these.)

INTERPRETERS

An interpreter is a language translator like a compiler. It differs from a compiler in that it executes the source program immediately rather than generating object code that is executed after translation is complete. In principle, any programming language can be either interpreted or compiled, but an interpreter may be preferred to a compiler depending on the language in use and the situation under which translation occurs. For example, BASIC is a language that is more usually interpreted than compiled. Similarly, functional languages such as LISP tend to be interpreted. Interpreters are also often used in educational and software development situations, where programs are likely to be translated and retranslated many times. On the other hand, a compiler is to be preferred if speed of execution is a primary consideration, since compiled object code is invariably faster than interpreted source code, sometimes by a factor of 10 or more. Interpreters, however, share many of their operations with compilers, and there can even be translators that are hybrids, lying somewhere between interpreters and compilers. We will discuss interpreters intermittently, but our main focus in this text will be on compilation.

ASSEMBLERS

An assembler is a translator for the assembly language of a particular computer. As we have already noted, assembly language is a symbolic form of the machine language of the computer and is particularly easy to translate. Sometimes, a compiler will generate assembly language as its target language and then rely on an assembler to finish the translation into object code.

LINKERS

Both compilers and assemblers often rely on a program called a linker, which collects code separately compiled or assembled in different object files into a file that is directly executable. In this sense, a distinction can be made between object code—machine code that has not yet been linked—and executable machine code. A linker also connects an object program to the code for standard library functions and to resources supplied by the operating system of the computer, such as memory allocators and input and output devices. It is interesting to note that linkers now perform the task that was originally one of the principal activities of a compiler (hence the use of the word *compile*—to construct by collecting from different sources). We will not study the linking process in this text, since it is extremely dependent on the details of the operating system and processor. We will also not always make a clear distinction between unlinked object code and executable code, since this distinction will not be important for our study of compilation techniques.

LOADERS

Often a compiler, assembler, or linker will produce code that is not yet completely fixed and ready to execute, but whose principal memory references are all made relative to an undetermined starting location that can be anywhere in memory. Such code is said to be **relocatable**, and a loader will resolve all relocatable addresses relative to a given base, or starting, address. The use of a loader makes executable code more flexible, but the loading process often occurs behind the scenes (as part of the operating environment) or in conjunction with linking. Rarely is a loader an actual separate program.

PREPROCESSORS

A preprocessor is a separate program that is called by the compiler before actual translation begins. Such a preprocessor can delete comments, include other files, and perform **macro** substitutions (a macro is a shorthand description of a repeated sequence of text). Preprocessors can be required by the language (as in C) or can be later add-ons that provide additional facilities (such as the Ratfor preprocessor for FORTRAN).

EDITORS

Compilers usually accept source programs written using any editor that will produce a standard file, such as an ASCII file. More recently, compilers have been bundled together with editors and other programs into an interactive development environment, or IDE. In such a case, an editor, while still producing standard files, may be oriented toward the format or structure of the programming language in question. Such editors are called **structure based** and already include some of the operations of a compiler, so that, for example, the programmer may be informed of errors as the program is written rather than when it is compiled. The compiler and its companion programs can also be called from within the editor, so that the programmer can execute the program without leaving the editor.

DEBUGGERS

A debugger is a program that can be used to determine execution errors in a compiled program. It is also often packaged with a compiler in an IDE. Running a program with a debugger differs from straight execution in that the debugger keeps track of most or all of the source code information, such as line numbers and names of variables and procedures. It can also halt execution at prespecified locations called **breakpoints** as well as provide information on what functions have been called and what the current values of variables are. To perform these functions, the debugger must be supplied with appropriate symbolic information by the compiler, and this can sometimes be difficult, especially in a compiler that tries to optimize the object code. Thus, debugging becomes a compiler question, which, however, is beyond the scope of this book.

PROFILERS

A profiler is a program that collects statistics on the behavior of an object program during execution. Typical statistics that may be of interest to the programmer are the number of times each procedure is called and the percentage of execution time spent in each procedure. Such statistics can be extremely useful in helping the programmer to improve the execution speed of the program. Sometimes the compiler will even use the output of the profiler to automatically improve the object code without intervention by the programmer.

PROJECT MANAGERS

Modern software projects are usually so large that they are undertaken by groups of programmers rather than a single programmer. In such cases, it is important that the files being worked on by different people are coordinated, and this is the job of a project manager program. For example, a project manager should coordinate the merging of separate versions of the same file produced by different programmers. It should also maintain a history of changes to each of a group of files, so that coherent versions of a program under development can be maintained (this is something that can also be useful to the one-programmer project). A project manager can be written in a language-independent way, but when it is bundled together with a compiler, it can maintain information on the specific compiler and linker operations needed to build a complete executable program. Two popular project manager programs on Unix systems are **sccs (source code control system)** and **rcs (revision control system)**.

1.3   THE TRANSLATION PROCESS

A compiler consists internally of a number of steps, or **phases**, that perform distinct logical operations. It is helpful to think of these phases as separate pieces within the compiler, and they may indeed be written as separately coded operations although in practice they are often grouped together. The phases of a compiler are shown in Figure 1.1, together with three auxiliary components that interact with some or all of

Figure 1.1

The phases of a compiler

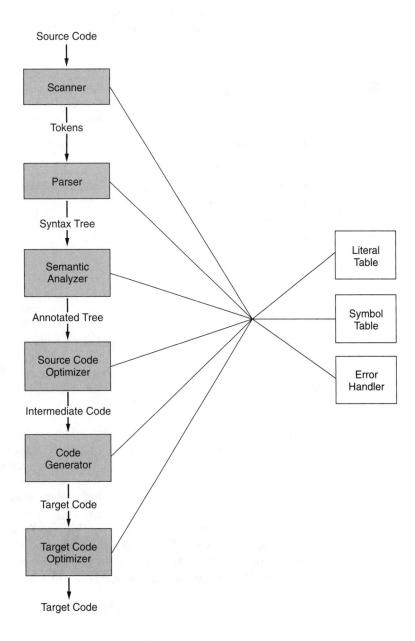

the phases: the literal table, the symbol table, and the error handler. We will briefly describe each phase here; they will be studied in greater detail in the following chapters. (The literal and symbol tables will be discussed in more detail in the next section and the error handler in Section 1.5.)

THE SCANNER

This phase of the compiler does the actual reading of the source program, which is usually in the form of a stream of characters. The scanner performs what is called **lexical analysis**: it collects sequences of characters into meaningful units called **tokens**, which are like the words of a natural language such as English. Thus, a scanner can be thought to perform a function similar to spelling.

As an example, consider the following line of code, which could be part of a C program:

```
a[index] = 4 + 2
```

This code contains 12 nonblank characters but only 8 tokens:

a	identifier
[	left bracket
index	identifier
]	right bracket
=	assignment
4	number
+	plus sign
2	number

Each token consists of one or more characters that are collected into a unit before further processing takes place.

A scanner may perform other operations along with the recognition of tokens. For example, it may enter identifiers into the symbol table, and it may enter **literals** into the literal table (literals include numeric constants such as 3.1415926535 and quoted strings of text such as "Hello, world!").

THE PARSER

The parser receives the source code in the form of tokens from the scanner and performs **syntax analysis**, which determines the structure of the program. This is similar to performing grammatical analysis on a sentence in a natural language. Syntax analysis determines the structural elements of the program as well as their relationships. The results of syntax analysis are usually represented as a **parse tree** or a **syntax tree**.

As an example, consider again the line of C code we have already given. It represents a structural element called an expression, which is an assignment expression consisting of a subscripted expression on the left and an integer arithmetic expression on the right. This structure can be represented as a parse tree in the following form:

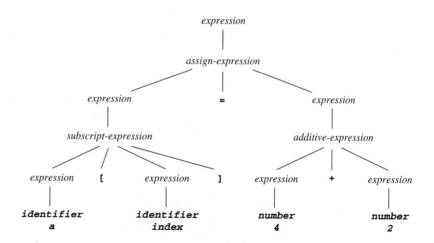

Note that the internal nodes of the parse tree are labeled by the names of the structures they represent and that the leaves of the parse tree represent the sequence of tokens from the input. (Names of structures are written in a different typeface to distinguish them from tokens.)

A parse tree is a useful aid to visualizing the syntax of a program or program element, but it is inefficient in its representation of that structure. Parsers tend to generate a syntax tree instead, which is a condensation of the information contained in the parse tree. (Sometimes syntax trees are called **abstract syntax trees**, since they represent a further abstraction from parse trees.) An abstract syntax tree for our example of a C assignment expression is as follows:

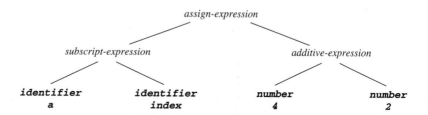

Note that in the syntax tree many of the nodes have disappeared (including token nodes). For example, if we know that an expression is a subscript operation, then it is no longer necessary to keep the brackets [and] that represent this operation in the original input.

THE SEMANTIC ANALYZER

The semantics of a program are its "meaning," as opposed to its syntax, or structure. The semantics of a program determine its runtime behavior, but most programming languages have features that can be determined prior to execution and yet cannot be conveniently expressed as syntax and analyzed by the parser. Such features are referred to as **static semantics**, and the analysis of such semantics is the task of the semantic analyzer. (The "dynamic" semantics of a program—those properties of a program that can only be determined by executing it—cannot be determined by a compiler, since it does not execute the program.) Typical static semantic features of common programming languages include declarations and type checking. The extra pieces of information (such as data types) computed by the semantic analyzer are called **attributes**, and these are often added to the tree as annotations, or "decorations." (Attributes may also be entered into the symbol table.)

In our running example of the C expression

```
a[index] = 4 + 2
```

typical type information that would be gathered prior to the analysis of this line might be that **a** is an array of integer values with subscripts from a subrange of the integers and that **index** is an integer variable. Then the semantic analyzer would annotate the syntax tree with the types of all the subexpressions and then check that the assignment makes sense for these types, declaring a type mismatch error if not. In our example, all the types make sense, and the result of semantic analysis on the syntax tree could be represented by the following annotated tree:

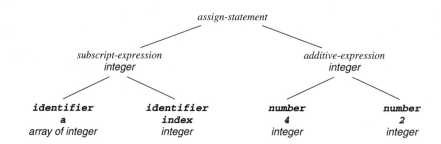

THE SOURCE CODE OPTIMIZER

Compilers often include a number of code improvement, or optimization, steps. The earliest point at which most optimization steps can be performed is just after semantic analysis, and there may be possibilities for code improvement that depend only on the source code. We indicate this possibility by providing this operation as a separate phase in the compilation process. Individual compilers exhibit a wide variation not only in the kinds of optimizations performed but also in the placement of the optimization phases.

In our example, we have included an opportunity for source-level optimization; namely, the expression **4 + 2** can be precomputed by the compiler to the result **6**. (This particular optimization is known as **constant folding**.) Of course, much more complex possibilities exist (some of these are mentioned in Chapter 8). In our example, this optimization can be performed directly on the (annotated) syntax tree by collapsing the right-hand subtree of the root node to its constant value:

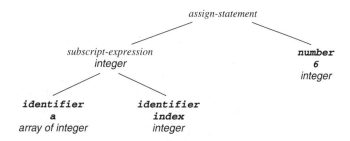

Many optimizations can be performed directly on the tree, but in a number of cases, it is easier to optimize a linearized form of the tree that is closer to assembly code. Many different varieties of such code exist, but a standard choice is **three-address code**, so called because it contains the addresses of (up to) three locations in memory. Another popular choice is **P-code**, which has been used in many Pascal compilers.

In our example, three-address code for the original C expression might look like this:

```
t = 4 + 2
a[index] = t
```

(Note the use of an extra temporary variable **t** to store the intermediate result of the addition.) Now the optimizer would improve this code in two steps, first computing the result of the addition

```
t = 6
a[index] = t
```

and then replacing **t** by its value to get the three-address statement

```
a[index] = 6
```

In Figure 1.1 we have indicated the possibility that the source code optimizer may use three-address code by referring to its output as **intermediate code**. Intermediate code historically referred to a form of code representation intermediate between source code and object code, such as three-address code or a similar linear representation. However, it can also more generally refer to *any* internal representation for the source code used by the compiler. In this sense, the syntax tree can also be referred to as intermediate code, and indeed the source code optimizer could continue to use this representation in its output. Sometimes this more general sense is indicated by referring to the intermediate code as the **intermediate representation**, or **IR**.

THE CODE GENERATOR

The code generator takes the intermediate code or IR and generates code for the target machine. In this text we will write target code in assembly language form for ease of understanding, although most compilers generate object code directly. It is in this phase of compilation that the properties of the target machine become the major factor. Not only is it necessary to use instructions as they exist on the target machine but decisions about the representation of data will now also play a major role, such as how many bytes or words variables of integer and floating-point data types occupy in memory.

In our example, we must now decide how integers are to be stored to generate code for the array indexing. For example, a possible sample code sequence for the given expression might be (in a hypothetical assembly language)

```
MOV    R0, index    ;; value of index -> R0
MUL    R0, 2        ;; double value in R0
MOV    R1, &a       ;; address of a -> R1
ADD    R1, R0       ;; add R0 to R1
MOV    *R1, 6       ;; constant 6 -> address in R1
```

In this code we have used a C-like convention for addressing modes, so that **&a** is the address of **a** (i.e., the base address of the array) and that ***R1** means indirect register addressing (so that the last instruction stores the value 6 to the address contained in R1). In this code we have also assumed that the machine performs byte addressing and that integers occupy two bytes of memory (hence the use of 2 as the multiplication factor in the second instruction).

THE TARGET CODE OPTIMIZER

In this phase, the compiler attempts to improve the target code generated by the code generator. Such improvements include choosing addressing modes to improve performance, replacing slow instructions by faster ones, and eliminating redundant or unnecessary operations.

In the sample target code given, there are a number of improvements possible. One is to use a shift instruction to replace the multiplication in the second instruction (which is usually expensive in terms of execution time). Another is to use a more powerful addressing mode, such as indexed addressing to perform the array store. With these two optimizations, our target code becomes

```
MOV R0, index    ;; value of index -> R0
SHL R0           ;; double value in R0
MOV &a[R0], 6    ;; constant 6 -> address a + R0
```

This completes our brief description of the phases of a compiler. We want to emphasize that this description is only schematic and does not necessarily represent the actual organization of a working compiler. Indeed, compilers exhibit a wide variation in their organizational details. Nevertheless, the phases we have described are present in some form in nearly all compilers.

We have also discussed only tangentially the data structures required to maintain the information needed by each phase, such as the syntax tree, the intermediate code (assuming these are not the same), the literal table, and the symbol table. We devote the next section to a brief overview of the major data structures in a compiler.

1.4   MAJOR DATA STRUCTURES IN A COMPILER

The interaction between the algorithms used by the phases of a compiler and the data structures that support these phases is, of course, a strong one. The compiler writer strives to implement these algorithms in as efficient a manner as possible, without incurring too much extra complexity. Ideally, a compiler should be capable of compiling a program in time proportional to the size of the program, that is, in $O(n)$ time, where n is a measure of program size (usually, the number of characters). In this section, we indicate a few of the principal data structures that are needed by the phases as part of their operation and that serve to communicate information among the phases.

TOKENS

When a scanner collects characters into a token, it generally represents the token symbolically, that is, as a value of an enumerated data type representing the set of tokens of the source language. Sometimes it is also necessary to preserve the string of characters itself or other information derived from it, such as the name associated with an identifier token or the value of a number token. In most languages the scanner needs only to generate one token at a time (this is called **single symbol lookahead**). In this case, a single global variable can be used to hold the token information. In other cases (most notably FORTRAN), an array of tokens may be needed.

THE SYNTAX TREE

If the parser does generate a syntax tree, it is usually constructed as a standard pointer-based structure that is dynamically allocated as parsing proceeds. The entire tree can then be kept as a single variable pointing to the root node. Each node in the structure is a record whose fields represent the information collected both by the parser and, later, by the semantic analyzer. For example, the data type of an expression may be kept as a field in the syntax tree node for the expression. Sometimes, to save space, these fields are also dynamically allocated, or they are stored in other data structures, such as the symbol table, that allow selective allocation and deallocation. Indeed, each syntax tree node itself may require different attributes to be stored, depending on the kind of language structure it represents (for example, an expression node has different requirements from a statement node or a declaration node). In this case, each node in the syntax tree may be represented by a variant record, with each node kind containing only the information necessary for that case.

THE SYMBOL TABLE

This data structure keeps information associated with identifiers: functions, variables, constants, and data types. The symbol table interacts with almost every phase of the compiler: the scanner, parser, or semantic analyzer may enter identifiers into the table; the semantic analyzer will add data type and other information; and the optimization and code generation phases will use the information provided by the symbol table to make appropriate object code choices. Since the symbol table will be accessed so frequently, insertion, deletion, and access operations need to be efficient, preferably constant-time operations. A standard data structure for this purpose is the hash table, although various tree structures can also be used. Sometimes several tables are used and maintained in a list or stack.

THE LITERAL TABLE

Quick insertion and lookup are essential as well to the literal table, which stores constants and strings used in a program. However, a literal table need not allow deletions, since its data applies globally to the program and a constant or string will appear only once in this table. The literal table is important in reducing the size of a program in memory by allowing the reuse of constants and strings. It is also needed by the code generator to construct symbolic addresses for literals and for entering data definitions in the target code file.

INTERMEDIATE CODE

Depending on the kind of intermediate code (e.g., three-address code and P-code) and the kinds of optimizations performed, this code may be kept as an array of text strings, a temporary text file, or as a linked list of structures. In compilers that perform complex optimizations, particular attention must be given to choosing representations that permit easy reorganization.

TEMPORARY FILES

Historically, computers did not possess enough memory for an entire program to be kept in memory during compilation. This problem was solved by using temporary files to hold the products of intermediate steps during translation or by compiling "on the fly," that is, keeping only enough information from earlier parts of the source program to enable translation to proceed. Memory constraints are now a much smaller problem, and it is possible to require that an entire compilation unit be maintained in memory, especially if separate compilation is available in the language. Still, compilers occasionally find it useful to generate intermediate files during some of the processing steps. Typical among these is the need to **backpatch** addresses during code generation. For example, when translating a conditional statement such as

```
if x = 0 then ... else ...
```

a jump from the test to the else-part must be generated before the location of the code for the else-part is known:

```
CMP X,0
JNE NEXT ;; location of NEXT not yet known
<code for then-part>
NEXT:
<code for else-part>
```

Typically, a blank must be left for the value of **NEXT**, which is filled in once that value becomes known. This is easily accomplished with the use of a temporary file.

1.5   OTHER ISSUES IN COMPILER STRUCTURE

The structure of a compiler may be viewed from many different angles. In Section 1.3 we described its phases, which represent the logical structure of a compiler. Other viewpoints are possible: the physical structure of the compiler, the sequencing of the operations, and so on. The compiler writer should be familiar with as many views of compiler structure as possible, since the structure of the compiler will have a major impact on its reliability, efficiency, usefulness, and maintainability. In this section we will consider other aspects of compiler structure and indicate how each view applies.

ANALYSIS AND SYNTHESIS

In this view, compiler operations that analyze the source program to compute its properties are classified as the **analysis** part of the compiler, while operations involved in producing translated code are called the **synthesis** part of the compiler. Naturally, lexical analysis, syntax analysis, and semantic analysis belong to the analysis part, while code generation is synthesis. Optimization steps may involve both analysis and synthesis. Analysis tends to be more mathematical and better understood, while synthesis requires more specialized techniques. Thus, it is helpful to separate analysis steps from synthesis steps so each can be changed independently of the other.

FRONT END AND BACK END

This view regards the compiler as separated into those operations that depend only on the source language (the **front end**) and those operations that depend only on the target language (the **back end**). This is similar to the division into analysis and synthesis: the scanner, parser, and semantic analyzer are part of the front end, while the code generator is part of the back end. However, some optimization analysis can be target dependent, and therefore part of the back end, while intermediate code synthesis is often target independent and thus part of the front end. Ideally, the compiler would be strictly divided into these two sections, with the intermediate representation as the medium of communication between them:

This structure is especially important for compiler **portability**, in which the compiler is designed with a view toward changing either the source code (which involves rewriting the front end) or the target code (which involves rewriting the back end). In practice this has proven difficult to achieve, and so-called portable compilers tend still to have features that depend on both source and target languages. In part, this can be blamed on rapid and fundamental changes in both programming languages and machine architectures, but it is also difficult to efficiently retain all the information one might need in moving to a new target language or in making the data structures suitably general to permit a change to a new source language. Nevertheless, a consistent attempt to separate front and back ends will pay off in easier portability.

PASSES

A compiler often finds it convenient to process the entire source program several times before generating code. These repetitions are referred to as **passes**. After the initial pass, which constructs a syntax tree or intermediate code from the source, a pass consists of processing the intermediate representation, adding information to it, altering its structure, or producing a different representation. Passes may or may not correspond to phases—often a pass will consist of several phases. Indeed, depending on the language, a compiler may be **one pass**, in that all phases occur during a single pass. This results in efficient compilation but also in (typically) less efficient target code. Pascal and C are both languages that permit one-pass compilation. (Modula-2 is a language whose structure requires that a compiler have at least two passes.) Most compilers with optimizations use more than one pass; a typical arrangement is one pass for scanning and parsing, one pass for semantic analysis and source-level optimization, and a third pass for code generation and target-level optimization. Heavily optimizing compilers may use even more passes: five, six, or even eight passes are not unknown.

LANGUAGE DEFINITION AND COMPILERS

We noted in Section 1.1 that the lexical and syntactic structures of a programming language are usually specified in formal terms and use regular expressions and context-free grammars. The semantics of a programming language, however, are still commonly specified using English (or other natural language) descriptions. These descriptions (together with the formal lexical and syntactic structure) are usually collected into a **language reference manual**, or **language definition**. With a new language, a language definition and a compiler are often developed simultaneously, since the techniques available to the compiler writer can have a major impact on the definition of the language. Similarly, the way in which a language is defined will have a major impact on the techniques that are needed to construct the compiler.

A more common situation for the compiler writer is that the language being implemented is well known and has an existing language definition. Sometimes this language definition has been raised to the level of a **language standard** that has been approved by one of the official standardization organizations, such as ANSI (American National Standards Institute) or ISO (International Organization for Standardization). For example, FORTRAN, Pascal, and C have ANSI standards. Ada has a standard approved by the U.S. government. In this case, the compiler writer must interpret the language definition and implement a compiler that conforms to the language definition. This is often not an easy task, but it is sometimes made easier by the existence of a set of standard test programs (a **test suite**) against which a compiler can be tested (such a test suite exists for Ada). The TINY example language used in the text has its lexical, syntactic, and semantic structure specified in Sections 2.5, 3.7, and 6.5, respectively. Appendix A contains a minimal language reference manual for the C-Minus compiler project language.

Occasionally, a language will have its semantics given by a **formal definition** in mathematical terms. Several methods that are currently used do this, and no one method has achieved the level of a standard, although so-called **denotational semantics** has become one of the more common methods, especially in the functional programming community. When a formal definition exists for a language, then it is (in theory) possible to give a mathematical proof that a compiler conforms to the definition. However, this is such a difficult undertaking that it is almost never done. In any case, the techniques for doing so are beyond the scope of this text, and formal semantic techniques will not be studied here.

One aspect of compiler construction that is particularly affected by the language definition is the structure and behavior of the runtime environment. Runtime environments are studied in detail in Chapter 7. It is worth noting here, however, that the structure of data allowed in a programming language, and particularly the kinds of function calls and returned values allowed, have a decisive effect on the complexity of the runtime system. In particular, the three basic types of runtime environments, in increasing order of complexity, are as follows:

First, FORTRAN77, with no pointers or dynamic allocation and no recursive function calls, allows a completely static runtime environment, where all memory allocation is done prior to execution. This makes the job of allocation particularly easy for the compiler writer, as no code needs to be generated to maintain the environment. Second, Pascal, C, and other so-called Algol-like languages allow a limited form of dynamic allocation and recursive function calls and require a "semi-dynamic" or stack-based runtime environment with an additional dynamic structure called a *heap* from which the programmer can schedule dynamic allocation. Finally, functional and most object-oriented languages, such as LISP and Smalltalk, require a "fully dynamic" environment in which all allocation is performed automatically by code generated by the compiler. This is complicated, because it requires that memory also be freed automatically, and this in turn requires complex "garbage collection" algorithms. We will survey such methods along with our study of runtime environments, but a complete account of this area is beyond the scope of this book.

COMPILER OPTIONS AND INTERFACES

An important aspect of compiler construction is the inclusion of mechanisms for interfacing with the operating system and for providing options to the user for various purposes. Examples of interface mechanisms are the provision of input and output facilities as well as access to the file system of the target machine. Examples of user options include the specification of listing characteristics (length, error messages, cross-reference tables) and code optimization options (performance of certain optimizations but not others). Both interfacing and options are collectively referred to as compiler **pragmatics**. Sometimes a language definition will specify that certain pragmatics must be provided. For example, Pascal and C both specify certain input/output procedures (in Pascal they are part of the language proper, whereas in C they are part of the specification of a standard library). In Ada, a number of compiler directives, called **pragmas**, are part of the language definition. For example, the Ada statements

```
pragma LIST(ON);
...
pragma LIST(OFF);
```

generate a compiler listing for the part of the program contained within the pragmas. In this text we will see compiler directives only in the context of generating listing information for compiler debugging purposes. Also, we will not treat issues in input/output and operating system interfacing, since these involve considerable detail and vary so much from one operating system to another.

ERROR HANDLING

One of the most important functions of a compiler is its response to errors in a source program. Errors can be detected during almost every phase of compilation. These **static** (or **compile-time**) **errors** must be reported by a compiler, and it is important that a compiler be able to generate meaningful error messages and resume compilation after each error. Each phase of a compiler will need a slightly different kind of error handling, and so an **error handler** must contain different operations, each appropriate for a specific phase and situation. Error handling techniques for each phase will therefore be studied separately in the appropriate chapter.

A language definition will usually require not only that static errors be caught by a compiler but also that certain execution errors be caught as well. This requires a compiler to generate extra code that will perform suitable runtime tests to guarantee that all such errors will cause an appropriate event during execution. The simplest such event will halt the execution of the program. Often, however, this is inadequate, and a language definition may require the presence of **exception handling** mechanisms. These can substantially complicate the management of a runtime system, especially if a program may continue to execute from the point where the error occurred. We will not consider the implementation of such a mechanism, but we will show how a compiler can generate test code to ensure that specified runtime errors will cause execution to halt.

1.6   BOOTSTRAPPING AND PORTING

We have discussed the source language and target language as determining factors in the structure of a compiler and the usefulness of separating source and target language issues into front and back ends. But we have not mentioned the third language involved in the compiler construction process: the language in which the compiler itself is written. For the compiler to execute immediately, this implementation (or **host**) language would have to be machine language. This was indeed how the first compilers were written, since essentially no compilers existed yet. A more reasonable approach today is to write the compiler in another language for which a compiler already exists. If the existing compiler already runs on the target machine, then we need only compile the new compiler using the existing compiler to get a running program:

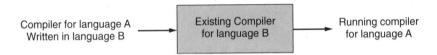

If the existing compiler for the language B runs on a machine different from the target machine, then the situation is a bit more complicated. Compilation then produces a **cross compiler**, that is, a compiler that generates target code for a different machine from the one on which it runs. This and other more complex situations are best described by drawing a compiler as a **T-diagram** (named after its shape). A compiler written in language H (for host language) that translates language S (for source language) into language T (for target language) is drawn as the following T-diagram:

Note that this is equivalent to saying that the compiler runs on "machine" H (if H is not machine code, then we consider it to be the executable code for a hypothetical machine). Typically, we expect H to be the same as T (that is, the compiler produces code for the same machine as the one on which it runs), but this needn't be the case.

T-diagrams can be combined in two ways. First, if we have two compilers that run on the same machine H, one of which translates language A to language B and the other of which translates language B to language C, then we can combine them by letting the output of the first be the input to the second. The result is a compiler from A to C on machine H. We express this as follows:

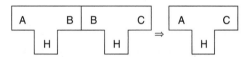

Second, we can use a compiler from "machine" H to "machine" K to translate the implementation language of another compiler from H to K. We express this as follows:

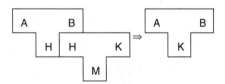

Now the first scenario we described previously—that is, using an existing compiler for language B on machine H to translate a compiler from language A to H written in B—can be viewed as the following diagram, which is just a special case of the previous diagram:

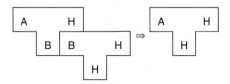

The second scenario we have described—where the compiler of language B runs on a different machine, which results in a cross compiler for A—can similarly be described as follows:

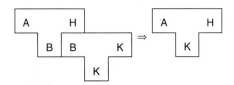

It is common to write a compiler in the same language that it is to compile:

While this appears to be a blunder of circularity—since, if no compiler for the source language yet exists, the compiler itself cannot be compiled—there are important advantages to be gained from this approach.

Consider, for example, how we might approach the circularity problem. We might write a "quick and dirty" compiler in assembly language, translating only those features of the language that are actually used in the compiler (having, of course, limited our use of those features when writing the "good" compiler). This "quick and dirty" compiler may also produce extremely inefficient code (it only needs to be correct!). Once we have the running "quick and dirty" compiler, we use it to compile the "good" compiler. Then we recompile the "good" compiler to produce the final version. This process is called **bootstrapping**. This process is illustrated in Figures 1.2(a) and 1.2(b).

After bootstrapping, we have a compiler in both source code and executing code. The advantage to this is that any improvement to the source code of the compiler can

Figure 1.2(a)
The first step in a bootstrap process

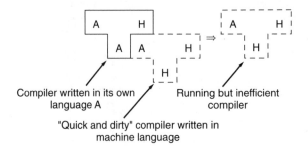

Figure 1.2(b)

The second step in a bootstrap process

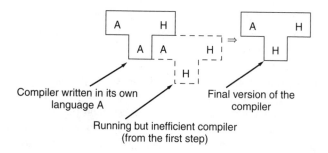

Compiler written in its own language A

Running but inefficient compiler (from the first step)

Final version of the compiler

be immediately bootstrapped to a working compiler by applying the same two-step process as before.

But there is another advantage. Porting the compiler to a new host computer now only requires that the back end of the source code be rewritten to generate code for the new machine. This is then compiled using the old compiler to produce a cross compiler, and the compiler is again recompiled by the cross compiler to produce a working version for the new machine. This is illustrated in Figures 1.3(a) and 1.3(b).

Figure 1.3(a)

Porting a compiler written in its own source language (step 1)

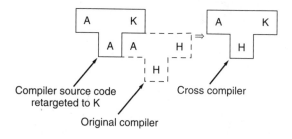

Compiler source code retargeted to K

Original compiler

Cross compiler

Figure 1.3(b)

Porting a compiler written in its own source language (step 2)

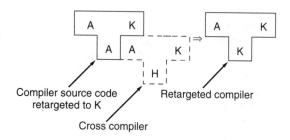

Compiler source code retargeted to K

Cross compiler

Retargeted compiler

1.7   THE TINY SAMPLE LANGUAGE AND COMPILER

A book on compiler construction would be incomplete without examples for each step in the compilation process. In many cases we will illustrate techniques with examples that are abstracted from existing languages, such as C, C++, Pascal, and Ada. These examples, however, are not enough to show how all the parts of a compiler fit together. For that, it is also necessary to exhibit a complete compiler and provide a commentary on its operation.

This requirement—that an actual compiler be demonstrated—is a difficult one. A "real" compiler—that is, one that we would expect to use in everyday programming— has far too much detail and would be overwhelming to study within the framework of a text. On the other hand, a compiler for a very small language, whose listing would comprise 10 or so pages of text, could not hope to demonstrate adequately all the features that a "real" compiler needs.

We will attempt to satisfy these requirements by giving complete source code in (ANSI) C for a small language whose compiler can be easily comprehended once the techniques are understood. We will call this language TINY and will use it as a running example for the techniques studied in each chapter. The code for its compiler will be discussed as the techniques are covered. In this section we will give an overview of the language and its compiler. The complete compiler code is collected in Appendix B.

A further problem is the choice of the machine language to use as the target language of the TINY compiler. Again, the complexity of using actual machine code for an exisiting processor makes such a choice difficult. But the choice of a specific processor also has the effect of limiting the execution of the resulting target code to these machines. Instead, we simplify the target code to be the assembly language for a simple hypothetical processor, which we will call the TM machine (for tiny machine). We will take a quick look at this machine here but will delay a more extensive description until Chapter 8 (code generation). A TM simulator listing in C appears in Appendix C.

1.7.1 The TINY Language

A program in TINY has a very simple structure: it is just a sequence of statements separated by semicolons in a syntax similar to that of Ada or Pascal. There are no procedures and no declarations. All variables are integer variables, and variables are declared simply by assigning values to them (somewhat like FORTRAN or BASIC). There are only two control statements: an if-statement and a repeat-statement. Both control statements may themselves contain statement sequences. An if-statement has an optional else part and must be terminated by the keyword **end**. There are also read and write statements that perform input/output. Comments are allowed within curly brackets; comments cannot be nested.

Expressions in TINY are also limited to Boolean and integer arithmetic expressions. A Boolean expression consists of a comparison of two arithmetic expressions using either of the two comparison operators **<** and **=**. An arithmetic expression may involve integer constants, variables, parentheses, and any of the four integer operators **+**, **−**, *****, and **/** (integer division), with the usual mathematical properties. Boolean expressions may appear only as tests in control statements—there are no Boolean variables, assignment, or I/O.

Figure 1.4 gives a sample program in this language for the well-known factorial function. We will use this program as a running example throughout the text.

Figure 1.4

A TINY language program that outputs the factorial of its input

```
{ Sample program
  in TINY language -
  computes factorial
}
read x; { input an integer }
if x > 0 then { don't compute if x <= 0 }
  fact := 1;
  repeat
    fact := fact * x;
    x := x - 1
  until x = 0;
  write fact { output factorial of x }
end
```

While TINY lacks many features necessary for real programming languages—procedures, arrays, and floating-point values are some of the more serious omissions—it is still large enough to exemplify most of the essential features of a compiler.

1.7.2 The TINY Compiler

The TINY compiler consists of the following C files, where we list header files (for inclusion) on the left and code files on the right:

globals.h	main.c
util.h	util.c
scan.h	scan.c
parse.h	parse.c
symtab.h	symtab.c
analyze.h	analyze.c
code.h	code.c
cgen.h	cgen.c

The source code for these files is listed in Appendix B, with line numbers, and in the order given, except that **main.c** is listed before **globals.h**. The **globals.h** header file is included in all the code files. It contains the definitions of data types and global variables used throughout the compiler. The file **main.c** contains the main program that drives the compiler, and it allocates and initializes the global variables. The remaining files consist of header/code file pairs, with the externally available function prototypes given in the header file and implemented (with possibly additional static local functions) in the associated code file. The **scan**, **parse**, **analyze**, and **cgen** files correspond exactly to the scanner, parser, semantic analyzer, and code generator phases of Figure 1.1. The **util** files contain utility functions needed to generate the internal representation of the source code (the syntax tree) and display listing and error information. The **symtab** files contain a hash-table implementation of a symbol table suitable for use with TINY. The **code** files contain utilities for code generation that are dependent on the target machine (the TM machine, described in Section 1.7.3). The remaining components of Figure 1.1 are absent: there is no separate error handler or literal table and there are no optimization phases. Also, there is no intermediate code separate from the syntax tree. Further, the symbol table interacts only with the semantic analyzer and the code generator (so we delay a discussion of it until Chapter 6).

To reduce the interaction among these files, we have also made the compiler four-pass: the first pass consists of the scanner and parser, which construct the syntax tree; the second and third passes undertake semantic analysis, with the second pass constructing the symbol table and the third pass performing type checking; the final pass is the code generator. The code in **main.c** that drives these passes is particularly simple. Ignoring flags and conditional compilation, the central code is as follows (see lines 69, 77, 79, and 94 of Appendix B):

```
syntaxTree = parse();
buildSymtab(syntaxTree);
typeCheck(syntaxTree);
codeGen(syntaxTree,codefile);
```

For flexibility, we have also built in conditional compilation flags that make it possible to build partial compilers. The flags, with their effect, are as follows:

FLAG	EFFECT IF SET	FILES NEEDED FOR COMPILATION (CUMULATIVE)
NO_PARSE	Builds a scanner-only compiler.	globals.h, main.c, util.h, util.c, scan.h, scan.c
NO_ANALYZE	Builds a compiler that parses and scans only.	parse.h, parse.c
NO_CODE	Builds a compiler that performs semantic analysis but generates no code.	symtab.h, symtab.c, analyze.h, analyze.c

Although this design for the TINY compiler is somewhat unrealistic, it has the pedagogical advantage that separate files correspond roughly to phases, and they can be discussed (and compiled and executed) individually in the chapters that follow.

The TINY compiler can be compiled by any ANSI C compiler. Assuming that the name of the executable file is **tiny**, it can be used to compile a TINY source program in the text file **sample.tny** by issuing the command

```
tiny sample.tny
```

(The compiler will also add the **.tny** suffix if it is omitted.) This will print a program listing to the screen (which can be redirected to a file) and (if code generation is activated) will also generate the target code file **sample.tm** (for use with the TM machine, described next).

There are several options for the information in the compilation listing. The following flags are available:

FLAG	EFFECT IF SET
EchoSource	Echoes the TINY source program to the listing together with line numbers.
TraceScan	Displays information on each token as the scanner recognizes it.
TraceParse	Displays the syntax tree in a linearized format.
TraceAnalyze	Displays summary information on the symbol table and type checking.
TraceCode	Prints code generation–tracing comments to the code file.

1.7.3 The TM Machine

We use the assembly language for this machine as the target language for the TINY compiler. The TM machine has just enough instructions to be an adequate target for a small language such as TINY. In fact, TM has some of the properties of Reduced Instruction Set Computers (or RISCs), in that all arithmetic and testing must take place in registers and the addressing modes are extremely limited. To give some idea of the simplicity of this machine, we translate the code for the C expression

```
a[index] = 6
```

into TM assembly language (compare this with the hypothetical assembly language for the same statement in Section 1.3, page 12):

```
LDC   1,0(0)          load 0 into reg 1
* the following instruction
* assumes index is at location 10 in memory
LD    0,10(1)         load val at 10+R1 into R0
LDC   1,2(0)          load 2 into reg 1
MUL   0,1,0           put R1*R0 into R0
LDC   1,0(0)          load 0 into reg 1
* the following instruction
* assumes a is at location 20 in memory
LDA   1,20(1)         load 20+R1 into R0
ADD   0,1,0           put R1+R0 into R0
LDC   1,6(0)          load 6 into reg 1
ST    1,0(0)          store R1 at 0+R0
```

We note that there are three addressing modes for the load operation, all given by different instructions: **LDC** is "load constant," **LD** is "load from memory," and **LDA** is "load address." We note also that addresses must always be given as "register+offset" values, as in **10(1)** (instruction 2 of the preceding code), which stands for the address computed by adding the offset 10 to the contents of register 1. (Since 0 was loaded into register 1 in the previous instruction, this actually refers to the absolute location 10.)[1] We also note that the arithmetic instructions **MUL** and **ADD** can have only register operands and are "three-address" instructions, in that the target register of the result can be specified independently of the operands (contrast this with the code in Section 1.3, page 12, where the operations were "two address").

Our simulator for the TM machine reads the assembly code directly from a file and executes it. Thus, we avoid the added complexity of translating the assembly language to machine code. However, our simulator is not a true assembler, in that there are no symbolic addresses or labels. Thus, the TINY compiler must still compute absolute addresses for jumps. Also, to avoid the extra complexity of linking with external input/output routines, the TM machine contains built-in I/O facilities for integers; these are read from and written to the standard devices during simulation.

The TM simulator can be compiled from the **tm.c** source code using any ANSI C compiler. Assuming the executable file is called **tm**, it can be used by issuing the command

```
tm sample.tm
```

where **sample.tm** is, for example, the code file produced by the TINY compiler from the **sample.tny** source file. This command causes the code file to be assembled and loaded; then the TM simulator can be run interactively. For example, if **sample.tny** is the sample program of Figure 1.4, then the factorial of 7 can be computed with the following interaction:

```
tm sample.tm
TM   simulation (enter h for help)...
Enter command: go
Enter value for IN instruction: 7
OUT instruction prints: 5040
HALT: 0,0,0
Halted
Enter command: quit
Simulation done.
```

1.8 C-MINUS: A LANGUAGE FOR A COMPILER PROJECT

A more extensive language than TINY, suitable for a compiler project, is described in Appendix A. It is a considerably restricted subset of C, which we will call C-Minus. It contains integers, integer arrays, and functions (including procedures, or void func-

---

1. The **LDC** command also requires a register+offset format, but the register is ignored and the offset itself is loaded as a constant. This is due to the simple uniform format of the TM assembler.

tions). It has local and global (static) declarations and (simple) recursive functions. It has an if-statement and a while-statement. It lacks almost everything else. A program consists of a sequence of function and variable declarations. A **main** function must be declared last. Execution begins with a call to **main**.[2]

As an example of a program in C-Minus, in Figure 1.5 we write the factorial program of Figure 1.4 using a recursive function. Input/output in this program is provided by a **read** function and a **write** function that can be defined in terms of the standard C functions **scanf** and **printf**.

C-Minus is a more complex language than TINY, particularly in its code generation requirements, but the TM machine is still a reasonable target for its compiler. In Appendix A we provide guidance on how to modify and extend the TINY compiler to C-Minus.

Figure 1.5
A C-Minus program that outputs the factorial of its input

```
int fact( int x )
/* recursive factorial function */
{ if (x > 1)
    return x * fact(x-1);
  else
    return 1;
}

void main( void )
{ int x;
  x = read();
  if (x > 0) write( fact(x) );
}
```

EXERCISES

1.1 Pick a familiar compiler that comes packaged with a development environment, and list all of the companion programs that are available with the compiler together with a brief description of their functions.

1.2 Given the C assignment

```
a[i+1] = a[i] + 2
```

draw a parse tree and a syntax tree for the expression, using the similar example in Section 1.3 as a guide.

1.3 Compilation errors can be loosely divided into two categories: syntax errors and semantic errors. Syntax errors include missing or incorrectly placed tokens, such as the missing

---

2. For consistency with other functions in C-Minus, **main** is declared as a **void** function with a **void** parameter list. While this differs from ANSI C, many C compilers will accept this notation.

right parenthesis in the arithmetic expression **(2+3** . Semantic errors include incorrect types in expressions and undeclared variables (in most languages), such as the assignment **x = 2**, where **x** is an array variable.

a. Give two more examples of errors of each kind in a language of your choice.

b. Pick a compiler with which you are familiar and determine if it lists all syntax errors before semantic errors or if syntax and semantic errors are intermixed. What implication does this have for the number of passes?

1.4 This question assumes that you have a compiler that has an option to produce assembly language output.

a. Determine if your compiler performs constant folding optimizations.

b. A related but more advanced optimization is that of constant propagation: a variable that currently has a constant value is replaced by that value in expressions. For example, the code (in C syntax)

```
x = 4;
y = x + 2;
```

would, using constant propagation (and constant folding), be replaced by the code

```
x = 4;
y = 6;
```

Determine if your compiler performs constant propagation.

c. Give as many reasons as you can why constant propagation is more difficult than constant folding.

d. A situation related to constant propagation and constant folding is the use of named constants in a program. Using a named constant **x** instead of a variable, we can translate the above example as the following C code:

```
const int x = 4;
...
y = x + 2;
...
```

Determine if your compiler performs propagation/folding under these circumstances. How is this different from part (b)?

1.5 If your compiler will accept input directly from the keyboard, determine if your compiler reads the entire program before generating error messages or generates error messages as it encounters them. What implication does this have for the number of passes?

1.6 Describe the tasks performed by the following programs, and explain how these programs resemble or are related to compilers:

a. A language preprocessor   **b.** A pretty-printer   **c.** A text formatter

1.7 Suppose you have a Pascal-to-C translator written in C and a working C compiler. Use T-diagrams to describe the steps you would take to create a working Pascal compiler.

1.8 We have used an arrow $\Rightarrow$ to indicate the reduction of a pattern of two T-diagrams to a single T-diagram. We may consider this arrow to be a "reduction relation" and form its transitive closure $\Rightarrow *$, in which we allow a sequence of reductions to take place. Given the following diagram, in which letters stand for arbitrary languages, determine which languages must be equal for the reduction to be valid, and show the single reduction steps that make it valid:

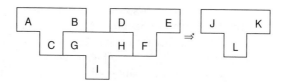

Give a practical example of the reduction described by this diagram.

1.9 An alternative to the method of porting a compiler described in Section 1.6 and Figure 1.3 is to use an interpreter for the intermediate code produced by the compiler and to do away with a back end altogether. Such a method is used by the **Pascal P-system**, which includes a Pascal compiler that produces P-code, a kind of assembly code for a "generic" stack machine, and a P-code interpreter that simulates the execution of the P-code. Both the Pascal compiler and the P-code interpreter are written in P-code.

a. Describe the steps needed to obtain a working Pascal compiler on an arbitrary machine, given a Pascal P-system.

b. Describe the steps needed to obtain a working native-code compiler from your system in (a) (i.e., a compiler that produces executable code for the host machine, rather than using the P-code interpreter).

1.10 The process of porting a compiler can be considered as two distinct operations: **retargeting** (modifying the compiler to produce target code for a new machine) and **rehosting** (modifying the compiler to run on a new machine). Discuss the distinctness of these two operations in terms of T-diagrams.

NOTES AND REFERENCES

Most of the topics mentioned in this chapter are treated in more detail in subsequent chapters, and the Notes and References of those chapters will provide suitable references. For instance, Lex is studied in Chapter 2; Yacc in Chapter 5; type checking, symbol tables, and attribute analysis in Chapter 6; code generation, three-address code, and P-code in Chapter 8; and error handling in Chapters 4 and 5.

A standard comprehensive reference on compilers is Aho [1986], particularly for theory and algorithms. A text that gives many useful implementation hints is Fischer and LeBlanc [1991]. Complete descriptions of C compilers can be found in Fraser and Hanson [1995] and Holub [1990]. A popular C/C++ compiler whose source code is widely available through the internet is the Gnu compiler. It is described in detail in Stallman [1994].

For a survey of programming language concepts, with information on their interactions with translators, see Louden [1993] or Sethi [1996].

A useful reference for automata theory from a mathematical view (as opposed to the practical view taken here) is Hopcroft and Ullman [1979]. More on the Chomsky hierarchy can also be found there (as well as in Chapter 3).

A description of the early FORTRAN compilers can be found in Backus [1957] and Backus [1981]. A description of an early Algol60 compiler can be found in Randell and Russell [1964]. Pascal compilers are described in Barron [1981], where a description of the Pascal P-system can also be found (Nori [1981]).

The Ratfor preprocessor mentioned in Section 1.2 is described in Kernighan [1975]. The T-diagrams of Section 1.6 were introduced by Bratman [1961].

This text focuses on standard translation techniques useful for the translation of most languages. Additional techniques may be needed for efficient translation of languages outside the main tradition of Algol-based imperative languages. In particular, the translation of functional languages such as ML and Haskell has been the source of many new techniques, some of which may become important general techniques in the future. Descriptions of these techniques can be found in Appel [1992], Peyton Jones [1992], and Peyton Jones [1987]. The latter contains a description of Hindley-Milner type checking (mentioned in Section 1.1).

Chapter 2

Scanning

The scanning, or **lexical analysis**, phase of a compiler has the task of reading the source program as a file of characters and dividing it up into tokens. Tokens are like the words of a natural language: each token is a sequence of characters that represents a unit of information in the source program. Typical examples are **keywords**, such as **if** and **while**, which are fixed strings of letters; **identifiers**, which are user-defined strings, usually consisting of letters and numbers and beginning with a letter; **special symbols**, such as the arithmetic symbols + and *; as well as a few multicharacter symbols, such as >= and <>. In each case a token represents a certain pattern of characters that is recognized, or matched, by the scanner from the beginning of the remaining input characters.

Since the task performed by the scanner is a special case of pattern matching, we need to study methods of pattern specification and recognition as they apply to the scanning process. These methods are primarily those of **regular expressions** and **finite automata**. However, a scanner is also the part of the compiler that handles the input of the source code, and since this input often involves a significant time overhead, the scanner must operate as efficiently as possible. Thus, we need also to pay close attention to the practical details of the scanner structure.

We divide the study of scanner issues as follows. First, we give an overview of the operation of a scanner and the structures and concepts involved. Then, we study regular expressions, a standard notation for representing the patterns in strings that form the lexical structure of a programming language. Following that, we study finite-state machines, or finite automata, which represent algorithms for recognizing string patterns given by regular expressions. We also study the process of constructing

31

finite automata out of regular expressions. We then turn to practical methods for writing programs that implement the recognition processes represented by finite automata, and we study a complete implementation of a scanner for the TINY language. Finally, we study the way the process of producing a scanner program can be automated through the use of a scanner generator, and we repeat the implementation of a scanner for TINY using Lex, which is a standard scanner generator available for use on Unix and other systems.

2.1 THE SCANNING PROCESS

It is the job of the scanner to read characters from the source code and form them into logical units to be dealt with by further parts of the compiler (usually the parser). The logical units the scanner generates are called **tokens**, and forming characters into tokens is much like forming characters into words in an English sentence and deciding which word is meant. In this it resembles the task of spelling.

Tokens are logical entities that are usually defined as an enumerated type. For example, tokens might be defined in C as[1]

```
typedef enum
    {IF,THEN,ELSE,PLUS,MINUS,NUM,ID,...}
    TokenType;
```

Tokens fall into several categories. These include the **reserved words**, such as **IF** and **THEN**, which represent the strings of characters "if" and "then." A second category is that of **special symbols**, such as the arithmetic symbols **PLUS** and **MINUS**, which represent the characters "+" and "−." Finally, there are tokens that can represent multiple strings. Examples are **NUM** and **ID**, which represent numbers and identifiers.

Tokens as logical entities must be clearly distinguished from the strings of characters that they represent. For example, the reserved word token **IF** must be distinguished from the string of two characters "if" that it represents. To make this distinction clearer, the string of characters represented by a token is sometimes called its **string value** or its **lexeme**. Some tokens have only one lexeme: reserved words have this property. A token may represent potentially infinitely many lexemes, however. Identifiers, for example, are all represented by the single token **ID**, but they have many different string values representing their individual names. These names cannot be ignored, since a compiler must keep track of them in a symbol table. Thus, a scanner must also construct the string values of at least some of the tokens. Any value associated to a token is called

---

1. In a language without enumerated types we would have to define tokens directly as symbolic numeric values. Thus, in old-style C one sometimes sees the following:

```
#define IF 256
#define THEN 257
#define ELSE 258
...
```

(These numbers begin at 256 to avoid confusion with numeric ASCII values.)

an **attribute** of the token, and the string value is an example of an attribute. Tokens may also have other attributes. For example, a **NUM** token may have a string value attribute such as "32767," which consists of five numeric characters, but it will also have a numeric value attribute that consists of the actual value 32767 computed from its string value. In the case of a special symbol token such as **PLUS**, there is not only the string value "+" but also the actual arithmetic operation + that is associated with it. Indeed, the token symbol itself may be viewed as simply another attribute, and the token viewed as the collection of all of its attributes.

A scanner needs to compute at least as many attributes of a token as necessary to allow further processing. For example, the string value of a **NUM** token needs to be computed, but its numeric value need not be computed immediately, since it is computable from its string value. On the other hand, if its numeric value is computed, then its string value may be discarded. Sometimes the scanner itself may perform the operations necessary to record an attribute in the appropriate place, or it may simply pass on the attribute to a later phase of the compiler. For example, a scanner could use the string value of an identifier to enter it into the symbol table, or it could pass it along to be entered at a later stage.

Since the scanner will have to compute possibly several attributes for each token, it is often helpful to collect all the attributes into a single structured data type, which we could call a **token record**. Such a record could be declared in C as

```
typedef struct
    { TokenType tokenval;
      char * stringval;
      int numval;
    } TokenRecord;
```

or possibly as a union

```
typedef struct
    { TokenType tokenval;
      union
      { char * stringval;
        int numval;
      } attribute;
    } TokenRecord;
```

(which assumes that the string value attribute is needed only for identifiers and the numeric value attribute only for numbers). A more common arrangement is for the scanner to return the token value only and place the other attributes in variables where they can be accessed by other parts of the compiler.

Although the task of the scanner is to convert the entire source program into a sequence of tokens, the scanner will rarely do this all at once. Instead, the scanner will operate under the control of the parser, returning the single next token from the input on demand via a function that will have a declaration similar to the C declaration

```
TokenType getToken(void);
```

The **getToken** function declared in this manner will, when called, return the next token from the input, as well as compute additional attributes, such as the string value of the token. The string of input characters is usually not made a parameter to this function, but is kept in a buffer or provided by the system input facilities.

As an example of the operation of **getToken**, consider the following line of C source code, which we used as an example in Chapter 1:

```
a[index] = 4 + 2
```

Suppose that this line of code is stored in an input buffer as follows, with the next input character indicated by the arrow:

A call to **getToken** will now need to skip the next four blanks, recognize the string "a" consisting of the single character *a* as the next token, and return the token value **ID** as the next token, leaving the input buffer as follows:

Thus, a subsequent call to **getToken** will begin the recognition process again with the left bracket character.

We turn now to the study of methods for defining and recognizing patterns in strings of characters.

2.2   REGULAR EXPRESSIONS

Regular expressions represent patterns of strings of characters. A regular expression *r* is completely defined by the set of strings that it matches. This set is called the **language generated by the regular expression** and is written as $L(r)$. Here the word *language* is used only to mean "set of strings" and has (at least at this stage) no specific relationship to a programming language. This language depends, first, on the character set that is available. Generally, this will be the set of ASCII characters or some subset of it. Sometimes the set will be more general than the ASCII character set, in which case the set elements are referred to as **symbols**. This set of legal symbols is called the **alphabet** and is usually written as the Greek symbol Σ (sigma).

A regular expression *r* will also contain characters from the alphabet, but such characters have a different meaning: in a regular expression, all symbols indicate *patterns*. In this chapter, we will distinguish the use of a character as a pattern by writing all patterns in boldface. Thus, **a** is the character *a* used as a pattern.

Last, a regular expression r may contain characters that have special meanings. Such characters are called **metacharacters** or **metasymbols**. These generally may not be legal characters in the alphabet, or we could not distinguish their use as metacharacter from their use as a member of the alphabet. Often, however, it is not possible to require such an exclusion, and a convention must be used to differentiate the two possible uses of a metacharacter. In many situations this is done by using an **escape character** that "turns off" the special meaning of a metacharacter. Common escape characters are the backslash and quotes. Note that escape characters are themselves metacharacters, if they are also legal characters in the alphabet.

2.2.1   Definition of Regular Expressions

We are now in a position to describe the meaning of regular expressions by stating which languages are generated by each pattern. We do this in several stages. First, we describe the set of basic regular expressions, which consist of individual symbols. Then, we describe operations that generate new regular expressions from existing ones. This is similar to the way arithmetic expressions are constructed: the basic arithmetic expressions are the numbers, such as 43 and 2.5. Then arithmetic operations, such as addition and multiplication, can be used to form new expressions from existing ones, as in 43 * 2.5 and 43 * 2.5 + 1.4.

The group of regular expressions that we describe here is minimal in the sense that it contains only the essential operations and metasymbols. Later we will consider extensions to this minimal set.

Basic Regular Expressions   These are just the single characters from the alphabet, which match themselves. Given any character a from the alphabet Σ, we indicate that the regular expression **a** matches the character a by writing $L(\mathbf{a}) = \{a\}$. There are two additional symbols that we will need in special situations. We need to be able to indicate a match of the **empty string**, that is, the string that contains no characters at all. We use the symbol ε (epsilon) to denote the empty string, and we define the metasymbol $\boldsymbol{\varepsilon}$ (boldface ε) by setting $L(\boldsymbol{\varepsilon}) = \{\varepsilon\}$. We also occasionally need to be able to write a symbol that matches no string at all, that is, whose language is the **empty set**, which we write as $\{\}$. We use the symbol $\boldsymbol{\phi}$ for this, and we write $L(\boldsymbol{\phi}) = \{\}$. Note the difference between $\{\}$ and $\{\varepsilon\}$: the set $\{\}$ contains no strings at all, while the set $\{\varepsilon\}$ contains the single string consisting of no characters.

Regular Expression Operations   There are three basic operations in regular expressions: (1) choice among alternatives, which is indicated by the metacharacter | (vertical bar); (2) concatenation, which is indicated by juxtaposition (without a metacharacter); and (3) repetition or "closure," which is indicated by the metacharacter *****. We discuss each of these in turn, giving the corresponding set construction for the languages of matched strings.

Choice Among Alternatives   If r and s are regular expressions, then $r|s$ is a regular expression which matches any string that is matched either by r or by s. In terms of languages, the language of $r|s$ is the **union** of the languages of r and s, or $L(r|s) = L(r) \cup L(s)$. As a simple example, consider the regular expression **a** | **b**: it matches either of the characters a or b, that is, $L(\mathbf{a} | \mathbf{b}) = L(\mathbf{a}) \cup L(\mathbf{b}) = \{a\} \cup \{b\} = \{a, b\}$. As a second example, the regular expression **a** | **ε** matches either the single character a or the empty string (consisting of no characters). In other words, $L(\mathbf{a} | \mathbf{ε}) = \{a, \varepsilon\}$.

Choice can be extended to more than one alternative, so that, for example, $L(\mathbf{a} | \mathbf{b} | \mathbf{c} | \mathbf{d}) = \{a, b, c, d\}$. We also sometimes write long sequences of choices with dots, as in **a** | **b** | **...** | **z**, which matches any of the lowercase letters a through z.

Concatenation   The concatenation of two regular expressions r and s is written as rs, and it matches any string that is the concatenation of two strings, the first of which matches r and the second of which matches s. For example, the regular expression **ab** matches only the string ab, while the regular expression **(a** | **b)c** matches the strings ac and bc. (The use of parentheses as metacharacters in this regular expression will be explained shortly.)

We can describe the effect of concatenation in terms of generated languages by defining the concatenation of two sets of strings. Given two sets of strings S_1 and S_2, the concatenated set of strings $S_1 S_2$ is the set of strings of S_1 appended by all the strings of S_2. For example, if $S_1 = \{aa, b\}$ and $S_2 = \{a, bb\}$, then $S_1 S_2 = \{aaa, aabb, ba, bbb\}$. Now the concatenation operation for regular expressions can be defined as follows: $L(rs) = L(r)L(s)$. Thus (using our previous example), $L((\mathbf{a} | \mathbf{b})\mathbf{c}) = L(\mathbf{a} | \mathbf{b})L(\mathbf{c}) = \{a, b\}\{c\} = \{ac, bc\}$.

Concatenation can also be extended to more than two regular expressions: $L(r_1 r_2 \ldots r_n) = L(r_1)L(r_2) \ldots L(r_n) =$ the set of strings formed by concatenating all strings from each of $L(r_1), \ldots, L(r_n)$.

Repetition   The repetition operation of a regular expression, sometimes also called **(Kleene) closure**, is written $r\mathbf{*}$, where r is a regular expression. The regular expression $r\mathbf{*}$ matches any finite concatenation of strings, each of which matches r. For example, **a*** matches the strings $\varepsilon, a, aa, aaa, \ldots$. (It matches ε because ε is the concatenation of *no* strings that match **a**.) We can define the repetition operation in terms of generated languages by defining a similar operation * for sets of strings. Given a set S of strings, let

$$S^* = \{\varepsilon\} \cup S \cup SS \cup SSS \cup \ldots$$

This is an infinite set union, but each element in it is a finite concatenation of strings from S. Sometimes the set S^* is written as follows:

$$S^* = \bigcup_{n=0}^{\infty} S^n$$

where $S^n = S \ldots S$ is the concatenation of S n-times. ($S^0 = \{\varepsilon\}$.)

Now we can define the repetition operation for regular expressions as follows:

$$L(r\mathbf{*}) = L(r)^*$$

As an example, consider the regular expression **(a|bb)***. (Again, the reason for the parentheses as metacharacters will be explained later.) This regular expression matches any of the following strings: ε, *a*, *bb*, *aa*, *abb*, *bba*, *bbbb*, *aaa*, *aabb*, and so on. In terms of languages, $L(\textbf{(a|bb)*}) = L(\textbf{a|bb})^* = \{a, bb\}^* = \{\varepsilon, a, bb, aa, abb, bba, bbbb, aaa, aabb, abba, abbbb, bbaa, \ldots\}$.

Precedence of Operations and Use of Parentheses   The foregoing description neglected the question of the precedence of the choice, concatenation, and repetition operations. For example, given the regular expression **a|b***, should we interpret this as **(a|b)*** or as **a|(b*)**? (There is a significant difference, since $L(\textbf{(a|b)*}) = \{\varepsilon, a, b, aa, ab, ba, bb, \ldots\}$, while $L(\textbf{a|(b*)}) = \{\varepsilon, a, b, bb, bbb, \ldots\}$.) The standard convention is that repetition should have higher precedence, so that the second interpretation is the correct one. Indeed, among the three operations, ***** is given the highest precedence, concatenation is given the next highest, and **|** is given the lowest. Thus, for example, **a|bc*** is interpreted as **a|(b(c*))**, and **ab|c*d** is interpreted as **(ab)|((c*)d)**.

When we wish to indicate a different precedence, we must use parentheses to do so. This is the reason we had to write **(a|b)c** to indicate that the choice operation should be given higher precedence than concatenation, for otherwise **a|bc** is interpreted as matching either *a* or *bc*. Similarly, without parentheses **(a|bb)*** would be interpreted as **a|bb***, which matches *a*, *b*, *bb*, *bbb*, ... This use of parentheses is entirely analogous to their use in arithmetic, where $(3 + 4) * 5 = 35$, but $3 + 4 * 5 = 23$, since * is assumed to have higher precedence than +.

Names for Regular Expressions   Often, it is helpful as a notational simplification to give a name to a long regular expression, so that we do not have to write the expression itself each time we wish to use it. As an example, if we want to develop a regular expression for a sequence of one or more numeric digits, then we could write

$$\textbf{(0|1|2|} \ldots \textbf{|9)(0|1|2|} \ldots \textbf{|9)*}$$

or we could write

    digit digit*

where

    ***digit* = 0|1|2|** . . . **|9**

is a **regular definition** of the name ***digit***.

The use of a regular definition is a great convenience, but it does introduce the added complication that the name itself then becomes a metasymbol and a means must be found to distinguish the name from the concatenation of its characters. In our case, we have made that distinction by using italics for the name. Note that a name cannot be used in its own definition (i.e., recursively)—we must be able to remove names by successively replacing them with the regular expressions for which they stand.

Before considering a series of examples to elaborate our definition of regular expressions, we collect all the pieces of the definition of a regular expression together.

Definition

A **regular expression** is one of the following:

1. A **basic** regular expression, consisting of a single character **a**, where a is from an alphabet Σ of legal characters; the metacharacter ε; or the metacharacter ϕ. In the first case, $L(\mathbf{a}) = \{a\}$; in the second, $L(\varepsilon) = \{\varepsilon\}$; in the third, $L(\phi) = \{\}$.

2. An expression of the form $\mathbf{r} \,|\, \mathbf{s}$, where r and s are regular expressions. In this case, $L(\mathbf{r} \,|\, \mathbf{s}) = L(r) \cup L(s)$.

3. An expression of the form rs, where r and s are regular expressions. In this case, $L(rs) = L(r)L(s)$.

4. An expression of the form $r\mathbf{*}$, where r is a regular expression. In this case, $L(r\mathbf{*}) = L(r)^*$.

5. An expression of the form (r), where r is a regular expression. In this case, $L((r)) = L(r)$. Thus, parentheses do not change the language. They are used only to adjust the precedence of the operations.

We note that, in this definition, the precedence of the operations in (2), (3), and (4) is in reverse order of their listing; that is, | has lower precedence than concatenation and concatenation has lower precedence than *. We also note that this definition gives a metacharacter meaning to the six symbols ϕ, ε, |, *, (,).

In the remainder of this section, we consider a series of examples designed to elaborate on the definition we have just given. These are somewhat artificial in that they do not usually appear as token descriptions in a programming language. In Section 2.2.3, we consider some common regular expressions that often appear as tokens in programming languages.

In the following examples, there generally is an English description of the strings to be matched, and the task is to translate the description into a regular expression. This situation, where a language manual contains descriptions of the tokens, is the most common one facing compiler writers. Occasionally, it may be necessary to reverse the direction, that is, move from a regular expression to an English description, so we also include a few exercises of this kind.

Example 2.1

Consider the simple alphabet consisting of just three alphabetic characters: $\Sigma = \{a, b, c\}$. Consider the set of all strings over this alphabet that contain exactly one b. This set is generated by the regular expression

```
(a|c)*b(a|c)*
```

Note that, even though **b** appears in the center of the regular expression, the letter b need not be in the center of the string being matched. Indeed, the repetition of a or c before and after the b may occur different numbers of times. Thus, all the following strings are matched by the above regular expression: b, abc, $abaca$, $baaaac$, $ccbaca$, $cccccb$. §

Example 2.2   With the same alphabet as before, consider the set of all strings that contain at most one *b*. A regular expression for this set can be obtained by using the solution to the previous example as one alternative (matching those strings with exactly one *b*) and the regular expression **(a|c)*** as the other alternative (matching no *b*'s at all). Thus, we have the following solution:

(a|c)*|(a|c)*b(a|c)*

An alternative solution would allow either *b* or the empty string to appear between the two repetitions of *a* or *c*:

(a|c)*(b|ε)(a|c)*

This example brings up an important point about regular expressions: the same language may be generated by many different regular expressions. Usually, we try to find as simple a regular expression as possible to describe a set of strings, though we will never attempt to prove that we have in fact found the "simplest"—for example, the shortest. There are two reasons for this. First, it rarely comes up in practical situations, where there is usually one standard "simplest" solution. Second, when we study methods for recognizing regular expressions, the algorithms there will be able to simplify the recognition process without bothering to simplify the regular expression first.   §

Example 2.3   Consider the set of strings *S* over the alphabet $\Sigma = \{a, b\}$ consisting of a single *b* surrounded by the same number of *a*'s:

$$S = \{b, aba, aabaa, aaabaaa, \ldots\} = \{a^n ba^n | n \neq 0\}$$

This set cannot be described by a regular expression. The reason is that the only repetition operation we have is the closure operation *****, which allows any number of repetitions. So if we write the expression **a*ba*** (about as close as we can get to a regular expression for *S*), then there is no guarantee that the number of *a*'s before and after the *b* will be the same. We express this by saying that "regular expressions can't count." To give a mathematical proof of this fact, however, would require the use of a famous theorem about regular expressions called the **pumping lemma**, which is studied in automata theory, but which we will not mention further here.

Clearly, not all sets of strings that we can describe in simple terms can be generated by regular expressions. A set of strings that *is* the language for a regular expression is, therefore, distinguished from other sets by calling it a **regular set**. Occasionally, nonregular sets appear as strings in programming languages that need to be recognized by a scanner. These are usually dealt with when they arise, and we will return to this matter again briefly in the section on practical scanner considerations.   §

Example 2.4   Consider the strings over the alphabet $\Sigma = \{a, b, c\}$ that contain no two consecutive *b*'s. Thus, between any two *b*'s there must be at least one *a* or *c*. We build up a regular expression for this set in several stages. First, we can force an *a* or *c* to come *after* every *b* by writing

(b(a|c))*

We can combine this with the expression **(a|c)***, which matches strings that have no *b*'s at all, and write

((a|c)*|(b(a|c))*)*

or, noting that $(r*|s*)*$ matches the same strings as $(r|s)*$

((a|c)|(b(a|c)))*

or

(a|c|ba|bc)*

(Warning! This is not yet the correct answer.)

The language generated by this regular expression does, indeed, have the property we seek, namely, that there are no two consecutive *b*'s (but isn't quite correct yet). Occasionally, we should prove such assertions, so we sketch a proof that all strings in $L(($**a|c|ba|bc**$)*)$ contain no two consecutive *b*'s. The proof is by induction on the length of the string (i.e., the number of characters in the string). Clearly, it is true for all strings of length 0, 1, or 2: these strings are precisely the strings ε, *a*, *c*, *aa*, *ac*, *ca*, *cc*, *ba*, *bc*. Now, assume it is true for all strings in the language of length $i < n$, and let *s* be a string in the language of length $n > 2$. Then, *s* contains more than one of the non-ε strings just listed, so $s = s_1 s_2$, where s_1 and s_2 are also in the language and are not ε. Hence, by the induction assumption, both s_1 and s_2 have no two consecutive *b*'s. Thus, the only way *s* itself could have two consecutive *b*'s would be for s_1 to end with a *b* and for s_2 to begin with a *b*. But this is impossible, since no string in the language can end with a *b*.

This last fact that we used in the proof sketch—that no string generated by the preceding regular expression can end with a *b*—also shows why our solution is not yet quite correct: it does not generate the strings *b*, *ab*, and *cb*, which contain no two consecutive *b*'s. We fix this by adding an optional trailing *b*, as follows:

(a|c|ba|bc)*(b|ε)

Note that the mirror image of this regular expression also generates the given language

(b|ε)(a|c|ab|cb)*

We could also generate this same language by writing

(*notb*|b *notb*)*(b|ε)

where ***notb*** = **a|c**. This is an example of the use of a name for a subexpression. This solution is in fact preferable in cases where the alphabet is large, since the definition of ***notb*** can be adjusted to include all characters except *b*, without complicating the original expression.   **§**

Example 2.5

This example is one where we are given the regular expression and are asked to determine a concise English description of the language it generates. Consider the alphabet $\Sigma = \{a, b, c\}$ and the regular expression

((b|c)*a(b|c)*a)*(b|c)*

This generates the language of all strings containing an even number of a's. To see this, consider the expression inside the outer left repetition:

(b|c)*a(b|c)*a

This generates those strings ending in a that contain exactly two a's (any number of b's and c's can appear before or between the two a's). Repeating these strings gives all strings ending in a whose number of a's is a multiple of 2 (i.e., even). Tacking on the repetition **(b|c)*** at the end (as in the previous example) gives the desired result.

We note that this regular expression could also be written as

(*nota* a nota* a*)* *nota** §

2.2.2   Extensions to Regular Expressions

We have given a definition of regular expressions that uses a minimal set of operations common to all applications, and we could limit ourselves to using only the three basic operations (together with parentheses) in all our examples. However, we have already seen in the examples so far that writing regular expressions using only these operators is sometimes unwieldy, creating regular expressions that are more complicated than they would be if a more expressive set of operations were available. For example, it would be useful to have a notation for a match of any character (we now have to list every character in the alphabet in a long alternative). In addition, it would help to have a regular expression for a range of characters and a regular expression for all characters except one character.

In the following paragraphs we will describe some extensions to the standard regular expressions already discussed, with corresponding new metasymbols, that cover these and similar common situations. In most of these cases no common terminology exists, so we will use a notation similar to that used by the scanner generator Lex, which is described later in this chapter. Indeed, many of the situations we are about to describe will appear again in our description of Lex. Not all applications that use regular expressions will include these operations, however, and even when they do, a different notation may be used.

We now proceed to our list of new operations.

ONE OR MORE REPETITIONS

Given a regular expression r, repetition of r is described using the standard closure operation, written $r*$. This allows r to be repeated 0 or more times. A typical situation that arises is the need for *one* or more repetitions instead of none, which guarantees that at least one string matching r appears, disallowing the empty string ε. An example is that of a natural number, where we want a sequence of digits, but we want at least one digit to appear. For example, if we want to match binary numbers, we could write **(0|1)***, but this will also match the empty string, which is not a number. We could, of course, write

(0|1)(0|1)*

but this situation occurs often enough that a relatively standard notation has been developed for it that uses **+** instead of *****: *r+* indicates one or more repetitions of *r*. Thus, our previous regular expression for binary numbers can now be written

(0|1)+

ANY CHARACTER

A common situation is the need to match any character in the alphabet. Without a special operation this requires that every character in the alphabet be listed in an alternative. A typical metacharacter that is used to express a match of any character is the period "**.**", which does not require that the alphabet actually be written out. Using this metacharacter, we can write a regular expression for all strings that contain at least one *b* as follows:

.*b.*

A RANGE OF CHARACTERS

Often, we need to write a range of characters, such as all lowercase letters or all digits. We have done this up to now by using the notation **a|b|...|z** for the lowercase letters or **0|1|...|9** for the digits. An alternative is to have a special notation for this situation, and a common one is to use square brackets and a hyphen, as in **[a-z]** for the lowercase letters and **[0-9]** for the digits. This can also be used for individual alternatives, so that **a|b|c** can be written as **[abc]**. Multiple ranges can be included as well, so that **[a-zA-Z]** represents all lowercase and uppercase letters. This general notation is referred to as **character classes**. Note that this notation may depend on the underlying order of the character set. For example, writing **[A-Z]** assumes that the characters *B*, *C*, and so on come between the characters *A* and *Z* (a reasonable assumption) and that *only* the uppercase characters are between *A* and *Z* (true for the ASCII character set). Writing **[A-z]** will *not* match the same characters as **[A-Za-z]**, however, even in the ASCII character set.

ANY CHARACTER NOT IN A GIVEN SET

As we have seen, it is often helpful to be able to exclude a single character from the set of characters to be matched. This can be achieved by designating a metacharacter to indicate the "not" or complement operation on a set of alternatives. For examples, a standard character representing "not" in logic is the tilde character **~**, and we could write a regular expression for a character in the alphabet that is not *a* as **~a** and a character that is not either *a* or *b* or *c* as

~(a|b|c)

An alternative to this notation is used in Lex, where the carat character **^** is used in conjunction with the character classes just described to form complements. For example, any character that is not *a* is written as **[^a]**, and any character that is not *a* or *b* or *c* is written as

[^abc]

OPTIONAL SUBEXPRESSIONS

A final common occurrence is for strings to contain optional parts that may or may not appear in any particular string. For example, a number may or may not have a leading sign, such as **+** or **-**. We can use alternatives to express this, as in the regular definitions

```
natural = [0-9]+
signedNatural = natural | + natural | - natural
```

This can quickly become cumbersome, however, and we introduce the question mark metacharacter *r***?** to indicate that strings matched by *r* are optional (or that 0 or 1 copies of *r* are present). Thus, the leading sign example becomes

```
natural = [0-9]+
signedNatural = (+|-)? natural
```

2.2.3   Regular Expressions for Programming Language Tokens

Programming language tokens tend to fall into several limited categories that are fairly standard across many different programming languages. One category is that of **reserved words**, sometimes also called **keywords**, which are fixed strings of alphabetic characters that have special meaning in the language. Examples include **if**, **while**, and **do** in such languages as Pascal, C, and Ada. Another category consists of the **special symbols**, including arithmetic operators, assignment, and equality. These can be a single character, such as **=**, or multiple characters, such as **:=** or **++**. A third category consists of **identifiers**, which commonly are defined to be sequences of letters and digits beginning with a letter. A final category consists of **literals** or **constants**, which can include numeric constants such as 42 and 3.14159, string literals such as "hello, world," and characters such as "a" and "b." We describe typical regular expressions for some of these here and discuss a few other issues related to the recognition of tokens. More detail on practical recognition issues appears later in the chapter.

Numbers   Numbers can be just sequences of digits (natural numbers), or decimal numbers, or numbers with an exponent (indicated by an e or E). For example, 2.71E-2 represents the number .0271. We can write regular definitions for these numbers as follows:

```
nat = [0-9]+
signedNat = (+|-)? nat
number = signedNat("." nat)?(E signedNat)?
```

Here we have written the decimal point inside quotes to emphasize that it should be matched directly and not be interpreted as a metacharacter.

Reserved Words and Identifiers   Reserved words are the simplest to write as regular expressions: they are represented by their fixed sequences of characters. If we wanted to collect all the reserved words into one definition, we could write something like

> **reserved = if | while | do | ...**

Identifiers, on the other hand, are strings of characters that are not fixed. Typically, an identifier must begin with a letter and contain only letters and digits. We can express this in terms of regular definitions as follows:

> **letter = [a-zA-Z]**
> **digit = [0-9]**
> **identifier = letter(letter|digit)***

Comments   Comments typically are ignored during the scanning process.[2] Nevertheless, a scanner must recognize comments and discard them. Thus, we will need to write regular expressions for comments, even though a scanner may have no explicit constant token (we could call these **pseudotokens**). Comments can have a number of different forms. Typically, they are either free format and surrounded by delimiters such as

> **{this is a Pascal comment}**
> **/* this is a C comment */**

or they begin with a specified character or characters and continue to the end of the line, as in

> **; this is a Scheme comment**
> **-- this is an Ada comment**

It is not hard to write a regular expression for comments that have single-character delimiters, such as the Pascal comment, or for those that reach from some specified character(s) to the end of the line. For example, the Pascal comment case can be written as

> **{(~})*}**

where we have written **~}** to indicate "not **}**" and where we have assumed that the character **}** has no meaning as a metacharacter. (A different expression must be written for Lex, which we discuss later in this chapter.) Similarly, an Ada comment can be matched by the regular expression

> **--(~newline)***

---

2. Sometimes they can contain compiler directives.

in which we assume that **newline** matches the end of a line (writable as **\n** on many systems), that the "**-**" character has no meaning as a metacharacter, and that the trailing end of the line is not included in the comment itself. (We will see how to write this in Lex in Section 2.6.)

It is much more difficult to write down a regular expression for the case of delimiters that are more than one character in length, such as C comments. To see this, consider the set of strings *ba. . .*(no appearances of *ab*)*. . .ab* (we use *ba. . .ab* instead of the C delimiters /*. . .*/, since the asterisk, and sometimes the forward slash, is a metacharacter that requires special handling). We cannot simply write

    ba(~(ab))*ab

because the "not" operator is usually restricted to single characters rather than strings of characters. We can try to write out a definition for **~(ab)** using **~a**, **~b**, and **~(a|b)**, but this is not trivial. One solution is

    b*(a*~(a|b)b*)*a*

but this is difficult to read (and to prove correct). Thus, a regular expression for C comments is so complicated that it is almost never written in practice. In fact, this case is usually handled by ad hoc methods in actual scanners, which we will see later in this chapter.

Finally, another complication in recognizing comments is that, in some programming languages, comments can be nested. For example, Modula-2 allows comments of the form

    (* this is (* a Modula-2 *) comment *)

Comment delimiters must be paired exactly in such nested comments, so that the following is not a legal Modula-2 comment:

    (* this is (* illegal in Modula-2 *)

Nesting of comments requires the scanner to count the numbers of delimiters. But we have noted in Example 2.3 (Section 2.2.1) that regular expressions cannot express counting operations. In practice, we use a simple counter scheme as an ad hoc solution to this problem (see the exercises).

Ambiguity, White Space, and Lookahead   Frequently, in the description of programming language tokens using regular expressions, some strings can be matched by several different regular expressions. For example, strings such as **if** and **while** could be either identifiers or keywords. Similarly, the string **<>** might be interpreted as representing either two tokens ("less than" and "greater than") or a single token ("not equal to"). A programming language definition must state which interpretation is to be observed, and the regular expressions themselves cannot do this. Instead, a language definition must give **disambiguating rules** that will imply which meaning is meant for each such case.

Two typical rules that handle the examples just given are the following. First, when a string can be either an identifier or a keyword, keyword interpretation is generally preferred. This is implied by using the term **reserved word**, which means simply a keyword that cannot also be an identifier. Second, when a string can be a single token or a sequence of several tokens, the single-token interpretation is typically preferred. This preference is often referred to as the **principle of longest substring**: the longest string of characters that could constitute a single token at any point is assumed to represent the next token.[3]

An issue that arises with the use of the principle of longest substring is the question of **token delimiters**, or characters that imply that a longer string at the point where they appear cannot represent a token. Characters that are unambiguously part of other tokens are delimiters. For example, in the string **xtemp=ytemp**, the equal sign delimits the identifier **xtemp**, since **=** cannot appear as part of an identifier. Blanks, newlines, and tab characters are generally also assumed to be token delimiters: **while x ...** is thus interpreted as containing the two tokens representing the reserved word **while** and the identifier with name **x**, since a blank separates the two character strings. In this situation it is often helpful to define a white space pseudotoken, similar to the comment pseudotoken, which simply serves the scanner internally to distinguish other tokens. Indeed, comments themselves usually serve as delimiters, so that, for example, the C code fragment

```
do/**/if
```

represents the two reserved words **do** and **if** rather than the identifier **doif**.

A typical definition of the white space pseudotoken in a programming language is

```
whitespace = (newline|blank|tab|comment)+
```

where the identifiers on the right stand for the appropriate characters or strings. Note that, other than acting as a token delimiter, white space is usually ignored. Languages that specify this behavior are called **free format**. Alternatives to free format include the fixed format of a few languages like FORTRAN and various uses of indentation, such as the **offside rule** (see the Notes and References section). A scanner for a free-format language must discard white space after checking for any token delimiting effects.

Delimiters end token strings but they are not part of the token itself. Thus, a scanner must deal with the problem of **lookahead**: when it encounters a delimiter, it must arrange that the delimiter is not removed from the rest of the input, either by returning it to the input string ("backing up") or by looking ahead before removing the character from the input. In most cases, it is only necessary to do this for a single character ("single-character lookahead"). For example, in the string **xtemp=ytemp**, the end of the identifier **xtemp** is found when the **=** is encountered, and the **=** must remain in the input, since it represents the next token to be recognized. Note also that lookahead may not be necessary to recognize a token. For example, the equal sign may be the only token that begins with the **=** character, in which case it can be recognized immediately without consulting the next character.

Sometimes a language may require more than single-character lookahead, and the scanner must be prepared to back up possibly arbitrarily many characters. In that case, buffering of input characters and marking places for backtracking become issues in the design of a scanner. (Some of these questions are dealt with later on in this chapter.)

---

3. Sometimes this is called the principle of "maximal munch."

FORTRAN is a good example of a language that violates many of the principles we have just been discussing. FORTRAN is a fixed-format language in which white space is removed by a preprocessor before translation begins. Thus, the FORTRAN line

```
I F ( X 2 . EQ. 0) THE N
```

would appear to a compiler as

```
IF(X2.EQ.0)THEN
```

so white space no longer functions as a delimiter. Also, there are no reserved words in FORTRAN, so all keywords can also be identifiers, and the position of the character string in each line of input is important in determining the token to be recognized. For example, the following line of code is perfectly correct FORTRAN:

```
IF(IF.EQ.0)THENTHEN=1.0
```

The first **IF** and **THEN** are keywords, while the second **IF** and **THEN** are identifiers representing variables. The effect of this is that a FORTRAN scanner must be able to backtrack to arbitrary positions within a line of code. Consider, for concreteness, the following well-known example:

```
DO99I=1,10
```

This initiates a loop comprising the subsequent code up to the line whose number is 99, with the same effect as the Pascal **for i := 1 to 10**. On the other hand, changing the comma to a period

```
DO99I=1.10
```

changes the meaning of the code completely: this assigns the value 1.1 to the variable with name **DO99I**. Thus, a scanner cannot conclude that the initial **DO** is a keyword until it reaches the comma (or period), in which case it may be forced to backtrack to the beginning of the line and start over.

2.3 FINITE AUTOMATA

Finite automata, or finite-state machines, are a mathematical way of describing particular kinds of algorithms (or "machines"). In particular, finite automata can be used to describe the process of recognizing patterns in input strings, and so can be used to construct scanners. There is also, of course, a strong relationship between finite automata and regular expressions, and we will see in the next section how to construct a finite automaton from a regular expression. Before we begin the study of finite automata proper, however, let us consider an elucidating example.

The pattern for identifiers as commonly defined in programming languages is given by the following regular definition (we assume that **letter** and **digit** have been already defined):

identifier = letter(letter|digit)*

This represents a string that begins with a letter and continues with any sequence of letters and/or digits. The process of recognizing such a string can be described by the diagram of Figure 2.1.

Figure 2.1

A finite automaton for identifiers

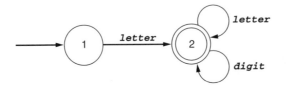

In that diagram, the circles numbered 1 and 2 represent **states**, which are locations in the process of recognition that record how much of the pattern has already been seen. The arrowed lines represent **transitions** that record a change from one state to another upon a match of the character or characters by which they are labeled. In the sample diagram, state 1 is the **start state**, or the state at which the recognition process begins. By convention, the start state is indicated by drawing an unlabeled arrowed line to it coming "from nowhere." State 2 represents the point at which a single letter has been matched (indicated by the transition from state 1 to state 2 labeled **letter**). Once in state 2, any number of letters and/or digits may be seen, and a match of these returns us to state 2. States that represent the end of the recognition process, in which we can declare success, are called **accepting states**, and are indicated by drawing a double-line border around the state in the diagram. There may be more than one of these. In the sample diagram state 2 is an accepting state, indicating that, after a letter is seen, any subsequent sequence of letters and digits (including none at all) represents a legal identifier.

The process of recognizing an actual character string as an identifier can now be indicated by listing the sequence of states and transitions in the diagram that are used in the recognition process. For example, the process of recognizing **xtemp** as an identifier can be indicated as follows:

$$\rightarrow 1 \xrightarrow{\ \mathbf{x}\ } 2 \xrightarrow{\ \mathbf{t}\ } 2 \xrightarrow{\ \mathbf{e}\ } 2 \xrightarrow{\ \mathbf{m}\ } 2 \xrightarrow{\ \mathbf{p}\ } 2$$

In this diagram, we have labeled each transition by the letter that is matched at each step.

2.3.1   Definition of Deterministic Finite Automata

Diagrams such as the one we have discussed are useful descriptions of finite automata, since they allow us to visualize easily the actions of the algorithm. Occasionally, however, it is necessary to have a more formal description of a finite automaton, and so we proceed now to give a mathematical definition. Most of the time, however, we will not need so abstract a view as this, and we will describe most examples in terms of the diagram alone. Other descriptions of finite automata are also possible, particularly tables, and these will be useful for turning the algorithms into working code. We will describe them as the need arises.

We should also note that what we have been describing are **deterministic** finite automata: automata where the next state is uniquely given by the current state and the current input character. A useful generalization of this is the **nondeterministic finite automaton**, which will be studied later on in this section.

Definition

A **DFA** (deterministic finite automaton) M consists of an alphabet Σ, a set of states S, a transition function $T: S \times \Sigma \to S$, a start state $s_0 \in S$, and a set of accepting states $A \subset S$. The language accepted by M, written $L(M)$, is defined to be the set of strings of characters $c_1 c_2 \ldots c_n$ with each $c_i \in \Sigma$ such that there exist states $s_1 = T(s_0, c_1)$, $s_2 = T(s_1, c_2), \ldots, s_n = T(s_{n-1}, c_n)$ with s_n an element of A (i.e., an accepting state).

We make the following notes about this definition. $S \times \Sigma$ refers to the Cartesian or cross product of S and Σ: the set of pairs (s, c), where $s \in S$ and $c \in \Sigma$. The function T records the transitions: $T(s, c) = s'$ if there is a transition from state s to state s' labeled by c. The corresponding piece of the diagram for M looks as follows:

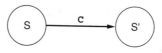

Acceptance as the existence of a sequence of states $s_1 = T(s_0, c_1)$, $s_2 = T(s_1, c_2), \ldots,$ $s_n = T(s_{n-1}, c_n)$ with s_n an accepting state thus means the same thing as the diagram

$$\to s_0 \xrightarrow{c_1} s_1 \xrightarrow{c_2} s_2 \longrightarrow \cdots \longrightarrow s_{n-1} \xrightarrow{c_n} s_n$$

We note a number of differences between the definition of a DFA and the diagram of the identifier example. First, we used numbers for the states in the identifier diagram, while the definition does not restrict the set of states to numbers. Indeed, we can use any system of identification we want for the states, including names. For example, we could write an equivalent diagram to that of Figure 2.1 as

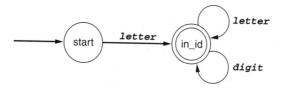

where we have now called the states **start** (since it is the start state) and in_id (since we have seen a letter and will be recognizing an identifier after any subsequent letters and numbers). The set of states for this diagram now becomes {start, in_id} instead of $\{1, 2\}$.

A second difference between the diagram and the definition is that we have not labeled the transitions with characters but with names representing a set of characters.

For instance, the name ***letter*** represents any letter of the alphabet according to the following regular definition:

    letter = [a-zA-Z]

This is a convenient extension of the definition, since it would be cumbersome to draw 52 separate transitions, one for each lowercase letter and one for each uppercase letter. We will continue to use this extension of the definition in the rest of the chapter.

A third and more essential difference between the definition and our diagram is that the definition represents transitions as a *function* $T: S \times \Sigma \to S$. This means that $T(s, c)$ must have a value *for every s and c*. But in the diagram we have $T(\text{start}, c)$ defined only if c is a letter, and $T(\text{in\_id}, c)$ is defined only if c is a letter or a digit. Where are the missing transitions? The answer is that they represent errors—that is, in recognizing an identifier we cannot accept any characters other than letters from the start state and letters or numbers after that.[4] The convention is that these **error transitions** are not drawn in the diagram but are simply assumed to always exist. If we were to draw them, the diagram for an identifier would look as in Figure 2.2.

Figure 2.2

A finite automaton for identifiers with error transitions

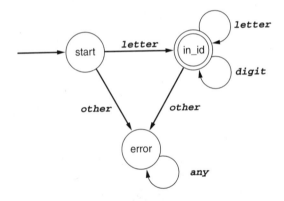

In that figure, we have labeled the new state **error** (since it represents an erroneous occurrence), and we have labeled the error transitions ***other***. By convention, ***other*** represents any character not appearing in any other transition from the state where it originates. Thus, the definition of ***other*** coming from the start state is

    other = ~letter

and the definition of ***other*** coming from the state in_id is

    other = ~(letter|digit)

---

4. In reality, these nonalphanumeric characters mean either that we do not have an identifier at all (if we are in the start state) or that we have encountered a delimiter that ends the recognition of an identifier (if we are in an accepting state). We will see how to handle these situations later in this section.

Note also that all transitions from the error state go back to itself (we have labeled these transitions **any** to indicate that any character results in this transition). Also, the error state is nonaccepting. Thus, once an error has occurred, we cannot escape from the error state, and we will never accept the string.

We now turn to a series of examples of DFAs, paralleling the examples of the previous section.

Example 2.6   The set of strings that contain exactly one *b* is accepted by the following DFA:

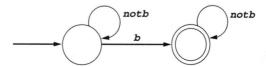

Note that we have not bothered to label the states. We will omit labels when it is not necessary to refer to the states by name.   §

Example 2.7   The set of strings that contain at most one *b* is accepted by the following DFA:

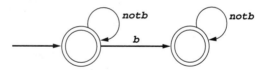

Note how this DFA is a modification of the DFA of the previous example, obtained by making the start state into a second accepting state.   §

Example 2.8   In the previous section we gave regular definitions for numeric constants in scientific notation as follows:

```
nat = [0-9]+
signedNat = (+|-)? nat
number = signedNat("." nat)?(E signedNat)?
```

We would like to write down DFAs for the strings matched by these definitions, but it is helpful to first rewrite them as follows:

```
digit = [0-9]
nat = digit+
signedNat = (+|-)? nat
number = signedNat("." nat)?(E signedNat)?
```

It is easy to write down a DFA for **nat** as follows (recall that **a+** = **aa*** for any **a**):

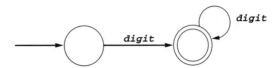

A **signedNat** is a little more difficult because of the optional sign. However, we may note that a **signedNat** begins either with a digit or a sign and a digit and then write the following DFA:

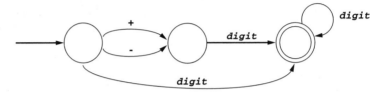

It is also easy to add the optional fractional part, as follows:

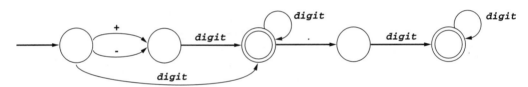

Note that we have kept both accepting states, reflecting the fact that the fractional part is optional.

Finally, we need to add the optional exponential part. To do this, we note that the exponential part must begin with the letter E and can occur only after we have reached either of the previous accepting states. The final diagram is given in Figure 2.3.

Figure 2.3   A finite automaton for floating-point numbers

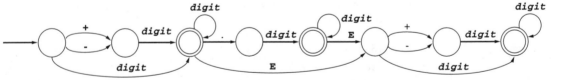

§

Example 2.9   Unnested comments can be described using DFAs. For example, comments surrounded by curly brackets are accepted by the following DFA:

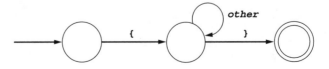

In this case ***other*** means all characters except the right curly bracket. This DFA corresponds to the regular expression **{ (~}) *}**, which we wrote down previously in Section 2.2.4.

We noted in that section that it was difficult to write down a regular expression for comments that are delimited by a sequence of two characters, such as C comments, which are of the form **/*...(no */s)...*/**. It is actually easier to write down a DFA that accepts such comments than it is to write a regular expression for them. A DFA for such C comments is given in Figure 2.4.

Figure 2.4

A finite automaton for C-style comments

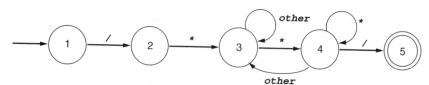

In that figure the ***other*** transition from state 3 to itself stands for all characters except *, while the ***other*** transition from state 4 to state 3 stands for all characters except * and /. We have numbered the states in this diagram for simplicity, but we could have given the states more meaningful names, such as the following (with the corresponding numbers in parentheses): start (1); entering_comment (2); in_comment (3); exiting_comment (4); and finish (5).

§

2.3.2 Lookahead, Backtracking, and Nondeterministic Automata

We have studied DFAs as a way of representing algorithms that accept character strings according to a pattern. As the reader may have already guessed, there is a strong relationship between a regular expression for a pattern and a DFA that accepts strings according to the pattern. We will explore this relationship in the next section. But, first, we need to study more closely the precise algorithms that DFAs represent, since we want eventually to turn these algorithms into the code for a scanner.

We have already noted that the diagram of a DFA does not represent everything a DFA needs but gives only an outline of its operation. Indeed, we saw that the mathematical definition implies that a DFA must have a transition for every state and character, and that those transitions that result in errors are usually left out of the diagram for the DFA. But even the mathematical definition does not describe every aspect of behavior of a DFA algorithm. For example, it does not specify what happens when an error does occur. It also does not specify the action that a program is to take upon reaching an accepting state, or even when matching a character during a transition.

A typical action that occurs when making a transition is to move the character from the input string to a string that accumulates the characters belonging to a single token (the token string value or lexeme of the token). A typical action when reaching an accepting state is to return the token just recognized, along with any associated attributes. A typical action when reaching an error state is to either back up in the input (backtracking) or to generate an error token.

Our original example of an identifier token exhibits much of the behavior that we wish to describe here, and so we return to the diagram of Figure 2.4. The DFA of that figure does not exhibit the behavior we want from a scanner for several reasons. First, the error state is not really an error at all, but represents the fact that either an identifier is not to be recognized (if we came from the start state) or a delimiter has been seen and we should now accept and generate an identifier token. Let us assume for the moment (which will in fact be correct behavior) that there are other transitions representing the nonletter transitions from the start state. Then we can indicate that a delimiter has been seen from the state in_id, and that an identifier token should be generated, by the diagram of Figure 2.5:

Figure 2.5

Finite automaton for an identifier with delimiter and return value

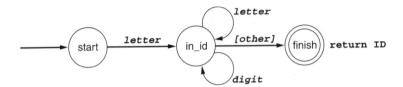

In the diagram we have surrounded the **other** transition with square brackets to indicate that the delimiting character should be considered lookahead, that is, that it should be returned to the input string and not consumed. In addition, the error state has become the accepting state in this diagram and there are no transitions out of the accepting state. This is what we want, since the scanner should recognize one token at a time and should begin again in its start state after each token is recognized.

This new diagram also expresses the principle of longest substring described in Section 2.2.4: the DFA continues to match letters and digits (in state in_id) until a delimiter is found. By contrast the old diagram allowed the DFA to accept at any point while reading an identifier string, something we certainly do not want to happen.

We turn our attention now to the question of how to arrive at the start state in the first place. In a typical programming language there are many tokens, and each token will be recognized by its own DFA. If each of these tokens begins with a different character, then it is easy to tie them together by simply uniting all of their start states into a single start state. For example, consider the tokens given by the strings $:=$, $<=$, and $=$. Each of these is a fixed string, and DFAs for them can be written as follows:

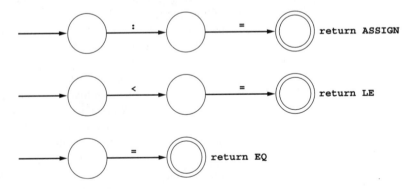

Since each of these tokens begins with a different character, we can simply identify their start states to get the following DFA:

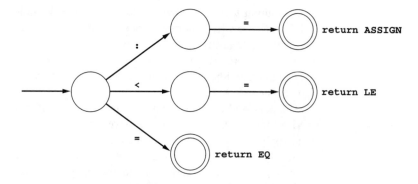

However, suppose we had several tokens that begin with the same character, such as <,
<=, and <>. Now we cannot simply write the following diagram, since it is not a
DFA (given a state and a character, there must always be a unique transition to a single new state):

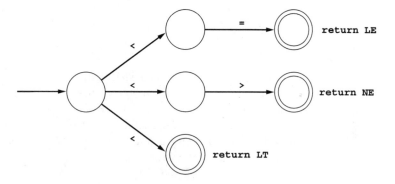

Instead, we must arrange it so that there is a unique transition to be made in each state,
such as in the following diagram:

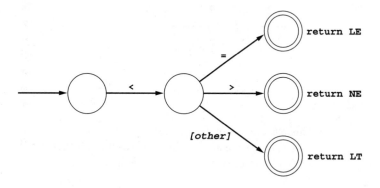

In principle, we should be able to combine all the tokens into one giant DFA in this
fashion. However, the complexity of such a task becomes enormous, especially if it is
done in an unsystematic way.

A solution to this problem is to expand the definition of a finite automaton to include the case where more than one transition from a state may exist for a particular character, while at the same time developing an algorithm for systematically turning these new, generalized finite automata into DFAs. We will describe these generalized automata here, while postponing the description of the translation algorithm until the next section.

The new kind of finite automaton is called a **nondeterministic finite automaton**, or **NFA** for short. Before we define it, we need one more generalization that will be useful in applying finite automata to scanners: the concept of the ε-transition.

An **ε-transition** is a transition that may occur without consulting the input string (and without consuming any characters). It may be viewed as a "match" of the empty string, which we have previously written as ε. In a diagram an ε-transition is written as though ε were actually a character:

This should not be confused with a match of the character ε in the input: if the alphabet includes such a character, it must be distinguished from the use of ε as a metacharacter to represent an ε-transition.

ε-transitions are somewhat counterintuitive, since they may occur "spontaneously," that is, without lookahead and without change to the input string, but they are useful in two ways. First, they can express a choice of alternatives in a way that does not involve combining states. For example, the choice of the tokens :=, <=, and = can be expressed by combining the automata for each token as follows:

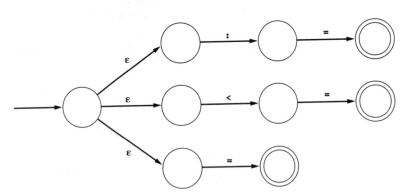

This has the advantage of keeping the original automata intact and only adding a new start state to connect them. The second advantage to ε-transitions is that they can explicitly describe a match of the empty string:

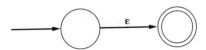

Of course, this is equivalent to the following DFA, which expresses that acceptance should occur without matching any characters:

But it is useful to have the previous, explicit notation.

We now proceed to a definition of a nondeterministic automaton. It is quite similar to that of a DFA, except that, according to the above discussion, we need to expand the alphabet Σ to include ε. We do this by writing $\Sigma \cup \{\varepsilon\}$ (the union of Σ and ε) where we used Σ before (this assumes that ε is not originally a member of Σ). We also need to expand the definition of T (the transition function) so that each character can lead to more than one state. We do this by letting the value of T be a *set* of states rather than a single state. For example, given the diagram

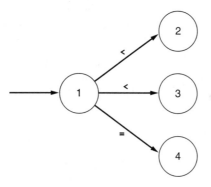

we have $T(1, <) = \{2, 3\}$. In other words, from state 1 we can move to either state 2 or state 3 on the input character $<$, and T becomes a function that maps state/symbol pairs to *sets of states*. Thus, the range of T is the **power set** of the set S of states (the set of all subsets of S); we write this as $\wp(S)$ (script p of S). We now state the definition.

Definition

An **NFA** (nondeterministic finite automaton) M consists of an alphabet Σ, a set of states S, a transition function $T: S \times (\Sigma \cup \{\varepsilon\}) \rightarrow \wp(S)$, a start state s_0 from S, and a set of accepting states A from S. The language accepted by M, written $L(M)$, is defined to be the set of strings of characters $c_1 c_2 \ldots c_n$ with each c_i from $\Sigma \cup \{\varepsilon\}$ such that there exist states s_1 in $T(s_0, c_1)$, s_2 in $T(s_1, c_2)$, $\ldots$, s_n in $T(s_{n-1}, c_n)$ with s_n an element of A.

Again, we need to note a few things about this definition. Any of the c_i in $c_1 c_2 \ldots c_n$ may be ε, and the string that is actually accepted is the string $c_1 c_2 \ldots c_n$ with the ε's removed (since the concatenation of s with ε is s itself). Thus, the string

$c_1 c_2 \ldots c_n$ may actually have fewer than n characters in it. Also, the sequence of states $s_1, \ldots, s_n$ are chosen from the *sets* of states $T(s_0, c_1), \ldots, T(s_{n-1}, c_n)$, and this choice will not always be uniquely determined. This is, in fact, why these automata are called *nondeterministic*: the sequence of transitions that accepts a particular string is not determined at each step by the state and the next input character. Indeed, arbitrary numbers of ε's can be introduced into the string at any point, corresponding to any number of ε-transitions in the NFA. Thus, an NFA does not represent an algorithm. However, it can be simulated by an algorithm that backtracks through every nondeterministic choice, as we will see later in this section.

First, however, we consider a couple of examples of NFAs.

Example 2.10   Consider the following diagram of an NFA.

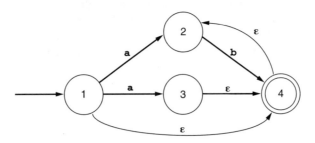

The string **abb** can be accepted by either of the following sequences of transitions:

$$\rightarrow 1 \xrightarrow{\ \mathbf{a}\ } 2 \xrightarrow{\ \mathbf{b}\ } 4 \xrightarrow{\ \varepsilon\ } 2 \xrightarrow{\ \mathbf{b}\ } 4$$

$$\rightarrow 1 \xrightarrow{\ \mathbf{a}\ } 3 \xrightarrow{\ \varepsilon\ } 4 \xrightarrow{\ \varepsilon\ } 2 \xrightarrow{\ \mathbf{b}\ } 4 \xrightarrow{\ \varepsilon\ } 2 \xrightarrow{\ \mathbf{b}\ } 4$$

Indeed the transitions from state 1 to state 2 on a, and from state 2 to state 4 on b, allow the machine to accept the string ab, and then, using the ε-transition from state 4 to state 2, all strings matching the regular expression **ab+**. Similarly, the transitions from state 1 to state 3 on a, and from state 3 to state 4 on ε, enable the acceptance of all strings matching **ab***. Finally, following the ε-transition from state 1 to state 4 enables the acceptance of all strings matching **b***. Thus, this NFA accepts the same language as the regular expression **ab+ | ab* | b***. A simpler regular expression that generates the same language is **(a | ε) b***. The following DFA also accepts this language:

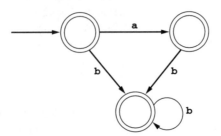

Example 2.11   Consider the following NFA:

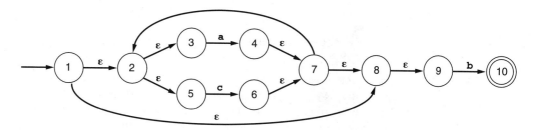

It accepts the string *acab* by making the following transitions:

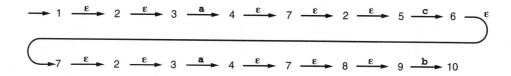

In fact, it is not hard to see that this NFA accepts the same language as that generated by the regular expression **(a|c)*b**.   §

2.3.3 Implementation of Finite Automata in Code

There are several ways to translate either a DFA or an NFA into code, and we will survey these in this section. Not all these methods will be useful for a compiler scanner, however, and the last two sections of this chapter will demonstrate the coding aspects appropriate for scanners in more detail.

Consider, again, our original example of a DFA that accepts identifiers consisting of a letter followed by a sequence of letters and/or digits, in its amended form that includes lookahead and the principle of longest substring (see Figure 2.5):

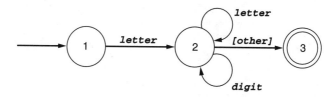

The first and easiest way to simulate this DFA is to write code in the following form:

```
{ starting in state 1 }
if the next character is a letter then
    advance the input;
    { now in state 2 }
    while the next character is a letter or a digit do
        advance the input; { stay in state 2 }
```

(continued)

```
   end while;
   { go to state 3 without advancing the input }
   accept;
else
   { error or other cases }
end if;
```

Such code uses the position in the code (nested within tests) to maintain the state implicitly, as we have indicated by the comments. This is reasonable if there are not too many states (requiring many levels of nesting), and if loops in the DFA are small. Code like this has been used to write small scanners. But there are two drawbacks to this method. The first is that it is ad hoc—that is, each DFA has to be treated slightly differently, and it is difficult to state an algorithm that will translate every DFA to code in this way. The second is that the complexity of the code increases dramatically as the number of states rises or, more specifically, as the number of different states along arbitrary paths rises. As one simple example of these problems, we consider the DFA from Example 2.9 as given in Figure 2.4 (page 53) that accepts C comments, which could be implemented by code in the following form:

```
{ state 1 }
if the next character is "/" then
   advance the input; { state 2 }
   if the next character is "*" then
      advance the input; { state 3 }
      done := false;
      while not done do
         while the next input character is not "*" do
            advance the input;
         end while;
         advance the input; { state 4 }
         while the next input character is "*" do
            advance the input;
         end while;
         if the next input character is "/" then
            done := true;
         end if;
         advance the input;
      end while;
      accept; { state 5 }
   else { other processing }
   end if;
else { other processing }
end if;
```

Notice the considerable increase in complexity, and the need to deal with the loop involving states 3 and 4 by using the Boolean variable *done*.

A substantially better implementation method is obtained by using a variable to maintain the current state and writing the transitions as a doubly nested case statement inside a loop, where the first case statement tests the current state and the nested second level tests the input character, given the state. For example, the previous DFA for identifiers can be translated into the code scheme of Figure 2.6.

Figure 2.6

Implementation of identifier
DFA using a state variable
and nested case tests.

```
state := 1; { start }
while state = 1 or 2 do
  case state of
   1:  case input character of
       letter : advance the input;
              state := 2;
       else state := . . . { error or other };
       end case;
   2:  case input character of
       letter, digit: advance the input;
                  state := 2; { actually unnecessary }
       else state := 3;
       end case;
   end case;
end while;
if state = 3 then accept else error ;
```

Notice how this code reflects the DFA directly: transitions correspond to assigning a new state to the *state* variable and advancing the input (except in the case of the "non-consuming" transition from state 2 to state 3).

Now the DFA for C comments (Figure 2.4) can be translated into the more readable code scheme of Figure 2.7. An alternative to this organization is to have the outer case based on the input character and the inner cases based on the current state (see the exercises).

In the examples we have just seen, the DFA has been "hardwired" right into the code. It is also possible to express the DFA as a data structure and then write "generic" code that will take its actions from the data structure. A simple data structure that is adequate for this purpose is a **transition table**, or two-dimensional array, indexed by state and input character that expresses the values of the transition function T:

	Characters in the alphabet c
States s	States representing transitions $T(s, c)$

As an example, the DFA for identifiers can be represented as the following transition table:

state \ input char	letter	digit	other
1	2		
2	2	2	3
3			

Figure 2.7

Implementation of DFA of
Figure 2.4

```
state := 1; { start }
while state = 1, 2, 3 or 4 do
  case state of
  1:  case input character of
      "/" : advance the input;
           state := 2;
      else state := ... { error or other };
      end case;
  2:  case input character of
      "*": advance the input;
           state := 3;
      else state := ... { error or other };
      end case;
  3:  case input character of
      "*": advance the input;
           state := 4;
      else advance the input { and stay in state 3 };
      end case;
  4:  case input character of
      "/" advance the input;
           state := 5;
      "*": advance the input; { and stay in state 4 }
      else advance the input;
           state := 3;
      end case;
  end case;
end while;
if state = 5 then accept else error ;
```

In this table, blank entries represent transitions that are not shown in the DFA diagram (i.e., they represent transitions to error states or other processing). We also assume that the first state listed is the start state. However, this table does not indicate which states are accepting and which transitions do not consume their inputs. This information can be kept either in the same data structure representing the table or in a separate data structure. If we add this information to the above transition table (using a separate column to indicate accepting states and brackets to indicate "noninput-consuming" transitions), we obtain the following table:

input char / state	letter	digit	other	Accepting
1	2			no
2	2	2	[3]	no
3				yes

As a second example of a transition table, we present the table for the DFA for C comments (our second example in the foregoing):

input char state	/	*	other	Accepting
1	2			no
2		3		no
3	3	4	3	no
4	5	4	3	no
5				yes

Now we can write code in a form that will implement any DFA, given the appropriate data structures and entries. The following code schema assumes that the transitions are kept in a transition array *T* indexed by states and input characters; that transitions that advance the input (i.e., those not marked with brackets in the table) are given by the Boolean array *Advance*, indexed also by states and input characters; and that accepting states are given by the Boolean array *Accept*, indexed by states. Here is the code scheme:

```
state := 1;
ch := next input character;
while not Accept[state] and not error(state) do
    newstate := T[state,ch];
    if Advance[state,ch] then ch := next input char;
    state := newstate;
end while;
if Accept[state] then accept;
```

Algorithmic methods such as we have just described are called **table driven**, since they use tables to direct the progress of the algorithm. Table-driven methods have certain advantages: the size of the code is reduced, the same code will work for many different problems, and the code is easier to change (maintain). The disadvantage is that the tables can become very large, causing a significant increase in the space used by the program. Indeed, much of the space in the arrays we have just described is wasted. Table-driven methods, therefore, often rely on table-compression methods such as sparse-array representations, although there is usually a time penalty to be paid for such compression, since table lookup becomes slower. Since scanners must be efficient, these methods are rarely used for them, though they may be used in scanner generator programs such as Lex. We will not study them further here.

Finally, we note that NFAs can be implemented in similar ways to DFAs, except that since NFAs are nondeterministic, there are potentially many different sequences of transitions that must be tried. Thus, a program that simulates an NFA must store up transitions that have not yet been tried and backtrack to them on failure. This is very similar to algorithms that attempt to find paths in directed graphs, except that the input string guides the search. Since algorithms that do a lot of backtracking tend to be inefficient, and a scanner must be as efficient as possible, we will not describe such algorithms further. Instead, the problem of simulating an NFA can be solved by using the method we study in the next section that converts an NFA into a DFA. We thus proceed to that section, where we will return briefly to the question of simulating an NFA.

2.4   FROM REGULAR EXPRESSIONS TO DFAs

In this section we will study an algorithm for translating a regular expression into a DFA. There also exists an algorithm for translating a DFA into a regular expression, so that the two notions are equivalent. However, because of the compactness of regular expressions, they are usually preferred to DFAs as token descriptions, and so scanner generation commonly begins with regular expressions and proceeds through the construction of a DFA to a final scanner program. For this reason, our interest will be only in an algorithm that performs this direction of the equivalence.

The simplest algorithm for translating a regular expression into a DFA proceeds via an intermediate construction, in which an NFA is derived from the regular expression, and then the NFA is used to construct an equivalent DFA. There exist algorithms that can translate a regular expression directly into a DFA, but they are more complex, and the intermediate construction is also of some interest. Thus, we concentrate on describing two algorithms, one that translates a regular expression into an NFA and a second that translates an NFA into a DFA. Combined with one of the algorithms to translate a DFA into a program described in the previous section, the process of constructing a scanner can be automated in three steps, as illustrated by the following picture:

2.4.1   From a Regular Expression
to an NFA

The construction we will describe is known as **Thompson's construction**, after its inventor. It uses ε-transitions to "glue together" the machines of each piece of a regular expression to form a machine that corresponds to the whole expression. Thus, the construction is inductive, and it follows the structure of the definition of a regular expression: we exhibit an NFA for each basic regular expression and then show how each regular expression operation can be achieved by connecting together the NFAs of the subexpressions (assuming these have already been constructed).

Basic Regular Expressions   A basic regular expression is of the form **a**, ε, or φ, where **a** represents a match of a single character from the alphabet, ε represents a match of the empty string, and φ represents a match of no strings at all. An NFA that is equivalent to the regular expression **a** (i.e., accepts precisely those strings in its language) is

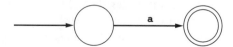

Similarly, an NFA that is equivalent to ε is

The case of the regular expression φ (which never occurs in practice in a compiler) is left as an exercise.

Concatenation We wish to construct an NFA equivalent to the regular expression *rs*, where *r* and *s* are regular expressions. We assume (inductively) that NFAs equivalent to *r* and *s* have already been constructed. We express this by writing

for the NFA corresponding to *r*, and similarly for *s*. In this drawing, the circle on the left inside the rounded rectangle indicates the start state, the double circle on the right indicates the accepting state, and the three dots indicate the states and transitions inside the NFA that are not shown. This picture assumes that the NFA corresponding to *r* has only one accepting state. This assumption will be justified if every NFA we construct has one accepting state. This is true for the NFAs of basic regular expressions, and it will be true for each of the following constructions.

We can now construct an NFA corresponding to *rs* as follows:

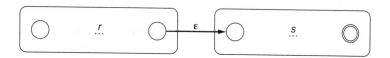

We have connected the accepting state of the machine of *r* to the start state of the machine of *s* by an ε-transition. The new machine has the start state of the machine of *r* as its start state and the accepting state of the machine of *s* as its accepting state. Clearly, this machine accepts $L(rs) = L(r)L(s)$ and so corresponds to the regular expression *rs*.

Choice Among Alternatives We wish to construct an NFA corresponding to *r*|*s* under the same assumptions as before. We do this as follows:

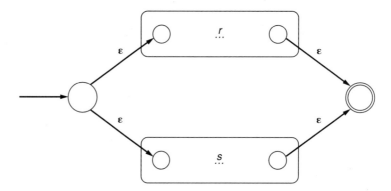

We have added a new start state and a new accepting state and connected them as shown using ε-transitions. Clearly, this machine accepts the language $L(r \mid s) = L(r) \cup L(s)$.

Repetition We want to construct a machine that corresponds to $r*$, given a machine that corresponds to r. We do this as follows:

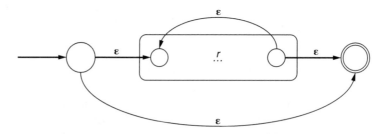

Here again we have added two new states, a start state and an accepting state. The repetition in this machine is afforded by the new ε-transition from the accepting state of the machine of r to its start state. This permits the machine of r to be traversed one or more times. To ensure that the empty string is also accepted (corresponding to zero repetitions of r), we must also draw an ε-transition from the new start state to the new accepting state.

This completes the description of Thompson's construction. We note that this construction is not unique. In particular, other constructions are possible when translating regular expression operations into NFAs. For example, in expressing concatenation rs, we could have eliminated the ε-transition between the machines of r and s and instead identified the accepting state of the machine of r with the start state of the machine of s, as follows:

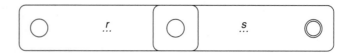

(This simplification depends, however, on the fact that in the other constructions, the accepting state has no transitions from it to other states—see the exercises.) Other simplifications are possible in the other cases. The reason we have expressed the translations as we have is that the machines are constructed according to very simple rules. First, each state has at most two transitions from it, and if there are two transitions, they must both be ε-transitions. Second, no states are deleted once they are constructed, and no transitions are changed except for the addition of transitions from the accepting state. These properties make it very easy to automate the process.

We conclude the discussion of Thompson's construction with a few examples.

Example 2.12   We translate the regular expression **ab|a** into an NFA according to Thompson's construction. We first form the machines for the basic regular expressions **a** and **b**:

We then form the machine for the concatenation **ab**:

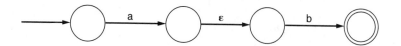

Now we form another copy of the machine for **a** and use the construction for choice to get the complete NFA for **ab|a**, which is shown in Figure 2.8.

Figure 2.8
NFA for the regular expression **ab|a** using Thompson's construction

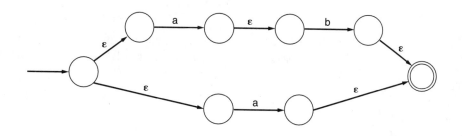

§

Example 2.13   We form the NFA of Thompson's construction for the regular expression **letter(letter|digit)***. As in the previous example, we form the machines for the regular expressions **letter** and **digit**:

We then form the machine for the choice **letter|digit**:

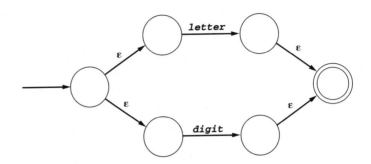

Now we form the NFA for the repetition **(letter|digit)*** as follows:

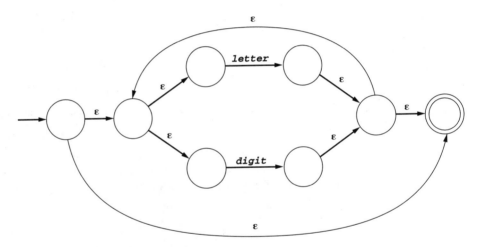

Finally, we construct the machine for the concatenation of **letter** with **(letter|digit)*** to get the complete NFA, as shown in Figure 2.9.

Figure 2.9
NFA for the reg-
ular expression
**letter(letter|
digit)*** using
Thompson's construction

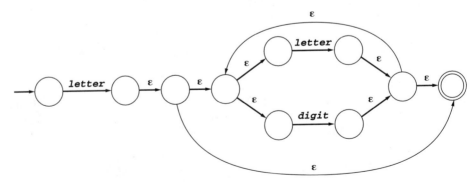

§

As a final example, we note that the NFA of Example 2.11 (Section 2.3.2) is exactly that corresponding to the regular expression **(a|c)*b** under Thompson's construction.

2.4.2   From an NFA to a DFA

We now wish to describe an algorithm that, given an arbitrary NFA, will construct an equivalent DFA (i.e., one that accepts precisely the same strings). To do this we will need some method for eliminating both ε-transitions and multiple transitions from a state on a single input character. Eliminating ε-transitions involves the construction of ε-closures, an **ε-closure** being the set of all states reachable by ε-transitions from a state or states. Eliminating multiple transitions on a single input character involves keeping track of the set of states that are reachable by matching a single character. Both these processes lead us to consider sets of states instead of single states. Thus, it is not surprising that the DFA we construct has as its states *sets of states* of the original NFA. Thus, this algorithm is called the **subset construction**. We first discuss the ε-closure in a little more detail and then proceed to a description of the subset construction.

The ε-Closure of a Set of States   We define the ε-closure of a single state s as the set of states reachable by a series of zero or more ε-transitions, and we write this set as $\bar{s}$. We leave a more mathematical statement of this definition to an exercise and proceed directly to an example. Note, however, that the ε-closure of a state always contains the state itself.

Example 2.14   Consider the following NFA corresponding to the regular expression **a*** under Thompson's construction:

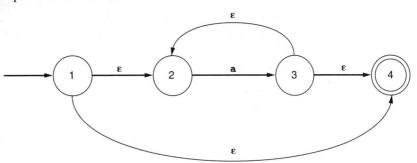

In this NFA, we have $\bar{1} = \{1, 2, 4\}$, $\bar{2} = \{2\}$, $\bar{3} = \{2, 3, 4\}$, and $\bar{4} = \{4\}$.   §

We now define the ε-closure of a set of states to be the union of the ε-closures of each individual state. In symbols, if S is a set of states, then we have

$$\bar{S} = \bigcup_{s \text{ in } S} \bar{s}$$

For instance, in the NFA of Example 2.14, $\overline{\{1, 3\}} = \overline{1} \cup \overline{3} = \{1, 2, 4\} \cup \{2, 3, 4\} = \{1, 2, 3, 4\}$.

The Subset Construction   We are now in a position to describe the algorithm for constructing a DFA from a given NFA M, which we will call $\overline{M}$. We first compute the ε-closure of the start state of M; this becomes the start state of $\overline{M}$. For this set, and for each subsequent set, we compute transitions on characters a as follows. Given a set S of states and a character a in the alphabet, compute the set $S'_a = \{\, t \mid$ for some s in S there is a transition from s to t on $a\, \}$. Then, compute $\overline{S'_a}$, the ε-closure of S'_a. This defines a new state in the subset construction, together with a new transition $S \xrightarrow{a} \overline{S'_a}$. Continue with this process until no new states or transitions are created. Mark as accepting those states constructed in this manner that contain an accepting state of M. This is the DFA $\overline{M}$. It contains no ε-transitions because every state is constructed as an ε-closure. It contains at most one transition from a state on a character a because each new state is constructed from *all* states of M reachable by transitions from a state on a single character a.

We illustrate the subset construction with a number of examples.

Example 2.15   Consider the NFA of Example 2.14. The start state of the corresponding DFA is $\overline{1} = \{1, 2, 4\}$. There is a transition from state 2 to state 3 on a, and no transitions from states 1 or 4 on a, so there is a transition on a from $\{1, 2, 4\}$ to $\overline{\{1, 2, 4\}_a} = \overline{\{3\}} = \{2, 3, 4\}$. Since there are no further transitions on a character from any of the states 1, 2, or 4, we turn our attention to the new state $\{2, 3, 4\}$. Again, there is a transition from 2 to 3 on a and no a-transitions from either 3 or 4, so there is a transition from $\{2, 3, 4\}$ to $\overline{\{2, 3, 4\}_a} = \overline{\{3\}} = \{2, 3, 4\}$. Thus, there is an a-transition from $\{2, 3, 4\}$ to itself. We have run out of states to consider, and so we have constructed the entire DFA. It only remains to note that state 4 of the NFA is accepting, and since both $\{1, 2, 4\}$ and $\{2, 3, 4\}$ contain 4, they are both accepting states of the corresponding DFA. We draw the DFA we have constructed as follows, where we name the states by their subsets:

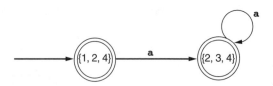

(Once the construction is complete, we could discard the subset terminology if we wished.)   §

Example 2.16   Consider the NFA of Figure 2.8, to which we add state numbers:

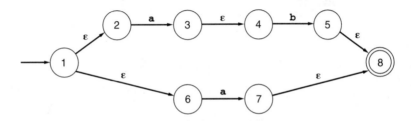

The DFA subset construction has as its start state $\overline{\{1\}} = \{1, 2, 6\}$. There is a transition on a from state 2 to state 3, and also from state 6 to state 7. Thus, $\{1, 2, 6\}_a = \overline{\{3, 7\}} = \{3, 4, 7, 8\}$, and we have $\{1, 2, 6\} \xrightarrow{a} \{3, 4, 7, 8\}$. Since there are no other character transitions from 1, 2, or 6, we go on to $\{3, 4, 7, 8\}$. There is a transition on b from 4 to 5 and $\{3, 4, 7, 8\}_b = \overline{\{5\}} = \{5, 8\}$, and we have the transition $\{3, 4, 7, 8\} \xrightarrow{b} \{5, 8\}$. There are no other transitions. Thus, the subset construction yields the following DFA equivalent to the previous NFA:

§

Example 2.17   Consider the NFA of Figure 2.9 (Thompson's construction for the regular expression **letter(letter|digit)***):

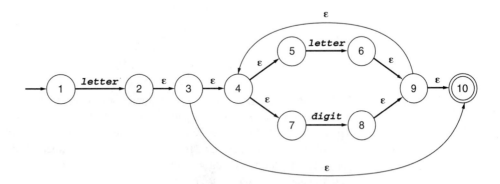

The subset construction proceeds as follows. The start state is $\overline{\{1\}} = \{1\}$. There is a transition on **letter** to $\overline{\{2\}} = \{2, 3, 4, 5, 7, 10\}$. From this state there is a transition on **letter** to $\overline{\{6\}} = \{4, 5, 6, 7, 9, 10\}$ and a transition on **digit** to $\overline{\{8\}} = \{4, 5, 7, 8, 9, 10\}$. Finally, each of these states also has transitions on **letter** and **digit**, either to itself or to the other. The complete DFA is given in the following picture:

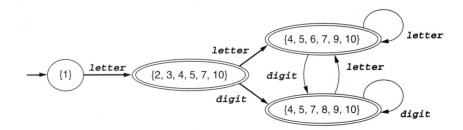

§

2.4.3 Simulating an NFA Using the Subset Construction

In the last section we briefly discussed the possibility of writing a program to simulate an NFA, a question that requires dealing with the nondeterminacy, or nonalgorithmic nature, of the machine. One way of simulating an NFA is to use the subset construction, but instead of constructing all the states of the associated DFA, we construct only the state at each point that is indicated by the next input character. Thus, we construct only those sets of states that will actually occur in a path through the DFA that is taken on the given input string. The advantage to this is that we may not need to construct the entire DFA. The disadvantage is that a state may be constructed many times, if the path contains loops.

For instance, in Example 2.16, if we have the input string consisting of the single character a, we will construct the start state $\{1, 2, 6\}$ and then the second state $\{3, 4, 7, 8\}$ to which we move and match the a. Then, since there is no following b, we accept without ever generating the state $\{5, 8\}$.

On the other hand, in Example 2.17, given the input string $r2d2$, we have the following sequence of states and transitions:

$$\{1\} \xrightarrow{\ r\ } \{2, 3, 4, 5, 7, 10\} \xrightarrow{\ 2\ } \{4, 5, 7, 8, 9, 10\}$$
$$\xrightarrow{\ d\ } \{4, 5, 6, 7, 9, 10\} \xrightarrow{\ 2\ } \{4, 5, 7, 8, 9, 10\}$$

If these states are constructed as the transitions occur, then all the states of the DFA have been constructed and the state $\{4, 5, 7, 8, 9, 10\}$ has even been constructed twice. Thus, this process is less efficient than constructing the entire DFA in the first place. For this reason, simulation of NFAs is not done in scanners. It does remain an option for pattern matching in editors and search programs, where regular expressions can be given dynamically by the user.

2.4.4 Minimizing the Number of States in a DFA

The process we have described of deriving a DFA algorithmically from a regular expression has the unfortunate property that the resulting DFA may be more complex than necessary. For instance, in Example 2.15 we derived the DFA for the regular expression **a***, whereas the DFA

will do as well. Since efficiency is extremely important in a scanner, we would like to be able to construct, if possible, a DFA that is minimal in some sense. In fact, an important result from automata theory states that, given any DFA, there is an equivalent DFA containing a minimum number of states, and that this minimum-state DFA is unique (except for renaming of states). It is also possible to directly obtain this minimum-state DFA from any given DFA, and we will briefly describe the algorithm here, without proof that it does indeed construct the minimum-state equivalent DFA (it should be easy for the reader to be informally convinced of this by reading the algorithm).

The algorithm proceeds by creating sets of states to be unified into single states. It begins with the most optimistic assumption possible: it creates two sets, one consisting of all the accepting states and the other consisting of all the nonaccepting states. Given this partition of the states of the original DFA, consider the transitions on each character a of the alphabet. If all accepting states have transitions on a to accepting states, then this defines an a-transition from the new accepting state (the set of all the old accepting states) to itself. Similarly, if all accepting states have transitions on a to nonaccepting states, then this defines an a-transition from the new accepting state to the new nonaccepting state (the set of all the old nonaccepting states). On the other hand, if there are two accepting states s and t that have transitions on a that land in different sets, then no a-transition can be defined for this grouping of the states. We say that a **distinguishes** the states s and t. In this case, the set of states under consideration (i.e., the set of all accepting states) must be split according to where their a-transitions land. Similar statements hold, of course, for each of the other sets of states, and once we have considered all characters of the alphabet, we must move on to them. Of course, if any further sets are split, we must return and repeat the process from the beginning. We continue this process of refining the partition of the states of the original DFA into sets until either all sets contain only one element (in which case, we have shown the original DFA to be minimal) or until no further splitting of sets occurs.

For the process we have just described to work correctly, we must also consider error transitions to an error state that is nonaccepting. That is, if there are accepting states s and t such that s has an a-transition to another accepting state, while t has no a-transition at all (i.e., an error transition), then a distinguishes s and t. Similarly, if a nonaccepting state s has an a-transition to an accepting state, while another nonaccepting state t has no a-transition, then a distinguishes s and t in this case too.

We conclude our discussion of state minimization with a couple of examples.

Example 2.18   Consider the DFA we constructed in the previous example, corresponding to the regular expression **letter(letter|digit)***. It had four states consisting of the start state and three accepting states. All three accepting states have transitions to other accepting states on both **letter** and **digit** and no other (nonerror) transitions. Thus, the three accepting states cannot be distinguished by any character, and the minimization algorithm results in combining the three accepting states into one, leaving the following minimum-state DFA (which we have already seen at the beginning of Section 2.3):

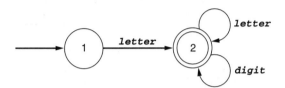

§

Example 2.19   Consider the following DFA, which we gave in Example 2.1 (Section 2.3.2) as equivalent to the regular expression **(a|ε)b***:

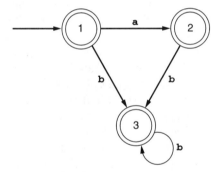

In this case, all the states (except the error state) are accepting. Consider now the character *b*. Each accepting state has a *b*-transition to another accepting state, so none of the states are distinguished by *b*. On the other hand, state 1 has an *a*-transition to an accepting state, while states 2 and 3 have no *a*-transition (or, rather, an error transition on *a* to the error nonaccepting state). Thus, *a* distinguishes state 1 from states 2 and 3, and we must repartition the states into the sets {1} and {2, 3}. Now we begin over. The set {1} cannot be split further, so we no longer consider it. Now the states 2 and 3 cannot be distinguished by either *a* or *b*. Thus, we obtain the minimum-state DFA:

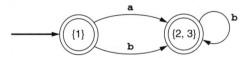

§

2.5   IMPLEMENTATION OF A TINY SCANNER

We want now to develop the actual code for a scanner to illustrate the concepts studied so far in this chapter. We do this for the TINY language that we introduced informally in Chapter 1 (Section 1.7). We then discuss a number of practical implementation issues raised by this scanner.

2.5.1   Implementing a Scanner for the Sample Language TINY

In Chapter 1 we gave only the briefest informal introduction to the TINY language. Our task here is to specify completely the lexical structure of TINY, that is, to define the tokens and their attributes. The tokens and token classes of TINY are summarized in Table 2.1.

The tokens of TINY fall into three typical categories: reserved words, special symbols, and "other" tokens. There are eight reserved words, with familiar meanings (though we do not need to know their semantics until much later). There are 10 special symbols, giving the four basic arithmetic operations on integers, two comparison operations (equal and less than), parentheses, semicolon, and assignment. All special symbols are one character long, except for assignment, which is two.

Table 2.1

Tokens of the TINY language

Reserved Words	Special Symbols	Other
if	+	*number*
then	–	(1 or more
else	*	digits)
end	/	
repeat	=	
until	<	*identifier*
read	(	(1 or more
write	)	letters)
	;	
	:=	

The other tokens are numbers, which are sequences of one or more digits, and identifiers, which (for simplicity) are sequences of one or more letters.

In addition to the tokens, TINY has the following lexical conventions. Comments are enclosed in curly brackets {...} and cannot be nested; the code is free format; white space consists of blanks, tabs, and newlines; and the principle of longest substring is followed in recognizing tokens.

In designing a scanner for this language, we could begin with regular expressions and develop NFAs and DFAs according to the algorithms of the previous section. Indeed regular expressions have been given previously for numbers, identifiers, and comments (TINY has particularly simple versions of these). Regular expressions for the other tokens are trivial, since they are all fixed strings. Instead of following this route, we will develop a DFA for the scanner directly, since the tokens are so simple. We do this in several steps.

First, we note that all the special symbols except assignment are distinct single characters, and a DFA for these symbols would look as follows:

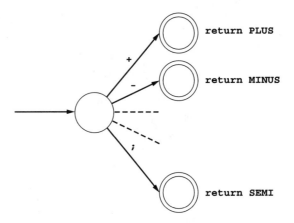

In this diagram, the different accepting states distinguish the token that is to be returned by the scanner. If we use some other indicator for the token to be returned (a variable in the code, say), then all the accepting states can be collapsed into one state that we will call **DONE**. If we combine this two-state DFA with DFAs that accept numbers and identifiers, we obtain the following DFA:

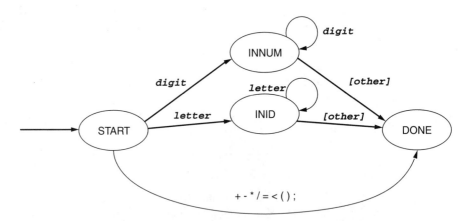

Note the use of the square brackets to indicate lookahead characters that should not be consumed.

We need to add comments, white space, and assignment to this DFA. White space is consumed by a simple loop from the start state to itself. Comments require an extra state, reached from the start state on left curly bracket and returning to it on right curly bracket. Assignment also requires an intermediate state, reached from the start state on semicolon. If an equal sign immediately follows, then an assignment token is generated. Otherwise, the next character should not be consumed, and an error token is generated.

Figure 2.10

DFA of the TINY scanner

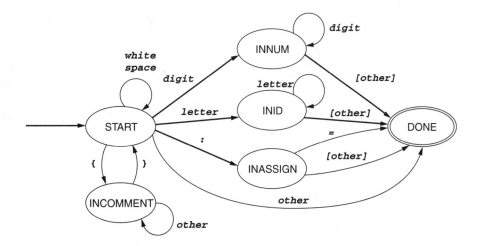

In fact, all single characters that are not in the list of special symbols, are not white space or comments, and are not digits or letters, should be accepted as errors, and we lump these in with the single-character symbols. The final DFA for our scanner is given in Figure 2.10.

We have not included reserved words in our discussion or in the DFA of Figure 2.10. This is because it is easiest from the point of view of the DFA to consider reserved words to be the same as identifiers, and then to look up the identifiers in a table of reserved words after acceptance. Indeed, the principle of the longest substring guarantees that the only action of the scanner that needs changing is the token that is returned. Thus, reserved words are considered only after an identifier has been recognized.

We turn now to a discussion of the code to implement this DFA, which is contained in the **scan.h** and **scan.c** files (see Appendix B). The principal procedure is **getToken** (lines 674–793), which consumes input characters and returns the next token recognized according to the DFA of Figure 2.10. The implementation uses the doubly nested case analysis we have described in Section 2.3.3, with a large case list based on the state, within which are individual case lists based on the current input character. The tokens themselves are defined as an enumerated type in **globals.h** (lines 174–186), which include all the tokens listed in Table 2.1, together with the bookkeeping tokens **EOF** (when the end of the file is reached) and **ERROR** (when an erroneous character is encountered). The states of the scanner are also defined as an enumerated type, but within the scanner itself (lines 612–614).

A scanner also needs in general to compute the attributes, if any, of each token, and sometimes also take other actions (such as inserting identifiers into a symbol table). In the case of the TINY scanner, the only attribute that is computed is the lexeme, or string value of the token recognized, and this is placed in the variable **tokenString**. This variable, together with **getToken** are the only services offered to other parts of the compiler, and their definitions are collected in the header file **scan.h** (lines 550–571). Note that **tokenString** is declared with a fixed length of 41, so that identifiers, for example, cannot be more than 40 characters (plus the ending null character). This is a limitation that is discussed later.

The scanner makes use of three global variables: the file variables **source** and **listing**, and the integer variable **lineno**, which are declared in **globals.h**, and allocated and initialized in **main.c**.

Additional bookkeeping done by the **getToken** procedure is as follows. The table **reservedWords** (lines 649–656) and the procedure **reservedLookup** (lines 658–666) perform a lookup of reserved words after an identifier is recognized by the principal loop of **getToken**, and the value of **currentToken** is changed accordingly. A flag variable **save** is used to indicate whether a character is to be added to **tokenString**; this is necessary, since white space, comments, and nonconsumed lookaheads should not be included.

Character input to the scanner is provided by the **getNextChar** function (lines 627–642), which fetches characters from **lineBuf**, a 256-character buffer internal to the scanner. If the buffer is exhausted, **getNextChar** refreshes the buffer from the **source** file using the standard C procedure **fgets**, assuming each time that a new source code line is being fetched (and incrementing **lineno**). While this assumption allows for simpler code, a TINY program with lines greater than 255 characters will not be handled quite correctly. We leave the investigation of the behavior of **getNextChar** in this case (and improvements to its behavior) to the exercises.

Finally, the recognition of numbers and identifiers in TINY requires that the transitions to the final state from **INNUM** and **INID** be nonconsuming (see Figure 2.10). We implement this by providing an **ungetNextChar** procedure (lines 644–647) that backs up one character in the input buffer. Again, this does not quite work for programs having very long source lines, and alternatives are explored in the exercises.

As an illustration of the behavior of the TINY scanner, consider the TINY program **sample.tny** in Figure 2.11 (the same program that was given as an example in Chapter 1). Figure 2.12 shows the listing output of the scanner, given this program as input, when **TraceScan** and **EchoSource** are set.

The remainder of this section will be devoted to an elaboration of some of the implementation issues raised by this scanner implementation.

Figure 2.11

Sample program in the TINY language

```
{ Sample program
  in TINY language -
  computes factorial
}
read x; { input an integer }
if 0 < x then { don't compute if x <= 0 }
  fact := 1;
  repeat
    fact := fact * x;
    x := x - 1
  until x = 0;
  write fact { output factorial of x }
end
```

Figure 2.12

Output of scanner given the
TINY program of Figure 2.11
as input

```
TINY COMPILATION: sample.tny
    1: { Sample program
    2:   in TINY language -
    3:   computes factorial
    4: }
    5: read x; { input an integer }
        5: reserved word: read
        5: ID, name= x
        5: ;
    6: if 0 < x then { don't compute if x <= 0 }
        6: reserved word: if
        6: NUM, val= 0
        6: <
        6: ID, name= x
        6: reserved word: then
    7:   fact := 1;
        7: ID, name= fact
        7: :=
        7: NUM, val= 1
        7: ;
    8:   repeat
        8: reserved word: repeat
    9:     fact := fact * x;
        9: ID, name= fact
        9: :=
        9: ID, name= fact
        9: *
        9: ID, name= x
        9: ;
   10:     x := x - 1
       10: ID, name= x
       10: :=
       10: ID, name= x
       10: -
       10: NUM, val= 1
   11:   until x = 0;
       11: reserved word: until
       11: ID, name= x
       11: =
       11: NUM, val= 0
       11: ;
   12:   write fact { output factorial of x }
       12: reserved word: write
       12: ID, name= fact
   13: end
       13: reserved word: end
       14: EOF
```

2.5.2   Reserved Words Versus Identifiers

Our TINY scanner recognizes reserved words by first considering them as identifiers and then looking them up in a table of reserved words. This is a common practice in scanners, but it means that the efficiency of the scanner depends on the efficiency of the lookup process in the reserved word table. In our scanner we have used a very simple method—linear search—in which the table is searched sequentially from beginning to end. This is not a problem for very small tables such as that for TINY, with only eight reserved words, but it becomes an unacceptable situation in scanners for real languages, which commonly have between 30 and 60 reserved words. In this case a faster lookup is required, and this can require the use of a better data structure than a linear list. One possibility is a binary search, which we could have applied had we written the list of reserved words in alphabetic order. Another possibility is to use a hash table. In this case we would like to use a hash function that has a very small number of collisions. Such a hash function can be developed in advance, since the reserved words are not going to change (at least not rapidly), and their places in the table will be fixed for every run of the compiler. Some research effort has gone into the determination of **minimal perfect hash functions** for various languages, that is, functions that distinguish each reserved word from the others, and that have the minimum number of values, so that a hash table no larger than the number of reserved words can be used. For instance, if there are only eight reserved words, then a minimal perfect hash function would always yield a value from 0 to 7, and each reserved word would yield a different value. (See the Notes and References section for more information.)

Another option in dealing with reserved words is to use the same table that stores identifiers, that is, the symbol table. Before processing is begun, all reserved words are entered into this table and are marked reserved (so that no redefinition is allowed). This has the advantage that only a single lookup table is required. In the TINY scanner, however, we do not construct the symbol table until after the scanning phase, so this solution is not appropriate for this particular design.

2.5.3   Allocating Space for Identifiers

A further flaw in the design of the TINY scanner is that token strings can only be a maximum of 40 characters. This is not a problem for most of the tokens, since their string sizes are fixed, but it is a problem for identifiers, since programming languages often require that arbitrarily long identifiers be allowed in programs. Even worse, if we allocate a 40-character array for each identifier, then much of the space is wasted, since most identifiers are short. This doesn't happen in the code of the TINY compiler, since token strings are copied using the utility function **copyString**, which dynamically allocates only the necessary space, as we will see in Chapter 4. A solution to the size limitation of **tokenString** would be similar: only allocate space on an as needed basis, possibly using the **realloc** standard C function. An alternative is to allocate an initial large array for all identifiers and then to perform do-it-yourself memory allocation within this array. (This is a special case of the standard dynamic memory management schemes discussed in Chapter 7.)

2.6 USE OF Lex TO GENERATE A SCANNER AUTOMATICALLY

In this section we repeat the development of a scanner for the TINY language carried out in the previous section, but now we will use the Lex scanner generator to generate a scanner from a description of the tokens of TINY as regular expressions. Since there are a number of different versions of Lex in existence, we confine our discussion to those features that are common to all or most of the versions. The most popular version of Lex is called **flex** (for Fast Lex). It is distributed as part of the **Gnu compiler package** produced by the Free Software Foundation, and is also freely available at many Internet sites.

Lex is a program that takes as its input a text file containing regular expressions, together with the actions to be taken when each expression is matched. Lex produces an output file that contains C source code defining a procedure **yylex** that is a table-driven implementation of a DFA corresponding to the regular expressions of the input file, and that operates like a **getToken** procedure. The Lex output file, usually called **lex.yy.c** or **lexyy.c**, is then compiled and linked to a main program to get a running program, just as the **scan.c** file was linked with the **tiny.c** file in the previous section.

In the following, we first discuss the Lex conventions for writing regular expressions and the format of a Lex input file. We then discuss the Lex input file for the TINY scanner given in Appendix B.

2.6.1 Lex Conventions for Regular Expressions

Lex conventions are very similar to those discussed in Section 2.2.3. Rather than list all of Lex's metacharacters and describe them individually, we will give an overview and then give the Lex conventions in a table.

Lex allows the matching of single characters, or strings of characters, simply by writing the characters in sequence, as we did in previous sections. Lex also allows metacharacters to be matched as actual characters by surrounding the characters in quotes. Quotes can also be written around characters that are not metacharacters, where they have no effect. Thus, it makes sense to write quotes around all characters that are to be matched directly, whether or not they are metacharacters. For example, we can write either **if** or **"if"** to match the reserved word **if** that begins an if-statement. On the other hand, to match a left parenthesis, we must write **"("**, since it is a metacharacter. An alternative is to use the backslash metacharacter ****, but this works only for single metacharacters: to match the character sequence **(*** we would have to write **\(***, repeating the backslash. Clearly, writing **"(*"** is preferable. Also using the backslash with regular characters may have a special meaning. For example, **\n** matches a newline and **\t** matches a tab (these are typical C conventions, and most such conventions carry over into Lex).

Lex interprets the metacharacters *****, **+**, **(**, **)**, and **|** in the usual way. Lex also uses the question mark as a metacharacter to indicate an optional part. As an example of the

Lex notation discussed so far, we can write a regular expression for the set of strings of *a*'s and *b*'s that begin with either *aa* or *bb* and have an optional *c* at the end as

    (aa|bb)(a|b)*c?

or as

    ("aa"|"bb")("a"|"b")*"c"?

The Lex convention for character classes (sets of characters) is to write them between square brackets. For example, **[abxz]** means any one of the characters *a*, *b*, *x*, or *z*, and we could write the previous regular expression in Lex as

    (aa|bb)[ab]*c?

Ranges of characters can also be written in this form using a hyphen. Thus, the expression **[0-9]** means in Lex any of the digits zero through nine. A period is a metacharacter that also represents a set of characters: it represents any character except a newline. Complementary sets—that is, sets that do *not* contain certain characters—can also be written in this notation, using the carat ^ as the first character inside the brackets. Thus, **[^0-9abc]** means any character that is not a digit and is not one of the letters *a*, *b*, or *c*.

As an example, we write a regular expression for the set of signed numbers that may contain a fractional part or an exponent beginning with the letter *E* (this expression was written in slightly different form in Section 2.2.4):

    ("+"|"-")?[0-9]+("."[0-9]+)?(E("+"|"-")?[0-9]+)?

One curious feature in Lex is that inside square brackets (representing a character class), most of the metacharacters lose their special status and do not need to be quoted. Even the hyphen can be written as a regular character if it is listed first. Thus, we could have written **[-+]** instead of **("+"|"-")** in the previous regular expression for numbers (but not **[+-]** because of the metacharacter use of **-** to express a range of characters). As another example, **[."?]** means any of the three characters period, quotation mark, or question mark (all three of these characters have lost their metacharacter meaning inside the brackets). Some characters, however, are still metacharacters even inside the square brackets, and to get the actual character, we must precede the character by a backslash (quotes cannot be used as they have lost their metacharacter meaning). Thus, **[\^\\]** means either of the actual characters ^ or \.

A further important metacharacter convention in Lex is the use of curly brackets to denote names of regular expressions. Recall that a regular expression can be given a name, and that these names can be used in other regular expressions as long as there are no recursive references. For example, we defined ***signedNat*** in Section 2.2.4 as follows:

    nat = [0-9]+
    signedNat = ("+"|"-")? nat

In this and other examples, we used italics to distinguish names from ordinary sequences of characters. Lex files, however, are ordinary text files, so italics are not available. Instead, Lex uses the convention that previously defined names are surrounded by curly brackets. Thus, the previous example would appear as follows in Lex (Lex also dispenses with the equal sign in defining names):

```
nat [0-9]+
signedNat (+|-)?{nat}
```

Note that the curly brackets do not appear when a name is defined, only when it is used.

Table 2.2 contains a summary list of the metacharacter conventions of Lex that we have discussed. There are a number of other metacharacter conventions in Lex that we will not use and we do not discuss them here (see the references at the end of the chapter).

Table 2.2

Metacharacter conventions in Lex

Pattern	Meaning
a	the character *a*
"a"	the character *a*, even if *a* is a metacharacter
\a	the character *a* when *a* is a metacharacter
a*	zero or more repetitions of *a*
a+	one or more repetitions of *a*
a?	an optional *a*
a|b	*a* or *b*
(a)	*a* itself
[abc]	any of the characters *a*, *b*, or *c*
[a-d]	any of the characters *a*, *b*, *c*, or *d*
[^ab]	any character except *a* or *b*
.	any character except a newline
{xxx}	the regular expression that the name *xxx* represents

2.6.2 The Format of a Lex Input File

A Lex input file consists of three parts, a collection of **definitions**, a collection of **rules**, and a collection of **auxiliary routines** or **user routines**. The three sections are separated by double percent signs that appear on separate lines beginning in the first column. Thus, the layout of a Lex input file is as follows:

```
{definitions}
%%
{rules}
%%
{auxiliary routines}
```

To properly understand how Lex interprets such an input file, we must keep in mind that some parts of the file will be regular expression information that Lex uses to guide its construction of the C output code, while other parts of the file will be actual C code that we are supplying to Lex, and that Lex will insert verbatim in the output code at the appropriate location. The precise rules Lex uses for this will be given after we have discussed each of the three sections and given a few examples.

The definition section occurs before the first **%%**. It contains two things. First, any C code that must be inserted external to any function should appear in this section between the delimiters **%{** and **%}**. (Note the order of these characters!) Second, names for regular expressions must also be defined in this section. A name is defined by writing it on a separate line starting in the first column and following it (after one or more blanks) by the regular expression it represents.

The second section contains the rules. These consist of a sequence of regular expressions followed by the C code that is to be executed when the corresponding regular expression is matched.

The third and final section contains C code for any auxiliary routines that are called in the second section and not defined elsewhere. This section may also contain a main program, if we want to compile the Lex output as a standalone program. This section can also be missing, in which case the second **%%** need not be written. (The first **%%** is always necessary.)

We give a series of examples to illustrate the format of a Lex input file.

Example 2.20   The following Lex input specifies a scanner that adds line numbers to text, sending its output to the screen (or a file, if redirected):

```
%{
/* a Lex program that adds line numbers
   to lines of text, printing the new text
   to the standard output
*/
#include <stdio.h>
int lineno = 1;
%}
line .*\n
%%
{line} { printf("%5d %s",lineno++,yytext); }
%%
main()
{ yylex(); return 0; }
```

For example, running the program obtained from Lex on this input file itself gives the following output:

```
1 %{
2 /* a Lex program that adds line numbers
```

```
 3      to lines of text, printing the new text
 4      to the standard output
 5 */
 6 #include <stdio.h>
 7 int lineno = 1;
 8 %}
 9 line .*\n
10 %%
11 {line} { printf("%5d %s",lineno++,yytext); }
12 %%
13 main()
14 { yylex(); return 0; }
```

We comment on this Lex input file using these line numbers. First, lines 1 through 8 are between the delimiters **%{** and **%}**. This causes these lines to be inserted directly into the C code produced by Lex, external to any procedure. In particular, the comment in lines 2 through 5 will be inserted near the beginning of the program, and the **#include** directive and the definition of the integer variable **lineno** on lines 6 and 7 will be inserted externally, so that **lineno** becomes a global variable and is initialized to the value 1. The other definition that appears before the first **%%** is the definition of the name **line** which is defined to be the regular expression **".*\n"**, which matches 0 or more characters (not including a newline), followed by a newline. In other words, the regular expression defined by **line** matches every line of input. Following the **%%** on line 10, line 11 comprises the action section of the Lex input file. In this case we have written a single action to be performed whenever a **line** is matched (**line** is surrounded by curly brackets to distinguish it as a name, according to the Lex convention). Following the regular expression is the **action**, that is, the C code that is to be executed whenever the regular expression is matched. In this example, the action consists of a single C statement, which is contained within the curly brackets of a C block. (Keep in mind that the curly brackets surrounding the name **line** have a completely different function from the curly brackets that form a block in the C code of the following action.) This C statement is to print the line number (in a five-space field, right justified) and the string **yytext**, after which **lineno** is incremented. The name **yytext** is the internal name Lex gives to the string matched by the regular expression, which in this case consists of each line of input (including the newline).[5] Finally, the C code after the second double percent (lines 13 and 14) is inserted as is at the end of the C code produced by Lex. In this example, the code consists of the definition of a **main** procedure that calls the function **yylex**. This allows the C code produced by Lex to be compiled into an executable program. (**yylex** is the name given to the procedure constructed by Lex that implements the DFA associated with the regular expressions and actions given in the action section of the input file.) §

---

5. We list the Lex internal names that are discussed in this section in a table at the end of the section.

Example 2.21   Consider the following Lex input file:

```
%{
/* a Lex program that changes all numbers
   from decimal to hexadecimal notation,
   printing a summary statistic to stderr
*/
#include <stdlib.h>
#include <stdio.h>
int count = 0;
%}
digit [0-9]
number {digit}+
%%
{number} { int n = atoi(yytext);
           printf("%x", n);
           if (n > 9) count++; }
%%
main()
{ yylex();
  fprintf(stderr,"number of replacements = %d",
                  count);
  return 0;
}
```

It is similar in structure to the previous example, except that the **main** procedure prints the count of the number of replacements to **stderr** after calling **yylex**. This example is also different in that not all text is matched. Indeed, only numbers are matched in the action section, where the C code for the action first converts the matched string (**yytext**) to an integer **n**, then prints it in hexadecimal form (**printf("%x",...)**), and finally increments **count** if the number is greater than 9. (If the number is smaller than or equal to 9, then it looks no different in hex.) Thus, the only action specified is for strings that are sequences of digits. Yet Lex generates a program that also matches all nonnumeric characters, and passes them through to the output. This is an example of a **default action** by Lex. If a character or string of characters matches none of the regular expressions in the action section, Lex will match it by default and echo it to the output. (Lex can also be forced to generate a runtime error, but we will not study this here.) The default action can also be specifically indicated through the Lex internally defined macro **ECHO**. (We study this use in the next example.)   §

Example 2.22   Consider the following Lex input file:

```
%{
/* Selects only lines that end or
   begin with the letter 'a'.
   Deletes everything else.
*/
```

```
#include <stdio.h>
%}
ends_with_a .*a\n
begins_with_a a.*\n
%%
{ends_with_a} ECHO;
{begins_with_a} ECHO;
.*\n ;
%%
main()
{ yylex(); return 0; }
```

This Lex input causes all input lines that begin or end with the character *a* to be written to the output. All other input lines are suppressed. The suppression of the input is caused by the rule below the **ECHO** rules. In this rule the "empty" action is specified for the regular expression `.*\n` by writing a semicolon for the C action code.

There is an additional feature of this Lex input that is worth noting. The listed rules are **ambiguous** in that a string may match more than one rule. In fact, *any* input line matches the expression `.*\n`, regardless of whether it is part of a line that begins or ends with an *a*. Lex has a priority system for resolving such ambiguities. First, Lex always matches the longest possible substring (so Lex always generates a scanner that follows the longest substring principle). Then, if the longest substring still matches two or more rules, Lex picks the first rule in the order they are listed in the action section. It is for this reason that the above Lex input file lists the **ECHO** actions first. If we had listed the actions in the following order,

```
.*\n ;
{ends_with_a} ECHO;
{begins_with_a} ECHO;
```

then the program produced by Lex would generate no output at all for any file, since every line of input will be matched by the first rule.   §

Example 2.23   In this example, Lex generates a program that will convert all uppercase letters to lowercase, except for letters inside C-style comments (that is, anything inside the delimiters `/*...*/`):

```
%{
/* Lex program to convert uppercase to
   lowercase except inside comments
*/
#include <stdio.h>
#ifndef FALSE
#define FALSE 0
#endif
#ifndef TRUE
#define TRUE 1
```

```
#endif
%}
%%
[A-Z]   {putchar(tolower(yytext[0]));
          /* yytext[0] is the single
             uppercase char found */
        }
"/*"    { char c;
          int done = FALSE;
          ECHO;
          do
          { while ((c=input())!='*')
              putchar(c);
            putchar(c);
            while ((c=input())=='*')
              putchar(c);
            putchar(c);
            if (c == '/') done = TRUE;
          } while (!done);
        }
%%
void main(void)
{ yylex();}
```

This example shows how code can be written to sidestep difficult regular expressions and implement a small DFA directly as a Lex action. Recall from the discussion in Section 2.2.4 that a regular expression for a C comment is extremely complex to write down. Instead, we write down a regular expression only for the string that begins a C comment—that is, `"/*"`—and then supply action code that will look for the ending string `"*/"`, while providing the appropriate action for other characters within the comment (in this case to just echo them without further processing). We do this by imitating the DFA from Example 2.9 (see Figure 2.4, page 53). Once we have recognized the string `"/*"`, we are in state 3, so our code picks up the DFA there. The first thing we do is cycle through characters (echoing them to the output) until we see an asterisk (corresponding to the *other* loop in state 3), as follows:

```
while ((c=input())!='*') putchar(c);
```

Here we have used yet another Lex internal procedure called **input**. The use of this procedure, rather than a direct input using **getchar**, ensures that the Lex input buffer is used, and that the internal structure of the input string is preserved. (Note, however, that we do use a direct output procedure **putchar**. This will be discussed further in Section 2.6.4.)

The next step in our code for the DFA corresponds to state 4. We loop again until we do *not* see an asterisk, and then, if the character is a forward slash, we exit; otherwise, we return to state 3.   §

We end this subsection with a summary of the Lex conventions we have introduced in the examples.

AMBIGUITY RESOLUTION

Lex's output will always first match the longest possible substring to a rule. If two or more rules cause substrings of equal length to be matched, then Lex's output will pick the rule listed first in the action section. If no rule matches any nonempty substring, then the default action copies the next character to the output and continues.

INSERTION OF C CODE

(1) Any text written between **%{** and **%}** in the definition section will be copied directly to the output program external to any procedure. (2) Any text in the auxiliary procedures section will be copied directly to the output program at the end of the Lex code. (3) Any code that follows a regular expression (by at least one space) in the action section (after the first **%%**) will be inserted at the appropriate place in the recognition procedure **yylex** and will be executed when a match of the corresponding regular expression occurs. The C code representing an action may be either a single C statement or a compound C statement consisting of any declarations and statements surrounded by curly brackets.

INTERNAL NAMES

Table 2.3 lists the Lex internal names that we discuss in this chapter. Most of these have been discussed in the previous examples.

Table 2.3

Some Lex internal names

Lex Internal Name	Meaning/Use
lex.yy.c or **lexyy.c**	Lex output file name
yylex	Lex scanning routine
yytext	string matched on current action
yyin	Lex input file (default: **stdin**)
yyout	Lex output file (default: **stdout**)
input	Lex buffered input routine
ECHO	Lex default action (print **yytext** to **yyout**)

We note one feature from this table not mentioned previously, which is that Lex has its own internal names for the files from which it takes input and to which it sends output: **yyin** and **yyout**. Using the standard Lex input routine **input** will automatically take input from the file **yyin**. However, in the foregoing examples, we have bypassed the internal output file **yyout** and just written to the standard output using **printf** and **putchar**. A better implementation, allowing the assignment of output to an arbitrary file, would replace these uses with **fprintf(yyout,...)** and **putc(...,yyout)**.

2.6.3   A TINY Scanner Using Lex

Appendix B gives a listing of a Lex input file **tiny.1** that will generate a scanner for the TINY language, whose tokens were described in Section 2.5 (see Table 2.1). In the following we make a few remarks about this input file (lines 3000–3072).

First, in the definitions section, the C code we insert directly into the Lex output consists of three **#include** directives (**globals.h**, **util.h**, and **scan.h**) and the definition of the **tokenString** attribute. This is necessary to provide the interface between the scanner and the rest of the TINY compiler.

The further contents of the definition section comprise the definitions of the names for the regular expressions that define the TINY tokens. Note that the definition of **number** uses the previously defined name **digit**, and the definition of **identifier** uses the previously defined **letter**. The definitions also distinguish between newlines and other white space (blanks and tabs, lines 3019 and 3020), since a newline will cause **lineno** to be incremented.

The action section of the Lex input consists of listing the various tokens, together with a **return** statement that returns the appropriate token as defined in **globals.h**. In this Lex definition we have listed the rules for reserved words before the rule for an identifier. Had we listed the identifier rule first, the ambiguity resolution rules of Lex would cause an identifier to always be recognized instead of a reserved word. We could also write code as in the scanner of the previous section, in which only identifiers are recognized, and then reserved words are looked up in a table. This would indeed be preferable in a real compiler, since separately recognized reserved words cause the size of the tables in the scanner code generated by Lex to grow enormously (and hence the size of memory used by the scanner).

One quirk of the Lex input is that we have to write code to recognize comments to ensure that **lineno** is updated correctly, even though the regular expression for TINY comments is easy to write. Indeed, the regular expression is

```
"{"[^\}]*"}"
```

(Note the use of the backslash inside the square brackets to remove the metacharacter meaning of right curly bracket—quotes will not work here.)[6]

We note also that there is no code written to return the **EOF** token on encountering the end of the input file. The Lex procedure **yylex** has a default behavior on encountering **EOF**—it returns the value 0. It is for this reason that the token **ENDFILE** was written first in the definition of **TokenType** in **globals.h** (line 179), so that it will have value 0.

Finally, the **tiny.1** file contains a definition of the **getToken** procedure in the auxiliary procedures section (lines 3056–3072). While this code contains some ad hoc initializations of Lex internals (such as **yyin** and **yyout**) that would be better performed directly in the main program, it does permit us to use the Lex-generated scanner directly, without changing any other files in the TINY compiler. Indeed, after gen-

---

6. Some versions of Lex have an internally defined variable **yylineno** that is automatically updated. Use of this variable instead of **lineno** would make it possible to eliminate the special code.

erating the C scanner file **lex.yy.c** (or **lexyy.c**), this file can be compiled and linked directly with the other TINY source files to produce a Lex-based version of the compiler. However, this version of the compiler lacks one service of the earlier version, in that no source code echoing with line numbers is provided (see Exercise 2.35).

EXERCISES

2.1 Write regular expressions for the following character sets, or give reasons why no regular expression can be written:

a. All strings of lowercase letters that begin and end in *a*.

b. All strings of lowercase letters that either begin or end in *a* (or both).

c. All strings of digits that contain no leading zeros.

d. All strings of digits that represent even numbers.

e. All strings of digits such that all the 2's occur before all the 9's.

f. All strings of *a*'s and *b*'s that contain no three consecutive *b*'s.

g. All strings of *a*'s and *b*'s that contain an odd number of *a*'s or an odd number of *b*'s (or both).

h. All strings of *a*'s and *b*'s that contain an even number of *a*'s and an even number of *b*'s.

i. All strings of *a*'s and *b*'s that contain exactly as many *a*'s as *b*'s.

2.2 Write English descriptions for the languages generated by the following regular expressions:

a. `(a|b)*a(a|b|`ε`)`

b. `(A|B|...|Z)(a|b|...|z)*`

c. `(aa|b)*(a|bb)*`

d. `(0|1|...|9|A|B|C|D|E|F)+(x|X)`

2.3 a. Many systems contain a version of **grep** (**g**lobal **r**egular **e**xpression **p**rint), a regular expression search program originally written for Unix.[7] Find a document describing your local grep, and describe its metasymbol conventions.

b. If your editor accepts some sort of regular expressions for its string searches, describe its metasymbol conventions.

2.4 In the definition of regular expressions, we described the precedence of the operations, but not their associativity. For example, we did not specify whether **a|b|c** meant **(a|b)|c** or **a|(b|c)** and similarly for concatenation. Why was this?

2.5 Prove that $L(r^{**}) = L(r^{*})$ for any regular expression *r*.

2.6 In describing the tokens of a programming language using regular expressions, it is not necessary to have the metasymbols ϕ (for the empty set) or ε (for the empty string). Why is this?

2.7 Draw a DFA corresponding to the regular expression ϕ.

2.8 Draw DFAs for each of the sets of characters of **(a)–(i)** in Exercise 2.1, or state why no DFA exists.

2.9 Draw a DFA that accepts the four reserved words **case, char, const,** and **continue** from the C language.

---

7. There are actually three versions of grep available on most Unix systems: "regular" grep, egrep (extended grep), and fgrep (fast grep).

2.10 Rewrite the pseudocode for the implementation of the DFA for C comments (Section 2.3.3) using the input character as the outer case test and the state as the inner case test. Compare your pseudocode to that of the text. When would you prefer to use this organization for code implementing a DFA?

2.11 Give a mathematical definition of the ε-closure of a set of states of an NFA.

2.12 a. Use Thompson's construction to convert the regular expression **(a|b)*a(a|b|ε)** into an NFA.

   b. Convert the NFA of part (a) into a DFA using the subset construction.

2.13 a. Use Thompson's construction to convert the regular expression **(aa|b)*(a|bb)*** into an NFA.

   b. Convert the NFA of part (a) into a DFA using the subset construction.

2.14 Convert the NFA of Example 2.1 (Section 2.3.2) into a DFA using the subset construction.

2.15 In Section 2.4.1 a simplification to Thompson's construction for concatenation was mentioned that eliminates the ε-transition between the two NFAs of the regular expressions being concatenated. It was also mentioned that this simplification needed the fact there were no transitions out of the accepting state in the other steps of the construction. Give an example to show why this is so. (Hint: Consider a new NFA construction for repetition that eliminates the new start and accepting states, and then consider the NFA for $r*s*$.)

2.16 Apply the state minimization algorithm of Section 2.4.4 to the following DFAs:

a.

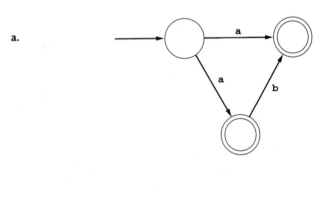

b.

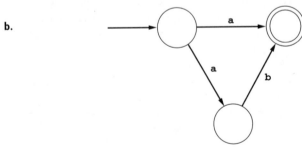

2.17 Pascal comments allow two distinct comment conventions: curly bracket pairs
{ ... } (as in TINY) and parentheses-asterisk pairs **(* ... *)**. Write a DFA
that recognizes both styles of comment.

2.18 **a.** Write out a regular expression for C comments in Lex notation. (Hint: See the discussion in Section 2.2.3.)

   b. Prove your answer in part (a) is correct.

2.19 The following regular expression has been given as a Lex definition of C comments (see
Schreiner and Friedman [1985, p. 25]):

"/*""/"*([^*/]|[^*]"/"|"*"[^/])*"*"*"*/"

Show that this expression is incorrect. (Hint: Consider the string **/*_/*/**.)

PROGRAMMING EXERCISES

2.20 Write a program that capitalizes all comments in a C program.

2.21 Write a program that capitalizes all reserved words outside of comments in a C program.
(A list of the reserved words of C can be found in Kernighan and Ritchie [1988,
p. 192].)

2.22 Write a Lex input file that will produce a program that capitalizes all comments in a C
program.

2.23 Write a Lex input file that will produce a program that capitalizes all reserved words
outside of comments in a C program (see Exercise 2.21).

2.24 Write a Lex input file that will produce a program that counts characters, words, and
lines in a text file and reports the counts. Define a word to be any sequence of letters
and/or digits, without punctuation or spaces. Punctuation and white space do not count
as words.

2.25 The Lex code of Example 2.23 (Section 2.6.2) can be shortened by using a global flag
inComment to distinguish behavior inside comments from behavior elsewhere. Rewrite
the code of the example to do this.

2.26 Add nested C comments to the Lex code of Example 2.23.

2.27 **a.** Rewrite the scanner for TINY to use binary search in the lookup of reserved words.

   b. Rewrite the scanner for TINY to use a hash table for the lookup of reserved words.

2.28 Remove the 40-character limit on identifiers in the TINY scanner by dynamically allocating space for **tokenString**.

2.29 **a.** Test the behavior of the TINY scanner when the source program has lines that
exceed the buffer size of the scanner, finding as many problems as you can.

   b. Rewrite the TINY scanner to remove the problems that you found in part (a) (or at
least improve its behavior). (This will require rewriting the **getNextChar** and
ungetNextChar procedures.)

2.30 An alternative to the use of the **ungetNextChar** procedure in the TINY scanner to
implement nonconsuming transitions is to use a Boolean flag to indicate that the current
character is to be consumed, so that no backup in the input is required. Rewrite the
TINY scanner to implement this method, and compare it to the existing code.

2.31 Add nested comments to the TINY scanner by using a counter called **nestLevel**.

2.32 Add Ada-style comments to the TINY scanner. (An Ada comment begins with two dashes and continues to the end of the line.)

2.33 Add the lookup of reserved words in a table to the Lex scanner for TINY (you may use linear search as in the handwritten TINY scanner or either of the search methods suggested in Exercise 2.27).

2.34 Add Ada-style comments to the Lex code for the TINY scanner. (An Ada comment begins with two dashes and continues to the end of the line.)

2.35 Add source code line echoing (using the **EchoSource** flag) to the Lex code for the TINY scanner, so that, when the flag is set, each line of source code is printed to the listing file with the line number. (This requires more extensive knowledge of Lex internals than we have studied.)

NOTES AND REFERENCES

The mathematical theory of regular expressions and finite automata is discussed in detail in Hopcroft and Ullman [1979], where some references to the historical development of the theory can be found. In particular, one can find there a proof of the equivalence of finite automata and regular expressions (we have used only one direction of the equivalence in this chapter). One can also find a discussion of the pumping lemma there, and its consequences for the limitations of regular expressions in describing patterns. A more detailed description of the state minimization algorithm can also be found there, together with a proof of the fact that such DFAs are essentially unique. The description of a one-step construction of a DFA from a regular expression (as opposed to the two-step approach described here) can be found in Aho, Hopcroft, and Ullman [1986]. A method for compressing tables in a table-driven scanner is also given there. A description of Thompson's construction using rather different NFA conventions from those described in this chapter is given in Sedgewick [1990], where descriptions of table lookup algorithms such as binary search and hashing for reserved word recognition can be found. (Hashing is also discussed in Chapter 6.) Minimal perfect hash functions, mentioned in Section 2.5.2, are discussed in Cichelli [1980] and Sager [1985]. A utility called **gperf** is distributed as part of the Gnu compiler package. It can quickly generate perfect hash functions for even large sets of reserved words. While these are generally not minimal, they are still quite useful in practice. Gperf is described in Schmidt [1990].

The original description of the Lex scanner generator is in Lesk [1975], which is still relatively accurate for more recent versions. Later versions, especially Flex (Paxson [1990]), have solved some efficiency problems and are competitive with even finely tuned handwritten scanners (Jacobson [1987]). A useful description of Lex can also be found in Schreiner and Friedman [1985], together with more examples of simple Lex programs to solve a variety of pattern-matching tasks. A brief description of the grep family of pattern matchers (Exercise 2.3) can be found in Kernighan and Pike [1984], and a more extensive discussion in Aho [1979]. The offside rule mentioned in Section 2.2.3 (a use of white space to provide formatting) is discussed in Landin [1966] and Hutton [1992].

Chapter 3

Context-Free Grammars and Parsing

Parsing is the task of determining the syntax, or structure, of a program. For this reason, it is also called **syntax analysis**. The syntax of a programming language is usually given by the **grammar rules** of a **context-free grammar**, in a manner similar to the way the lexical structure of the tokens recognized by the scanner is given by regular expressions. Indeed, a context-free grammar uses naming conventions and operations very similar to those of regular expressions. The major difference is that the rules of a context-free grammar are **recursive**. For instance, the structure of an if-statement must in general allow other if-statements to be nested inside it, something that is not allowed in regular expressions. The consequences of this seemingly elementary change to the power of the representation are enormous. The class of structures recognizable by context-free grammars is increased significantly over those of regular expressions. The algorithms used to recognize these structures are also quite different from scanning algorithms, in that they must use recursive calls or an explicitly managed parsing stack. The data structures used to represent the syntactic structure of a language must now also be recursive rather than linear (as they are for lexemes and tokens). The basic structure used is usually some kind of tree, called a **parse tree** or **syntax tree**.

In a similar manner to the previous chapter, we need to study the theory of context-free grammars before we study parsing algorithms and the details of actual parsers using these algorithms. However, contrary to the situation with scanners, where there is essentially only one algorithmic method (represented by finite automata), parsing involves a choice from among a number of different methods, each of which has distinct properties and capabilities. There are in fact two general categories of algorithms: **top-down parsing** and **bottom-up parsing** (from the way they construct the parse or syntax tree). We postpone a detailed discussion of these parsing methods to subsequent chapters. In this chapter, we will give a general description of the parsing process and then study the basic theory of context-free grammars. A final section gives the syntax of the TINY language in terms of a context-free grammar. The reader familiar with the theory of context-free grammars and syntax trees may wish to skip the middle sections of this chapter (or use them as a review).

3.1 THE PARSING PROCESS

It is the task of the parser to determine the syntactic structure of a program from the tokens produced by the scanner and, either explicitly or implicitly, to construct a parse tree or syntax tree that represents this structure. Thus, the parser may be viewed as a function that takes as its input the sequence of tokens produced by the scanner and produces as its output the syntax tree

$$sequence\ of\ tokens \xrightarrow{\text{parser}} syntax\ tree$$

Usually the sequence of tokens is not an explicit input parameter, but the parser calls a scanner procedure such as **getToken** to fetch the next token from the input as it is needed during the parsing process. Thus, the parsing step of the compiler reduces to a call to the parser as follows:

```
syntaxTree = parse();
```

In a single-pass compiler the parser will incorporate all the other phases of a compiler, including code generation, and so no explicit syntax tree needs to be constructed (the parser steps themselves will represent the syntax tree implicitly), and thus a call

```
parse();
```

will do. More commonly, a compiler will be multipass, in which case the further passes will use the syntax tree as their input.

The structure of the syntax tree is heavily dependent on the particular syntactic structure of the language. This tree is usually defined as a dynamic data structure, in which each node consists of a record whose fields include the attributes needed for the remainder of the compilation process (i.e., not just those computed by the parser). Often the node structure will be a variant record to save space. Attribute fields may also be structures that are dynamically allocated as needed, as a further space-saving tool.

One problem that is more difficult for the parser than the scanner is the treatment of errors. In the scanner, if a character is encountered that cannot be part of a legal token, then it is sufficiently simple to generate an error token and consume the offending character. (In a sense, by generating an error token, the scanner passes off the difficulty onto the parser.) The parser, on the other hand, must not only report an error message, but it must **recover** from the error and continue parsing (to find as many errors as possible). Sometimes, a parser may perform **error repair**, in which it infers a possible corrected code version from the incorrect version presented to it.

(This is usually done only in simple cases.) One particularly important aspect of error recovery is the reporting of meaningful error messages and the resumption of parsing as close to the actual error as possible. This is not easy, since the parser may not discover an error until well after the actual error has occurred. Since error recovery techniques depend on the particular parsing algorithm used, a study of them is delayed until subsequent chapters.

3.2 CONTEXT-FREE GRAMMARS

A context-free grammar is a specification for the syntactic structure of a programming language. Such a specification is very similar to the specification of the lexical structure of a language using regular expressions, except that a context-free grammar involves recursive rules. As a running example, we will use simple integer arithmetic expressions with addition, subtraction, and multiplication operations. These expressions can be given by the following grammar:

$$exp \rightarrow exp \; op \; exp \mid (\; exp \;) \mid \textbf{number}$$
$$op \rightarrow \textbf{+} \mid \textbf{-} \mid \textbf{*}$$

3.2.1 Comparison to Regular Expression Notation

Consider how the above sample context-free grammar compares to the regular expression rules given for **number** in the previous chapter:

```
number = digit digit*
digit = 0|1|2|3|4|5|6|7|8|9
```

In basic regular expression rules we have three operations: choice (given by the vertical bar metasymbol), concatenation (with no metasymbol), and repetition (given by the asterisk metasymbol). We also use the equal sign to represent the definition of a name for a regular expression, and we write the name in italics to distinguish it from a sequence of actual characters.

Grammar rules use similar notations. Names are written in italic (but now in a different font, so we can tell them from names for regular expressions). The vertical bar still appears as the metasymbol for choice. Concatenation is also used as a standard operation. There is, however, no metasymbol for repetition (like the ***** of regular expressions), a point to which we shall return shortly. A further difference in notation is that we now use the arrow symbol → instead of equality to express the definitions of names. This is because names cannot now simply be replaced by their definitions, but a more complex defining process is implied, as a result of the recursive nature of the definitions.[1] In our example, the rule for *exp* is recursive, in that the name *exp* appears to the right of the arrow.

Note, also, that the grammar rules use regular expressions as components. In the rules for *exp* and *op* there are actually six regular expressions representing tokens in the

---

1. But see the discussion later in the chapter on grammar rules as equations.

language. Five of these are single-character tokens: **+**, **-**, *****, **(**, and **)**. One is the name ***number***, the name of a token representing sequences of digits.

Grammar rules in a similar form to this example were first used in the description of the Algol60 language. The notation was developed by John Backus and adapted by Peter Naur for the Algol60 report. Thus, grammar rules in this form are usually said to be in **Backus-Naur form**, or **BNF**.

3.2.2 Specification of Context-Free Grammar Rules

Like regular expressions, grammar rules are defined over an alphabet, or set of symbols. In the case of regular expressions, these symbols are usually characters. In the case of grammar rules, the symbols are usually tokens representing strings of characters. In the last chapter we defined the tokens in a scanner using an enumerated type in C. In this chapter, to avoid the details of the way tokens are represented in a specific implementation language (such as C), we will use the regular expressions themselves to represent the tokens. In the case where a token is a fixed symbol, as in the reserved word **while** or the special symbols such as **+** or **:=**, we write the string itself in the code font used in Chapter 2. In the case of tokens such as identifiers and numbers, which represent more than one string, we use code font in italics, just as though the token is a name for a regular expression (which it usually does represent). For example, we will represent the alphabet of tokens for the TINY language as the set

```
{if,then,else,end,repeat,until,read,write,
identifier,number,+,-,*,/,=,<,(,),;,:=}
```

instead of the set of tokens (as defined in the TINY scanner):

```
{IF,THEN,ELSE,END,REPEAT,UNTIL,READ,WRITE,ID,NUM,
PLUS,MINUS,TIMES,OVER,EQ,LT,LPAREN,RPAREN,SEMI,ASSIGN}
```

Given an alphabet, a **context-free grammar rule in BNF** consists of a string of symbols. The first symbol is a name for a structure. The second symbol is the meta-symbol "→". This symbol is followed by a string of symbols, each of which is either a symbol from the alphabet, a name for a structure, or the metasymbol "|".

In informal terms, a grammar rule in BNF is interpreted as follows. The rule defines the structure whose name is to the left of the arrow. The structure is defined to consist of one of the choices on the right-hand side separated by the vertical bars. The sequences of symbols and structure names within each choice defines the layout of the structure. For instance, consider the grammar rules of our previous example:

$$exp \rightarrow exp \; op \; exp \mid (\; exp \;) \mid \textbf{number}$$
$$op \rightarrow \textbf{+} \mid \textbf{-} \mid \textbf{*}$$

The first rule defines an expression structure (with name *exp*) to consist of either an expression followed by an operator and another expression, or an expression within parentheses, or a number. The second rule defines an operator (with name *op*) to consist of one of the symbols **+**, **-**, or *****.

The metasymbols and conventions we have used here are similar to those in wide use, but we should note that there is no universal standard for these conventions.

Indeed, common alternatives for the arrow metasymbol "→" include "=" (the equal sign), ":" (the colon), and "::=" ("double-colon-equals"). In normal text files, it is also necessary to find a replacement for the use of italics. This is often done by surrounding structure names with angle brackets <...> and by writing italicized token names in uppercase. Thus, with different conventions, the above grammar rules might appear as

```
<exp> ::= <exp> <op> <exp> | ( <exp> ) | NUMBER
<op> ::= + | - | *
```

Each author will also have other variations on these notations. A few of the more significant (some of which we will occasionally use) will be discussed later in this section. Two additional small notational issues are worth discussing immediately.

It is sometimes useful to include parentheses in the metasymbols of the BNF notation, much as parentheses are useful to rearrange precedence in regular expressions. For example, it is possible to rewrite the grammar rules above as a single grammar rule as follows:

$$exp \rightarrow exp\ (\text{``}+\text{''} \mid \text{``}-\text{''} \mid \text{``}*\text{''})\ exp \mid \text{``}(\text{''}\ exp\ \text{``})\text{''} \mid \mathbf{number}$$

In this rule the parentheses are necessary to group the choices of operators between the expressions on the right-hand side, since concatenation takes precedence over choice (as in regular expressions). Thus, the following rule would have a different (and incorrect) meaning:

$$exp \rightarrow exp\ \text{``}+\text{''} \mid \text{``}-\text{''} \mid \text{``}*\text{''}\ exp \mid \text{``}(\text{''}\ exp\ \text{``})\text{''} \mid \mathbf{number}$$

Note also that, when parentheses are included as a metasymbol, it is necessary to distinguish the parentheses tokens from the metasymbols, and we have done this by surrounding them in quotes, as we would in the case of regular expressions. (We have surrounded the operator symbols with quotes as well, for consistency.)

Parentheses are not absolutely necessary as metasymbols in BNF, since it is always possible to separate parenthesized parts into a new grammar rule. In fact, the choice operation given by the vertical bar metasymbol is also not necessary in grammar rules, if we allow the same name to appear any number of times to the left of the arrow. For example, our simple expression grammar could be written as follows:

$$exp \rightarrow exp\ op\ exp$$
$$exp \rightarrow (\ exp\ )$$
$$exp \rightarrow \mathbf{number}$$
$$op \rightarrow +$$
$$op \rightarrow -$$
$$op \rightarrow *$$

However, we will usually write grammar rules so that all the choices for each structure are listed in a single rule, and each structure name appears only once to the left of the arrow.

Sometimes we will want to give examples of grammar rules in a shortened notation for simplicity. In these cases, we will use uppercase letters for structure names and lowercase letters for individual token symbols (which often are just single characters). Thus, our simple expression grammar might be written in this shorthand as

$$E \rightarrow E\,O\,E \mid (\,E\,) \mid \mathbf{n}$$
$$O \rightarrow \mathbf{+} \mid \mathbf{-} \mid \mathbf{*}$$

Occasionally, we will also simplify the notation when we are using just characters as tokens and write them without using code font:

$$E \rightarrow E\,O\,E \mid (\,E\,) \mid a$$
$$O \rightarrow + \mid - \mid *$$

3.2.3 Derivations and the Language Defined by a Grammar

We turn now to a description of how grammar rules determine a "language," or set of legal strings of tokens.

Context-free grammar rules determine the set of syntactically legal strings of token symbols for the structures defined by the rules. For example, the arithmetic expression

    (34-3)*42

corresponds to the legal string of seven tokens

    (number - number) * number

where the **number** tokens have their structure determined by the scanner and the string itself is legally an expression because each part corresponds to choices given by the grammar rules

$$exp \rightarrow exp\ op\ exp \mid (\ exp\ ) \mid \mathbf{number}$$
$$op \rightarrow \mathbf{+} \mid \mathbf{-} \mid \mathbf{*}$$

On the other hand, the string

    (34-3*42

is not a legal expression, because there is a left parenthesis that is not matched by a right parenthesis and the second choice in the grammar rule for an *exp* requires that parentheses be generated in pairs.

Grammar rules determine the legal strings of token symbols by means of derivations. A **derivation** is a sequence of replacements of structure names by choices on the right-hand sides of grammar rules. A derivation begins with a single structure name and ends with a string of token symbols. At each step in a derivation, a single replacement is made using one choice from a grammar rule.

As an example, Figure 3.1 gives a derivation for the expression **(34-3)*42** using the grammar rules as given in our simple expression grammar. At each step the grammar rule choice used for the replacement is given on the right. (We have also numbered the steps for later reference.)

Figure 3.1

A derivation for the arithmetic expression **(34-3)*42**

(1) $exp \Rightarrow exp\ op\ exp$	$[exp \rightarrow exp\ op\ exp]$
(2) $\Rightarrow exp\ op\ \textbf{number}$	$[exp \rightarrow \textbf{number}]$
(3) $\Rightarrow exp\ \textbf{*}\ \textbf{number}$	$[op \rightarrow \textbf{*}\ ]$
(4) $\Rightarrow \textbf{(}\ exp\ \textbf{)}\ \textbf{*}\ \textbf{number}$	$[exp \rightarrow \textbf{(}\ exp\ \textbf{)}]$
(5) $\Rightarrow \textbf{(}\ exp\ op\ exp\ \textbf{)}\ \textbf{*}\ \textbf{number}$	$[exp \rightarrow exp\ op\ exp]$
(6) $\Rightarrow \textbf{(}exp\ op\ \textbf{number)}\ \textbf{*}\ \textbf{number}$	$[exp \rightarrow \textbf{number}]$
(7) $\Rightarrow \textbf{(}exp\ \textbf{-}\ \textbf{number)}\ \textbf{*}\ \textbf{number}$	$[op \rightarrow\ \textbf{-}\ ]$
(8) $\Rightarrow \textbf{(number}\ \textbf{-}\ \textbf{number)*number}$	$[exp \rightarrow \textbf{number}]$

Note that derivation steps use a different arrow from the arrow metasymbol in the grammar rules. This is because there is a difference between a derivation step and a grammar rule: grammar rules **define**, while derivation steps **construct** by replacement. In the first step of Figure 3.1, the single *exp* is replaced by the string *exp op exp* from the right-hand side of the rule *exp → exp op exp* (the first choice in the BNF for *exp*). In the second step, the rightmost *exp* in the string *exp op exp* is replaced by the symbol **number** from the right-hand side of the choice *exp →* **number** to obtain the string *exp op* **number**. In the third step, the *op* is replaced by the symbol ***** from the right-hand side of the rule *op →* ***** (the third of the choices in the BNF for *op*) to obtain the string *exp* *** number**. And so on.

The set of all strings of token symbols obtained by derivations from the *exp* symbol is the **language defined by the grammar** of expressions. This language contains all syntactically legal expressions. We can write this symbolically as

$$L(G) = \{\ s\ |\ exp \Rightarrow^* s\ \}$$

where G represents the expression grammar, s represents an arbitrary string of token symbols (sometimes called a **sentence**), and the symbols $\Rightarrow^*$ stand for a derivation consisting of a sequence of replacements as described earlier. (The asterisk is used to indicate a sequence of steps, much as it indicates repetition in regular expressions.) Grammar rules are sometimes called **productions** because they "produce" the strings in $L(G)$ via derivations.

Each structure name in a grammar defines its own language of syntactically legal strings of tokens. For example, the language defined by *op* in our simple expression grammar defines the language {**+, -, ***} consisting of just three symbols. Usually, we are most interested in the language defined by the most general structure in a grammar. The grammar for a programming language often defines a structure called *program*, and the language of this structure is the set of all syntactically legal programs of the programming language (note we have used the word "language" in two separate senses here).

For example, a BNF for Pascal will begin with grammar rules such as

$program \rightarrow program\text{-}heading$ **;** $program\text{-}block$ **.**
$program\text{-}heading \rightarrow \ldots$
$program\text{-}block \rightarrow \ldots$
   $\ldots$

(The first rule says that a program consists of a program heading, followed by a semi-colon, followed by a program block, followed by a period.) In languages with separate compilation such as C, the most general structure is often called a *compilation-unit*. In every case, we assume that the most general structure is listed first in the grammar rules, unless we specify otherwise. (In the mathematical theory of context-free grammars, this structure is called the **start symbol**.)

One further piece of terminology allows us to distinguish more clearly between structure names and the symbols of the alphabet (which we have been calling token symbols, since they usually are tokens in compiler applications). Structure names are also called **nonterminals**, since they always must be replaced further on in a derivation (they do not terminate a derivation). By contrast, symbols in the alphabet are called **terminals**, since they terminate a derivation. Since terminals are usually tokens in compiler applications, we will use both names as being essentially synonymous. Often, terminals and nonterminals are both referred to as symbols.

We consider now a few examples of languages generated by grammars.

Example 3.1

Consider the grammar G with the single grammar rule

$$E \rightarrow (E) \mid a$$

This grammar has one nonterminal E and three terminals (,), and a. This grammar generates the language $L(G) = \{ a, (a), ((a)), (((a))), \ldots \} = \{ (^n a)^n \mid n \text{ an integer} \geq 0 \}$, that is, the strings consisting of 0 or more left parentheses, followed by an a, followed by the same number of right parentheses as left parentheses. As an example of a derivation for one of these strings, we give a derivation for $((a))$:

$$E \Rightarrow (E) \Rightarrow ((E)) \Rightarrow ((a)) \qquad \S$$

Example 3.2

Consider the grammar G with the single grammar rule

$$E \rightarrow (E)$$

This is the same as the grammar of the previous example, except that the option $E \rightarrow a$ is missing. This grammar generates no strings at all, so its language is empty: $L(G) = \{\}$. The reason is that any derivation beginning with E will generate strings that always contain an E. Thus, there is no way we can derive a string consisting only of terminals. Indeed, as with all recursive processes (such as induction proofs or recursive functions), a grammar rule that defines a structure recursively must always have at least one nonrecursive case (which we could call a **base case**). The grammar rule of this example has no such case, and any potential derivation is doomed to infinite recursion.   §

Example 3.3   Consider the grammar G with the single grammar rule

$$E \rightarrow E + a \mid a$$

This grammar generates all strings consisting of a's separated by $+$'s:

$$L(G) = \{\, a, a + a, a + a + a, a + a + a + a, \ldots \}$$

To see this (informally), consider the effect of the rule $E \rightarrow E + a$: it causes the string $+ a$ to be repeated on the right in a derivation:

$$E \Rightarrow E + a \Rightarrow E + a + a \Rightarrow E + a + a + a \Rightarrow \ldots$$

Finally, we must replace the E on the left using the base case $E \rightarrow a$.

More formally, we can prove this by induction as follows. First, we show that every string $a + a + \cdots + a$ is in $L(G)$ by induction on the number of a's. The derivation $E \Rightarrow a$ shows that a is in $L(G)$; assume now that $s = a + a + \cdots + a$, with $n - 1$ a's, is in $L(G)$. Thus, there is a derivation $E \Rightarrow^* s$: Now the derivation $E \Rightarrow E + a \Rightarrow^* s + a$ shows that the string $s + a$, with $n + a$'s, is in $L(G)$. Conversely, we also show that any string s from $L(G)$ must be of the form $a + a + \cdots + a$. We show this by induction on the length of a derivation. If the derivation has length 1, then it is of the form $E \Rightarrow a$, and so s is of the correct form. Now, assume the truth of the hypothesis for all strings with derivations of length $n - 1$, and let $E \Rightarrow^* s$ be a derivation of length $n > 1$. This derivation must begin with the replacement of E by $E + a$, and so is of the form $E \Rightarrow E + a \Rightarrow^* s' + a = s$. Then, s' has a derivation of length $n - 1$, and so is of the form $a + a + \cdots + a$. Hence, s itself must have this same form.   §

Example 3.4   Consider the following extremely simplified grammar of statements:

$$statement \rightarrow \textit{if-stmt} \mid \textbf{other}$$
$$\textit{if-stmt} \rightarrow \textbf{if (} exp \textbf{)} statement$$
$$\mid \textbf{if (} exp \textbf{)} statement \textbf{ else } statement$$
$$exp \rightarrow \textbf{0} \mid \textbf{1}$$

The language of this grammar consists of nested if-statements in a C-like form. (We have simplified the logical test expressions to either 0 or 1, and all statements other than the if-statement are grouped into the terminal **other**.) Examples of strings in this language are

```
other
if (0) other
if (1) other
```

```
if (0) other else other
if (1) other else other
if (0) if (0) other
if (0) if (1) other else other
if (1) other else if (0) other else other
. . .
```

Note how the optional else-part of the if-statement is indicated by a separate choice in the grammar rule for *if-stmt*.   §

We noted previously that grammar rules in BNF provide for concatenation and choice but have no specific repetition operation equivalent to the ***** of regular expressions. Such an operation is in fact unnecessary, since repetition can be achieved by recursion (as programmers in functional languages know). For example, either the grammar rule

$$A \rightarrow A\,a \mid a$$

or the grammar rule

$$A \rightarrow a\,A \mid a$$

generates the language $\{a^n \mid n$ an integer $\geq 1\}$ (the set of all strings of one or more a's), which is the same language as that generated by the regular expression **a+**. For instance, the string *aaaa* can be generated by the first grammar rule with the derivation

$$A \Rightarrow Aa \Rightarrow Aaa \Rightarrow Aaaa \Rightarrow aaaa$$

A similar derivation works for the second grammar rule. The first of these grammar rules is **left recursive**, since the nonterminal A appears as the first symbol on the right-hand side of the rule defining A.[2] The second grammar rule is **right recursive**.

Example 3.3 is another example of a left recursive grammar rule, which causes the repetition of the string "$+\ a$". This and the previous example can be generalized as follows. Consider a rule of the form

$$A \rightarrow A\,\alpha \mid \beta$$

where α and β represent arbitrary strings and β does not begin with A. This rule generates all strings of the form β, $\beta\alpha$, $\beta\alpha\alpha$, $\beta\alpha\alpha\alpha$, . . . (all strings beginning with a β, followed by 0 or more α's). Thus, this grammar rule is equivalent in its effect to the regular expression $\beta\alpha*$. Similarly, the right recursive grammar rule

$$A \rightarrow \alpha\,A \mid \beta$$

(where β does not end in A) generates all strings β, $\alpha\beta$, $\alpha\alpha\beta$, $\alpha\alpha\alpha\beta$, ...

---

2. This is a special case of left recursion called **immediate left recursion**. More general cases are discussed in the next chapter.

If we want to write a grammar that generates the same language as the regular expression **a***, then we must have a notation for a grammar rule that generates the empty string (since the regular expression **a*** matches the empty string). Such a grammar rule must have an empty right-hand side. We could simply write nothing on the right-hand side, as in

$$empty \rightarrow$$

but most often we will use the epsilon metasymbol for the empty string (similar to its use in regular expressions):

$$empty \rightarrow \varepsilon$$

Such a grammar rule is called an **ε-production** (an "epsilon production"). A grammar that generates a language containing the empty string must have at least one ε-production.

We can now write a grammar that is equivalent to the regular expression **a*** either as

$$A \rightarrow A\, a \mid \varepsilon$$

or

$$A \rightarrow a\, A \mid \varepsilon$$

Both grammars generate the language $\{a^n \mid n \text{ an integer} \geq 0\} = L(\mathbf{a*})$. ε-productions are also useful in defining structures that are optional, as we shall soon see.

We conclude this subsection with a few more examples.

Example 3.5

Consider the grammar

$$A \rightarrow (\,A\,)\,A \mid \varepsilon$$

This grammar generates the strings of all "balanced parentheses." For example, the string (( ) (( ))) ( ) is generated by the following derivation (the ε-production is used to make A disappear as needed):

$$A \Rightarrow (\,A\,)\,A \Rightarrow (\,A\,)\,(\,A\,)\,A \Rightarrow (\,A\,)\,(\,A\,) \Rightarrow (\,A\,)\,(\,) \Rightarrow (\,(\,A\,)\,A\,)\,(\,)$$
$$\Rightarrow (\,(\,)\,A\,)\,(\,) \Rightarrow (\,(\,)\,(\,A\,)\,A\,)\,(\,) \Rightarrow (\,(\,)\,(\,A\,)\,)\,(\,)$$
$$\Rightarrow (\,(\,)\,(\,(\,A\,)\,A\,)\,)\,(\,) \Rightarrow (\,(\,)\,(\,(\,)\,A\,)\,)\,(\,) \Rightarrow (\,(\,)\,(\,(\,)\,)\,)\,(\,) \qquad §$$

Example 3.6

The statement grammar of Example 3.4 can be written in the following alternative way using an ε-production:

$$statement \rightarrow if\text{-}stmt \mid \mathbf{other}$$
$$if\text{-}stmt \rightarrow \mathbf{if}\ (\ exp\ )\ statement\ else\text{-}part$$
$$else\text{-}part \rightarrow \mathbf{else}\ statement \mid \varepsilon$$
$$exp \rightarrow \mathbf{0} \mid \mathbf{1}$$

Note how the ε-production indicates that the structure *else-part* is optional. §

Example 3.7   Consider the following grammar G for a sequence of statements:

$$stmt\text{-}sequence \rightarrow stmt \; ; \; stmt\text{-}sequence \mid stmt$$
$$stmt \rightarrow \mathbf{s}$$

This grammar generates sequences of one or more statements separated by semicolons (statements have been abstracted into the single terminal **s**):

$$L(G) = \{ \; \mathbf{s}, \; \mathbf{s;s}, \; \mathbf{s;s;s}, \ldots \}$$

If we want to allow statement sequences to also be empty, we could write the following grammar G':

$$stmt\text{-}sequence \rightarrow stmt \; \mathbf{;} \; stmt\text{-}sequence \mid \varepsilon$$
$$stmt \rightarrow \mathbf{s}$$

but this turns the semicolon into a statement **terminator** rather than a statement **separator**:

$$L(G') = \{ \; \varepsilon, \; \mathbf{s;}, \; \mathbf{s;s;}, \; \mathbf{s;s;s;}, \ldots \}$$

If we want to allow statement sequences to be empty, but also retain the semicolon as a statement separator, we must write the grammar as follows:

$$stmt\text{-}sequence \rightarrow nonempty\text{-}stmt\text{-}sequence \mid \varepsilon$$
$$nonempty\text{-}stmt\text{-}sequence \rightarrow stmt \; \mathbf{;} \; nonempty\text{-}stmt\text{-}sequence \mid stmt$$
$$stmt \rightarrow \mathbf{s}$$

This example shows that care must be taken in the placement of the ε-production when constructing optional structures.   §

3.3   PARSE TREES AND ABSTRACT SYNTAX TREES

3.3.1   Parse Trees

A derivation provides a method for constructing a particular string of terminals from a starting nonterminal. But derivations do not uniquely represent the structure of the strings they construct. In general, there are many derivations for the same string. For example, we constructed the string of tokens

```
( number - number ) * number
```

from our simple expression grammar using the derivation in Figure 3.1. A second derivation for this string is given in Figure 3.2. The only difference between the two derivations is the order in which the replacements are supplied, and this is in fact a superficial difference. To make this clear, we need a representation for the structure of a string of terminals that abstracts the essential features of a derivation while factoring out superficial differences in ordering. The representation that does this is a tree structure, and is called a parse tree.

Figure 3.2

Another derivation for the expression **(34-3)*42**

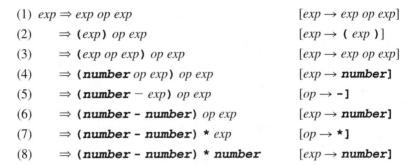

(1) *exp* ⇒ *exp op exp*   [*exp* → *exp op exp*]

(2)   ⇒ **(***exp***)** *op exp*   [*exp* → **(** *exp* **)**]

(3)   ⇒ **(***exp op exp***)** *op exp*   [*exp* → *exp op exp*]

(4)   ⇒ **(number** *op exp***)** *op exp*   [*exp* → **number**]

(5)   ⇒ **(number** − *exp***)** *op exp*   [*op* → **-**]

(6)   ⇒ **(number - number)** *op exp*   [*exp* → **number**]

(7)   ⇒ **(number - number) *** *exp*   [*op* → *****]

(8)   ⇒ **(number - number) * number**   [*exp* → **number**]

A **parse tree** corresponding to a derivation is a labeled tree in which the interior nodes are labeled by nonterminals, the leaf nodes are labeled by terminals, and the children of each internal node represent the replacement of the associated nonterminal in one step of the derivation.

To give a simple example, the derivation

$$exp \Rightarrow exp\ op\ exp$$
$$\Rightarrow \textbf{number}\ op\ exp$$
$$\Rightarrow \textbf{number + } exp$$
$$\Rightarrow \textbf{number + number}$$

corresponds to the parse tree

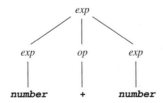

The first step in the derivation corresponds to the three children of the root node. The second step corresponds to the single **number** child of the leftmost *exp* below the root, and similarly for the remaining two steps. We can make this correspondence explicit by numbering the internal nodes of the parse tree by the step number in which its associated nonterminal is replaced in a corresponding derivation. Thus, if we number the previous derivation as follows:

(1) $exp \Rightarrow exp \; op \; exp$

(2) $\Rightarrow \textbf{number} \; op \; exp$

(3) $\Rightarrow \textbf{number} + exp$

(4) $\Rightarrow \textbf{number} + \textbf{number}$

we can number the internal nodes of the parse tree correspondingly:

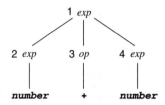

Note that this numbering of the internal nodes of the parse tree is actually a **preorder numbering**.

This same parse tree also corresponds to the derivations

$$exp \Rightarrow exp \; op \; exp$$
$$\Rightarrow exp \; op \; \textbf{number}$$
$$\Rightarrow exp + \textbf{number}$$
$$\Rightarrow \textbf{number} + \textbf{number}$$

and

$$exp \Rightarrow exp \; op \; exp$$
$$\Rightarrow exp + exp$$
$$\Rightarrow \textbf{number} + exp$$
$$\Rightarrow \textbf{number} + \textbf{number}$$

but that different numberings of the internal nodes would apply. Indeed the former of these two derivations corresponds to the following numbering:

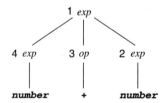

(We leave it to the reader to construct the numbering of the other.) In this case, the numbering is the reverse of a **postorder numbering** of the internal nodes of the parse tree. (A postorder traversal would visit the internal nodes in the order 4, 3, 2, 1.)

A parse tree corresponds in general to many derivations, all of which represent the same basic structure for the parsed string of terminals. However, it is possible to distinguish particular derivations that are uniquely associated with the parse tree. A **leftmost derivation** is a derivation in which the leftmost nonterminal is replaced at each step in the derivation. Correspondingly, a **rightmost derivation** is a derivation in which the rightmost nonterminal is replaced at each step in the derivation. A leftmost derivation corresponds to the preorder numbering of the internal nodes of its associated parse tree, while a rightmost derivation corresponds to a postorder numbering in reverse.

Indeed, we have seen this correspondence in the three derivations and the parse tree of the example just given. The first of the three derivations we gave is a leftmost derivation, while the second is a rightmost derivation. (The third derivation is neither leftmost nor rightmost.)

As a more complex example of a parse tree and leftmost and rightmost derivations, we return to the expression **(34-3)*42** and the derivations we gave in Figures 3.1 and 3.2. This parse tree for this expression is given in Figure 3.3, where we have also numbered the nodes according to the derivation of Figure 3.1. This derivation is in fact a rightmost derivation, and the corresponding numbering of the parse tree is a reverse postorder numbering. The derivation of Figure 3.2, on the other hand, is a leftmost derivation. (We invite the reader to supply a preorder numbering of the parse tree corresponding to this derivation.)

Figure 3.3

Parse tree for the arithmetic expression **(34-3)*42**

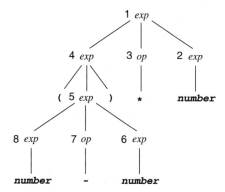

3.3.2 Abstract Syntax Trees

A parse tree is a useful representation of the structure of a string of tokens, in that the tokens appear as the leaves of the parse tree (from left to right), and the internal nodes of the parse tree represent the steps in a derivation (in some order). However, a parse tree contains much more information than is absolutely necessary for a compiler to produce executable code. To see this, consider the parse tree for the expression **3+4** according to our simple expression grammar:

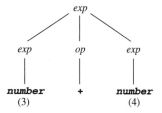

This is the parse tree from a previous example. We have augmented the tree to show the actual numeric value of each of the **number** tokens (this is an attribute of the token that is computed either by the scanner or the parser). The **principle of syntax-directed translation** states that the meaning, or semantics, of the string **3+4** should be directly related to its syntactic structure as represented by the parse tree. In this case, the principle of syntax-directed translation means that the parse tree should imply that the value 3 and the value 4 are to be added. Indeed, we can view the tree as implying this as follows. The root represents the operation of adding the values of the two child *exp* subtrees. Each of these subtrees, on the other hand, represents the value of its single **number** child. There is, however, a much simpler way to represent this same information, namely, as the tree

Here, the root node is simply labeled by the operation it represents, and the leaf nodes are labeled by their values (rather than the **number** tokens). Similarly, the expression **(34-3)*42** whose parse tree is given in Figure 3.3 can be represented more simply by the tree

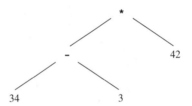

In this tree the parentheses tokens have actually disappeared, yet it still represents precisely the semantic content of subtracting 3 from 34, and then multiplying by 42.

Such trees represent abstractions of the actual source code token sequences, and the token sequences cannot be recovered from them (unlike parse trees). Nevertheless they contain all the information needed for translation, in a more efficient form than parse trees. Such trees are called **abstract syntax trees**, or **syntax trees** for short. A parser will go through all the steps represented by a parse tree, but will usually only construct an abstract syntax tree (or its equivalent).

Abstract syntax trees can be thought of as a tree representation of a shorthand notation called **abstract syntax**, much as a parse tree is a representation for the structure of ordinary syntax (also called **concrete syntax** when comparing it to abstract syntax). For example, the abstract syntax for the expression **3+4** might be written as *OpExp(Plus,ConstExp(3),ConstExp(4))*, and the abstract syntax for the expression **(34-3)*42** might be written as

$$OpExp(Times,OpExp(Minus,ConstExp(34),ConstExp(3)),ConstExp(42))$$

Indeed, abstract syntax can be given a formal definition using a BNF-like notation, just like concrete syntax. For example, we could write the following BNF-like rules for the abstract syntax of our simple arithmetic expressions as

$$exp \rightarrow OpExp(op,exp,exp) \mid ConstExp(integer)$$
$$op \rightarrow Plus \mid Minus \mid Times$$

We will not pursue this further. Our main interest is in the actual syntax tree structure that will be used by the parser, and this will be given by a data type declaration.[3] For example, the abstract syntax trees for our simple arithmetic expressions can be given by the C data type declarations

```
typedef enum {Plus,Minus,Times} OpKind;
typedef enum {OpKind,ConstKind} ExpKind;
typedef struct streenode
     { ExpKind kind;
       OpKind op;
       struct streenode *lchild,*rchild;
       int val;
     } STreeNode;
typedef STreeNode *SyntaxTree;
```

Note that we have used enumerated types for the two different kinds of syntax tree nodes (integer constants and operations), as well as for the operations (plus, minus, times) themselves. In fact, we would probably use the tokens to represent the operations, rather than defining a new enumerated type. We could also have used a C **union** type to save space, since a node cannot be both an operator node and a constant node simultaneously. Finally, we remark that these tree node declarations only include the attributes that are directly needed for this example. In practical situations there will be many more fields for the compile-time attributes, such as data type, symbol table information, and so on, as examples later on in this chapter and in subsequent chapters will make clear.

We conclude this section with a number of examples of parse and syntax trees using grammars we have considered in previous examples.

Example 3.8   Consider the grammar for simplified if-statements of Example 3.4:

$$statement \rightarrow if\text{-}stmt \mid \textbf{other}$$
$$if\text{-}stmt \rightarrow \textbf{if} \; (\; exp \;) \; statement$$
$$\mid \textbf{if} \; (\; exp \;) \; statement \; \textbf{else} \; statement$$
$$exp \rightarrow \textbf{0} \mid \textbf{1}$$

---

3. There are languages for which the abstract syntax just given is essentially a type declaration. See the exercises.

The parse tree for the string

if (0) other else other

is as follows:

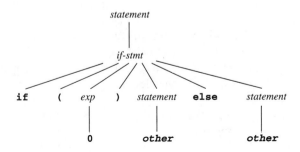

Using the grammar of Example 3.6,

$$statement \rightarrow if\text{-}stmt \mid \textbf{other}$$
$$if\text{-}stmt \rightarrow \textbf{if (}\, exp \,\textbf{)}\, statement \; else\text{-}part$$
$$else\text{-}part \rightarrow \textbf{else}\; statement \mid \varepsilon$$
$$exp \rightarrow \textbf{0} \mid \textbf{1}$$

this same string has the following parse tree:

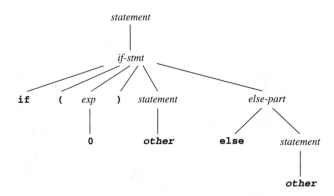

An appropriate abstract syntax tree for if-statements would dispense with all except the three subordinate structures of the if-statement: the test expression, the then-part, and the else-part (if present). Thus, a syntax tree for the previous string (using either the grammar of Example 3.4 or 3.6) would be:

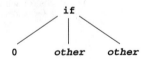

Here, we have used the remaining tokens **if** and **other** as labels to distinguish the kind of statement node in the syntax tree. This would more properly be done using an enumerated type. For example, a set of C declarations that would be appropriate for the structure of the statements and expressions in this example is as follows:

```
typedef enum {ExpK,StmtK} NodeKind;
typedef enum {Zero,One} ExpKind;
typedef enum {IfK,OtherK} StmtKind;
typedef struct streenode
  {NodeKind kind;
   ExpKind ekind;
   StmtKind skind;
   struct streenode
      *test,*thenpart,*elsepart;
  } STreeNode;
typedef STreeNode * SyntaxTree;
```
§

Example 3.9   Consider the grammar of a sequence of statements separated by semicolons from Example 3.7:

$$stmt\text{-}sequence \rightarrow stmt \; ; \; stmt\text{-}sequence \mid stmt$$
$$stmt \rightarrow \mathbf{s}$$

The string **s;s;s** has the following parse tree with respect to this grammar:

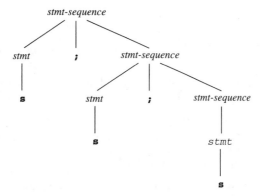

A possible syntax tree for this same string is

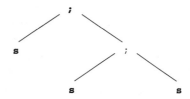

In this tree the semicolon nodes are similar to operator nodes (like the **+** nodes of arithmetic expressions), except that they "operate" only by binding the statements together in a sequence. We could instead try to bind all the statement nodes in a sequence together with just one node, so that the previous syntax tree would become

The problem with this is that a **seq** node may have an arbitrary number of children, and this is difficult to provide for in a data type declaration. The solution is to use the standard **leftmost-child right-sibling** representation for a tree (presented in most data structures texts). In this representation, the only physical link from the parent to its children is to the leftmost child. The children are then linked together from left to right in a standard linked list, which are called **sibling** links to distinguish them from parent-child links. The previous tree now becomes, in the leftmost-child right-sibling arrangement:

With this arrangement, we can also do away with the connecting **seq** node, and the syntax tree then becomes simply:

$$s \;\text{—}\; s \;\text{—}\; s$$

This is clearly the simplest and easiest representation for a sequence of things in a syntax tree. The complication is that the links here are sibling links that must be distinguished from child links, and that require a new field in the syntax tree declaration. **§**

3.4   AMBIGUITY

3.4.1   Ambiguous Grammars

Parse trees and syntax trees uniquely express the structure of syntax, as do leftmost and rightmost derivations, but not derivations in general. Unfortunately, it is possible for a grammar to permit a string to have more than one parse tree. Consider, for example, the simple integer arithmetic grammar we have been using as a standard example

$$exp \rightarrow exp \; op \; exp \mid (\; exp \;) \mid \textbf{\textit{number}}$$
$$op \rightarrow \textbf{+} \mid \textbf{--} \mid \textbf{*}$$

and consider the string **34-3*42**. This string has two different parse trees

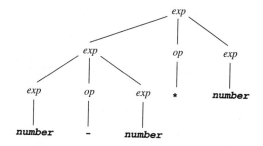

and

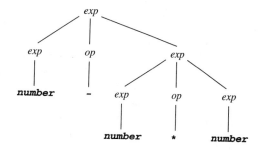

corresponding to the two leftmost derivations

$exp \Rightarrow exp \; op \; exp$ $[exp \rightarrow exp \; op \; exp]$

$\Rightarrow exp \; op \; exp \; op \; exp$ $[exp \rightarrow exp \; op \; exp]$

$\Rightarrow \mathbf{number} \; op \; exp \; op \; exp$ $[exp \rightarrow \mathbf{number}]$

$\Rightarrow \mathbf{number} - exp \; op \; exp$ $[op \rightarrow \mathtt{-}]$

$\Rightarrow \mathbf{number} - \mathbf{number} \; op \; exp$ $[exp \rightarrow \mathbf{number}]$

$\Rightarrow \mathbf{number} - \mathbf{number} * exp$ $[op \rightarrow \mathtt{*}]$

$\Rightarrow \mathbf{number} - \mathbf{number} * \mathbf{number}$ $[exp \rightarrow \mathbf{number}]$

and

$exp \Rightarrow exp \; op \; exp$ $[exp \rightarrow exp \; op \; exp]$

$\Rightarrow \mathbf{number} \; op \; exp$ $[exp \rightarrow \mathbf{number}]$

$\Rightarrow \mathbf{number} - exp$ $[op \rightarrow \mathtt{-}]$

$\Rightarrow \mathbf{number} - exp \; op \; exp$ $[exp \rightarrow exp \; op \; exp]$

$\Rightarrow \mathbf{number} - \mathbf{number} \; op \; exp$ $[exp \rightarrow \mathbf{number}]$

$\Rightarrow \mathbf{number} - \mathbf{number} * exp$ $[op \rightarrow \mathtt{*}]$

$\Rightarrow \mathbf{number} - \mathbf{number} * \mathbf{number}$ $[exp \rightarrow \mathbf{number}]$

The associated syntax trees are

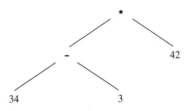

and

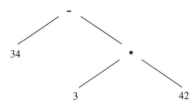

A grammar that generates a string with two distinct parse trees is called an **ambiguous grammar**. Such a grammar represents a serious problem for a parser, since it does not specify precisely the syntactic structure of a program (even though the legal strings themselves—the members of the language of the grammar—are completely determined). In some sense, an ambiguous grammar is like a nondeterministic automaton, in which two separate paths can accept the same string. However, ambiguity in grammars cannot be removed nearly as easily as nondeterminism in finite automata, since there is no algorithm for doing so, unlike the situation in the case of automata (the subset construction, discussed in the previous chapter).[4]

An ambiguous grammar must therefore be considered to be an incomplete specification of the syntax of a language, and as such should be avoided. Fortunately, ambiguous grammars always fail the tests that we introduce later for the standard parsing algorithms, and a body of standard techniques have been developed to deal with typical ambiguities that come up in programming languages.

Two basic methods are used to deal with ambiguities. One is to state a rule that specifies in each ambiguous case which of the parse trees (or syntax trees) is the correct one. Such a rule is called a **disambiguating rule**. The usefulness of such a rule is that it corrects the ambiguity without changing (and possibly complicating) the grammar. The disadvantage is that the syntactic structure of the language is no longer given by the grammar alone. The alternative is to change the grammar into a form that forces the construction of the correct parse tree, thus removing the ambiguity. Of course, in either method we must first decide which of the trees in an ambiguous case is the correct one. This involves again the principle of syntax-directed translation. The parse (or syntax) tree that we want is the one that correctly reflects the later meaning we will apply to the construct in order to translate it into object code.

---

4. The situation is actually even worse, since there is no algorithm to determine whether a grammar is ambiguous in the first place. See Section 3.2.7.

Which of the two previously given syntax trees represent the correct interpretation of the string **34-3*42**? The first tree indicates, by making the subtraction node a child of the multiplication node, that we intend the expression to be evaluated by first evaluating the subtraction $(34 - 3 = 31)$ and then the multiplication $(31 * 42 = 1302)$. The second tree, on the other hand, indicates that the multiplication is to be performed first $(3 * 42 = 126)$ and then the subtraction $(34 - 126 = -92)$. Which tree we choose depends on which of these calculations we view as the correct one. Standard mathematical convention dictates that the second interpretation is correct. This is because multiplication is said to have **precedence** over subtraction. Usually, both multiplication and division have precedence over both addition and subtraction.

To remove the given ambiguity in our simple expression grammar, we could now simply state a disambiguating rule that establishes the relative precedences of the three operations represented. The standard solution is to give addition and subtraction the same precedence, and to give multiplication a higher precedence.

Unfortunately, this rule still does not completely remove the ambiguity of the grammar. Consider the string **34-3-42**. This string also has two possible syntax trees:

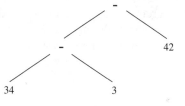

and

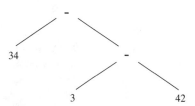

The first represents the computation $(34 - 3) - 42 = -11$, while the second represents the computation $34 - (3 - 42) = 73$. Again, which computation is correct is a matter of convention. Standard mathematics dictates that the first choice is correct. This is because subtraction is considered to be **left associative**; that is, a series of subtraction operations is performed from left to right.

Thus, a further ambiguity requiring a disambiguating rule is the associativity of each of the operations of addition, subtraction, and multiplication. It is common to specify that all three of these operations are left associative. This does indeed remove the remaining ambiguities of our simple expression grammar (though we will not be able to prove this until later).

It is also possible to choose to specify that an operation is **nonassociative**, in that a sequence of more than one operator in an expression is not allowed. We could, for instance, have written our simple expression grammar in the following form:

$$exp \rightarrow factor\ op\ factor \mid factor$$
$$factor \rightarrow (\ exp\ ) \mid \mathbf{number}$$
$$op \rightarrow \mathbf{+} \mid \mathbf{-} \mid \mathbf{*}$$

In this case, strings such as **34-3-42** and even **34-3*42** are now illegal, and must instead be written with parentheses, such as **(34-3)-42** and **34-(3*42)**. Such **fully parenthesized expressions** have no need for the specification of associativity or, indeed, precedence. The above grammar is unambiguous as written. Of course, we have not only changed the grammar, we have also changed the language being recognized.

We turn now to methods for rewriting the grammar to remove the ambiguity rather than stating disambiguating rules. Note that we must find methods that do not change the basic strings being recognized (as the example of fully parenthesized expressions did).

3.4.2 Precedence and Associativity

To handle the precedence of operations in the grammar, we must group the operators into groups of equal precedence, and for each precedence we must write a different rule. For example, the precedence of multiplication over addition and subtraction can be added to our simple expression grammar as follows:

$$exp \rightarrow exp\ addop\ exp \mid term$$
$$addop \rightarrow \mathbf{+} \mid \mathbf{-}$$
$$term \rightarrow term\ mulop\ term \mid factor$$
$$mulop \rightarrow \mathbf{*}$$
$$factor \rightarrow (\ exp\ ) \mid \mathbf{number}$$

In this grammar, multiplication is grouped under the *term* rule, while addition and subtraction are grouped under the *exp* rule. Since the base case for an *exp* is a *term*, this means that addition and subtraction will appear "higher" (that is, closer to the root) in the parse and syntax trees, and thus receive lower precedence. Such a grouping of operators into different precedence levels is a standard method in syntactic specification using BNF. We call such a grouping a **precedence cascade**.

This last grammar for simple arithmetic expressions still does not specify the associativity of the operators and is still ambiguous. The reason is that the recursion on both sides of the operator allows either side to match repetitions of the operator in a derivation (and, hence, in the parse and syntax trees). The solution is to replace one of the recursions with the base case, forcing the repetitive matches on the side with the remaining recursion. Thus, replacing the rule

$$exp \rightarrow exp\ addop\ exp \mid term$$

by

$$exp \rightarrow exp\ addop\ term \mid term$$

makes addition and subtraction left associative, while writing

$$exp \rightarrow term\ addop\ exp \mid term$$

makes them right associative. In other words, a left recursive rule makes its operators associate on the left, while a right recursive rule makes them associate on the right.

To complete the removal of ambiguity in the BNF rules for our simple arithmetic expressions, we write the rules to make all the operations left associative:

$$exp \rightarrow exp\ addop\ term \mid term$$
$$addop \rightarrow + \mid -$$
$$term \rightarrow term\ mulop\ factor \mid factor$$
$$mulop \rightarrow *$$
$$factor \rightarrow (\ exp\ ) \mid \textbf{number}$$

Now the parse tree for the expression **34-3*42** is

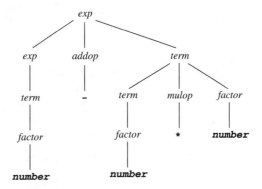

and the parse tree for the expression **34-3-42** is

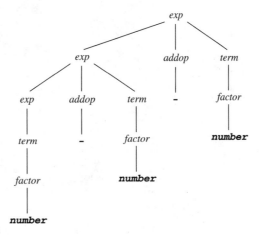

Note that the precedence cascades cause the parse trees to become much more complex. The syntax trees, however, are not affected.

3.4.3   The Dangling Else Problem

Consider the grammar from Example 3.4 (page 103):

$$
\begin{aligned}
statement &\rightarrow \textit{if-stmt} \mid \textbf{other} \\
\textit{if-stmt} &\rightarrow \textbf{if (} exp \textbf{) } statement \\
&\qquad \mid \textbf{if (} exp \textbf{)} statement \textbf{ else } statement \\
exp &\rightarrow \textbf{0} \mid \textbf{1}
\end{aligned}
$$

This grammar is ambiguous as a result of the optional else. To see this, consider the string

    if (0) if (1) other else other

This string has the two parse trees:

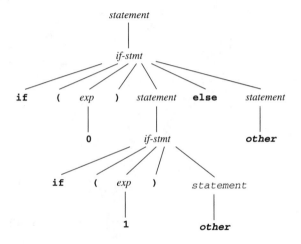

and

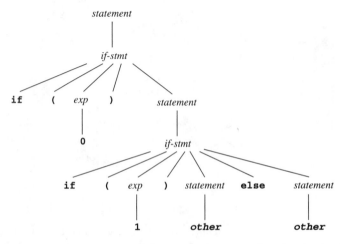

Which one is correct depends on whether we want to associate the single else-part with the first or the second if-statement: the first parse tree associates the else-part with the first if-statement; the second parse tree associates it with the second if-statement. This ambiguity is called the **dangling else problem**. To see which parse tree is correct, we must consider the implications for the meaning of the if-statement. To get a clearer idea of this, consider the following piece of C code

```
if (x != 0)
    if (y == 1/x) ok = TRUE;
    else z = 1/x;
```

In this code, whenever **x** is 0, a division by zero error will occur if the else-part is associated with the first if-statement. Thus, the implication of this code (and indeed the implication of the indentation of the else-part) is that an else-part should always be associated with the nearest if-statement that does not yet have an associated else-part. This disambiguating rule is called the **most closely nested rule** for the dangling else problem, and it implies that the second parse tree above is the correct one. Note that, if we wanted we *could* associate the else-part with the first if-statement by using brackets **{...}** in C, as in

```
if (x != 0)
    {if (y == 1/x) ok = TRUE;}
else z = 1/x;
```

A solution to the dangling else ambiguity in the BNF itself is more difficult than the previous ambiguities we have seen. A solution is as follows:

statement → *matched-stmt* | *unmatched-stmt*
matched-stmt → **if** **(** *exp* **)** *matched-stmt* **else** *matched-stmt* | **other**
unmatched-stmt → **if** **(** *exp* **)** *statement*
              | **if** **(** *exp* **)** *matched-stmt* **else** *unmatched-stmt*
exp → **0** | **1**

This works by permitting only a *matched-stmt* to come before an **else** in an if-statement, thus forcing all else-parts to be matched as soon as possible. For instance, the associated parse tree for our sample string now becomes

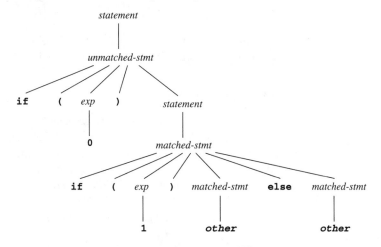

which indeed associates the else-part with the second if-statement.

Building the most closely nested rule into the BNF is usually not undertaken. Instead, the disambiguating rule is preferred. One reason is the added complexity of the new grammar, but the principal reason is that parsing methods are easy to configure in such a way that the most closely nested rule is obeyed. (Precedence and associativity are a little harder to achieve automatically without rewriting the grammar.)

The dangling else problem has its origins in the syntax of Algol60. It is possible to design the syntax in such a way that the dangling else problem does not appear. One way is to *require* the presence of the else-part, and this method has been used in LISP and other functional languages (where a value must also be returned). Another solution is to use a **bracketing keyword** for the if-statement. Languages that use this solution include Algol68 and Ada. In Ada, for example, the programmer writes

```
if x /= 0 then
  if y = 1/x then ok := true;
  else z := 1/x;
  end if;
end if;
```

to associate the else-part with the second if-statement. Alternatively, the programmer writes

```
if x /= 0 then
  if y = 1/x then ok := true;
  end if;
else z := 1/x;
end if;
```

to associate it with the first if-statement. The corresponding BNF in Ada (somewhat simplified) is

$$if\text{-}stmt \rightarrow \textbf{if } condition \textbf{ then } statement\text{-}sequence \textbf{ end if}$$
$$| \textbf{ if } condition \textbf{ then } statement\text{-}sequence$$
$$\textbf{else } statement\text{-}sequence \textbf{ end if}$$

Thus, the two keywords **end if** are the bracketing keyword in Ada. In Algol68 the bracketing keyword is **fi** (**if** written backwards).

3.4.4   Inessential Ambiguity

Sometimes a grammar may be ambiguous and yet always produce unique abstract syntax trees. Consider, for example, the statement sequence grammar of Example 3.9 (page 113), where we could choose a simple sibling list as the syntax tree. In that case, either a right recursive or left recursive grammar rule would still result in the same syntax tree structure, and we could write the grammar ambiguously as

$$stmt\text{-}sequence \rightarrow stmt\text{-}sequence \textbf{ ; } stmt\text{-}sequence \mid stmt$$
$$stmt \rightarrow \textbf{s}$$

and still obtain unique syntax trees. Such an ambiguity could be called an **inessential ambiguity**, since the associated semantics do not depend on what disambiguating rule is used. A similar situation arises with binary operators, such as arithmetic addition or string concatenation, that represent **associative operations** (a binary operator · is associative if $(a \cdot b) \cdot c = a \cdot (b \cdot c)$ for all values a, b, and c). In this case the syntax trees are still distinct, but represent the same semantic value, and we may not care which one we use. Nevertheless, a parsing algorithm will need to apply some disambiguating rule that the compiler writer may need to supply.

3.5 EXTENDED NOTATIONS: EBNF AND SYNTAX DIAGRAMS
3.5.1 EBNF Notation

Repetitive and optional constructs are extremely common in programming languages, and thus in BNF grammar rules as well. Therefore, it should not be surprising that the BNF notation is sometimes extended to include special notations for these two situations. These extensions comprise a notation that is called **extended BNF**, or **EBNF**.

Consider, first, the case of repetition, such as that of statement sequences. We have seen that repetition is expressed by recursion in grammar rules and that either left or right recursion might be used, indicated by the generic rules

$$A \rightarrow A \; \alpha \mid \beta \quad \text{(left recursive)}$$

and

$$A \rightarrow \alpha \; A \mid \beta \quad \text{(right recursive)}$$

where α and β are arbitrary strings of terminals and nonterminals and where in the first rule β does not begin with A and in the second β does not end with A.

It would be possible to use the same notation for repetition that regular expressions use, namely, the asterisk * (also called Kleene closure in regular expressions). Then these two rules would be written as the nonrecursive rules

$$A \rightarrow \beta \; \alpha^*$$

and

$$A \rightarrow \alpha^* \; \beta$$

Instead, EBNF opts to use curly brackets {...} to express repetition (thus making clear the extent of the string to be repeated), and we write

$$A \rightarrow \beta \; \{\alpha\}$$

and

$$A \rightarrow \{\alpha\} \; \beta$$

for the rules.

The problem with any repetition notation is that it obscures how the parse tree is to be constructed, but, as we have seen, we often do not care. Take for example, the case of statement sequences (Example 3.9). We wrote the grammar as follows, in right recursive form:

$$stmt\text{-}sequence \rightarrow stmt \text{ ; } stmt\text{-}sequence \mid stmt$$
$$stmt \rightarrow \mathbf{s}$$

This rule has the form $A \rightarrow \alpha\,A \mid \beta$, with $A = stmt\text{-}sequence$, $\alpha = stmt \text{ ; }$, and $\beta = stmt$. In EBNF this would appear as

$$stmt\text{-}sequence \rightarrow \{ \ stmt \text{ ; } \} \ stmt \quad \text{(right recursive form)}$$

We could equally as well have used a left recursive rule and obtained the EBNF

$$stmt\text{-}sequence \rightarrow stmt \ \{ \text{ ; } stmt \ \} \quad \text{(left recursive form)}$$

In fact, the second form is the one generally used (for reasons we shall discuss in the next chapter).

A more significant problem occurs when the associativity matters, as it does for binary operations such as subtraction and division. For example, consider the first grammar rule in the simple expression grammar of the previous subsection:

$$exp \rightarrow exp \ addop \ term \mid term$$

This has the form $A \rightarrow A\,\alpha \mid \beta$, with $A = exp$, $\alpha = addop \ term$, and $\beta = term$. Thus, we write this rule in EBNF as

$$exp \rightarrow term \ \{ \ addop \ term \ \}$$

We must now also assume that this implies left associativity, although the rule itself does not explicitly state it. We might assume that a right associative rule would be implied by writing

$$exp \rightarrow \{ \ term \ addop \ \} \ term$$

but this is not the case. Instead, a right recursive rule such as

$$stmt\text{-}sequence \rightarrow stmt \text{ ; } stmt\text{-}sequence \mid stmt$$

is viewed as being a *stmt* followed by an optional semicolon and *stmt-sequence*.

Optional constructs in EBNF are indicated by surrounding them with square brackets [. . .]. This is similar in spirit to the regular expression convention of putting a question mark after an optional part, but has the advantage of surrounding the optional part without requiring parentheses. For example, the grammar rules for if-statements with optional else-parts (Examples 3.4 and 3.6) would be written as follows in EBNF:

$$statement \rightarrow \textit{if-stmt} \mid \textbf{other}$$
$$\textit{if-stmt} \rightarrow \textbf{if} \ (\ exp \ ) \, statement \ [\ \textbf{else} \ statement \ ]$$
$$exp \rightarrow \textbf{0} \mid \textbf{1}$$

Also, a right recursive rule such as

$$\textit{stmt-sequence} \rightarrow stmt \ \textbf{;} \ \textit{stmt-sequence} \mid stmt$$

is written as

$$\textit{stmt-sequence} \rightarrow stmt \ [\ \textbf{;} \ \textit{stmt-sequence} \ ]$$

(contrast this to the use of curly brackets previously to write this rule in left recursive form).

If we wished to write an arithmetic operation such as addition in right associative form, we would write

$$exp \rightarrow \textit{term} \ [\ \textit{addop} \ exp \ ]$$

instead of using curly brackets.

3.5.2 Syntax Diagrams

Graphical representations for visually representing EBNF rules are called **syntax diagrams**. They consist of boxes representing terminals and nonterminals, arrowed lines representing sequencing and choices, and nonterminal labels for each diagram representing the grammar rule defining that nonterminal. A round or oval box is used to indicate terminals in a diagram, while a square or rectangular box is used to indicate nonterminals.

As an example, consider the grammar rule

$$factor \rightarrow (\ exp \ ) \mid \textbf{number}$$

This is written as a syntax diagram in the following way:

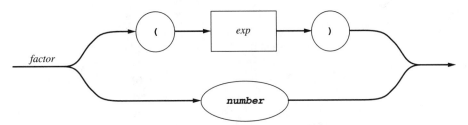

Note that *factor* is not placed inside a box, but is used as a label for the syntax diagram, indicating the diagram represents the definition of the structure of that name. Note, also, the use of the arrowed lines to indicate choice and sequencing.

Syntax diagrams are written from the EBNF rather than the BNF, so we need diagrams representing repetition and optional constructs. Given a repetition such as

$$A \rightarrow \{ \, B \, \}$$

the corresponding syntax diagram is usually drawn as follows:

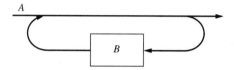

Note that the diagram must allow for no B's at all to appear.
   An optional construct such as

$$A \rightarrow [\, B \,]$$

is drawn as

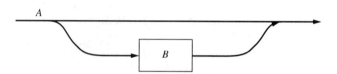

We conclude our discussion of syntax diagrams with some examples using previous EBNF examples.

Example 3.10   Consider our running example of simple arithmetic expressions. This has the BNF (including associativity and precedence).

$$
\begin{aligned}
exp &\rightarrow exp \; addop \; term \mid term \\
addop &\rightarrow \textbf{+} \mid \textbf{--} \\
term &\rightarrow term \; mulop \; factor \mid factor \\
mulop &\rightarrow \textbf{*} \\
factor &\rightarrow \textbf{(} \; exp \; \textbf{)} \mid \textbf{number}
\end{aligned}
$$

The corresponding EBNF is

$$
\begin{aligned}
exp &\rightarrow term \; \{ \, addop \; term \, \} \\
addop &\rightarrow \textbf{+} \mid \textbf{--} \\
term &\rightarrow factor \; \{ \, mulop \; factor \, \} \\
mulop &\rightarrow \textbf{*} \\
factor &\rightarrow \textbf{(} \; exp \; \textbf{)} \mid \textbf{number}
\end{aligned}
$$

The corresponding syntax diagrams are given in Figure 3.4 (the syntax diagram for *factor* was given previously).

Figure 3.4

Syntax diagrams for the grammar of Example 3.10

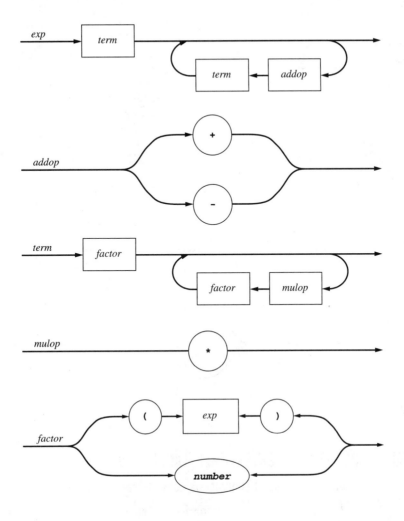

Example 3.11   Consider the grammar of simplified if-statements from Example 3.4 (page 103). This has the BNF

$$statement \rightarrow if\text{-}stmt \mid \mathbf{other}$$
$$if\text{-}stmt \rightarrow \mathbf{if} \ (\ exp \ ) \, statement$$
$$\mid \mathbf{if} \ (\ exp \ ) \, statement \ \mathbf{else} \ statement$$
$$exp \rightarrow \mathbf{0} \mid \mathbf{1}$$

and the EBNF

$$statement \rightarrow if\text{-}stmt \mid \mathbf{other}$$
$$if\text{-}stmt \rightarrow \mathbf{if} \ (\ exp \ ) \, statement \ [\ \mathbf{else} \ statement \ ]$$
$$exp \rightarrow \mathbf{0} \mid \mathbf{1}$$

The corresponding syntax diagrams are given in Figure 3.5.

Figure 3.5

Syntax diagrams for the grammar of Example 3.11

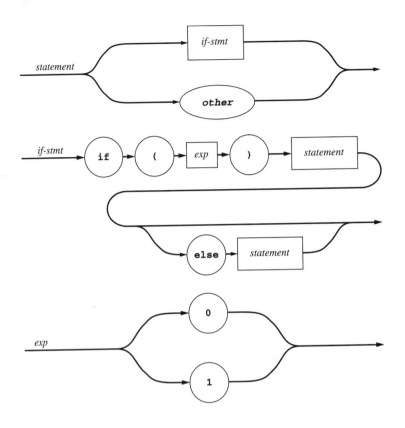

§

3.6   FORMAL PROPERTIES OF CONTEXT-FREE LANGUAGES

3.6.1   A Formal Definition of Context-Free Languages

We present here in a more formal and mathematical way some of the terminology and definitions that we have introduced previously in this chapter. We begin by stating a formal definition of a context-free grammar.

Definition

A **context-free grammar** consists of the following:

1. A set T of **terminals**.
2. A set N of **nonterminals** (disjoint from T).
3. A set P of **productions**, or **grammar rules**, of the form $A \rightarrow \alpha$, where A is an element of N and α is an element of $(T \cup N)^*$ (a possibly empty sequence of terminals and nonterminals).
4. A **start symbol** S from the set N.

Let G be a grammar as defined above, so that $G = (T, N, P, S)$. A **derivation step** over G is of the form $\alpha A \gamma \Rightarrow \alpha \beta \gamma$, where α and γ are elements of $(T \cup N)^*$ and

$A \to \beta$ is in P. (The union $T \cup N$ of the sets of terminals and nonterminals is sometimes called the **set of symbols** of G, and a string α in $(T \cup N)^*$ is called a **sentential form**.) The relation $\alpha \Rightarrow^* \beta$ is defined to be the transitive closure of the derivation step relation $\Rightarrow$; that is, $\alpha \Rightarrow^* \beta$ if and only if there is a sequence of 0 or more derivation steps $(n \geq 0)$

$$\alpha_1 \Rightarrow \alpha_2 \Rightarrow \cdots \Rightarrow \alpha_{n-1} \Rightarrow \alpha_n$$

such that $\alpha = \alpha_1$ and $\beta = \alpha_n$. (If $n = 0$, then $\alpha = \beta$.) A **derivation** over the grammar G is of the form $S \Rightarrow^* w$, where $w \in T^*$ (i.e., w is a string of terminals only, called a **sentence**) and S is the start symbol of G.

The **language generated by** G, written $L(G)$, is defined as the set $L(G) = \{w \in T^* \mid$ there exists a derivation $S \Rightarrow^* w$ of $G\}$. That is, $L(G)$ is the set of sentences derivable from S.

A **leftmost derivation** $S \Rightarrow^*_{lm} w$ is a derivation in which each derivation step $\alpha A \gamma \Rightarrow \alpha \beta \gamma$ is such that $\alpha \in T^*$; that is, α consists only of terminals. Similarly, a **rightmost derivation** is one in which each derivation step $\alpha A \gamma \Rightarrow \alpha \beta \gamma$ has the property that $\gamma \in T^*$.

A **parse tree** over the grammar G is a rooted labeled tree with the following properties:

1. Each node is labeled with a terminal or a nonterminal or ε.
2. The root node is labeled with the start symbol S.
3. Each leaf node is labeled with a terminal or with ε.
4. Each nonleaf node is labeled with a nonterminal.
5. If a node with label $A \in N$ has n children with labels $X_1, X_2, \ldots, X_n$ (which may be terminals or nonterminals), then $A \to X_1 X_2 \ldots X_n \in P$ (a production of the grammar).

Each derivation gives rise to a parse tree such that each step $\alpha A \gamma \Rightarrow \alpha \beta \gamma$ in the derivation, with $\beta = X_1 X_2 \ldots X_n$ corresponds to the construction of n children with labels $X_1, X_2, \ldots, X_n$ of the node with label A. In general, many derivations may give rise to the same parse tree. Each parse tree, however, has a unique leftmost and rightmost derivation that give rise to it. The leftmost derivation corresponds to a preorder traversal of the parse tree, while the rightmost derivation corresponds to the reverse of a postorder traversal of the parse tree.

A set of strings L is said to be a **context-free language** if there is context-free grammar G such that $L = L(G)$. In general, many different grammars generate the same context-free language, but the strings in the language will have different parse trees depending on the grammar used.

A grammar G is **ambiguous** if there exists a string $w \in L(G)$ such that w has two distinct parse trees (or leftmost or rightmost derivations).

3.6.2 Grammar Rules as Equations

At the beginning of this section, we noted that grammar rules use the arrow symbol instead of an equal sign to represent the definition of names for structures (nonterminals), unlike our notation for regular expressions, where we used the equal sign in defining names for regular expressions. The reason given was that the recursive nature of grammar rules makes the defining relations (the grammar rules) less like equality, and we did indeed see that the strings defined by grammar rules result from derivations, where a left-to-right replacement method is used that follows the direction of the arrow in the BNF.

There is a sense, however, in which equality of left- and right-hand sides in a grammar rule still holds, but the defining process of the language that results from this view is different. This view is important for the theory of programming language semantics and is worth studying briefly for its insight into recursive processes such as parsing, even though the parsing algorithms we study are not based on it.

Consider, for example, the following grammar rule, which is extracted (in simplified form) from our simple expression grammar:

$$exp \rightarrow exp + exp \mid \texttt{number}$$

We have already seen that a nonterminal name like exp defines a set of strings of terminals (which is the language of the grammar if the nonterminal is the start symbol). Suppose we call this set $\mathbf{E}$, and let $\mathbf{N}$ be the set of natural numbers (corresponding to the regular expression name $\texttt{number}$). Then, the given grammar rule can be interpreted as the set equation

$$\mathbf{E} = (\mathbf{E} + \mathbf{E}) \cup \mathbf{N}$$

where $\mathbf{E} + \mathbf{E}$ is the set of strings $\{u + v \mid u,v \in \mathbf{E} \}$. (We are not *adding* the strings u and v here but, rather, are concatenating them with the symbol $+$ in between.)

This is a recursive equation for the set $\mathbf{E}$. Consider how this may define $\mathbf{E}$. First, the set $\mathbf{N}$ is contained in $\mathbf{E}$ (the base case), since $\mathbf{E}$ is the union of $\mathbf{N}$ and $\mathbf{E} + \mathbf{E}$. Next, the fact that $\mathbf{E} + \mathbf{E}$ is also contained in $\mathbf{E}$ implies that $\mathbf{N} + \mathbf{N}$ is contained in $\mathbf{E}$. But then, since both $\mathbf{N}$ and $\mathbf{N} + \mathbf{N}$ are contained in $\mathbf{E}$, so is $\mathbf{N} + \mathbf{N} + \mathbf{N}$, and so on. We can view this as an inductive construction of longer and longer strings, and the union of all these sets is the desired result:

$$\mathbf{E} = \mathbf{N} \cup (\mathbf{N} + \mathbf{N}) \cup (\mathbf{N} + \mathbf{N} + \mathbf{N}) \cup (\mathbf{N} + \mathbf{N} + \mathbf{N} + \mathbf{N}) \cup \ldots$$

In fact, it can be proved that this $\mathbf{E}$ does satisfy the equation in question. Indeed, $\mathbf{E}$ is the *smallest* set that does. If we view the right-hand side of the equation for $\mathbf{E}$ as a (set) function of $\mathbf{E}$, so that we define $f(s) = (s + s) \cup \mathbf{N}$, then the equation for $\mathbf{E}$ becomes $\mathbf{E} = f(\mathbf{E})$. In other words, $\mathbf{E}$ is a **fixed point** of the function f and (according to our previous comment) is indeed the smallest such fixed point. We say that $\mathbf{E}$ as defined by this method is given **least-fixed-point semantics**.

Recursively defined programming language structures, such as syntax, recursive data types, and recursive functions, can all be shown to have least-fixed-point semantics when they are implemented according to the usual algorithms that we will study further on in this book. This is an important point, because methods such as this may be used in the future to verify the correctness of compilers. At present, compilers are rarely proved to be correct. Instead, testing of compiler code assures only an approximation of correctness, and substantial errors often remain, even in commercially produced compilers.

3.6.3   The Chomsky Hierarchy and the Limits of Syntax as Context-Free Rules

When representing the syntactic structure of a programming language, context-free grammars in BNF or EBNF are a useful and powerful tool. But it is also important to know what can or should be represented by the BNF. We have already seen a situation in which the grammar may be left ambiguous intentionally (the dangling else problem), and thus not express the complete syntax directly. Other situations can arise where we may try to express too much in the grammar, or where it may be essentially impossible to express a requirement in the grammar. In this section, we discuss a few of the common cases.

A frequent question that arises when writing the BNF for a language is the extent to which the lexical structure should be expressed in the BNF rather than in a separate description (possibly using regular expressions). The previous discussion has shown that context-free grammars can express concatenation, repetition, and choice, just as regular expressions can. We could, therefore, write out grammar rules for the construction of all the tokens from characters and dispense with regular expressions altogether.

For example, consider the definition of a number as a sequence of digits using regular expressions:

```
digit = 0|1|2|3|4|5|6|7|8|9
number = digit digit*
```

We can write this definition using BNF, instead, as

$$digit \rightarrow 0 \mid 1 \mid 2 \mid 3 \mid 4 \mid 5 \mid 6 \mid 7 \mid 8 \mid 9$$
$$number \rightarrow number\ digit \mid digit$$

Note that the recursion in the second rule is used to express repetition only. A grammar with this property is said to be a **regular grammar**, and regular grammars can express everything that regular expressions can. A consequence of this is that we could design a parser that would accept characters directly from the input source file and dispense with the scanner altogether.

Why isn't this a good idea? Efficiency would be compromised. A parser is a more powerful machine than a scanner but is correspondingly less efficient. Nevertheless, it may be reasonable and useful to include a definition of the tokens in the BNF itself—the grammar would then express the complete syntactic structure, including the lexical structure. Of course, the language implementor would be expected to extract these definitions from the grammar and turn them into a scanner.

A different situation occurs with respect to **context rules**, which occur frequently in programming languages. We have been using the term context-free without explaining why such rules are in fact "free of context." The simple reason is that nonterminals appear by themselves to the left of the arrow in context-free rules. Thus, a rule

$$A \rightarrow \alpha$$

says that A may be replaced by α *anywhere*, regardless of where the A occurs. On the other hand, we could informally define a **context** as a pair of strings (of terminals and nonterminals) β, γ, such that a rule would apply only if β occurs before and γ occurs after the nonterminal. We would write this as

$$\beta\ A\ \gamma \rightarrow \beta\alpha\gamma$$

Such a rule in which $\alpha \neq \varepsilon$ is called a **context-sensitive grammar rule**. Context-sensitive grammars are more powerful than context-free grammars but are also much more difficult to use as the basis for a parser.

What kind of requirements in programming languages require context-sensitive rules? Typical examples involve the use of names. The C rule requiring **declaration before use** is a typical example. Here, a name must appear in a declaration before its use in a statement or expression is allowed:

```
{int x;
  ...
  ...x...
  ...
}
```

If we were to try to deal with this requirement using BNF rules, we would, first, have to include the name strings themselves in the grammar rules rather than include all names as identifier tokens that are indistinguishable. Second, for each name we would have to write a rule establishing its declaration prior to a potential use. But in many languages, the length of an identifier is unrestricted, and so the number of possible identifiers is (at least potentially) infinite. Even if names are allowed to be only two characters long, we have the potential for hundreds of new grammar rules. Clearly, this is an impossible situation. The solution is similar to that of a disambiguating rule: we simply state a rule (declaration before use) that is not explicit in the grammar. There is a difference, however: such a rule cannot be enforced by the parser itself, since it is beyond the power of (reasonable) context-free rules to express. Instead, this rule becomes part of semantic analysis, because it depends on the use of the symbol table (which records which identifiers have been declared).

The body of language rules that are beyond the scope of the parser to check, but that are still capable of being checked by the compiler, are referred to as the **static semantics** of the language. These include type checking (in a statically typed language) and such rules as declaration before use. Henceforth, we will regard as *syntax* only those rules that can be expressed by BNF rules. Everything else we regard as semantics.

There is one more kind of grammar that is even more general than the context-sensitive grammars. These grammars are called **unrestricted grammars** and have grammar rules of the form $\alpha \rightarrow \beta$, where there are no restrictions on the form of the strings α and β (except that α cannot be ε). The four kinds of grammars—unrestricted, context sensitive, context free, and regular—are also called type 0, type 1, type 2, and type 3 grammars, respectively. The language classes they construct are also referred to as the **Chomsky hierarchy**, after Noam Chomsky, who pioneered their use to describe natural languages. These grammars represent distinct levels of computational power.

Indeed, the unrestricted (or type 0) grammars are equivalent to Turing machines in the same way regular grammars are equivalent to finite automata, and thus represent the most general kind of computation known. Context-free grammars also have a corresponding equivalent machine, called a pushdown automaton, but we will not need the full power of such a machine for our parsing algorithms and do not discuss it further.

We should also be aware that certain computationally intractable problems are associated with context-free languages and grammars. For example, in dealing with ambiguous grammars, it would be nice if we could state an algorithm that would convert an ambiguous grammar into an unambiguous one without changing the underlying language. Unfortunately, this is known to be an undecidable problem, so that such an algorithm cannot possibly exist. In fact, there even exist context-free languages for which *no* unambiguous grammar exists (these are called **inherently ambiguous languages**), and determining even whether a language is inherently ambiguous is undecidable.

Fortunately, complications such as inherent ambiguity do not as a rule arise in programming languages, and the ad hoc techniques for removing ambiguity that we have described usually prove to be adequate in practical cases.

3.7 SYNTAX OF THE TINY LANGUAGE

3.7.1 A Context-Free Grammar for TINY

The grammar for TINY is given in BNF in Figure 3.6. From it, we make the following observations. A TINY program is simply a sequence of statements. There are five kinds of statements: if-statements, repeat-statements, read-statements, write-statements, and assignment-statements. These have a Pascal-like syntax, except that the if-statement uses **end** as a bracketing keyword (so that there is no dangling else ambiguity in TINY) and that if-statements and repeat-statements allow statement sequences as bodies, so brackets or **begin-end** pairs are unnecessary (and **begin** is not even a reserved word

Figure 3.6
Grammar of the TINY
language in BNF

$$
\begin{aligned}
&program \rightarrow stmt\text{-}sequence \\
&stmt\text{-}sequence \rightarrow stmt\text{-}sequence \; ; \; statement \mid statement \\
&statement \rightarrow if\text{-}stmt \mid repeat\text{-}stmt \mid assign\text{-}stmt \mid read\text{-}stmt \mid write\text{-}stmt \\
&if\text{-}stmt \rightarrow \textbf{if } exp \textbf{ then } stmt\text{-}sequence \textbf{ end} \\
&\qquad \mid \textbf{if } exp \textbf{ then } stmt\text{-}sequence \textbf{ else } stmt\text{-}sequence \textbf{ end} \\
&repeat\text{-}stmt \rightarrow \textbf{repeat } stmt\text{-}sequence \textbf{ until } exp \\
&assign\text{-}stmt \rightarrow \textbf{identifier := } exp \\
&read\text{-}stmt \rightarrow \textbf{read identifier} \\
&write\text{-}stmt \rightarrow \textbf{write } exp \\
&exp \rightarrow simple\text{-}exp \; comparison\text{-}op \; simple\text{-}exp \mid simple\text{-}exp \\
&comparison\text{-}op \rightarrow \textbf{<} \mid \textbf{=} \\
&simple\text{-}exp \rightarrow simple\text{-}exp \; addop \; term \mid term \\
&addop \rightarrow \textbf{+} \mid \textbf{-} \\
&term \rightarrow term \; mulop \; factor \mid factor \\
&mulop \rightarrow \textbf{*} \mid \textbf{/} \\
&factor \rightarrow \textbf{(} exp \textbf{)} \mid \textbf{number} \mid \textbf{identifier}
\end{aligned}
$$

in TINY). The input/output statements are begun by the reserved words **read** and **write**. A read-statement can read only one variable at a time, and a write-statement can write only one expression at a time.

TINY expressions are of two varieties: Boolean expressions using the comparison operators = and < that appear in the tests of if- and repeat-statements and arithmetic expressions (denoted by *simple-exp* in the grammar) that include the standard integer operators +, -, *, and / (which stands for integer division, sometimes known as **div**). The arithmetic operations are left associative and have the usual precedences. The comparison operations, by contrast, are nonassociative: only one comparison operation is allowed per unparenthesized expression. The comparison operations also have lower precedence than any of the arithmetic operations.

Identifiers in TINY refer to simple integer variables. There are no structured variables such as arrays or records. There are also no variable declarations in TINY: a variable is declared implicitly by appearing on the left of an assignment. Also, there is only one (global) scope—and no procedures or functions (and hence also no calls).

One final note about the grammar of TINY. Statement sequences *must* contain semicolons separating statements, and a semicolon after the final statement in a statement sequence is illegal. This is because there are no empty statements in TINY (unlike Pascal and C). Also, we wrote the BNF rule for *stmt-sequence* as a left recursive rule, but we really don't care about the associativity of statement sequences, since the intent is simply that they be executed in order. Thus, we could have just as well written the *stmt-sequence* rule right recursively instead. This view will also be represented in the syntax tree structure of a TINY program, where statement sequences will be represented by lists rather than trees. We turn now to a discussion of this structure.

3.7.2 Syntax Tree Structure for the TINY Compiler

In TINY there are two basic kinds of structures: statements and expressions. There are five kinds of statements (if-statements, repeat-statements, assign-statements, read-statements, and write-statements) and three kinds of expressions (operator-expressions, constant-expressions, and identifier-expressions). A syntax tree node will, therefore, be classified primarily as to whether it is a statement or expression and secondarily as to the kind of statement or expression. A tree node will have a maximum of three child structures (all three are needed only in the case of an if-statement with an else-part). Statements will be sequenced via a sibling field instead of using a child field.

Attributes that must be kept in the tree nodes are as follows (aside from the fields already mentioned). Each kind of expression node needs a special attribute. A constant node needs a field for the integer constant that it represents. An identifier node needs a field to contain the name of the identifier. And an operator node needs a field to contain the name of the operator. Statement nodes generally do not need attributes (other than the kind of node they are). For simplicity, however, in the case of assign-statements and read-statements, we will keep the name of the variable being assigned or read right in the statement node itself (rather than as an expression child node).

The tree node structure we have just described can be achieved by the C declarations given in Figure 3.7, which are repeated from the listing of the **globals.h** file in Appendix B (lines 198–217). Note that we have used unions in these declarations to help conserve space. These also help to remind us which attributes go with each node kind. Two additional attributes are present in the declaration that we have not yet mentioned. The first is the bookkeeping attribute **lineno**; this allows us to print source code line numbers with errors that may occur in later stages of translation. The second is the **type** field, which will be needed later for type checking of expressions (and only expressions). It is declared to be of the enumerated type **ExpType**; this will be discussed fully in Chapter 6.

Figure 3.7

C declarations for a TINY syntax tree node

```
typedef enum {StmtK,ExpK} NodeKind;
typedef enum {IfK,RepeatK,AssignK,ReadK,WriteK}
             StmtKind;
typedef enum {OpK,ConstK,IdK} ExpKind;


/* ExpType is used for type checking */
typedef enum {Void,Integer,Boolean} ExpType;


#define MAXCHILDREN 3

typedef struct treeNode
   { struct treeNode * child[MAXCHILDREN];
     struct treeNode * sibling;
     int lineno;
     NodeKind nodekind;
     union { StmtKind stmt; ExpKind exp;} kind;
     union { TokenType op;
             int val;
             char * name; } attr;
     ExpType type; /* for type checking of exps */
   } TreeNode;
```

We want now to give a visual description of the syntax tree structure and show visually the syntax tree for a sample program. To do this, we use rectangular boxes to indicate statement nodes and round or oval boxes to indicate expression nodes. The kind of statement or expression will be given as a label inside the box, and additional attributes will also be listed there in parentheses. Sibling pointers will be drawn to the right of node boxes, while child pointers will be drawn below the boxes. We will also indicate additional, unspecified tree structures in diagrams by triangles, with dashed lines to indicate structures that may or may not appear. A sequence of statements connected by sibling fields would thus look as follows (potential subtrees are indicated by the dashed lines and triangles).

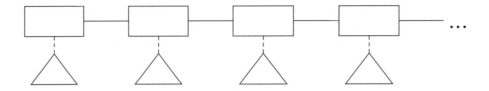

An if-statement (with potentially three children) will look as follows.

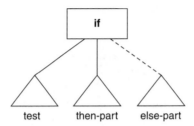

A repeat-statement will have two children. The first is the statement sequence representing its body; the second is the test expression:

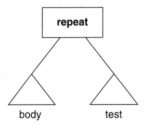

An assign-statement has one child representing the expression whose value is assigned (the variable name being assigned is kept in the statement node):

A write-statement also has one child, representing the expression whose value is to be written:

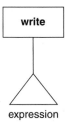

An operator expression has two children, representing the left and right operand expressions:

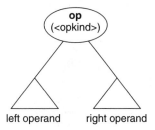

All other nodes (read-statements, identifier-expressions, and constant-expressions) are leaf nodes.

We are finally ready to show the tree of a TINY program. The sample program from Chapter 1 that computes the factorial of an integer is repeated in Figure 3.8. Its syntax tree is shown in Figure 3.9.

Figure 3.8

Sample program in the TINY language

```
{ Sample program
  in TINY language—
  computes factorial
}
read x; { input an integer }
if 0 < x then { don't compute if x <= 0 }
  fact := 1;
  repeat
    fact := fact * x;
    x := x - 1
  until x = 0;
  write fact { output factorial of x }
end
```

Figure 3.9

Syntax tree for the TINY
program of Figure 3.8

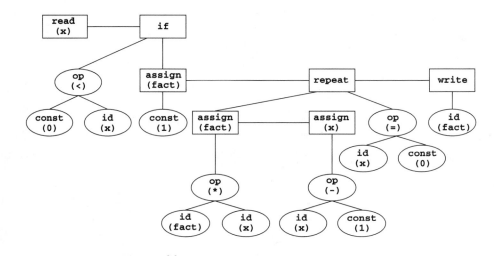

EXERCISES

3.1 a. Write down an unambiguous grammar that generates the set of strings
   $\{\mathtt{s;}, \mathtt{s;s;}, \mathtt{s;s;s;}, \ldots\}$.

   b. Give a leftmost and rightmost derivation for the string $\mathtt{s;s;}$ using your grammar.

3.2 Given the grammar $A \rightarrow AA \mid (A) \mid \varepsilon,$

   a. Describe the language it generates.

   b. Show that it is ambiguous.

3.3 Given the grammar

$$exp \rightarrow exp\ addop\ term \mid term$$
$$addop \rightarrow + \mid -$$
$$term \rightarrow term\ mulop\ factor \mid factor$$
$$mulop \rightarrow *$$
$$factor \rightarrow (\ exp\ ) \mid \mathbf{\textit{number}}$$

write down leftmost derivations, parse trees, and abstract syntax trees for the following
expressions:

   a. $\mathtt{3+4*5-6}$ **b.** $\mathtt{3*(4-5+6)}$ **c.** $\mathtt{3-(4+5*6)}$

3.4 The following grammar generates all regular expressions over the alphabet of letters (we
have used quotes to surround operators, since the vertical bar is an operator as well as a
metasymbol):

$$rexp \rightarrow rexp\ \text{``}|\text{''}\ rexp$$
$$\mid rexp\ rexp$$
$$\mid rexp\ \text{``}*\text{''}$$
$$\mid \text{``}(\text{''}\ rexp\ \text{``})\text{''}$$
$$\mid \mathbf{\textit{letter}}$$

    a. Give a derivation for the regular expression **(ab|b)** * using this grammar.

    b. Show that this grammar is ambiguous.

    c. Rewrite this grammar to establish the correct precedences for the operators (see Chapter 2).

    d. What associativity does your answer in part (c) give to the binary operators? Why?

3.5 Write a grammar for Boolean expressions that includes the constants **true** and **false**, the operators **and**, **or**, and **not**, and parentheses. Be sure to give **or** a lower precedence than **and** and **and** a lower precedence than **not** and to allow repeated **not**'s, as in the Boolean expression **not not true**. Also be sure your grammar is not ambiguous.

3.6 Consider the following grammar representing simplified LISP-like expressions:

$$lexp \rightarrow atom \mid list$$
$$atom \rightarrow \mathbf{number} \mid \mathbf{identifier}$$
$$list \rightarrow (\ lexp\text{-}seq\ )$$
$$lexp\text{-}seq \rightarrow lexp\text{-}seq\ lexp \mid lexp$$

    a. Write a leftmost and a rightmost derivation for the string **(a 23 (m x y))**.

    b. Draw a parse tree for the string of part (a).

3.7 **a.** Write C type declarations for an abstract syntax tree structure for the grammar of Exercise 3.6.

    b. Draw the syntax tree for the string **(a 23 (m x y))** that would result from your declarations of part (a).

3.8 Given the following grammar

$$statement \rightarrow if\text{-}stmt \mid \mathbf{other} \mid \varepsilon$$
$$if\text{-}stmt \rightarrow \mathbf{if}\ (\ exp\ )\ statement\ else\text{-}part$$
$$else\text{-}part \rightarrow \mathbf{else}\ statement \mid \varepsilon$$
$$exp \rightarrow \mathbf{0} \mid \mathbf{1}$$

    a. Draw a parse tree for the string

        if(0) if(1) *other* **else else** *other*

    b. What is the purpose of the two **else**'s?

    c. Is similar code permissible in C? Explain.

3.9 (Aho, Sethi, and Ullman) Show that the following attempt to solve the dangling else ambiguity is still ambiguous (compare with the solution on page 121):

$$statement \rightarrow \mathbf{if}\ (\ exp\ )\ statement \mid matched\text{-}stmt$$
$$matched\text{-}stmt \rightarrow \mathbf{if}\ (\ exp\ )\ matched\text{-}stmt\ \mathbf{else}\ statement \mid \mathbf{other}$$
$$exp \rightarrow \mathbf{0} \mid \mathbf{1}$$

3.10 **a.** Translate the grammar of Exercise 3.6 into EBNF.

    b. Draw syntax diagrams for the EBNF of part (a).

3.11 Given the set equation $\mathbf{X} = (\mathbf{X} + \mathbf{X}) \cup \mathbf{N}$ ($\mathbf{N}$ is the set of natural numbers; see Section 3.6.2, page 129).

    a. Show that the set $\mathbf{E} = \mathbf{N} \cup (\mathbf{N} + \mathbf{N}) \cup (\mathbf{N} + \mathbf{N} + \mathbf{N}) \cup (\mathbf{N} + \mathbf{N} + \mathbf{N} + \mathbf{N}) \cup \dots$
    satisfies the equation.

    b. Show that, given any set $\mathbf{E}'$ that satisfies the equation, $\mathbf{E} \subset \mathbf{E}'$.

3.12 Unary minuses can be added in several ways to the simple arithmetic expression grammar of Exercise 3.3. Revise the BNF for each of the cases that follow so that it satisfies the stated rule.

    a. At most one unary minus is allowed in each expression, and it must come at the beginning of an expression, so **-2-3** is legal[5] (and evaluates to -5) and **-2-(-3)** is legal, but **-2--3** is not.

    b. At most one unary minus is allowed before a number or left parenthesis, so **-2--3** is legal but **--2** and **-2---3** are not.

    c. Arbitrarily many unary minuses are allowed before numbers and left parentheses, so everything above is legal.

3.13 Consider the following simplification of the grammar of Exercise 3.6.

$$lexp \rightarrow \textbf{number} \mid (\; op \; lexp\text{-}seq\;)$$
$$op \rightarrow + \mid - \mid *$$
$$lexp\text{-}seq \rightarrow lexp\text{-}seq \; lexp \mid lexp$$

This grammar can be thought of as representing simple integer arithmetic expressions in LISP-like prefix form. For example, the expression **34-3*42** would be written in this grammar as **(- 34 (* 3 42))**.

    a. What interpretation should be given to the legal expressions **(- 2 3 4)** and **(- 2)**? What about the expressions **(+ 2)** and **(* 2)**?

    b. Are precedence and associativity a problem with this grammar? Is the grammar ambiguous?

3.14 a. Write C-type declarations for a syntax tree structure for the grammar of the previous exercise.

    b. Draw the syntax tree for the expression **(- 34 (* 3 42))** using your answer to part (a).

3.15 It was mentioned on page 111 that the BNF-like description of an abstract syntax tree

$$exp \rightarrow OpExp(op,exp,exp) \mid ConstExp(integer)$$
$$op \rightarrow Plus \mid Minus \mid Times$$

is close to an actual type declaration in some languages. Two such languages are ML and Haskell. This exercise is for those readers who know either of those two languages.

    a. Write data type declarations that implement the above abstract syntax.

    b. Write an abstract syntax expression for the expression **(34*(42-3))**.

3.16 Rewrite the syntax tree **typedef** at the beginning of Section 3.3.2 (page 111) to use a **union**.

3.17 Prove that the grammar of Example 3.5 (page 105) generates the set of all strings of

---

5. Note that the second minus in this expression is a *binary* minus, not a unary minus.

balanced parentheses, where w is a string of balanced parentheses provided it has the following two properties:

1. w contains exactly the same number of left and right parentheses.

2. Every prefix u of w ($w = ux$ for some x) has at least as many left parentheses as right parentheses.

(Hint: Prove by induction on the length of a derivation.)

3.18 a. Write a context-sensitive grammar that generates strings of the form xcx, where x is a string of a's and b's.

b. Is it possible to write a context-free grammar for the strings of part (a)? Explain.

3.19 In some languages (Modula-2 and Ada are examples), a procedure declaration is expected to be terminated by syntax that includes the name of the procedure. For example, in Modula-2 a procedure is declared as follows:

```
PROCEDURE P;
BEGIN
    ...
END P;
```

Note the use of the procedure name **P** after the closing **END**. Can such a requirement be checked by a parser? Explain.

3.20 a. Write a regular expression that generates the same language as the following grammar:

$$A \rightarrow aA \mid B \mid \varepsilon$$
$$B \rightarrow bB \mid A$$

b. Write a grammar that generates the same language as the following regular expression:

```
(a|c|ba|bc)*(b|ε)
```

3.21 A **unit production** is a grammar rule choice of the form $A \rightarrow B$, where both A and B are nonterminals.

a. Show that unit productions can be systematically eliminated from a grammar to yield a grammar with no unit productions that generates the same language as the original grammar.

b. Do you expect unit productions to appear often in the definition of programming languages? Explain.

3.22 A **cyclic grammar** is one in which there is a derivation $A \Rightarrow^* A$ for some nonterminal A.

a. Show that a cyclic grammar is ambiguous.

b. Would you expect grammars that define programming languages to be often cyclic? Explain.

3.23 Rewrite the TINY grammar of Figure 3.6 into EBNF.

3.24 For the TINY program

```
read x;
x := x+1;
write x
```

   a. Draw the TINY parse tree.

   b. Draw the TINY syntax tree.

3.25 Draw the TINY syntax tree for the following program:

```
read u;
read v; { input two integers }
if v = 0 then v := 0 { do nothing }
else
  repeat
    temp := v;
    v := u - u/v*v;
    u := temp
  until v = 0
end;
write u { output gcd of original u & v }
```

NOTES AND REFERENCES

Much of the theory of context-free grammars can be found in Hopcroft and Ullman [1979], where proofs of many properties, such as the undecidability of inherent ambiguity may be found. It also contains an account of the Chomsky hierarchy. Additional information is in Ginsburg [1966, 1975]. Chomsky [1956, 1959] was responsible for much of the early theory, applying it to the study of natural languages. Only later was the importance of the subject for programming languages understood, and the first use of context-free grammars came in the definition of Algol60 (Naur [1963]). The solution on page 121 to the dangling else problem using context-free rules was taken from Aho, Hopcroft, and Ullman [1986], as was Exercise 3.9. The view of context-free grammars as recursive equations (Section 3.6.2) is that taken by denotational semantics. For a study, see Schmidt [1986].

Chapter 4

Top-Down Parsing

A **top-down** parsing algorithm parses an input string of tokens by tracing out the steps in a leftmost derivation. Such an algorithm is called top-down because the implied traversal of the parse tree is a preorder traversal and, thus, occurs from the root to the leaves (see Section 3.3 of Chapter 3). Top-down parsers come in two forms: **backtracking parsers** and **predictive parsers**. A predictive parser attempts to predict the next construction in the input string using one or more lookahead tokens, while a backtracking parser will try different possibilities for a parse of the input, backing up an arbitrary amount in the input if one possibility fails. While backtracking parsers are more powerful than predictive parsers, they are also much slower, requiring exponential time in general and, therefore, are unsuitable for practical compilers. We do not study backtracking parsers here (but see the Notes and References section and the exercises for a few hints and pointers on this topic).

The two kinds of top-down parsing algorithms that we do study here are called **recursive-descent parsing** and **LL(1) parsing**. Recursive-descent parsing is quite versatile and is the most suitable method for a handwritten parser, so we study it first. LL(1) parsing is studied next; while it is no longer often used in practice, it is useful to study as a simple scheme with an explicit stack, and it may serve as a prelude to the more powerful (but also more complex) bottom-up algorithms of the next chapter. It also aids in formalizing some of the problems that appear in recursive-descent. The LL(1) parsing method gets its name as follows. The first "L" refers to the fact that it processes the input from left to right (some old parsers used to process input from right to left, but it is unusual today). The second "L" refers to the fact that it traces out a leftmost derivation for the input string. The number 1 in parentheses means that it uses only one symbol of input to predict the direction of the parse. (It is also possible to have LL(k) parsing, using k symbols of lookahead, and we study this briefly later in the chapter, but one symbol of lookahead is the most common case.)

Both recursive-descent parsing and LL(1) parsing require in general the computation of lookahead sets that are called **First** and **Follow** sets.[1] Since simple top-down parsers can be constructed without constructing these sets explicitly, we delay a discussion of them until after the basic algorithms have been introduced. We then proceed to a discussion of a TINY parser constructed by recursive-descent and close the chapter with a description of error recovery methods in top-down parsing.

4.1 TOP-DOWN PARSING BY RECURSIVE-DESCENT

4.1.1 The Basic Method of Recursive-Descent

The idea of recursive-descent parsing is extremely simple. We view the grammar rule for a nonterminal A as a definition for a procedure that will recognize an A. The right-hand side of the grammar rule for A specifies the structure of the code for this procedure: the sequence of terminals and nonterminals in a choice correspond to matches of the input and calls to other procedures, while choices correspond to alternatives (case- or if-statements) within the code.

As a first example, consider the expression grammar from the previous chapter:

$$exp \rightarrow exp\ addop\ term \mid term$$
$$addop \rightarrow + \mid -$$
$$term \rightarrow term\ mulop\ factor \mid factor$$
$$mulop \rightarrow *$$
$$factor \rightarrow (\ exp\ ) \mid \mathbf{number}$$

and consider the grammar rule for a *factor*. A recursive-descent procedure that recognizes a *factor* (and which we will call by the same name) can be written in pseudocode as follows:

```
procedure factor ;
begin
  case token of
  ( :    match( ( ) ;
         exp ;
         match( ) ) ;
  number :
         match(number) ;
  else error ;
  end case ;
end factor ;
```

In this pseudocode we have assumed that there is a *token* variable that keeps the current next token in the input (so that this example uses one symbol of lookahead). We have also assumed that there is a *match* procedure that matches the current next token with its parameter, advances the input if it succeeds, and declares error if it does not:

---

1. These sets are also needed in some of the bottom-up parsing algorithms studied in the next chapter.

```
procedure match ( expectedToken ) ;
begin
  if token = expectedToken then
    getToken ;
  else
    error ;
  end if ;
end match ;
```

For the moment we leave unspecified the *error* procedure that is called in both *match* and *factor*. It can be assumed to print an error message and exit.

Note that in the calls *match*(**(**) and *match*(**number**) in *factor*, the variables *expectedToken* and *token* are known to be the same. However, in the call *match*(**)**), *token* cannot be assumed to be a right parenthesis, so a test is necessary. The code for *factor* also assumes that a procedure *exp* has been defined that it can call. In a recursive-descent parser for the expression grammar, the *exp* procedure will call *term*, the term procedure will call *factor*, and the *factor* procedure will call *exp*, so all these procedures must be able to call each other. Unfortunately, writing recursive-descent procedures for the remaining rules in the expression grammar is not as easy as for *factor* and requires the use of EBNF, as we now shall see.

4.1.2   Repetition and Choice: Using EBNF

Consider as a second example the (simplified) grammar rule for an if-statement:

$$if\text{-}stmt \rightarrow \textbf{if } \textbf{(} \ exp \ \textbf{)} \ statement$$
$$|\ \textbf{if } \textbf{(} \ exp \ \textbf{)} \ statement \ \textbf{else} \ statement$$

This can be translated into the procedure

```
procedure ifStmt ;
begin
  match (if) ;
  match (( ) ;
  exp ;
  match ( )) ;
  statement ;
  if token = else then
    match (else) ;
    statement ;
  end if ;
end ifStmt ;
```

In this example, we could not immediately distinguish the two choices on the right-hand side of the grammar rule (they both start with the token **if**). Instead, we must put off the decision on whether to recognize the optional else-part until we see the token **else** in the input. Thus, the code for the if-statement corresponds more to the EBNF

$$if\text{-}stmt \rightarrow \textbf{if } \textbf{(} \ exp \ \textbf{)} \ statement \ [\ \textbf{else} \ statement \ ]$$

than the BNF, where the square brackets of the EBNF translate into a test in the code for *ifStmt*. In fact, EBNF notation is designed to mirror closely the actual code of a recursive-descent parser, so a grammar should always be translated into EBNF if recursive-descent is to be used. Note also that, even though this grammar is ambiguous (see the previous chapter), it is natural to write a parser that matches each **else** token as soon as it is encountered in the input. This corresponds precisely to the most closely nested disambiguating rule.

Consider now the case of an *exp* in the grammar for simple arithmetic expressions in BNF:

$$exp \rightarrow exp \; addop \; term \mid term$$

If we were to try to turn this into a recursive *exp* procedure according to our plan, the first thing we might try to do is to call *exp* itself, and this would lead to an immediate infinite recursive loop. Trying to test for which choice to use (*exp* → *exp addop term* or *exp* → *term*) is just as problematic, since both *exp* and *term* can begin with the same tokens (a number or left parenthesis).

The solution is to use the EBNF rule

$$exp \rightarrow term \; \{ \; addop \; term \; \}$$

instead. The curly brackets expressing repetition can be translated into the code for a loop, as follows:

```
procedure exp ;
begin
   term ;
   while token = + or token = - do
      match (token) ;
      term ;
   end while ;
end exp ;
```

Similarly, the EBNF rule for *term*:

$$term \rightarrow factor \; \{ \; mulop \; factor \; \}$$

becomes the code

```
procedure term ;
begin
   factor ;
   while token = * do
      match (token) ;
      factor ;
   end while ;
end term ;
```

Here we have eliminated the nonterminals *addop* and *mulop* as separate procedures, since their only function is to match the operators:

$$addop \rightarrow + \mid -$$
$$mulop \rightarrow *$$

We do this matching inside *exp* and *term* instead.

A question that arises with this code is whether the left associativity implied by the curly brackets (and explicit in the original BNF) can still be maintained. Suppose, for example, that we want to write a recursive-descent calculator for the simple integer arithmetic of our grammar. We can ensure that the operations are left associative by performing the operations as we cycle through the loop (we assume now that the parsing procedures are functions that return an integer result):

```
function exp : integer ;
var temp : integer ;
begin
   temp := term ;
   while token = + or token = - do
      case token of
        + : match (+) ;
            temp := temp + term ;
        - : match (-) ;
            temp := temp - term ;
      end case ;
   end while ;
   return temp ;
end exp ;
```

and similarly for *term*. We have used these ideas to create a working simple calculator whose C code is given in Figure 4.1 (pages 148–149), where instead of writing a full scanner, we have opted to use calls to **getchar** and **scanf** in place of a **getToken** procedure.

This method of turning grammar rules in EBNF into code is quite powerful, and we use it to give a complete parser for the TINY language in Section 4.4. However, there are a few pitfalls, and care must be taken in scheduling the actions within the code. One example of this is in the previous pseudocode for *exp*, where a match of the operations had to occur before the repeated calls to *term* (otherwise *term* would see an operation as its first token, which would generate an error). Indeed, the following protocol for keeping the global *token* variable current must be rigidly adhered to: *token* must be set before the parse begins, and *getToken* (or its equivalent) must be called just after a successful test of a token (we put this into the *match* procedure in the pseudocode).

The same care must also be taken in scheduling the actions during the construction of a syntax tree. We saw that left associativity in an EBNF with repetition can be maintained for calculation purposes by performing the calculation as the loop is executed.

Figure 4.1 (beginning)

Recursive-descent calculator

for simple integer arithmetic

```
/* Simple integer arithmetic calculator
   according to the EBNF:

   <exp> -> <term> { <addop> <term> }
   <addop> -> + | -
   <term> -> <factor> { <mulop> <factor> }
   <mulop> -> *
   <factor> -> ( <exp> ) | Number

   Inputs a line of text from stdin
   Outputs "Error" or the result.
*/

#include <stdio.h>
#include <stdlib.h>

char token; /* global token variable */

/* function prototypes for recursive calls */
int exp(void);
int term(void);
int factor(void);

void error(void)
{ fprintf(stderr,"Error\n");
  exit(1);
}

void match( char expectedToken)
{ if (token==expectedToken) token = getchar();
  else error();
}

main()
{ int result;
  token = getchar(); /* load token with first
                        character for lookahead */
  result = exp();
  if (token=='\n') /* check for end of line */
    printf("Result = %d\n",result);
  else error(); /* extraneous chars on line */
  return 0;
}
```

Figure 4.1 (conclusion)
Recursive-descent calculator
for simple integer arithmetic

```c
int exp(void)
{ int temp = term();
  while ((token=='+')||(token=='-'))
    switch (token) {
    case '+': match('+');
              temp+=term();
              break;
    case '-': match('-');
              temp-=term();
              break;
    }
  return temp;
}

int term(void)
{ int temp = factor();
  while (token=='*') {
    match('*');
    temp*=factor();
  }
  return temp;
}

int factor(void)
{ int temp;
  if (token=='(') {
    match('(');
    temp = exp();
    match(')');
  }
  else if (isdigit(token)) {
    ungetc(token,stdin);
    scanf("%d",&temp);
    token = getchar();
  }
  else error();
  return temp;
}
```

This no longer corresponds to a top-down construction of the parse or syntax tree, however. Indeed, if we consider the expression **3+4+5**, with syntax tree

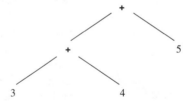

the node representing the sum of 3 and 4 must be created (or processed) before the root node (the node representing its sum with 5). Translating this into actual syntax tree construction, we have the following pseudocode for the *exp* procedure:

```
function exp : syntaxTree ;
var temp, newtemp : syntaxTree ;
begin
   temp := term ;
   while token = + or token = - do
      case token of
        + : match (+) ;
            newtemp := makeOpNode(+) ;
            leftChild(newtemp) := temp ;
            rightChild(newtemp) := term ;
            temp := newtemp ;
        - : match (-) ;
            newtemp := makeOpNode(-) ;
            leftChild(newtemp) := temp ;
            rightChild(newtemp) := term ;
            temp := newtemp ;
      end case ;
   end while ;
   return temp ;
end exp ;
```

or the simpler

```
function exp : syntaxTree ;
var temp, newtemp : syntaxTree ;
begin
   temp := term ;
   while token = + or token = - do
      newtemp := makeOpNode(token) ;
      match (token) ;
      leftChild(newtemp) := temp ;
      rightChild(newtemp) := term ;
      temp := newtemp ;
   end while ;
   return temp ;
end exp ;
```

In this code we have used a new function *makeOpNode* that receives an operator token as a parameter and returns a newly constructed syntax tree node. We have also indicated assignment of a syntax tree *p* as a left or right child of a syntax tree *t* by writing *leftChild*(*t*) := *p* or *rightChild*(*t*) := *p*. With this pseudocode, the *exp* procedure does indeed construct the syntax tree and not the parse tree. This is because a call to *exp* does not invariably construct a new tree node; if there are no operators, *exp* simply passes back the tree received from the initial call to *term* as its own value. Corresponding pseudocode for *term* and *factor* can also be written (see the exercises).

By contrast, the syntax tree for an if-statement can be constructed in strict top-down fashion by a recursive-descent parser:

```
function ifStatement : syntaxTree ;
var temp : syntaxTree ;
begin
    match (if) ;
    match (( ) ;
    temp := makeStmtNode(if) ;
    testChild(temp) := exp ;
    match ( )) ;
    thenChild(temp) := statement ;
    if token = else then
        match (else) ;
        elseChild(temp) := statement ;
    else
        elseChild(temp) := nil ;
    end if ;
end ifStatement ;
```

The flexibility of recursive-descent parsing in allowing the programmer to adjust the scheduling of the actions makes it the method of choice for hand-generated parsers.

4.1.3 Further Decision Problems

The recursive-descent method we have described is quite powerful but still ad hoc. With a small, carefully designed language (such as TINY or even C), these methods are adequate to construct a complete parser. We should be aware that more formal methods may be necessary in complex situations. Several problems can arise. First, it may be difficult to convert a grammar originally written in BNF into EBNF form. An alternative to the use of EBNF is studied in the next section, where a transformed BNF is constructed that is essentially equivalent to EBNF. Second, when formulating a test to distinguish two or more grammar rule options

$$A \rightarrow \alpha \mid \beta \mid \dots$$

it may be difficult to decide when to use the choice $A \rightarrow \alpha$ and when to use the choice $A \rightarrow \beta$, if both α and β begin with nonterminals. Such a decision problem requires the computation of the **First** sets of α and β: the set of tokens that can legally begin each string. We formalize the details of this computation in Section 4.3. Third, in writing code for an ε-production

$$A \rightarrow \varepsilon$$

it may be necessary to know what tokens can legally come after the nonterminal A, since such tokens indicate that A may appropriately disappear at this point in the parse. This set is called the **Follow** set of A. The computation of this set is also made precise in Section 4.3.

A final concern that may require the computation of First and Follow sets is early error detection. Consider, for example, the calculator program of Figure 4.1. Given the input **)3-2)**, the parser will descend from **exp** to **term** to **factor** before an error is reported, while it would be possible to declare the error already in **exp**, since a right parenthesis is not a legal first character in an expression. The First set of *exp* would tell us this, allowing for earlier error detection. (Error detection and recovery is discussed in more detail at the end of the chapter.)

4.2 LL(1) PARSING

4.2.1 The Basic Method of LL(1) Parsing

LL(1) parsing uses an explicit stack rather than recursive calls to perform a parse. It is helpful to represent this stack in a standard way, so that the actions of an LL(1) parser can be visualized quickly and easily. In this introductory discussion, we use the very simple grammar that generates strings of balanced parentheses:

$$S \rightarrow (S) S \mid \varepsilon$$

(see Example 3.5 of the previous chapter).

Table 4.1 shows the actions of a top-down parser given this grammar and the string **( )**. In this table are four columns. The first column numbers the steps for later reference. The second column shows the contents of the parsing stack, with the bottom of the stack to the left and the top of the stack to the right. We mark the bottom of the stack with a dollar sign. Thus, a stack containing the nonterminal S at the top appears as

$$\$\ S$$

and additional stack items would be pushed on the right. The third column of Table 4.1 shows the input. The input symbols are listed from left to right. A dollar sign is used to mark the end of the input (this corresponds to an EOF token generated by a scanner). The fourth column of the table gives a shorthand description of the action taken by the parser, which will change the stack and (possibly) the input, as given in the next row of the table.

Table 4.1

Parsing actions of a top-down parser

	Parsing stack	Input	Action
1	$\$\ S$	( ) $\$$	$S \rightarrow (S) S$
2	$\$\ S\ )\ S\ ($	( ) $\$$	match
3	$\$\ S\ )\ S$	) $\$$	$S \rightarrow \varepsilon$
4	$\$\ S\ )$	) $\$$	match
5	$\$\ S$	$\$$	$S \rightarrow \varepsilon$
6	$\$$	$\$$	accept

A top-down parser begins by pushing the start symbol onto the stack. It accepts an input string if, after a series of actions, the stack and the input become empty. Thus, a general schematic for a successful top-down parse is

$StartSymbol   InputString $
         . . .   . . .
         . . .   . . .
$ $ accept

In the case of our example, the start symbol is S, and the input string is ( ) .

A top-down parser parses by replacing a nonterminal at the top of the stack by one of the choices in the grammar rule (in BNF) for that nonterminal. It does this with a view to producing the current input token on the top of the parsing stack, whence it has matched the input token and can discard it from both the stack and the input. These two actions,

1. Replace a nonterminal A at the top of the stack by a string α using the grammar rule choice $A \rightarrow \alpha$, and
2. Match a token on top of the stack with the next input token,

are the two basic actions in a top-down parser. The first action could be called **generate**; we indicate this action by writing the BNF choice used in the replacement (whose left-hand side must be the nonterminal currently at the top of the stack). The second action matches a token at the top of the stack with the next token in the input (and throws both away by popping the stack and advancing the input); we indicate this action by writing the word *match*. It is important to note that in the *generate* action, the replacement string α from the BNF must be pushed *in reverse* onto the stack (since that ensures that the string α will come to the top of the stack in left to right order).

For example, at step 1 of the parse in Table 4.1, the stack and input are

$S   ( ) $

and the rule we use to replace S on the top of the stack is $S \rightarrow$ (S) S, so that the string S) S (is pushed onto the stack to obtain

$S) S (( ) $

Now we have generated the next input terminal, namely a left parenthesis, on the top of the stack, and we perform a *match* action to obtain the following situation:

$S) S   ) $

The list of generating actions in Table 4.1 corresponds precisely to the steps in a leftmost derivation of the string ( ) :

$$S \Rightarrow (S)S \quad [S \rightarrow (S) S]$$
$$\Rightarrow ()S \quad [S \rightarrow \varepsilon]$$
$$\Rightarrow () \quad [S \rightarrow \varepsilon]$$

This is characteristic of top-down parsing. If we want to construct a parse tree as the parse proceeds, we can add node construction actions as each nonterminal or terminal is pushed onto the stack. Thus, the root node of the parse tree (corresponding to the start symbol) is constructed at the beginning of the parse. And in step 2 of Table 4.1, when

S is replaced by (S) S, the nodes for each of the four replacement symbols are constructed as the symbols are pushed onto the stack and are connected as children to the node of S that they replace on the stack. To make this effective, we have to modify the stack to contain pointers to these constructed nodes, rather than simply the nonterminals or terminals themselves. Further on, we shall see how this process can be modified to yield a construction of the syntax tree instead of the parse tree.

4.2.2   The LL(1) Parsing Table and Algorithm

Using the parsing method just described, when a nonterminal A is at the top of the parsing stack, a decision must be made, based on the current input token (the lookahead), which grammar rule choice for A to use when replacing A on the stack. By contrast, no decision is necessary when a token is at the top of the stack, since it is either the same as the current input token, and a match occurs, or it isn't, and an error occurs.

We can express the choices that are possible by constructing an **LL(1) parsing table**. Such a table is essentially a two-dimensional array indexed by nonterminals and terminals containing production choices to use at the appropriate parsing step (including $ to represent the end of the input). We call this table $M[N, T]$. Here N is the set of nonterminals of the grammar, T is the set of terminals or tokens (for convenience, we suppress the fact that $ must be added to T), and M can be thought of as the table of "moves." We assume that the table $M[N, T]$ starts out with all its entries empty. Any entries that remain empty after the construction represent potential errors that may occur during a parse.

We add production choices to this table according to the following rules:

1. If $A \rightarrow \alpha$ is a production choice, and there is a derivation $\alpha \Rightarrow^* a \beta$, where a is a token, then add $A \rightarrow \alpha$ to the table entry $M[A, a]$.
2. If $A \rightarrow \alpha$ is a production choice, and there are derivations $\alpha \Rightarrow^* \varepsilon$ and $S \, \$ \Rightarrow^* \beta A a \gamma$, where S is the start symbol and a is a token (or $), then add $A \rightarrow \alpha$ to the table entry $M[A, a]$.

The idea behind these rules is as follows. In rule 1, given a token a in the input, we wish to select a rule $A \rightarrow \alpha$ if α can produce an a for matching. In rule 2, if A derives the empty string (via $A \rightarrow \alpha$), and if a is a token that can legally come after A in a derivation, then we want to select $A \rightarrow \alpha$ to make A disappear. Note that a special case of rule 2 is when $\alpha = \varepsilon$.

These rules are difficult to implement directly, and in the next section we will develop algorithms for doing so, involving the First and Follow sets already mentioned. In extremely simple cases, however, these rules can be carried out by hand.

Consider as a first example the grammar for balanced parentheses used in the previous subsection. There is one nonterminal (S), three tokens (left parenthesis, right parenthesis, and $), and two production choices. Since there is only one nonempty production for S, namely, $S \rightarrow$ (S) S, every string derivable from S must be either empty or begin with a left parenthesis, and this production choice is added to the entry $M[S, (]$ (and only there). This completes all the cases under rule 1. Since $S \Rightarrow$ (S) S, rule 2 applies with $\alpha = \varepsilon$, $\beta = ($, $A = S$, $a =)$, and $\gamma = S \, \$$, so $S \rightarrow \varepsilon$ is added to $M[S,)]$. Since $S \, \$ \Rightarrow^* S \, \$$ (the empty derivation), $S \rightarrow \varepsilon$ is also added to $M[S, \$]$. This completes the construction of the LL(1) parsing table for this grammar, which we can write in the following form:

M[N, T]	(	)	$
S	$S \rightarrow (S) S$	$S \rightarrow \varepsilon$	$S \rightarrow \varepsilon$

To complete the LL(1) parsing algorithm, this table must give unique choices for each nonterminal-token pair. Thus, we state the following

Definition

A grammar is an **LL(1) grammar** if the associated LL(1) parsing table has at most one production in each table entry.

An LL(1) grammar cannot be ambiguous, since the definition implies that an unambiguous parse can be constructed using the LL(1) parsing table. Indeed, given an LL(1) grammar, a parsing algorithm that uses the LL(1) parsing table is given in Figure 4.2. This algorithm results in precisely those actions described in the example of the previous subsection.

While the algorithm of Figure 4.2 requires that the parsing table entries have at most one production each, it is possible to build disambiguating rules into the table construction for simple ambiguous cases such as the dangling else problem, in a similar way to recursive-descent.

Figure 4.2

Table-based LL(1) parsing algorithm

```
(* assumes $ marks the bottom of the stack and the end of the input *)
push the start symbol onto the top of the parsing stack ;
while the top of the parsing stack ≠ $ and the next input token ≠ $ do
    if the top of the parsing stack is terminal a
        and the next input token = a
    then (* match *)
        pop the parsing stack ;
        advance the input ;
    else if the top of the parsing is nonterminal A
        and the next input token is terminal a
        and parsing table entry M[A, a] contains
                production A → X₁X₂ . . . Xₙ
    then (* generate *)
        pop the parsing stack ;
        for i := n downto 1 do
            push Xᵢ onto the parsing stack ;
    else error ;
    if the top of the parsing stack = $
            and the next input token = $
    then accept
    else error ;
```

Consider, for example, the simplified grammar of if-statements (see Example 3.6 in Chapter 3):

$$statement \rightarrow \textit{if-stmt} \mid \textbf{other}$$
$$\textit{if-stmt} \rightarrow \textbf{if (} \textit{exp} \textbf{)} \textit{statement else-part}$$
$$\textit{else-part} \rightarrow \textbf{else} \textit{ statement} \mid \varepsilon$$
$$exp \rightarrow \textbf{0} \mid \textbf{1}$$

Constructing the LL(1) parsing table gives the result shown in Table 4.2, where we do not list the parentheses terminals **(** or **)** in the table, since they do not cause any actions. (The construction of this table will be explained in detail in the next section.)

Table 4.2

LL(1) parsing table for (ambiguous) if-statements

M[N, T]	if	other	else	0	1	$
statement	*statement* → *if-stmt*	*statement* → **other**				
if-stmt	*if-stmt* → **if (** *exp* **)** *statement* *else-part*					
else-part			*else-part* → **else** *statement* *else-part* → ε			*else-part* → ε
exp				*exp* → **0**	*exp* → **1**	

In Table 4.2, the entry M[*else-part*, **else**] contains two entries, corresponding to the dangling else ambiguity. As in recursive-descent, when constructing this table, we could apply a disambiguating rule that would always prefer the rule that generates the current lookahead token over any other, and thus the production

$$\textit{else-part} \rightarrow \textbf{else} \textit{ statement}$$

would be preferred over the production *else-part* → ε. This corresponds in fact to the most closely nested disambiguating rule. With this modification, Table 4.2 becomes unambiguous, and the grammar can be parsed as if it were an LL(1) grammar. For example, Table 4.3 shows the parsing actions of the LL(1) parsing algorithm, given the string

if(0) if(1) *other* else *other*

(For conciseness, we use the following abbreviations in that figure: *statement* = S, *if-stmt* = I, *else-part* = L, *exp* = E, **if** = **i**, **else** = **e**, ***other*** = *o*.)

Table 4.3

LL(1) parsing actions for if-statements using the most closely nested disambiguating rule

Parsing stack	Input	Action
$\$\,S$	i(0)i(1)oeo$\$$	$S \rightarrow I$
$\$\,I$	i(0)i(1)oeo$\$$	$I \rightarrow$ i (E) $S\,L$
$\$\,L\,S$) E (i	i(0)i(1)oeo$\$$	match
$\$\,L\,S$) E (	(0)i(1)oeo$\$$	match
$\$\,L\,S$) E	0)i(1)oeo$\$$	$E \rightarrow 0$
$\$\,L\,S$) 0	0)i(1)oeo$\$$	match
$\$\,L\,S$)	)i(1)oeo$\$$	match
$\$\,L\,S$	i(1)oeo$\$$	$S \rightarrow I$
$\$\,L\,I$	i(1)oeo$\$$	$I \rightarrow$ i (E) $S\,L$
$\$\,L\,L\,S$) E (i	i(1)oeo$\$$	$I \rightarrow$ i (E) $S\,L$
$\$\,L\,L\,S$) E (i	i(1)oeo$\$$	match
$\$\,L\,L\,S$) E (	(1)oeo$\$$	match
$\$\,L\,L\,S$) E	1)oeo$\$$	$E \rightarrow 1$
$\$\,L\,L\,S$)	)oeo$\$$	match
$\$\,L\,L\,S$	oeo$\$$	$S \rightarrow$ o
$\$\,L\,L$ o	oeo$\$$	match
$\$\,L\,L$	eo$\$$	$L \rightarrow$ e S
$\$\,L\,S$ e	eo$\$$	match
$\$\,L\,S$	o$\$$	$S \rightarrow$ o
$\$\,L$ o	o$\$$	match
$\$\,L$	$\$$	$L \rightarrow \varepsilon$
$\$$	$\$$	accept

4.2.3 Left Recursion Removal and Left Factoring

Repetition and choice in LL(1) parsing suffer from similar problems to those that occur in recursive-descent parsing, and for that reason we have not yet been able to give an LL(1) parsing table for the simple arithmetic expression grammar of previous sections. We solved these problems for recursive-descent using EBNF notation. We cannot apply the same ideas to LL(1) parsing; instead, we must rewrite the grammar within the BNF notation into a form that the LL(1) parsing algorithm can accept. The two standard techniques that we apply are **left recursion removal** and **left factoring**. We consider each of these techniques. It must be emphasized that there is no guarantee that the application of these techniques will turn a grammar into an LL(1) grammar, just as EBNF is not guaranteed to solve all problems in writing a recursive-descent parser. Nevertheless, they are very useful in most practical situations and have the advantage that their application can be automated, so that, assuming a successful result, an LL(1) parser can be automatically generated using them (see the Notes and References section).

Left Recursion Removal   Left recursion is commonly used to make operations left associative, as in the simple expression grammar, where

$$exp \rightarrow exp\ addop\ term\ |\ term$$

makes the operations represented by *addop* left associative. This is the simplest case of left recursion, where there is only a single left recursive production choice. Only slightly more complex is the case when more than one choice is left recursive, which happens if we write out *addop*:

$$exp \rightarrow exp \; \mathbf{+} \; term \mid exp \; \mathbf{-} \; term \mid term$$

Both these cases involve **immediate left recursion**, where the left recursion occurs only within the production of a single nonterminal (like *exp*). A more difficult case is *indirect* left recursion, such as in the rules

$$A \rightarrow B \, b \mid \ldots$$
$$B \rightarrow A \, a \mid \ldots$$

Such rules almost never occur in actual programming language grammars, but we include a solution to this case for completeness. We consider immediate left recursion first.

CASE 1: Simple immediate left recursion

In this case the left recursion is present only in grammar rules of the form

$$A \rightarrow A \, \alpha \mid \beta$$

where α and β are strings of terminals and nonterminals and β does not begin with A. We saw in Section 3.2.3 that this grammar rule generates strings of the form $\beta \alpha^n$, for $n \geq 0$. The choice $A \rightarrow \beta$ is the base case, while $A \rightarrow A \, \alpha$ is the recursive case.

To remove the left recursion, we rewrite this grammar rule into two rules: one that generates β first and one that generates the repetitions of α, using right recursion instead of left recursion:

$$A \rightarrow \beta \, A'$$
$$A' \rightarrow \alpha \, A' \mid \varepsilon$$

Example 4.1

Consider again the left recursive rule from the simple expression grammar:

$$exp \rightarrow exp \; addop \; term \mid term$$

This is of the form $A \rightarrow A \, \alpha \mid \beta$, with $A = exp$, $\alpha = addop \; term$, and $\beta = term$. Rewriting this rule to remove left recursion, we obtain

$$exp \rightarrow term \; exp'$$
$$exp' \rightarrow addop \; term \; exp' \mid \varepsilon$$

§

CASE 2: General immediate left recursion

This is the case where we have productions of the form

$$A \rightarrow A \, \alpha_1 \mid A \, \alpha_2 \mid \ldots \mid A \, \alpha_n \mid \beta_1 \mid \beta_2 \mid \ldots \mid \beta_m$$

where none of the $\beta_1, \ldots, \beta_m$ begin with A. In this case, the solution is similar to the simple case, with the choices expanded accordingly:

$$A \rightarrow \beta_1 A' \mid \beta_2 A' \mid \ldots \mid \beta_m A'$$
$$A' \rightarrow \alpha_1 A' \mid \alpha_2 A' \mid \ldots \mid \alpha_n A' \mid \varepsilon$$

Example 4.2   Consider the grammar rule

$$exp \rightarrow exp + term \mid exp - term \mid term$$

We remove the left recursion as follows:

$$exp \rightarrow term \; exp'$$
$$exp' \rightarrow + term \; exp' \mid - term \; exp' \mid \varepsilon \qquad \S$$

CASE 3: General left recursion   The algorithm we describe here is guaranteed to work only in the case of grammars with no ε-productions and with no cycles, where a **cycle** is a derivation of at least one step that begins and ends with the same nonterminal: $A \Rightarrow \alpha \Rightarrow^* A$. A cycle is almost certain to cause a parser to go into an infinite loop, and grammars with cycles never appear as programming language grammars. Programming language grammars do have ε-productions, but usually in very restricted forms, so this algorithm will almost always work for these grammars too.

The algorithm works by picking an arbitrary order for all the nonterminals of the language, say, $A_1, \ldots, A_m$, and then eliminating all left recursion that does not increase the index of the A_i's. This eliminates all rules of the form $A_i \rightarrow A_j \gamma$ with $j \leq i$. If we do this for each i from 1 to m, then no recursive loop can be left, since every step in such a loop would only increase the index, and thus the original index cannot be reached again. The algorithm is given in detail in Figure 4.3.

Figure 4.3

Algorithm for general left recursion removal

> **for** $i := 1$ **to** n **do**
>   **for** $j := 1$ **to** $i-1$ **do**
>   *replace each grammar rule choice of the form $A_i \rightarrow A_j \beta$ by the rule*
> $A_i \rightarrow \alpha_1 \beta \mid \alpha_2 \beta \mid \ldots \mid \alpha_k \beta$, where $A_j \rightarrow \alpha_1 \mid \alpha_2 \mid \ldots \mid \alpha_k$ is
>   *the current rule for A_j*
>   *remove, if necessary, immediate left recursion involving A_i*

Example 4.3   Consider the following grammar:

$$A \rightarrow B \, a \mid A \, a \mid c$$
$$B \rightarrow B \, b \mid A \, b \mid d$$

(This grammar is completely artificial, since this situation does not occur in any standard programming language.)

We consider B to have a higher number than A for purposes of the algorithm (that is, $A_1 = A$ and $A_2 = B$). Since $n = 2$, the outer loop of the algorithm of Figure 4.3 executes twice, once for $i = 1$ and once for $i = 2$. When $i = 1$, the inner loop (with index j) does not execute, so the only action is to remove the immediate left recursion of A. The resulting grammar is

$$A \to B\,a\,A' \mid c\,A'$$
$$A' \to a\,A' \mid \varepsilon$$
$$B \to B\,b \mid A\,b \mid d$$

Now the outer loop executes for $i = 2$, and the inner loop executes once, with $j = 1$. In this case we eliminate the rule $B \to A\,b$ by replacing A with its choices from the first rule. Thus, we obtain the grammar

$$A \to B\,a\,A' \mid c\,A'$$
$$A' \to a\,A' \mid \varepsilon$$
$$B \to B\,b \mid B\,a\,A'\,b \mid c\,A'\,b \mid d$$

Finally, we remove the immediate left recursion of B to obtain

$$A \to B\,a\,A' \mid c\,A'$$
$$A' \to a\,A' \mid \varepsilon$$
$$B \to c\,A'\,b\,B' \mid d\,B'$$
$$B' \to b\,B' \mid a\,A'\,b\,B' \mid \varepsilon$$

This grammar has no left recursion.   §

Left recursion removal does not change the language being recognized, but it does change the grammar and thus also the parse trees. Indeed, this change causes a complication for the parser (and for the parser designer). Consider, for example, the simple expression grammar that we have been using as a standard example. As we saw, the grammar is left recursive, so as to express the left associativity of the operations. If we remove the immediate left recursion as in Example 4.1, we obtain the grammar given in Figure 4.4.

Figure 4.4

Simple arithmetic expression grammar with left recursion removed

$$exp \to term\ exp'$$
$$exp' \to addop\ term\ exp' \mid \varepsilon$$
$$addop \to + \mid -$$
$$term \to factor\ term'$$
$$term' \to mulop\ factor\ term' \mid \varepsilon$$
$$mulop \to *$$
$$factor \to (\ exp\ ) \mid \textbf{number}$$

Now consider the parse tree for the expression **3 - 4 - 5**:

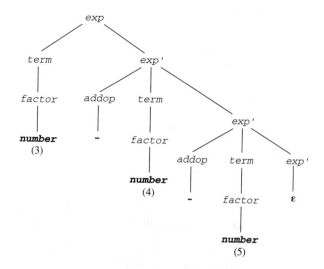

This tree no longer expresses the left associativity of subtraction. Nevertheless, a parser should still construct the appropriate left associative syntax tree:

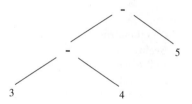

It is not completely trivial to do this using the new grammar. To see how, consider instead the somewhat simpler question of computing the value of the expression using the given parse tree. To do this, the value 3 must be passed from the root *exp* node to its right child *exp'*. This *exp'* node must then subtract 4 and pass the new value −1 down to *its* rightmost child (another *exp'*). This *exp'* node in its turn must subtract 5 and pass the value −6 to the final *exp'* node. This node has an ε child only and simply passes the value −6 back. This value is then returned up the tree to the root *exp* node and is the final value of the expression.

Consider how this would work in a recursive-descent parser. The grammar with its left recursion removed would give rise to the procedures *exp* and *exp'* as follows:

```
procedure exp ;
begin
    term ;
    exp' ;
end exp ;
```

```
procedure exp' ;
begin
  case token of
    + : match (+) ;
        term ;
        exp' ;
    - : match (-) ;
        term ;
        exp' ;
  end case ;
end exp' ;
```

To get these procedures to actually compute the value of the expression, we would rewrite them as follows:

```
function exp : integer ;
var temp : integer ;
begin
  temp := term ;
  return exp'(temp) ;
end exp ;
```

```
function exp' ( valsofar : integer ) : integer ;
begin
  if token = + or token = - then
    case token of
      + : match (+) ;
          valsofar := valsofar + term ;
      - : match (-) ;
          valsofar := valsofar - term ;
    end case ;
    return exp'(valsofar) ;
  else return valsofar ;
end exp' ;
```

Note how the *exp'* procedure now needs a parameter passed from the *exp* procedure. A similar situation occurs if these procedures are to return a (left associative) syntax tree. The code we gave in Section 4.1 used a simpler solution based on EBNFs, which does not require the extra parameter.

Finally, we note that the new expression grammar of Figure 4.4 is indeed an LL(1) grammar. The LL(1) parsing table is given in Table 4.4. As with previous tables, we will return to its construction in the next section.

Left Factoring   Left factoring is required when two or more grammar rule choices share a common prefix string, as in the rule

$$A \rightarrow \alpha \, \beta \mid \alpha \, \gamma$$

Table 4.4

LL(1) parsing table for the grammar of Figure 4.4

M[N, T]	(	*number*	)	+	-	*	$
exp	*exp →* *term exp'*	*exp →* *term exp'*					
exp'			*exp' → ε*	*exp' →* *addop* *term exp'*	*exp' →* *addop* *term exp'*		*exp' → ε*
addop				*addop →* **+**	*addop →* **-**		
term	*term →* *factor* *term'*	*term →* *factor* *term'*					
term'			*term' →* *ε*	*term' ε*	*term' → ε*	*term' →* *mulop* *factor* *term'*	*term' →* *ε*
mulop						*mulop →* *****	
factor	*factor →* *(exp)*	*factor →* **number**					

Examples are the right recursive rule for statement sequences (Example 3.7, of Chapter 3):

$$stmt\text{-}sequence \rightarrow stmt \textbf{ ; } stmt\text{-}sequence \mid stmt$$
$$stmt \rightarrow \textbf{s}$$

and the following version of the if-statement:

$$if\text{-}stmt \rightarrow \textbf{if } (\ exp \ ) \, statement$$
$$\mid \textbf{if } (\ exp \ ) \, statement \ \textbf{else} \ statement$$

Obviously, an LL(1) parser cannot distinguish between the production choices in such a situation. The solution in this simple case is to "factor" the α out on the left and rewrite the rule as two rules

$$A \rightarrow \alpha A'$$
$$A' \rightarrow \beta \mid \gamma$$

(If we wanted to use parentheses as metasymbols in grammar rules, we could also write $A \rightarrow \alpha \, (\beta \mid \gamma)$, which looks exactly like factoring in arithmetic.) For left factoring to work properly, we must make sure that α is in fact the longest string shared by the right-hand sides. It is also possible for there to be more than two options that share a prefix. We state the general algorithm in Figure 4.5 and then apply it to a number of examples. Note that as the algorithm proceeds, the number of production choices for each nonterminal that can share a prefix is reduced by at least one at each step, so the algorithm is guaranteed to terminate.

Figure 4.5

Algorithm for left factoring a grammar

> **while** *there are changes to the language* **do**
>   **for** *each nonterminal A* **do**
>   *let α be a prefix of maximal length that is shared*
>   *by two or more production choices for A*
>   **if** $\alpha \neq \varepsilon$ **then**
>   *let $A \rightarrow \alpha_1 \mid \alpha_2 \mid \ldots \mid \alpha_n$ be all the production choices for A*
>   *and suppose that $\alpha_1, \ldots, \alpha_k$ share α, so that*
>   *$A \rightarrow \alpha\, \beta_1 \mid \ldots \mid \alpha\, \beta_k \mid \alpha_{k+1} \mid \ldots \mid \alpha_n$, the β_j's share*
>   *no common prefix, and the $\alpha_{k+1}, \ldots, \alpha_n$ do not share α*
>   *replace the rule $A \rightarrow \alpha_1 \mid \alpha_2 \mid \ldots \mid \alpha_n$ by the rules*
>   *$A \rightarrow \alpha\, A' \mid \alpha_{k+1} \mid \ldots \mid \alpha_n$*
>   *$A' \rightarrow \beta_1 \mid \ldots \mid \beta_k$*

Example 4.4

Consider the grammar for statement sequences, written in right recursive form:

$$\textit{stmt-sequence} \rightarrow \textit{stmt} \; \texttt{;} \; \textit{stmt-sequence} \mid \textit{stmt}$$
$$\textit{stmt} \rightarrow \mathbf{s}$$

The grammar rule for *stmt-sequence* has a shared prefix that can be left factored as follows:

$$\textit{stmt-sequence} \rightarrow \textit{stmt stmt-seq}'$$
$$\textit{stmt-seq}' \rightarrow \texttt{;} \; \textit{stmt-sequence} \mid \varepsilon$$

Notice that if we had written the *stmt-sequence* rule left recursively instead of right recursively,

$$\textit{stmt-sequence} \rightarrow \textit{stmt-sequence} \; \texttt{;} \; \textit{stmt} \mid \textit{stmt}$$

then removing the immediate left recursion would result in the rules

$$\textit{stmt-sequence} \rightarrow \textit{stmt stmt-seq}'$$
$$\textit{stmt-seq}' \rightarrow \texttt{;} \; \textit{stmt stmt-seq}' \mid \varepsilon$$

This is almost identical to the result we obtained from left factoring, and indeed making the substitution of *stmt-sequence* for *stmt stmt-seq'* in the last rule makes the two results identical.   §

Example 4.5

Consider the following (partial) grammar for if-statements:

$$\textit{if-stmt} \rightarrow \mathbf{if} \; (\; \textit{exp} \;) \; \textit{statement}$$
$$\mid \mathbf{if} \; (\; \textit{exp} \;) \; \textit{statement} \; \mathbf{else} \; \textit{statement}$$

The left factored form of this grammar is

$$if\text{-}stmt \rightarrow \mathbf{if}\ (\ exp\ )\ statement\ else\text{-}part$$
$$else\text{-}part \rightarrow \mathbf{else}\ statement\ |\ \varepsilon$$

This is precisely the form in which we used it in Section 4.2.2 (see Table 4.2).   §

Example 4.6   Suppose we wrote an arithmetic expression grammar in which we gave an arithmetic operation right associativity instead of left associativity (we use **+** here just to have a concrete example):

$$exp \rightarrow term\ \mathbf{+}\ exp\ |\ term$$

This grammar needs to be left factored, and we obtain the rules

$$exp \rightarrow term\ exp'$$
$$exp' \rightarrow \mathbf{+}\ exp\ |\ \varepsilon$$

Now, continuing as in Example 4.4, suppose we substitute *term exp'* for *exp* in the second rule (this is legal, since this expansion would take place at the next step in a derivation anyway). We then obtain

$$exp \rightarrow term\ exp'$$
$$exp' \rightarrow \mathbf{+}\ term\ exp'\ |\ \varepsilon$$

This is identical to the grammar obtained from the left recursive rule by left recursion removal. Thus, both left factoring and left recursion removal can obscure the semantics of the language structure (in this case, they both obscure the associativity).

  If, for example, we wished to preserve the right associativity of the operation from the above grammar rules (in either form), then we must arrange that each **+** operation is applied at the end rather than at the beginning. We leave it to the reader to write this out for recursive-descent procedures.   §

Example 4.7   Here is a typical case where a programming language grammar fails to be LL(1), because procedure calls and assignments both begin with an identifier. We write out the following representation of this problem:

$$statement \rightarrow assign\text{-}stmt\ |\ call\text{-}stmt\ |\ \mathbf{other}$$
$$assign\text{-}stmt \rightarrow \mathbf{identifier}\ \mathbf{:=}\ exp$$
$$call\text{-}stmt \rightarrow \mathbf{identifier}\ (\ exp\text{-}list\ )$$

This grammar is not LL(1) because **identifier** is shared as the first token of both *assign-stmt* and *call-stmt* and, thus, could be the lookahead token for either. Unfortunately, the grammar is not in a form that can be left factored. What we must do is first replace *assign-stmt* and *call-stmt* by the right-hand sides of their defining productions, as follows:

$$statement \rightarrow \textbf{\textit{identifier}} \textbf{ :=} \; exp$$
$$| \; \textbf{\textit{identifier}} \textbf{ (} \; exp\text{-}list \textbf{)}$$
$$| \; \textbf{\textit{other}}$$

Then we left factor to obtain

$$statement \rightarrow \textbf{\textit{identifier}} \; statement'$$
$$| \; \textbf{\textit{other}}$$
$$statement' \rightarrow \textbf{ :=} \; exp \; | \; \textbf{ (} \; exp\text{-}list \textbf{)}$$

Note how this obscures the semantics of call and assignment by separating the identifier (the variable to be assigned to or the procedure to be called) from the actual call or assign action (represented by *statement'*). An LL(1) parser must fix this up by making the identifier available to the call or assign step in some way (as a parameter, say) or by otherwise adjusting the syntax tree.   §

Finally, we note that all the examples to which we have applied left factoring do indeed become LL(1) grammars after the transformation. We will construct the LL(1) parsing tables for some of them in the next section. Others are left for the exercises.

4.2.4   Syntax Tree Construction in LL(1) Parsing

It remains to comment on how LL(1) parsing may be adapted to construct syntax trees rather than parse trees. (We described in Section 4.2.1 how parse trees can be constructed using the parsing stack.) We saw in the section on recursive descent parsing that adapting that method to syntax tree construction was relatively easy. By contrast, LL(1) parsers are more difficult to adapt. This is partially because, as we have seen, the structure of the syntax tree (such as left associativity) can be obscured by left factoring and left recursion removal. Mainly, however, it is due to the fact that the parsing stack represents only predicted structures, not structures that have been actually seen. Thus, the construction of syntax tree nodes must be delayed to the point when structures are removed from the parsing stack, rather than when they are first pushed. In general, this requires that an extra stack be used to keep track of syntax tree nodes and that "action" markers be placed in the parsing stack to indicate when and what actions on the tree stack should occur. Bottom-up parsers (the next chapter) are easier to adapt to the construction of syntax trees using a parsing stack and are, therefore, preferred as table-driven stack-based parsing methods. Thus, we give only a brief example of the details of how this can be done for LL(1) parsing.

Example 4.8   We use as our grammar a barebones expression grammar with only an addition operation. The BNF is

$$E \rightarrow E \textbf{ + } \textbf{n} \; | \; \textbf{n}$$

This causes addition to be applied left associatively. The corresponding LL(1) grammar with left recursion removed is

$$E \rightarrow \mathbf{n}\, E'$$
$$E' \rightarrow +\, \mathbf{n}\, E' \mid \varepsilon$$

We show now how this grammar can be used to compute the arithmetic value of the expression. Construction of a syntax tree is similar.

To compute a value for the result of an expression, we will use a separate stack to store the intermediate values of the computation, which we call the **value stack**. We must schedule two operations on that stack. The first operation is a push of a number when it is matched in the input. The second is the addition of two numbers in the stack. The first can be performed by the *match* procedure (based on the token it is matching). The second needs to be scheduled on the parsing stack. We will do this by pushing a special symbol on the parsing stack, which, when popped, will indicate that an addition is to be performed. The symbol that we use for this purpose is the pound sign (#). This symbol now becomes a new stack symbol and must also be added to the grammar rule that matches a **+**, namely, the rule for E':

$$E' \rightarrow +\, \mathbf{n}\, \#\, E' \mid \varepsilon$$

Note that the addition is scheduled just *after* the next number, but before any more E' nonterminals are processed. This guarantees left associativity. Now let us see how the computation of the value of the expression **3+4+5** takes place. We indicate the parsing stack, input, and action as before, but list the value stack on the right (it grows toward the left). The actions of the parser are given in Table 4.5.

Table 4.5

Parsing stack with value stack actions for Example 4.8

Parsing stack	Input	Action	Value stack
$\$\, E$	3 + 4 + 5 $	$E \rightarrow \mathbf{n}\, E'$	$
$\$\, E'\, \mathbf{n}$	3 + 4 + 5 $	match/push	$
$\$\, E'$	+ 4 + 5 $	$E' \rightarrow +\, \mathbf{n}\, \#\, E'$	3 $
$\$\, E'\, \#\, \mathbf{n}\, +$	+ 4 + 5 $	match	3 $
$\$\, E'\, \#\, \mathbf{n}$	4 + 5 $	match/push	3 $
$\$\, E'\, \#$	+ 5 $	addstack	4 3 $
$\$\, E'$	+ 5 $	$E' \rightarrow +\, \mathbf{n}\, \#\, E'$	7 $
$\$\, E'\, \#\, \mathbf{n}\, +$	+ 5 $	match	7 $
$\$\, E'\, \#\, \mathbf{n}$	5 $	match/push	7 $
$\$\, E'\, \#$	$	addstack	5 7 $
$\$\, E'$	$	$E' \rightarrow \varepsilon$	12 $
$\$$	$	accept	12 $

Note that when an addition takes place, the operands are in reverse order on the value stack. This is typical of such stack-based evaluation schemes.   §

4.3 FIRST AND FOLLOW SETS

To complete the LL(1) parsing algorithm, we develop an algorithm to construct the LL(1) parsing table. As we have already indicated at several points, this involves computing the First and Follow sets, and we turn in this section to the definition and construction of these sets, after which we give a precise description of the construction of an LL(1) parsing table. At the end of this section we briefly consider how the construction can be extended to more than one symbol of lookahead.

4.3.1 First Sets

Definition

Let X be a grammar symbol (a terminal or nonterminal) or ε. Then the set **First(X)** consisting of terminals, and possibly ε, is defined as follows.

1. If X is a terminal or ε, then First(X) = $\{X\}$.
2. If X is a nonterminal, then for each production choice $X \rightarrow X_1 X_2 \ldots X_n$, First($X$) contains First($X_1$) $-$ $\{\varepsilon\}$. If also for some $i < n$, all the sets First(X_1), . . . , First(X_i) contain ε, then First(X) contains First(X_{i+1}) $-$ $\{\varepsilon\}$. If all the sets First(X_1), . . . , First(X_n) contain ε, then First(X) also contains ε.

Now define **First(α)** for any string $\alpha = X_1 X_2 \ldots X_n$ (a string of terminals and nonterminals), as follows. First(α) contains First(X_1) $-$ $\{\varepsilon\}$. For each $i = 2, \ldots, n$, if First(X_k) contains ε for all $k = 1, \ldots, i - 1$, then First(α) contains First(X_i) $-$ $\{\varepsilon\}$. Finally, if for all $i = 1, \ldots, n$, First(X_i) contains ε, then First(α) contains ε.

This definition can be easily turned into an algorithm. Indeed, the only difficult case is to compute First(A) for every nonterminal A, since the First set of a terminal is trivial and the first set of a string α is built up from the first sets of individual symbols in at most n steps, where n is the number of symbols in α. We thus state the pseudocode for the algorithm only in the case of nonterminals, and this is given in Figure 4.6.

Figure 4.6

Algorithm for computing First(A) for all nonterminals A

```
for all nonterminals A do First(A) := { };
while there are changes to any First(A) do
    for each production choice A → X₁X₂ . . . Xₙ do
        k := 1 ; Continue := true ;
        while Continue = true and k <= n do
            add First(Xₖ)−{ε} to First(A);
            if ε is not in First(Xₖ) then Continue := false ;
            k := k + 1 ;
        if Continue = true then add ε to First(A) ;
```

It is also easy to see how this definition can be interpreted in the absence of ε-productions: simply keep adding First(X_1) to First(A) for each nonterminal A and production choice $A \rightarrow X_1 \ldots$ until no further additions take place. In other words, we consider only the case $k = 1$ in Figure 4.6, and the inner while-loop is not needed. We state this algorithm separately in Figure 4.7. In the presence of ε-productions, the situation is more complicated, since we must also ask whether ε is in First(X_1), and if so continuing with the same process for X_2, and so on. The process will still finish after finitely many steps, however. Indeed, not only does this process compute the terminals that may appear as the first symbols in a string derived from a nonterminal, but it also determines whether a nonterminal can derive the empty string (i.e., disappear). Such nonterminals are called nullable:

Figure 4.7

Simplified algorithm of Figure 4.6 in the absence of ε-productions

> **for** *all nonterminals A* **do** *First(A)* := { };
> **while** *there are changes to any First(A)* **do**
>   **for** *each production choice $A \rightarrow X_1 X_2 \ldots X_n$* **do**
>   *add First(X_1) to First(A)*;

Definition

A nonterminal A is **nullable** if there exists a derivation $A \Rightarrow^* \varepsilon$.

Now we show the following theorem.

Theorem

A nonterminal A is nullable if and only if First(A) contains ε.

Proof: We show that if A is nullable, then First(A) contains ε. The converse can be proved in a similar manner. We use induction on the length of a derivation. If $A \Rightarrow \varepsilon$, then there must be a production $A \rightarrow \varepsilon$, and by definition, First(A) contains First(ε) = {ε}. Assume now the truth of the statement for derivations of length $< n$, and let $A \Rightarrow X_1 \ldots X_k \Rightarrow^* \varepsilon$ be a derivation of length n (using a production choice $A \rightarrow X_1 \ldots X_k$). If any of the X_i are terminals, they cannot derive ε, so all the X_i must be nonterminals. Indeed, the existence of the above derivation of which they are a part implies that each $X_i \Rightarrow^* \varepsilon$, and in fewer than n steps. Thus, by the induction assumption, for each i, First(X_i) contains ε. Finally, by definition, First(A) must contain ε

We give several examples of the computation of First sets for nonterminals.

Example 4.9   Consider our simple integer expression grammar:[2]

$$exp \rightarrow exp \ addop \ term \mid term$$
$$addop \rightarrow \texttt{+} \mid \texttt{-}$$
$$term \rightarrow term \ mulop \ factor \mid factor$$
$$mulop \rightarrow \texttt{*}$$
$$factor \rightarrow \texttt{(} \ exp \ \texttt{)} \mid \textbf{\texttt{number}}$$

We write out each choice separately so that we may consider them in order (we also number them for reference):

(1) $exp \rightarrow exp \ addop \ term$
(2) $exp \rightarrow term$
(3) $addop \rightarrow \texttt{+}$
(4) $addop \rightarrow \texttt{-}$
(5) $term \rightarrow term \ mulop \ factor$
(6) $term \rightarrow factor$
(7) $mulop \rightarrow \texttt{*}$
(8) $factor \rightarrow \texttt{(} \ exp \ \texttt{)}$
(9) $factor \rightarrow \textbf{\texttt{number}}$

This grammar contains no ε-productions, so we may use the simplified algorithm of Figure 4.7. We also note that the left recursive rules 1 and 5 will add nothing to the computation of First sets.[3] For example, grammar rule 1 states only that First(exp) should be added to First(exp). Thus, we could delete these productions from the computation. In this example, however, we will retain them in the list for clarity.

Now we apply the algorithm of Figure 4.7, considering the productions in the order just given. Production 1 makes no changes. Production 2 adds the contents of First($term$) to First(exp). But First($term$) is currently empty, so this also changes nothing. Rules 3 and 4 add **+** and **-** to First($addop$), respectively, so First($addop$) = {**+**, **-**}. Rule 5 adds nothing. Rule 6 adds First($factor$) to First($term$), but First($factor$) is currently still empty, so no change occurs. Rule 6 adds ***** to First($mulop$) so First($mulop$) = {*****}. Rule 8 adds **(** to First($factor$), and rule 9 adds **number** to First($factor$), so First($factor$) = { **(**, **number** }. We now begin again with rule 1, since there have been changes. Now rules 1 through 5 make no changes (First($term$) is still empty). Rule 6 adds First($factor$) to First($term$), and First($factor$) = { **(**, **number** }, so now also First($term$) = { **(**, **number** }. Rules 8 and 9 make no more changes. Again, we must begin with rule 1, since one set has changed. Rule 2 will finally add the new contents of First($term$) to First(exp), and First(exp) = { **(**, **number** }. One more pass through the grammar rules is necessary, and no more changes occur, so after four passes we have computed the following First sets:

---

2. This grammar has left recusion and is not LL(1), so we will not be able to build an LL(1) parsing table for it. However, it is still a useful example of how to compute First sets.

3. In the presence of ε-productions, left recursive rules may contribute to First sets.

$$\text{First}(exp) = \{\, (,\ \textbf{number}\,\}$$
$$\text{First}(term) = \{\, (,\ \textbf{number}\,\}$$
$$\text{First}(factor) = \{\, (,\ \textbf{number}\,\}$$
$$\text{First}(addop) = \{\, \textbf{+},\ \textbf{-}\,\}$$
$$\text{First}(mulop) = \{\, \textbf{*}\,\}$$

(Note that if we had listed the grammar rules for *factor* first instead of last, we could have reduced the number of passes from four to two.) We indicate this computation in Table 4.6. In that table, only changes are recorded, in the appropriate box where they occur. Blank entries indicate that no set has changed at that step. We also suppress the last pass, since no changes occur.

Table 4.6

Computation of First sets for the grammar of Example 4.9

Grammar rule	Pass 1	Pass 2	Pass 3
exp → *exp addop term*			
exp → *term*			First(*exp*) = { (, **number** }
addop → **+**	First(*addop*) = { **+** }		
addop → **-**	First(*addop*) = { **+**, **-** }		
term → *term mulop factor*			
term → *factor*		First(*term*) = { (, **number** }	
mulop → *****	First(*mulop*) = { ***** }		
factor → **(** *exp* **)**	First(*factor*) = { **(** }		
factor → **number**	First(*factor*) = { (, **number** }		

§

Example 4.10

Consider the (left-factored) grammar of if-statements (Example 4.5):

$$statement \rightarrow \textit{if-stmt} \mid \textbf{other}$$
$$\textit{if-stmt} \rightarrow \textbf{if} \ (\ exp\ )\ statement\ \textit{else-part}$$
$$\textit{else-part} \rightarrow \textbf{else}\ statement \mid \varepsilon$$
$$exp \rightarrow \textbf{0} \mid \textbf{1}$$

This grammar does have an ε-production, but only the *else-part* nonterminal is nullable, so the complications to the computation are minimal. Indeed, we will only need to add ε at one step, and all the other steps will remain unaffected, since none begin with a nonterminal whose First set contains ε. This is fairly typical for actual programming language grammars, where the ε-productions are almost always very limited and seldom exhibit the complexity of the general case.

As before, we write out the grammar rule choices separately and number them:

(1) *statement* → *if-stmt*
(2) *statement* → **other**
(3) *if-stmt* → **if (** *exp* **)** *statement else-part*
(4) *else-part* → **else** *statement*
(5) *else-part* → ε
(6) *exp* → **0**
(7) *exp* → **1**

Again, we proceed to step through the production choices one by one, making a new pass whenever a First set has changed in the previous pass. Grammar rule 1 begins by making no changes, since First(*if-stmt*) is still empty. Rule 2 adds the terminal **other** to First(*statement*), so First(*statement*) = {**other**}. Rule 3 adds **if** to First(*if-stmt*), so First(*if-stmt*) = {**if**}. Rule 4 adds **else** to First(*else-part*), so First(*else-part*) = {**else**}. Rule 5 adds ε to First(*else-part*), so First(*else-part*) = {**else**, ε}. Rules 6 and 7 add **0** and **1** to First(*exp*), so First(*exp*) = {**0**, **1**}. Now we make a second pass, beginning with rule 1. This rule now adds **if** to First(*statement*), since First(*if-stmt*) contains this terminal. Thus, First(*statement*) = {**if**, **other**}. No other changes occur during the second pass, and a third pass results in no changes whatsoever. Thus, we have computed the following First sets:

First(*statement*) = {**if**, **other**}
First(*if-stmt*) = {**if**}
First(*else-part*) = {**else**, ε}
First(*exp*) = {**0**, **1**}

Table 4.7 displays this computation in a similar manner to Table 4.6. As before, the table displays only changes, and the final pass (where no changes occur) is not displayed.

Table 4.7

Computation of First sets for the grammar of Example 4.10

Grammar rule	Pass 1	Pass 2
statement → *if-stmt*		First(*statement*) = {**if**, **other**}
statement → **other**	First(*statement*) = {**other**}	
if-stmt → **if (** *exp* **)** *statement else-part*	First(*if-stmt*) = {**if**}	
else-part → **else** *statement*	First(*else-part*) = {**else**}	
else-part → ε	First(*else-part*) = {**else**, ε}	
exp → **0**	First(*exp*) = {**0**}	
exp → **1**	First(*exp*) = {**0**, **1**}	

§

Example 4.11

Consider the following grammar for statement sequences (see Example 4.4):

$$stmt\text{-}sequence \rightarrow stmt\ stmt\text{-}seq'$$
$$stmt\text{-}seq' \rightarrow \texttt{;}\ stmt\text{-}sequence\ |\ \varepsilon$$
$$stmt \rightarrow \texttt{s}$$

Again, we list the production choices individually:

(1) *stmt-sequence* → *stmt stmt-seq'*
(2) *stmt-seq'* → **;** *stmt-sequence*
(3) *stmt-seq'* → ε
(4) *stmt* → **s**

On the first pass rule 1 adds nothing. Rules 2 and 3 result in First(*stmt-seq'*) = {**;**, ε}. Rule 4 results in First(*stmt*) = {**s**}. On the second pass, rule 1 now results in First(*stmt-sequence*) = First(*stmt*) = {**s**}. No other changes are made, and a third pass also results in no changes. We have computed the following First sets:

$$\text{First}(stmt\text{-}sequence) = \{\texttt{s}\}$$
$$\text{First}(stmt) = \{\texttt{s}\}$$
$$\text{First}(stmt\text{-}seq') = \{\texttt{;}, \varepsilon\}$$

We leave it to the reader to construct a table similar to those in Tables 4.6 and 4.7. §

4.3.2 Follow Sets

Definition

Given a nonterminal A, the set **Follow(A)**, consisting of terminals, and possibly $, is defined as follows.

1. If A is the start symbol, then $ is in Follow(A).
2. If there is a production $B \rightarrow \alpha A \gamma$, then First($\gamma$) − {ε} is in Follow($A$).
3. If there is a production $B \rightarrow \alpha A \gamma$ such that ε is in First (γ), then Follow(A) contains Follow(B).

We first examine the content of this definition and then write down the algorithm for the computation of the Follow sets that results from it. The first thing to notice is that the $, used to mark the end of the input, behaves as if it were a token in the computation of the Follow set. Without it, we would not have a symbol to follow the entire string to be matched. Since such a string is generated by the start symbol of the grammar, the $ must always be added to the Follow set of the start symbol. (It will be the only member of the Follow set of the start symbol if the start symbol never appears on the right-hand side of a production.)

The second thing to notice is that the empty "pseudotoken" ε is never an element of a Follow set. This makes sense because ε was used in First sets only to mark those strings that can disappear. It cannot actually be recognized in the input. Follow symbols, on the other hand, will always be matched against existing input tokens (including the $ symbol, which will match an EOF generated by the scanner).

We also note that Follow sets are defined only for nonterminals, while First sets are also defined for terminals and for strings of terminals and nonterminals. We *could* extend the definition of Follow sets to strings of symbols, but it is unnecessary, since in constructing LL(1) parsing tables we will only need the Follow sets of nonterminals.

Finally, we note that the definition of Follow sets works "on the right" in productions, while the definition of the First sets works "on the left." By this we mean that a production $A \rightarrow \alpha$ has *no* information about the Follow set of A if α does not contain A. Only appearances of A on right-hand sides of productions will contribute to Follow(A). As a consequence, each grammar rule choice will in general make contributions to the Follow sets of *each* nonterminal that appears in the right-hand side, unlike the case of First sets, where each grammar rule choice adds to the First set of only one nonterminal (the one on the left).

Furthermore, given a grammar rule $A \rightarrow \alpha B$, Follow(B) will include Follow(A) by case (3) of the definition. This is because, in any string that contains A, A could be replaced by αB (this is "context-freeness" in action). This property is, in a sense, the opposite of the situation for First sets, where if $A \rightarrow B \alpha$, then First(A) includes First(B) (except possibly for ε).

In Figure 4.8 we give the algorithm for the computation of the Follow sets that results from the definition of Follow sets. We use this algorithm to compute Follow sets for the same three grammars for which we have just computed First sets. (As with the First sets, in the absence of ε-productions, the algorithm simplifies. We leave the simplification to the reader.)

Figure 4.8

Algorithm for the computation of Follow sets

> *Follow(start-symbol)* := {$} ;
> **for** *all nonterminals A ≠ start-symbol* **do** *Follow(A)* := {} ;
> **while** *there are changes to any Follow sets* **do**
>   **for** *each production $A \rightarrow X_1 X_2 \ldots X_n$* **do**
>   **for** *each X_i that is a nonterminal* **do**
>   *add First($X_{i+1} X_{i+2} \ldots X_n$) − {$\varepsilon$} to Follow($X_i$)*
>   (* *Note: if i=n, then $X_{i+1} X_{i+2} \ldots X_n = \varepsilon$* *)
>   **if** *ε is in First($X_{i+1} X_{i+2} \ldots X_n$)* **then**
>   *add Follow(A) to Follow(X_i)*

Example 4.12   Consider again the simple expression grammar whose First sets we computed in Example 4.9, as follows:

$$\text{First}(exp) = \{\, (,\ \textbf{number} \,\}$$
$$\text{First}(term) = \{\, (,\ \textbf{number} \,\}$$
$$\text{First}(factor) = \{\, (,\ \textbf{number} \,\}$$
$$\text{First}(addop) = \{\, \textbf{+},\ \textbf{-} \,\}$$
$$\text{First}(mulop) = \{\, \textbf{*} \,\}$$

We again write out the production choices with numbering:

(1) *exp* → *exp addop term*
(2) *exp* → *term*
(3) *addop* → **+**
(4) *addop* → **-**
(5) *term* → *term mulop factor*
(6) *term* → *factor*
(7) *mulop* → *****
(8) *factor* → **(** *exp* **)**
(9) *factor* → **number**

Rules 3, 4, 7, and 9 all have no nonterminals on their right-hand sides, so they add nothing to the computation of Follow sets. We consider the other rules in order. Before we begin we set Follow(*exp*) = {$}; all other Follow sets are initialized to empty.

Rule 1 affects the Follow sets of three nonterminals: *exp*, *addop*, and *term*. First(*addop*) is added to Follow(*exp*), so now Follow(*exp*) = {$, **+**, **-**}. Next, First(*term*) is added to Follow(*addop*), so Follow(*addop*) = { **(**, **number**}. Finally, Follow(*exp*) is added to Follow(*term*), so Follow(*term*) = {$, **+**, **-**}.

Rule 2 again causes Follow(*exp*) to be added to Follow(*term*), but this has just been done by rule 1, so no change to the Follow sets occurs.

Rule 5 has three effects. First(*mulop*) is added to Follow(*term*), so Follow(*term*) = {$, **+**, **-**, *****}. Then First(*factor*) is added to Follow(*mulop*), so Follow(*mulop*) = { **(**, **number**}. Finally, Follow(*term*) is added to Follow(*factor*), so Follow(*factor*) = {$, **+**, **-**, *****}.

Rule 6 has the same effect as the last step for rule 5, and so makes no changes.

Finally, rule 8 adds First(**)**) = { **)** } to Follow(*exp*), so Follow(*exp*) = {$, **+**, **-**, **)** }.

On the second pass, rule 1 adds **)** to Follow(*term*) (so Follow(*term*) = {$, **+**, **-**, *****, **)** }), and rule 5 adds **)** to Follow(*factor*) (so Follow(*factor*) = {$, **+**, **-**, *****, **)** }). A third pass results in no further changes, and the algorithm finishes. We have computed the following Follow sets:

Follow(*exp*) = {$, **+**, **-**, **)** }
Follow(*addop*) = { **(**, **number** }
Follow(*term*) = {$, **+**, **-**, *****, **)** }
Follow(*mulop*) = { **(**, **number** }
Follow(*factor*) = {$, **+**, **-**, *****, **)** }

As in the computation of First sets, we display the progress of this computation in Table 4.8. As before, we omit the concluding pass in this table and only indicate changes to the Follow sets when they occur. We also omit the four grammar rule choices that have no possibility of affecting the computation. (We include the two rules *exp* → *term* and *term* → *factor* because they have a potential effect, even though they have no actual effect.)

Table 4.8

Computation of Follow sets for the grammar of Example 4.12

Grammar rule	Pass 1	Pass 2
$exp \rightarrow exp \ addop$ $term$	Follow(exp) = {$\$, +, -$} Follow($addop$) = {$($, **number**} Follow($term$) = {$\$, +, -$}	Follow($term$) = {$\$, +, -, *,)$}
$exp \rightarrow term$		
$term \rightarrow term \ mulop$ $factor$	Follow($term$) = {$\$, +, -, *$} Follow($mulop$) = {$($, **number**} Follow($factor$) = {$\$, +, -, *$}	Follow($factor$) = {$\$, +, -, *,)$}
$term \rightarrow factor$		
$factor \rightarrow (\ exp \ )$	Follow(exp) = {$\$, +, -,)$}	

§

Example 4.13

Consider again the simplified grammar of if-statements, whose First sets we computed in Example 4.10, as follows:

$$\text{First}(statement) = \{\textbf{if}, \textbf{other}\}$$
$$\text{First}(if\text{-}stmt) = \{\textbf{if}\}$$
$$\text{First}(else\text{-}part) = \{\textbf{else}, \varepsilon\}$$
$$\text{First}(exp) = \{\textbf{0}, \textbf{1}\}$$

We repeat here the production choices with numbering:

(1) $statement \rightarrow if\text{-}stmt$
(2) $statement \rightarrow \textbf{other}$
(3) $if\text{-}stmt \rightarrow \textbf{if} \ (\ exp \ ) \ statement \ else\text{-}part$
(4) $else\text{-}part \rightarrow \textbf{else} \ statement$
(5) $else\text{-}part \rightarrow \varepsilon$
(6) $exp \rightarrow \textbf{0}$
(7) $exp \rightarrow \textbf{1}$

Rules 2, 5, 6, and 7 have no effect on the computation of Follow sets, so we ignore them. We begin by setting Follow($statement$) = {$\$$} and initializing Follow of the other nonterminals to empty. Rule 1 now adds Follow($statement$) to Follow($if\text{-}stmt$), so Follow($if\text{-}stmt$) = {$\$$}. Rule 3 affects the Follow sets of exp, $statement$, and $else\text{-}part$. First, Follow(exp) gets First($)$) = {$)$}, so Follow(exp) = {$)$}. Then Follow($statement$) gets First($else\text{-}part$) − {ε}, so Follow($statement$) = {$\$$, **else**}. Finally, Follow ($if\text{-}stmt$) is added to both Follow($else\text{-}part$) and Follow($statement$) (this is because *if-stmt* can disappear). The first addition gives Follow(*else-part*) = {$}, but the second results in no change. Finally, rule 4 causes Follow(*else-part*) to be added to Follow(*statement*), also resulting in no change.

In the second pass, rule 1 again adds Follow(*statement*) to Follow(*if-stmt*), resulting in Follow(*if-stmt*) = {$, **else**}. Rule 3 now causes the terminal **else** to be added to Follow(*else-part*), so Follow(*else-part*) = {$, **else**}. Finally, rule 4 causes no additional changes. The third pass also results in no more changes, and we have computed the following Follow sets:

$$Follow(statement) = \{\$, \textbf{else}\}$$
$$Follow(if\text{-}stmt) = \{\$, \textbf{else}\}$$
$$Follow(else\text{-}part) = \{\$, \textbf{else}\}$$
$$Follow(exp) = \{\,\textbf{)}\,\}$$

We leave it to the reader to construct a table of this computation as in the previous example. §

Example 4.14

We compute the Follow sets for the simplified statement sequence grammar of Example 4.11, with the grammar rule choices:

(1) *stmt-sequence* → *stmt stmt-seq'*
(2) *stmt-seq'* → **;** *stmt-sequence*
(3) *stmt-seq'* → ε
(4) *stmt* → **s**

In Example 4.11, we computed the following First sets:

$$First(stmt\text{-}sequence) = \{\textbf{s}\}$$
$$First(stmt) = \{\textbf{s}\}$$
$$First(stmt\text{-}seq') = \{\textbf{;}, \varepsilon\}$$

Grammar rules 3 and 4 make no contribution to the Follow set computation. We start with Follow(*stmt-sequence*) = {$} and the other Follow sets empty. Rule 1 results in Follow(*stmt*) = {**;**} and Follow(*stmt-seq'*) = {$}. Rule 2 has no effect. A second pass results in no further changes. Thus, we have computed the Follow sets

$$Follow(stmt\text{-}sequence) = \{\$\}$$
$$Follow(stmt) = \{\textbf{;}\}$$
$$Follow(stmt\text{-}seq') = \{\$\}$$
§

4.3.3 Constructing LL(1) Parsing Tables

Consider now the original construction of the entries of the LL(1) parsing table, as given in Section 4.2.2:

1. If $A \rightarrow \alpha$ is a production choice, and there is a derivation $\alpha \Rightarrow^* a \beta$, where a is a token, then add $A \rightarrow \alpha$ to the table entry $M[A, a]$.
2. If $A \rightarrow \varepsilon$ is an ε-production and there is a derivation $S \$ \Rightarrow^* \alpha A a \beta$, where S is the start symbol and a is a token (or \$), then add $A \rightarrow \varepsilon$ to the table entry $M[A, a]$.

Clearly, the token a in rule 1 is in First(α), and the token a of rule 2 is in Follow(A). Thus, we have arrived at the following algorithmic construction of the LL(1) parsing table:

Construction of the LL(1) parsing table $M[N, T]$

Repeat the following two steps for each nonterminal A and production choice $A \rightarrow \alpha$.

1. For each token a in First(α), add $A \rightarrow \alpha$ to the entry $M[A, a]$.
2. If ε is in First(α), for each element a of Follow(A) (a token or \$), add $A \rightarrow \alpha$ to $M[A, a]$.

The following theorem is essentially a direct consequence of the definition of an LL(1) grammar and the parsing table construction just given, and we leave its proof to the exercises:

Theorem

A grammar in BNF is **LL(1)** if the following conditions are satisfied.

1. For every production $A \rightarrow \alpha_1 \mid \alpha_2 \mid \ldots \mid \alpha_n$, First($\alpha_i$) $\cap$ First(α_j) is empty for all i and j, $1 \le i, j \le n$, $i \ne j$.
2. For every nonterminal A such that First(A) contains ε, First(A) $\cap$ Follow(A) is empty.

We now look at some examples of parsing tables for grammars we have previously seen.

Example 4.15

Consider the simple expression grammar we have been using as a standard example throughout this chapter. This grammar as originally given (see Example 4.9 earlier) is left recursive. In the last section we wrote out an equivalent grammar using left recursion removal, as follows:

$$exp \rightarrow term\ exp'$$
$$exp' \rightarrow addop\ term\ exp' \mid \varepsilon$$
$$addop \rightarrow + \mid -$$
$$term \rightarrow factor\ term'$$
$$term' \rightarrow mulop\ factor\ term' \mid \varepsilon$$
$$mulop \rightarrow *$$
$$factor \rightarrow (\ exp\ ) \mid \mathbf{number}$$

We must compute First and Follow sets for the nonterminals for this grammar. We leave this computation for the exercises and simply state the result:

First(*exp*) = { **(**, **number**}   Follow(*exp*) = {\$, **)** }

First(*exp'*) = {**+**, **-**, *ε*}   Follow(*exp'*) = {\$, **)** }

First(*addop*) = {**+**, **-**}   Follow(*addop*) = { **(**, **number**}

First(*term*) = { **(**, **number**}   Follow(*term*) = {\$, **)**, **+**, **-**}

First(*term'*) = { *****, *ε*}   Follow(*term'*) = {\$, **)**, **+**, **-**}

First(*mulop*) = { *****}   Follow(*mulop*) = { **(**, **number**}

First(*factor*) = { **(**, **number**}   Follow(*factor*) = {\$, **)**, **+**, **-**, *****}

Applying the LL(1) parsing table construction just described, we get the table as given in Table 4.4, page 163.   §

Example 4.16   Consider the simplified grammar of if-statements

$$statement \rightarrow \textit{if-stmt} \mid \textbf{other}$$
$$\textit{if-stmt} \rightarrow \textbf{if (} exp \textbf{)} statement \ \textit{else-part}$$
$$\textit{else-part} \rightarrow \textbf{else} \ statement \mid ε$$
$$exp \rightarrow \textbf{0} \mid \textbf{1}$$

The First sets of this grammar were computed in Example 4.10 and the Follow sets were computed in Example 4.13. We list these sets again here:

First(*statement*) = {**if**, **other**}   Follow(*statement*) = {\$, **else**}

First(*if-stmt*) = {**if**}   Follow(*if-stmt*) = {\$, **else**}

First(*else-part*) = {**else**, *ε*}   Follow(*else-part*) = {\$, **else**}

First(*exp*) = {**0**, **1**}   Follow(*exp*) = { **)** }

Constructing the LL(1) parsing table gives Table 4.3, page 156.   §

Example 4.17   Consider the grammar of Example 4.4 (with left factoring applied):

$$\textit{stmt-sequence} \rightarrow \textit{stmt stmt-seq'}$$
$$\textit{stmt-seq'} \rightarrow \textbf{;} \ \textit{stmt-sequence} \mid ε$$
$$\textit{stmt} \rightarrow \textbf{s}$$

This grammar has the following First and Follow sets

First(*stmt-sequence*) = {**s**}   Follow(*stmt-sequence*) = {\$}

First(*stmt*) = {**s**}   Follow(*stmt*) = {**;**}

First(*stmt-seq'*) = {**;**, *ε*}   Follow(*stmt-seq'*) = {\$}

and the LL(1) parsing table at the top of the next page.

M[N, T]	s	;	$
stmt-sequence	*stmt-sequence* → *stmt stmt-seq'*		
stmt	*stmt* → **s**		
stmt-seq'		*stmt-seq'* → **;** *stmt-sequence*	*stmt-seq'* → ε

§

4.3.4 Extending the Lookahead: LL(*k*) Parsers

The previous work can be extended to *k* symbols of lookahead. For example, we can define First$_k(\alpha)$ = { w_k | $\alpha \Rightarrow^* w$ }, where *w* is a string of tokens and w_k = the first *k* tokens of *w* (or *w*, if *w* has fewer than *k* tokens). Similarly, we can define Follow$_k(A)$ = { w_k | $S\$ \Rightarrow^* \alpha Aw$ }. While these definitions are less "algorithmic" than our definitions for the case *k* = 1, algorithms to compute these sets can be developed, and the construction of the LL(*k*) parsing table can be performed as before.

Several complications occur in LL(*k*) parsing, however. First, the parsing table becomes much larger, since the number of columns increases exponentially with *k*. (To a certain extent this can be countered by using table compression methods.) Second, the parsing table itself does not express the complete power of LL(*k*) parsing, essentially because the Follow strings do not all occur in all contexts. Thus, parsing using the table as we have constructed it is distinguished from LL(*k*) parsing by calling it **Strong LL(*k*) parsing, or SLL(*k*) parsing**. We refer the reader to the Notes and References section for more information.

LL(*k*) and SLL(*k*) parsers are uncommon, partially because of the added complexity, but primarily because of the fact that a grammar that fails to be LL(1) is in practice likely not to be LL(*k*) for any *k*. For instance, a grammar with left recursion is never LL(*k*), no matter how large the *k*. Recursive-descent parsers, however, are able to selectively use larger lookaheads when needed and even, as we have seen, use ad hoc methods to parse grammars that are not LL(*k*) for any *k*.

4.4 A RECURSIVE-DESCENT PARSER FOR THE TINY LANGUAGE

In this section we discuss the complete recursive-descent parser for the TINY language listed in Appendix B. The parser constructs a syntax tree as described in Section 3.7 of the previous chapter and, additionally, prints a representation of the syntax tree to the listing file. The parser uses the EBNF as given in Figure 4.9, corresponding to the BNF of Chapter 3, Figure 3.6.

Figure 4.9

Grammar of the TINY
language in EBNF

$program \rightarrow stmt\text{-}sequence$

$stmt\text{-}sequence \rightarrow statement \{ \; ; \; statement \}$

$statement \rightarrow if\text{-}stmt \mid repeat\text{-}stmt \mid assign\text{-}stmt \mid read\text{-}stmt \mid write\text{-}stmt$

$if\text{-}stmt \rightarrow$ **if** exp **then** $stmt\text{-}sequence \; [$ **else** $stmt\text{-}sequence \;]$ **end**

$repeat\text{-}stmt \rightarrow$ **repeat** $stmt\text{-}sequence$ **until** exp

$assign\text{-}stmt \rightarrow$ **identifier** $:= exp$

$read\text{-}stmt \rightarrow$ **read identifier**

$write\text{-}stmt \rightarrow$ **write** exp

$exp \rightarrow simple\text{-}exp \; [\; comparison\text{-}op \; simple\text{-}exp \;]$

$comparison\text{-}op \rightarrow$ **<** $\mid$ **=**

$simple\text{-}exp \rightarrow term \{ \; addop \; term \}$

$addop \rightarrow$ **+** $\mid$ **-**

$term \rightarrow factor \{ \; mulop \; factor \}$

$mulop \rightarrow$ ***** $\mid$ **/**

$factor \rightarrow$ **(** exp **)** $\mid$ **number** $\mid$ **identifier**

The TINY parser follows closely the outline of recursive descent parsing given in Section 4.1. The parser consists of two code files, **parse.h** and **parse.c**. The **parse.h** file (Appendix B, lines 850–865) is extremely simple: it consists of a single declaration

```
TreeNode * parse(void);
```

defining the main parse routine **parse** that returns a pointer to the syntax tree constructed by the parser. The **parse.c** file is given in Appendix B, lines 900–1114. It consists of 11 mutually recursive procedures that correspond directly to the EBNF grammar of Figure 4.9: one for *stmt-sequence*, one for *statement*, one each for the five different kinds of statements, and four for the different precedence levels of expressions. Operator nonterminals are not included as procedures, but are recognized as part of their associated expressions. There is also no procedure corresponding to *program*, since a program is just a statement sequence, so the **parse** routine simply calls **stmt_sequence**.

The parser code also includes a static variable **token** that keeps the lookahead token, a **match** procedure that looks for a specific token, calling **getToken** if it finds it and declaring error otherwise, and a **syntaxError** procedure that prints an error message to the listing file. The main **parse** procedure initializes **token** to the first token in the input, calls **stmt_sequence**, and then checks for the end of the source file before returning the tree constructed by **stmt_sequence**. (If there are more tokens after **stmt_sequence** returns, this is an error.)

The contents of each recursive procedure should be relatively self-explanatory, with the possible exception of **stmt_sequence**, which has been written in a somewhat more complex form to improve error handling; this will be explained in the discussion of error handling given shortly. The recursive parsing procedures make use of three utility procedures, which are gathered for simplicity into the file **util.c** (Appendix

B, lines 350–526), with interface **util.h** (Appendix B, lines 300–335). These procedures are

1. **newStmtNode** (lines 405–421), which takes a parameter indicating the kind of statement, and allocates a new statement node of that kind, returning a pointer to the newly allocated node;
2. **newExpNode** (lines 423–440), which takes a parameter indicating the kind of expression and allocates a new expression node of that kind, returning a pointer to the newly allocated node; and
3. **copyString** (lines 442–455), which takes a string parameter, allocates sufficient space for a copy, and copies the string, returning a pointer to the newly allocated copy.

The **copyString** procedure is made necessary by the fact that the C language does not automatically allocate space for strings and by the fact that the scanner reuses the same space for the string values (or lexemes) of the tokens it recognizes.

A procedure **printTree** (lines 473–506) is also included in **util.c** that writes a linear version of the syntax tree to the listing, so that we may view the result of a parse. This procedure is called from the main program, under the control of the global **traceParse** variable.

The **printTree** procedure operates by printing node information and then indenting to print child information. The actual tree can be reconstructed from this indentation. The syntax tree of the sample TINY program (see Chapter 3, Figures 3.8 and 3.9, pp. 137–138) is printed to the listing file by **traceParse** as shown in Figure 4.10.

Figure 4.10

Display of a TINY syntax tree by the **printTree** procedure

```
Read: x
If
   Op: <
      const: 0
      Id: x
   Assign to: fact
      const: 1
   Repeat
      Assign to: fact
         Op: *
            Id: fact
            Id: x
      Assign to: x
         Op: -
            Id: x
            const: 1
      Op: =
         Id: x
         const: 0
   Write
      Id: fact
```

4.5   ERROR RECOVERY IN TOP-DOWN PARSERS

The response of a parser to syntax errors is often a critical factor in the usefulness of a compiler. Minimally, a parser must determine whether a program is syntactically correct or not. A parser that performs this task alone is called a **recognizer**, since all it does is recognize strings in the context-free language generated by the grammar of the programming language in question. It is worth stating that at a minimum, any parser must behave like a recognizer—that is, if a program contains a syntax error, the parser must indicate that *some* error exists, and conversely, if a program contains no syntax errors, then the parser should not claim that an error exists.

Beyond this minimal behavior, a parser can exhibit many different levels of responses to errors. Usually, a parser will attempt to give a meaningful error message, at least for the first error encountered, and also attempt to determine as closely as possible the location where that error has occurred. Some parsers may go so far as to attempt some form of **error correction** (or, perhaps more appropriately, **error repair**), where the parser attempts to infer a correct program from the incorrect one given. If this is attempted, most of the time it is limited to easy cases, such as missing punctuation. There exists a body of algorithms that can be applied to find a correct program that is closest in some sense to the one given (usually in terms of number of tokens that must be inserted, deleted, or changed). Such **minimal distance error correction** is usually too inefficient to be applied to every error and, in any case, results in error repair that is often very far from what the programmer actually intended. Thus, it is seldom seen in actual parsers. Compiler writers find it difficult enough to generate meaningful error messages without trying to do error correction.

Most of the techniques for error recovery are ad hoc, in the sense that they apply to specific languages and specific parsing algorithms, with many special cases for individual situations. General principles are hard to come by. Some important considerations that apply are the following.

1. A parser should try to determine that an error has occurred *as soon as possible*. Waiting too long before declaring error means the location of the actual error may have been lost.
2. After an error has occurred, the parser must pick a likely place to resume the parse. A parser should always try to parse as much of the code as possible, in order to find as many real errors as possible during a single translation.
3. A parser should try to avoid the **error cascade problem**, in which one error generates a lengthy sequence of spurious error messages.
4. A parser must avoid infinite loops on errors, in which an unending cascade of error messages is generated without consuming any input.

Some of these goals conflict with each other, so that a compiler writer is forced to make trade-offs during the construction of an error handler. For example, avoiding the error cascade and infinite loop problems can cause the parser to skip some of the input, compromising the goal of processing as much of the input as possible.

4.5.1   Error Recovery in Recursive-Descent Parsers

A standard form of error recovery in recursive-descent parsers is called **panic mode**. The name derives from the fact that, in complex situations, the error handler will consume a possibly large number of tokens in an attempt to find a place to resume parsing (in the worst case, it might even consume the entire rest of the program, in which case it is no better than simply exiting after the error). However, when implemented with some care, this can be a much better method for error recovery than its name implies.[4] Panic mode has the added attraction that it virtually ensures that the parser cannot get into an infinite loop during error recovery.

The basic mechanism of panic mode is to provide each recursive procedure with an extra parameter consisting of a set of **synchronizing tokens**. As parsing proceeds, tokens that may function as synchronizing tokens are added to this set as each call occurs. If an error is encountered, the parser **scans ahead**, throwing away tokens until one of the synchronizing set of tokens is seen in the input, whence parsing is resumed. Error cascades are avoided (to a certain extent) by not generating new error messages while this forward scan takes place.

The important decisions to be made in this error recovery method are what tokens to add to the synchronizing set at each point in the parse. Generally, Follow sets are important candidates for such synchronizing tokens. First sets may also be used to prevent the error handler from skipping important tokens that begin major new constructs (like statements or expressions). First sets are also important, in that they allow a recursive descent parser to detect errors early in the parse, which is always helpful in any error recovery. It is important to realize that panic mode works best when the compiler "knows" when *not* to panic. For example, missing punctuation symbols such as semicolons or commas, and even missing right parentheses, should not always cause an error handler to consume tokens. Of course, care must be taken to ensure that an infinite loop cannot occur.

We illustrate panic mode error recovery by sketching in pseudocode its implementation in the recursive descent calculator of Section 4.1.2 (see also Figure 4.1). In addition to the *match* and *error* procedures, which remain essentially the same (except that *error* no longer exits immediately), we have two more procedures, *checkinput*, which performs the early lookahead checking, and *scanto*, which is the panic mode token consumer proper:

```
procedure scanto ( synchset ) ;
begin
  while not ( token in synchset ∪ { $ }) do
    getToken ;
end scanto ;

procedure checkinput ( firstset, followset ) ;
begin
  if not ( token in firstset ) then
    error ;
    scanto ( firstset ∪ followset ) ;
  end if ;
end;
```

Here the $ refers to the end of input (EOF).

---

4. Wirth [1976], in fact, calls panic mode the "don't panic" rule, presumably in an attempt to improve its image.

These procedures are used as follows in the *exp* and *factor* procedures (which now take a *synchset* parameter):

```
procedure exp ( synchset ) ;
begin
  checkinput ( { (, number }, synchset ) ;
  if not ( token in synchset ) then
    term ( synchset ) ;
    while token = + or token = - do
      match (token) ;
      term ( synchset ) ;
    end while ;
    checkinput ( synchset, { (, number }) ;
  end if;
end exp ;


procedure factor ( synchset ) ;
begin
  checkinput ( { (, number }, synchset ) ;
  if not ( token in synchset ) then
    case token of
    ( :  match( ( ) ;
         exp ( { ) } ) ;
         match( ) ) ;
    number :
         match(number) ;
    else error ;
    end case ;
    checkinput ( synchset, { (, number }) ;
  end if ;
end factor ;
```

Note how *checkinput* is called twice in each procedure: once to verify that a token in the First set is the next token in the input and a second time to verify that a token in the Follow set (or *synchset*) is the next token on exit.

This form of panic mode will generate reasonable errors (useful error messages can also be added as parameters to *checkinput* and *error*). For example, the input string **(2+-3)*4-+5** will generate exactly two error messages (one at the first minus sign and one at the second plus sign).

We note that, in general, *synchset* is to be passed down in the recursive calls, with new synchronizing tokens added as appropriate. In the case of *factor*, an exception is made after a left parenthesis is seen: *exp* is called with right parenthesis only as its follow set (*synchset* is discarded). This is typical of the kind of ad hoc analysis that accompanies panic mode error recovery. (We did this so that, for example, the expression **(2+*)** would not generate a spurious error message at the right parenthesis.) We leave an analysis of the behavior of this code, and its implementation in C, to the exercises. Unfortunately, to obtain the best error messages and error recovery, virtually every token test must be examined for the possibility that a more general test, or an earlier test, may improve error behavior.

4.5.2   Error Recovery in LL(1) Parsers

Panic mode error recovery can be implemented in LL(1) parsers in a similar manner to the way it is implemented in recursive-descent parsing. Since the algorithm is nonrecursive, a new stack is required to keep the *synchset* parameters, and a call to *checkinput* must be scheduled by the algorithm before each generate action of the algorithm (when a nonterminal is at the top of the stack).[5] Note that the primary error situation occurs with a nonterminal A at the top of the stack and the current input token is not in First(A) (or Follow(A), if ε is in First(A)). The case where a token is at the top of the stack, and it is not the same as the current input token, does not normally occur, since tokens are, in general, only pushed onto the stack when they are actually seen in the input (table compression methods may compromise this slightly). We leave the modifications to the parsing algorithm of Figure 4.2, page 155, to the exercises.

An alternative to the use of an extra stack is to statically build the sets of synchronizing tokens directly into the LL(1) parsing table, together with the corresponding actions that *checkinput* would take. Given a nonterminal A at the top of the stack and an input token that is not in First(A) (or Follow(A), if ε is in First(A)), there are three possible alternatives:

1. Pop A from the stack.
2. Successively pop tokens from the input until a token is seen for which we can restart the parse.
3. Push a new nonterminal onto the stack.

We choose alternative 1 if the current input token is $ or is in Follow(A) and alternative 2 if the current input token is not $ and is not in First(A) $\cup$ Follow(A). Option 3 is occasionally useful in special situations, but is rarely appropriate (we shall discuss one case shortly). We indicate the first action in the parsing table by the notation *pop* and the second by the notation *scan*. (Note that a *pop* action is equivalent to a reduction by an ε-production.)

With these conventions, the LL(1) parsing table (Table 4.4) looks as in Table 4.9. The behavior of an LL(1) parser using this table, given the string **(2+*)**, is shown in Table 4.10. In that table, the parse is shown only from the first error on (so the prefix **(2+** has already been successfully matched). We also use the abbreviations E for *exp*, E' for *exp'*, and so on. Note that there are two adjacent error moves before the parse resumes successfully. We can arrange to suppress an error message on the second error move by requiring, after the first error, that the parser make one or more successful moves before generating any new error messages. Thus, error message cascades would be avoided.

There is (at least) one problem in this error recovery method that calls for special action. Since many error actions pop a nonterminal from the stack, it is possible for the stack to become empty, with some input still to parse. A simple case of this in the example just given is any string beginning with a right parenthesis: this will cause E to be immediately popped, leaving the stack empty with all the input yet to be consumed.

---

5. Calls to *checkinput* at the end of a match, as in the recursive-descent code, can also be scheduled by a special stack symbol in a similar fashion to the value computation scheme of Section 4.2.4, page 167.

One possible action that the parser can take in this situation is to push the start symbol onto the stack and scan forward in the input until a symbol in the First set of the start symbol is seen.

Table 4.9

LL(1) parsing table (Table 4.4) with error recovery entries

M[N, T]	(	**number**	)	+	-	*	$
exp	*exp →* *term exp'*	*exp →* *term exp'*	pop	scan	scan	scan	pop
exp'	scan	scan	*exp' → ε*	*exp' →* *addop* *term exp'*	*exp' →* *addop* *term exp'*	scan	*exp' → ε*
addop	pop	pop	scan	*addop →* **+**	*addop →* **-**	scan	pop
term	*term →* *factor* *term'*	*term →* *factor* *term'*	pop	pop	pop	scan	pop
term'	scan	scan	*term' → ε*	*term' → ε*	*term' → ε*	*term' →* *mulop* *factor* *term'*	*term' → ε*
mulop	pop	pop	scan	scan	scan	*mulop →* *****	pop
factor	*factor →* *(exp)*	*factor →* **number**	pop	pop	pop	pop	pop

Table 4.10

Moves of an LL(1) parser using Table 4.9

Parsing stack	Input	Action
$ E' T') E' T	*****) $	scan (error)
$ E' T') E' T	) $	pop (error)
$ E' T') E'	) $	$E' → ε$
$ E' T')	) $	match
$ E' T'	$	$T' → ε$
$ E'	$	$E' → ε$
$	$	accept

4.5.3   Error Recovery in the TINY Parser

The error handling of the TINY parser, as given in Appendix B, is extremely rudimentary: only a very primitive form of panic mode recovery is implemented, without the synchronizing sets. The **match** procedure simply declares error, stating which token it found that it did not expect. In addition, the procedures **statement** and **factor** declare error when no correct choice is found. Also the **parse** procedure declares error if a token other than end of file is found after the parse finishes. The principal error message generated is "unexpected token," which can be very unhelpful to the user. In addition, the parser makes no attempt to avoid error cascades. For example, the sample program with a semicolon added after the write-statement

```
 . . .
  5: read x ;
  6: if 0 < x then
  7:    fact := 1;
  8:    repeat
  9:       fact := fact * x;
 10:       x := x - 1
 11:    until x = 0;
 12:    write fact; {<- - BAD SEMICOLON! }
 13: end
 14:
```

causes the following *two* error messages to be generated (when only one error has occurred):

```
Syntax error at line 13: unexpected token -> reserved word: end
Syntax error at line 14: unexpected token -> EOF
```

And the same program with the comparison < deleted in the second line of code

```
 . . .
  5: read x ;
  6: if 0 x then { <- - COMPARISON MISSING HERE! }
  7:    fact := 1;
  8:    repeat
  9:       fact := fact * x;
 10:       x := x - 1
 11:    until x = 0;
 12:    write fact
 13: end
 14:
```

causes *four* error messages to be printed in the listing:

```
Syntax error at line 6: unexpected token -> ID, name = x
Syntax error at line 6: unexpected token -> reserved word: then
Syntax error at line 6: unexpected token -> reserved word: then
Syntax error at line 7: unexpected token -> ID, name = fact
```

On the other hand, some of the TINY parser's behavior is reasonable. For example, a missing (rather than an extra) semicolon will generate only one error message, and the parser will go on to build the correct syntax tree as if the semicolon had been there all along, thus performing a rudimentary form of error correction in this one case. This behavior results from two coding facts. The first is that the **match** procedure does not consume a token, which results in behavior that is identical to inserting a missing token. The second is that the **stmt_sequence** procedure has been written so as to connect up as much of the syntax tree as possible in the case of an error. In particular, care was taken to make sure that the sibling pointers are connected up whenever a non-nil pointer is found (the parser procedures are designed to return a nil syntax tree pointer if an error is found). Also, the obvious way of writing the body of **stmt_sequence** based on the EBNF

```
statement();
while (token==SEMI)
{ match(SEMI);
  statement();
}
```

is instead written with a more complicated loop test:

```
statement();
while ((token!=ENDFILE) && (token!=END) &&
       (token!=ELSE) && (token!=UNTIL))
{ match(SEMI);
  statement();
}
```

The reader may note that the four tokens in this negative test comprise the Follow set for *stmt-sequence*. This is not an accident, as a test may either look for a token in the First set (as do the procedures for *statement* and *factor*) or look for a token *not* in the Follow set. This latter is particularly effective in error recovery, since if a First symbol is missing, the parse would stop. We leave to the exercises a trace of the program behavior to show that a missing semicolon would indeed cause the rest of the program to be skipped if **stmt_sequence** were written in the first form given.

Finally, we note that the parser has also been written in such a way that it cannot get into an infinite loop when it encounters errors (the reader should have worried about this when we noted that **match** does not consume an unexpected token). This is because, in an arbitrary path through the parsing procedures, eventually either the default case of **statement** or **factor** must be encountered, and both of these *do* consume a token while generating an error message.

EXERCISES

4.1 Write pseudocode for *term* and *factor* corresponding to the pseudocode for *exp* in Section 4.1.2 (page 150) that constructs a syntax tree for simple arithmetic expressions.

4.2 Given the grammar $A \rightarrow (A) A \mid \varepsilon$, write pseudocode to parse this grammar by recursive-descent.

4.3 Given the grammar

$$statement \rightarrow assign\text{-}stmt \mid call\text{-}stmt \mid \textbf{other}$$
$$assign\text{-}stmt \rightarrow \textbf{identifier} := exp$$
$$call\text{-}stmt \rightarrow \textbf{identifier} (exp\text{-}list)$$

write pseudocode to parse this grammar by recursive-descent.

4.4 Given the grammar

$$lexp \rightarrow \textbf{number} \mid (\ op \ lexp\text{-}seq \ )$$
$$op \rightarrow \texttt{+} \mid \texttt{-} \mid \texttt{*}$$
$$lexp\text{-}seq \rightarrow lexp\text{-}seq \ lexp \mid lexp$$

write pseudocode to compute the numeric value of an *lexp* by recursive-descent (see Exercise 3.13 of Chapter 3).

4.5 Show the actions of an LL(1) parser that uses Table 4.4 (page 163) to recognize the following arithmetic expressions:

a. 3+4*5-6   **b. 3*(4-5+6)**   **c. 3-(4+5*6)**

4.6 Show the actions of an LL(1) parser that uses the table of Section 4.2.2, page 155, to recognize the following strings of balanced parentheses:

a. (( )) ( )   **b. (( ) ( ))**   **c. ( ) (( ))**

4.7 Given the grammar $A \rightarrow (A) A \mid \varepsilon$,

   a. Construct First and Follow sets for the nonterminal A.
   b. Show this grammar is LL(1).

4.8 Consider the grammar

$$lexp \rightarrow atom \mid list$$
$$atom \rightarrow \textbf{number} \mid \textbf{identifier}$$
$$list \rightarrow (\ lexp\text{-}seq \ )$$
$$lexp\text{-}seq \rightarrow lexp\text{-}seq \ lexp \mid lexp$$

   a. Remove the left recursion.
   b. Construct First and Follow sets for the nonterminals of the resulting grammar.
   c. Show that the resulting grammar is LL(1).
   d. Construct the LL(1) parsing table for the resulting grammar.
   e. Show the actions of the corresponding LL(1) parser, given the input string
      (a (b (2)) (c)).

4.9 Consider the following grammar (similar, but not identical to the grammar of Exercise 4.8):

$$lexp \rightarrow atom \mid list$$
$$atom \rightarrow \textbf{number} \mid \textbf{identifier}$$
$$list \rightarrow (\ lexp\text{-}seq \ )$$
$$lexp\text{-}seq \rightarrow lexp \ \texttt{,} \ lexp\text{-}seq \mid lexp$$

   a. Left factor this grammar.
   b. Construct First and Follow sets for the nonterminals of the resulting grammar.
   c. Show that the resulting grammar is LL(1).
   d. Construct the LL(1) parsing table for the resulting grammar.
   e. Show the actions of the corresponding LL(1) parser, given the input string
      (a, (b, (2)), (c)).

4.10 Consider the following grammar of simplified C declarations:

$$declaration \rightarrow type\ var\text{-}list$$
$$type \rightarrow \textbf{int} \mid \textbf{float}$$
$$var\text{-}list \rightarrow \textbf{identifier}, var\text{-}list \mid \textbf{identifier}$$

    a. Left factor this grammar.

    b. Construct First and Follow sets for the nonterminals of the resulting grammar.

    c. Show that the resulting grammar is LL(1).

    d. Construct the LL(1) parsing table for the resulting grammar.

    e. Show the actions of the corresponding LL(1) parser, given the input string
       `int x,y,z`.

4.11 An LL(1) parsing table such as that of Table 4.4 (page 163) generally has many blank entries representing errors. In many cases, all the blank entries in a row can be replaced by a single **default entry**, thus decreasing the size of the table considerably. Potential default entries occur in nonterminal rows when a nonterminal has a single production choice or when it has an ε-production. Apply these ideas to Table 4.4. What are the drawbacks of such a scheme, if any?

4.12 **a.** Can an LL(1) grammar be ambiguous? Why or why not?

    b. Can an ambiguous grammar be LL(1)? Why or why not?

    c. Must an unambiguous grammar be LL(1)? Why or why not?

4.13 Show that a left-recursive grammar cannot be LL(1).

4.14 Prove the theorem on page 178 that concludes a grammar is LL(1) from two conditions on its First and Follow sets.

4.15 Define the operator $\oplus$ on two sets of token strings S_1 and S_2 as follows: $S_1 \oplus S_2 =$ { $\text{First}(xy) \mid x \in S_1, y \in S_2$ }.

    a. Show that, for any two nonterminals A and B, $\text{First}(AB) = \text{First}(A) \oplus \text{First}(B)$.

    b. Show that the two conditions of the theorem on page 178 can be replaced by the single condition: if $A \rightarrow \alpha$ and $A \rightarrow \beta$, then $(\text{First}(\alpha) \oplus \text{Follow}(A)) \cap (\text{First}(\beta) \oplus \text{Follow}(A))$ is empty.

4.16 A nonterminal A is **useless** if there is no derivation from the start symbol to a string of tokens in which A appears.

    a. Give a mathematical formulation of this property.

    b. Is it likely that a programming language grammar will have a useless symbol? Explain.

    c. Show that, if a grammar has a useless symbol, the computation of First and Follow sets as given in this chapter may produce sets that are too large to accurately construct an LL(1) parsing table.

4.17 Give an algorithm that removes useless nonterminals (and associated productions) from a grammar without changing the language recognized. (See the previous exercise.)

4.18 Show that the converse of the theorem on page 178 is true, if a grammar has no useless nonterminals (see Exercise 4.16).

4.19 Give details of the computation of the First and Follow sets listed in Example 4.15 (page 178).

4.20 **a.** Construct the First and Follow sets for the nonterminals of the left-factored grammar of Example 4.7 (page 165).

    b. Construct the LL(1) parsing table using your results of part (a).

4.21 Given the grammar $A \rightarrow a\,A\,a \mid \varepsilon$,

    a. Show that this grammar is not LL(1).

    b. An attempt to write a recursive-descent parser for this grammar is represented by the following pseudocode.

```
procedure A ;
begin
  if token = a then
    getToken ;
    A ;
    if token = a then getToken ;
    else error ;
  else if token <> $ then error ;
end A ;
```

    Show that this procedure will not work correctly.

    c. A **backtracking** recursive-descent parser for this language *can* be written but requires the use of an *unGetToken* procedure that takes a token as a parameter and returns that token to the front of the stream of input tokens. It also requires that the procedure A be written as a Boolean function that returns success or failure, so that when A calls itself, it can test for success before consuming another token, and so that, if the $A \rightarrow a\,A\,a$ choice fails, the code can go on to try the $A \rightarrow \varepsilon$ alternative. Rewrite the pseudocode of part (b) according to this recipe, and trace its operation on the string *aaaa*$.

4.22 In the TINY grammar of Figure 4.9 (page 181), a clear distinction is not made between Boolean and arithmetic expressions. For instance, the following is a syntactically legal TINY program:

```
if 0 then write 1>0 else x := (x<1)+1 end
```

Rewrite the TINY grammar so that only Boolean expressions (expressions containing comparison operators) are allowed as the test of an if- or repeat-statement, and only arithmetic expressions are allowed in write- or assign-statements or as operands of any of the operators.

4.23 Add the Boolean operators **and**, **or**, and **not** to the TINY grammar of Figure 4.9 (page 181). Give them the properties described in Exercise 3.5 (page 139), as well as lower precedence than all arithmetic operators. Make sure any expression can be either Boolean or integer.

4.24 The changes to the TINY syntax in Exercise 4.23 have made the problem described in Exercise 4.22 worse. Rewrite the answer to Exercise 4.23 to rigidly distinguish between Boolean and arithmetic expressions, and incorporate this into the solution to Exercise 4.22.

4.25 The panic mode error recovery for the simple arithmetic expression grammar, as described in Section 4.5.1, still suffers from some drawbacks. One is that the while-loops that test for operators should continue to operate under certain circumstances. For instance, the expression **(2)(3)** is missing its operator in between the factors, but the error handler consumes the second factor without restarting the parse. Rewrite the pseudocode to improve its behavior in this case.

4.26 Trace the actions of an LL(1) parser on the input **(2+-3)*4-+5**, using the error recovery as given in Table 4.9 (page 187).

4.27 Rewrite the LL(1) parsing algorithm of Figure 4.2 (page 155) to implement full panic mode error recovery, and trace its behavior on the input **(2+-3)*4-+5**.

4.28 **a.** Trace the operation of the **stmt_sequence** procedure in the TINY parser to verify that the correct syntax tree is constructed for the following TINY program, despite the missing semicolon:

```
x := 2
y := x + 2
```

b. What syntax tree is constructed for the following (incorrect) program:

```
x 2
y := x + 2
```

c. Suppose that the **stmt_sequence** procedure was written instead using the simpler code sketched on page 189:

```
statement();
while (token==SEMI)
{ match(SEMI);
  statement();
}
```

What syntax trees are constructed for the programs in parts (a) and (b) using this version of the **stmt_sequence** procedure?

PROGRAMMING EXERCISES

4.29 Add the following to the simple integer arithmetic recursive-descent calculator of Figure 4.1, pages 148–149 (make sure they have the correct associativity and precedence):
  a. Integer division with the symbol **/**.
  b. Integer mod with the symbol **%**.
  c. Integer exponentiation with the symbol **^**. (Warning: This operator has higher precedence than multiplication and is right associative.)
  d. Unary minus with the symbol **–**. (See Exercise 3.12, page 140.)

4.30 Rewrite the recursive-descent calculator of Figure 4.1 (pages 148–149) so that it computes with floating-point numbers instead of integers.

4.31 Rewrite the recursive-descent calculator of Figure 4.1 so that it *distinguishes* between floating-point and integer values, rather than simply computing everything as integers or floating-point numbers. (Hint: A "value" is now a record with a flag indicating whether it is integer or floating point.)

4.32 **a.** Rewrite the recursive-descent calculator of Figure 4.1 so that it returns a syntax tree according to the declarations of Section 3.3.2 (page 111).
  b. Write a function that takes as a parameter the syntax tree produced by your code of part (a) and returns the calculated value by traversing the tree.

4.33 Write a recursive-descent calculator for simple integer arithmetic similar to that of Figure 4.1, but use the grammar of Figure 4.4 (page 160).

4.34 Consider the following grammar:

$$lexp \rightarrow \textbf{number} \mid (\ op \ lexp\text{-}seq \ )$$
$$op \rightarrow + \mid - \mid *$$
$$lexp\text{-}seq \rightarrow lexp\text{-}seq \ lexp \mid lexp$$

This grammar can be thought of as representing simple integer arithmetic expressions in LISP-like prefix form. For example, the expression **34-3*42** would be written in this grammar as **(- 34 (* 3 42))**.

Write a recursive-descent calculator for the expressions given by this grammar.

4.35 a. Devise a syntax tree structure for the grammar of the previous exercise and write a recursive-descent parser for it that returns a syntax tree.

b. Write a function that takes as a parameter the syntax tree produced by your code of part (a) and returns the calculated value by traversing the tree.

4.36 a. Use the grammar for regular expressions of Exercise 3.4, page 138 (appropriately disambiguated) to construct a recursive-descent parser that reads a regular expression and performs Thompson's construction of an NFA (see Chapter 2).

b. Write a procedure that takes an NFA data structure as produced by the parser of part (a) and constructs an equivalent DFA according to the subset construction.

c. Write a procedure that takes the data structure as produced by your procedure of part (b) and finds longest substrings matches in a text file according to the DFA it represents. (Your program has now become a "compiled" version of grep!)

4.37 Add the comparison operators **<=** (less than or equal to), **>** (greater than), **>=** (greater than or equal to), and **<>** (not equal to) to the TINY parser. (This will require adding these tokens and changing the scanner as well, but should not require a change to the syntax tree.)

4.38 Incorporate your grammar changes from Exercise 4.22 into the TINY parser.

4.39 Incorporate your grammar changes from Exercise 4.23 into the TINY parser.

4.40 a. Rewrite the recursive-descent calculator program of Figure 4.1 (pages 148–149) to implement panic mode error recovery as outlined in Section 4.5.1.

b. Add useful error messages to your error handling of part (a).

4.41 One of the reasons that the TINY parser produces poor error messages is that the **match** procedure is limited to printing only the current token when an error occurs, rather than printing both the current token and the expected token, and that no special error message is passed to the **match** procedure from its call sites. Rewrite the **match** procedure so that it prints the expected token as well as the current token and also passes along an error message to the **syntaxError** procedure. This will require a rewrite of the **syntaxError** procedure, as well as changes to the calls of **match** to include an appropriate error message.

4.42 Add synchronizing sets of tokens and panic mode error recovery to the TINY parser, as described on page 184.

4.43 (From Wirth [1976]) Data structures based on syntax diagrams can be used by a "generic" recursive-descent parser that will parse any set of LL(1) grammar rules. A suitable data structure is given by the following C declarations:

```
typedef struct rulerec
      { struct rulerec *next,*other;
        int isToken;
        union
        { Token name;
          struct rulerec *rule;
        } attr;
      } Rulerec;
```

The **next** field is used to point to the next item in the grammar rule, and the **other** field is used to point to alternatives given by the | metasymbol. Thus, the data structure for the grammar rule

$$factor \rightarrow (\; exp \;) \; | \; \textbf{number}$$

would look as follows

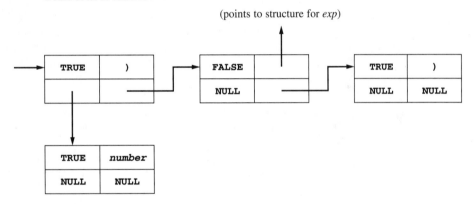

where the fields of the record structure are shown as follows

isToken	name/rule
other	next

a. Draw the data structures for the rest of the grammar rules in Figure 4.4, page 160 (Hint: You will need a special token to represent ε internally in the data structure.)

b. Write a generic parse procedure that uses these data structures to recognize an input string.

c. Write a parser generator that reads BNF rules (either from a file or standard input) and generates the preceding data structures.

NOTES AND REFERENCES

Recursive-descent parsing has been a standard method for parser construction since the early 1960s and the introduction of BNF rules in the Algol60 report [Naur, 1963]. For an early description of the method, see Hoare [1962]. Backtracking recursive-descent parsers have recently become popular in strongly typed lazy functional languages such as Haskell and Miranda, where this form of recursive-descent parsing is called combinator parsing. For a description of this method see Peyton Jones and Lester [1992] or Hutton [1992]. The use of EBNF in conjunction with recursive-descent parsing has been popularized by Wirth [1976].

LL(1) parsing was studied extensively in the 1960s and early 1970s. For an early description see Lewis and Stearns [1968]. A survey of LL(k) parsing may be found in Fischer and LeBlanc [1991], where an example of an LL(2) grammar that is not SLL(2) can be found. For practical uses of LL(k) parsing, see Parr, Dietz, and Cohen [1992].

There are, of course, many more top-down parsing methods than just the two we have studied in this chapter. For an example of another, more general, method, see Graham, Harrison, and Ruzzo [1980].

Panic mode error recovery is studied in Wirth [1976] and Stirling [1985]. Error recovery in LL(k) parsers is studied in Burke and Fisher [1987]. More sophisticated error repair methods are studied in Fischer and LeBlanc [1991] and Lyon [1974].

This chapter did not discuss automatic tools for generating top-down parsers, primarily because the most widely used tool, Yacc, will be discussed in the next chapter. However, good top-down parser generators do exist. One such is called Antlr and is part of the Purdue Compiler Construction Tool Set (PCCTS). See Parr, Dietz, and Cohen [1992] for a description. Antlr generates a recursive-descent parser from an EBNF description. It has a number of useful features, including a built-in mechanism for constructing syntax trees. For an overview of an LL(1) parser generator called LLGen, see Fischer and LeBlanc [1991].

Chapter 5

Bottom-Up Parsing

In the previous chapter we covered the basic top-down parsing algorithms of recursive-descent and predictive parsing. In this chapter, we will describe the major bottom-up parsing techniques and their associated constructions. As with top-down parsing, we restrict ourselves primarily to the study of those parsing algorithms that make use of at most one symbol of lookahead, with a few comments on how to extend the algorithms.

In terminology similar to that of LL(1) parsers, the most general bottom-up algorithm is called **LR(1) parsing** (the L indicates that the input is processed from left to right, the R indicates that a rightmost derivation is produced, and the number 1 indicates that one symbol of lookahead is used). A consequence of the power of bottom-up parsing is the fact that it is also meaningful to talk about **LR(0) parsing**, where *no* lookahead is consulted in making parsing decisions. (This is possible because a lookahead token can be examined *after* it appears on the parsing stack, and if this happens it does not count as lookahead.) An improvement on LR(0) parsing that does make some use of lookahead is called **SLR(1) parsing** (for *simple* LR(1) parsing). A method that is slightly more powerful than SLR(1) parsing but less complex than general LR(1) parsing is called **LALR(1) parsing** (for *lookahead* LR(1) parsing).

We will treat the constructions necessary for each of these parsing methods in the following sections. This will include the construction of the DFAs of LR(0) and LR(1) items; descriptions of the SLR(1), LR(1), and LALR(1) parsing algorithms; and the construction of the associated parsing tables. We will also describe the use of Yacc, an LALR(1) parser generator, and will use Yacc to generate a parser for the

TINY language that constructs the same syntax trees as the recursive-descent parser that we developed in the previous chapter.

Bottom-up parsing algorithms are in general more powerful than top-down methods. (For example, left recursion is not a problem in bottom-up parsing.) Not unexpectedly, the constructions involved in these algorithms are also more complex. Thus, we will need to proceed carefully in their description, and we will need to use very simple examples of grammars to introduce them. We will give two such examples early in the chapter, which we will use throughout the rest of the chapter. We will also continue with the use of some of the recurrent examples of the previous chapter (integer arithmetic expressions, if-statements, etc.). We will not carry out by hand *any* of the bottom-up parsing algorithms for the full TINY language, however, since this would be tremendously complex. Indeed, all of the important bottom-up methods are really too complex for hand coding, but are well suited for parser generators like Yacc. Nevertheless, it is important to understand the operation of the methods so that the behavior of a parser generator can be properly analyzed by the compiler writer. The designer of a programming language can also benefit from this information, since a parser generator can identify potential problems with a proposed language syntax in BNF.

Previously covered topics that will be needed in order to understand the operation of bottom-up parsing algorithms include the properties of finite automata and the subset construction of a DFA from an NFA (Chapter 2, Sections 2.3 and 2.4) and general properties of context-free grammars, derivations, and parse trees (Chapter 3, Sections 3.2 and 3.3). Follow sets (Chapter 4, Section 4.3) will also be needed occasionally. We begin this chapter with a general overview of bottom-up parsing.

5.1 OVERVIEW OF BOTTOM-UP PARSING

A bottom-up parser uses an explicit stack to perform a parse, similar to a nonrecursive top-down parser. The parsing stack will contain both tokens and nonterminals, and also some extra state information that we will discuss later. The stack is empty at the beginning of a bottom-up parse and will contain the start symbol at the end of a successful parse. A schematic for bottom-up parsing is, therefore,

$$\$ \qquad\qquad InputString \; \$$$

$$\cdots \qquad\qquad \cdots$$

$$\cdots \qquad\qquad \cdots$$

$$\$ \; StartSymbol \qquad\qquad \$ \qquad accept$$

where the parsing stack is on the left, the input is in the center, and the actions of the parser are on the right (in this case, "accept" is the only action indicated).

A bottom-up parser has two possible actions (besides "accept"):

1. **Shift** a terminal from the front of the input to the top of the stack.
2. **Reduce** a string α at the top of the stack to a nonterminal A, given the BNF choice $A \rightarrow \alpha$.

A bottom-up parser is thus sometimes called a **shift-reduce** parser.[1] Shift actions are indicated by writing the word *shift*. Reduce actions are indicated by writing the word *reduce* and giving the BNF choice used in the reduction.[2] One further feature of bottom-up parsers is that, for technical reasons to be discussed later, grammars are always **augmented** with a new start symbol. This means that if S is the start symbol, a new start symbol S' is added to the grammar, with a single unit production to the previous start symbol:

$$S' \to S$$

We proceed immediately to two examples, and then discuss some of the properties of bottom-up parsing displayed by these examples.

Example 5.1

Consider the following augmented grammar for balanced parentheses:

$$S' \to S$$
$$S \to (S) \ S \mid \varepsilon$$

A bottom-up parse of the string **()** using this grammar is given in Table 5.1.

Table 5.1

Parsing actions of a bottom-up parser for the grammar of Example 5.1

	Parsing stack	Input	Action
1	$	( ) $	shift
2	$ (	) $	reduce $S \to \varepsilon$
3	$ (S	) $	shift
4	$ (S)	$	reduce $S \to \varepsilon$
5	$ (S) S	$	reduce $S \to (S) S$
6	$ S	$	reduce $S' \to S$
7	$ S'	$	accept

§

Example 5.2

Consider the following augmented grammar for rudimentary arithmetic expressions (no parentheses and one operation):

$$E' \to E$$
$$E \to E + \boldsymbol{n} \mid \boldsymbol{n}$$

A bottom-up parse of the string $\boldsymbol{n} + \boldsymbol{n}$ using this grammar is given in Table 5.2.

---

1. Top-down parsers could be called generate-match parsers for the same reason, but this is not customary.

2. In the case of a reduction, we could simply write the BNF choice by itself, as we did for a *generate* action in top-down parsing, but it is customary to add the *reduce*.

Table 5.2

Parsing actions of a
bottom-up parser for the
grammar of Example 5.2

	Parsing stack	Input	Action
1	$	$n + n$ \$	shift
2	\$ n	$+ n$ \$	reduce $E \rightarrow n$
3	\$ E	$+ n$ \$	shift
4	\$ E +	n \$	shift
5	\$ $E + n$	\$	reduce $E \rightarrow E + n$
6	\$ E	\$	reduce $E' \rightarrow E$
7	\$ E'	\$	accept

§

Bottom-up parsers have less difficulty than top-down parsers with lookahead. Indeed, a bottom-up parser can shift input symbols onto the stack until it determines what action to perform (assuming that an action can be determined that does not require the symbols to be shifted back to the input). However, a bottom-up parser may need to look deeper into the stack than just the top in order to determine what action to perform. For example, in Table 5.1, line 5 has S on the top of the stack, and the parser performs a reduction by the production $S \rightarrow (S) S$, while line 6 also has S on the top of the stack, but the parser performs a reduction by $S' \rightarrow S$. To be able to know that $S \rightarrow (S) S$ is a valid reduction at step 5, we must know that the stack actually does contain the string $(S) S$ at that point. Thus, bottom-up parsing requires arbitrary "stack lookahead." This is not nearly as serious as input lookahead, since the parser itself builds the stack and can arrange for the appropriate information to be available. The mechanism that will do this is a deterministic finite automaton of "items" that will be described in the next section.

Of course, keeping track of the stack contents alone is not enough to be able to uniquely determine the next step in a shift-reduce parse—the next token in the input may also need to be consulted as a lookahead. For example, in line 3 of Table 5.2, E is on the stack and a shift occurs, while in line 6, E is again on the stack but a reduction by $E' \rightarrow E$ occurs. The difference is that in line 3 the next token in the input is + , while in line 6 the next input token is \$. Thus, any algorithm that performs that parse must make use of the next input token (the lookahead) to determine the appropriate action. Different shift-reduce parsing methods use the lookahead in different ways, and this results in parsers of varying power and complexity. Before we look at the individual algorithms, we make some general observations on how the intermediate stages in a bottom-up parse may be characterized.

First, we note again that a shift-reduce parser traces out a rightmost derivation of the input string, but the steps of the derivation occur in reverse order. In Table 5.1 there are four reductions, corresponding in reverse to the four steps of the rightmost derivation:

$$S' \Rightarrow S \Rightarrow (S) S \Rightarrow (S) \Rightarrow ()$$

In Table 5.2, the corresponding derivation is

$$E' \Rightarrow E \Rightarrow E + n \Rightarrow n + n$$

Each of the intermediate strings of terminals and nonterminals in such a derivation is called a **right sentential form**. Each such sentential form is split between the parsing stack and the input during a shift-reduce parse. For example, the right sentential form

$E + n$, which occurs in the third step of the previous derivation, occurs in steps 3, 4, and 5 of Table 5.2. If we indicate where the top of the stack is at each moment by the symbol $\|$ (that is, where the split occurs between the stack and the input), then step 3 of Table 5.2 is given by $E \| + n$ and step 4 is given by $E + \| n$. In each case, the sequence of symbols on the parsing stack is called a **viable prefix** of the right sentential form. Thus, E, $E +$, and $E + n$ are all viable prefixes of the right sentential form $E + n$, while the right sentential form $n + n$ has ε and n as its viable prefixes (steps 1 and 2 of Table 5.2). Note that $n +$ is not a viable prefix of $n + n$.

A shift-reduce parser will shift terminals from the input to the stack until it is possible to perform a reduction to obtain the next right sentential form. This will occur when the string of symbols on the top of the stack matches the right-hand side of the production that is used in the next reduction. This string, together with the position in the right sentential form where it occurs, and the production used to reduce it, is called the **handle** of the right sentential form.[3] For example, in the right sentential form $n + n$, the handle is the string consisting of the leftmost single token n, together with the production $E \rightarrow n$ that is used to reduce it to yield the new right sentential form $E + n$. The handle of this new sentential form is the entire string $E + n$ (a viable prefix), together with the production $E \rightarrow E + n$. Sometimes, by abuse of notation, we refer to the string by itself as the handle.

Determining the next handle in a parse is the main task of a shift-reduce parser. Note that the string of a handle always forms a complete right-hand side for its production (the production used in the next reduction) and that the rightmost position of the handle string will correspond to the top of the stack when the reduction is to take place. Thus, it seems plausible that a shift-reduce parser will want to determine its actions based on positions in right-hand sides of productions. When these positions reach the right-hand end of a production, then this production is a candidate for a reduction, and it is possible that the handle is at the top of the stack. To be the handle, however, it is not enough for the string at the top of the stack to match the right-hand side of a production. Indeed, if an ε-production is available for reduction, as in Example 5.1, then its right-hand side (the empty string) is always at the top of the stack. Reductions occur only when the resulting string is indeed a right sentential form. For example, in step 3 of Table 5.1 a reduction by $S \rightarrow \varepsilon$ could be performed, but the resulting string $(S S)$ is not a right sentential form, and thus ε is not the handle at this position in the sentential form (S).

5.2   FINITE AUTOMATA OF LR(0) ITEMS AND LR(0) PARSING

5.2.1   LR(0) Items

An **LR(0) item** (or just **item** for short) of a context-free grammar is a production choice with a distinguished position in its right-hand side. We will indicate this distinguished position by a period (which, of course, becomes a metasymbol, not to be confused with

---

3. If the grammar is ambiguous, so that more than one derivation may exist, then there may be more than one handle in a right sentential form. If the grammar is unambiguous, then handles are unique.

an actual token). Thus, if $A \rightarrow \alpha$ is a production choice, and if β and γ are any two strings of symbols (including the empty string ε) such that $\beta\gamma = \alpha$, then $A \rightarrow \beta \,.\, \gamma$ is an LR(0) item. These are called LR(0) items because they contain no explicit reference to lookahead.

Example 5.3   Consider the grammar of Example 5.1:

$$S' \rightarrow S$$
$$S \rightarrow (S) S \mid \varepsilon$$

This grammar has three production choices and eight items:

$$S' \rightarrow .S$$
$$S' \rightarrow S.$$
$$S \rightarrow .(S)S$$
$$S \rightarrow (.S)S$$
$$S \rightarrow (S.)S$$
$$S \rightarrow (S).S$$
$$S \rightarrow (S)S.$$
$$S \rightarrow .$$

§

Example 5.4   The grammar of Example 5.2 has the following eight items:

$$E' \rightarrow .E$$
$$E' \rightarrow E.$$
$$E \rightarrow .E + \mathbf{n}$$
$$E \rightarrow E.+ \mathbf{n}$$
$$E \rightarrow E +.\mathbf{n}$$
$$E \rightarrow E + \mathbf{n}.$$
$$E \rightarrow .\mathbf{n}$$
$$E \rightarrow \mathbf{n}.$$

§

The idea behind the concept of an item is that an item records an intermediate step in the recognition of the right-hand side of a particular grammar rule choice. In particular, the item $A \rightarrow \beta \,.\, \gamma$ constructed from the grammar rule choice $A \rightarrow \alpha$ (with $\alpha = \beta\gamma$) means that β has already been seen and that it may be possible to derive the next input tokens from γ. In terms of the parsing stack, this means that β must appear at the top of the stack. An item $A \rightarrow .\alpha$ means that we may be about to recognize an A by using the grammar rule choice $A \rightarrow \alpha$ (we call such items **initial items**). An item $A \rightarrow \alpha.$ means that α now resides on the top of the parsing stack and may be the handle, if $A \rightarrow \alpha$ is to be used for the next reduction (we call such items **complete items**).

5.2.2   Finite Automata of Items

The LR(0) items can be used as the states of a finite automaton that maintains information about the parsing stack and the progress of a shift-reduce parse. This will start out as a nondeterministic finite automaton. From this NFA of LR(0) items we can construct the DFA of sets of LR(0) items using the subset construction of Chapter 2. As we will see, it is also easy to construct the DFA of sets of LR(0) items directly.

What are the transitions of the NFA of LR(0) items? Consider the item $A \rightarrow \alpha \, . \, \gamma$, and suppose γ begins with the symbol X, which may be either a token or a nonterminal, so that the item can be written as $A \rightarrow \alpha \, . \, X\eta$. Then there is a transition on the symbol X from the state represented by this item to the state represented by the item $A \rightarrow \alpha X \, . \, \eta$. In graphical form we write this as

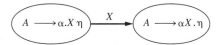

If X is a token, then this transition corresponds to a shift of X from the input to the top of the stack during a parse. On the other hand, if X is a nonterminal, then the interpretation of this transition is more complex, since X will never appear as an input symbol. In fact, such a transition will still correspond to the pushing of X onto the stack during a parse, but this can only occur during a reduction by a production $X \rightarrow \beta$. Now, since such a reduction must be preceded by the recognition of a β, and the state given by the initial item $X \rightarrow .\beta$ represents the beginning of this process (the dot indicating that we are about to recognize a β), then for every item $A \rightarrow \alpha . X\eta$ we must add an ε-transition

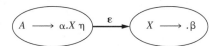

for every production choice $X \rightarrow \beta$ of X, indicating that X can be produced by recognizing any of the right-hand sides of its production choices.

These two cases represent the only transitions in the NFA of LR(0) items. It remains to discuss the choice of initial state and accepting states of the NFA. The start state of the NFA should correspond to the initial state of the parser: the stack is empty, and we are about to recognize an S, where S is the start symbol of the grammar. Thus, any initial item $S \rightarrow .\alpha$ constructed from a production choice for S could serve as a start state. Unfortunately, there may be many such production choices for S. How can we tell which one to use? In fact, we can't. The solution is to **augment** the grammar by a single production $S' \rightarrow S$, where S' is a new nonterminal. S' then becomes the start state of the **augmented grammar**, and the initial item $S' \rightarrow .S$ becomes the start state of the NFA. This is the reason we have augmented the grammars of the previous examples.

What states should become accepting states in this NFA? Here we must remember that the purpose of the NFA is to keep track of the state of a parse, not to recognize strings outright, as the automata in Chapter 2 are designed to do. Thus, the parser itself will decide when to accept, and the NFA need not contain that information, so the NFA will in fact have no accepting states at all. (The NFA *will* have some information on acceptance but not in the form of an accepting state. We will discuss this when we describe the parsing algorithms that use the automaton.)

This completes the description of the NFA of LR(0) items. We now turn to the simple grammars of the two previous examples and construct their NFAs of LR(0) items.

Example 5.5

In Example 5.3 we listed the eight LR(0) items of the grammar of Example 5.1. The NFA, therefore, has eight states; it is shown in Figure 5.1. Note that every item in the figure with a dot before the nonterminal S has an ε-transition to every initial item of S.

Figure 5.1

The NFA of LR(0) items for the grammar of Example 5.6

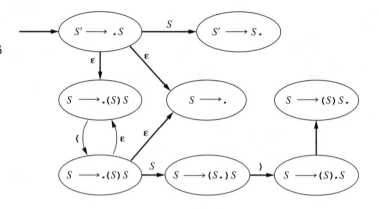

§

Example 5.6

In Example 5.4 we listed the LR(0) items associated with the grammar of Example 5.2. The NFA of items appears in Figure 5.2. Note that the initial item $E \rightarrow . E + n$ has an ε-transition to itself. (This situation will occur in all grammars with immediate left recursion.)

Figure 5.2

The NFA of LR(0) items for the grammar of Example 5.6

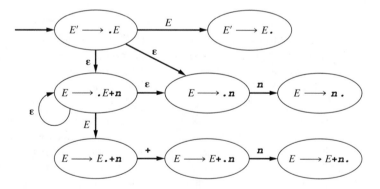

§

To complete the description of the use of items to keep track of the parsing state, we must construct the DFA of sets of items corresponding to the NFA of items according to the subset construction of Chapter 2. We will then be able to state the LR(0) parsing algorithm. We perform the subset construction for the two examples of NFAs that we have just given.

Example 5.7

Consider the NFA of Figure 5.1. The start state of the associated DFA is the ε-closure of the set consisting of the item $S' \rightarrow . S$, and this is the set of three items { $S' \rightarrow . S$,

$S \rightarrow .(S) S, S \rightarrow .$}. Since there is a transition from $S' \rightarrow . S$ to $S' \rightarrow S .$ on S, there is a corresponding transition from the start state to the DFA state { $S' \rightarrow S .$ } (there being no ε-transitions from $S' \rightarrow S .$ to any other item). There is also a transition on **(** from the start state to the DFA state { $S \rightarrow (. S) S , S \rightarrow .(S) S , S \rightarrow .$} (the ε-closure of { $S \rightarrow (. S) S$ }). The DFA state { $S \rightarrow (. S) S , S \rightarrow .(S) S , S \rightarrow .$} has transitions to itself on **(** and to { $S \rightarrow (S .) S$ } on S. This state has a transition to the state { $S \rightarrow (S). S , S \rightarrow .(S) S , S \rightarrow .$} on **)**. Finally, this last state has transitions on **)** to the previously constructed state { $S \rightarrow (. S) S, S \rightarrow .(S) S, S \rightarrow .$} and a transition on S to the state { $S \rightarrow (S) S .$}. The complete DFA is given in Figure 5.3, where we have numbered the states for reference (state 0 being traditionally the start state).

Figure 5.3

The DFA of sets of items corresponding to the NFA of Figure 5.1

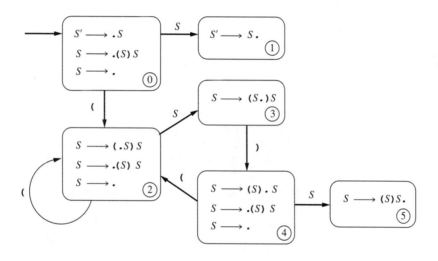

§

Example 5.8

Consider the NFA of Figure 5.2. The start state of the associated DFA consists of the set of three items $\{E' \rightarrow .E , E \rightarrow .E + \boldsymbol{n} , E \rightarrow .\boldsymbol{n}\}$. There is a transition from the item $E' \rightarrow .E$ to the item $E' \rightarrow E .$ on E, but there is also a transition on E from the item $E \rightarrow .E + \boldsymbol{n}$ to the item $E \rightarrow E .+ \boldsymbol{n}$. Thus, there is a transition on E from the start state of the DFA to the closure of the set $\{E' \rightarrow E . , E \rightarrow E .+ \boldsymbol{n}\}$. Since there are no ε-transitions from either of these items, this set is its own ε-closure and forms a complete DFA state. There is one other transition from the start state, corresponding to the transition on the symbol $\boldsymbol{n}$ from $E \rightarrow .\boldsymbol{n}$ to $E \rightarrow \boldsymbol{n}.$. Since there are no ε-transitions from the item $E \rightarrow \boldsymbol{n}.$, this item is its own ε-closure and forms the DFA state $\{E \rightarrow \boldsymbol{n}.\}$. There are no transitions from this state, so the only transitions still to be computed are from the set $\{E' \rightarrow E ., E \rightarrow E .+ \boldsymbol{n}\}$. There is only one transition from this set, corresponding to the transition from the item $E \rightarrow E .+ \boldsymbol{n}$ to the item $E \rightarrow E +.\boldsymbol{n}$ on the symbol **+**. The item $E \rightarrow E +.\boldsymbol{n}$ also has no ε-transitions and so forms a singleton set in the DFA. Finally, there is a transition on $\boldsymbol{n}$ from the set $\{E \rightarrow E +.\boldsymbol{n}\}$ to the set $\{E \rightarrow E + \boldsymbol{n}.\}$. The entire DFA is given in Figure 5.4.

Figure 5.4

The DFA of sets of items corresponding to the NFA of Figure 5.2

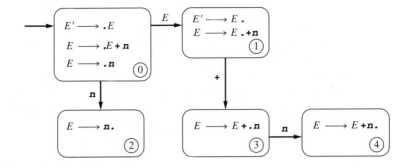

§

In the construction of the DFA of sets of LR(0) items, a distinction is sometimes made between those items that are added to a state during the ε-closure step and those that originate the state as targets of non-ε-transitions. The former are called **closure items**, while the latter are called **kernel items**. In state 0 of Figure 5.4, $E' \to .E$ is a kernel item (the only one), and $E \to .E + n$ and $E \to .n$ are closure items. In state 2 of Figure 5.3, $S \to (.S) S$ is a kernel item, and $S \to .(S) S$ and $S \to .$ are closure items. By definition of the ε-transitions of the NFAs of items, all closure items are initial items.

The importance of the distinction between kernel and closure items is that, given the grammar, the kernel items uniquely determine the state and its transitions. Thus, only kernel items need to be specified to completely characterize the DFA of sets of items. Parser generators that construct the DFA may, therefore, only report the kernel items (this is true of Yacc, for instance).

A further simplification occurs if the DFA of sets of items is computed directly, rather than first computing the NFA of items and then applying the subset construction. Indeed, from a set of items it is easy to determine immediately what the ε-transitions are, and to which initial items they point. Therefore, parser generators like Yacc always compute the DFA directly from the grammar, and we will do this also for the remainder of the chapter.

5.2.3   The LR(0) Parsing Algorithm

We are now ready to state the LR(0) parsing algorithm. Since the algorithm depends on keeping track of the current state in the DFA of sets of items, we must modify the parsing stack to store not only symbols but also state numbers. We do this by pushing the new state number onto the parsing stack after each push of a symbol. In fact, the states themselves contain all the information about the symbols, so we could dispense with the symbols altogether and keep only state numbers on the parsing stack. We will, however, retain the symbols on the stack for convenience and clarity.

To begin a parse, we push the bottom marker $ and the start state 0 onto the stack, so that at the beginning of the parse, the situation can be represented as

Parsing stack	Input
$ 0	*InputString* $

Suppose now that the next step is to shift a token n onto the stack and go to state 2 (this will in fact happen when the DFA is as in Figure 5.4 and n is the next token in the input). This is represented as follows:

Parsing stack	Input
$ 0 n 2	*Rest of InputString* $

The LR(0) parsing algorithm chooses an action based on the current DFA state, which is always the state that appears at the top of the stack.

Definition

The LR(0) parsing algorithm. Let s be the current state (at the top of the parsing stack). Then actions are defined as follows:

1. If state s contains any item of the form $A \rightarrow \alpha . X \beta$, where X is a terminal, then the action is to shift the current input token onto the stack. If this token is X, and state s contains item $A \rightarrow \alpha . X \beta$, then the new state to be pushed on the stack is the state containing the item $A \rightarrow \alpha X . \beta$. If this token is not X for some item in state s of the form just described, an error is declared.

2. If state s contains any complete item (an item of the form $A \rightarrow \alpha .$), then the action is to reduce by the rule $A \rightarrow \alpha$. A reduction by the rule $S' \rightarrow S$, where S is the start state, is equivalent to acceptance, provided the input is empty, and error if the input is not empty. In all other cases, the new state is computed as follows. Remove the string α and all of its corresponding states from the parsing stack (the string α must be at the top of the stack, according to the way the DFA is constructed). Correspondingly, back up in the DFA to the state from which the construction of α began (this must be the state uncovered by the removal of α). Again, by the construction of the DFA, this state must contain an item of the form $B \rightarrow \alpha . A \beta$. Push A onto the stack, and push (as the new state) the state containing the item $B \rightarrow \alpha A . \beta$. (Note that this corresponds to following the transition on A in the DFA, which is indeed reasonable, since we are pushing A onto the stack.)

A grammar is said to be an **LR(0) grammar** if the above rules are unambiguous. This means that if a state contains a complete item $A \rightarrow \alpha .$, then it can contain no other items. Indeed, if such a state also contains a "shift" item $A \rightarrow \alpha . X \beta$ (X a terminal), then an ambiguity arises as to whether action (1) or action (2) is to be performed. This situation is called a **shift-reduce conflict**. Similarly, if such a state contains another complete item $B \rightarrow \beta .$, then an ambiguity arises as to which production to use for the reduction ($A \rightarrow \alpha$ or $B \rightarrow \beta$). This situation is called a **reduce-reduce conflict**. Thus, a grammar is LR(0) if and only if each state is a shift state (a state containing only "shift" items) or a reduce state containing a single complete item.

We note that neither of the two grammars we have been using as our examples are LR(0) grammars. In Figure 5.3 states 0, 2, and 4 all contain shift-reduce conflicts for the LR(0) parsing algorithm, while in the DFA of Figure 5.4, state 1 contains a shift-reduce conflict. This is not surprising, since almost all "real" grammars are not LR(0). We present, however, the following example of a grammar that is LR(0).

Example 5.9   Consider the grammar

$$A \rightarrow (A) \mid \mathbf{a}$$

The augmented grammar has the DFA of sets of items shown in Figure 5.5, which is LR(0). To see how the LR(0) parsing algorithm works, consider the string **((a))**. A parse of this string according to the LR(0) parsing algorithm is given by the steps in Table 5.3. The parse begins in state 0, which is a shift state, so the first token **(** is shifted onto the stack. Then, since the DFA indicates a transition from state 0 to state 3 on the symbol **(**, state 3 is pushed onto the stack. State 3 is also a shift state, so the next **(** is shifted onto the stack, and the transition on **(** returns to state 3. Shifting again places **a** on the stack, and the transition on **a** from state 3 goes to state 2. We are now at step 4 in Table 5.3, and we have reached the first reduce state. Here state 2 and symbol **a** are popped from the stack, backing up to state 3 in the process. A is then pushed onto the stack and the A transition from state 3 to state 4 is taken. State 4 is a shift state, so **)** is shifted onto the stack and the transition on **)** takes the parse to state 5. Here a reduction by the rule $A \rightarrow (A)$ occurs, popping states 5, 4, 3, and symbols **)**, A, **(** from the stack. The parse is now in state 3, and again A and state 4 are pushed onto the stack. Again, **)** is shifted onto the stack, and state 5 is pushed. Another reduction by $A \rightarrow (A)$ removes the string **(** 3 A 4 **)** 5 (backwards) from the stack, leaving the parse in state 0. Now A is pushed and the A transition from state 0 to state 1 is taken. State 1 is the accepting state. Since the input is now empty, the parse algorithm accepts.

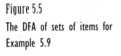

Figure 5.5

The DFA of sets of items for Example 5.9

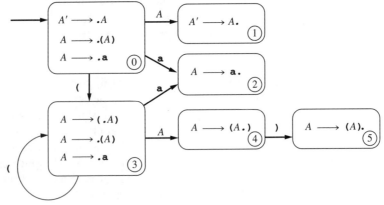

Table 5.3

Parsing actions for
Example 5.9

	Parsing stack	Input	Action
1	$ 0	((a)) $	shift
2	$ 0 (3	(a)) $	shift
3	$ 0 (3 (3	a)) $	shift
4	$ 0 (3 (3 a 2	)) $	reduce $A \rightarrow a$
5	$ 0 (3 (3 A 4	)) $	shift
6	$ 0 (3 (3 A 4) 5	) $	reduce $A \rightarrow (A)$
7	$ 0 (3 A 4	) $	shift
8	$ 0 (3 A 4) 5	$	reduce $A \rightarrow (A)$
9	$ 0 A 1	$	accept

§

The DFA of sets of items and the actions specified by the LR(0) parsing algorithm can be combined into a parsing table, so that LR(0) parsing becomes a table-driven parsing method. A typical organization is for the table rows to be labeled with the states of the DFA, and the columns to be labeled as follows. Since LR(0) parsing states are either "shift" states or "reduce" states, one column is reserved to indicate this for each state. In the case of a "reduce" state, a further column is used to indicate the grammar rule choice to be used in the reduction. In the case of a shift state, the symbol to be shifted determines the next state (via the DFA), and so there must be a column for every token, whose entries are the new states to be entered on a shift of that token. Transitions on nonterminals (which are pushed during a reduction) represent a special case, since they are not actually seen in the input, although the parser acts as though they have been shifted. Thus, in a "shift" state there needs also to be a column for each nonterminal, and traditionally these columns are listed in a separate part of the table called the **goto** section.

An example of such a parsing table is Table 5.4, which is the table for the grammar of Example 5.9. The reader is encouraged to verify that this table leads to the parsing actions for that example as given in Table 5.3.

Table 5.4

Parsing table for the
grammar of Example 5.9

State	Action	Rule	Input (	Input a	Input)	Goto A
0	shift		3	2		1
1	reduce	$A' \rightarrow A$				
2	reduce	$A \rightarrow a$				
3	shift		3	2		4
4	shift				5	
5	reduce	$A \rightarrow (A)$				

We note that empty entries in such a parsing table represent errors. In practical situations where error recovery is necessary, we will need to precisely specify what action the parser takes for each of these blank entries. We delay this discussion until a later section.

5.3   SLR(1) PARSING

5.3.1   The SLR(1) Parsing Algorithm

Simple LR(1), or SLR(1), parsing uses the DFA of sets of LR(0) items as constructed in the previous section. It increases the power of LR(0) parsing significantly, however, by using the next token in the input string to direct its actions. It does so in two ways. First, it consults the input token *before* a shift to make sure that an appropriate DFA transition exists. Second, it uses the Follow set of a nonterminal, as constructed in Section 4.3, to decide if a reduction should be performed. Surprisingly, this simple use of lookahead is powerful enough to parse almost all commonly occurring language constructs.

Definition

The SLR(1) parsing algorithm. Let s be the current state (at the top of the parsing stack). Then actions are defined as follows:

1. If state s contains any item of the form $A \to \alpha . X \beta$, where X is a terminal, and X is the next token in the input string, then the action is to shift the current input token onto the stack, and the new state to be pushed on the stack is the state containing the item $A \to \alpha X . \beta$.
2. If state s contains the complete item $A \to \gamma .$, and the next token in the input string is in Follow(A), then the action is to reduce by the rule $A \to \gamma$. A reduction by the rule $S' \to S$, where S is the start state, is equivalent to acceptance; this will happen only if the next input token is \$.[4] In all other cases, the new state is computed as follows. Remove the string α and all of its corresponding states from the parsing stack. Correspondingly, back up in the DFA to the state from which the construction of α began. By construction, this state must contain an item of the form $B \to \gamma . A \beta$. Push A onto the stack, and push the state containing the item $B \to \alpha A . \beta$.
3. If the next input token is such that neither of the above two cases applies, an error is declared.

We say that a grammar is an **SLR(1) grammar** if the application of the above SLR(1) parsing rules results in no ambiguity. In particular, a grammar is SLR(1) if and only if, for any state s, the following two conditions are satisfied:

---

4. Indeed, the Follow set for the augmented start state S' of any grammar is always the set consisting only of \$, since S' appears only in the grammar rule $S' \to S$.

1. For any item $A \rightarrow \alpha . X \beta$ in s with X a terminal, there is no complete item $B \rightarrow \gamma.$ in s with X in Follow(B).
2. For any two complete items $A \rightarrow \alpha.$ and $B \rightarrow \beta.$ in s, Follow(A) $\cap$ Follow(B) is empty.

A violation of the first of these conditions represents a **shift-reduce conflict**. A violation of the second of these conditions represents a **reduce-reduce conflict**.

These two conditions are similar in spirit to the two conditions for LL(1) parsing stated in the previous chapter, except that, as with all shift-reduce parsing methods, decisions on which grammar rule to use can be delayed until the last possible moment, resulting in a more powerful parser.

A parsing table for SLR(1) parsing can also be constructed in a manner similar to that for LR(0) parsing described in the previous section. The differences are as follows. Since a state can have both shifts and reduces in an SLR(1) parser (depending on the lookahead), each entry in the input section must now have a "shift" or "reduce" label, and grammar rule choices must also be placed in entries marked "reduce." This also makes the action and rule columns unnecessary. Since the end of input symbol $ can also be a legal lookahead, a new column must be created for this symbol in the input section. We demonstrate the construction of the SLR(1) parsing table along with our first example of SLR(1) parsing.

Example 5.10   Consider the grammar of Example 5.8, whose DFA of sets of items is given in Figure 5.4. As we stated, this grammar is not LR(0), but it is SLR(1). The Follow sets for the nonterminals are Follow(E') = {$} and Follow($E$) = {$, +}. The SLR(1) parsing table is given in Table 5.5. In the table a shift is indicated by the letter s in the entry, and a reduce by the letter r. Thus, in state 1 on input +, a shift is indicated, together with a transition to state 3. In state 2 on input +, on the other hand, a reduction by production $E \rightarrow n$ is indicated. We have also written the action "accept" in state 1 on input $ instead of r ($E' \rightarrow E$).

Table 5.5

SLR(1) parsing table for Example 5.10

State	Input			Goto
	n	+	$	E
0	s2			1
1		s3	accept	
2		r ($E \rightarrow n$)	r ($E \rightarrow n$)	
3	s4			
4		r ($E \rightarrow E + n$)	r ($E \rightarrow E + n$)	

We finish this example with a parse of the string $n + n + n$. The parsing steps are given in Table 5.6. Step 1 in this figure begins in state 0 on input token n, and the parsing table indicates the action "s2," that is, shift the token onto the stack and go into state 2. We indicate this in Table 5.6 with the phrase "shift 2." In step 2 of the figure, the parser is in state 2 with input token **+**, and the table indicates a reduction by the rule $E \rightarrow \textbf{\textit{n}}$. In this case state 2 and token **n** are popped from the stack, exposing state 0. The symbol E is pushed and the Goto for E is taken from state 0 to state 1. In step 3 the parser is in state 1 with input token **+**, and the table indicates a shift and a transition to state 3. In state 3 on input **n** the table also indicates a shift and a transition to state 4. In state 4 on input **+** the table indicates a reduction by the rule $E \rightarrow E + \textbf{\textit{n}}$. This reduction is accomplished by popping the string $E + \textbf{\textit{n}}$ and its associated states from the stack, exposing state 0 again, pushing E and taking the Goto to state 1. The remaining steps in the parse are similar.

Table 5.6

Parsing actions for Example 5.10

	Parsing stack	Input	Action
1	$\$\ 0$	$\textbf{\textit{n}} + \textbf{\textit{n}} + \textbf{\textit{n}}\ \$$	shift 2
2	$\$\ 0\ \textbf{\textit{n}}\ 2$	$+ \textbf{\textit{n}} + \textbf{\textit{n}}\ \$$	reduce $E \rightarrow \textbf{\textit{n}}$
3	$\$\ 0\ E\ 1$	$+ \textbf{\textit{n}} + \textbf{\textit{n}}\ \$$	shift 3
4	$\$\ 0\ E\ 1 + 3$	$\textbf{\textit{n}} + \textbf{\textit{n}}\ \$$	shift 4
5	$\$\ 0\ E\ 1 + 3\ \textbf{\textit{n}}\ 4$	$+ \textbf{\textit{n}}\ \$$	reduce $E \rightarrow E + \textbf{\textit{n}}$
6	$\$\ 0\ E\ 1$	$+ \textbf{\textit{n}}\ \$$	shift 3
7	$\$\ 0\ E\ 1 + 3$	$\textbf{\textit{n}}\ \$$	shift 4
8	$\$\ 0\ E\ 1 + 3\ \textbf{\textit{n}}\ 4$	$\$$	reduce $E \rightarrow E + \textbf{\textit{n}}$
9	$\$\ 0\ E\ 1$	$\$$	accept

§

Example 5.11

Consider the grammar of balanced parentheses, whose DFA of LR(0) items is given in Figure 5.3 (page 205). A straightforward computation yields Follow(S') = {$} and Follow($S$) = {$, **)** }. The SLR(1) parsing table is given in Table 5.7. Note how the non-LR(0) states 0, 2, and 4 have both shifts and reductions by the ε-production $S \rightarrow \varepsilon$. Table 5.8 gives the steps that the SLR(1) parsing algorithm takes to parse the string **( ) ( )**. Note how the stack continues to grow until the final reductions. This is characteristic of bottom-up parsers in the presence of right-recursive rules such as $S \rightarrow$ **(** S **)** S. Thus, right recursion can cause stack overflow, and so is to be avoided if possible.

Table 5.7

SLR(1) parsing table for Example 5.11

State	Input			Goto
	(	**)**	**$**	S
0	s2	r ($S \rightarrow \varepsilon$)	r ($S \rightarrow \varepsilon$)	1
1		s3	accept	
2	s2	r ($S \rightarrow \varepsilon$)	r ($S \rightarrow \varepsilon$)	3
3		s4		
4	s2	r ($S \rightarrow \varepsilon$)	r ($S \rightarrow \varepsilon$)	5
5		r ($S \rightarrow$ **(** S **)** S)	r ($S \rightarrow$ **(** S **)** S)	

Table 5.8

Parsing actions for
Example 5.11

	Parsing stack	Input	Action
1	$ 0	( ) ( ) $	shift 2
2	$ 0 (2	) ( ) $	reduce $S \to \varepsilon$
3	$ 0 (2 S 3	( ) $	shift 4
4	$ 0 (2 S 3) 4	( ) $	shift 2
5	$ 0 (2 S 3) 4 (2	) $	reduce $S \to \varepsilon$
6	$ 0 (2 S 3) 4 (2 S 3	) $	shift 4
7	$ 0 (2 S 3) 4 (2 S 3) 4	$	reduce $S \to \varepsilon$
8	$ 0 (2 S 3) 4 (2 S 3) 4 S 5	$	reduce $S \to (S) S$
9	$ 0 (2 S 3) 4 S 5	$	reduce $S \to (S) S$
10	$ 0 S 1	$	accept

§

5.3.2 Disambiguating Rules for Parsing Conflicts

Parsing conflicts in SLR(1) parsing, as with all shift-reduce parsing methods, can be of two kinds: shift-reduce conflicts and reduce-reduce conflicts. In the case of shift-reduce conflicts, there is a natural disambiguating rule, which is to always prefer the shift over the reduce. Most shift-reduce parsers therefore automatically resolve shift-reduce conflicts by preferring the shift over the reduce. The case of reduce-reduce conflicts is more difficult; such conflicts often (but not always) indicate an error in the design of the grammar. (Examples of such conflicts will be given later.) Prefering the shift over the reduce in a shift-reduce conflict automatically incorporates the most closely nested rule for the dangling else ambiguity in if-statements, as the following example shows. This is one reason for letting the ambiguity remain in a programming language grammar.

Example 5.12   Consider the grammar of simplified if statements used in the previous chapters (see, e.g., Chapter 3, Section 3.4.3):

$$statement \to if\text{-}stmt \mid \textbf{other}$$
$$if\text{-}stmt \to \textbf{if} \textbf{ (} exp \textbf{)} statement$$
$$\mid \textbf{if} \textbf{ (} exp \textbf{)} statement \textbf{ else } statement$$
$$exp \to \textbf{0} \mid \textbf{1}$$

Since this is an ambiguous grammar, there must be a parsing conflict somewhere in any parsing algorithm. To see this in an SLR(1) parser, we simplify the grammar even further, to make the construction of the DFA of sets of items more manageable. We even eliminate the test expression altogether and write the grammar as follows (it still contains the dangling else ambiguity):

$$S \to I \mid \textbf{other}$$
$$I \to \textbf{if } S \mid \textbf{if } S \textbf{ else } S$$

The DFA of sets of items is shown in Figure 5.6. To construct the SLR(1) parsing actions we need the Follow sets for S and I. These are

$$\text{Follow}(S) = \text{Follow}(I) = \{\$, \textbf{else}\}$$

Now we can see the parsing conflict caused by the dangling else problem. It occurs in state 5 of the DFA, where the complete item $I \to \textbf{if } S.$ indicates that a reduction by the rule $I \to \textbf{if } S$ is to take place on inputs **else** and $\$$, while the item $I \to \textbf{if } S. \textbf{else}$ S indicates that a shift of the input token is to take place on **else**. Thus, the dangling else will result in a shift-reduce conflict in the SLR(1) parsing table. Clearly, a disambiguating rule that prefers the shift over the reduce will remove the conflict and parse according to the most closely nested rule. (Indeed, if the reduction were preferred over the shift, there would be no way of entering states 6 or 7 in the DFA, which would result in spurious parsing errors.)

Figure 5.6

DFA of sets of LR(0) items

for Example 5.12

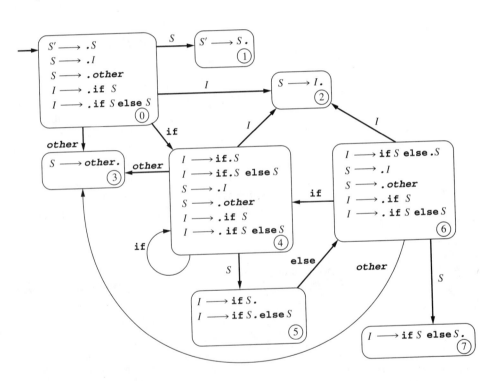

The SLR(1) parsing table that results from this grammar is shown in Table 5.9. In that table we have used a numbering scheme for the grammar rule choices in the reduce actions instead of writing out the rules themselves. The numbering is

(1) $S \to I$
(2) $S \to \textbf{other}$
(3) $I \to \textbf{if } S$
(4) $I \to \textbf{if } S \textbf{ else } S$

Note that it is not necessary to number the augmentation production $S' \rightarrow S$, since a reduction by this rule corresponds to acceptance and is written as "accept" in the table.

We warn the reader that the production numbers used in reduce entries are easy to confuse with state numbers used in shift and Goto entries. For example, in the table of Table 5.9, in state 5 the entry under input **else** is s6, indicating a shift and a transition to state 6, while the entry under input $ is r3, indicating a reduction by production number 3 (that is, $I \rightarrow$ **if** S).

In Table 5.9 we have also removed the shift-reduce conflict in the table in favor of the shift. We have shaded the entry in the table to show where the conflict would have occurred.

Table 5.9

SLR(1) parsing table for
Example 5.12 (with
parsing conflict removed)

State	Input				Goto	
	if	**else**	**other**	**$**	S	I
0	s4		s3		1	2
1				accept		
2		r1		r1		
3		r2		r2		
4	s4		s3		5	2
5		s6		r3		
6	s4		s3		7	2
7		r4		r4		

§

5.3.3 Limits of SLR(1) Parsing Power

SLR(1) parsing is a simple, effective extension of LR(0) parsing that is powerful enough to handle almost all practical language structures. Unfortunately, there are a few situations in which SLR(1) parsing is not quite powerful enough, and this will lead us to study the more powerful general LR(1) and LALR(1) parsing. The next example is a typical situation in which SLR(1) parsing fails.

Example 5.13

Consider the following grammar rules for statements, extracted and simplified from Pascal (a similar situation occurs in C):

$$\begin{aligned}
stmt &\rightarrow call\text{-}stmt \mid assign\text{-}stmt \\
call\text{-}stmt &\rightarrow \textbf{identifier} \\
assign\text{-}stmt &\rightarrow var \; \textbf{:=} \; exp \\
var &\rightarrow var \; \textbf{[} \; exp \; \textbf{]} \mid \textbf{identifier} \\
exp &\rightarrow var \mid \textbf{number}
\end{aligned}$$

This grammar models statements which can be either calls to parameterless procedures, or assignments of expressions to variables. Note that both assignments and procedure calls begin with an identifier. It is not until either the end of the statement or the token **:=** is seen that a parser can decide whether the statement is an assignment or a call. We simplify this situation to the following grammar, where we have removed the alternative choices for a variable, and simplified the statement options, without changing the basic situation:

$$S \rightarrow \textbf{id} \mid V \textbf{ := } E$$
$$V \rightarrow \textbf{id}$$
$$E \rightarrow V \mid \textbf{n}$$

To show how this grammar results in a parsing conflict in SLR(1) parsing, consider the start state of the DFA of sets of items:

$$S' \rightarrow . \, S$$
$$S \rightarrow . \textbf{id}$$
$$S \rightarrow . \, V \textbf{ := } E$$
$$V \rightarrow . \textbf{id}$$

This state has a shift transition on **id** to the state

$$S \rightarrow \textbf{id}.$$
$$V \rightarrow \textbf{id}.$$

Now, Follow(S) = {\$} and Follow(V) = { **:=** , \$} (**:=** because of the rule $V \rightarrow V$ **:=** E, and \$ because an E can be a V). Thus, the SLR(1) parsing algorithm calls for a reduction in this state by both the rule $S \rightarrow \textbf{id}$ and the rule $V \rightarrow \textbf{id}$ under input symbol \$. (This is a reduce-reduce conflict.) This parsing conflict is actually a "phony" problem caused by the weakness of the SLR(1) method. Indeed, the reduction by $V \rightarrow \textbf{id}$ should *never* be made in this state when the input is \$, since a variable can never occur at the end of a statement until after the token **:=** is seen and shifted.   §

In the following two sections we show how this parsing problem can be removed by the use of more powerful parsing methods.

5.3.4   SLR(k) Grammars

As with other parsing algorithms, the SLR(1) parsing algorithm can be extended to SLR(k) parsing where parsing actions are based on $k \geq 1$ symbols of lookahead. Using the sets First$_k$ and Follow$_k$ as defined in the previous chapter, an SLR(k) parser uses the following two rules:

1. If state s contains an item of the form $A \rightarrow \alpha.X\beta$ (X a token), and $Xw \in$ First$_k(X \beta)$ are the next k tokens in the input string, then the action is to shift the current input token onto the stack, and the new state to be pushed on the stack is the state containing the item $A \rightarrow \alpha X . \beta$.
2. If state s contains the complete item $A \rightarrow \alpha.$, and $w \in$ Follow$_k(A)$ are the next k tokens in the input string, then the action is to reduce by the rule $A \rightarrow \alpha$.

SLR(k) parsing is more powerful than SLR(1) parsing when $k > 1$, but at a substantial cost in complexity, since the parsing table grows exponentially in size with k.

Typical language constructs that are not SLR(1) are handled better by using an LALR(1) parser, by using standard disambiguating rules, or by rewriting the grammar. While it is true that the simple non-SLR(1) grammar of Example 5.13 does happen to be SLR(2), the programming language problem that it came from is not SLR(*k*) for any *k*.

5.4   GENERAL LR(1) AND LALR(1) PARSING

In this section we study the most general form of LR(1) parsing, sometimes called **canonical** LR(1) parsing. This method overcomes the problem with SLR(1) parsing described at the end of the previous section, but at a cost of substantially increased complexity. Indeed, general LR(1) parsing is usually considered too complex to use in the construction of parsers in most situations. Fortunately, a modification of general LR(1) parsing, called LALR(1) (for "lookahead" LR parsing), retains most of the benefit of general LR(1) parsing, while preserving the efficiency of the SLR(1) method. The LALR(1) method has become the method of choice for parser generators such as Yacc, and we study it later in this section. However, to understand that method we must first study the general method.

5.4.1   Finite Automata of LR(1) Items

The difficulty with the SLR(1) method is that it applies lookaheads *after* the construction of the DFA of LR(0) items, a construction that ignores lookaheads. The power of the general LR(1) method is that it uses a new DFA that has the lookaheads built into its construction from the start. This DFA uses items that are an extension of LR(0) items. They are called **LR(1) items** because they include a single lookahead token in each item. More precisely, an LR(1) item is a pair consisting of an LR(0) item and a lookahead token. We write LR(1) items using square brackets as

$$[A \rightarrow \alpha.\beta, a]$$

where $A \rightarrow \alpha.\beta$ is an LR(0) item and a is a token (the lookahead).

To complete the definition of the automaton used for general LR(1) parsing, we need to define the transitions between LR(1) items. These are similar to the LR(0) transitions except that they also keep track of lookaheads. As with LR(0) items they include ε-transitions, and it is necessary to build a DFA whose states are sets of items that are ε-closures. The major difference between the LR(0) and LR(1) automata comes in the definition of the ε-transitions. We give the definition of the easier case (the non-ε-transitions) first, which are essentially identical to those of the LR(0) case.

Definition

Definition of LR(1) transitions (part 1). Given an LR(1) item $[A \rightarrow \alpha.X\gamma, a]$, where X is any symbol (terminal or nonterminal), there is a transition on X to the item $[A \rightarrow \alpha X.\gamma, a]$.

Note that in this case the same lookahead a appears in both items. Thus, these transitions do not cause new lookaheads to appear. Only ε-transitions "create" new lookaheads, as follows.

Definition

Definition of LR(1) transitions (part 2). Given an LR(1) item $[A \rightarrow \alpha.B\,\gamma, a]$, where B is a nonterminal, there are ε-transitions to items $[B \rightarrow .\beta, b]$ for every production $B \rightarrow \beta$ and *for every token b in* First(γa).

Note how these ε-transitions keep track of the context in which the structure B needs to be recognized. Indeed, the item $[A \rightarrow \alpha.B\,\gamma, a]$ says that at this point in the parse we may want to recognize a B, but *only* if this B is followed by a string derivable from the string γa, and such strings must begin with a token in First(γa). Since the string γ follows B in the production $A \rightarrow \alpha B\gamma$, if a is constructed to be in Follow(A), then First(γa) $\subset$ Follow(B), and the b's in the items $[B \rightarrow .\beta, b]$ will always be in Follow(B). The power of the general LR(1) method lies in the fact that the set First(γa) may be a *proper* subset of Follow(B). (An SLR(1) parser essentially takes the lookaheads b from the entire Follow set.) Note also that the original lookahead a appears as one of the b's only if γ can derive the empty string. Much of the time (especially in practical situations), this will only occur if γ is itself ε, in which case we get the special case of an ε-transition from $[A \rightarrow \alpha.B, a]$ to $[B \rightarrow .\beta, a]$.

To complete the description of the construction of the DFA of sets of LR(1) items, it remains to specify the start state. We do this as in the LR(0) case by augmenting the grammar with a new start symbol S' and a new production $S' \rightarrow S$ (where S is the original start symbol). Then the start symbol of the NFA of LR(1) items becomes the item $[S' \rightarrow .S, \$]$, where the \$ represents the end marker (and is the only symbol in Follow(S')). In effect, this says that we start by recognizing a string derivable from S, followed by the \$ symbol.

We now look at several examples of the construction of the DFA of LR(1) items.

Example 5.14   Consider the grammar

$$A \rightarrow (\ A \ ) \mid \mathbf{a}$$

of Example 5.9. We begin the construction of its DFA of sets of LR(1) items by augmenting the grammar and forming the initial LR(1) item $[A' \rightarrow .A, \$]$. The ε-closure of this item is the start state of the DFA. Since A is not followed by any symbols in this item (in the terminology of the previous discussion of transitions, the string γ is ε), there are ε-transitions to items $[A \rightarrow . (\ A \ ), \$]$ and $[A \rightarrow .\mathbf{a}, \$]$ (that is, First$(\gamma\$)$ = {\$}, in the terminology of the previous discussion). The start state (state 0) is then the set of these three items:

State 0: $[A' \rightarrow .A, \$]$
$[A \rightarrow .(\ A \ ), \$]$
$[A \rightarrow .\mathbf{a}, \$]$

From this state there is a transition on A to the closure of the set containing the item $[A' \rightarrow A., \$]$, and since there are no transitions from complete items, this state contains just the single item $[A' \rightarrow A., \$]$. There are no transitions out of this state, and we will number it state 1:

$$\text{State 1:} \qquad [A' \rightarrow A., \$]$$

(This is the state from which the LR(1) parsing algorithm will generate accept actions.)

Returning to state 0, there is also a transition on the token **(** to the closure of the set consisting of the item $[A \rightarrow (. A), \$]$. Since there are ε-transitions from this item, this closure is nontrivial. Indeed, there are ε-transitions from this item to the items $[A \rightarrow . (A),)]$ and $[A \rightarrow .\mathbf{a},)]$. This is because, in the item $[A \rightarrow (. A), \$]$, A is being recognized in the right-hand side *in the context of parentheses*. That is, the Follow of the right-hand A is First(**)** $\$$) = { **)** }. Thus, we have obtained a new look-ahead token in this situation, and the new DFA state consists of the following items:

$$\begin{aligned} \text{State 2:} \qquad &[A \rightarrow (. A), \$] \\ &[A \rightarrow . (A),)] \\ &[A \rightarrow .\mathbf{a},)] \end{aligned}$$

We return once more to state 0, where we find a last transition to the state generated by the item $[A \rightarrow \mathbf{a}., \$]$. Since this is a complete item, it is a state of one item:

$$\text{State 3:} \qquad [A \rightarrow \mathbf{a}., \$]$$

Now we return to state 2. From this state there is a transition on A to the ε-closure of $[A \rightarrow (A .), \$]$, which is a state with one item:

$$\text{State 4:} \qquad [A \rightarrow (A .), \$]$$

There is also a transition on **(** to the ε-closure of $[A \rightarrow (. A),)]$. Here, we also generate the closure items $[A \rightarrow . (A),)]$ and $[A \rightarrow .\mathbf{a},)]$, for the same reasons as in the construction of state 2. Thus, we obtain the new state:

$$\begin{aligned} \text{State 5:} \qquad &[A \rightarrow (. A),)] \\ &[A \rightarrow . (A),)] \\ &[A \rightarrow .\mathbf{a},)] \end{aligned}$$

Note that this state is the same as state 2, except for the lookahead of the first item.

Finally, we have a transition on the token **a** from state 2 to state 6:

$$\text{State 6:} \qquad [A \rightarrow \mathbf{a}.,)]$$

Note again that this is almost the same as state 3, differing from it only in the lookahead.

The next state that has a transition is state 4, which has a transition on the token **)** to the state

$$\text{State 7:} \qquad [A \rightarrow (A)., \$]$$

Returning to state 5, we have a transition from this state to itself on **(**, a transition on *A* to the state

$$\text{State 8:} \qquad [A \rightarrow (A .),)]$$

and a transition to the already constructed state 6 on **a**.

Finally, there is a transition on **)** from state 8 to

$$\text{State 9:} \qquad [A \rightarrow (A) .,)].$$

Thus, the DFA of LR(1) items for this grammar has ten states. The complete DFA is shown in Figure 5.7. Comparing this with the DFA of sets of LR(0) items for the same grammar (see Figure 5.5, page 208), we see that the DFA of LR(1) items is almost twice as large. This is not unusual. Indeed, the number of LR(1) states can exceed the number of LR(0) states by a factor of 10 in complex situations with many lookahead tokens.

Figure 5.7

The DFA of sets of LR(1) items for Example 5.14

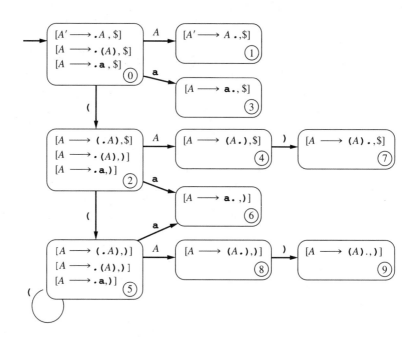

§

5.4.2   The LR(1) Parsing Algorithm

Before considering additional examples, we need to complete the discussion of general LR(1) parsing by restating the parsing algorithm based on the new DFA construction. This is easy to do, since it is just a restatement of the SLR(1) parsing algorithm, except that it uses the lookahead tokens in the LR(1) items instead of the Follow sets.

The General LR(1) parsing algorithm Let s be the current state (at the top of the parsing stack). Then actions are defined as follows:

1. If state s contains any LR(1) item of the form $[A \rightarrow \alpha.X \beta, a]$, where X is a terminal, and X is the next token in the input string, then the action is to shift the current input token onto the stack, and the new state to be pushed on the stack is the state containing the LR(1) item $[A \rightarrow \alpha X.\beta, a]$.

2. If state s contains the complete LR(1) item $[A \rightarrow \alpha., a]$, and the next token in the input string is a, then the action is to reduce by the rule $A \rightarrow \alpha$. A reduction by the rule $S' \rightarrow S$, where S is the start state, is equivalent to acceptance. (This will happen only if the next input token is \$.) In the other cases, the new state is computed as follows. Remove the string α and all of its corresponding states from the parsing stack. Correspondingly, back up in the DFA to the state from which the construction of α began. By construction, this state must contain an LR(1) item of the form $[B \rightarrow \alpha.A \beta, b]$. Push A onto the stack, and push the state containing the item $[B \rightarrow \alpha A.\beta, b]$.

3. If the next input token is such that neither of the above two cases applies, an error is declared.

As with the previous methods, we say that a grammar is an **LR(1) grammar** if the application of the above general LR(1) parsing rules results in no ambiguity. In particular, a grammar is LR(1) if and only if, for any state s, the following two conditions are satisfied:

1. For any item $[A \rightarrow \alpha.X \beta, a]$ in s with X a terminal, there is no item in s of the form $[B \rightarrow \beta., X]$ (otherwise there is a shift-reduce conflict).

2. There are no two items in s of the form $[A \rightarrow \alpha., a]$ and $[B \rightarrow \beta., a]$ (otherwise, there is a reduce-reduce conflict).

We remark also that a parsing table can be constructed from the DFA of sets of LR(1) items that expresses the general LR(1) parsing algorithm. This table has exactly the same form as the table for SLR(1) parsers, as the next example shows.

Example 5.15

We give the general LR(1) parsing table for the grammar of Example 5.14 in Table 5.10. It can be easily constructed from the DFA of Figure 5.7. In the table we have used the following numbering for the grammar rule choices in the reduction actions:

$$(1) \ A \rightarrow (\ A \ )$$
$$(2) \ A \rightarrow \mathbf{a}$$

Thus, the entry r2 in state 3 with lookahead \$ indicates a reduction by the rule $A \rightarrow \mathbf{a}$.

Since the steps in the parse of a particular string in general LR(1) parsing are just as they would be in SLR(1) or LR(0) parsing, we omit an example of such a parse. In

Table 5.10

General LR(1) parsing table for Example 5.14

State	Input				Goto
	(	**a**	**)**	**$**	**A**
0	s2	s3			1
1				accept	
2	s5	s6			4
3				r2	
4			s7		
5	s5	s6			8
6			r2		
7				r1	
8			s9		
9			r1		

§

subsequent examples in this section, we will also omit the explicit construction of the parsing table, since it is so easily supplied from the DFA.

In practice, almost all reasonable programming language grammars are LR(1), unless they are ambiguous. It is, of course, possible to construct examples of nonambiguous grammars that fail to be LR(1), but we shall not do so here (see the Exercises). Such examples tend to be contrived and can usually be avoided in practical situations. In fact, a programming language rarely even needs the power that general LR(1) parsing provides. Indeed, the example we have used to introduce LR(1) parsing (Example 5.14) is already an LR(0) grammar (and, hence, also SLR(1)).

The next example shows that general LR(1) parsing solves the lookahead problem for the grammar of Example 5.13 that failed to be SLR(1).

Example 5.16   The grammar of Example 5.13 in simplified form is as follows:

$$S \rightarrow \textbf{\textit{id}} \mid V \textbf{ := } E$$
$$V \rightarrow \textbf{\textit{id}}$$
$$E \rightarrow V \mid \textbf{n}$$

We construct the DFA of sets of LR(1) items for this grammar. The start state is the closure of the item $[S' \rightarrow .S, \$]$. It contains the items $[S \rightarrow . \textbf{\textit{id}}, \$]$ and $[S \rightarrow .V \textbf{ := } E, \$]$. This last item also gives rise to the closure item $[V \rightarrow . \textbf{\textit{id}}, \textbf{:=}]$, since $S \rightarrow .V \textbf{ :=} E$ indicates that a V may be recognized, but only if it is followed by an assignment token. Thus, the token $\textbf{:=}$ appears as the lookahead of the initial item $V \rightarrow . \textbf{\textit{id}}$. Summarizing, the start state consists of the following LR(1) items:

State 0: $[S' \rightarrow . S, \$]$
             $[S \rightarrow . \textbf{\textit{id}}, \$]$
             $[S \rightarrow .V \textbf{ := } E, \$]$
             $[V \rightarrow . \textbf{\textit{id}}, \textbf{:=}]$

From this state there is a transition on S to the state of one item

State 1: $[S' \rightarrow S\,., \$]$

and a transition on **id** to the state of two items

State 2: $[S \rightarrow .\,\mathbf{id}, \$]$
$[V \rightarrow .\,\mathbf{id}, :=]$

There is also a transition on V from state 0 to the state of one item

State 3: $[S \rightarrow V\,.:= E\,, \$]$

From states 1 and 2 there are no transitions, but there is a transition from state 3 on **:=** to the closure of item $[S \rightarrow V := .\ E\,, \$]$. Since E has no symbols following it in this item, this closure includes the items $[E \rightarrow .V\,, \$]$ and $[E \rightarrow .\,\mathbf{n}, \$]$. Finally, the item $[E \rightarrow .V, \$]$ leads to the closure item $[V \rightarrow .\,\mathbf{id}, \$]$, since V also has no symbols following it in this case. (Contrast this to the situation in state 0, where a V was followed by an assignment. Here V *cannot* be followed by an assignment, because an assignment token has already been seen.) The complete state is then

State 4: $[S \rightarrow V := .\ E\,, \$]$
$[E \rightarrow .V\,, \$]$
$[E \rightarrow .\,\mathbf{n}, \$]$
$[V \rightarrow .\,\mathbf{id}, \$]$

The remaining states and transitions are easy to construct, and we leave it to the reader to do so. The complete DFA of sets of LR(1) items is shown in Figure 5.8.

Now consider state 2. This was the state that gave rise to the SLR(1) parsing conflict. The LR(1) items clearly distinguish the two reductions by their lookaheads: reduce by $S \rightarrow \mathbf{id}$ on $\$$ and by $V \rightarrow \mathbf{id}$ on **:=**. Thus, this grammar is LR(1).

Figure 5.8

The DFA of sets of LR(1) items for Example 5.16

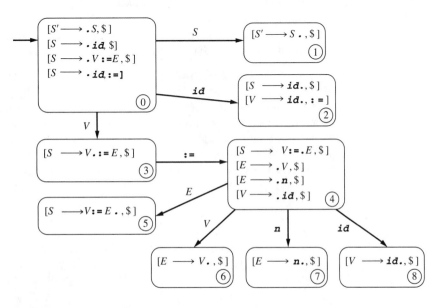

§

5.4.3   LALR(1) Parsing

LALR(1) parsing is based on the observation that, in many cases, the size of the DFA of sets of LR(1) items is due in part to the existence of many different states that have the same set of first components in their items (the LR(0) items), while differing only in their second components (the lookahead symbols). For example, the DFA of LR(1) items of Figure 5.7 has 10 states, while the corresponding DFA of LR(0) items (Figure 5.5) has only 6. Indeed, in Figure 5.7 each state of the pairs of states 2 and 5, 4 and 8, 7 and 9, and 3 and 6 differs from the other only in the lookahead components of its items. Consider, for instance, states 2 and 5. These two states differ only in their first item, and only in the lookahead of that item: state 2 has the first item $[A \rightarrow (.A), \$]$, with $\$$ as lookahead, while state 5 has the first item $[A \rightarrow (.A),)]$, with) as lookahead.

The LALR(1) parsing algorithm expresses the fact that it makes sense to identify all such states and combine their lookaheads. In doing so, we always must end up with a DFA that is identical to the DFA of LR(0) items, except that each state consists of items with sets of lookaheads. In the case of complete items these lookahead sets are often smaller than the corresponding Follow sets. Thus, LALR(1) parsing retains some of the benefit of LR(1) parsing over SLR(1) parsing, while preserving the smaller size of the DFA of LR(0) items.

Formally, the **core** of a state of the DFA of LR(1) items is the set of LR(0) items consisting of the first components of all LR(1) items in the state. Since the construction of the DFA of LR(1) items uses transitions that are the same as in the construction of the DFA of LR(0) items, except for their effect on the lookahead parts of the items, we obtain the following two facts, which form the basis for the LALR(1) parsing construction.

FIRST PRINCIPLE OF LALR(1) PARSING
The core of a state of the DFA of LR(1) items is a state of the DFA of LR(0) items.

SECOND PRINCIPLE OF LALR(1) PARSING
Given two states s_1 and s_2 of the DFA of LR(1) items that have the same core, suppose there is a transition on the symbol X from s_1 to a state t_1. Then there is also a transition on X from state s_2 to a state t_2, and the states t_1 and t_2 have the same core.

Taken together, these two principles allow us to construct the **DFA of LALR(1) items**, which is constructed from the DFA of LR(1) items by identifying all states that have the same core and forming the union of the lookahead symbols for each LR(0) item. Thus, each LALR(1) item in this DFA will have an LR(0) item as its first component and a set of lookahead tokens as its second component.[5] In subsequent examples we will denote multiple lookaheads by writing a / between them. Thus, the LALR(1) item $[A \rightarrow \alpha.\beta, a \ / \ b \ / \ c]$ has a lookahead set consisting of the symbols a, b, and c.

---

5. DFAs of LR(1) items could, in fact, also use sets of lookahead symbols to represent multiple items in the same state that share their first components, but we find it convenient to use this representation for the LALR(1) construction, where it is most appropriate.

We give an example to demonstrate this construction.

Example 5.17

Consider the grammar of Example 5.14, whose DFA of LR(1) items is given in Figure 5.7. Identifying states 2 and 5, 4 and 8, 7 and 9, and 3 and 6 gives the DFA of LALR(1) items in Figure 5.9. In that figure we have retained the numbering of the states 2, 3, 4, and 7, and added the lookaheads from states 5, 6, 8, and 9. As we expect, this DFA is identical to the DFA of LR(0) items (Figure 5.5), except for the lookaheads.

Figure 5.9

The DFA of sets of LALR(1) items for Example 5.17

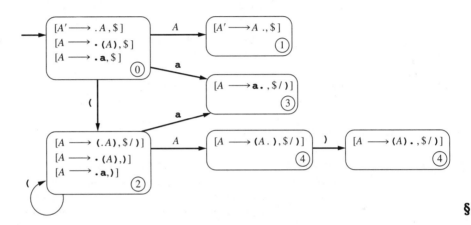

§

The algorithm for LALR(1) parsing using the condensed DFA of LALR(1) items is identical to the general LR(1) parsing algorithm described in the previous section. As before, we call a grammar an **LALR(1) grammar** if no parsing conflicts arise in the LALR(1) parsing algorithm. It is possible for the LALR(1) construction to create parsing conflicts that do not exist in general LR(1) parsing, but this rarely happens in practice. Indeed, if a grammar is LR(1), then the LALR(1) parsing table cannot have any shift-reduce conflicts; there may be reduce-reduce conflicts, however (see the Exercises). Nevertheless, if a grammar is SLR(1), then it certainly is LALR(1), and LALR(1) parsers often do as well as general LR(1) parsers in removing typical conflicts that occur in SLR(1) parsing. For example, the non-SLR(1) grammar of Example 5.16 is LALR(1): the DFA of LR(1) items of Figure 5.8 is also the DFA of LALR(1) items. If, as in this example, the grammar is already LALR(1), the only consequence of using LALR(1) parsing over general LR parsing is that, in the presence of errors, some spurious reductions may be made before error is declared. For example, we see from Figure 5.9 that, given the erroneous input string **a)**, an LALR(1) parser will perform the reduction $A \rightarrow$ **a** before declaring error, while a general LR(1) parser will declare error immediately after a shift of the token **a**.

Combining LR(1) states to form the DFA of LALR(1) items solves the problem of large parsing tables, but it still requires the entire DFA of LR(1) items to be computed. In fact, it is possible to compute the DFA of LALR(1) items directly from the DFA of LR(0) items through a process of **propagating lookaheads**. Though we will not describe this process formally, it is instructive to see how this can be done relatively easily.

Consider the LALR(1) DFA of Figure 5.9. We begin constructing lookaheads by adding the endmarker $ to the lookahead of the augmentation item $A' \rightarrow .A$ in state 0. (The $ lookahead is said to be **spontaneously generated**.) Then by the rules of ε-closure, the $ propagates to the two closure items (the A on the right-hand side of the kernel item $A' \rightarrow .A$ is followed by the empty string). By following the three transitions from state 0, the $ propagates to the kernel items of states 1, 3, and 2. Continuing with state 2, the closure items get the lookahead **)**, again by spontaneous generation (because A on the right-hand side of the kernel item $A \rightarrow (.A)$ comes before a right parenthesis). Now the transition on **a** to state 3 causes the **)** to be propagated to the lookahead of the item in that state. Also, the transition on **(** from state 2 to itself causes the **)** to be propagated to the lookahead of the kernel item (this is why the kernel item has both $ and **)** in its lookahead set). Now the lookahead set $/**)** propagates to state 4 and then to state 7. Thus, through this process, we have obtained the DFA of LALR(1) items of Figure 5.9 directly from the DFA of LR(0) items.

5.5   Yacc: AN LALR(1) PARSER GENERATOR

A **parser generator** is a program that takes as its input a specification of the syntax of a language in some form, and produces as its output a parse procedure for that language. Historically, parser generators were called **compiler-compilers**, since traditionally all compilation steps were performed as actions included within the parser. The modern view is to consider the parser to be just one part of the compilation process, so this term is out of date. One widely used parser generator that incorporates the LALR(1) parsing algorithm is called **Yacc** (for yet another compiler-compiler). We will give an overview of Yacc in this section, and then in the following section we will use Yacc to develop a parser for the TINY language. Since there are a number of different implementations of Yacc, as well as several public domain versions commonly called **Bison**,[6] there are numerous variations in the details of their operation, which may differ somewhat from the version presented here.[7]

5.5.1   Yacc Basics

Yacc takes a specification file (usually with a **.y** suffix) and produces an output file consisting of C source code for the parser (usually in a file called **y.tab.c** or **ytab.c** or, more recently <filename>**.tab.c**, where <filename>**.y** is the input file). A Yacc specification file has the basic format

---

6. One popular version, Gnu Bison, is part of the Gnu software distributed by the Free Software Foundation—see the Notes and References section.

7. Indeed, we have used several different versions to generate subsequent examples.

```
{definitions}
%%
{rules}
%%
{auxiliary routines}
```

Thus, there are three sections—the definitions section, the rules section, and the auxiliary routines section—separated by lines containing double percent signs.

The definitions section contains information about the tokens, data types, and grammar rules that Yacc needs to build the parser. It also includes any C code that must go directly into the output file at its beginning (primarily **#include** directives of other source code files). This section of the specification file can be empty.

The rules section contains grammar rules in a modified BNF form, together with actions in C code that are to be executed whenever the associated grammar rule is recognized (i.e., used in a reduction, according to the LALR(1) parsing algorithm). The metasymbol conventions used in the grammar rules are as follows. As usual, the vertical bar is used for alternatives (alternatives may also be written out separately). The arrow symbol → that we have used to separate the left and right sides of a grammar rule is replaced in Yacc by a colon. Also, a semicolon must end each grammar rule.

The third, auxiliary routines, section contains procedure and function declarations that may not be available otherwise through **#include** files and that are needed to complete the parser and/or the compiler. This section can be empty, in which case the second double percent metasymbol can be omitted from the specification file. Thus, a minimal Yacc specification file would consist only of **%%** followed by grammar rules and actions (actions may also be missing if our intent is just to analyze the grammar, a subject treated later in this section).

Yacc also permits C-style comments to be inserted in the specification file at any point where they do not interfere with the basic format.

We explain the contents of the Yacc specification file in more detail by using a simple example. The example is a calculator for simple integer arithmetic expressions with the grammar

$$exp \rightarrow exp\ addop\ term \mid term$$
$$addop \rightarrow \texttt{+} \mid \texttt{-}$$
$$term \rightarrow term\ mulop\ factor \mid factor$$
$$mulop \rightarrow \texttt{*}$$
$$factor \rightarrow \texttt{(}\ exp\ \texttt{)} \mid \textbf{\texttt{number}}$$

This grammar was used extensively as an example in previous chapters. In Section 4.1.2 we developed a recursive descent calculator program for this grammar. A completely equivalent Yacc specification is given in Figure 5.10. We discuss the contents of each of the three sections of this specification in turn.

In the definitions section of Figure 5.10 there are two items. The first consists of code to be inserted at the beginning of the Yacc output. This code consists of two typical **#include** directives and is set off from other Yacc declarations in this section by the surrounding delimiters **%{** and **%}**. (Note that the percent signs come before the brackets.) The second item in the definitions section is a declaration of the token **NUMBER**, which is to represent a sequence of digits.

Figure 5.10
Yacc definition for a simple
calculator program

```
%{
#include <stdio.h>
#include <ctype.h>
%}

%token NUMBER

%%

command : exp      { printf("%d\n",$1);}
        ; /* allows printing of the result */

exp     : exp '+' term   {$$ = $1 + $3;}
        | exp '-' term   {$$ = $1 - $3;}
        | term   {$$ = $1;}
        ;

term    : term '*' factor {$$ = $1 * $3;}
        | factor  {$$ = $1;}
        ;

factor      : NUMBER       {$$ = $1;}
            | '(' exp ')'   {$$ = $2;}
            ;
%%

main()
{ return yyparse();
}

int yylex(void)
{ int c;
  while((c = getchar()) == ' ');
  /* eliminates blanks */
  if ( isdigit(c) ) {
    ungetc(c,stdin);
    scanf("%d",&yylval);
    return(NUMBER);
  }
  if (c == '\n') return 0;
  /* makes the parse stop */
  return(c);
}

void yyerror(char * s)
{ fprintf(stderr,"%s\n",s);
} /* allows for printing of an error message */
```

Yacc has two ways of recognizing tokens. First, any character inside single quotes in a grammar rule will be recognized as itself. Thus, single-character tokens may be included directly in grammar rules in this fashion, as in fact the operator tokens **+**, **-**, and ***** are in Figure 5.10 (as well as the parentheses tokens). Second, symbolic tokens may be declared in a Yacc **%token** declaration, as the token **NUMBER** is in Figure 5.10. Such tokens are assigned a numeric value by Yacc that does not conflict with any character value. Typically, Yacc begins assigning token values with the number 258. Yacc inserts these token definitions as **#define** statements in the output code. Thus, in the output file we would likely find the line

```
#define NUMBER 258
```

as Yacc's response to the **%token NUMBER** declaration in the specification file. Yacc insists on defining all symbolic tokens itself, rather than importing a definition from elsewhere. However, it is possible to specify the numeric value that will be assigned to the token by writing a value after the token name in the token declaration. For example, writing

```
%token NUMBER 18
```

assigns **NUMBER** the numeric value 18 (instead of 258).

In the rules section of Figure 5.10, we see the rules for the nonterminals *exp*, *term*, and *factor*. Since we also want to print the value of an expression, we have an additional rule, which we call *command*, and to which we associate the printing action. Because the rule for *command* is listed first, *command* is taken to be the start symbol of the grammar. Alternatively, we could have included the line

```
%start command
```

in the definitions section, in which case we would not have to put the rule for *command* first.

Actions are specified in Yacc by writing them as actual C code (inside curly brackets) within each grammar rule. Typically, action code is placed at the end of each grammar rule choice (but before the vertical bar or semicolon), although it is also possible to write **embedded actions** within a choice (we will discuss these shortly). In writing the actions, we may take advantage of Yacc **pseudovariables**. When a grammar rule is recognized, each symbol in the rule possesses a value, which is assumed to be an integer unless changed by the programmer (we will see later how to do this). These values are kept on a **value stack** by Yacc, which is maintained parallel to the parsing stack. Each symbol's value on the stack may be referred to by using a pseudovariable that begins with a $. **$$** represents the value of the nonterminal that has just been recognized, that is, the symbol on the left-hand side of the grammar rule. The pseudovariables **$1**, **$2**, **$3**, and so on, represent the values of each symbol in succession on the right-hand side of the grammar rule. Thus, in Figure 5.10 the grammar rule and action

```
exp    : exp '+' term {$$ = $1 + $3;}
```

means that when we recognize the rule *exp* → *exp* **+** *term* we assign the value of the *exp* on the left to be the sum of the values of the *exp* and the *term* on the right.

All nonterminals achieve their values by such user-supplied actions. Tokens may also be assigned values, but this is done during the scanning process. Yacc assumes that the value of a token is assigned to the variable **yylval**, which is defined internally by Yacc, and which must be assigned when the token is recognized. Thus, in the grammar rule and action

```
factor    : NUMBER    {$$ = $1;}
```

the value **$1** refers to the value of the **NUMBER** token that was previously assigned to **yylval** when the token was recognized.

The third section of Figure 5.10 (the auxiliary routines section) contains the definition of three procedures. The first is a definition of **main**, which is included so that the resulting Yacc output can be compiled directly to an executable program. Procedure **main** calls **yyparse**, which is the name Yacc gives to the parsing procedure it produces. This procedure is declared to return an integer value, which is always 0 if the parse succeeds, and 1 if it does not (i.e., an error has occurred and no error recovery has been performed). The Yacc-generated **yyparse** procedure, in its turn, calls a scanner procedure, which it assumes has the name **yylex**, for purposes of compatibility with the Lex scanner generator (see Chapter 2). Thus, the Yacc specification of Figure 5.10 also includes a definition for **yylex**. In this particular situation, the **yylex** procedure is very simple. All it needs to do is return the next nonblank character, unless this character is a digit, in which case it must recognize the single multicharacter token **NUMBER** and return its value in the variable **yylval**. The one exception to this is when the scanner has reached the end of the input. In this case, the end of the input is indicated by a newline character ('**\n**' in C), since we are assuming that an expression is entered on a single line. Yacc expects the end of the input to be signaled by a return of the null value 0 by **yylex** (again, this is a convention shared with Lex). Finally, a **yyerror** procedure is defined. Yacc uses this procedure to print an error message when an error is encountered during the parse (typically Yacc prints the string "syntax error," but this behavior can be changed by the user).

5.5.2   Yacc Options

Usually there will be many auxiliary procedures that Yacc will need access to in addition to **yylex** and **yyerror**, and these are often placed into external files rather than put directly in the Yacc specification file. It is easy to give Yacc access to these procedures by writing appropriate header files and putting **#include** directives into the definitions section of the Yacc specification. More difficult is making Yacc-specific definitions available to other files. This is particularly true of the token definitions, which, as we have said, Yacc insists on generating itself (rather than importing), but which must be available to many other parts of a compiler (particularly the scanner). For this reason, Yacc has an option available that will automatically produce a header file containing this information, which can then be included in any other files that need the definitions. This header file is usually named **y.tab.h** or **ytab.h**, and is produced with the **-d** option (for heaDer file).

For example, if the Yacc specification of Figure 5.10 is contained in the file **calc.y**, then the command

```
yacc -d calc.y
```

will produce (in addition to the **y.tab.c** file) the file **y.tab.h** (or similar name), whose contents vary, but typically include such things as the following:

```
#ifndef YYSTYPE
#define YYSTYPE int
#endif
#define     NUMBER      258


extern YYSTYPE yylval;
```

(We will describe the meaning of **YYSTYPE** in more detail shortly.) This file can be used to place the code for **yylex** into a different file by inserting the line

```
#include y.tab.h
```

into that file.[8]

A second, extremely useful Yacc option is the **verbose option**, activated by the **-v** flag in the command line. This option produces yet another file, with the name **y.output** (or similar name). This file contains a textual description of the LALR(1) parsing table that is used by the parser. Reading this file allows the user to determine exactly what action the Yacc-generated parser will take in any situation, and this can be an extremely effective way to track down ambiguities and inaccuracies in a grammar. Indeed, it is a good idea to run Yacc with this option on the grammar alone, before adding the actions or auxiliary procedures to the specification, to make sure that the Yacc-generated parser will indeed perform as intended.

As an example, consider the Yacc specification of Figure 5.11. This is just a skeletal version of the Yacc specification of Figure 5.10. Both of these specifications will generate the same output file when Yacc is used with the verbose option:

```
yacc -v calc.y
```

Figure 5.11

A skeletal Yacc specification for use with the **-v** option.

```
%token NUMBER
%%
command     : exp
            ;
exp         : exp '+' term
            | exp '-' term
            | term
            ;
term        : term '*' factor
            | factor
            ;
factor      : NUMBER
            | '(' exp ')'
            ;
```

---

8. Older versions of Yacc may only place the token definitions (and not that of **yylval**) in **y.tab.h**. This may then require manual workarounds or rearrangement of the code.

A typical **y.output** file is listed in its entirety for this grammar in Figure 5.12.[9] We discuss the interpretation of this file in the following paragraphs.

The Yacc output file consists of a listing of all states in the DFA, followed by a summary of internal statistics. The states are numbered beginning with 0. Under each state the output file first lists the kernel items (closure items are not listed), then the actions corresponding to various lookaheads, and finally the goto actions on various nonterminals. Yacc typically uses an underscore character _ to mark the distinguished position in an item, instead of the period that we have been using in this chapter. Yacc uses the period instead to indicate a default, or "don't care" lookahead token in the action section of each state's listing.

Yacc begins in state 0 by listing the initial item of the augmentation production, which is always the only kernel item in the start state of the DFA. In the output file of our example, this item is written as

```
$accept : _command $end
```

This corresponds to the item *command'* → . *command* in our own terminology. Yacc gives the augmentation nonterminal the name **$accept**. It also lists the end-of-input pseudotoken explicitly as **$end**.

Let us briefly look at the action section of state 0, which follows the list of kernel items:

```
NUMBER shift 5
( shift 6
. error
command goto 1
exp goto 2
term goto 3
factor goto 4
```

The above list specifies that the DFA shifts into state 5 on lookahead token **NUMBER**, shifts into state 6 on lookahead token (, and declares error on all other lookahead tokens. Four goto transitions are also listed, for use during reductions to the given nonterminals. These actions are exactly as they would appear in a parsing table constructed by hand using the methods of this chapter.

Consider now state 2, with the output listing

```
state 2
        command : exp_   (1)
        exp : exp_+ term
        exp : exp_- term

        + shift 7
        - shift 8
        . reduce 1
```

---

9. Newer versions of Bison produce a substantially different format in the output files, but the contents are essentially the same.

Figure 5.12 (beginning)
A typical `y.output` file generated for the Yacc specification of Figure 5.10 using the verbose option

```
state 0
     $accept :  _command $end

     NUMBER   shift 5
     (   shift 6
     .   error

     command   goto 1
     exp   goto 2
     term   goto 3
     factor   goto 4

state 1
     $accept :   command_$end

     $end   accept
     .   error

state 2
     command :  exp_    (1)
     exp :   exp_+ term
     exp :   exp_- term

     +   shift 7
     -   shift 8
     .   reduce 1

state 3
     exp :   term_    (4)
     term :   term_* factor

     *   shift 9
     .   reduce 4

state 4
     term :   factor_    (6)

     .   reduce 6

state 5
     factor :  NUMBER_    (7)

     .   reduce 7
```

```
state 6
     factor :   (_exp )

     NUMBER   shift 5
     (   shift 6
     .   error

     exp   goto 10
     term   goto 3
     factor   goto 4

state 7
     exp :   exp +_term

     NUMBER   shift 5
     (   shift 6
     .   error

     term   goto 11
     factor   goto 4

state 8
     exp :   exp -_term

     NUMBER   shift 5
     (   shift 6
     .   error

     term   goto 12
     factor   goto 4

state 9
     term :   term *_factor

     NUMBER   shift 5
     (   shift 6
     .   error

     factor   goto 13
```

Figure 5.12 (conclusion)

A typical `y.output` file generated for the Yacc specification of Figure 5.10 using the verbose option

```
state 10
    exp  :   exp_+ term
    exp  :   exp_- term
    factor :   ( exp_)

    +  shift 7
    -  shift 8
    )  shift 14
    .  error

state 11
    exp  :   exp + term_     (2)
    term :   term_* factor

    *  shift 9
    .  reduce 2
```

```
state 12
    exp  :   exp - term_     (3)
    term :   term_* factor

    *  shift 9
    .  reduce 3

state 13
    term :   term * factor_   (5)

    .  reduce 5

state 14
    factor :   ( exp )_      (8)

    .  reduce 8
```

```
8/127 terminals, 4/600 nonterminals
9/300 grammar rules, 15/1000 states
0 shift/reduce, 0 reduce/reduce conflicts reported
9/601 working sets used
memory: states, etc. 36/2000, parser 11/4000
9/601 distinct lookahead sets
6 extra closures
18 shift entries, 1 exceptions
8 goto entries
4 entries saved by goto default
Optimizer space used: input 50/2000, output 218/4000
218 table entries, 202 zero
maximum spread: 257, maximum offset: 43
```

Here the kernel item is a complete item, so there will be a reduction by the associated production choice in the action section. To remind us of the number of the production being used for the reduction, Yacc lists the number after the complete item. In this case the production number is 1, and there is a **reduce 1** action, which indicates a reduction by the production *command → exp*. Yacc always numbers the productions in the order in which they are listed in the specification file. In our example there are eight productions (one for *command*, three for *exp*, two for *term*, and two for *factor*).

Note that the reduction action in this state is a *default* action: a reduction will be performed on any lookahead other than + and -. Here Yacc differs from a pure LALR(1) parser (and even an SLR(1) parser) in that no attempt is made to check for legal lookaheads on reductions (other than to decide among several reductions). A Yacc parser will generally make a number of reductions on errors before finally declaring error (which it eventually must do before any more shifts occur). This means that error messages may not be as informative as they might be, but the parsing table becomes considerably simpler, since fewer cases occur (this point will be discussed again in Section 5.7).

We conclude this example by constructing a parsing table from the Yacc output file, exactly as we would have written it by hand earlier in this chapter. The parsing table appears in Table 5.11.

Table 5.11

Parsing table corresponding to the Yacc output of Figure 5.12

State	Input							Goto			
	NUMBER	**(**	**+**	**–**	*****	**)**	**$**	*command*	*exp*	*term*	*factor*
0	s5	s6						1	2	3	4
1							accept				
2	r1	r1	s7	s8	r1	r1	r1				
3	r4	r4	r4	r4	s9	r4	r4				
4	r6	r6	r6	r6	r6	r6	r6				
5	r7	r7	r7	r7	r7	r7	r7				
6	s5	s6							10	3	4
7	s5	s6								11	4
8	s5	s6								12	4
9	s5	s6									13
10			s7	s8		s14					
11	r2	r2	r2	r2	s9	r2	r2				
12	r3	r3	r3	r3	s9	r3	r3				
13	r5	r5	r5	r5	r5	r5	r5				
14	r8	r8	r8	r8	r8	r8	r8				

5.5.3 Parsing Conflicts and Disambiguating Rules

One of the important uses of the verbose option is to investigate parsing conflicts, which Yacc will report in the **y.output** file. Yacc has disambiguating rules built into it that will allow it to produce a parser even in the presence of parsing conflicts (thus, even for ambiguous grammars). Often these disambiguating rules do the right thing, but sometimes they do not. Examining the **y.output** file allows the user to determine what the parsing conflicts are, and whether the parser produced by Yacc will resolve them correctly.

In the example of Figure 5.10 there were no parsing conflicts, and Yacc reported this fact in the summary information at the end of the output file as

0 shift/reduce, 0 reduce/reduce conflicts reported

A more interesting example is the ambiguous dangling else grammar of Example 5.12 (page 213). In Table 5.9 (page 215) we gave the SLR(1) parsing table for this grammar, with the shift-reduce conflict in state 5 removed by preferring the shift over the reduce (this corresponds to the most closely nested disambiguating rule). Yacc reports the ambiguity in exactly the same terms, and resolves the ambiguity by the same disambiguating rule. Indeed, the parsing table reported by Yacc is identical to Table 5.9, except for the default reductions Yacc inserts into error entries. For example, Yacc reports the state 5 actions as follows in the **y.output** file (the tokens were defined in uppercase in the specification file to avoid conflicts with the reserved words of C):

```
5: shift/reduce conflict (shift 6, red'n 3) on ELSE
state 5
        I : IF S_   (3)
        I : IF S_ELSE S

    ELSE shift 6
    . reduce 3
```

In the summary information, Yacc also reports the single shift-reduce conflict:

```
1 shift/reduce, 0 reduce/reduce conflicts reported
```

In the case of a reduce-reduce conflict, Yacc disambiguates by preferring the reduction by the grammar rule listed first in the specification file. This is more likely to be an error in the grammar, although it can also result in a correct parser. We offer the following simple example.

Example 5.18   Consider the following grammar:

$$S \rightarrow A \mid B$$
$$A \rightarrow a$$
$$B \rightarrow a$$

This is an ambiguous grammar, since the single legal string a has the two derivations $S \Rightarrow A \Rightarrow a$ and $S \Rightarrow B \Rightarrow a$. The complete **y.output** file for this grammar is given in Figure 5.13. Note the reduce-reduce conflict in state 4, which is resolved by preferring the rule $A \rightarrow a$ over the rule $B \rightarrow a$. This results in this latter rule never being used in a reduction (which clearly indicates a problem with the grammar), and Yacc reports this fact at the end with the line

```
Rule not reduced:   B : a
```

Figure 5.13

Yacc output file for the grammar of Example 5.18

```
state 0
        $accept : _S $end

        a    shift 4
        .    error

        S    goto 1
        A    goto 2
        B    goto 3
```

Figure 5.13   continued
Yacc output file for the
grammar of Example 5.18

```
state 1
      $accept :   S_$end

      $end   accept
      .   error

state 2
      S :   A_     (1)

      .   reduce 1

state 3
      S :   B_     (2)

      .   reduce 2

4: reduce/reduce conflict (red'ns 3 and 4 ) on $end
state 4
      A :   a_     (3)
      B :   a_     (4)

      .   reduce 3

Rule not reduced:   B :   a

3/127 terminals, 3/600 nonterminals
5/300 grammar rules, 5/1000 states
0 shift/reduce, 1 reduce/reduce conflicts reported
...
```

§

Yacc has, in addition to the disambiguating rule already mentioned, several ad hoc mechanisms for specifying operator precedence and associativity separately from a grammar that is otherwise ambiguous. This has several advantages. First, the grammar need not contain explicit constructions that specify associativity and precedence, and this means that the grammar can be shorter and simpler. Second, the associated parsing table can also be smaller and the resulting parser more efficient.

Consider, for example, the Yacc specification of Figure 5.14. In that figure the grammar is written in ambiguous form with no precedence or associativity of the operators. Instead, the precedence and associativity of the operators is specified in the definitions section by writing the lines

```
%left '+' '-'
%left '*'
```

These lines indicate to Yacc that the operators + and – have the same precedence and are left associative and that the operator * is left associative and has higher precedence than **+** and **–** (since it is listed after these operators in the declarations). The other possible Yacc operator specifications are **%right** and **%nonassoc** ("nonassoc" means that repeated operators are not allowed at the same level).

Figure 5.14

Yacc specification for a simple calculator with ambiguous grammar and precedence and associativity rules for operators

```
%{
#include <stdio.h>
#include <ctype.h>
%}

%token NUMBER

%left '+' '-'
%left '*'

%%

command : exp          { printf("%d\n",$1);}
        ;

exp     : NUMBER        {$$ = $1;}
        | exp '+' exp   {$$ = $1 + $3;}
        | exp '-' exp   {$$ = $1 - $3;}
        | exp '*' exp   {$$ = $1 * $3;}
        | '(' exp ')'   {$$ = $2;}
        ;

%%
/* auxiliary procedure declarations as in Figure 5.10 */
```

5.5.4   Tracing the Execution of a Yacc Parser

In addition to the verbose option that displays the parsing table in the **y.output** file, it is also possible to get a Yacc-generated parser to print a trace of its execution, including a description of the parsing stack and parser actions similar to the descriptions we have given earlier in this chapter. This is done by compiling **y.tab.c** with the symbol **YYDEBUG** defined (by using the **-DYYDEBUG** compiler option, for example) and by setting the Yacc integer variable **yydebug** to 1 at the point where trace information is desired. For example, adding the following lines to the beginning of the **main** procedure of Figure 5.10

```
extern int yydebug;
yydebug = 1;
```

will cause the parser to produce an output resembling that in Figure 5.15, given the expression **2+3** as input. We invite the reader to construct a hand trace of the actions of the parser using the parsing table of Table 5.11 and compare it to this output.

Figure 5.15

Tracing output using **yydebug** for the Yacc parser generated by Figure 5.10, given the input **2+3**

```
Starting parse
Entering state 0
Input: 2+3
Next token is NUMBER
Shifting token NUMBER, Entering state 5
Reducing via rule 7, NUMBER -> factor
state stack now 0
Entering state 4
Reducing via rule 6, factor -> term
state stack now 0
Entering state 3
Next token is '+'
Reducing via rule 4, term -> exp
state stack now 0
Entering state 2
Next token is '+'
Shifting token '+', Entering state 7
Next token is NUMBER
Shifting token NUMBER, Entering state 5
Reducing via rule 7, NUMBER -> factor
state stack now 0 2 7
Entering state 4
Reducing via rule 6, factor -> term
state stack now 0 2 7
Entering state 11
Now at end of input.
Reducing via rule 2, exp '+' term -> exp
state stack now 0
Entering state 2
Now at end of input.
Reducing via rule 1, exp -> command
5
state stack now 0
Entering state 1
Now at end of input.
```

5.5.5 Arbitrary Value Types in Yacc

In Figure 5.10 we specified the actions of a calculator by using the Yacc pseudovariables associated with each grammar symbol in a grammar rule. For example, we wrote **$$ = $1 + $3** to set the value of an expression to be the sum of the values of its two subexpressions (in positions 1 and 3 on the right-hand side of the grammar rule *exp* → *exp* **+** *term*). This is fine as long as the values we are dealing with are integers, since the Yacc default type of these values is always integer. However, this is inadequate if, for example, we want a calculator to compute with floating-point values. In this case, we must include a redefinition of the value type of the Yacc pseudovariables in the specification file. This data type is always defined in Yacc by the C preprocessor symbol **YYSTYPE**. Redefining this symbol will appropriately change the type of the Yacc value stack. Thus, if we want a calculator that computes floating-point values, we must add the line

```
#define YYSTYPE double
```

inside the brackets **%{...%}** in the definitions section of the Yacc specification file.

In more complicated situations, we may need different values for different grammar rules. For example, suppose we wished to separate the recognition of a selection of operators from the rule that computes with those operators, as in the rules

$$exp \rightarrow exp\ addop\ term\ |\ term$$
$$addop \rightarrow +\ |\ -$$

(These were in fact the original rules of the expression grammar, which we changed to recognize the operators directly in the rules for *exp* in Figure 5.10.) Now *addop* must return the operator (a character), while *exp* must return the computed value (a **double**, say), and these two data types are different. What we need to do is to define **YYSTYPE** to be a union of **double** and **char**. There are two ways to do this. One is to declare the union directly in the Yacc specification using the **%union** Yacc declaration:

```
%union { double val;
         char op; }
```

Now Yacc needs to be told the return type of each nonterminal, and this is accomplished by using the **%type** directive in the definitions section:

```
%type <val> exp term factor
%type <op> addop mulop
```

Note how the names of the union fields are surrounded by angle brackets in the Yacc **%type** declaration. Then, the Yacc specification of Figure 5.10 would be modified to begin as follows (we leave the details to the exercises):

```
...
%token NUMBER

%union { double val;
         char op; }

%type <val> exp term factor NUMBER
```

```
%type <op> addop mulop

%%
command : exp          { printf("%d\n",$1);}
          ;
exp     : exp op term { switch ($2) {
                            case '+': $$ = $1 + $3; break;
                            case '-': $$ = $1 - $3; break;
                            }
                        }
        | term   {$$ = $1;}
          ;
op : '+' { $$ '+'; }
   | '-' { $$ '-'; }
     ;
```

The second alternative is to define a new data type in a separate include file (for example, a header file) and then define **YYSTYPE** to be this type. Then the appropriate values must be constructed by hand in the associated action code. An example of this is the TINY parser of the next section.

5.5.6 Embedded Actions in Yacc

Sometimes it is necessary to execute some code prior to the complete recognition of a grammar rule choice during parsing. As an example, consider the case of simple declarations:

$$decl \rightarrow type\ var\text{-}list$$
$$type \rightarrow \textbf{int} \mid \textbf{float}$$
$$var\text{-}list \rightarrow var\text{-}list\ \textbf{, id} \mid \textbf{id}$$

We would like, when recognizing a *var-list*, to tag each variable identifier with the current type (integer or floating point). We might do this in Yacc as follows:

```
decl  : type { current_type = $1; }
        var_list
      ;
type  : INT { $$ = INT_TYPE; }
      | FLOAT { $$ = FLOAT_TYPE; }
      ;
var_list : var_list ',' ID
            { setType(tokenString,current_type);}
         | ID
            { setType(tokenString,current_type);}
         ;
```

Note how **current_type** (which needs to be declared a static variable in the declarations section) is set by an embedded action before the recognition of the variables in the **decl** rule. Additional examples of embedded actions will be seen in the following sections.

Yacc interprets an embedded action

```
A : B {/* embedded action */} C ;
```

as being equivalent to the creation of a new placeholder nonterminal and an ε-production for that nonterminal that, when reduced, performs the embedded action:

```
A : B E C ;
E : {/* embedded action */} ;
```

To close this section, we summarize in Table 5.12 the Yacc definition mechanisms and internal names that we have discussed.

Table 5.12

Yacc internal names and definition mechanisms

Yacc internal name	Meaning/Use
y.tab.c	Yacc output file name
y.tab.h	Yacc-generated header file containing token definitions
yyparse	Yacc parsing routine
yylval	value of current token in stack
yyerror	user-defined error message printer used by Yacc
error	Yacc error pseudotoken
yyerrok	procedure that resets parser after error
yychar	contains the lookahead token that caused an error
YYSTYPE	preprocessor symbol that defines the value type of the parsing stack
yydebug	variable which, if set by the user to 1, causes the generation of runtime information on parsing actions

Yacc definition mechanism	Meaning/Use
%token	defines token preprocessor symbols
%start	defines the start nonterminal symbol
%union	defines a union **YYSTYPE**, allowing values of different types on parser stack
%type	defines the variant union type returned by a symbol
%left %right %nonassoc	defines the associativity and precedence (by position) of operators

5.6 GENERATION OF A TINY PARSER USING Yacc

The syntax of TINY was given in Section 3.7, and a handwritten parser was described in Section 4.4; we refer the reader to those descriptions. Here we will describe the Yacc specification file **tiny.y**, together with the changes needed to the global definitions **globals.h** (we have taken steps to minimize changes to other files, and this will also be discussed). The entire **tiny.y** file is listed in Appendix B, lines 4000–4162.

We begin with a discussion of the definitions section of the Yacc specification of TINY. The use of the flag **YYPARSER** (line 4007) will be described later. There are four **#include** files, representing the information needed by Yacc from elsewhere in the program (lines 4009–4012). The definitions section has four other declarations. The first (line 4014) is a definition of **YYSTYPE**, which defines the values returned by Yacc parsing procedures to be pointers to node structures (**TreeNode** itself is defined in **globals.h**). This allows the Yacc parser to construct a syntax tree. The second declaration is of a static global **savedName** variable, which is used to temporarily store identifier strings that need to be inserted in tree nodes that are not yet constructed when the strings are seen in the input (in TINY this is only necessary in assignments). The variable **savedLineNo** is used for the same purpose, so that proper source code line numbers will be associated with the identifiers. Finally, **savedTree** is used to temporarily store the syntax tree produced by the **yyparse** procedure (**yyparse** itself can only return an integer flag).

We proceed to a discussion of the actions associated with each of the grammar rules of TINY (these rules are slight variations of the BNF grammar given in Chapter 3, Figure 3.6). In most cases these actions represent the construction of the syntax tree corresponding to the parse tree at that point. Specifically, new nodes need to be allocated by calls to **newStmtNode** and **newExpNode** from the **util** package (these were described on page 182), and appropriate child nodes of the new tree node need to be assigned. For example, the actions corresponding to the TINY **write_stmt** (lines 4082ff) are as follows:

```
write_stmt : WRITE exp
             { $$ = newStmtNode(WriteK);
               $$->child[0] = $2;
             }
        ;
```

The first instruction calls **newStmtNode** and assigns its returned value as the value of the **write_stmt**. Then it assigns the previously constructed value of **exp** (the Yacc pseudovariable **$2**, which is a pointer to the tree node of the expression to be printed) to be the first child of the tree node of the write statement. The action code for other statements and expressions is quite similar.

The actions for **program**, **stmt_seq**, and **assign_stmt** deal with small problems associated with each of these constructs. In the case of the grammar rule for **program**, the associated action (line 4029) is

```
{ savedTree = $1;}
```

This assigns the tree constructed for the **stmt_seq** to the static variable **savedTree**. This is necessary so that the syntax tree can later be returned by the **parse** procedure.

In the case of **assign_stmt**, we have already mentioned that we need to store the identifier string of the variable that is the target of the assignment so that it will be available when the node is constructed (as well as its line number for later tracing). This is achieved by using the static **savedName** and **saveLineNo** variables (lines 4067ff):

```
assign_stmt : ID { savedName = copyString(tokenString);
                    savedLineNo = lineno; }
              ASSIGN exp
                { $$ = newStmtNode(AssignK);
                  $$->child[0] = $4;
                  $$->attr.name = savedName;
                  $$->lineno = saveLineNo;
                }
            ;
```

The identifier string and line number must be saved as an embedded action before the recognition of the **ASSIGN** token, since as new tokens are matched, the values of **tokenString** and **lineno** are changed by the scanner. Yet the new node for the assignment cannot be fully constructed until the **exp** is recognized. Hence, the need for **savedName** and **saveLineNo**. (The use of the utility procedure **copyString** ensures no sharing of memory for these strings. Note also that the **exp** value is referred to as **$4**. This is because Yacc counts embedded actions as additional places in the right-hand sides of grammar rules—see the discussion in the previous section.)

In the case of **stmt_seq** (lines 4031–4039), the problem is that statements are strung together in a TINY syntax tree using sibling pointers instead of child pointers. Since the rule for statement sequences is written left recursively, this requires that the code chase down the already constructed sibling list for the left sublist in order to attach the current statement at the end. This is inefficient and can be avoided by rewriting the rule right recursively, but this solution has its own problem, in that the parsing stack will grow large as long statement sequences are processed.

Finally, the auxiliary procedure section of the Yacc specification (lines 4144–4162) contains the definition of three procedures, **yyerror**, **yylex**, and **parse**. The **parse** procedure, which is called from the main program, calls the Yacc-defined parse procedure **yyparse** and then returns the saved syntax tree. The **yylex** procedure is needed because Yacc assumes this is the name of the scanner procedure, and this was defined externally as **getToken**. We wrote this definition so that the Yacc-generated parser would work with the TINY compiler with a minimum of changes to other code files. One might wish to make the appropriate changes to the scanner and eliminate this definition, particularly if the Lex version of the scanner is being used. The **yyerror** procedure is called by Yacc when an error occurs; it prints some useful information, such as the line number, to the listing file. It uses an internal Yacc variable **yychar** that contains the token number of the token that caused the error.

It remains to describe the changes to the other files in the TINY parser that are made necessary by the use of Yacc to produce the parser. As we have noted, we have aimed to keep these changes to a minimum, and have confined all changes to the **globals.h** file. The revised file is listed in Appendix B, lines 4200–4320. The basic problem is that the header file generated by Yacc, containing the token definitions, must be included into most of the other code files, but cannot be included directly in the Yacc-generated parser, since that would repeat the internal definitions. The solution is to begin the Yacc declaration section with the definition of a flag **YYPARSER** (line 4007), which will be included in the Yacc parser and will indicate when the C compiler is inside the parser. We use that flag (lines 4226–4236) to selectively include the Yacc-generated header file **y.tab.h** into **globals.h**.

A second problem occurs with the **ENDFILE** token, which the scanner generates to indicate the end of the input file. Yacc assumes this token always has the value 0. We thus provide a direct definition of this token (line 4234) and include it in the selectively compiled section controlled by **YYPARSER**, since it is not needed internally by Yacc.

The final change to the **globals.h** file is to redefine **TokenType** to be a synonym for **int** (line 4252), since the Yacc tokens all have integer values. This avoids unnecessary replacements of the previous enumerated type **TokenType** in other files.

5.7   ERROR RECOVERY IN BOTTOM-UP PARSERS

5.7.1   Detecting Errors in Bottom-Up Parsing

A bottom-up parser will detect an error when a blank (or error) entry is detected in the parsing table. Obviously, it makes sense that errors should be detected as soon as possible, since error messages can be more meaningful and specific. Thus, a parsing table should have as many blank entries as possible.

Unfortunately, this goal conflicts with an equally important one: reducing the size of the parsing table. We have already seen (Table 5.11) that Yacc fills in as many table entries as it can with default reductions, so that a large number of reductions may take place on the parsing stack before an error is declared. This obscures the precise source of the error and may lead to uninformative error messages.

An additional feature of bottom-up parsing is that the power of the particular algorithm used can affect the ability of the parser to detect errors early. An LR(1) parser can, for example, detect errors earlier than an LALR(1) or SLR(1) parser, and these latter can detect errors earlier than an LR(0) parser. As a simple example of this, compare the LR(0) parsing table of Table 5.4 (page 209) with the LR(1) parsing table of Table 5.10 (page 222) for the same grammar. Given the incorrect input string **(a** $, the LR(1) parsing table of Table 5.10 will shift **(** and **a** onto the stack and move to state 6. In state 6 there is no entry under $, so an error will be reported. By contrast, the LR(0) algorithm (and the SLR(1) algorithm as well) will reduce by $A \to$ **a** before discovering the lack of a balancing right parenthesis. Similarly, given the incorrect string **a)** $, the general LR(1) parser will shift **a** and then declare error from state 3 on right parenthesis, while the LR(0) parser will again reduce by $A \to$ **a** before declaring error. Of course, any bottom-up parser will always report the error eventually, after perhaps a number of "erroneous" reductions. None of these parsers will ever shift a token on error.

5.7.2   Panic Mode Error Recovery

As in top-down parsing, it is possible to achieve reasonably good error recovery in bottom-up parsers by judiciously removing symbols from either the parsing stack or the input or both. Similar to LL(1) parsers, there are three possible alternative actions that might be contemplated:

1. Pop a state from the stack.
2. Successively pop tokens from the input until a token is seen for which we can restart the parse.
3. Push a new state onto the stack.

One particularly effective method for choosing which of these actions to take when an error occurs is as follows:

1. Pop states from the parsing stack until a state is found with nonempty Goto entries.
2. If there is a legal action on the current input token from one of the Goto states, push that state onto the stack and restart the parse. If there are several such states, prefer a shift to a reduce. Among the reduce actions, prefer one whose associated nonterminal is least general.
3. If there is no legal action on the current input token from one of the Goto states, advance the input until there is a legal action or the end of the input is reached.

These rules have the effect of forcing the recognition of a construct which was in the process of being recognized when the error occurred, and restarting the parse immediately thereafter. Error recovery that uses these or similar rules could be called **panic mode** error recovery, since it is similar to the top-down panic mode described in Section 4.5.

Unfortunately, these rules can result in an infinite loop, since step 2 pushes new states onto the stack. In that case, there are several possible solutions. One is to insist on a shift action from a Goto state in step 2. This may be too restrictive, however. Another solution is, if the next legal move is a reduction, to set a flag that causes the parser to keep track of the sequence of states during the following reductions, and if the same state recurs, to pop stack states until the original state is removed at which the error occurred, and begin again with step 1. If, at any time, a shift action occurs, the parser resets the flag and continues with a normal parse.

Example 5.19

Consider the simple arithmetic expression grammar whose Yacc parsing table is given in Table 5.11 (page 235). Now consider the erroneous input (2+*). The parse proceeds normally until the * is seen. At that point, panic mode would cause the following actions to take place on the parsing stack:

Parsing stack	Input	Action
. . .	. . .	. . .
$ 0 (6 E 10 + 7	*) $	error:
		push T, goto 11
$ 0 (6 E 10 + 7 T 11	*) $	shift 9
$ 0 (6 E 10 + 7 T 11 * 9	) $	error:
		push F, goto 13
$ 0 (6 E 10 + 7 T 11 * 9 F 13	) $	reduce $T \to T * F$
. . .	. . .	. . .

At the first error, the parser is in state 7, which has legal Goto states 11 and 4. Since state 11 has a shift on the next input token *****, that Goto is preferred, and the token is shifted. At that point the parser is in state 9, with a right parenthesis on the input. This is again an error. In state 9 there is a single Goto entry (to state 11), and state 11 does have a legal action on **)** (albeit a reduction). The parse then proceeds normally to its conclusion.   §

5.7.3 Error Recovery in Yacc

An alternative to panic mode is to use so-called **error productions**. An error production is a production that contains the pseudotoken **error** as the only symbol on its right-hand side. An error production marks a context in which erroneous tokens can be deleted until appropriate synchronizing tokens are seen, whence the parse can be restarted. In effect, error productions allow the programmer to manually mark those nonterminals whose Goto entries are to be used for error recovery.

Error productions are the principal method available in Yacc for error recovery. The behavior of a Yacc parser in the presence of errors, and its handling of error productions, is as follows.

1. When the parser detects an error during a parse (that is, it encounters an empty entry in the parsing table), it pops states from the parsing stack until it reaches a state in which the **error** pseudotoken is a legal lookahead. The effect is to discard input to the left of the error, and to view the input as containing the **error** pseudotoken. If there are no error productions, then **error** is never a legal lookahead for a shift, and the parser stack will be emptied, aborting the parse at the first error. (This is the behavior of the parser generated by the Yacc input of Figure 5.10, page 228.)

2. Once the parser has found a state on the stack in which **error** is a legal lookahead, it continues in normal fashion with shifts and reduces. The effect is as though **error** were seen in the input, followed by the original lookahead (that is, the lookahead that caused the error). If desired, the Yacc macro **yyclearin** can be used to discard the token that caused the error, and to use the token following it as the next lookahead (after **error**).

3. If, after an error occurs, the parser discovers further errors, then the input tokens causing the errors are silently discarded, until three successive tokens are shifted legally onto the parsing stack. During this time the parser is said to be in an "error state." This behavior is designed to avoid cascades of error messages caused by the same error. This can, however, result in large amounts of input being thrown away before the parser exits the error state (just as with panic mode). The compiler writer can override this behavior by using the Yacc macro **yyerrok** to remove the parser from the error state, so that no further input will be discarded without a new error recovery.

We describe a few simple examples of this behavior, based on the Yacc input of Figure 5.10.

Example 5.20   Consider the following replacement for the rule for *command* in Figure 5.10:

```
command : exp        { printf("%d\n",$1);}
        | error      { yyerror("incorrect expression"); }
        ;
```

Consider also the erroneous input **2++3**. The parse of this string proceeds normally until the erroneous second **+** is reached. At that point the parse is given by the following parsing stack and input (we use Table 5.11 to describe this, although the addition of the error production will actually result in a slightly different parse table):

PARSING STACK	INPUT
$0 *exp* 2 + 7	+3$

Now the parser enters the error "state" (generating an error message such as "syntax error"), and begins popping states from the stack, until state 0 is uncovered. At this point the error production for *command* provides that **error** is a legal lookahead, and it will be shifted onto the parsing stack, and immediately reduced to *command*, causing the associated action to be executed (which prints the message "incorrect expression"). The resulting situation is now as follows:

PARSING STACK	INPUT
$0 *command* 1	+3$

At this point the only legal lookahead is the end of input (indicated by $ here, corresponding to the return of 0 by **yylex**), and the parser will delete the remaining input tokens **+3** before exiting (while still in the "error state"). Thus, the addition of the error production has essentially the same effect as the version in Figure 5.10, except that we are now able to supply our own error message.

An even better error mechanism than this would allow the user to reenter the line after the erroneous input. In this case, a synchronizing token is needed, and the end of line marker is the only sensible one. Thus, the scanner must be modified to return the newline character (instead of 0), and with this modification we may write (but see Exercise 5.32):

```
command : exp '\n'   { printf("%d\n",$1); exit(0);}
        | error '\n'
          { yyerrok;
             printf("reenter expression: "); }
          command
        ;
```

This code has the effect that, when an error occurs, the parser will skip all tokens up to a newline, when it will execute the action represented by **yyerrok** and the **printf** statement. Then it will attempt to recognize another *command*. The call to **yyerrok** is needed here to cancel the "error state" after the newline is seen, since otherwise if a new error occurs right after the newline, Yacc will silently delete tokens until it finds a sequence of three correct tokens.

§

Example 5.21

Consider what would happen if an error production were added to the Yacc definition of Figure 5.10 as follows:

```
factor    : NUMBER          {$$ = $1;}
          | '(' exp ')'     {$$ = $2;}
          | error {$$ = 0;}
          ;
```

Consider first the erroneous input **2++3** as in the previous example. (We continue to use Table 5.11, although the additional error production results in a slightly different table.) As before, the parser will reach the following point:

PARSING STACK	INPUT
$0 *exp* 2 **+** 7	**+3**$

Now the error production for *factor* will provide that **error** is a legal lookahead in state 7 and **error** will be immediately shifted onto the stack and reduced to *factor*, causing the value 0 to be returned. Now the parser has reached the following point:

PARSING STACK	INPUT
$0 *exp* 2 **+** 7 *factor* 4	**+3**$

This is a normal situation, and the parser will continue to execute normally to the end. The effect is to interpret the input as **2+0+3**—the 0 between the two **+** symbols is there because that is where the **error** pseudotoken is inserted, and by the action for the error production, **error** is viewed as equivalent to a factor with value 0.

Now consider the erroneous input **2 3** (that is, two numbers with a missing operator). Here the parser reaches the position

PARSING STACK	INPUT
$0 *exp* 2	**3**$

At this point (if the rule for *command* has not been changed), the parser will (erroneously) reduce by the rule *command* → *exp* (and print the value 2), even though a number is not a legal follow symbol for *command*. The parser then reaches the position

PARSING STACK	INPUT
$0 *command* 1	**3**$

Now an error is detected, and state 1 is popped from the parsing stack, uncovering state 0. At this point the error production for *factor* allows for **error** to be a legal lookahead from state 0, and **error** is shifted onto the parsing stack, resulting in another cascade of reductions and the printing of the value 0 (the value returned by the error production). Now the parser is back at the same position in the parse, with the number **3** still in the input! Fortunately, the parser is already in the "error state" and will not shift **error** again, but throws away the number **3**, uncovering the correct lookahead for state 1, whereupon the parser exits.[10] The result is that the parser prints the following (we repeat the user input on the first line):

```
> 2 3
2
syntax error
incorrect expression
0
```

This behavior gives a glimpse of the difficulties of good error recovery in Yacc. (See the exercises for more examples.)   §

5.7.4   Error Recovery in TINY

The Yacc specification file **tiny.y** in Appendix B contains two error productions, one for **stmt** (line 4047) and one for **factor** (line 4139), whose associated actions are to return the null syntax tree. These error productions provide a level of error handling similar to that of the recursive-descent TINY parser in the previous chapter, except that no attempt is made to build a significant syntax tree in the presence of errors. Also, these error productions provide no special synchronization for the restart of the parse, so in the presence of multiple errors many tokens may be skipped.

EXERCISES   **5.1** Consider the following grammar:

$$E \rightarrow (L) \mid \mathbf{a}$$
$$L \rightarrow L , E \mid E$$

   a. Construct the DFA of LR(0) items for this grammar.
   b. Construct the SLR(1) parsing table.
   c. Show the parsing stack and the actions of an SLR(1) parser for the input string **((a),a,(a,a))**.
   d. Is this grammar an LR(0) grammar? If not, describe the LR(0) conflict. If so, construct the LR(0) parsing table, and describe how a parse might differ from an SLR(1) parse.

5.2 Consider the grammar of the previous exercise.
   a. Construct the DFA of LR(1) items for this grammar.
   b. Construct the general LR(1) parsing table.
   c. Construct the DFA of LALR(1) items for this grammar.
   d. Construct the LALR(1) parsing table.

---

10. Some versions of Yacc pop the parsing stack again before deleting any input. This can result in even more complicated behavior. See the exercises.

   e. Describe any differences that might occur between the actions of a general LR(1) parser and an LALR(1) parser.

5.3 Consider the following grammar:

$$A \to A \ (\ A \ ) \ | \ \varepsilon$$

   a. Construct the DFA of LR(0) items for this grammar.
   b. Construct the SLR(1) parsing table.
   c. Show the parsing stack and the actions of an SLR(1) parser for the input string (( ) ( )).
   d. Is this grammar an LR(0) grammar? If not, describe the LR(0) conflict. If so, construct the LR(0) parsing table, and describe how a parse might differ from an SLR(1) parse.

5.4 Consider the grammar of the previous exercise.
   a. Construct the DFA of LR(1) items for this grammar.
   b. Construct the general LR(1) parsing table.
   c. Construct the DFA of LALR(1) items for this grammar.
   d. Construct the LALR(1) parsing table.
   e. Describe any differences that might occur between the actions of a general LR(1) parser and an LALR(1) parser.

5.5 Consider the following grammar of simplified statement sequences:

$$stmt\text{-}sequence \to stmt\text{-}sequence \ ; \ stmt \ | \ stmt$$
$$stmt \to \mathbf{s}$$

   a. Construct the DFA of LR(0) items for this grammar.
   b. Construct the SLR(1) parsing table.
   c. Show the parsing stack and the actions of an SLR(1) parser for the input string **s;s;s**.
   d. Is this grammar an LR(0) grammar? If not, describe the LR(0) conflict. If so, construct the LR(0) parsing table, and describe how a parse might differ from an SLR(1) parse.

5.6 Consider the grammar of the previous exercise.
   a. Construct the DFA of LR(1) items for this grammar.
   b. Construct the general LR(1) parsing table.
   c. Construct the DFA of LALR(1) items for this grammar.
   d. Construct the LALR(1) parsing table.
   e. Describe any differences that might occur between the actions of a general LR(1) parser and an LALR(1) parser.

5.7 Consider the following grammar:

$$E \to (\ L \ ) \ | \ \mathbf{a}$$
$$L \to E \ L \ | \ E$$

   a. Construct the DFA of LR(0) items for this grammar.
   b. Construct the SLR(1) parsing table.

    c. Show the parsing stack and the actions of an SLR(1) parser for the input string
        `((a)a(a a))`.

    d. Construct the DFA of LALR(1) items by propagating the lookaheads through the
        DFA of LR(0) items.

    e. Construct the LALR(1) parsing table.

5.8 Consider the following grammar

$$declaration \rightarrow type\ var\text{-}list$$
$$type \rightarrow \texttt{int} \mid \texttt{float}$$
$$var\text{-}list \rightarrow \texttt{identifier,}\ var\text{-}list \mid \texttt{identifier}$$

    a. Rewrite it in a form more suitable for bottom-up parsing.

    b. Construct the DFA of LR(0) items for the rewritten grammar.

    c. Construct the SLR(1) parsing table for the rewritten grammar.

    d. Show the parsing stack and the actions of an SLR(1) parser for the input string
        `int x,y,z` using the table of part (c).

    e. Construct the DFA of LALR(1) items by propagating the lookaheads through the
        DFA of LR(0) items of part (b).

    f. Construct the LALR(1) parsing table for the rewritten grammar.

5.9 Write down a formal description of the algorithm for constructing the DFA of LALR(1)
items by propagating lookaheads through the DFA of LR(0) items. (This algorithm was
informally described in Section 5.4.3.)

5.10 All the parsing stacks shown in this chapter have included both state numbers and grammar symbols (for clarity). However, the parsing stack need only store the state numbers—the tokens and nonterminals need not be stored in the stack. Describe the SLR(1)
parsing algorithm if only the state numbers are kept in the stack.

5.11 a. Show that the following grammar is not LR(1):

$$A \rightarrow a\,A\,a \mid \varepsilon$$

    b. Is this grammar ambiguous? Why or why not?

5.12 Show that the following grammar is LR(1) but not LALR(1):

$$S \rightarrow a\,A\,d \mid b\,B\,d \mid a\,B\,e \mid b\,A\,e$$
$$A \rightarrow c$$
$$B \rightarrow c$$

5.13 Show that an LR(1) grammar that is not LALR(1) must have only reduce-reduce conflicts.

5.14 Show that a prefix of a right sentential form is a viable prefix if and only if it does not
extend beyond the handle.

5.15 Can there be an SLR(1) grammar that is not LALR(1)? Why or why not?

5.16 Show that a general LR(1) parser will make no reduction before an error is declared, if
the next input token cannot eventually be shifted.

5.17 Can an SLR(1) parser make more or fewer reductions than an LALR(1) parser before
declaring error? Explain.

5.18 The following ambiguous grammar generates the same strings as the grammar of Exercise 5.3 (namely, all strings of nested parentheses):

$$A \rightarrow AA \mid (A) \mid \varepsilon$$

Will a Yacc-generated parser using this grammar recognize all legal strings? Why or why not?

5.19 Given a state in which there are two possible reductions (on different lookaheads), Yacc will choose one of the reductions as its default action. Describe the rule Yacc uses for making this choice. (Hint: Use the grammar of Example 5.16, page 222, as a test case.)

5.20 Suppose we remove the associativity and precedence specifications of the operators from the Yacc specification of Figure 5.14, page 238 (thus leaving an ambiguous grammar). Describe what associativity and precedences result from Yacc's default disambiguation rules.

5.21 As described in the footnote on page 250, some Yacc parsers pop the parsing stack again before discarding any input while in "error state." Describe the behavior of such a parser for the Yacc specification of Example 5.21, given the erroneous input **2 3**.

5.22 a. Trace the behavior of a panic mode error recovery mechanism as described in Section 5.7.1, using the parsing Table 5.11, page 235, and the string **(*2** .

   b. Suggest an improvement to the behavior in part (a).

5.23 Suppose the rule for **command** in the Yacc calculator specification of Figure 5.10, page 228, is replaced by the following rule for a **list** starting nonterminal:

```
list    :       list '\n' {exit(0);}
        |       list exp '\n' {printf("%d\n",$2);}
        |       list error '\n' {yyerrok;}
        ;
```

and the **yylex** procedure in that figure has the line

```
if (c == '\n') return 0;
```

deleted.

   a. Explain the differences in the behavior of this version of the simple calculator from that of the version in Figure 5.10.

   b. Explain the reason for the **yyerrok** in the last line of this rule. Give an example to show what would happen if it were not there.

5.24 a. Suppose the rule for **command** in the Yacc calculator specification of Figure 5.10 is replaced by the following rule:

```
command : exp error {printf("%d\n",$1);}
```

Explain precisely the behavior of the Yacc parser, given the input **2 3**.

   b. Suppose the rule for **command** in the Yacc calculator specification of Figure 5.10 is replaced instead by the following rule:

```
command : error exp {printf("%d\n",$2);}
```

Explain precisely the behavior of the Yacc parser, given the input **2 3**.

5.25 Suppose the Yacc error production of Example 5.21, page 249, was replaced by the following rule:

```
factor  : NUMBER          {$$ = $1;}
        | '(' exp ')'     {$$ = $2;}
        | error {yyerrok; $$ = 0;}
        ;
```

    a. Explain the behavior of the Yacc parser given the erroneous input **2++3**.

    b. Explain the behavior of the Yacc parser given the erroneous input **2   3**.

5.26 Compare the error recovery of the Yacc-generated TINY parser to that of the recursive-descent parser of the previous chapter, using the test programs of Section 4.5.3. Explain the differences in behavior.

PROGRAMMING EXERCISES

5.27 Rewrite the Yacc specification of Figure 5.10, page 235, to use the following grammar rules (instead of **scanf**) to calculate the value of a number (and, hence, do away with the **NUMBER** token):

$$number \rightarrow number\ digit \mid digit$$
$$digit \rightarrow 0 \mid 1 \mid 2 \mid 3 \mid 4 \mid 5 \mid 6 \mid 7 \mid 8 \mid 9$$

5.28 Add the following to the Yacc integer calculator specification of Figure 5.10 (make sure they have the correct associativity and precedence):

    a. Integer division with the symbol **/**.

    b. Integer mod with the symbol **%**.

    c. Integer exponentiation with the symbol **^**. (Warning: This operator has higher precedence than multiplication and is right associative.)

    d. Unary minus with the symbol **-**. (See Exercise 3.12.)

5.29 Redo the Yacc calculator specification of Figure 5.10 so that the calculator will accept floating-point numbers (and perform floating-point calculations).

5.30 Rewrite the Yacc calculator specification of Figure 5.10 so that it *distinguishes* between floating-point and integer values, rather than simply computing everything as integers or floating-point numbers. (Hint: A "value" is now a record with a flag indicating whether it is integer or floating point.)

5.31 **a.** Rewrite Yacc calculator specification of Figure 5.10 so that it returns a syntax tree according to the declarations of Section 3.3.2.

    b. Write a function that takes as a parameter the syntax tree produced by your code of part (a) and returns the calculated value by traversing the tree.

5.32 The simple error recovery technique suggested for the calculator program on page 248 was flawed in that it could cause stack overflow after many errors. Rewrite it to remove this problem.

5.33 Rewrite the Yacc calculator specification of Figure 5.10 to add the following useful error messages:

        "missing right parenthesis," generated by the string **(2+3**

        "missing left parenthesis," generated by the string **2+3)**

        "missing operator," generated by the string **2   3**

        "missing operand," generated by the string **(2+)**

5.34 The following grammar represents simple arithmetic expressions in a LISP-like prefix notation:

$$lexp \rightarrow \textbf{number} \mid (\; op \; lexp\text{-}seq \;)$$
$$op \rightarrow \textbf{+} \mid \textbf{-} \mid \textbf{*}$$
$$lexp\text{-}seq \rightarrow lexp\text{-}seq \; lexp \mid lexp$$

For example, the expression **(* (-2) 3 4)** has value -24. Write a Yacc specification for a program that will compute and print the value of expressions in this syntax. (Hint: This will require rewriting the grammar, as well as the use of a mechanism for passing the operator to an *lexp-seq*.)

5.35 The following (ambiguous) grammar represents the simple regular expressions discussed in Chapter 2:

$$rexp \rightarrow rexp \text{ "}|\text{" } rexp$$
$$\mid rexp \; rexp$$
$$\mid rexp \text{ "}*\text{"}$$
$$\mid \text{ "}(\text{" } rexp \text{ "}) \text{"}$$
$$\mid \textbf{letter}$$

a. Write a skeleton Yacc specification (i.e., without actions) that expresses the correct associativity and precedence of the operations.

b. Extend your specification of part (a) to include all actions and auxiliary procedures needed to produce a "regular expression compiler," that is, a program that will take a regular expression as input and output a C program that, when compiled, will search an input string for the first occurrence of a substring that matches the regular expression. (Hint: A table, or two-dimensional array, can be used to represent the states and transitions of the associated NFA. The NFA can then be simulated using a queue to store states. Only the table needs to be generated by the Yacc actions; the rest of the code will be always the same. See Chapter 2.)

5.36 Rewrite the Yacc specification for TINY (Appendix B, lines 4000–4162) in a more compact form

a. by using an ambiguous grammar for expressions (with Yacc disambiguating rules for precedence and associativity), and

b. by collapsing the recognition of operators into a single rule, as in

$$exp \rightarrow exp \; op \; exp \mid \dots$$
$$op \rightarrow \textbf{+} \mid \textbf{-} \mid \dots$$

and by using the **%union** Yacc declaration (allowing *op* to return the operator, while *exp* and other nonterminals return pointers to tree nodes). Make sure your parser produces the same syntax trees as before.

5.37 Add the comparison operators **<=** (less than or equal to), **>** (greater than), **>=** (greater than or equal to), and **<>** (not equal to) to the Yacc specification for the TINY parser. (This will require adding these tokens and changing the scanner as well, but should not require a change to the syntax tree.)

5.38 Add the Boolean operators **and**, **or**, and **not** to the Yacc specification for the TINY parser. Give them the properties described in Exercise 3.5, as well as lower precedence than all arithmetic operators. Make sure any expression can be either Boolean or integer.

5.39 Rewrite the Yacc specification for the TINY parser to improve its error recovery.

NOTES AND REFERENCES

General LR parsing was invented by Knuth [1965], but it was thought to be impractical until the SLR and LALR techniques were developed by DeRemer [1969, 1971]. We have echoed the conventional wisdom that LR(1) parsers are too complicated for practical use. In fact it is possible to build practical LR(1) parsers using more delicate state merging techniques than those of LALR(1) parsing [Pager, 1977]. Nevertheless, the added power is rarely needed. A thorough study of the theory of LR parsing techniques can be found in Aho and Ullman [1972].

Yacc was developed by Steve Johnson at AT&T Bell Labs in the mid-1970s and is included in most Unix implementations [Johnson, 1975]. It was used to develop the portable C compiler [Johnson, 1978] and many other compilers. Bison was developed by Richard Stallman and others; Gnu Bison is a part of the Gnu software distribution of the Free Software Foundation and is available from many Internet sites. An example of the use of Yacc to develop a powerful, yet compact, calculator program is given in Kernighan and Pike [1984]. An in-depth study of the use of Yacc can be found in Schreiner and Friedman [1985].

LR error recovery techniques are studied in Graham, Haley, and Joy [1979]; Penello and DeRemer [1978]; and Burke and Fisher [1987]. An LR error repair technique is described in Fischer and LeBlanc [1991]. The basic ideas of the panic mode technique described in Section 5.7.2 are attributed by Fischer and LeBlanc to James [1972].

Chapter 6

———

Semantic Analysis

———

———

In this chapter we investigate the phase of the compiler that computes additional information needed for compilation once the syntactic structure of a program is known. This phase is referred to as semantic analysis because it involves computing information that is beyond the capabilities of context-free grammars and standard parsing algorithms and, therefore, is not regarded as syntax.[1] The information computed is also closely related to the eventual meaning, or semantics, of the program being translated. Since the analysis performed by a compiler is by definition static (it takes place prior to execution), such semantic analysis is also called **static semantic analysis**. In a typical statically typed language such as C, semantic analysis involves building a symbol table to keep track of the meanings of names established in declarations and performing type inference and type checking on expressions and statements to determine their correctness within the type rules of the language.

Semantic analysis can be divided into two categories. The first is the analysis of a program required by the rules of the programming language to establish its correctness and to guarantee proper execution. The amount of such analysis required by a language definition varies tremendously from language to language. In dynamically oriented languages such as LISP and Smalltalk, there may be no static semantic analysis at all, while in a language such as Ada there are strong requirements that a program must meet to be executable. Other languages fall in between these extremes (Pascal, for instance, being not quite as strict in its static requirements as Ada and C being not quite as permissive as LISP).

———

1. This point was discussed in some detail in Section 3.6.3 of Chapter 3.

The second category of semantic analysis is the analysis performed by a compiler to enhance the efficiency of execution of the translated program. This kind of analysis is usually included in discussions of "optimization," or code improving techniques. We will survey some of these methods in the chapter on code generation, while in this chapter we focus on the common analyses that are required by a language definition for correctness. It should be noted that the techniques studied here apply to both situations. Also, the two categories are not mutually exclusive, since correctness requirements, such as static type checking, also allow a compiler to generate more efficient code than for a language without these requirements. In addition, it is worth noting that the correctness requirements discussed here can never establish the complete correctness of a program, but only a kind of partial correctness. Such requirements are still useful in that they provide the programmer with information to improve the security and robustness of the program.

Static semantic analysis involves both the **description** of the analyses to perform and the **implementation** of the analyses using appropriate algorithms. In this, it is similar to lexical and syntactic analysis. In syntactic analysis, for example, we used context-free grammars in Backus-Naus Form (BNF) to describe the syntax and various top-down and bottom-up parsing algorithms to implement the syntax. In semantic analysis, the situation is not as clear, partially because there is no standard method (like BNF) used to specify the static semantics of a language and partially because the amount and kind of static semantic analysis varies so widely from language to language. One method of describing semantic analysis that is frequently used to good effect by compiler writers is to identify **attributes**, or properties, of language entities that must be computed and to write **attribute equations**, or **semantic rules**, that express how the computation of such attributes is related to the grammar rules of the language. Such a set of attributes and equations is called an **attribute grammar**. Attribute grammars are most useful for languages that obey the principle of **syntax-directed semantics**, which asserts that the semantic content of a program is closely related to its syntax. All modern languages have this property. Unfortunately, the compiler writer must usually construct an attribute grammar by hand from the language manual, since it is rarely given by the language designer. Worse yet, the construction of an attribute grammar may be made unnecessarily complicated by its very adherence to the explicit syntactic structure of the language. A much better basis for the expression of semantic computations is the abstract syntax, as represented by an abstract syntax tree. Yet the specification of the abstract syntax is also usually left to the compiler writer by the language designer.

Algorithms for the implementation of semantic analysis are also not as clearly expressible as parsing algorithms. Again, this is partially due to the same problems that were just mentioned regarding the specification of semantic analysis. There is, however, an additional problem caused by the timing of the analysis during the compilation process. If semantic analysis can be suspended until all the syntactic analysis (and the construction of an abstract syntax tree) is complete, then the task of implementing semantic analysis is made considerably easier and consists essentially of specifying an order for a traversal of the syntax tree, together with the computations to be performed each time a node is encountered in the traversal. This, however, implies that the compiler must be multipass. If, on the other hand, it is necessary for the compiler to perform all its operations in a single pass (including code generation), then the implementation of semantic analysis becomes much more an ad hoc process of finding a correct order and method for computing semantic information (assuming such a correct order actually exists). Fortunately, modern practice increasingly permits the compiler writer to use multiple passes to simplify the processes of semantic analysis and code generation.

Despite this somewhat disorderly state of semantic analysis, it is extremely useful to study attribute grammars and specification issues, since this will pay off in an ability to write clearer, more concise, less error-prone code for semantic analysis, as well as permit an easier understanding of that code.

The chapter begins, therefore, with a study of attributes and attribute grammars. It continues with techniques for implementing the computations specified by an attribute grammar, including the inferring of an order for the computations and accompanying tree traversals. Two subsequent sections concentrate on the major areas of semantic analysis: symbol tables and type checking. The last section describes a semantic analyzer for the TINY programming language introduced in previous chapters.

Unlike previous chapters, this chapter contains no description of a **semantic analyzer generator** or general tool for constructing semantic analyzers. Though a number of such tools have been constructed, none has achieved the wide use and availability of Lex or Yacc. In the Notes and References section at the end of the chapter, we mention a few of these tools and provide references to the literature for the interested reader.

6.1 ATTRIBUTES AND ATTRIBUTE GRAMMARS

An **attribute** is any property of a programming language construct. Attributes can vary widely in the information they contain, their complexity, and particularly the time during the translation/execution process when they can be determined. Typical examples of attributes are

- The data type of a variable
- The value of an expression
- The location of a variable in memory
- The object code of a procedure
- The number of significant digits in a number

Attributes may be fixed prior to the compilation process (or even the construction of a compiler). For instance, the number of significant digits in a number may be fixed (or at least given a minimum value) by the definition of a language. Also, attributes may be only determinable during program execution, such as the value of a (nonconstant) expression, or the location of a dynamically allocated data structure. The process of computing an attribute and associating its computed value with the language construct in question is referred to as the **binding** of the attribute. The time during the compilation/execution process when the binding of an attribute occurs is called its **binding time**. Binding times of different attributes vary, and even the same attribute can have quite different binding times from language to language. Attributes that can be bound prior to execution are called **static**, while attributes that can only be bound during execution are **dynamic**. A compiler writer is, of course, interested in those static attributes that are bound at translation time.

Consider the previously given sample list of attributes. We discuss the binding time and significance during compilation of each of the attributes in the list.

- In a statically typed language like C or Pascal, the data type of a variable or expression is an important compile-time attribute. A **type checker** is a semantic analyzer that computes the data type attribute of all language entities for which data types are defined and verifies that these types conform to the type rules of the language. In a language like C or Pascal, a type checker is an important part of semantic analysis. In a language like LISP, however, data types are dynamic, and a LISP compiler must generate code to compute types and perform type checking during program execution.
- The values of expressions are usually dynamic, and a compiler will generate code to compute their values during execution. However, some expressions may, in fact, be constant (3 + 4 * 5, for example), and a semantic analyzer may choose to evaluate them during compilation (this process is called **constant folding**).
- The allocation of a variable may be either static or dynamic, depending on the language and the properties of the variable itself. For example, in FORTRAN77 all variables are allocated statically, while in LISP all variables are allocated dynamically. C and Pascal have a mixture of static and dynamic variable allocation. A compiler will usually put off computations associated with allocation of variables until code generation, since such computations depend on the runtime environment and, occasionally, on the details of the target machine. (The next chapter treats this in more detail.)
- The object code of a procedure is clearly a static attribute. The code generator of a compiler is wholly concerned with the computation of this attribute.
- The number of significant digits in a number is an attribute that is often not explicitly treated during compilation. It is implicit in the way the compiler writer implements representations for values, and this is usually considered as part of the runtime environment, discussed in the next chapter. However, even the scanner may need to know the number of allowable significant digits if it is to translate constants correctly.

As we see from these examples, attribute computations are extremely varied. When they appear explicitly in a compiler, they may occur at any time during compilation: even though we associate attribute computation most strongly with the semantic analysis phase, both the scanner and the parser may need to have attribute information available to them, and some semantic analysis may need to be performed at the same time as parsing. In this chapter, we focus on typical computations that occur prior to code generation and after parsing (but see Section 6.2.5 for information on semantic analysis during parsing). Attribute analysis that directly applies to code generation will be discussed in Chapter 8.

6.1.1 Attribute Grammars

In **syntax-directed semantics**, attributes are associated directly with the grammar symbols of the language (the terminals and nonterminals).[2] If X is a grammar symbol, and a is an attribute associated to X, then we write $X.a$ for the value of a associated to X. This notation is reminiscent of a record field designator of Pascal or (equivalently) a structure member operation of C. Indeed, a typical way of implementing attribute calculations is to put attribute values into the nodes of a syntax tree using record fields (or structure members). We will see this in more detail in the next section.

Given a collection of attributes $a_1, \ldots, a_k$, the principle of syntax-directed semantics implies that for each grammar rule $X_0 \to X_1 X_2 \ldots X_n$ (where X_0 is a nonterminal and the other X_i are arbitrary symbols), the values of the attributes $X_i.a_j$ of each grammar symbol X_i are related to the values of the attributes of the other symbols in the rule. Should the same symbol X_i appear more than once in the grammar rule, then each occurrence must be distinguished from the other occurrences by suitable subscripting, so that the attribute values of different occurrences may be distinguished. Each relationship is specified by an **attribute equation** or **semantic rule**[3] of the form

$$X_i.a_j = f_{ij}(X_0.a_1, \ldots, X_0.a_k, X_1.a_1, \ldots, X_1.a_k, \ldots, X_n.a_1, \ldots, X_n.a_k)$$

where f_{ij} is a mathematical function of its arguments. An **attribute grammar** for the attributes $a_1, \ldots, a_k$ is the collection of all such equations, for all the grammar rules of the language.

In this generality, attribute grammars may appear to be extremely complex. In practice the functions f_{ij} are usually quite simple. Also, it is rare for attributes to depend on large numbers of other attributes, and so attributes can be separated into small independent sets of interdependent attributes, and attribute grammars can be written separately for each set.

Typically, attribute grammars are written in tabular form, with each grammar rule listed with the set of attribute equations, or semantic rules associated to that rule, as follows:[4]

---

2. Syntax-directed semantics could just as easily be called **semantics-directed syntax**, since in most languages the syntax is designed with the (eventual) semantics of the construct already in mind.

3. In later work we will view semantic rules as being somewhat more general than attribute equations. For now, the reader can consider them to be identical.

4. We will always use the heading "semantic rules" in these tables instead of "attribute equations" to allow for a more general interpretation of semantic rules later on.

Grammar Rule	Semantic Rules
Rule 1	Associated attribute equations
.	.
.	.
.	.
Rule n	Associated attribute equations

We proceed immediately to several examples.

Example 6.1   Consider the following simple grammar for unsigned numbers:

$$number \rightarrow number\ digit \mid digit$$
$$digit \rightarrow 0 \mid 1 \mid 2 \mid 3 \mid 4 \mid 5 \mid 6 \mid 7 \mid 8 \mid 9$$

The most significant attribute of a number is its value, to which we give the name *val*. Each digit has a value which is directly computable from the actual digit it represents. Thus, for example, the grammar rule *digit* → **0** implies that *digit* has value 0 in this case. This can be expressed by the attribute equation $digit.val = 0$, and we associate this equation with the rule *digit* → **0**. Furthermore, each number has a value based on the digits it contains. If a number is derived using the rule

$$number \rightarrow digit$$

then the number contains just one digit, and its value is the value of this digit. The attribute equation that expresses this fact is

$$number.val = digit.val$$

If a number contains more than one digit, then it is derived using the grammar rule

$$number \rightarrow number\ digit$$

and we must express the relationship between the value of the symbol on the left-hand side of the grammar rule and the values of the symbols on the right-hand side. Note that the two occurrences of *number* in the grammar rule must be distinguished, since the *number* on the right will have a different value from that of the *number* on the left. We distinguish them by using subscripts, and we write the grammar rule as follows:

$$number_1 \rightarrow number_2\ digit$$

Now consider a number such as **34**. A (leftmost) derivation of this number is as follows: *number* $\Rightarrow$ *number digit* $\Rightarrow$ *digit digit* $\Rightarrow$ **3** *digit* $\Rightarrow$ **34**. Consider the use of the grammar rule $number_1 \rightarrow number_2\ digit$ in the first step of this derivation. The nonterminal $number_2$ corresponds to the digit **3**, while *digit* corresponds to the digit **4**. The values of each are 3 and 4, respectively. To obtain the value of $number_1$ (that is, 34), we must multiply the value of $number_2$ by 10 and add the value of *digit*: 34 = 3 * 10 + 4. In other words, we shift the 3 one decimal place to the left and add 4. This corresponds to the attribute equation

$$number_1\ .val = number_2\ .val * 10 + digit.val$$

A complete attribute grammar for the *val* attribute is given in Table 6.1.

The meaning of the attribute equations for a particular string can be visualized using the parse tree for the string. For example, the parse tree for the number **345** is given in Figure 6.1. In this figure the calculation corresponding to the appropriate attribute equation is shown below each interior node. Viewing the attribute equations as computations on the parse tree is important for algorithms to compute attribute values, as we shall see in the next section.[5]

In both Table 6.1 and Figure 6.1 we have emphasized the difference between the syntactic representation of a digit and the value, or semantic content, of the digit by using different fonts. For instance, in the grammar rule *digit* $\rightarrow$ **0**, the digit **0** is a token or character, while *digit.val* = 0 means that the digit has the numeric value 0.

Table 6.1

Attribute grammar for
Example 6.1

Grammar Rule	Semantic Rules
$number_1 \rightarrow$ $\quad number_2\ digit$	$number_1\ .val =$ $\quad number_2\ .val * 10 + digit.val$
$number \rightarrow digit$	$number.val = digit.val$
$digit \rightarrow$ **0**	$digit.val = 0$
$digit \rightarrow$ **1**	$digit.val = 1$
$digit \rightarrow$ **2**	$digit.val = 2$
$digit \rightarrow$ **3**	$digit.val = 3$
$digit \rightarrow$ **4**	$digit.val = 4$
$digit \rightarrow$ **5**	$digit.val = 5$
$digit \rightarrow$ **6**	$digit.val = 6$
$digit \rightarrow$ **7**	$digit.val = 7$
$digit \rightarrow$ **8**	$digit.val = 8$
$digit \rightarrow$ **9**	$digit.val = 9$

---

5. In fact, numbers are usually recognized as tokens by the scanner, and their numeric values are easily computed at the same time. In doing so, however, the scanner is likely to use implicitly the attribute equations specified here.

Figure 6.1
Parse tree showing
attribute computations for
Example 6.1

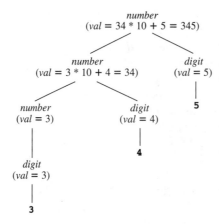

§

Example 6.2   Consider the following grammar for simple integer arithmetic expressions:

$$exp \rightarrow exp + term \mid exp - term \mid term$$
$$term \rightarrow term * factor \mid factor$$
$$factor \rightarrow (\, exp \,) \mid \mathbf{number}$$

This grammar is a slightly modified version of the simple expression grammar studied extensively in previous chapters. The principal attribute of an *exp* (or *term* or *factor*) is its numeric value, which we write as *val*. The attribute equations for the *val* attribute are given in Table 6.2.

Table 6.2

Attribute grammar for
Example 6.2

Grammar Rule	Semantic Rules
$exp_1 \rightarrow exp_2 + term$	$exp_1.val = exp_2.val + term.val$
$exp_1 \rightarrow exp_2 - term$	$exp_1.val = exp_2.val - term.val$
$exp \rightarrow term$	$exp.val = term.val$
$term_1 \rightarrow term_2 * factor$	$term_1.val = term_2.val * factor.val$
$term \rightarrow factor$	$term.val = factor.val$
$factor \rightarrow (\, exp \,)$	$factor.val = exp.val$
$factor \rightarrow \mathbf{number}$	$factor.val = \mathbf{number}.val$

These equations express the relationship between the syntax of the expressions and the semantics of the arithmetic computations to be performed. Note, for example, the difference between the syntactic symbol + (a token) in the grammar rule

$$exp_1 \rightarrow exp_2 + term$$

and the arithmetic addition operation + to be performed in the equation

$$exp_1.val = exp_2.val + term.val$$

Note also that there is no equation with **number**.*val* on the left-hand side. As we shall see in the next section, this implies that **number**.*val* must be computed prior to any semantic analysis that uses this attribute grammar (e.g., by the scanner). Alternatively, if we want this value to be explicit in the attribute grammar, we must add grammar rules and attribute equations to the attribute grammar (for instance, the equations of Example 6.1).

We can also express the computations implied by this attribute grammar by attaching equations to nodes in a parse tree, as in Example 6.1. For instance, given the expression **(34-3)*42**, we can express the semantics of its value on its parse tree as in Figure 6.2. §

Figure 6.2

Parse tree for **(34-3)*42** showing *val* attribute computations for the attribute grammar of Example 6.2

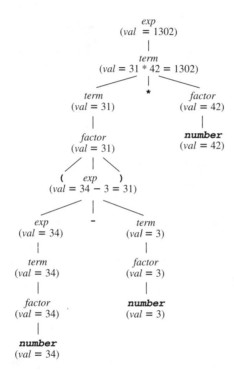

Example 6.3

Consider the following simple grammar of variable declarations in a C-like syntax:

$$decl \rightarrow type \; var\text{-}list$$
$$type \rightarrow \textbf{int} \mid \textbf{float}$$
$$var\text{-}list \rightarrow \textbf{id}, var\text{-}list \mid \textbf{id}$$

We want to define a data type attribute for the variables given by the identifiers in a declaration and write equations expressing how the data type attribute is related to the type of the declaration. We do this by constructing an attribute grammar for a *dtype* attribute (we use the name *dtype* to distinguish the attribute from the nonterminal *type*). The attribute grammar for *dtype* is given in Table 6.3. We make the following remarks about the attribute equations in that figure.

First, the values of *dtype* are from the set {*integer*, *real*}, corresponding to the tokens **int** and **float**. The nonterminal *type* has a *dtype* given by the token it represents. This *dtype* corresponds to the *dtype* of the entire *var-list*, by the equation associated to the grammar rule for *decl*. Each **id** in the list has this same *dtype*, by the equations associated to *var-list*. Note that there is no equation involving the *dtype* of the nonterminal *decl*. Indeed, a *decl* need not have a *dtype*—it is not necessary for the value of an attribute to be specified for all grammar symbols.

As before, the attribute equations can be displayed on a parse tree. An example is given in Figure 6.3.   §

Table 6.3

Attribute grammar for Example 6.3

Grammar Rule	Semantic Rules
decl → *type var-list*	*var-list.dtype* = *type.dtype*
type → **int**	*type.dtype* = *integer*
type → **float**	*type.dtype* = *real*
var-list$_1$ → **id,** *var-list$_2$*	**id** *.dtype* = *var-list$_1$.dtype*
	var-list$_2$.dtype = *var-list$_1$.dtype*
var-list → **id**	**id** *.dtype* = *var-list.dtype*

Figure 6.3

Parse tree for the string **float x,y** showing the *dtype* attribute as specified by the attribute grammar of Table 6.3.

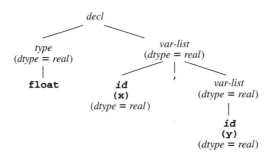

In the examples so far, there was only one attribute. Attribute grammars may involve several interdependent attributes. The next example is a simple situation where there are interdependent attributes.

Example 6.4

Consider a modification of the number grammar of Example 6.1, where numbers may be octal or decimal. Suppose this is indicated by a one-character suffix **o** (for octal) or **d** (for decimal). Then we have the following grammar:

$$based\text{-}num \rightarrow num\ basechar$$
$$basechar \rightarrow \textbf{o} \mid \textbf{d}$$
$$num \rightarrow num\ digit \mid digit$$
$$digit \rightarrow \textbf{0} \mid \textbf{1} \mid \textbf{2} \mid \textbf{3} \mid \textbf{4} \mid \textbf{5} \mid \textbf{6} \mid \textbf{7} \mid \textbf{8} \mid \textbf{9}$$

In this case *num* and *digit* require a new attribute *base*, which is used to compute the *val* attribute. The attribute grammar for *base* and *val* is given in Table 6.4.

Table 6.4

Attribute grammar for Example 6.4

Grammar Rule	Semantic Rules
based-num → *num basechar*	*based-num.val = num.val* *num.base = basechar.base*
basechar → **o**	*basechar.base* = 8
basechar → **d**	*basechar.base* = 10
$num_1 \rightarrow num_2\ digit$	num_1 *.val =* **if** *digit.val = error* **or** num_2 *.val = error* **then** *error* **else** num_2 *.val* * num_1 *.base + digit.val* num_2 *.base =* num_1 *.base* *digit.base =* num_1 *.base*
num → *digit*	*num.val = digit.val* *digit.base = num.base*
digit → **0**	*digit.val* = 0
digit → **1**	*digit.val* = 1
. . .	. . .
digit → **7**	*digit.val* = 7
digit → **8**	*digit.val =* **if** *digit.base* = 8 **then** *error* **else** 8
digit → **9**	*digit.val =* **if** *digit.base* = 8 **then** *error* **else** 9

Two new features should be noted in this attribute grammar. First, the BNF grammar does not itself eliminate the erroneous combination of the (non-octal) digits **8** and **9** with the **o** suffix. For instance, the string **189o** is syntactically correct according to the above BNF, but cannot be assigned any value. Thus, a new *error* value is needed for such cases. Additionally, the attribute grammar must express the fact that the inclusion of **8** or **9** in a number with an **o** suffix results in an *error* value. The easiest way to do this is to use an **if-then-else** expression in the functions of the appropriate attribute equations. For instance, the equation

$$num_1\ .val =$$
$$\textbf{if } digit.val = error \textbf{ or } num_2\ .val = error$$
$$\textbf{then } error$$
$$\textbf{else } num_2\ .val * num_1\ .base + digit.val$$

corresponding to the grammar rule $num_1 \rightarrow num_2\ digit$ expresses the fact that if either of num_2 *.val* or *digit.val* are *error* then num_1 *.val* must also be *error*, and only if that is not the case is num_1 *.val* given by the formula num_2 *.val* * num_1 *.base + digit.val*.

To conclude this example, we again show the attribute calculations on a parse tree. Figure 6.4 gives a parse tree for the number **345o**, together with the attribute values computed according to the attribute grammar of Table 6.4.

Figure 6.4

Parse tree showing attribute computations for Example 6.4

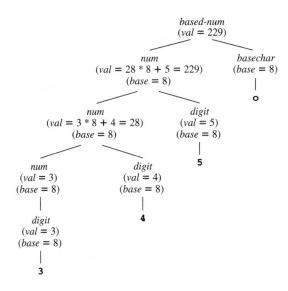

§

6.1.2   Simplifications and Extensions to Attribute Grammars

The use of an **if-then-else** expression extends the kinds of expressions that can appear in an attribute equation in a useful way. The collection of expressions allowable in an attribute equation is called the **metalanguage** for the attribute grammar. Usually we want a metalanguage whose meaning is clear enough that confusion over its own semantics does not arise. We also want a metalanguage that is close to an actual programming language, since, as we shall see shortly, we want to turn the attribute equations into working code in a semantic analyzer. In this book we use a metalanguage that is limited to arithmetic, logical, and a few other kinds of expressions, together with an **if-then-else** expression, and occassionally a **case** or **switch** expression.

An additional feature useful in specifying attribute equations is to add to the metalanguage the use of functions whose definitions may be given elsewhere. For instance, in the grammars for numbers we have been writing out attribute equations for each of the choices of *digit*. Instead, we could adopt a more concise convention by writing the grammar rule for *digit* as *digit* → **D** (where **D** is understood to be one of the digits) and then writing the corresponding attribute equation as

$$digit.val = numval(\mathbf{D})$$

Here *numval* is a function whose definition must be specified elsewhere as a supplement to the attribute grammar. For instance, we might give the following definition of *numval* as C code:

```
int numval(char D)
{ return (int)D - (int)'0';}
```

A further simplification that can be useful in specifying attribute grammars is to use an ambiguous, but simpler, form of the original grammar. In fact, since the parser is assumed to have already been constructed, all ambiguity will have been dealt with at that stage, and the attribute grammar can be freely based on ambiguous constructs, without implying any ambiguity in the resulting attributes. For instance, the arithmetic expression grammar of Example 6.2 has the following simpler, but ambiguous, form:

$$exp \rightarrow exp + exp \mid exp - exp \mid exp * exp \mid (\ exp\ ) \mid \textbf{number}$$

Using this grammar, the *val* attribute can be defined by the table in Table 6.5 (compare this with Table 6.2).

Table 6.5

Defining the *val* attribute for an expression using an ambiguous grammar

Grammar Rule	Semantic Rules
$exp_1 \rightarrow exp_2 + exp_3$	$exp_1 .val = exp_2 .val + exp_3 .val$
$exp_1 \rightarrow exp_2 - exp_3$	$exp_1 .val = exp_2 .val - exp_3 .val$
$exp_1 \rightarrow exp_2 * exp_3$	$exp_1 .val = exp_2 .val * exp_3 .val$
$exp_1 \rightarrow (\ exp_2\ )$	$exp_1 .val = exp_2 .val$
$exp \rightarrow \textbf{number}$	$exp.val = \textbf{number}.val$

A simplification can also be made in displaying attribute values by using an abstract syntax tree instead of a parse tree. An abstract syntax tree must always have enough structure so that the semantics defined by an attribute grammar can be expressed. For instance, the expression **(34-3)*42**, whose parse tree and *val* attributes were shown in Figure 6.2, can have its semantics completely expressed by the abstract syntax tree of Figure 6.5.

It is not surprising that the syntax tree itself can be specified by an attribute grammar as the next example shows.

Figure 6.5

Abstract syntax tree for **(34-3)*42** showing *val* attribute computations for the attribute grammar of Table 6.2 or Table 6.5.

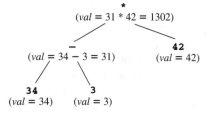

Example 6.5   Given the grammar for simple integer arithmetic expressions of Example 6.2 (page 264), we can define an abstract syntax tree for expressions by the attribute grammar given in Table 6.6. In this attribute grammar we have used two auxiliary functions *mkOpNode* and *mkNumNode*. The *mkOpNode* function takes three parameters (an operator token and two syntax trees) and constructs a new tree node whose operator label is the first parameter, and whose children are the second and third parameters. The *mkNumNode* function takes one parameter (a numeric value) and constructs a leaf node

representing a number with that value. In Table 6.6 we have written the numeric value as **number**.*lexval* to indicate that it is constructed by the scanner. In fact, this could be the actual numeric value of the number, or its string representation, depending on the implementation. (Compare the equations in Table 6.6 with the recursive descent construction of the TINY syntax tree in Appendix B.)

Table 6.6

Attribute grammar for abstract syntax trees of simple integer arithmetic expressions

Grammar Rule	Semantic Rules
$exp_1 \rightarrow exp_2$ **+** *term*	exp_1 .*tree* = $mkOpNode$ (**+**, exp_2 .*tree*, *term.tree*)
$exp_1 \rightarrow exp_2$ **-** *term*	exp_1 .*tree* = $mkOpNode$(**-**, exp_2 .*tree*, *term.tree*)
$exp \rightarrow term$	$exp.tree = term.tree$
$term_1 \rightarrow term_2$ ***** *factor*	$term_1$.*tree* = $mkOpNode$(*****, $term_2$.*tree*, *factor.tree*)
$term \rightarrow factor$	$term.tree = factor.tree$
$factor \rightarrow$ **(** exp **)**	$factor.tree = exp.tree$
$factor \rightarrow$ **number**	$factor.tree = mkNumNode($**number**.*lexval*$)$

§

One question that is central to the specification of attributes using attribute grammars is: How can we be sure that a particular attribute grammar is consistent and complete, that is, that it uniquely defines the given attributes? The simple answer is that so far we cannot. This is a question similar to that of determining whether a grammar is ambiguous. In practice, it is the parsing algorithms that we use that determine the adequacy of a grammar, and a similar situation occurs in the case of attribute grammars. Thus, the algorithmic methods for computing attributes that we study in the next section will determine whether an attribute grammar is adequate to define the attribute values.

6.2 ALGORITHMS FOR ATTRIBUTE COMPUTATION

In this section we study the ways an attribute grammar can be used as a basis for a compiler to compute and use the attributes defined by the equations of the attribute grammar. Basically, this amounts to turning the attribute equations into computation rules. Thus, the attribute equation

$$X_i.a_j = f_{ij}(X_0.a_1, \ldots, X_0.a_k, X_1.a_1, \ldots, X_1.a_k, \ldots, X_n.a_1, \ldots, X_n.a_k)$$

is viewed as an assignment of the value of the functional expression on the right-hand side to the attribute $X_i.a_j$. For this to succeed, the values of all the attributes that appear on the right-hand side must already exist. This requirement can be ignored in the specification of attribute grammars, where the equations can be written in arbitrary order without affecting their validity. The problem of implementing an algorithm corresponding to an attribute grammar consists primarily in finding an order for the evaluation and assignment of attributes that ensures that all attribute values used in each computation are available when each computation is performed. The attribute equations themselves indicate the order constraints on the computation of the attributes, and the first task is to make the order constraints explicit by using directed graphs to represent these constraints. These directed graphs are called dependency graphs.

6.2.1   Dependency Graphs and Evaluation Order

Given an attribute grammar, each grammar rule choice has an **associated dependency graph**. This graph has a node labeled by each attribute $X_i.a_j$ of each symbol in the grammar rule, and for each attribute equation

$$X_i.a_j = f_{ij}(\dots , X_m.a_k, \dots)$$

associated to the grammar rule there is an edge from each node $X_m.a_k$ in the right-hand side to the node $X_i.a_j$ (expressing the dependency of $X_i.a_j$ on $X_m.a_k$). Given a legal string in the language generated by the context-free grammar, the **dependency graph** of the string is the union of the dependency graphs of the grammar rule choices representing each (nonleaf) node of the parse tree of the string.

In drawing the dependency graph for each grammar rule or string, the nodes associated to each symbol X are drawn in a group, so that the dependencies can be viewed as structured around a parse tree.

Example 6.6   Consider the grammar of Example 6.1, with the attribute grammar as given in Table 6.1. There is only one attribute, *val*, so for each symbol there is only one node in each dependency graph, corresponding to its *val* attribute. The grammar rule choice $number_1$ $\rightarrow number_2$ *digit* has the single associated attribute equation

$$number_1 .val = number_2 .val * 10 + digit.val$$

The dependency graph for this grammar rule choice is

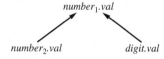

(In future dependency graphs, we will omit the subscripts for repeated symbols, since the graphical representation clearly distinguishes the different occurrences as different nodes.)

Similarly, the dependency graph for the grammar rule *number* $\rightarrow$ *digit* with the attribute equation *number.val* = *digit.val* is

$$number.val$$
$$\uparrow$$
$$digit.val$$

For the remaining grammar rules of the form *digit* → **D** the dependency graphs are trivial (there are no edges), since *digit.val* is computed directly from the right-hand side of the rule.

Finally, the string **345** has the following dependency graph corresponding to its parse tree (see Figure 6.1):

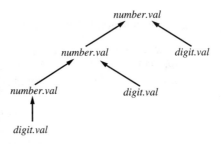

§

Example 6.7   Consider the grammar of Example 6.3, with the attribute grammar for the attribute *dtype* given in Table 6.3. In this example the grammar rule *var-list₁* → **id,** *var-list₂* has the two associated attribute equations

$$id\ dtype = var\text{-}list_1.dtype$$
$$var\text{-}list_2.dtype = var\text{-}list_1.dtype$$

and the dependency graph

Similarly, the grammar rule *var-list* → **id** has the dependency graph

The two rules *type* → **int** and *type* → **float** have trivial dependency graphs.

Finally, the rule *decl* → *type var-list* with the associated equation *var-list.dtype* = *type.dtype* has the dependency graph

$$type.dtype \quad \longrightarrow \quad var\text{-}list.dtype$$

In this case, since *decl* is not directly involved in the dependency graph, it is not completely clear which grammar rule has this graph associated to it. For this reason (and a few other reasons that we discuss later), we often draw the dependency graph superimposed over a parse tree segment corresponding to the grammar rule. Thus, the above dependency graph can be drawn as

and this makes clearer the grammar rule to which the dependency is associated. Note, too, that when we draw the parse tree nodes we suppress the dot notation for the attributes, and represent the attributes of each node by writing them next to their associated node. Thus, the first dependency graph in this example can also be written as

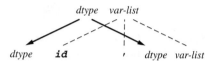

Finally, the dependency graph for the string **float x,y** is

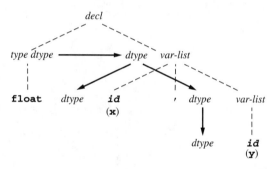

§

Example 6.8   Consider the grammar of based numbers of Example 6.4, with the attribute grammar for the attributes *base* and *val* as given in Table 6.4. We will draw the dependency graphs for the four grammar rules

$$based\text{-}num \rightarrow num\ basechar$$
$$num \rightarrow num\ digit$$
$$num \rightarrow digit$$
$$digit \rightarrow 9$$

and for the string **345o**, whose parse tree is given in Figure 6.4.

   We begin with the dependency graph for the grammar rule *based-num* → *num basechar*:

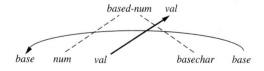

This graph expresses the dependencies of the two associated equations *based-num.val* = *num.val* and *num.base* = *basechar.base*.

Next we draw the dependency graph corresponding to the grammar rule *num* → *num digit*:

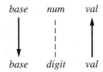

This graph expresses the dependencies of the three attribute equations

num_1 .*val* =
     if *digit.val* = *error* **or** num_2 .*val* = *error*
     then *error*
     else num_2 .*val* * num_1 .*base* + *digit.val*
num_2 .*base* = num_1 .*base*
digit.base = num_1 .*base*

The dependency graph for the grammar rule *num* → *digit* is similar:

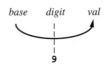

Finally, we draw the dependency graph for the grammar rule *digit* → **9**:

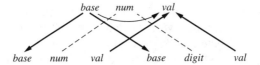

This graph expresses the dependency created by the equation *digit.val* = **if** *digit.base* = 8 **then** *error* **else** 9, namely, that *digit.val* depends on *digit.base* (it is part of the test in the **if**-expression). It remains to draw the dependency graph for the string **345o**. This is done in Figure 6.6.

Figure 6.6

Dependency graph for the string **345o** (Example 6.8)

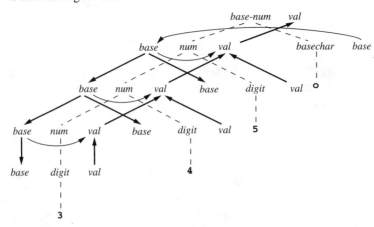

§

Suppose now that we wish to determine an algorithm that computes the attributes of an attribute grammar using the attribute equations as computation rules. Given a particular string of tokens to be translated, the dependency graph of the parse tree of the string gives a set of order constraints under which the algorithm must operate to compute the attributes for that string. Indeed, any algorithm must compute the attribute at each node in the dependency graph *before* it attempts to compute any successor attributes. A traversal order of the dependency graph that obeys this restriction is called a **topological sort**, and a well-known necessary and sufficient condition for a topological sort to exist is that the graph must be **acyclic**. Such graphs are called **directed acyclic graphs**, or **DAGs**.

Example 6.9

The dependency graph of Figure 6.6 is a DAG. In Figure 6.7 we number the nodes of the graph (and erase the underlying parse tree for ease of visualization). One topological sort is given by the node order in which the nodes are numbered. Another topological sort is given by the order

12 6 9 1 2 11 3 8 4 5 7 10 13 14

Figure 6.7

Dependency graph for the string **3450** (Example 6.9)

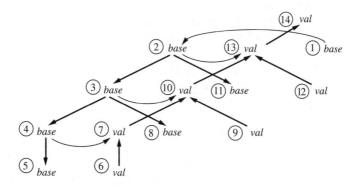

§

One question that arises in the use of a topological sort of the dependency graph to compute attribute values is how attribute values are found at the roots of the graph (a **root** of a graph is a node that has no predecessors). In Figure 6.7, nodes 1, 6, 9, and 12 are all roots of the graph.[6] Attribute values at these nodes do not depend on any other attribute, and so must be computed using information that is directly available. This information is often in the form of tokens that are children of the corresponding parse tree nodes. In Figure 6.7, for instance, the *val* of node 6 depends on the token **3** that is the child of the *digit* node that *val* corresponds to (see Figure 6.6). Thus, the attribute value at node 6 is 3. All such root values need to be computable prior to the computation of any other attribute values. Such computations are frequently performed by the scanner or the parser.

---

6. A root of the dependency graph should not be confused with the root of the parse tree.

It is possible to base an algorithm for attribute analysis on a construction of the dependency graph during compilation and a subsequent topological sort of the dependency graph to determine an order for the evaluation of the attributes. Since the construction of the dependency graph is based on the specific parse tree at compile time, this method is sometimes called a **parse tree method**. It is capable of evaluating the attributes in any attribute grammar that is **noncircular**, that is, an attribute grammar for which *every* possible dependency graph is acyclic.

There are several problems with this method. First, there is the added complexity required by the compile-time construction of the dependency graph. Second, while this method can determine whether a dependency graph is acyclic at compile time, it is generally inadequate to wait until compile time to discover a circularity, since a circularity almost certainly represents an error in the original attribute grammar. Instead, an attribute grammar should be tested in advance for noncircularity. There is an algorithm to do this (see the Notes and References section), but it is an exponential-time algorithm. Of course, this algorithm only needs to be run once, at compiler construction time, so this is not an overwhelming argument against it (at least for the purposes of compiler construction). The complexity of this approach is a more compelling argument.

The alternative to the above approach to attribute evaluation, and one adopted by practically every compiler, is for the compiler writer to analyze the attribute grammar and fix an order for attribute evaluation at compiler construction time. Although this method still uses the parse tree as a guide for attribute evaluation, the method is referred to as a **rule-based method**, since it depends on an analysis of the attribute equations, or semantic rules. Attribute grammars for which an attribute evaluation order can be fixed at compiler construction time form a class that is less general than the class of all noncircular attribute grammars, but in practice all reasonable attribute grammars have this property. They are sometimes called **strongly noncircular** attribute grammars. We proceed to a discussion of rule-based algorithms for this class of attribute grammars, after the following example.

Example 6.10

Consider again the dependency graphs of Example 6.8 and the topological sorts of the dependency graph discussed in Example 6.9 (see Figure 6.7). Even though nodes 6, 9, and 12 of Figure 6.7 are roots of the DAG, and thus all could occur at the beginning of a topological sort, in a rule-based method this is not possible. The reason is that any *val* might depend on the *base* of its associated *digit* node, if the corresponding token is **8** or **9**. For example, the dependency graph for *digit* → **9** is

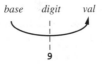

Thus, in Figure 6.7, node 6 might have depended on node 5, node 9 might have depended on node 8, and node 12 might have depended on node 11. In a rule-based method, these nodes would be constrained to be evaluated after any nodes that they

might potentially depend on. Therefore, an evaluation order that, say, evaluates node 12 first (see Example 6.9), while correct for the particular tree of Figure 6.7, is not a valid order for a rule-based algorithm, since it would violate the order for other parse trees.

§

6.2.2   Synthesized and Inherited Attributes

Rule-based attribute evaluation depends on an explicit or implicit traversal of the parse or syntax tree. Different kinds of traversals vary in power in terms of the kinds of attribute dependencies that can be handled. To study the differences, we must first classify attributes by the kinds of dependencies they exhibit. The simplest kind of dependency to handle is that of synthesized attributes, defined next.

Definition

An attribute is **synthesized** if all its dependencies point from child to parent in the parse tree. Equivalently, an attribute a is synthesized if, given a grammar rule $A \to X_1 X_2 \ldots X_n$, the only associated attribute equation with an a on the left-hand side is of the form

$$A.a = f(X_1.a_1, \ldots, X_1.a_k, \ldots, X_n.a_1, \ldots, X_n.a_k)$$

An attribute grammar in which all the attributes are synthesized is called an **S-attributed grammar**.

We have already seen a number of examples of synthesized attributes and S-attributed grammars. The *val* attribute of numbers in Example 6.1 is synthesized (see the dependency graphs in Example 6.6, page 262), as is the *val* attribute of the simple integer arithmetic expressions in Example 6.2, page 271.

Given that a parse or syntax tree has been constructed by a parser, the attribute values of an S-attributed grammar can be computed by a single bottom-up, or postorder, traversal of the tree. This can be expressed by the following pseudocode for a recursive postorder attribute evaluator:

```
procedure PostEval ( T: treenode );
begin
   for each child C of T do
      PostEval ( C );
   compute all synthesized attributes of T;
end;
```

Example 6.11

Consider the attribute grammar of Example 6.2 for simple arithmetic expressions, with the synthesized attribute *val*. Given the following structure for a syntax tree (such as that of Figure 6.5, page 269)

```
typedef enum {Plus,Minus,Times} OpKind;
typedef enum {OpKind,ConstKind} ExpKind;
typedef struct streenode
      { ExpKind kind;
       OpKind op;
       struct streenode *lchild,*rchild;
        int val;
      } STreeNode;
typedef STreeNode *SyntaxTree;
```

the PostEval pseudocode would translate into the C code of Figure 6.8 for a left-to-right traversal.

Figure 6.8

C code for the postorder attribute evaluator for Example 6.11

```
void postEval(SyntaxTree t)
{ int temp;
  if (t->kind = OpKind)
  { postEval(t->lchild);
    postEval(t->rchild);
    switch (t->op)
    { case Plus:
        t->val = t->lchild->val + t->rchild->val;
        break;
      case Minus:
        t->val = t->lchild->val - t->rchild->val;
        break;
      case Minus:
        t->val = t->lchild->val * t->rchild->val;
        break;
    } /* end switch */
  } /* end if */
} /* end postEval */
```

§

Not all attributes are synthesized, of course.

Definition

An attribute that is not synthesized is called an **inherited** attribute.

Examples of inherited attributes that we have already seen include the *dtype* attribute of Example 6.3 (page 265) and the *base* attribute of Example 6.4 (page 266). Inherited attributes have dependencies that flow either from parent to children in the parse tree (the reason for the name) or from sibling to sibling. Figures 6.9(a) and (b) illustrate the two basic kinds of dependency of inherited attributes. Both of these kinds of dependency occur in Example 6.7 for the *dtype* attribute. The reason that both are classified as inherited is that in algorithms to compute inherited attributes, sibling inheritance is often implemented in such a way that attribute values are passed from sibling to sibling *via* the parent. Indeed, this is necessary if syntax tree edges only point from parent to child (a child thus cannot access its parent or siblings directly). On the other hand, if some structures in a syntax tree are implemented via sibling pointers, then sibling inheritance can proceed directly along a sibling chain, as depicted in Figure 6.9(c).

Figure 6.9
Different kinds of inherited dependencies

(a) Inheritance from parent to siblings   **(b) Inheritance from sibling to sibling**

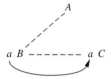

(c) Sibling inheritance via sibling pointers

We turn now to algorithmic methods for the evaluation of inherited attributes. Inherited attributes can be computed by a preorder traversal, or combined preorder/ inorder traversal of the parse or syntax tree. Schematically, this can be represented by the following pseudocode:

```
procedure PreEval ( T: treenode );
begin
    for each child C of T do
        compute all inherited attributes of C;
        PreEval ( C );
end;
```

Unlike synthesized attributes, the order in which the inherited attributes of the children are computed is important, since inherited attributes may have dependencies among the attributes of the children. The order in which each child *C* of *T* in the foregoing pseudocode is visited must therefore adhere to any requirements of these dependencies. In the next two examples, we demonstrate this using the *dtype* and *base* inherited attributes of previous examples.

Example 6.12   Consider the grammar of Example 6.3, which has the inherited attribute *dtype* and whose dependency graphs are given in Example 6.7, page 272 (see the attribute grammar in Table 6.3, page 266). Let us assume first that a parse tree has been explicitly constructed from the grammar, which for ease of reference we repeat here:

$$decl \rightarrow type \; var\text{-}list$$
$$type \rightarrow \textbf{int} \mid \textbf{float}$$
$$var\text{-}list \rightarrow \textbf{id,} \; var\text{-}list \mid \textbf{id}$$

Then the pseudocode for a recursive procedure that computes the *dtype* attribute at all required nodes is as follows:

```
procedure EvalType ( T: treenode );
begin
    case nodekind of T of
    decl:
            EvalType ( type child of T );
            Assign dtype of type child of T to var-list child of T;
            EvalType ( var-list child of T );
    type:
            if child of T = int then T.dtype := integer
            else T.dtype := real;
    var-list:
            assign T.dtype to first child of T;
            if third child of T is not nil then
                assign T.dtype to third child;
                EvalType ( third child of T );
        end case;
    end EvalType;
```

Notice how preorder and inorder operations are mixed, depending on the different kind of node being processed. For instance, a *decl* node requires that the *dtype* of its first child be computed first and then assigned to its second child before a recursive call of *EvalType* on that child; this is an in-order process. On the other hand, a *var-list* node assigns *dtype* to its children before making any recursive calls; this is a preorder process.

In Figure 6.10 we show the parse tree for the string **float x,y** together with the dependency graph for the *dtype* attribute, and we number the nodes in the order in which *dtype* is computed according to the above pseudocode.

Figure 6.10

Parse tree showing traversal order for Example 6.12

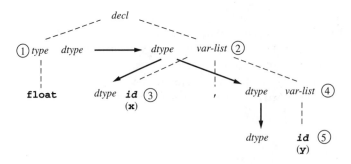

To give a completely concrete form to this example, let us convert the previous pseudocode into actual C code. Also, rather than using an explicit parse tree, let us assume that a syntax tree has been constructed, in which *var-list* is represented by a sibling list of **id** nodes. Then a declaration string such as **float x,y** would have the syntax tree (compare this with Figure 6.10)

and the evaluation order of the children of the *decl* node would be left to right (the *type* node first, then the **x** node, and finally the **y** node). Note that in this tree we have already included the *dtype* of the *type* node; we assume this has been precomputed during the parse.

The syntax tree structure is given by the following C declarations:

```
typedef enum {decl,type,id} nodekind;
typedef enum {integer,real} typekind;
typedef struct treeNode
  { nodekind kind;
    struct treeNode
       * lchild, * rchild, * sibling;
    typekind dtype;
    /* for type and id nodes */
    char * name;
    /* for id nodes only */
  } * SyntaxTree;
```

The *EvalType* procedure now has the corresponding C code:

```
void evalType (SyntaxTree t)
{ switch (t->kind)
  { case decl:
      t->rchild->dtype = t->lchild->dtype;
      evalType(t->rchild);
      break;
    case id:
      if (t->sibling != NULL)
      { t->sibling->dtype = t->dtype;
        evalType(t->sibling);
      }
      break;
  } /* end switch */
} /* end evalType */
```

This code can be simplified to the following nonrecursive procedure, which operates entirely at the level of the root (**decl**) node:

```
void evalType (SyntaxTree t)
{ if (t->kind == decl)
  { SyntaxTree p = t->rchild;
    p->dtype = t->lchild->dtype;
    while (p->sibling != NULL)
    { p->sibling->dtype = p->dtype;
      p = p->sibling;
    }
  } /* end if */
} /* end evalType */
```

§

Example 6.13   Consider the grammar of Example 6.4 (page 266), which has the inherited attribute *base* (the dependency graphs are given in Example 6.8, page 273). We repeat the grammar of that example here:

$$based\text{-}num \rightarrow num\ basechar$$
$$basechar \rightarrow \mathbf{o} \mid \mathbf{d}$$
$$num \rightarrow num\ digit \mid digit$$
$$digit \rightarrow \mathbf{0} \mid \mathbf{1} \mid \mathbf{2} \mid \mathbf{3} \mid \mathbf{4} \mid \mathbf{5} \mid \mathbf{6} \mid \mathbf{7} \mid \mathbf{8} \mid \mathbf{9}$$

This grammar has two new features. First, there are two attributes, the synthesized attribute *val*, and the inherited attribute *base*, on which *val* depends. Second, the *base* attribute is inherited from the right child to the left child of a *based-num* (that is, from *basechar* to *num*). Thus, in this case, we must evaluate the children of a *based-num* from right to left instead of left to right. We proceed to give the pseudocode for an *EvalWithBase* procedure that computes both *base* and *val*. In this case, *base* is computed in preorder and *val* in postorder during a single pass (we discuss the question of multiple attributes and passes shortly). The pseudocode is as follows (see the attribute grammar in Table 6.4, page 267).

procedure *EvalWithBase* (*T*: *treenode*);
begin
   case *nodekind of T* **of**
   based-num:
      EvalWithBase (*right child of T*);
      assign base of right child of T to base of left child;
      EvalWithBase (*left child of T*);
      assign val of left child of T to T.val;
   num:
      assign T.base to base of left child of T;
      EvalWithBase (*left child of T*);
      if *right child of T is not nil* **then**
         assign T.base to base of right child of T;
         EvalWithBase (*right child of T*);
         if *vals of left and right children* $\neq$ *error* **then**
            T.val := *T.base**(*val of left child*) + *val of right child*
         else *T.val* := *error*;
      else *T.val* := *val of left child*;

> *basechar*:
>   **if** *child of T* = **o then** *T.base* := 8
>   **else** *T.base* := 10;
> *digit*:
>   **if** *T.base* = **8 and** *child of T* = **8 or 9 then** *T.val* := *error*
>   **else** *T.val* := *numval* (*child of T*);
>   **end case;**
> **end** *EvalWithBase*;

We leave to the exercises the construction of C declarations for an appropriate syntax tree and a translation of the pseudocode for *EvalWithBase* into C code. §

In attribute grammars with combinations of synthesized and inherited attributes, if the synthesized attributes depend on the inherited attributes (as well as other synthesized attributes) but the inherited attributes do not depend on any synthesized attributes, then it is possible to compute all the attributes in a single pass over the parse or syntax tree. The previous example is a good example of how this is done, and the order of evaluation may be summarized by combining the *PostEval* and *PreEval* pseudocode procedures:

> **procedure** *CombinedEval* (*T: treenode*);
> **begin**
>   **for** *each child C of T* **do**
>   *compute all inherited attributes of C*;
>   *CombinedEval* (*C*);
>   *compute all synthesized attributes of T*;
> **end;**

Situations in which inherited attributes depend on synthesized attributes are more complex and require more than one pass over the parse or syntax tree, as the following example shows.

Example 6.14   Consider the following simple version of an expression grammar:

$$exp \rightarrow exp \text{ / } exp \mid \textbf{num} \mid \textbf{num}.\textbf{num}$$

This grammar has a single operation, division, indicated by the token **/**. It also has two versions of numbers: integer numbers consisting of sequences of digits, which we indicate by the token **num**, and floating-point numbers, which we indicate by the token **num.num**. The idea of this grammar is that operations may be interpreted differently, depending on whether they are floating-point or strictly integer operations. Division, in particular, is quite different, depending on whether fractions are allowed. If not, division is often called a **div** operation, and the value of **5/4** is 5 **div** 4 = 1. If floating-point division is meant, then **5/4** has value 1.2.

Suppose now that a programming language requires mixed expressions to be promoted to floating-point expressions throughout, and the appropriate operations to be used in their semantics. Thus, the meaning of the expression **5/2/2.0** (assuming left associativity of division) is 1.25, while the meaning of **5/2/2** is 1.[7] To describe these semantics requires three attributes: a synthesized Boolean attribute *isFloat* which indicates if any part of an expression has a floating-point value; an inherited attribute *etype*, with two values *int* and *float*, which gives the type of each subexpression and which depends on *isFloat*; and, finally, the computed *val* of each subexpression, which depends on the inherited *etype*. This situation also requires that the top-level expression be identified (so that we know there are no more subexpressions to be considered). We do this by augmenting the grammar with a start symbol:

$$S \rightarrow exp$$

The attribute equations are given in Table 6.7. In the equations for the grammar rule $exp \rightarrow \mathbf{num}$, we have used $Float(\mathbf{num}.val)$ to indicate a function that converts the integer value $\mathbf{num}.val$ into a floating-point value. We have also used / for floating-point division and **div** for integer division.

The *isFloat*, *etype*, and *val* attributes in this example can be computed by two passes over the parse or syntax tree. The first pass computes the synthesized attribute *isFloat* by a postorder traversal. The second pass computes both the inherited attribute *etype* and the synthesized attribute *val* in a combined preorder/postorder traversal. We leave the description of these passes and the corresponding attribute computations for the expression 5/2/2.0 to the exercises, as well as the construction of pseudocode or C code to perform the successive passes on the syntax tree.

Table 6.7

Attribute grammar for Example 6.14

Grammar Rule	Semantic Rules
$S \rightarrow exp$	$exp.etype =$ **if** $exp.isFloat$ **then** *float* **else** int $S.val = exp.val$

$exp_1 \rightarrow exp_2 \, / \, exp_3$	$exp_1.isFloat =$
	    $exp_2.isFloat$ **or** $exp_3.isFloat$
	$exp_2.etype = exp_1.etype$
	$exp_3.etype = exp_1.etype$
	$exp_1.val =$
	    if $exp_1.etype = int$
	    then $exp_2.val$ **div** $exp_3.val$
	    else $exp_2.val \, / \, exp_3.val$

$exp \rightarrow \mathbf{num}$	$exp.isFloat = \mathbf{false}$
	$exp.val =$
	    if $exp.etype = int$ **then** $\mathbf{num}.val$
	    else $Float(\mathbf{num}.val)$

$exp \rightarrow \mathbf{num.num}$	$exp.isFloat = \mathbf{true}$ $exp.val = \mathbf{num.num}.val$

§

---

7. This rule is not the same rule as the one used in C. For instance, the value of **5/2/2.0** is 1.0 in C, not 1.25.

6.2.3 Attributes as Parameters and Returned Values

Often when computing attributes, it makes sense to use parameters and returned function values to communicate attribute values rather than to store them as fields in a syntax tree record structure. This is particularly true if many of the attribute values are the same or are only used temporarily to compute other attribute values. In this case, it makes little sense to use space in the syntax tree to store attribute values at each node. A single recursive traversal procedure that computes inherited attributes in preorder and synthesized attributes in postorder can, in fact, pass the inherited attribute values as parameters to recursive calls on children and receive synthesized attribute values as returned values of those same calls. Several examples of this have already occurred in previous chapters. In particular, the computation of the synthesized value of an arithmetic expression can be done by a recursive parsing procedure that returns the value of the current expression. Similarly, the syntax tree as a synthesized attribute must itself be computed by returned value during parsing, since until it has been constructed, no data structure yet exists in which to record itself as an attribute.

In more complex situations, for instance when more than one synthesized attribute must be returned, it may be necessary to use a record structure or union as a returned value, or one may split up the recursive procedure into several procedures to cover different cases. We illustrate this with an example.

Example 6.15 Consider the recursive procedure *EvalWithBase* of Example 6.13. In this procedure, the *base* attribute of a number is computed only once and then is used for all subsequent computations of the *val* attribute. Similarly, the *val* attribute of a part of the number is only used as a temporary in the computation of the value of the complete number. It makes sense to turn *base* into a parameter (as an inherited attribute) and *val* into a returned value. The modified *EvalWithBase* procedure is as follows:

```
function EvalWithBase ( T: treenode; base: integer ): integer;
var temp, temp2: integer;
begin
    case nodekind of T of
    based-num:
        temp := EvalWithBase ( right child of T );
        return EvalWithBase ( left child of T, temp );
    num:
        temp := EvalWithBase ( left child of T, base );
        if right child of T is not nil then
            temp2 := EvalWithBase ( right child of T, base );
            if temp ≠ error and temp2 ≠ error then
                return base*temp + temp2
            else return error;
        else return temp;
    basechar:
        if child of T = o then return 8
        else return 10;
    digit:
        if base = 8 and child of T = 8 or 9 then return error
        else return numval ( child of T );
    end case;
end EvalWithBase;
```

Of course, this only works because the *base* attribute and the *val* attribute have the same *integer* data type, since in one case *EvalWithBase* returns the *base* atttribute (when the parse tree node is a *basechar* node), and in the other cases *EvalWithBase* returns the *val* attribute. It is also somewhat irregular that the first call to *EvalWithBase* (on the root *based_num* parse tree node) must have a *base* value supplied, even though one does not yet exist, and which is subsequently ignored. For example, to start the computation, one would have to make a call such as

$$EvalWithBase(rootnode,0);$$

with a dummy base value 0. It would be more rational, therefore, to distinguish three cases—the *based_num* case, the *basechar* case, and the *num* and *digit* case—and write three separate procedures for these three cases. The pseudocode would then appear as follows:

```
function EvalBasedNum ( T: treenode ): integer;
(* only called on root node *)
begin
   return EvalNum ( left child of T, EvalBase(right child of T) );
end EvalBasedNum;

function EvalBase ( T: treenode ): integer;
(* only called on basechar node *)
begin
   if child of T = o then return 8
   else return 10;
end EvalBase;

function EvalNum ( T: treenode; base: integer ): integer;
var temp, temp2: integer;
begin
   case nodekind of T of
   num:
        temp := EvalWithBase ( left child of T, base );
        if right child of T is not nil then
           temp2 := EvalWithBase ( right child of T, base );
           if temp ≠ error and temp2 ≠ error then
              return base*temp + temp2
           else return error;
        else return temp;
    digit:
        if base = 8 and child of T = 8 or 9 then return error
        else return numval ( child of T );
   end case;
end EvalNum;                                                    §
```

6.2.4   The Use of External Data Structures to Store Attribute Values

In those cases where attribute values do not lend themselves easily to the method of parameters and returned values (particularly true when attribute values have significant structure and may be needed at arbitrary points during translation), it may still not be reasonable to store attribute values in the syntax tree nodes. In such cases, data structures such as lookup tables, graphs, and other structures may be useful to obtain the correct behavior and accessibility of attribute values. The attribute grammar itself can be modified to reflect this need by replacing attribute equations (representing assignments of attribute values) by calls to procedures representing operations on the appropriate data structures used to maintain the attribute values. The resulting semantic rules then no longer represent an attribute grammar, but are still useful in describing the semantics of the attributes, as long as the operation of the procedures is made clear.

Example 6.16   Consider the previous example with the *EvalWithBase* procedure using parameters and returned values. Since the *base* attribute, once it is set, is fixed for the duration of the value computation, we may use a nonlocal variable to store its value, rather than passing it as a parameter each time. (If *base* were not fixed, this would be risky or even incorrect in such a recursive process.) Thus, we can alter the pseudocode for *EvalWithBase* as follows:

```
function EvalWithBase ( T: treenode ): integer;
var temp, temp2: integer;
begin
    case nodekind of T of
    based-num:
            SetBase ( right child of T );
            return EvalWithBase ( left child of T );
    num:
            temp := EvalWithBase ( left child of T );
            if right child of T is not nil then
                temp2 := EvalWithBase ( right child of T );
                if temp ≠ error and temp2 ≠ error then
                    return base*temp + temp2
                else return error;
            else return temp;
    digit:
            if base = 8 and child of T = 8 or 9 then return error
            else return numval ( child of T );
    end case;
end EvalWithBase;

procedure SetBase ( T: treenode );
begin
    if child of T = o then base := 8
    else base := 10;
end SetBase ;
```

Here we have separated out the process of assigning to the nonlocal *base* variable in the procedure *SetBase*, which is only called on a *basechar* node. The rest of the code of *EvalWithBase* then simply refers to *base* directly, without passing it as a parameter.

We can also change the semantic rules to reflect the use of the nonlocal *base* variable. In this case, the rules would look something like the following, where we have used assignment to explicitly indicate the setting of the nonlocal *base* variable:

Grammar Rule	Semantic Rules
based-num → *num basechar*	*based-num.val* = *num.val*
basechar → **o**	*base* := 8
basechar → **d**	*base* := 10
num_1 → num_2 *digit*	num_1 *.val* = **if** *digit.val* = *error* **or** num_2 *.val* = error **then** *error* **else** num_2 *.val* * *base* + *digit.val*
etc.	etc.

Now *base* is no longer an attribute in the sense in which we have used it up to now, and the semantic rules no longer form an attribute grammar. Nevertheless, if *base* is known to be a variable with the appropriate properties, then these rules still adequately define the semantics of a *based-num* for the compiler writer.   §

One of the prime examples of a data structure external to the syntax tree is the **symbol table**, which stores attributes associated to declared constants, variables, and procedures in a program. A symbol table is a dictionary data structure with operations such as *insert*, *lookup*, and *delete*. In the next section we discuss issues surrounding the symbol table in typical programming languages. We content ourselves in this section with the following simple example.

Example 6.17   Consider the attribute grammar of simple declarations of Table 6.3 (page 266), and the attribute evaluation procedure for this attribute grammar given in Example 6.12 (page 279). Typically, the information in declarations is inserted into a symbol table using the declared identifiers as keys and stored there for later lookup during the translation of other parts of the program. Let us, therefore, assume for this attribute grammar that a symbol table exists that will store the identifier name together with its declared data type and that name-data type pairs are inserted into the symbol table via an *insert* procedure declared as follows:

procedure *insert* (*name*: *string*; *dtype*: *typekind*);

Thus, instead of storing the data type of each variable in the syntax tree, we insert it into the symbol table using this procedure. Also, since each declaration has only one associated type, we can use a nonlocal variable to store the constant *dtype* of each declaration during processing. The resulting semantic rules are as follows:

Grammar Rule	Semantic Rules
decl → *type var-list*	
type → **int**	*dtype* = *integer*
type → **float**	*dtype* = *real*
$var\text{-}list_1$ → **id** , $var\text{-}list_2$	*insert*(**id** *.name, dtype*)
var-list → **id**	*insert*(**id** *.name, dtype*)

In the calls to *insert* we have used **id** *.name* to refer to the identifier string, which we assume to be computed by the scanner or parser. These semantic rules are quite different from the corresponding attribute grammar; the grammar rule for a *decl* has, in fact, no semantic rules at all. Dependencies are not as clearly expressed, although it is clear that the *type* rules must be processed before the associated *var-list* rules, since the calls to *insert* depend on *dtype*, which is set in the *type* rules.

The corresponding pseudocode for an attribute evaluation procedure *EvalType* is as follows (compare this with the code on page 280):

```
procedure EvalType ( T: treenode );
begin
    case nodekind of T of
    decl:
            EvalType ( type child of T );
            EvalType ( var-list child of T );
    type:
            if child of T = int then dtype := integer
            else dtype := real;
    var-list:
            insert(name of first child of T, dtype)
            if third child of T is not nil then
                EvalType ( third child of T );
    end case;
end EvalType;                                                                    §
```

6.2.5   The Computation of Attributes During Parsing

A question that naturally occurs is to what extent attributes can be computed at the same time as the parsing stage, without waiting to perform further passes over the source code by recursive traversals of the syntax tree. This is particularly important with regard to the syntax tree itself, which is a synthesized attribute that must be constructed during the parse, if it is to be used for further semantic analysis. Historically, the possibility of computing all attributes during the parse was of even greater interest, since considerable emphasis was placed on the capability of a compiler to perform one-pass translation. Nowadays this is less important, so we do not provide an exhaustive analysis of all the special techniques that have been developed. However, a basic overview of the ideas and requirements is worthwile.

Which attributes can be successfully computed during a parse depends to great extent on the power and properties of the parsing method employed. One important restriction is provided by the fact that all the major parsing methods process the input program from left to right (this is the content of the first L in the LL and LR parsing techniques studied in the previous two chapters). This is equivalent to the requirement that the attributes be capable of evaluation by a left-to-right traversal of the parse tree. For synthesized attributes this is not a restriction, since the children of a node can be processed in arbitrary order, in particular from left to right. But, for inherited attributes, this means that there may be no "backward" dependencies in the dependency graph (dependencies pointing from right to left in the parse tree). For example, the attribute grammar of Example 6.4 (page 266) violates this property, since a *based-num* has its base given by the suffix **o** or **d**, and the *val* attribute cannot be computed until the suffix is seen and processed at the end of the string. Attribute grammars that *do* satisfy this property are called L-attributed (for left to right), and we make the following definition.

Definition

An attribute grammar for attributes $a_1, \ldots, a_k$ is **L-attributed** if, for each inherited attribute a_j and each grammar rule

$$X_0 \rightarrow X_1 X_2 \ldots X_n$$

the associated equations for a_j are all of the form

$$X_i.a_j = f_{ij}(X_0.a_1, \ldots, X_0.a_k, X_1.a_1, \ldots, X_1.a_k, \ldots, X_{i-1}.a_1, \ldots, X_{i-1}.a_k)$$

That is, the value of a_j at X_i can only depend on attributes of the symbols $X_0, \ldots, X_{i-1}$ that occur to the left of X_i in the grammar rule.

As a special case, we have already noted that an S-attributed grammar is L-attributed.

Given an L-attributed grammar in which the inherited attributes do not depend on the synthesized attributes, a recursive-descent parser can evaluate all the attributes by turning the inherited attributes into parameters and synthesized attributes into returned values, as previously described. Unfortunately, LR parsers, such as a Yacc-generated LALR(1) parser, are suited to handling primarily synthesized attributes. The reason lies, ironically, in the greater power of LR parsers over LL parsers. Attributes only become computable when the grammar rule to be used in a derivation becomes known, since only then are the equations for the attribute computation determined. LR parsers, however, put off deciding which grammar rule to use in a derivation until the right-hand side of a grammar rule is fully formed. This makes it difficult for inherited attributes to be made available, unless their properties remain fixed for all possible right-hand side choices. We will briefly discuss the use of the parsing stack to compute attributes in the most common cases, with applications to Yacc. Sources for more complex techniques are mentioned in the Notes and References section.

Computing Synthesized Attributes During LR Parsing   This is the easy case for an LR parser. An LR parser will generally have a **value stack** in which the synthesized attributes are stored (perhaps as unions or structures, if there is more than one attribute for each grammar symbol). The value stack will be manipulated in parallel with the parsing stack, with new values being computed according to the attribute equations each time a shift or a reduction on the parsing stack occurs. We illustrate this in Table 6.8 for the attribute grammar of Table 6.5 (page 269), which is the ambiguous version of the simple arithmetic expression grammar. For simplicity, we use abbreviated notation for the grammar and ignore some of the details of an LR parsing algorithm in the table. In particular, we do not indicate state numbers, we do not show the augmented start symbol, and we do not express the implicit disambiguating rules. The table contains two new columns in addition to the usual parsing actions: the value stack and semantic actions. The semantic actions indicate how computations occur on the value stack as reductions occur on the parsing stack. (Shifts are viewed as pushing the token values on both the parsing stack and the value stack, though this may differ in individual parsers.)

As an example of a semantic action, consider step 10 in Table 6.8. The value stack contains the integer values 12 and 5, separated by the token **+**, with 5 at the top of the stack. The parsing action is to reduce by $E \rightarrow E + E$, and the corresponding semantic action from Table 6.5 is to compute according to the equation $E_1 .val = E_2 .val + E_3 .val$. The corresponding actions on the value stack taken by the parser are as follows (in pseudocode):

pop t3	{ get $E_3 .val$ from the value stack }
pop	{ discard the + token }
pop t2	{ get $E_2 .val$ from the value stack }
t1 = t2 + t3	{ add }
push t1	{ push the result back onto the value stack }

In Yacc the situation represented by the reduction at step 10 would be written as the rule

```
E : E + E { $$ = $1 + $3; }
```

Here the pseudovariables **$i** represent positions in the right-hand side of the rule being reduced and are converted to value stack positions by counting backward from the right. Thus, **$3**, corresponding to the rightmost **E**, is to be found at the top of the stack, while **$1** is to be found two positions below the top.

Table 6.8

Parsing and semantic actions for the expression **3*4+5** during an LR parse

	Parsing Stack	Input	Parsing Action	Value Stack	Semantic Action
1	$	3*4+5 $	shift	$	
2	$ *n*	*4+5 $	reduce $E \rightarrow n$	$ *n*	$E .val = n .val$
3	$ E	*4+5 $	shift	$ 3	
4	$ E *	4+5 $	shift	$ 3 *	
5	$ E * *n*	+5 $	reduce $E \rightarrow n$	$ 3 * *n*	$E .val = n .val$
6	$ E * E	+5 $	reduce $E \rightarrow E * E$	$ 3 * 4	$E_1 .val = E_2 .val * E_3 .val$
7	$ E	+5 $	shift	$ 12	
8	$ E +	5 $	shift	$ 12 +	
9	$ E + *n*	$	reduce $E \rightarrow n$	$ 12 + *n*	$E .val = n .val$
10	$ E + E	$	reduce $E \rightarrow E + E$	$ 12 + 5	$E_1 .val = E_2 .val + E_3 .val$
11	$ E	$		$ 17	

Inheriting a Previously Computed Synthesized Attribute During LR Parsing   Because of the left-to-right evaluation strategy of LR parsing, an action associated to a nonterminal in the right-hand side of a rule can make use of synthesized attributes of the symbols to the left of it in the rule, since these values have already been pushed onto the value stack. To illustrate this briefly, consider the production choice $A \rightarrow B\ C$, and suppose that C has an inherited attribute i that depends in some way on the synthesized attribute s of B: $C.i = f(B.s)$. The value of $C.i$ can be stored in a variable prior to the recognition of C by introducing an ε-production between B and C that schedules the storing of the top of the value stack:

Grammar Rule	Semantic Rules
$A \rightarrow B\ D\ C$	
$B \rightarrow \ldots$	{ compute $B.s$ }
$D \rightarrow \varepsilon$	$saved\_i = f(valstack[top])$
$C \rightarrow \ldots$	{ now $saved\_i$ is available }

In Yacc this process is made even easier, since the ε-production need not be introduced explicitly. Instead, the action of storing the computed attribute is simply written at the place in the rule where it is to be scheduled:

```
A : B { saved_i = f($1); } C ;
```

(Here the pseudovariable **$1** refers to the value of **B**, which is at the top of the stack when the action is executed.) Such embedded actions in Yacc were studied in Section 5.5.6 of the previous chapter.

An alternative to this strategy is available when the position of a previously computed synthesized attribute in the value stack can always be predicted. In this case, the value need not be copied into a variable, but can be accessed directly on the value stack. Consider, for example, the following L-attributed grammar with an inherited *dtype* attribute:

Grammar Rule	Semantic Rules
decl → *type var-list*	*var-list.dtype* = *type.dtype*
type → **int**	*type.dtype* = *integer*
type → **float**	*type.dtype* = *real*
var-list$_1$ → *var-list*$_2$ **,id**	*insert*(**id**.*name*, *var-list*$_1$.*dtype*)
	var-list$_2$.*dtype* = *var-list*$_1$.*dtype*
var-list → **id**	*insert*(**id**.*name*, *var-list.dtype*)

In this case, the *dtype* attribute, which is a synthesized attribute for the *type* nonterminal, can be computed onto the value stack just before the first *var-list* is recognized. Then, when each rule for *var-list* is reduced, *dtype* can be found at a fixed position in the value stack by counting backward from the top: when *var-list* → **id** is reduced, *dtype* is just below the stack top, while when *var-list*$_1$ → *var-list*$_2$ **,id** is reduced, *dtype* is three positions below the top of the stack. We can implement this in an LR parser by eliminating the two **copy rules** for *dtype* in the above attribute grammar and accessing the value stack directly:

Grammar Rule	Semantic Rules
decl → type var-list	
type → **int**	*type.dtype = integer*
type → **float**	*type.dtype = real*
var-list$_1$ → var-list$_2$ **,id**	*insert(**id**.name, valstack[top−3])*
var-list → **id**	*insert(**id**.name, valstack[top−1])*

(Note that, since *var-list* has no synthesized *dtype* attribute, the parser must push a dummy value onto the stack to retain the proper placement in the stack.)

There are several problems with this method. First, it requires the programmer to directly access the value stack during a parse, and this may be risky in automatically generated parsers. Yacc, for instance, has no pseudovariable convention for accessing the value stack below the current rule being recognized, as would be required by the above method. Thus, to implement such a scheme in Yacc, one would have to write special code to do this. The second problem is that this technique only works if the position of the previously computed attribute is predictable from the grammar. If, for example, we had written the above declaration grammar so that *var-list* was right recursive (as we did in Example 6.17), then an arbitrary number of **id**'s could be on the stack, and the position of *dtype* in the stack would be unknown.

By far the best technique for dealing with inherited attributes in LR parsing is to use external data structures, such as a symbol table or nonlocal variables, to hold inherited attribute values, and to add ε-productions (or embedded actions as in Yacc) to allow for changes to these data structures to occur at appropriate moments. For example, a solution to the *dtype* problem just discussed can be found in the discussion of embedded actions in Yacc (Section 5.5.6).

We should be aware, however, that even this latter method is not without pitfalls: adding ε-productions to a grammar can add parsing conflicts, so that an LALR(1) grammar can turn into a non-LR(k) grammar for any k (see Exercise 6.15 and the Notes and References section). In practical situations, this rarely happens, however.

6.2.6   The Dependence of Attribute Computation on the Syntax

As the final topic in this section, it is worth noting that the properties of attributes depend heavily on the structure of the grammar. It can happen that modifications to the grammar that do not change the legal strings of the language can make the computation of attributes simpler or more complex. Indeed, we have the following:

Theorem

(From Knuth [1968]). Given an attribute grammar, all inherited attributes can be changed into synthesized attributes by suitable modification of the grammar, without changing the language of the grammar.

We give one example of how an inherited attribute can be turned into a synthesized attribute by modification of the grammar.

Example 6.18

Consider the grammar of simple declarations considered in the previous examples:

$$decl \rightarrow type \ var\text{-}list$$
$$type \rightarrow \textbf{int} \ | \ \textbf{float}$$
$$var\text{-}list \rightarrow \textbf{id ,} \ var\text{-}list \ | \ \textbf{id}$$

The *dtype* attribute of the attribute grammar of Table 6.3 is inherited. If, however, we rewrite the grammar as follows,

$$decl \rightarrow var\text{-}list \ \textbf{id}$$
$$var\text{-}list \rightarrow var\text{-}list \ \textbf{id ,} \ | \ type$$
$$type \rightarrow \textbf{int} \ | \ \textbf{float}$$

then the same strings are accepted, but the *dtype* attribute now becomes synthesized, according to the following attribute grammar:

Grammar Rule	Semantic Rules
$decl \rightarrow var\text{-}list \ \textbf{id}$	$\textbf{id}.dtype = var\text{-}list.dtype$
$var\text{-}list_1 \rightarrow var\text{-}list_2 \ \textbf{id ,}$	$\textbf{id}.dtype = var\text{-}list_2.dtype$
	$var\text{-}list_1.dtype = var\text{-}list_2.dtype$
$var\text{-}list \rightarrow type$	$var\text{-}list.dtype = type.dtype$
$type \rightarrow \textbf{int}$	$type.dtype = integer$
$type \rightarrow \textbf{float}$	$type.dtype = real$

We illustrate how this change in the grammar affects the parse tree and the *dtype* attribute computation in Figure 6.11, which shows the parse tree for the string **float x,y**, together with the attribute values and dependencies. The dependencies of the two **id** .*dtype* values on the values of the parent or sibling are drawn as dashed lines in the figure. While these dependencies appear to be violations of the claim that there are no inherited attributes in this attribute grammar, in fact these dependencies are always to leaves in the parse tree (that is, not recursive) and may be achieved by operations at the appropriate parent nodes. Thus, these dependencies are not viewed as inheritances. §

Figure 6.11

Parse tree for the string **float x,y** showing the *dtype* attribute as specified by the attribute grammar of Example 6.18

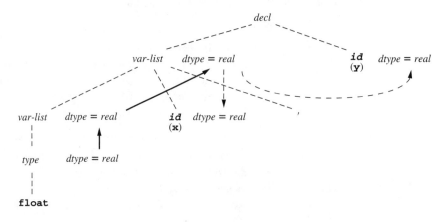

In fact, the stated theorem is less useful than it might seem. Changing the grammar in order to turn inherited attributes into synthesized attributes often makes the grammar and the semantic rules much more complex and difficult to understand. It is, therefore, not a recommended way to deal with the problems of computing inherited attributes. On the other hand, if an attribute computation seems unnaturally difficult, it may be because the grammar is defined in an unsuitable way for its computation, and a change in the grammar may be worthwhile.

6.3   THE SYMBOL TABLE

The symbol table is the major inherited attribute in a compiler and, after the syntax tree, forms the major data structure as well. Although we have, with a few exceptions, delayed a discussion of the symbol table to this point, where it fits best into the conceptual framework of the semantic analysis phase, the reader should be aware that in practical compilers the symbol table is often intimately involved with the parser and even the scanner, either of which may need to enter information directly into the symbol table or consult it to resolve ambiguities (for one such example from C, see Exercise 6.22). Nevertheless, in a very carefully designed language such as Ada or Pascal, it is possible and even reasonable to put off symbol table operations until after a complete parse, when the program being translated is known to be syntactically correct. We have done this, for example, in the TINY compiler, whose symbol table will be studied later in this chapter.

The principal symbol table operations are *insert*, *lookup*, and *delete*; other operations may also be necessary. The *insert* operation is used to store the information provided by name declarations when processing these declarations. The *lookup* operation is needed to retrieve the information associated to a name when that name is used in the associated code. The *delete* operation is needed to remove the information provided by a declaration when that declaration no longer applies.[8] The properties of these operations are dictated by the rules of the programming language being translated. In particular, what information needs to be stored in the symbol table is a function of the structure and purpose of the declarations. Typically this includes data type information, information on region of applicability (scope, discussed below), and information on eventual location in memory.

In this section we discuss, first, the organization of the symbol table data structure for speed and ease of access. Subsequently, we describe some typical language requirements and the effect they have on the operation of the symbol table. Last, we give an extended example of the use of a symbol table with an attribute grammar.

6.3.1   The Structure of the Symbol Table

The symbol table in a compiler is a typical dictionary data structure. The efficiency of the three basic operations *insert*, *lookup*, and *delete* vary according to the organization of the data structure. The analysis of this efficiency for different organizations, and the

---

8. Rather than destroying this information, a *delete* operation is more likely to remove it from view, either by storing it elsewhere, or by marking it as no longer active.

investigation of good organization strategies, is one of the major topics of a data structures course. Therefore, we will not treat this subject in great detail in this text, but refer the reader desiring more information to the sources mentioned in the Notes and References section at the end of this chapter. We will, however, give an overview here of the most useful data structures for these tables in compiler construction.

Typical implementations of dictionary structures include linear lists, various search tree structures (binary search trees, AVL trees, B trees), and hash tables. Linear lists are a good basic data structure that can provide easy and direct implementations of the three basic operations, with a constant-time *insert* operation (by always inserting at the front or rear) and *lookup* and *delete* operations that are linear time in the size of the list. This may be good enough for a compiler implementation in which compilation speed is not a major concern, such as a prototype or experimental compiler, or an interpreter for very small programs. Search tree structures are somewhat less useful for the symbol table, partially because they do not provide best case efficiency, but also because of the complexity of the *delete* operation. The hash table often provides the best choice for implementing the symbol table, since all three operations can be performed in almost constant time, and is used most frequently in practice. We, therefore, discuss the hash table case in somewhat more detail.

A hash table is an array of entries, called **buckets**, indexed by an integer range, usually from 0 to the table size minus one. A **hash function** turns the search key (in this case, the identifier name, consisting of a string of characters) into an integer hash value in the index range, and the item corresponding to the search key is stored in the bucket at this index. Care must be taken so that the hash function distributes the key indices as uniformly as possible over the index range, since hash **collisions** (where two keys are mapped to the same index by the hash function) cause a performance degradation in the *lookup* and *delete* operations. The hash function also needs to operate in constant time, or at least time that is linear in the size of the key (this amounts to constant time if there is an upper bound on the size of the key). We will investigate hash functions shortly.

An important question is how a hash table deals with collisions (this is called **collision resolution**). One method allocates only enough space for a single item in each bucket and resolves collisions by inserting new items in successive buckets (this is sometimes called **open addressing**). In this case, the contents of the hash table are limited by the size of the array used for the table and, as the array fills collisions become more and more frequent, causing a significant degradation in performance. A further problem with this method, at least for compiler construction, is that it is difficult to implement a *delete* operation and that deletions do not improve subsequent table performance.

Perhaps the best scheme for compiler construction is the alternative to open addressing, called **separate chaining**. In this method each bucket is actually a linear list, and collisions are resolved by inserting the new item into the bucket list. Figure 6.12 shows a simple example of this scheme, with a hash table of size 5 (unrealistically small, for demonstration purposes). In that table, we have assumed that four identifiers have been inserted (**i**, **j**, **size**, and **temp**) and that **size** and **j** have the same hash value (namely, 1). In the picture we show **size** before **j** in the list of bucket number 1; the order of the items in the list depends on the order of insertion and how the list is maintained. A common method is to always insert at the beginning of the list, so that **size** would have been inserted after **j** using this method.

Figure 6.12

Separately chained hash table
showing collision resolution

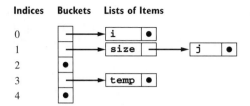

Figure 6.12 also shows the lists in each bucket implemented as linked lists (solid dots are used to indicate null pointers). These can be allocated using the dynamic pointer allocation of the compiler implementation language, or they can be allocated by hand from an array of space within the compiler itself.

One question the compiler writer must answer is how large to make the initial bucket array. Usually, this size will be fixed at compiler construction time.[9] Typical sizes range from a few hundred to over a thousand. If dynamic allocation is used for the actual entries, even small arrays will still allow the compilation of very large programs, at the cost of extra compile time. In any case, the actual size of the bucket array should be chosen to be a prime number, since this makes typical hash functions behave better. For example, if one wishes a bucket array of size 200, one should choose 211 as the size instead of 200 itself (211 is the smallest prime number greater than 200).

We turn now to a description of common hash functions. A hash function, for use in a symbol table implementation, converts a character string (the identifier name) into an integer in the range $0..size - 1$. Typically, this is done by a three-step process. First, each character in the character string is converted to a nonnegative integer. Then, these integers are combined in some way to form a single integer. Finally, the resulting integer is scaled to the range $0..size - 1$.

Converting each character to a nonnegative integer is usually done by using the built-in conversion mechanism of the compiler implementation language. For example, the **ord** function of Pascal converts a character into an integer, usually its ASCII value. Similarly, the C language will automatically convert a character to an integer if it is used in an arithmetic expression or assigned to an integer variable.

Scaling a nonnegative integer to fall in the range $0..size - 1$ is also easily done using the **modulo** function of mathematics, which returns the remainder of dividing *size* into the number. This function is called **mod** in Pascal and **%** in C. When using this method, it is important that *size* be a prime number. Otherwise, a randomly distributed set of integers may not have their scaled values as randomly distributed within the range $0..size - 1$.

It remains for the hash table implementor to choose a method for combining the different integer values of the characters into a single nonnegative integer. One simple method is to ignore many of the characters and to add together only the values of the first few, or the first, middle, and last, characters. This is inadequate for a compiler, since programmers tend to assign variable names in groups, like **temp1**, **temp2**, or **m1tmp**, **m2tmp**, and so on, and this method will cause frequent collisions among such

---

9. Methods do exist for increasing the size of the array (and changing the hash function) on the fly if the hash table grows too large, but these are complex and rarely used.

names. Thus, the chosen method should involve all the characters in each name. Another popular but inadequate method is simply to add up the values of all the characters. Using that method, all permutations of the same characters, such as **tempx** and **xtemp**, will cause collisions.

One good solution to these problems is to repeatedly use a constant number α as a multiplying factor when adding in the value of the next character. Thus, if c_i is the numeric value of the ith character, and h_i is the partial hash value computed at the ith step, then the h_i's are computed according to the recursive formulas $h_0 = 0$, and $h_{i+1} = \alpha h_i + c_i$, with the final hash value h computed as $h = h_n \bmod size$, where n is the number of characters in the name being hashed. This is equivalent to the formula

$$h = (\alpha^{n-1}c_1 + \alpha^{n-2}c_2 + \cdots + \alpha c_{n-1} + c_n) \bmod size = \left(\sum_{i=1}^{n} \alpha^{n-i}c_i \right) \bmod size$$

The choice of α in this formula has, of course, a significant effect on the outcome. A resonable choice for α is a power of two, such as 16 or 128, so that the multiplication can be performed as a shift. Indeed, choosing $\alpha = 128$ has the effect of viewing the character string as a number in base 128, assuming that the character values c_i all are less than 128 (true for the ASCII characters). Other possibilities mentioned in the literature are various prime numbers (see the Notes and References section).

Sometimes overflow can be a problem in the formula for h, especially for large values of α on machines with two-byte integers. If integer values are used for the computations, overflow may result in negative values (in two's complement representation), which will cause execution errors. In that case, it is possible to achieve the same effect by performing the **mod** operation within the summation loop. Sample C code for a hash function h that does this using the previous formula and a value of 16 for α (a bit shift of 4, since $16 = 2^4$) is given in Figure 6.13.

Figure 6.13

Hash function for a symbol table

```
#define SIZE ...
#define SHIFT 4

int hash ( char * key )
{ int temp = 0;
  int i = 0;
  while (key[i] != '\0')
  { temp = ((temp << SHIFT) + key[i]) % SIZE;
    ++i;
  }
  return temp;
}
```

6.3.2 Declarations

The behavior of a symbol table depends heavily on the properties of declarations of the language being translated. For example, how the *insert* and *delete* operations act on the symbol table, when these operations need to be called, and what attributes are inserted into the table, all vary widely from language to language. Even the time during the translation/execution process when the symbol table can be built, and how long the symbol table needs to exist, can be quite different from language to language. In this section we indicate a few of the language issues involved in declarations that affect the behavior and implementation of the symbol table.

There are four basic kinds of declarations that occur frequently in programming languages: constant declarations, type declarations, variable declarations, and procedure/function declarations.

Constant declarations include the **const** declarations of C, such as

```
const int SIZE = 199;
```

(C also has a **#define** mechanism for creating constants, but that is handled by a preprocessor rather than the compiler proper.)

Type declarations include the type declarations of Pascal, such as

```
type Table = array [1..SIZE] of Entry;
```

and **struct** and **union** declarations of C such as

```
struct Entry
{ char * name;
  int count;
  struct Entry * next;
};
```

which defines a structure type with name **Entry**. C also has a **typedef** mechanism for declaring names that are aliases for types

```
typedef struct Entry * EntryPtr;
```

Variable declarations are the most common form of declaration and include FORTRAN declarations such as

```
integer a,b(100)
```

and C declarations such as

```
int a,b[100];
```

Finally, there are **procedure/function declarations**, such as the C function defined in Figure 6.13. These are really nothing more than constant declaration of procedure/function type, but they are usually singled out in language definitions because of their special nature. These declarations are **explicit**, in that a special language construct is used for declarations. It is also possible to have **implicit** declarations, in which declarations are attached to executable instructions without explicit mention. FORTRAN and BASIC, for example, allow variables to be used without explicit declaration. In such implicit declarations, conventions are used to provide the information that would otherwise be given by an explicit declaration. FORTRAN, for example, has the type convention that variables beginning with the letters I through N are automatically integers if used without an explicit declaration, while all others are automatically reals. Implicit declarations can also be called **declaration by use**, since the first use of a variable not explicitly declared can be viewed as implicitly containing its declaration.

Often it is easiest to use one symbol table to hold the names from all the different kinds of declarations, particularly when the language prohibits the use of the same name in different kinds of declarations. Occasionally, it is easier to use a different symbol table for each kind of declaration, so that, for example, all type declarations are contained in one symbol table, while all variable declarations are contained in another. With certain languages, particularly the Algol-derived languages such as C, Pascal, and Ada, we may wish to associate separate symbol tables with different regions of a program (such as procedures) and link them together according to the semantic rules of the language (we will discuss this in more detail shortly).

The attributes bound to a name by a declaration vary with the kind of the declaration. Constant declarations associate values to names; sometimes constant declarations are called **value bindings** for this reason. The values that can be bound determine how the compiler treats them. Pascal and Modula-2, for example, require that the values in a constant declaration be static and, hence, computable by the compiler. The compiler can then use the symbol table to replace the constant names with their values during compilation. Other languages, such as C and Ada, permit constants to be dynamic—that is, only computable during execution. Such constants must be treated more like variables, in that code must be generated to compute their values during execution. However, such constants are **single assignment**: once their values have been determined they cannot change. Constant declarations may also implicitly or explicitly bind data types to names. In Pascal, for example, data types of constants are implicitly determined from their (static) values, while in C the data types are explicitly given, as in variable declarations.

Type declarations bind names to newly constructed types and may also create aliases for existing named types. Type names are usually used in conjunction with a type equivalence algorithm to perform type checking of a program according to the rules of the language. We devote a later section in this chapter to type checking, so we will not discuss type declarations further.

Variable declarations most often bind names to data types, as in the C

```
Table symtab;
```

which binds the data type represented by the name **Table** to the variable with name **symtab**. Variable declarations may also bind other attributes implicitly. One such attribute that has a major effect on the symbol table is the **scope** of a declaration or the region of the program where the declaration applies (i.e., where the variables defined by the declaration are accessible). Scope is usually implied by the position of the declaration within the program, but it may also be affected by explicit syntactic notations and interactions with other declarations. Scope can also be a property of constant, type, and procedure declarations. We discuss scope rules in more detail shortly.

An attribute of variables related to scope that is also implicitly or explicitly bound by a declaration is the allocation of memory for the declared variable, and the duration during execution of the allocation (sometimes called the **lifetime** or **extent** of the declaration). For example, in C, all variables whose declarations are external to functions are allocated **statically** (that is, prior to the beginning of execution) and so have extent equal to the entire execution time of the program, while variables declared within functions are allocated only for the duration of each function call (so-called **automatic** allocation). C also allows for the extent of a declaration within a function to be changed from automatic to static by the use of the keyword **static** in the declaration, as in

```
int count(void)
{ static int counter = 0;
  return ++counter;
}
```

The function **count** has a static local variable **counter** that retains its value from call to call, so that **count** returns as its value the current number of times it has been called.

C also distinguishes between declarations that are used to control memory allocation and those that are used to check types. In C, any variable declaration that begins with the keyword **extern** is not used to perform allocation. Thus, if the previous function were written as

```
int count(void)
{ extern int counter;
  return ++counter;
}
```

the **counter** variable would have to be allocated (and initialized) elsewhere in the program. The C language refers to declarations that allocate memory as **definitions**, while reserving the word "declaration" for declarations that do not allocate memory. Thus, a declaration beginning with the keyword **extern** is not a definition, but a standard declaration of a variable such as

```
int x;
```

is a definition. In C, there can be many declarations of the same variable, but only one definition.

Memory allocation strategies, like type checking, form a complex and important area in compiler design that is part of the structure of the **runtime environment**. We devote the entire next chapter to a study of environments, and so will not study allocation further here. Instead, we turn to an analysis of scope and strategies for maintaining scope in a symbol table.

6.3.3 Scope Rules and Block Structure

Scope rules in programming languages vary widely, but there are several rules that are common to many languages. In this section, we discuss two of these rules, declaration before use and the most closely nested rule for block structure.

Declaration before use is a common rule, used in C and Pascal, that requires that a name be declared in the text of a program prior to any references to the name. Declaration before use permits the symbol table to be built as parsing proceeds and for lookups to be performed as soon as a name reference is encountered in the code; if the lookup fails, a violation of declaration before use has occurred, and the compiler will issue an appropriate error message. Thus, declaration before use promotes one-pass compilation. Some languages do not require declaration before use (Modula-2 is one example), and in such languages a separate pass for symbol table construction is required; one-pass compilation is not possible.

Block structure is a common property of modern languages. A **block** in a programming language is any construct that can contain declarations. For example, in Pascal, the blocks are the main program and procedure/function declarations. In C, the blocks are the compilation units (i.e., the code files), procedure/function declarations, and the compound statements (statement sequences surrounded by curly brackets **{...}**). Structures and unions in C (records in Pascal) can also be viewed as blocks, since they contain field declarations. Similarly, the class declarations of object-oriented programming languages are blocks. A language is **block structured** if it permits the nesting of blocks inside other blocks and if the scope of declarations in a block are limited to that block and other blocks contained in that block, subject to the **most closely nested rule**: given several different declarations for the same name, the declaration that applies to a reference is the one in the most closely nested block to the reference.

To see how block structure and the most closely nested rule affect the symbol table, consider the C code fragment of Figure 6.14. In this code, there are five blocks. First, there is the block of the entire code, which contains the declarations of the integer variables **i** and **j** and the function **f**. Second, there is the declaration of **f** itself, which contains the declaration of the parameter **size**. Third, there is the compound statement of the body of **f**, which contains the declarations of the character variables **i** and **temp**. (The function declaration and its associated body can alternately be viewed as representing a single block.) Fourth, there is the compound statement containing the declaration **double j**. Finally, there is the compound statement containing the declaration **char * j**. Inside function **f** there are single declarations of variables **size** and **temp** in the symbol table, and all uses of these names refer to these declarations. In the case of the name **i**, there is a local declaration of **i** as a **char** inside the compound statement of **f**, and by the most closely nested rule, this declaration supersedes the nonlocal declaration of **i** as an **int** in the surrounding code file block. (The nonlocal **int i** is said to have a **scope hole** inside **f**.) Similarly, the declarations of **j** in the two subsequent compound statements within **f** supersede the nonlocal declaration of **j** as an **int** within their respective blocks. In each case the original declarations of **i** and **j** are recovered when the blocks of the local declarations are exited.

Figure 6.14
C code fragment illustrating
nested scopes

```
int i,j;

int f(int size)
{ char i, temp;
  ...
  { double j;
    ...
  }
  ...
  { char * j;
    ...
  }
}
```

In many languages, such as Pascal and Ada (but not C), procedures and functions can also be nested. This presents a complicating factor in the runtime environment for such languages (studied in the next chapter), but presents no particular complications for nested scopes. For example, the Pascal code of Figure 6.15 contains nested procedures **g** and **h**, but has essentially the same symbol table structure as that of the C code in Figure 6.14 (except, of course, for the additional names **g** and **h**).

Figure 6.15

Pascal code fragment illustrating nested scopes

```
program Ex;
var i,j: integer;

function f(size: integer): integer;
var i,temp: char;

    procedure g;
    var j: real;
    begin
      ...
    end;

    procedure h;
    var j: ^char;
    begin
      ...
    end;

begin (* f *)
  ...
end;

begin (* main program *)
  ...
end.
```

To implement nested scopes and the most closely nested rule, the symbol table *insert* operation must not overwrite previous declarations, but must temporarily hide them, so that the *lookup* operation only finds the most recently inserted declaration for a name. Similarly, the *delete* operation must not delete all declarations corresponding to a name, but only the most recent one, uncovering any previous declarations. Then the symbol table construction can proceed by performing *insert* operations for all declared names on entry into each block and perform corresponding *delete* operations of the same names on exit from the block. In other words, the symbol table behaves in a stacklike manner during the processing of nested scopes.

To see how this structure can be maintained in a practical way, consider the hash table implementation of a symbol table described earlier. If we make simplifying assumptions similar to those of Figure 6.12 (page 297), then after the declarations of the body of procedure **f** in Figure 6.14 are processed, the symbol table might look as in Figure 6.16(a). During the processing of the second compound statement within the body of **f** (the one containing the declaration **char * j**), the symbol table would look as in Figure 6.16(b). Finally, after the block of function **f** is exited, the symbol table would look as in Figure 6.16(c). Note how, for each name, the linked lists in each bucket behave as a stack for the different declarations of that name.

Figure 6.16

Symbol table contents at various places in the code of Figure 6.14

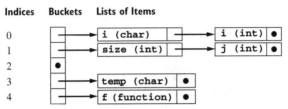

(a) After processing the declarations of the body of f

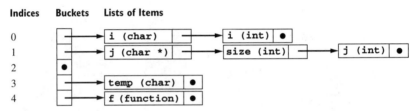

(b) After processing the declaration of the second nested compound statement within the body of f

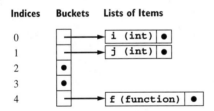

(c) After exiting the body of f (and deleting its declarations)

A number of alternatives to this implementation of nested scopes are possible. One solution is to build a new symbol table for each scope and to link the tables from inner to outer scopes together, so that the *lookup* operation will automatically continue the search with an enclosing table if it fails to find a name in the current table. Leaving a scope then requires less effort, in that the declarations need not be reprocessed using *delete* operations. Instead, the entire symbol table corresponding to the scope can be released in one step. An example of this structure corresponding to Figure 6.16(b) is given in Figure 6.17. In that figure there are three tables, one for each scope, linked from innermost to outermost. Leaving a scope simply requires resetting the access pointer (indicated on the left) to the next outermost scope.

Figure 6.17

Symbol table structure
corresponding to Figure
6.16(b) using separate tables
for each scope

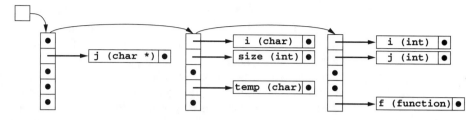

Additional processing and attribute computation may also be necessary during the construction of the symbol table, depending on the language and the details of the compiler operation. One example is the requirement in Ada that a nonlocal name still be visible within a scope hole, where it can be referenced by using a notation similar to record field selection, using the name associated to the scope in which the nonlocal name is declared. For example, in the Pascal code of Figure 6.15, inside function **f** the global integer variable **i** would, in Ada, still be visible as the variable **Ex.i** (using the program name to identify the global scope). Thus, it may make sense, while building the symbol table, to identify each scope by a name and to prefix each name declared within a scope by its accumulated nested scope names. Thus, all occurrences of the name **j** in Figure 6.15 would be distinguished as **Ex.j**, **Ex.f.g.j**, and **Ex.f.h.j**. Additionally or alternatively, one may need to assign a **nesting level** or **nesting depth** to each scope and record in each symbol table entry the nesting level of each name. Thus, in Figure 6.15, the global scope of the program has nesting level 0, the declarations of **f** (its parameters and local variables) have nesting level 1, and the local declarations of both **g** and **h** have nesting level 2.

A mechanism that is similar to the scope selection feature of Ada just described is the **scope resolution operator :: ** of C++. This operator allows the scope of a class declaration to be accessed from outside the declaration itself. This can be used to complete the definition of member functions from outside the class declaration:

```
class A
{ ... int f();...}; // f is a member function

A::f() // this is the definition of f in A
{ ... }
```

Classes, procedures (in Ada), and record structures can all be viewed as representing a named scope, with the set of local declarations as an attribute. In situations where these scopes can be referenced externally, it is advantageous to build a separate symbol table for each scope (as in Figure 6.17).

So far we have been discussing the standard scope rule that follows the textual structure of the program. Sometimes this is called **lexical scope** or **static scope** (since the symbol table is built statically). An alternative scope rule that is used in some dynamically oriented languages (older versions of LISP, SNOBOL, and some database query languages) is called **dynamic scope**. This rule requires that the application of nested scopes follow the execution path, rather than the textual layout of the program. A simple example that shows the difference between the two rules is the C code of Figure 6.18. This code prints 1 using the standard scope rule of C, since the scope of the variable **i** at the file level extends to procedure **f**. If dynamic scope were used, then the program would print 2, since **f** is called from **main**, and **main** contains a declaration of **i** (with value 2) that extends to **f** if we use the sequence of calls to resolve nonlocal references. Dynamic scope requires that the symbol table be built during execution by performing *insert* and *delete* operations as scopes are entered and exited at runtime. Thus, using dynamic scope requires that the symbol table become part of the environment and that code be generated by a compiler to maintain it, rather than having the symbol table built directly (and statically) by the compiler. Also, dynamic scope compromises the readability of programs, since nonlocal references cannot be resolved without simulating the execution of the program. Finally, dynamic scope is incompatible with static type checking, since the data types of variables must be maintained by the symbol table. (Note the problem that occurs in the code of Figure 6.18 if the **i** inside **main** is declared to be a **double**.) Thus, dynamic scope is rarely used in modern languages, and we will not discuss it further.

Figure 6.18

C code illustrating the difference between static and dynamic scope

```
#include <stdio.h>

int i = 1;

void f(void)
{ printf("%d\n",i);}

void main(void)
{ int i = 2;
  f();
  return 0;
}
```

Finally, we should note that the *delete* operation has been shown in Figure 6.16 to altogether eliminate declarations from the symbol table. It may in fact be necessary to keep the declarations in the table (or at least not to deallocate their memory), since other parts of the compiler may need to refer to them again later. If they must be kept in the symbol table, then the *delete* operation would need to simply mark them as no longer active, and then *lookup* will skip over such marked declarations while searching the table.

6.3.4   Interaction of Same-Level Declarations

One more issue that relates to scope is the interaction among declarations at the same nesting level (that is, associated to a single block). These can vary with the kind of declaration, and with the language being translated. One typical requirement in many languages (C, Pascal, Ada) is that there can be no reuse of the same name in declarations at the same level. Thus, in C, the following consecutive declarations will cause a compilation error:

```
typedef int i;
int i;
```

To check this requirement, a compiler must perform a *lookup* before each *insert* and determine by some mechanism (nesting level, for example) whether any preexisting declarations with the same name are at the same level or not.

Somewhat more difficult is the question of how much information the declarations in a sequence at the same level have available about each other. For example, consider the C code fragment

```
int i = 1;

void f(void)
{ int i = 2, j = i+1;
  ...
}
...
```

The question is whether **j** inside **f** is initialized to the value 2 or 3, that is, whether the local declaration for **i** or the nonlocal declaration for **i** is used. It may seem natural that the most recent declaration—the local one—is used, by the most closely nested rule. This is in fact the way C behaves. But this presupposes that each declaration is added to the symbol table as it is processed and is called **sequential declaration**. It is possible instead for all declarations to be processed "simultaneously" and added at once to the symbol table at the end of the declaration section. Then any names in expressions within the declarations would refer to previous declarations, not to the new declarations being processed. Such a declaration structure is called **collateral declaration**, and some functional languages, such as ML and Scheme, have a declaration structure like this. Such a rule for declarations requires that declarations not be added immediately to the existing symbol table, but accumulated in a new table (or temporary structure), and then added to the existing table after all declarations have been processed.

Finally, there is the case of the **recursive declaration** structure, in which declarations may refer to themselves or each other. This is particularly necessary for procedure/function declarations, where groups of mutually recursive functions are common (e.g., in a recursive-descent parser). In its simplest form, a recursive function calls itself, as in the following C code for a function that computes the greatest common divisor of two integers:

```
int gcd(int n, int m)
{ if (m == 0) return n;
  else return gcd(m,n % m);
}
```

For this to be compiled correctly, the compiler must add the function name **gcd** to the symbol table *before* processing the body of the function. Otherwise, the name **gcd** will not be found (or not have the correct meaning) when the recursive call is encountered. In more complex cases of a group of mutually recursive functions, such as in the C code fragment

```
void f(void)
{... g() ...}

void g(void)
{... f() ...}
```

simply adding each function to the symbol table before its body is processed is insuffi-cient. Indeed, the above C code fragment will produce an error during compilation at the call to **g** inside **f**. In C, this problem is removed by adding a so-called **function prototype** declaration for **g** before the declaration of **f**:

```
void g(void); /* function prototype
                         declaration */


void f(void)
{... g() ...}

void g(void)
{... f() ...}
```

Such a declaration can be seen as a **scope modifier**, extending the scope of the name **g** to include **f**. Thus, the compiler adds **g** to the symbol table when the (first) prototype declaration for **g** is reached (together with its own positional scope attribute). Of course, the body of **g** does not exist until the main declaration (or definition) of **g** is reached. Also, all prototypes of **g** must be type checked to make sure they are identical in structure.

Different solutions to the problem of mutual recursion are possible. For example, in Pascal a **forward** declaration is provided as a procedure/function scope extender. In Modula-2, the scope rule for procedures and functions (as well as variables) extends their scopes to include the entire block of their declarations, so that they are naturally mutually recursive and no additional language mechanism is necessary. This does require a processing step in which all procedures and functions are added to the sym-bol table before processing any of their bodies. Similar mutually recursive declarations are also available in a number of other languages.

6.3.5   An Extended Example of an Attribute Grammar Using a Symbol Table

We now want to consider an example demonstrating a number of the properties of dec-larations we have described and develop an attribute grammar that makes these prop-erties explicit in the behavior of the symbol table. The grammar we use for this exam-ple is the following condensation of the simple arithmetic expression grammar, together with an extension involving declarations:

$$
\begin{aligned}
&S \rightarrow exp \\
&exp \rightarrow (\ exp \ ) \mid exp + exp \mid id \mid num \mid let \ dec\text{-}list \ in \ exp \\
&dec\text{-}list \rightarrow dec\text{-}list \ , \ decl \mid decl \\
&decl \rightarrow id = exp
\end{aligned}
$$

This grammar includes a top-level start symbol S, since the attribute grammar contains inherited attributes that will need initialization at the root of the syntax tree. The gram-mar contains only one operation (addition, with token **+**) to make it very simple. It is also ambiguous, and we assume that a parser has already constructed a syntax tree or otherwise dealt with the ambiguities (we leave to the exercises the construction of an equivalent unambiguous grammar). We nevertheless include parentheses, so that we may write expressions unambiguously in this grammar if we wish. As in previous examples using similar grammars, we assume that **num** and **id** are tokens whose structure is determined by a scanner (**num** can be assumed to be a sequence of digits and **id** a sequence of characters).

The addition to the grammar that involves declarations is the **let** **expression**:

$$exp \rightarrow \textbf{let } \textit{dec-list } \textbf{in } exp$$

In a *let* expression, the declarations consist of a comma-separated sequence of declarations of the form **id** **=** *exp*. An example is

```
let x = 2+1, y = 3+4 in x + y
```

Informally, the semantics of a *let* expression are as follows. The declarations after the **let** token establish names for expressions which, when these names appear in the *exp* after the token **in**, stand for the values of the expressions they represent. (The *exp* is the **body** of the *let* expression.) The value of the *let* expression is the value of its body, which is computed by replacing each name in the declarations by the value of its corresponding *exp* and then computing the value of the body according to the rules of arithmetic. For instance, in the previous example, **x** stands for the value 3 (the value of **2+1**), and **y** stands for the value 7 (the value of **3+4**). Thus, the *let* expression itself has value 10 (= the value of **x+y** when **x** has value 3 and **y** has value 7).

From the semantics just given, we see that the declarations inside a *let* expression represent a kind of constant declaration (or binding) and that the *let* expressions represent the blocks of this language. To complete the informal discussion of the semantics of these expressions, we need to describe the scope rules and interactions of the declarations in the *let* expressions. Note that the grammar allows arbitrary nestings of *let* expressions inside each other, as, for example, in the expression

```
let x = 2, y = 3 in
  (let x = x+1, y=(let z=3 in x+y+z)
   in (x+y)
  )
```

We establish the following scope rules for the declarations of *let* expressions. First, there shall be no redeclaration of the same name within the same *let* expression. Thus, an expression of the form

```
let x=2,x=3 in x+1
```

is illegal, and results in an error. Second, if any name is not declared in some surrounding *let* expression, then an error also results. Thus, the expression

```
let x=2 in x+y
```

is erroneous. Third, the scope of each declaration in a *let* expression extends over the body of the *let* according to the most closely nested rule for block structure. Thus, the value of the expression

```
let x=2 in (let x=3 in x)
```

is 3, not 2 (since the **x** in the inner *let* refers to the declaration **x=3**, not the declaration **x=2**).

Finally, we define the interaction of the declarations in a list of declarations in the same *let* to be sequential. That is, each declaration uses the previous declarations to resolve names within its own expression. Thus, in the expression

```
let x=2,y=x+1 in (let x=x+y,y=x+y in y)
```

the first **y** has value 3 (using the previous declaration of **x**), the second **x** has value 5 (using the declarations of the enclosing *let*), and the second **y** has value 8 (using the enclosing declaration of **y** and the value of the just-declared **x**). Thus, the entire expression has value 8. We invite the reader to similarly compute the value of the triply nested *let* expression on the previous page.

We want now to develop attribute equations that use a symbol table to keep track of the declarations in *let* expressions and that express the scope rules and interactions just described. For simplicity, we only use the symbol table to determine whether an expression is erroneous or not. We will not write equations for computing the value of the expressions, but leave this to an exercise. Instead, we compute the synthesized Boolean attribute *err* that has the value **true** if the expression is erroneous and **false** if the expression is correct according to the previously stated rules. To do this, we need both an inherited atttribute *symtab*, representing the symbol table, and an inherited attribute *nestlevel* to determine whether two declarations are within the same *let* block. The value of *nestlevel* is a nonnegative integer that expresses the current nesting level of the *let* blocks. It is initialized with the value 0 at the outermost level.

The *symtab* attribute will need typical symbol table operations. Since we want to write attribute equations, we express the symbol table operations in a way free of side effects by writing the *insert* operation as taking a symbol table as a parameter and returning a new symbol table with the new information added, but with the original symbol table left unchanged. Thus, *insert*(*s*, *n*, *l*) returns a new symbol table containing all the information from symbol table *s* and in addition associating the name *n* with the nesting level *l*, without changing *s*. (Since we are determining only correctness, it is not necessary to associate a value to *n*, just a nesting level.) Since this notation guarantees that we can recover the original symbol table *s*, an explicit *delete* operation is unnecessary. Finally, to test for the two criteria that must be satisfied for correctness (that all names that appear in expressions have been previously declared and that no redeclarations occur at the same level), we must be able to test for the presence of a name in a symbol table, and also retrieve the nesting level associated with a name that is present. We do this with the two operations *isin*(*s*, *n*), which returns a Boolean value depending on whether *n* is in symbol table *s* or not, and *lookup*(*s*, *n*), which returns an integer value giving the nesting level of the most recent declaration of *n*, if it exists, or −1, if *n* is not in the symbol table *s* (this allows us to express equations using *lookup* without first having to perform an *isin* operation). Finally, we must have a notation for an initial symbol table that has no entries; we write this as *emptytable*.

With these operations and conventions for symbol tables, we now turn to writing the attribute equations for the three attributes *symtab*, *nestlevel*, and *err* of expressions. The complete attribute grammar is collected in Table 6.9.

Table 6.9

Attribute grammar for expressions with *let* blocks

Grammar Rule	Semantic Rules
$S \rightarrow exp$	$exp.symtab = emptytable$ $exp.nestlevel = 0$ $S.err = exp.err$
$exp_1 \rightarrow exp_2 + exp_3$	$exp_2.symtab = exp_1.symtab$ $exp_3.symtab = exp_1.symtab$ $exp_2.nestlevel = exp_1.nestlevel$ $exp_3.nestlevel = exp_1.nestlevel$ $exp_1.err = exp_2.err$ **or** $exp_3.err$
$exp_1 \rightarrow (exp_2)$	$exp_2.symtab = exp_1.symtab$ $exp_2.nestlevel = exp_1.nestlevel$ $exp_1.err = exp_2.err$
$exp \rightarrow$ **id**	$exp.err =$ **not** $isin(exp.symtab, \mathbf{id}.name)$
$exp \rightarrow$ **num**	$exp.err =$ **false**
$exp_1 \rightarrow$ **let** $dec\text{-}list$ **in** exp_2	$dec\text{-}list.intab = exp_1.symtab$ $dec\text{-}list.nestlevel = exp_1.nestlevel + 1$ $exp_2.symtab = dec\text{-}list.outtab$ $exp_2.nestlevel = dec\text{-}list.nestlevel$ $exp_1.err = (decl\text{-}list.outtab = errtab)$ **or** $exp_2.err$
$dec\text{-}list_1 \rightarrow dec\text{-}list_2 , decl$	$dec\text{-}list_2.intab = dec\text{-}list_1.intab$ $dec\text{-}list_2.nestlevel = dec\text{-}list_1.nestlevel$ $decl.intab = dec\text{-}list_2.outtab$ $decl.nestlevel = dec\text{-}list_2.nestlevel$ $dec\text{-}list_1.outtab = decl.outtab$
$dec\text{-}list \rightarrow decl$	$decl.intab = dec\text{-}list.intab$ $decl.nestlevel = dec\text{-}list.nestlevel$ $dec\text{-}list.outtab = decl.outtab$

$decl \rightarrow$ **id** $= exp$	$exp.symtab = decl.intab$
	$exp.nestlevel = decl.nestlevel$
	$decl.outtab =$
	    if $(decl.intab = errtab)$ **or** $exp.err$
	    then $errtab$
	    else if $lookup(decl.intab, \mathbf{id}.name) =$
	        $decl.nestlevel)$
	    then $errtab$
	    else $insert(decl.intab, \mathbf{id}.name, decl.nestlevel)$

At the topmost level, we assign the values of the two inherited attributes and lift the value of the synthesized attribute. Thus, the grammar rule $S \rightarrow exp$ has the three associated attribute equations

$$exp.symtab = emptytable$$
$$exp.nestlevel = 0$$
$$S.err = exp.err$$

Similar rules hold for the grammar rule $exp \rightarrow (exp)$.

For the rule $exp_1 \rightarrow exp_2$ + exp_3 (as usual we number the nonterminals when writing attribute equations), the following rules express the fact that the right-hand expressions inherit the attributes *symtab* and *nestlevel* from the left-hand expression and the left-hand expression contains an error if at least one of the right-hand expressions contains an error:

$$exp_2 \; .symtab = exp_1 \; .symtab$$
$$exp_3 \; .symtab = exp_1 \; .symtab$$
$$exp_2 \; .nestlevel = exp_1 \; .nestlevel$$
$$exp_3 \; .nestlevel = exp_1 \; .nestlevel$$
$$exp_1 \; .err = exp_2 \; .err \textbf{ or } exp_3 \; .err$$

The rule $exp \rightarrow \textbf{\textit{id}}$ produces an error only if the name of the **id** cannot be found in the current symbol table (we write **id** *.name* for the name of the identifier and assume that it is computed by the scanner or parser), so the associated attribute equation is

$$exp.err = \textbf{not } isin(exp.symtab, \textbf{\textit{id}} \; .name)$$

On the other hand, the rule $exp \rightarrow \textbf{\textit{num}}$ can never produce an error, so the attribute equation is

$$exp.err = \textbf{false}$$

We now turn to a discussion of *let* expressions, with grammar rule

$$exp_1 \rightarrow \textbf{let } \textit{dec-list } \textbf{in } exp_2$$

and the associated rules for declarations. In the rule for *let* expressions, the *decl-list* consists of a number of declarations that must be added to the current symbol table. We express this by associating two separate symbol tables with *decl-list*: the incoming table *intab*, which is inherited from exp_1, and the outgoing table *outtab*, which contains the new declarations (as well as the old) and which must be passed on to exp_2. Since the new declarations may contain errors (such as redeclaration of the same names), we must express this by allowing for a special *errtab* symbol table to be passed from a *dec-list*. Finally, the *let* expression has an error only if either *dec-list* contains an error (in which case its *outtab* is *errtab*) or the body exp_2 of the *let* expression contains an error. The attribute equations are

$$dec\text{-}list.intab = exp_1 \; .symtab$$
$$dec\text{-}list.nestlevel = exp_1 \; .nestlevel + 1$$
$$exp_2 \; .symtab = dec\text{-}list.outtab$$
$$exp_2 \; .nestlevel = dec\text{-}list.nestlevel$$
$$exp_1 \; .err = (decl\text{-}list.outtab = errtab) \textbf{ or } exp_2 \; .err$$

Note that the nesting level has also increased by one as soon as the *let* block is entered.

It remains to develop equations for declaration lists and for individual declarations. A declaration list must, by the sequential rule for declarations, accumulate individual declarations as processing of the list proceeds. Thus, given the rule

$$dec\text{-}list_1 \rightarrow dec\text{-}list_2 \text{ , } decl$$

the *outtab* from *dec-list$_2$* is passed as the *intab* to *decl*, thus giving *decl* access to the declarations that precede it in the list. In the case of a single declaration (*dec-list* → *decl*), the standard inheritance and lifting are performed. The complete equations are in Table 6.9.

Finally, we discuss the case of an individual declaration

$$decl \rightarrow \textbf{\textit{id}} = exp$$

In this case the inherited *decl.intab* is passed immediately to *exp* (since declarations in this language are not recursive, so *exp* should find only previous declarations of the name of this **id**, not the current one). Then, if there are no errors, **id**.*name* is inserted into the table with the current nesting level, and this is passed back as the synthesized *outtab* of the declaration. Errors can occur in three ways. First, an error may already have occurred in a previous declaration, in which case *decl.intab* is *errtab*; this *errtab* must be passed on as *outtab*. Second, an error may occur within the *exp*; this is indicated by *exp.err* and, if true, must also cause *outtab* to be *errtab*. Third, the declaration may be a redeclaration of a name at the same nesting level. This must be checked by performing a *lookup*, and this error must also be reported by forcing *outtab* to be *errtab*. (Note that if *lookup* fails to find **id**.*name*, then it returns −1, which never matches the current nesting level, so no error is generated.) The complete equation for *decl.outtab* is given in Table 6.9.

This concludes our discussion of the attribute equations.

6.4 DATA TYPES AND TYPE CHECKING

One of the principal tasks of a compiler is the computation and maintenance of information on data types (**type inference**) and the use of such information to ensure that each part of a program makes sense under the type rules of the language (**type checking**). Usually, these two tasks are closely related, performed together, and referred to simply as type checking. Data type information may be either static or dynamic, or a mixture of the two. In most dialects of LISP, type information is entirely dynamic. In such a language, a compiler must generate code to perform type inference and type checking during execution. In more traditional languages such as Pascal, C, and Ada, type information is primarily static, and is used as the principal mechanism for checking the correctness of a program prior to execution. Static type information is also used to determine the size of memory needed for the allocation of each variable and the way that memory can be accessed, and this can be used to simplify the runtime environment. (We will discuss this in the next chapter.) In this section we will only be concerned with static type checking.

Data type information can occur in a program in several different forms. Theoretically, a **data type** is a set of values, or more precisely, a set of values with certain operations on those values. For instance, the data type **integer** in a programming language refers to a subset of the mathematical integers, together with the arithmetic operations, such as + and *, that are provided for by the language definition. In the practical realm of compiler construction, these sets are usually described by a **type expression**, which is a type name, such as **integer**, or a structured expression, such as **array [1..10] of real**, whose operations are usually assumed or implied. Type expressions can occur in several places in a program. These include variable declarations, such as

```
var x: array [1..10] of real;
```

which associates a type to a variable name, and type declarations, such as

```
type RealArray = array [1..10] of real;
```

which defines a new type name for use in subsequent type or variable declarations. Such type information is **explicit**. It is also possible for type information to be **implicit**, as for example in the Pascal constant declaration

```
const greeting = "Hello!";
```

where the type of **greeting** is implicitly **array [1..6] of char** according to the rules of Pascal.

Type information, either explicit or implicit, that is contained in declarations, is maintained in the symbol table and retrieved by the type checker whenever the associated names are referenced. New types are then inferred from these types and are associated to the appropriate nodes in the syntax tree. For instance, in the expression

```
a[i]
```

the data types of the names **a** and **i** are fetched from the symbol table. If **a** has type **array [1..10] of real** and i has type **integer**, then the subexpression **a[i]** is determined to be type correct and has type **real**. (The question of whether **i** has a value that is between 1 and 10 is a **range checking** question that is not in general statically determinable.)

The way data types are represented by a compiler, the way a symbol table maintains type information, and the rules used by a type checker to infer types, all depend on the kinds of type expressions available in a language and the type rules of the language that govern the use of these type expressions.

6.4.1 Type Expressions and Type Constructors

A programming language always contains a number of built-in types, with names like **int** and **double**. These **predefined** types correspond either to numeric data types that are provided internally by various machine architectures, and whose operations already exist as machine instructions, or are elementary types like **boolean** or **char** whose behavior is easy to implement. Such data types are **simple types**, in that their values exhibit no explicit internal structure. A typical representation for integers is two- or four-byte two's complement form. A typical representation for real, or floating-point, numbers is four or eight bytes, with a sign bit, an exponent field, and a fraction (or mantissa) field. A typical representation for characters is as one-byte ASCII codes, and for Boolean values is as one byte, only the least significant bit of which is used (1 = true, 0 = false). Sometimes a language will impose restrictions on how these predefined types are to be implemented. For instance, the C language standard requires that a **double** floating-point type has at least 10 decimal digits of precision.

An interesting predefined type in the C language is the **void** type. This type has no values, and so represents the empty set. It is used to represent a function that returns no value (i.e., a procedure), as well as to represent a pointer that (as yet) points to no known type.

In some languages, it is possible to define new simple types. Typical examples of these are **subrange types** and **enumerated types**. For instance, in Pascal the subrange of the integers consisting of the values 0 through 9 can be declared as

```
type Digit = 0..9;
```

while an enumerated type consisting of the named values **red**, **green**, and **blue** can be declared in C as

```
typedef enum {red,green,blue} Color;
```

Implementations of both subranges and enumerations could be as integers, or a smaller amount of memory could be used that is sufficient to represent all the values.

Given a set of predefined types, new data types can be created using **type constructors**, such as **array** and **record** or **struct**. Such constructors can be viewed as functions that take existing types as parameters and return new types with a structure that depends on the constructor. Such types are often called **structured types**. In the classification of such types, it is important to understand the nature of the set of values that such a type represents. Often, a type constructor will correspond closely to a set operation on the underlying sets of values of its parameters. We illustrate this by listing a number of common constructors and compare them to set operations.

Array   The array type constructor takes two type parameters, one the **index type** and the other the **component type** and produces a new array type. In Pascal-like syntax we write

$$\textbf{array} \; [\textit{index-type}] \; \textbf{of} \; \textit{component-type}$$

For example, the Pascal type expression

```
array [Color] of char;
```

creates an array type whose index type is **Color** and whose component type is **char**. Often there are restrictions on the types that can occur as index types. For example, in Pascal an index type is limited to so-called **ordinal types**: types for which every value has an immediate predecessor and an immediate successor. Such types include integer and character subranges and enumerated types. In C by contrast, only integer ranges beginning at 0 are allowed, and only the size is specified in place of the index type. Indeed there is no keyword corresponding to **array** in C—array types are declared by simply suffixing a range inside brackets. Thus there is no direct equivalent in C to the foregoing Pascal type expression, but the C type declaration

```
typedef char Ar[3];
```

defines a type **Ar** that has an equivalent type structure to the foregoing type (assuming that **Color** has three values).

An array represents values that are sequences of values of the component type, indexed by values of the index type. That is, if *index-type* has set of values *I* and *component-type* has set of values *C*, then the set of values corresponding to the type **array [***index-type***] of** *component-type* is the set of finite sequences of elements of *C* indexed by elements of *I*, or in mathematical terms, the set of functions $I \rightarrow C$. The associated operations on values of the array type consist of the single operation of subscripting, which can be used to either assign values to components or fetch component values: **x := a[red]** or **a[blue] := y**.

Arrays are commonly allocated contiguous storage from smaller to larger indexes, to allow for the use of automatic offset calculations during execution. The amount of memory needed is *n* * *size*, where *n* is the number of values in the index type and *size* is the amount of memory needed for a value of the component type. Thus, a variable of type **array [0..9] of integer** needs 40 bytes of storage if each integer occupies 4 bytes.

One complication in the declaration of arrays is that of **multidimensioned arrays**. These can often be declared using either repeated applications of the array type constructor, as in

```
array [0..9] of array [Color] of integer;
```

or in a shorter version in which the index sets are listed together:

```
array [0..9,Color] of integer;
```

Subscripting in the first case appears as **a[1][red]**, while in the second case we write **a[1,red]**. One problem with multiple subscripts is that the sequence of values can be organized in different ways in memory depending on whether the indexing is done first on the first index, and then on the second index, or vice versa. Indexing on the first index results in a sequencing in memory that looks like **a[0,red]**, **a[1,red]**, **a[2,red]**, . . . , **a[9,red]**, **a[0,blue]**, **a[1,blue]**, . . . , and so on (this is called **column-major form**), while indexing on the second index results in the memory order **a[0,red]**, **a[0,blue]**, **a[0,green]**, **a[1,red]**, **a[1,blue]**, **a[1,green]**, . . . , and so on (this is called **row-major form**). If the repeated version of multidimensional array declaration is to be equivalent to the shortened version (i.e., **a[0,red]** = **a[0][red]**), then row-major form must be used, since the different indices can be added separately: **a[0]** must have type **array [Color] of integer** and must refer to a contiguous portion of memory. The FORTRAN language, in which there is no partial indexing of multidimensional arrays, has traditionally been implemented using column-major form.

Occasionally, a language will permit the use of an array whose index range is unspecified. Such an **open-indexed array** is especially useful in the declaration of array parameters to functions, so that the function can handle arrays of different sizes. For example, the C declaration

```
void sort (int a[], int first, int last)
```

can be used to define a sorting procedure that will work on any sized array **a**. (Of course, some method must be used to determine the actual size at the time of call. In this example, other parameters do this.)

Record A **record** or **structure** type constructor takes a list of names and associated types and constructs a new type, as in the C

```
struct
{ double r;
  int i;
}
```

Records differ from arrays in that components of different types may be combined (in an array all the components have the same type) and that names (rather than indices) are used to access the different components. The values of a record type correspond roughly to the Cartesian product of the values of its component types, except that names rather than positions are used to access the components. For example, the previously given record corresponds roughly to the Cartesian product $R \times I$, where R is the set corresponding to the **double** type and I is the set corresponding to **int**. More precisely, the given record corresponds to the Cartesian product $(\mathbf{r} \times R) \times (\mathbf{i} \times I)$, where the names **r** and **i** identify the components. These names are usually used with a **dot notation** to select their corresponding components in expressions. Thus, if **x** is a variable of the given record type, then **x.r** refers to its first component and **x.i** to its second.

Some languages have pure Cartesian product type constructors. Such a language is ML, where **int*real** is the notation for the Cartesian product of the integers and the real numbers. Values of type **int*real** are written as tuples, such as **(2,3.14)**, and the components are accessed by projection functions **fst** and **snd** (for first and second): **fst(2,3.14) = 2** and **snd(2,3.14) = 3.14**.

The standard implementation method for a record or Cartesian product is to allocate memory sequentially, with a block of memory for each component type. Thus, if a real number requires four bytes and an integer two bytes, then the previously given record structure needs six bytes of storage, which is allocated as follows:

Union A union type corresponds to the set union operation. It is available directly in C via the **union** declaration, as for example the declaration

```
union
{ double r;
  int i;
}
```

which defines a type that is the union of the real numbers and the integers. Strictly speaking, this is a **disjoint union**, since each value is viewed as either a real or an integer, but never both. Which interpretation is desired is made clear by the component name used to access the value: if **x** is a variable of the given union type, then **x.r** means the value of **x** as a real number, while **x.i** means the value of **x** as an integer. Mathematically, this union is defined by writing $(\mathbf{r} \times R) \cup (\mathbf{i} \times I)$.

The standard implementation method for a union is to allocate memory in parallel for each component, so that the memory for each component type overlaps with all the others. Thus, if a real number requires four bytes and an integer two bytes, then the previously given union structure needs only four bytes of storage (the maximum of the memory requirements of its components), and this memory is allocated as follows:

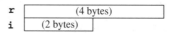

Such an implementation requires, in fact, that the union be interpreted as a disjoint union, since the representation of an integer will not agree with its corresponding representation as a real. Indeed, without some means for a programmer to distinguish the values, such a union leads to errors in data interpretation, and also provides a way to circumvent a type checker. For example, in C if **x** is a variable that has the given union type, then writing

```
x.r = 2.0;
printf("%d",x.i);
```

will not cause a compilation error, but will not print the value 2, but a garbage value instead.

This insecurity in union types has been addressed by many different language designs. In Pascal, for instance, a union type is declared using a so-called **variant record**, in which values from an ordinal type are recorded in a **discriminant** component and used to distinguish the intended values. Thus, the previous union type can be written in Pascal as

```
record case isReal: boolean of
   true:(r: real);
   false:(i: integer);
end;
```

Now a variable **x** of this type has three components: **x.isReal** (a Boolean value), **x.r** and **x.i**, and the **isReal** field is allocated a separate nonoverlapping space in memory. When assigning a real value such as **x.r := 2.0**, one should then also make the assignment **x.isReal := true**. In reality, this mechanism is relatively useless (at least for the use of the compiler in type checking) since the discriminant can be assigned separately from the values being discriminated. Indeed, Pascal permits the discriminant component (but not the use of its values to distinguish cases) to be dropped by deleting its name in the declaration, as in

```
record case boolean of
   true:(r: real);
   false:(i: integer);
end;
```

which no longer causes space for the discriminant to be allocated in memory. Thus, Pascal compilers almost never make any attempt to use the discriminant as a legality check. Ada, on the other hand, has a similar mechanism, but insists that whenever a union component is assigned, the discriminant must be simultaneously assigned with a value that can be checked for legality.

A different approach is taken by functional languages such as the language ML. In that language, a union type is defined using a vertical bar to indicate union, and by giving names to each component to discriminate them, as in

> `IsReal of real | IsInteger of int`

Now the names **IsReal** and **IsInteger** must also be used whenever a value of this type is used, as in (**IsReal 2.0**) or (**IsInteger 2**). The names **IsReal** and **IsIntegers** are called **value constructors**, since they "construct" values of this type. Since they must always be used when referring to values of this type, no error of interpretation can occur.

Pointer   A pointer type consists of values that are references to values of another type. Thus, a value of a pointer type is a memory address whose location holds a value of its base type. Pointer types are frequently thought of as numeric types, since arithmetic calculations, such as adding offsets and multiplying by scale factors, can be performed on them. Yet they are not really simple types, since they are constructed from existing types by applying a pointer type constructor. There is also no standard set operation that directly corresponds to the pointer type constructor, as Cartesian product corresponds to the record constructor. Thus, pointer types occupy a somewhat special position in a type system.

In Pascal the character ^ corresponds to the pointer type constructor, so that the type expression ^**integer** means "pointer to integer." In C, an equivalent type expression is **int***. The standard basic operation on a value of a pointer type is the **dereference** operation. For example, in Pascal, the ^ stands for the dereference operator (as well as the pointer type constructor), and if **p** is a variable of type ^**integer**, then **p^** is the dereferenced value of **p** and has type **integer**. A similar rule holds in C, where * dereferences a pointer variable and is written ***p**.

Pointer types are most useful in describing recursive types, which we discuss shortly. In doing so, the pointer type constructor is most often applied to record types.

Pointer types are allocated space based on the address size of the target machine. Usually, this is four, or occasionally eight, bytes. Sometimes a machine architecture will force a more complex allocation scheme. In DOS-based PCs, for instance, a distinction is made between **near** pointers (for addresses within a segment, with size two bytes) and **far** pointers (addresses that may be outside a single segment, with size four bytes).

Function   We have already noted that an array can be viewed as a function from its index set to its component set. Many languages (but not Pascal or Ada) have a more general ability to describe function types. For example, in Modula-2 the declaration

> `VAR f: PROCEDURE (INTEGER): INTEGER;`

declares the variable **f** to be of function (or procedure) type, with an integer parameter and yielding an integer result. In mathematical notation, this set would be described as the set of functions $\{ f: I \to I \}$, where I is the set of integers. In the language ML this same type would be written as `int -> int`. The C language also has function types, but they must be written as "pointer to function," in a somewhat awkward notation. For instance, the Modula-2 declaration just given must be written in C as

```
int (*f) (int);
```

Function types are allocated space according to the address size of the target machine. Depending on the language and the organization of the runtime environment, a function type may need to be allocated space for a code pointer alone (pointing to the code implementing the function) or a code pointer and an environment pointer (pointing to a location in the runtime environment). The role of the environment pointer is discussed in the next chapter.

Class   Most object-oriented languages have a class declaration that is similar to a record declaration, except that it includes the definition of operations, called **methods** or **member functions**. Class declarations may or may not create new types in an object-oriented language (in C++ they do). Even if this is the case, class declarations are not *just* types, since they permit the use of features that are beyond the type system, such as inheritance and dynamic binding.[10] These latter properties must be maintained by separate data structures, such as the **class hierarchy** (a directed acyclic graph), which implements inheritance, and the **virtual method table**, which implements dynamic binding. We shall discuss these structures again in the next chapter.

6.4.2   Type Names, Type Declarations, and Recursive Types

Languages that have a rich set of type constructors usually also have a mechanism for a programmer to assign names to type expressions. Such **type declarations** (sometimes also called **type definitions**) include the `typedef` mechanism of C and the type definitions of Pascal. For example, the C code

```
typedef struct
      { double r;
        int i;
      } RealIntRec;
```

defines the name **RealIntRec** as a name for the record type constructed by the `struct` type expression that precedes it. In the language ML, a similar declaration (but without the field names) is

```
type RealIntRec = real*int;
```

---

10. In some languages, such as C++, inheritance is mirrored in the type system, since subclasses are viewed as **subtypes** (a type S is a subtype of type T if all of its values can be viewed as values of T, or, in set terminology, if $S \subset T$).

The C language has an additional type naming mechanism in which a name can be associated directly with a **struct** or **union** constructor, without using a **typedef** directly. For example, the C code

```
struct RealIntRec
      { double r;
        int i;
      };
```

also declares a type name **RealIntRec**, but it must be used with the **struct** constructor name in variable declarations:

```
struct RealIntRec x; /* declares x a var
                          of RealIntRec type */
```

Type declarations cause the declared type names to be entered into the symbol table just as variable declarations cause variable names to be entered. One question that arises is whether type names can be reused as variable names or not. Usually this is not permitted (except as allowed by the scope nesting rules). The C language has a small exception to this rule in that names associated to **struct** or **union** declarations can be reused as **typedef** names:

```
struct RealIntRec
      { double r;
        int i;
      };
typedef struct RealIntRec RealIntRec;
/* a legal declaration ! */
```

This can be achieved by considering the type name introduced by the **struct** declaration to be the entire string "**struct RealIntRec**," which is different from the type name **RealIntRec** introduced by the **typedef**.

Type names are associated with attributes in the symbol table in a similar way to variable declarations. These attributes include the scope (which can be inherent in the structure of the symbol table) and the type expression corresponding to the type name. Since type names can appear in type expressions, questions arise about the recursive use of type names that are similar to the recursive definition of functions, discussed in the previous section. Such **recursive data types** are extremely important in modern programming languages and include lists, trees, and many other structures.

Languages divide into two general groups in their handling of recursive types. The first group consists of those languages that permit the direct use of recursion in type declarations. Such a language is ML. In ML, for instance, a binary search tree containing integers can be declared as

```
datatype intBST = Nil | Node of int*intBST*intBST
```

This can be viewed as a definition of **intBST** as the union of the value **Nil** with the Cartesian product of the integers with two copies of **intBST** itself (one for the left subtree and one for the right subtree). An equivalent C declaration (in slightly altered form) is

```
struct intBST
{ int isNull;
  int val;
  struct intBST left,right;
};
```

This declaration will, however, generate an error message in C, which is caused by the recursive use of the type name **intBST**. The problem is that these declarations do not determine the size of the memory needed to allocate a variable of type **intBST**. The class of languages, such as ML, that can accept such declarations are those languages that do not need such information in advance of execution and those are the languages that provide a general automatic memory allocation and deallocation mechanism. Such memory management facilities are part of the runtime environment and are discussed in the next chapter. C does not have such a mechanism, and so must make such recursive type declarations illegal. C is representative of the second group of languages—those that do not permit the direct use of recursion in type declarations.

The solution for such languages is to allow recursion only **indirectly**, through pointers. A correct declaration for **intBST** in C is

```
struct intBST
{ int val;
  struct intBST *left,*right;
};
typedef struct intBST * intBST;
```

or

```
typedef struct intBST * intBST;
struct intBST
{ int val;
  intBST left,right;
};
```

(In C, recursive declarations require the use of the **struct** or **union** form for the declaration of the recursive type name.) In these declarations the memory size of each type is directly computable by a compiler, but space for values must be allocated manually by the programmer through the use of allocation procedures such as **malloc**.

6.4.3   Type Equivalence

Given the possible type expressions of a language, a type checker must frequently answer the question of when two type expressions represent the same type. This is the question of **type equivalence**. There are many possible ways for type equivalence to be defined by a language. In this section we briefly discuss only the most common forms of equivalence. In this discussion we represent type equivalence as it would be in a compiler semantic analyzer, namely, as a function

function *typeEqual* **(** *t1, t2* : *TypeExp* **)** : *Boolean*;

which takes two type expressions and returns *true* if they represent the same type according to the type equivalence rules of the language and *false* otherwise. We will give several different pseudocode descriptions of this function for different type equivalence algorithms.

One issue that relates directly to the description of type equivalence algorithms is the way type expressions are represented within a compiler. One straightforward method is to use a syntax tree representation, since this makes it easy to translate directly from the syntax in declarations to the internal representation of the types. To have a concrete example of such representations, consider the grammar for type expressions and variable declarations given in Figure 6.19. Simple versions of many of the type structures we have discussed appear there. There are, however, no type declarations that permit the association of new type names to type expressions (and hence no recursive types are possible, despite the presence of pointer types). We want to describe a possible syntax tree structure for type expressions corresponding to the grammar rules in that figure.

Consider, first, the type expression

```
record
   x: pointer to real;
   y: array [10] of int
end
```

This type expression can be represented by the syntax tree

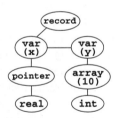

Here the child nodes of the record are represented as a sibling list, since the number of components of a record is arbitrary. Note that the nodes representing simple types form the leaves of the tree.

Figure 6.19

A simple grammar for type expressions

$$
\begin{aligned}
&\textit{var-decls} \rightarrow \textit{var-decls} \textbf{ ; } \textit{var-decl} \mid \textit{var-decl} \\
&\textit{var-decl} \rightarrow \textbf{id : } \textit{type-exp} \\
&\textit{type-exp} \rightarrow \textit{simple-type} \mid \textit{structured-type} \\
&\textit{simple-type} \rightarrow \textbf{int} \mid \textbf{bool} \mid \textbf{real} \mid \textbf{char} \mid \textbf{void} \\
&\textit{structured-type} \rightarrow \textbf{array [num] of } \textit{type-exp} \mid \\
&\qquad\qquad \textbf{record } \textit{var-decls} \textbf{ end} \mid \\
&\qquad\qquad \textbf{union } \textit{var-decls} \textbf{ end} \mid \\
&\qquad\qquad \textbf{pointer to } \textit{type-exp} \mid \\
&\qquad\qquad \textbf{proc (} \textit{type-exps} \textbf{) } \textit{type-exp} \\
&\textit{type-exps} \rightarrow \textit{type-exps} \textbf{ , } \textit{type-exp} \mid \textit{type-exp}
\end{aligned}
$$

Similarly, the type expression

```
proc(bool,union a:real; b:char end,int):void
```

can be represented by the syntax tree

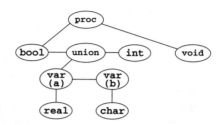

Note that the parameter types are also given as a sibling list, while the result type (**void**, in this example) is distinguished by making it directly a child of **proc**.

The first kind of type equivalence that we describe, and the only one available in the absence of names for types, is **structural equivalence**. In this view of equivalence, two types are the same if and only if they have the same structure. If syntax trees are used to represent types, this rule says that two types are equivalent if and only if they have syntax trees that are identical in structure. As an example of how structural equivalence is checked in practice, Figure 6.20 gives a pseudocode description of the *typeEqual* function for the structural equivalence of two type expressions given by the grammar of Figure 6.19, using the syntax tree structure we have just described.

We note from the pseudocode of Figure 6.20 that this version of structural equivalence implies that two arrays are not equivalent unless they have the same size and component type and two records are not equivalent unless they have the same components with the same names and in the same order. It is possible for different choices to be made in a structural equivalence algorithm. For instance, the size of the array could be ignored in determining equivalence, and it would also be possible to allow the components of a structure or union to occur in a different order.

A much more restrictive type equivalence can be defined when new type names for type expressions can be declared in a type declaration. In Figure 6.21, we have modified the grammar of Figure 6.19 to include type declarations, and we have also restricted variable declarations and type subexpressions to simple types and type names. With these declarations one can no longer write

```
record
   x: pointer to real;
   y: array [10] of int
end
```

but must write instead

```
t1 = pointer to real;
t2 = array [10] of int;
t3 = record
        x: t1;
        y: t2
end
```

Figure 6.20

Pseudocode for a *typeEqual* function that tests structural equivalence of type expressions from the grammar of Figure 6.19

```
function typeEqual ( t1, t2 : TypeExp ) : Boolean;
var temp : Boolean ;
    p1, p2 : TypeExp ;
begin
  if t1 and t2 are of simple type then return t1 = t2
  else if t1.kind = array and t2.kind = array then
      return t1.size = t2.size and typeEqual ( t1.child1, t2.child1)
  else if t1.kind = record and t2.kind = record
      or t1.kind = union and t2.kind = union then
  begin
    p1 := t1.child1 ;
    p2 := t2.child1 ;
    temp := true ;
    while temp and p1 ≠ nil and p2 ≠ nil do
        if p1.name ≠ p2.name then
          temp := false
        else if not typeEqual ( p1.child1 , p2.child1 )
        then temp := false
        else begin
          p1 := p1.sibling ;
          p2 := p2.sibling ;
        end;
    return temp and p1 = nil and p2 = nil ;
  end
  else if t1.kind = pointer and t2.kind = pointer then
      return typeEqual ( t1.child1 , t2.child1 )
  else if t1.kind = proc and t2.kind = proc then
  begin
    p1 := t1.child1 ;
    p2 := t2.child1 ;
    temp := true ;
    while temp and p1 ≠ nil and p2 ≠ nil do
        if not typeEqual ( p1.child1 , p2.child1 )
        then temp := false
        else begin
          p1 := p1.sibling ;
          p2 := p2.sibling ;
        end;
    return temp and p1 = nil and p2 = nil
            and typeEqual ( t1.child2 , t2.child2 )
  end
  else return false ;
end ; (* typeEqual *)
```

$var\text{-}decls \rightarrow var\text{-}decls$ **;** $var\text{-}decl \mid var\text{-}decl$
$var\text{-}decl \rightarrow$ **id** **:** $simple\text{-}type\text{-}exp$
$type\text{-}decls \rightarrow type\text{-}decls$ **;** $type\text{-}decl \mid type\text{-}decl$
$type\text{-}decl \rightarrow$ **id** **=** $type\text{-}exp$
$type\text{-}exp \rightarrow simple\text{-}type\text{-}exp \mid structured\text{-}type$
$simple\text{-}type\text{-}exp \rightarrow simple\text{-}type \mid$ **id**
$simple\text{-}type \rightarrow$ **int** $\mid$ **bool** $\mid$ **real** $\mid$ **char** $\mid$ **void**
$structured\text{-}type \rightarrow$ **array** **[num]** **of** $simple\text{-}type\text{-}exp \mid$
            record $var\text{-}decls$ **end** $\mid$
            union $var\text{-}decls$ **end** $\mid$
            pointer to $simple\text{-}type\text{-}exp \mid$
            proc($type\text{-}exps$ **)** $simple\text{-}type\text{-}exp$
$type\text{-}exps \rightarrow type\text{-}exps$ **,** $simple\text{-}type\text{-}exp \mid simple\text{-}type\text{-}exp$

Now we can define type equivalence based on type names, and this form of type equivalence is called **name equivalence**: two type expressions are equivalent if and only if they are either the same simple type or are the same type name. This is a very strong sort of type equivalence, since now given the type declarations

```
t1 = int;
t2 = int
```

the types **t1** and **t2** are not equivalent (since they are different names) and are also not equivalent to **int**. Pure name equivalence is very easy to implement, since a *typeEqual* function can be written in a few lines:

function *typeEqual* (*t1, t2* : *TypeExp*) : *Boolean*;
var *temp* : *Boolean* ;
     p1, p2 : *TypeExp* ;
begin
   if *t1 and t2 are of simple type* **then**
       return *t1* = *t2*
   else if *t1 and t2 are type names* **then**
       return *t1* = *t2*
   else return *false* ;
end;

Of course, the actual type expressions corresponding to type names must be entered into the symbol table to permit the later calculation of memory size for storage allocation and to check the validity of operations such as pointer dereferencing and component selection.

One complication in name equivalence is when type expressions other than simple types or type names continue to be allowed in variable declarations, or as subexpressions of type expressions. In such cases, a type expression may have no explicit name given to it, and a compiler will have to generate an internal name for the type expression that is different from any other names. For example, given the variable declarations

```
x: array [10] of int;
y: array [10] of int;
```

the variables **x** and **y** are assigned different (and unique) type names corresponding to the type expression **array [10] of int**.

It is possible to retain structural equivalence in the presence of type names. In this case, when a name is encountered, its corresponding type expression must be fetched from the symbol table. This can be accomplished by adding the following case to the code of Figure 6.20,

> **else if** *t1 and t2 are type names* **then**
>   **return** *typeEqual(getTypeExp(t1), getTypeExp(t2))*

where *getTypeExp* is a symbol table operation that returns the type expression structure associated to its parameter (which must be a type name). This requires that each type name be inserted into the symbol table with a type expression representing its structure, or at least that chains of type names resulting from type declarations such as

```
t2 = t1;
```

lead eventually back to a type structure in the symbol table.

Care must be taken in implementing structural equivalence when recursive type references are possible, since the algorithm just described can result in an infinite loop. This can be avoided by modifying the behavior of the call *typeEqual(t1, t2)* in the case where *t1* and *t2* are type names to include the assumption that they are already potentially equal. Then if the *typeEqual* function ever returns to the same call, success can be declared at that point. Consider, for example, the type declarations

```
t1 = record
        x: int;
        t: pointer to t2;
     end;

t2 = record
        x: int;
        t: pointer to t1;
     end;
```

Given the call *typeEqual(t1, t2)*, the *typeEqual* function will assume that *t1* and *t2* are potentially equal. Then the structures of both *t1* and *t2* will be fetched, and the algorithm will proceed successfully until the call *typeEqual(t2, t1)* is made to analyze the child types of the pointer declarations. This call will then immediately return *true*, because of the assumption of potential equality made in the original call. In general, this algorithm will need to make successive assumptions that pairs of type names may be equal and accumulate the assumptions in a list. Eventually, of course, the algorithm must either succeed or fail (i.e., it cannot get into an infinite loop), because there are only finitely many type names in any given program. We leave the details of the modifications to the *typeEqual* pseudocode to an exercise (see also the Notes and References section).

A final variation on type equivalence is a weaker version of name equivalence used by Pascal and C, called **declaration equivalence**. In this method type, declarations such as

```
t2 = t1;
```

are interpreted as establishing type **aliases**, rather than new types (as in name equivalence). Thus, given the declarations

```
t1 = int;
t2 = int
```

both **t1** and **t2** are equivalent to **int** (that is, they are just aliases for the type name **int**). In this version of type equivalence, every type name is equivalent to some base type name, which is either a predefined type or is given by a type expression resulting from the application of a type constructor. For example, given the declarations

```
t1 = array [10] of int;
t2 = array [10] of int;
t3 = t1;
```

the type names **t1** and **t3** are equivalent under declaration equivalence, but neither is equivalent to **t2**.

To implement declaration equivalence, a new operation *getBaseTypeName* must be provided by the symbol table, which fetches the base type name rather than the associated type expression. A type name can be distinguished in the symbol table as being a base type name if it is either a predefined type or is given by a type expression that is not simply another type name. Note that declaration equivalence, similar to name equivalence, solves the problem of infinite loops in checking recursive types, since two base type names can only be declaration equivalent if they are the same name.

Pascal uniformly uses declaration equivalence, while C uses declaration equivalence for structures and unions, but structural equivalence for pointers and arrays.

Occasionally, a language will offer a choice of structural, declaration, or name equivalence, where different type declarations are used for different forms of equivalence. For instance, the ML language allows type names to be declared as aliases using the reserved word **type**, as in the declaration

```
type RealIntRec = real*int;
```

This declares **RealIntRec** to be an alias of the Cartesian product type **real*int**. On the other hand, the **datatype** declaration creates a completely new type, as in the declaration

```
datatype intBST = Nil | Node of int*intBST*intBST
```

Note that a **datatype** declaration must also contain value constructor names (**Nil** and **Node** in the given declaration), unlike a **type** declaration. This makes the values of the new type distinguishable from the values of existing types. Thus, given the declaration

```
datatype NewRealInt = Prod of real*int;
```

the value **(2.7,10)** is of type **RealIntRec** or **real*int**, while the value **Prod(2.7,10)** is of type **NewRealInt** (but not **real*int**).

6.4.4   Type Inference and Type Checking

We proceed now to describe a type checker for a simple language in terms of semantic actions, based on a representation of types and a *typeEqual* operation as discussed in previous sections. The language we use has the grammar given in Figure 6.22, which includes a small subset of the type expressions of Figure 6.19, with a small number of expressions and statements added. We also assume the availability of a symbol table that contains variable names and associated types, with operations *insert*, which inserts a name and a type into the table, and *lookup*, which returns the associated type of a name. We will not specify the properties of these operations themselves in the attribute grammar. We discuss the type inference and type checking rules for each kind of language construct individually. The complete list of semantic actions is given in Table 6.10 (page 330). These actions are not given in pure attribute grammar form, and we use the symbol := rather than equality in the rules of Table 6.10 to indicate this.

Figure 6.22

A simple grammar to
illustrate type checking

$program \rightarrow var\text{-}decls \; \textbf{;} \; stmts$
$var\text{-}decls \rightarrow var\text{-}decls \; \textbf{;} \; var\text{-}decl \mid var\text{-}decl$
$var\text{-}decl \rightarrow \textbf{id} \; \textbf{:} \; type\text{-}exp$
$type\text{-}exp \rightarrow \textbf{int} \mid \textbf{bool} \mid \textbf{array} \; \textbf{[num]} \; \textbf{of} \; type\text{-}exp$
$stmts \rightarrow stmts \; \textbf{;} \; stmt \mid stmt$
$stmt \rightarrow \textbf{if} \; exp \; \textbf{then} \; stmt \mid \textbf{id} \; \textbf{:=} \; exp$

Declarations   Declarations cause the type of an identifier to be entered into the symbol table. Thus, the grammar rule

$$var\text{-}decl \rightarrow \textbf{id} \; \textbf{:} \; type\text{-}exp$$

has the associated semantic action

$$insert(\textbf{id}.name, type\text{-}exp.type)$$

which inserts an identifier into the symbol table and associates a type to it. The associated type in this insertion is constructed according to the grammar rules for *type-exp*.

Table 6.10

Attribute grammar for type checking of the simple grammar of Figure 6.22

Grammar Rule	Semantic Rules
var-decl → **id** : type-exp	insert(**id** .name, type-exp.type)
type-exp → **int**	type-exp.type := integer
type-exp → **bool**	type-exp.type := boolean
type-exp$_1$ → **array** [**num**] **of** type-exp$_2$	type-exp$_1$ .type := makeTypeNode(array, **num** .size, type-exp$_2$ .type)
stmt → **if** exp **then** stmt	**if not** typeEqual(exp.type, boolean) **then** type-error(stmt)
stmt → **id** **:=** exp	**if not** typeEqual(lookup(**id** .name), exp.type) **then** type-error(stmt)
exp$_1$ → exp$_2$ **+** exp$_3$	**if not** (typeEqual(exp$_2$ .type, integer) **and** typeEqual(exp$_3$ .type, integer)) **then** type-error(exp$_1$) ; exp$_1$ .type := integer
exp$_1$ → exp$_2$ **or** exp$_3$	**if not** (typeEqual(exp$_2$ .type, boolean) **and** typeEqual(exp$_3$ .type, boolean)) **then** type-error(exp$_1$) ; exp$_1$ .type := boolean
exp$_1$ → exp$_2$ [exp$_3$]	**if** isArrayType(exp$_2$ .type) **and** typeEqual(exp$_3$ .type, integer) **then** exp$_1$ .type := exp$_2$ .type.child1 **else** type-error(exp$_1$)
exp → **num**	exp.type := integer
exp → **true**	exp.type := boolean
exp → **false**	exp.type := boolean
exp → **id**	exp.type := lookup(**id** .name)

Types are assumed to be kept as some kind of tree structure, so that the one structured type **array** in the grammar of Figure 6.22 corresponds to the semantic action

$$makeTypeNode(array, size, type)$$

which constructs a type node

where the child of the array node is the type tree given by the *type* parameter. The simple types *integer* and *boolean* are assumed to be constructed as standard leaf nodes in the tree representation.

Statements   Statements do not themselves have types, but substructures will need to be checked for type correctness. Typical situations are shown by the two statement rules in the sample grammar, the if-statement and the assignment statement. In the case of the if-statement, the conditional expression must have Boolean type. This is indicated by the rule

$$\textbf{if not } typeEqual(exp.type, boolean) \textbf{ then } type\text{-}error(stmt)$$

where *type-error* indicates an error reporting mechanism whose behavior will be described shortly.

In the case of the assignment statement, the requirement is that the variable being assigned must have the same type as the expression whose value it is to receive. This depends on the type equivalence algorithm as expressed by the *typeEqual* function.

Expressions   Constant expressions, such as numbers and the Boolean values **true** and **false**, have implicitly defined *integer* and *boolean* types. Variable names have their types determined by a *lookup* in the symbol table. Other expressions are formed by operators, such as the arithmetic operator **+**, the Boolean operator **or**, and the subscript operator **[]**. In each case the subexpressions must be of the correct type for the indicated operation. In the case of subscripting, this is indicated by the rule

$$\textbf{if } isArrayType(exp_2.type)$$
$$\textbf{and } typeEqual(exp_3.type, integer)$$
$$\textbf{then } exp_1.type := exp_2.type.child1 \textbf{ else } type\text{-}error(exp_1)$$

Here the function *isArrayType* tests that its parameter is an array type, that is, that the tree representation of the type has a root node that represents the array type constructor. The type of the resulting subscript expression is the base type of the array, which is the type represented by the (first) child of the root node in the tree representation of an array type, and this is indicated by writing $exp_2.type.child1$.

It remains to describe the behavior of such a type checker in the presence of errors, as indicated by the *type-error* procedure in the semantic rules of Table 6.10. The primary issues are when to generate an error message and how to continue to check types in the presence of errors. An error message should *not* be generated every time a type error occurs; otherwise, a single error could cause a cascade of many errors to be printed (something that can also happen with parse errors). Instead, if the *type-error* procedure can determine that a type error must already have occurred in a related place, then the generation of an error message should be suppressed. This can be signaled by having a special internal error type (which can be represented by a null type tree). If *typeError* encounters this error type in a substructure, then no error message is generated. At the same time, if a type error also means that the type of a structure cannot be determined, then the type checker can use the error type as its (actually unknown) type. For instance, in the semantic rules of Table 6.10, given a subscripted expression $exp_1 \rightarrow exp_2[exp_3]$, if exp_2 is not an array type, then exp_1 cannot be assigned a valid type, and there is no assignment of a type in the semantic actions. This assumes that type fields have been initialized to some error type. On the other hand, in the case of the operations **+** and **or**, even in the presence of a type error, the assumption can be made that the result is meant to be of integer or Boolean type, and the rules of Table 6.10 use that fact to assign a type to the result.

6.4.5   Additional Topics in Type Checking

In this subsection we briefly discuss some of the common extensions to the type checking algorithms that we have discussed.

Overloading   An operator is **overloaded** if the same operator name is used for two different operations. A common example of overloading is the case of the arithmetic operators, which often represent operations on different numeric values. For instance, **2+3** represents integer addition, while **2.1+3.0** represents floating-point addition, which must be implemented internally by a different instruction or set of instructions. Such overloading can be extended to user-defined functions and procedures, where the same name might be used for related operations, but defined for parameters of different types. For example, we might want to define a maximum value procedure for both integer and real values:

```
procedure max (x,y: integer): integer;
procedure max (x,y: real): real;
```

In Pascal and C this is illegal, since it represents a redeclaration of the same name within the same scope. However, in Ada and C++, such a declaration is legal, since the type checker can decide which **max** procedure is meant based on the types of the parameters. Such a use of type checking to disambiguate multiple meanings of names can be implemented in a number of ways, depending on the language rules. One way would be to augment the *lookup* procedure of the symbol table with type parameters, allowing the symbol table to find the right match. A different solution is for the symbol table to maintain sets of possible types for names and to return the set to the type checker for disambiguation. This is useful in more complex situations, where a unique type may not be immediately determinable.

Type Conversion and Coercion   A common extension of the type rules of a language is to allow arithmetic expressions of mixed type, such as **2.1 + 3**, where a real number and an integer are added. In such cases, a common type must be found that is compatible with all the types of the subexpressions, and operations must be applied to convert the values at runtime to the appropriate representations before applying the operator. For example, in the expression **2.1 + 3**, the integer value **3** must be converted to floating point before the addition, and the resulting expression will have floating-point type. There are two approaches a language can take to such conversions. Modula-2, for instance, requires that the programmer supply a conversion function, so that the example just given must be written as **2.1 + FLOAT(3)**, or it will cause a type error. The other possibility (used in the C language) is for the type checker to supply the conversion operation automatically, based on the types of the subexpressions. Such an automatic conversion is called **coercion**. Coercion can be implicitly expressed by the type checker, in that the inferred type of an expression changes from that of a subexpression, as in

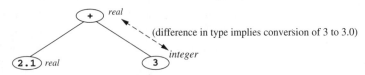

This requires that a code generator later examine the types of expressions to determine whether a conversion must be applied. Alternatively, conversion can be explicitly supplied by the type checker by inserting a conversion node into the syntax tree, as in

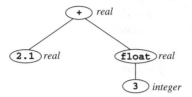

Type conversions and coercions also apply to assignments, such as

```
r = i;
```

in C, which, if **r** is a **double** and **i** is an **int**, coerces the value of **i** to a **double** before it is stored as the value of **r**. Such assignments can lose information during the conversion, as would happen if the assignment were done in the opposite direction (also legal in C):

```
i = r;
```

A similar situation occurs in object-oriented languages, where assignment of objects of subclasses to objects of superclasses is usually permitted (with a corresponding loss of information). For example, in C++ if **A** is a class and **B** is a subclass, and if **x** is an **A** and **y** is a **B**, then the assignment **x=y** is permitted, but not vice versa. (This is called the **subtype principle**.)

Polymorphic Typing   A language is **polymorphic** if it allows language constructs to have more than one type. Up to now we have discussed type checking for a language that is essentially **monomorphic** in that all names and expressions are required to have unique types. A relaxation of this monomorphism requirement is overloading. But overloading, though a form of polymorphism, applies only to situations where a number of separate declarations apply to the same name. A different situation occurs when a single declaration might apply to any type. For example, a procedure that swaps the values of two variables could in principle apply to variables of any type (as long as they have the same type):

```
procedure swap (var x,y:anytype);
```

The type of this **swap** procedure is said to be **parametrized** by the type **anytype**, and **anytype** is considered to be a **type variable**, which can assume any actual type. We might express the type of this procedure as

$$procedure(var\ anytype,\ var\ anytype): void$$

where every occurrence of *anytype* refers to the same (but unspecified) type. Such a type is actually a **type pattern** or **type scheme** rather than an actual type, and a type checker must in every situation where **swap** is used determine an actual type that matches this type pattern or declare a type error. For instance, given the code

```
var x,y: integer;
    a,b: char;
. . .
swap(x,y);
swap(a,b);
swap(a,x);
```

in the call **swap(x,y)**, the **swap** procedure is "specialized" from its given polymorphic type pattern to the (monomorphic) type

$$procedure(var\ integer,\ var\ integer):\ void$$

while in the call **swap(a,b)** it is specialized to the type

$$procedure(var\ char,\ var\ char):\ void$$

On the other hand, in the call **swap(a,x)**, the **swap** procedure would have to be of the type

$$procedure(var\ char,\ var\ integer):\ void$$

and this is a type that cannot be generated from the type pattern of **swap** by replacement of the type variable *anytype*. Type checking algorithms exist for such general polymorphic type checking, most notably in modern functional languages such as ML, but they involve sophisticated pattern matching techniques that we do not study here. (See the Notes and References section.)

6.5 A SEMANTIC ANALYZER FOR THE TINY LANGUAGE

In this section we develop the code for a semantic analyzer for the TINY language, based on the parsers for TINY that were constructed in previous chapters. The syntax of TINY and the structure of the syntax tree on which we base the semantic analyzer was described in Section 3.7.

The TINY language is extremely simple in its static semantic requirements, and the semantic analyzer will reflect that simplicity. There are no explicit declarations in TINY, and there are no named constants, data types, or procedures: names can only refer to variables. Variables are declared implicitly by use, and all variables have integer data type. There are also no nested scopes, so that a variable name has the same meaning throughout a program, and the symbol table does not need to maintain any scope information.

Type checking is also extremely simple in TINY. There are only two simple types: integer and Boolean. The only Boolean values are those that result from the comparison of two integer values. Since there are no Boolean operators or variables, a Boolean value can only appear in the test expression of an if- or repeat-statement, and not as the operand of an operator or the value in an assignment. Finally, a Boolean value cannot be output using a write-statement.

We separate the discussion of the code for the TINY semantic analyzer into two parts. First, we discuss the structure of the symbol table and its associated operations. Then we describe the operation of the semantic analyzer itself, including the construction of the symbol table and type checking.

6.5.1   A Symbol Table for TINY

In the design of the symbol table for the TINY semantic analyzer, we must first determine what information needs to be held in the table. In typical cases this information includes data type and scope information. Since TINY has no scope information, and since all variables have integer data type, a TINY symbol table does not need to contain this information. During code generation, however, the variables will need to be allocated memory locations, and, since there are no declarations in the syntax tree, the symbol table is the logical place to store these locations. For now, locations can be viewed simply as integer indices that are incremented each time a new variable is encountered. To make the symbol table more interesting and more useful, we also use the symbol table to generate a cross-reference listing of line numbers where variables are accessed.

As an example of the information that will be generated by the symbol table, consider the sample TINY program (with line numbers added):

```
 1: { Sample program
 2:    in TINY language --
 3:    computes factorial
 4: }
 5: read x; { input an integer }
 6: if 0 < x then { don't compute if x <= 0 }
 7:    fact := 1;
 8:    repeat
 9:      fact := fact * x;
10:      x := x - 1
11:    until x = 0;
12:    write fact { output factorial of x }
13: end
```

After the generation of the symbol table for this program, the semantic analyzer will output (with **TraceAnalyze = TRUE**) the following information to the listing file:

Symbol table:

Variable Name	Location	Line Numbers					
x	0	5	6	9	10	10	11
fact	1	7	9	9	12		

Note that multiple references in the same line generate multiple entries for that line in the symbol table.

The code for the symbol table is contained in the **symtab.h** and **symtab.c** files listed in Appendix B (lines 1150–1179 and 1200–1321, respectively).

The structure we use for the symbol table is the separately chained hash table as described in Section 6.3.1, and the hash function is the one given in Figure 6.13 (page 298). Since there is no scope information, there is no need for a *delete* operation, and the *insert* operation needs only line number and location parameters, in addition to the identifier. The two other operations needed are a procedure to print the summary information as just shown to the listing file, and a *lookup* operation to fetch location numbers from the table (needed later by the code generator, and also by the symbol table builder to check whether a variable has been seen already). Therefore, the header file **symtab.h** contains the following declarations:

```
void st_insert( char * name, int lineno, int loc );
int st_lookup ( char * name );
void printSymTab(FILE * listing);
```

Since there is only one symbol table, its structure does not need to be declared in the header file, nor does it need to appear as a parameter to these procedures.

The associated implementation code in **symtab.c** uses a dynamically allocated linked list with type name **LineList** (lines 1236–1239) to store the line numbers associated to each identifier record in the hash table. The identifier records themselves are kept in a bucket list with type name **BucketList** (lines 1247–1252). The **st_insert** procedure (lines 1262–1295) adds new identifier records to the front of each bucket list, but the line numbers are added at the end of each list of line numbers, in order to preserve numerical order. (The efficiency of **st_insert** could be improved by using a circular list or front/rear pointers for the list of line numbers; see the exercises.)

6.5.2   A Semantic Analyzer for TINY

The static semantics of TINY share with standard programming languages the properties that the symbol table is an inherited attribute, while the data type of an expression is a synthesized attribute. Thus, the symbol table can be built by a preorder traversal of the syntax tree, and type checking can be performed by a postorder traversal. While these two traversals can easily be combined into a single traversal, to make clear the distinctness of the operations of both processing steps, we separate them into two separate passes over the syntax tree. Thus, the interface of the semantic analyzer to the rest of the compiler, which we put into the file **analyze.h** (Appendix B, lines 1350–1370), consists of two procedures, given by the declarations

```
void buildSymtab(TreeNode *);
void typeCheck(TreeNode *);
```

The first procedure performs a preorder traversal of the syntax tree, calling the symbol table **st_insert** procedure as it encounters variable identifiers in the tree. After the traversal is complete, it then calls **printSymTab** to print out the stored information to the listing file. The second procedure performs a postorder traversal of the syntax tree, inserting data types into tree nodes as they are computed and reporting any type checking errors to the listing file. The code for these procedures and their auxiliary procedures is contained in the file **analyze.c** (Appendix B, lines 1400–1558).

To emphasize the standard tree traversal techniques involved, we implement both **buildSymtab** and **typeCheck** using the same generic traversal function **traverse** (lines 1420–1441) that takes two procedures (as well as the syntax tree) as parameters, one to perform preorder processing of each node and one to perform postorder processing:

```
static void traverse( TreeNode * t,
                void (* preProc) (TreeNode *),
                void (* postProc) (TreeNode *) )
{ if (t != NULL)
  { preProc(t);
    { int i;
      for (i=0; i < MAXCHILDREN; i++)
        traverse(t->child[i],preProc,postProc);
    }
    postProc(t);
    traverse(t->sibling,preProc,postProc);
  }
}
```

Given this procedure, to obtain a preorder traversal, we need to define a procedure that provides preorder processing and pass it to **traverse** as **preproc**, while passing a "do-nothing" procedure as **postproc**. In the case of the TINY symbol table, the preorder processor is called **insertNode**, since it performs insertions into the symbol table. The "do-nothing" procedure is called **nullProc** and is defined with an empty body (lines 1438–1441). Then the preorder traversal that builds the symbol table is accomplished by the single call

```
traverse(syntaxTree,insertNode,nullProc);
```

within the **buildSymtab** procedure (lines 1488–1494). Similarly, the postorder traversal required by **typeCheck** (lines 1556–1558) can be achieved by the single call

```
traverse(syntaxTree,nullProc,checkNode);
```

where **checkNode** is an appropriately defined procedure that computes and checks type at each node. It remains to describe the operation of the procedures **insertNode** and **checkNode**.

The **insertNode** procedure (lines 1447–1483) must determine when to insert an identifier (together with its line number and location) into the symbol table, based on the kind of syntax tree node it receives through its parameter (a pointer to a syntax tree node). In the case of statement nodes, the only nodes that contain variable references are assignment nodes and read nodes, where the variable name being assigned to or read is contained in the **attr.name** field of the node. In the case of expression nodes, the only nodes of interest are identifier nodes, where again the name is stored in **attr.name**. Thus, in those three places, the **insertNode** procedure contains a call

```
st_insert(t->attr.name,t->lineno,location++);
```

if the variable has not yet been seen (which stores and increments the location counter as well as the line number) and

```
st_insert(t->attr.name,t->lineno,0);
```

if the variable is already in the symbol table (which stores the line number but not the location).

Finally, after the symbol table has been built, the **buildSymtab** performs a call to **printSymTab** to write the line number information to the listing file, under the control of the **TraceAnalyze** flag (which is set in **main.c**).

The **checkNode** procedure of the type checking pass has two tasks. First, it must determine if, based on the types of the child nodes, a type error has occurred. Second, it must infer a type for the current node (if it has a type) and assign this type to a new field in the tree node. This field is called the **type** field in **TreeNode** (defined in **globals.h**; see Appendix B, line 216). Since only expression nodes have types, this type inference only occurs for expression nodes. In TINY there are only two types, integer and Boolean, and these types are defined in an enumerated type in the global declarations (see Appendix B, line 203):

```
typedef enum {Void,Integer,Boolean} ExpType;
```

Here the type **Void** is a "no-type" type that is used only in initialization and for error checking. When an error occurs, the **checkNode** procedure calls the **typeError** procedure, which prints an error message to the listing file, based on the current node.

It remains to catalog the actions of **checkNode**. In the case of an expression node, the node is either a leaf node (a constant or an identifier, of kind **ConstK** or **IdK**) or an operator node (of kind **OpK**). In the case of a leaf node (lines 1517–1520), the type is always **Integer** (and no type checking occurs). In the case of an operator node (lines 1508–1516), the two child subexpressions must be of type **Integer** (and their types have already been computed, since a postorder traversal is being performed). The type of the **OpK** node is then determined from the operator itself (regardless of whether a type error has occurred): if the operator is a comparison operator (**<** or **=**), then the type is **Boolean**; otherwise, it is **Integer**.

In the case of a statement node, no type is inferred, but in all but one case, some type checking must be performed. That case is that of a **ReadK** statement, where the variable being read must automatically be of **Integer** type, so no type checking is necessary. All four other statement kinds need some form of type checking: **IfK** and **RepeatK** statements need their test expressions checked to make sure they have **Boolean** type (lines 1527–1530 and 1539–1542), and the **WriteK** and **AssignK** statements need a check (lines 1531–1538) that the expression being written or assigned is not Boolean (since variables can only hold integer values, and only integer values can be written):

```
x := 1 < 2; { error - Boolean value
                  cannot be assigned }
write 1 = 2; { also an error }
```

EXERCISES **6.1** Write an attribute grammar for the integer value of a number given by the following grammar:

$$number \rightarrow digit\ number\ |\ digit$$
$$digit \rightarrow 0\ |\ 1\ |\ 2\ |\ 3\ |\ 4\ |\ 5\ |\ 6\ |\ 7\ |\ 8\ |\ 9$$

6.2 Write an attribute grammar for the floating point value of a decimal number given by the following grammar. (Hint: Use a *count* attribute to count the number of digits to the right of the decimal point.)

$$dnum \rightarrow num.num$$
$$num \rightarrow num\ digit\ |\ digit$$
$$digit \rightarrow 0\ |\ 1\ |\ 2\ |\ 3\ |\ 4\ |\ 5\ |\ 6\ |\ 7\ |\ 8\ |\ 9$$

6.3 The grammar for decimal numbers of the previous exercise can be rewritten so that a *count* attribute is unnecessary (and equations involving exponents are avoided). Rewrite the grammar to do this and give a new attribute grammar for the value of a *dnum*.

6.4 Consider an expression grammar as it would be written for a predictive parser with left recursion removed:

$$exp \rightarrow term\ exp'$$
$$exp' \rightarrow +\ term\ exp'\ |\ -\ term\ exp'\ |\ \varepsilon$$
$$term \rightarrow factor\ term'$$
$$term' \rightarrow *\ factor\ term'\ |\ \varepsilon$$
$$factor \rightarrow (\ exp\ )\ |\ \textbf{number}$$

Write an attribute grammar for the value of an expression given by this grammar.

6.5 Rewrite the attribute grammar of Table 6.2 to compute a *postfix* string attribute instead of *val*, containing the postfix form for the simple integer expression. For example, the *postfix* attribute for **(34-3)*42** is "34 3 − 42 + *." You may assume a concatenation operator || and the existence of a **number**.*strval* attribute.

6.6 Consider the following grammar for integer binary trees (in linearized form):

$$btree \rightarrow (\ \textbf{number}\ btree\ btree\ )\ |\ \textbf{nil}$$

Write an attribute grammar to check that a binary tree is ordered, that is, that the values of the numbers of the first subtree are ≤ the value of the current number and the values of all the numbers of the second subtree are ≥ the value of the current number. For example, **(2 (1 nil nil) (3 nil nil))** is ordered, but **(1 (2 nil nil) (3 nil nil))** is not.

6.7 Consider the following grammar for simple Pascal-style declarations:

$$decl \rightarrow var\text{-}list : type$$
$$var\text{-}list \rightarrow var\text{-}list\ ,\ \textbf{id}\ |\ \textbf{id}$$
$$type \rightarrow \textbf{integer}\ |\ \textbf{real}$$

Write an attribute grammar for the type of a variable.

6.8 Consider the grammar of Exercise 6.7. Rewrite the grammar so that the type of a variable can be defined as a purely synthesized attribute, and give a new attribute grammar for the type that has this property.

6.9 Rewrite the grammar and attribute grammar of Example 6.4 (page 266) so that value of a *based-num* is computed by synthesized attributes alone.

6.10 a. Draw dependency graphs corresponding to each grammar rule of Example 6.14 (page 283), and for the expression **5/2/2.0**.

  b. Describe the two passes required to compute the attributes on the syntax tree of **5/2/2.0**, including a possible order in which the nodes could be visited and the attribute values computed at each point.

  c. Write pseudocode for procedures that would perform the computations described in part (b).

6.11 Draw dependency graphs corresponding to each grammar rule for the attribute grammar of Exercise 6.4, and for the string **3*(4+5)*6**.

6.12 Draw dependency graphs corresponding to each grammar rule for the attribute grammar of Exercise 6.7, and draw a dependency graph for the declaration **x,y,z:real**.

6.13 Consider the following attribute grammar:

Grammar Rule	Semantic Rules
$S \rightarrow A\ B\ C$	$B.u = S.u$
	$A.u = B.v + C.v$
	$S.v = A.v$
$A \rightarrow a$	$A.v = 2 * A.u$
$B \rightarrow b$	$B.v = B.u$
$C \rightarrow c$	$C.v = 1$

  a. Draw the parse tree for the string *abc* (the only string in the language), and draw the dependency graph for the associated attributes. Describe a correct order for the evaluation of the attributes.

  b. Suppose that $S.u$ is assigned the value 3 before attribute evaluation begins. What is the value of $S.v$ when evaluation has finished?

  c. Suppose the attribute equations are modified as follows:

Grammar Rule	Semantic Rules
$S \rightarrow A\ B\ C$	$B.u = S.u$
	$C.u = A.v$
	$A.u = B.v + C.v$
	$S.v = A.v$
$A \rightarrow a$	$A.v = 2 * A.u$
$B \rightarrow b$	$B.v = B.u$
$C \rightarrow c$	$C.v = C.u - 2$

What value does $S.v$ have after attribute evaluation, if $S.u = 3$ before evaluation begins?

6.14 Show that, given the attribute grammar,

Grammar Rule	Semantic Rules
$decl \rightarrow type\ var\text{-}list$	$var\text{-}list.dtype = type.dtype$
$type \rightarrow$ **int**	$type.dtype = integer$
$type \rightarrow$ **float**	$type.dtype = real$
$var\text{-}list_1 \rightarrow$ **id** , $var\text{-}list_2$	**id**$.dtype = var\text{-}list_1.dtype$
	$var\text{-}list_2.dtype = var\text{-}list_1.dtype$
$var\text{-}list \rightarrow$ **id**	**id**$.dtype = var\text{-}list.dtype$

if the attribute *type.dtype* is kept on the value stack during an LR parse, then this value cannot be found at a fixed position in the stack when reductions to a *var-list* occur.

6.15 a. Show that the grammar $B \rightarrow B\ b \mid a$ is SLR(1), but that the grammar

$$B \rightarrow A\ B\ b \mid a$$
$$A \rightarrow \varepsilon$$

(constructed from the previous grammar by adding a single ε-production) is not LR(k) for any k.

b. Given the grammar of part (a) (with the ε-production), what strings would a Yacc-generated parser accept?

c. Is this situation likely to occur during the semantic analysis of a "real" programming language? Explain.

6.16 Rewrite the expression grammar of Section 6.3.5 into an unambiguous grammar, in such a way that the expressions written in that section remain legal, and rewrite the attribute grammar of Table 6.9 (page 311) for this new grammar.

6.17 Rewrite the attribute grammar of Table 6.9 to use collateral declarations instead of sequential declarations. (See page 307).

6.18 Write an attribute grammar that computes the value of each expression for the expression grammar of Section 6.3.5.

6.19 Modify the pseudocode for the *typeEqual* function of Figure 6.20 (page 325) to incorporate type names and the suggested algorithm for determining structural equivalence of recursive types as described on page 327.

6.20 Consider the following (ambiguous) grammar of expressions:

$$exp \rightarrow exp + exp \mid exp - exp \mid exp * exp \mid exp / exp$$
$$\mid (\ exp\ ) \mid num \mid num.num$$

Suppose that the rules of C are followed in computing the value of any such expression: if two subexpressions are of mixed type, then the integer subexpression is converted to floating point, and the floating-point operator is applied. Write an attribute grammar that will convert such expressions into expressions that are legal in Modula-2: conversions from integer to floating point are expressed by applying the **FLOAT** function, and the division operator / is considered to be **div** if both its operands are integer.

6.21 Consider the following extension of the grammar of Figure 6.22 (page 329) to include function declarations and calls:

$$\begin{aligned}
\textit{program} &\rightarrow \textit{var-decls} \textbf{;} \textit{fun-decls} \textbf{;} \textit{stmts} \\
\textit{var-decls} &\rightarrow \textit{var-decls} \textbf{;} \textit{var-decl} \mid \textit{var-decl} \\
\textit{var-decl} &\rightarrow \textbf{id} \textbf{:} \textit{type-exp} \\
\textit{type-exp} &\rightarrow \textbf{int} \mid \textbf{bool} \mid \textbf{array [num] of} \textit{type-exp} \\
\textit{fun-decls} &\rightarrow \textbf{fun id} \textbf{(} \textit{var-decls} \textbf{)} \textbf{:} \textit{type-exp} \textbf{;} \textit{body} \\
\textit{body} &\rightarrow \textit{exp} \\
\textit{stmts} &\rightarrow \textit{stmts} \textbf{;} \textit{stmt} \mid \textit{stmt} \\
\textit{stmt} &\rightarrow \textbf{if} \textit{exp} \textbf{then} \textit{stmt} \mid \textbf{id} \textbf{:=} \textit{exp} \\
\textit{exp} &\rightarrow \textit{exp} \textbf{+} \textit{exp} \mid \textit{exp} \textbf{ or } \textit{exp} \mid \textit{exp} \textbf{[} \textit{exp} \textbf{]} \mid \textbf{id} \textbf{(} \textit{exps} \textbf{)} \\
&\quad \mid \textbf{num} \mid \textbf{true} \mid \textbf{false} \mid \textbf{id} \\
\textit{exps} &\rightarrow \textit{exps} \textbf{,} \textit{exp} \mid \textit{exp}
\end{aligned}$$

a. Devise a suitable tree structure for the new function type structures, and write a *typeEqual* function for two function types.

b. Write semantic rules for the type checking of function declarations and function calls (represented by the rule $\textit{exp} \rightarrow \textbf{id} \textbf{(} \textit{exps} \textbf{)}$), similar to the rules of Table 6.10 (page 330).

6.22 Consider the following ambiguity in C expressions. Given the expression

```
(A)-x
```

if **x** is an integer variable and **A** is defined in a **typedef** as equivalent to **double**, then this expression casts the value of **-x** to **double**. On the other hand, if **A** is an integer variable, then this computes the integer difference of the two variables.

a. Describe how the parser might use the symbol table to disambiguate these two interpretations.

b. Describe how the scanner might use the symbol table to disambiguate these two interpretations.

6.23 Write an attribute grammar corresponding to the type constraints enforced by the TINY type checker.

6.24 Write an attribute grammar for the symbol table construction of the TINY semantic analyzer.

PROGRAMMING EXERCISES

6.25 Write C declarations for a syntax tree for the based numbers of Example 6.4 (page 266), and use these declarations to translate the *EvalWithBase* pseudocode of Example 6.13 (page 282) into C code.

6.26 a. Rewrite the recursive-descent evaluator of Figure 4.1 (page 148) so that it prints the postfix translation instead of the value of an expression (see Exercise 6.5).

b. Rewrite the recursive-descent evaluator so that it prints *both* the value and the postfix translation.

6.27 a. Rewrite the Yacc specification of Figure 5.10 (page 228) for a simple integer calculator so that it prints a postfix translation instead of the value (see Exercise 6.5).

b. Rewrite the Yacc specification so that it prints *both* the value and the postfix translation.

6.28 Write a Yacc specification that will print the Modula-2 translation of a given expression for the grammar of Exercise 6.20.

6.29 Write a Yacc specification for a program that will compute the value of an expression with let-blocks (Table 6.9, page 311). (You may abbreviate the tokens **let** and **in** to single characters and restrict identifiers as well or use Lex to generate a suitable scanner.)

6.30 Write a Yacc and Lex specification of a program to type check the language whose grammar is given in Figure 6.22 (page 329).

6.31 Rewrite the implementation of the symbol table for the TINY semantic analyzer to add a rear pointer to the data structure **LineList** and improve the efficiency of the **insert** operation.

6.32 Rewrite the TINY semantic analyzer so that it makes only a single pass over the syntax tree.

6.33 The TINY semantic analyzer makes no attempt to ensure that a variable has been assigned to before it is used. Thus, the following TINY code is considered semantically correct:

```
y := 2+x;
x := 3;
```

Rewrite the TINY analyzer so that it makes "reasonable" checks that an assignment to a variable has occurred before a use of that variable in an expression. What prevents such checks from being foolproof?

6.34 a. Rewrite the TINY semantic analyzer to allow Boolean values to be stored in variables. This will require that variables be given data type Boolean or integer in the symbol table and that type checking include a symbol table lookup. The type correctness of a TINY program now must include the requirement that all assignments to (and uses of) a variable must be consistent in their data types.

b. Write an attribute grammar for the TINY type checker as modified in part (a).

NOTES AND REFERENCES

The principal early work on attribute grammars is Knuth [1968]. Extensive studies of the use of attribute grammars in compiler construction appear in Lorho [1984]. The use of attribute grammars to formally specify the semantics of programming languages is studied in Slonneger and Kurtz [1995], where a complete attribute grammar is given for the static semantics of a language similar to TINY. Additional mathematical properties of attribute grammars can be found in Mayoh [1981]. A test for noncircularity can be found in Jazayeri, Ogden, and Rounds [1975].

The question of the evaluation of attributes during parsing is studied in somewhat more detail in Fischer and LeBlanc [1991]. Conditions that ensure that this can be done during an LR parse appear in Jones [1980]. The question of maintaining deterministic LR parsing while adding new ε-productions to schedule actions (as in Yacc) is studied in Purdom and Brown [1980].

Data structures for symbol table implementation, including hash tables, and analyses of their efficiency, can be found in many texts; see, for example, Aho, Hopcroft, and Ullman [1983] or Cormen, Leiserson, and Rivest [1990]. A careful study of the choice of a hash function appears in Knuth [1973].

Type systems, type correctness, and type inference form one of the major fields of study of theoretical computer science, with applications to many languages. For a traditional overview, see Louden [1993]. For a deeper perspective, see Cardelli and Wegner [1985]. C and Ada use mixed forms of type equivalence similar to the declaration equivalence of Pascal that are difficult to describe succinctly. Older languages, such as FORTRAN77, Algol60, and Algol68 use structural equivalence. Modern functional languages like ML and Haskell use strict name equivalence, with type synonyms taking the place of structural equivalence. The algorithm for structural equivalence described in Section 6.4.3 can be found in Koster [1969]; a modern application of a similar algorithm is in Amadio and Cardelli [1993]. Polymorphic type systems and type inference algorithms are described in Peyton Jones [1987] and Reade [1989]. The version of polymorphic type inference used in ML and Haskell is called **Hindley-Milner type inference** [Hindley, 1969; Milner, 1978].

In this chapter we have not described any tools for the automatic construction of attribute evaluators, since none are in general use (unlike the scanner and parser generators Lex and Yacc). Some interesting tools based on attribute grammars are LINGUIST [Farrow, 1984] and GAG [Kastens, Hutt, and Zimmermann, 1982]. The Synthesizer Generator [Reps and Teitelbaum, 1989] is a mature tool for the generation of context-sensitive editors based on attribute grammars. One of the interesting things that can be done with this tool is to construct a language editor that automatically supplies variable declarations based on use.

Chapter 7

Runtime Environments

In previous chapters we have studied the phases of a compiler that perform static analysis of the source language. This has included scanning, parsing, and static semantic analysis. This analysis depends only on the properties of the source language—it is completely independent of the target (assembly or machine) language and the properties of the target machine and its operating system.

In this chapter and the next we turn to the task of studying how a compiler generates executable code. This can involve additional analysis, such as that performed by an optimizer, and some of this can be machine independent. But much of the task of code generation is dependent on the details of the target machine. Nevertheless, the general characteristics of code generation remain the same across a wide variety of architectures. This is particularly true for the **runtime environment**, which is the structure of the target computer's registers and memory that serves to manage memory and maintain the information needed to guide the execution process. In fact, almost all programming languages use one of three kinds of runtime environment, whose essential structure does not depend on the specific details of the target machine. These three kinds of environments are the **fully static environment** characteristic of FORTRAN77; the **stack-based environment** of languages like C, C++, Pascal, and Ada; and the **fully dynamic environment** of functional languages like LISP. Hybrids of these are also possible.

In this chapter, we will discuss each of these kinds of environments in turn, together with the language features that dictate which environments are feasible, and what their properties must be. This includes scoping and allocation issues, the nature of procedure calls, and the varieties of parameter passing mechanisms. Here, the focus will be on the general structure of the environment, while in the next chapter, the focus will be on the actual code that needs to be generated to maintain

345

the environment. In this regard, it is important to keep in mind that a compiler can maintain an environment only indirectly, in that it must generate code to perform the necessary maintenance operations during program execution. By contrast, an interpreter has an easier task, since it can maintain the environment directly within its own data structures.

The first section of this chapter contains a discussion of the general characteristics of all runtime environments and their relationship to the architecture of the target machine. The next two sections discuss the static and stack-based environments, together with examples of their operation during execution. Since the stack-based environment is the most common, some detail is given about the different varieties and structure of a stack-based system. A subsequent section discusses dynamic memory issues, including fully dynamic environments and object-oriented environments. Following that is a discussion of the effect of various parameter passing techniques on the operation of an environment. The chapter closes with a brief description of the simple environment needed to implement the TINY language.

7.1 MEMORY ORGANIZATION DURING PROGRAM EXECUTION

The memory of a typical computer is divided into a register area and a slower directly addressable random access memory (RAM). The RAM area may be further divided into a code area and a data area. In most compiled languages, it is not possible to make changes to the code area during execution, and the code and data area can be viewed as conceptually separate. Further, since the code area is fixed prior to execution, all code addresses are computable at compile time, and the code area can be visualized as follows:

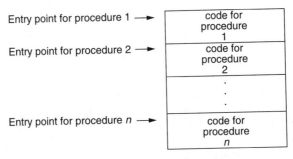

Code memory

In particular, the entry point of each procedure and function is known at compile time.[1] The same cannot be said for the allocation of data, only a small part of which can be assigned fixed locations in memory before execution begins. Much of the rest of the chapter will be taken up with how to deal with nonfixed, or dynamic, data allocation.

---

1. More likely, the code is loaded by a loader into an area in memory that is assigned at the beginning of execution and, thus, is not absolutely predictable. However, all actual addresses are then automatically computed by offset from a fixed base load address, so the principle of fixed addresses remains the same. Sometimes, the compiler writer must take care to generate so-called **relocatable code**, in which jumps, calls, and references are all performed relative to some **base**, usually a register. Examples of this will be given in the next chapter.

There *is* one class of data that can be fixed in memory prior to execution and that comprises the global and/or static data of a program. (In FORTRAN77, unlike most languages, all data are in this class.) Such data are usually allocated separately in a fixed area in a similar fashion to the code. In Pascal, global variables are in this class, as are the external and static variables of C.

One question that arises in the organization of the global/static area involves constants that are known at compile time. These include the **const** declarations of C and Pascal, as well as literal values used in the code itself, such as the string **"Hello %d\n"** and the integer value 12345 in the C statement

```
printf("Hello %d\n",12345);
```

Small compile-time constants such as 0 and 1 are usually inserted directly into the code by the compiler and are not allocated any data space. Also, no space needs to be allocated in the global data area for global functions or procedures, since their entry points are known to the compiler and can be inserted directly into the code as well. However, large integer values, floating-point values, and particularly string literals are usually allocated memory in the global/static area, stored once on start-up and then are fetched from those locations by the executing code. (Indeed, in C string literals are viewed as pointers, so they must be stored in this way.)

The memory area used for the allocation of dynamic data can be organized in many different ways. A typical organization divides this memory into a **stack** area and a **heap** area, with the stack area used for data whose allocation occurs in LIFO (last-in, first-out) fashion and the heap area used for dynamic allocation that does not conform to a LIFO protocol (pointer allocation in C, for example).[2] Often the architecture of the target machine will include a processor stack, and using this stack makes it possible to use processor support for procedure calls and returns (the principal mechanism that uses stack-based memory allocation). Sometimes, a compiler will have to arrange for the explicit allocation of the processor stack in an appropriate place in memory.

A general organization of runtime storage that has all of the described memory categories might look as follows:

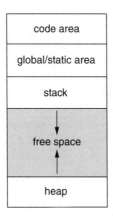

---

2. It should be noted that the heap is usually a simple linear memory area. It is called a heap for historical reasons and is unrelated to the heap data structure used in algorithms such as heapsort.

The arrows in this picture indicate the direction of growth of the stack and heap. Traditionally, the stack is pictured as growing downward in memory, so that its top is actually at the bottom of its pictured area. Also, the heap is pictured as being similar to the stack, but it is not a LIFO structure and its growth and shrinkage is more complicated than the arrow indicates (see Section 7.4). In some organizations the stack and heap are allocated separate sections of memory, rather than occupying the same area.

An important unit of memory allocation is the **procedure activation record**, which contains memory allocated for the local data of a procedure or function when it is called, or activated. An activation record, at a minimum, must contain the following sections:

space for arguments (parameters)
space for bookkeeping information, including return address
space for local data
space for local temporaries

We emphasize here (and repeatedly in following sections) that this picture only illustrates the general organization of an activation record. Specific details, including the order of the data it contains, will depend on the architecture of target machine, the properties of the language being compiled, and even the taste of the compiler writer.

Some parts of an activation record have the same size for all procedures—the space for bookkeeping information, for example. Other parts, like the space for arguments and local data, may remain fixed for each individual procedure, but will vary from procedure to procedure. Also, some parts of the activation record may be allocated automatically by the processor on procedure calls (storing the return address, for example). Other parts (like the local temporary space) may need to be allocated explicitly by instructions generated by the compiler. Depending on the language, activation records may be allocated in the static area (FORTRAN77), the stack area (C, Pascal), or the heap area (LISP). When activation records are kept in the stack, they are sometimes referred to as **stack frames**.

Processor registers are also part of the structure of the runtime environment. Registers may be used to store temporaries, local variables, or even global variables. When a processor has many registers, as in the newer RISC processors, the entire static area and whole activation records may be kept entirely in registers. Processors also have special-purpose registers to keep track of execution, such as the **program counter (pc)** and **stack pointer (sp)** in most architectures. There may also be registers specifically designed to keep track of procedure activations. Typical such registers are the **frame pointer (fp)**, which points to the current activation record, and the **argument pointer** (**ap**), which points to the area of the activation record reserved for arguments (parameter values).[3]

A particularly important part of the design of a runtime environment is the determination of the sequence of operations that must occur when a procedure or function is called. Such operations may include the allocation of memory for the activation record, the computation and storing of the arguments, and the storing and setting of the necessary registers to effect the call. These operations are usually referred to as the **calling sequence**. The additional operations needed when a procedure or function returns, such as the placing of the return value where it can be accessed by the caller, the readjustment of registers, and the possible releasing of activation record memory, are commonly also considered to be part of the calling sequence. If necessary, we will refer to the part of the calling sequence that is performed during a call as the **call sequence** and the part that is performed on return the **return sequence**.

Important aspects of the design of the calling sequence are (1) how to divide the calling sequence operations between the caller and callee (that is, how much of the code of the calling sequence to place at the point of call and how much to place at the beginning of the code of each procedure) and (2) to what extent to rely on processor support for calls rather that generating explicit code for each step of the calling sequence. Point (1) is a particularly thorny issue, since it is usually easier to generate calling sequence code at the point of call rather than inside the callee, but doing so causes the size of the generated code to grow, since the same code must be duplicated at each call site. These issues will be handled in more detail later on.

At a minimum, the caller is responsible for computing the arguments and placing them in locations where they may be found by the callee (perhaps directly in the activation record of the callee). In addition, the state of the machine at the point of call, including the return address and, possibly, registers that are in use, must be saved, either by the caller or the callee, or partially by both. Finally, any additional bookkeeping information must also be set up, again in some possibly cooperative manner between caller and callee.

7.2 FULLY STATIC RUNTIME ENVIRONMENTS

The simplest kind of a runtime environment is that in which all data are static, remaining fixed in memory for the duration of program execution. Such an environment can be used to implement a language in which there are no pointers or dynamic allocation, and in which procedures may not be called recursively. The standard example of such a language is FORTRAN77.

In a fully static environment not only the global variables, but *all* variables are allocated statically. Thus, each procedure has only a single activation record, which is allocated statically prior to execution. All variables, whether local or global, can be accessed directly via fixed addresses, and the entire program memory can be visualized as follows:

---

3. These names are taken from the VAX architecture, but similar names occur in other architectures.

code for main procedure	
code for procedure 1	**Code area**
. . .	
code for procedure *n*	
global data area	
activation record of main procedure	**Data area**
activation record of procedure 1	
. . .	
activation record of procedure *n*	

In such an environment there is relatively little overhead in terms of bookkeeping information to retain in each activation record, and no extra information about the environment (other than possibly the return address) needs to be kept in an activation record. The calling sequence for such an environment is also particularly simple. When a procedure is called, each argument is computed and stored into its appropriate parameter location in the activation of the procedure being called. Then the return address in the code of the caller is saved, and a jump is made to the beginning of the code of the called procedure. On return, a simple jump is made to the return address.[4]

Example 7.1   As a concrete example of this kind of environment, consider the FORTRAN77 program of Figure 7.1. This program has a main procedure and a single additional procedure **QUADMEAN**.[5] There is a single global variable given by the **COMMON MAXSIZE** declaration in both the main procedure and **QUADMEAN**.[6]

---

4. In most architectures, a subroutine jump automatically saves the return address; this address is also automatically reloaded when a return instruction is executed.

5. We ignore the library function **SQRT**, which is called by **QUADMEAN** and which is linked in prior to execution.

6. In fact, FORTRAN77 allows COMMON variables to have different names in different procedures, while still referring to the same memory location. From now on in this example, we will silently ignore such complexities.

Figure 7.1
A FORTRAN77 sample
program

```
PROGRAM TEST
COMMON MAXSIZE
INTEGER MAXSIZE
REAL TABLE(10),TEMP
MAXSIZE = 10
READ *, TABLE(1),TABLE(2),TABLE(3)
CALL QUADMEAN(TABLE,3,TEMP)
PRINT *, TEMP
END

SUBROUTINE QUADMEAN(A,SIZE,QMEAN)
COMMON MAXSIZE
INTEGER MAXSIZE,SIZE
REAL A(SIZE),QMEAN, TEMP
INTEGER K
TEMP = 0.0
IF ((SIZE.GT.MAXSIZE).OR.(SIZE.LT.1)) GOTO 99
DO 10 K = 1,SIZE
    TEMP = TEMP + A(K)*A(K)
10  CONTINUE
99  QMEAN = SQRT(TEMP/SIZE)
RETURN
END
```

Ignoring the possible size difference between integer and floating-point values in memory, we show a runtime environment for this program in Figure 7.2 (page 352).[7] In this picture we have drawn in arrows to indicate the values that the parameters **A**, **SIZE**, and **QMEAN** of procedure **QUADMEAN** have during the call from the main procedure. In FORTRAN77, parameter values are implicitly memory references, so the locations of the arguments of the call (**TABLE**, **3**, and **TEMP**) are copied into the parameter locations of **QUADMEAN**. This has several consequences. First, an extra dereference is required to access parameter values. Second, array parameters do not need to be reallocated and copied (thus, array parameter **A** in **QUADMEAN** is allocated only one space, which points to the base location of **TABLE** during the call). Third, constant arguments, such as the value 3 in the call, must be stored to a memory location and this location used during the call. (Parameter passing mechanisms are more fully discussed in Section 7.5.)

There is one more feature of Figure 7.2 that requires explanation, and that is the unnamed location allocated at the end of the activation record of **QUADMEAN**. This location is a "scratch" location used to store temporary values during the computation of arithmetic expressions. There are two computations in **QUADMEAN** where this may

---

7. Again we emphasize that the details of this picture are meant to be illustrative only. Actual implementations may differ substantially from those given here.

be needed. The first is the computation of **TEMP + A(K)*A(K)** in the loop, and the second is the computation of **TEMP/SIZE** as the parameter in the call to **SQRT**. We have already discussed the need to allocate space for parameter values (although in a call to a library function the convention may in fact be different). The reason a temporary memory location may also be needed for the loop computation is that each arithmetic operation must be applied in a single step, so that **A(K)*A(K)** is computed and then added to the value of **TEMP** in the next step. If there are not enough registers available to hold this temporary value, or if a call is made requiring this value to be saved, then the value will be stored in the activation record prior to the completion of the computation. A compiler can always predict whether this will be necessary during execution, and arrange for the allocation of the appropriate number (and size) of temporary locations.

Figure 7.2

A runtime environment for the program of Figure 7.1

Global area

Activation record of main procedure

Activation record of procedure **QUADMEAN**

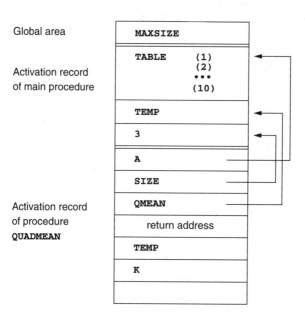

§

7.3   STACK-BASED RUNTIME ENVIRONMENTS

In a language in which recursive calls are allowed, and in which local variables are newly allocated at each call, activation records cannot be allocated statically. Instead, activation records must be allocated in a stack-based fashion, in which each new activation record is allocated at the top of the stack as a new procedure call is made (a **push** of the activation record) and deallocated again when the call exits (a **pop** of the activation record). The **stack of activation records** (also referred to as the **runtime stack** or **call stack**) then grows and shrinks with the chain of calls that have occurred in the executing program. Each procedure may have several different activation records on the call stack at one time, each representing a distinct call. Such an environment requires a more complex strategy for bookkeeping and variable access than a fully static environment. In particular, additional bookkeeping information must be kept in the activation records, and the calling sequence must also include the steps necessary to set up and maintain this extra information. The correctness of a stack-based environment, and the amount of bookkeeping information required, depends heavily on the properties of the language being compiled. In this section we will consider the organization of stack-based environments in order of increasing complexity, classified by the language properties involved.

7.3.1 Stack-Based Environments Without Local Procedures

In a language where all procedures are global (such as the C language), a stack-based environment requires two things: the maintenance of a pointer to the current activation record to allow access to local variables and a record of the position or size of the immediately preceding activation record (the caller's activation record) to allow that activation record to be recovered (and the current activation to be discarded) when the current call ends. The pointer to the current activation is usually called the **frame pointer**, or **fp**, and is usually kept in a register (often also referred to as the fp). The information about the previous activation is commonly kept in the current activation as a pointer to the previous activation record and is referred to as the **control link** or **dynamic link** (*dynamic*, since it points to the caller's activation record during execution). Sometimes this pointer is called the **old fp**, since it represents the previous value of the fp. Typically, this pointer is kept somewhere in the middle of the stack, between the parameter area and the local variable area, and points to the location of the control link of the previous activation record. Additionally, there may be a **stack pointer**, or **sp**, which always points to the last location allocated on the call stack (sometimes this is called the **top of stack** pointer, or **tos**).

We consider some examples.

Example 7.2

Consider the simple recursive implementation of Euclid's algorithm to compute the greatest common divisor of two nonnegative integers, whose code (in C) is given in Figure 7.3.

Figure 7.3
C code for Example 7.2

```
#include <stdio.h>

int x,y;

int gcd( int u, int v)
{ if (v == 0) return u;
   else return gcd(v,u % v);
}

main()
{ scanf("%d%d",&x,&y);
  printf("%d\n",gcd(x,y));
  return 0;
}
```

Suppose the user inputs the values 15 and 10 to this program, so that **main** initially makes the call **gcd(15,10)**. This call results in a second, recursive call **gcd(10,5)** (since 15 % 10 = 5), and this results in a third call **gcd(5,0)** (since 10 % 5 = 0), which then returns the value 5. During the third call the runtime environment may be visualized as in Figure 7.4. Note how each call to **gcd** adds a new activation record of exactly the same size to the top of the stack, and in each new activation record, the control link points to the control link of the previous activation record. Note also that the fp points to the control link of the current activation record, so on the next call the current fp becomes the control link of the next activation record.

Figure 7.4

Stack-based environment for Example 7.2

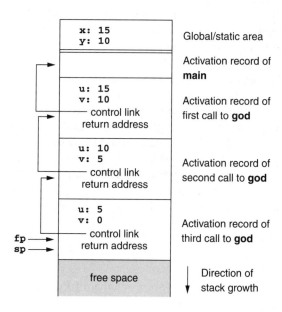

After the final call to **gcd**, each of the activations is removed in turn from the stack, so that when the **printf** statement is executed in **main**, only the activation record for **main** and the global/static area remain in the environment. (We have shown the activation record of **main** as empty. In reality, it would contain information that would be used to transfer control back to the operating system.)

Finally, we remark that no space in the caller is needed for the argument values in the calls to **gcd** (unlike the constant 3 in the FORTRAN77 environment of Figure 7.2), since the C language uses value parameters. This point will be discussed in more detail in Section 7.5.   §

Example 7.3   Consider the C code of Figure 7.5. This code contains variables that will be used to illustrate further points later in this section, but its basic operation is as follows. The

Figure 7.5

C program of Example 7.3

```
int x = 2;

void g(int); /* prototype */

void f(int n)
{ static int x = 1;
  g(n);
  x--;
}

void g(int m)
{ int y = m--1;
  if (y > 0)
  { f(y);
    x--;
    g(y);
  }
}


main()
{ g(x);
  return 0;
}
```

first call from **main** is to **g(2)** (since **x** has the value 2 at that point). In this call, **m** becomes 2, and **y** becomes 1. Then, **g** makes the call **f(1)**, and **f** in turn makes the call **g(1)**. In this call to **g**, **m** becomes 1, and **y** becomes 0, so no further calls are made. The runtime environment at this point (during the second call to **g**) is shown in Figure 7.6(a) (page 356).

Now the calls to **g** and **f** exit (with **f** decrementing its static local variable **x** before returning), their activation records are popped from the stack, and control is returned to the point directly following the call to **f** in the first call to **g**. Now **g** decrements the external variable **x** and makes a further call **g(1)**, which sets **m** to 2 and **y** to 1, resulting in the runtime environment shown in Figure 7.6(b). After that no further calls are made, the remaining activation records are popped from the stack, and the program exits.

Note how, in Figure 7.6(b), the activation record of the third call to **g** occupies (and overwrites) the area of memory previously occupied by the activation record of **f**. Note, also, that the static variable **x** in **f** cannot be allocated in an activation record of **f**, since it must persist across all calls to **f**. Thus, it must be allocated in the global/static area along with the external variable **x**, even though it is not a global variable. There can in fact be no confusion with the external **x**, since the symbol table will always distinguish them and determine the correct variable to access at each point in the program.

Figure 7.6

(a) Runtime environment of the program of Figure 7.5 during the second call to **g**

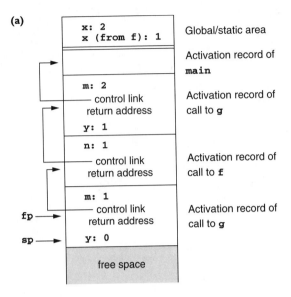

(a)

x: 2 x (from f): 1	Global/static area
	Activation record of **main**
m: 2 control link return address y: 1	Activation record of call to **g**
n: 1 control link return address	Activation record of call to **f**
m: 1 control link return address y: 0	Activation record of call to **g**
free space	

fp → (points to m: 1 control link)
sp → (points to y: 0)

(b) Runtime environment of the program of Figure 7.5 during the third call to **g**

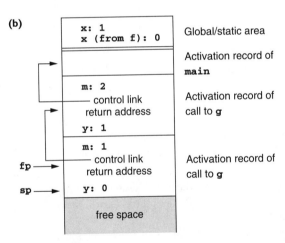

(b)

x: 1 x (from f): 0	Global/static area
	Activation record of **main**
m: 2 control link return address y: 1	Activation record of call to **g**
m: 1 control link return address	Activation record of call to **g**
y: 0	
free space	

fp → (points to m: 1 control link)
sp → (points to y: 0)

§

A useful tool for the analysis of complex calling structures in a program is the **activation tree**: each activation record (or call) becomes a node in this tree, and the descendants of each node represent all the calls made during the call corresponding to that node. For example, the activation tree of the program of Figure 7.3 is linear and is depicted (for the inputs 15 and 10) in Figure 7.7(a), while the activation tree of the program of Figure 7.5 is depicted in Figure 7.7(b). Note that the environments shown in Figures 7.4 and 7.6 represent the environments during the calls represented by each of the leaves of the activation trees. In general, the stack of activation records at the beginning of a particular call has a structure equivalent to the path from the corresponding node in the activation tree to the root.

Access to Names   In a stack-based environment, parameters and local variables can no longer be accessed by fixed addresses as in a fully static environment. Instead, they

Figure 7.7

Activation trees for the programs of Figures 7.3 and 7.5

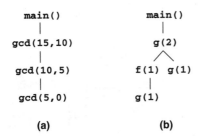

(a)   (b)

must be found by offset from the current frame pointer. In most languages, the offset for each local declaration is still statically computable by the compiler, since the declarations of a procedure are fixed at compile time and the memory size to be allocated for each declaration is fixed by its data type.

Consider the procedure **g** in the C program of Figure 7.5 (see also the runtime environments pictured in Figure 7.6). Each activation record of **g** has exactly the same form, and the parameter **m** and the local variable **y** are always in exactly the same relative location in the activation record. Let us call these distances **mOffset** and **yOffset**. Then, during any call to **g**, we have the following picture of the local environment

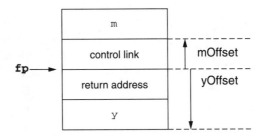

Both **m** and **y** can be accessed by their fixed offsets from the fp. For instance, assume for concreteness that the runtime stack grows from higher to lower memory addresses, that integer variables require 2 bytes of storage, and that addresses require 4 bytes. With the organization of an activation record as shown, we have **mOffset** = +4 and **yOffset** = −6, and references to **m** and **y** can be written in machine code (assuming standard assembler conventions) as **4(fp)** and **−6(fp)**, respectively.

Local arrays and structures are no more difficult to allocate and compute addresses for than are simple variables, as the following example demonstrates.

Example 7.4   Consider the C procedure

```
void f(int x, char c)
{ int a[10];
  double y;
  ...
}
```

The activation record for a call to **f** would appear as

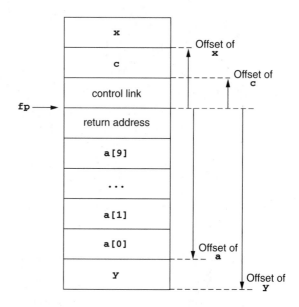

and, assuming two bytes for integers, four bytes for addresses, one byte for characters, and eight bytes for double-precision floating point, we would have the following offset values (again assuming a negative direction of growth for the stack), which are all computable at compile time:

Name	Offset
x	+5
c	+4
a	−24
y	−32

Now an access of, say, **a[i]** would require the computation of the address

(-24+2*i)(fp)

(here the factor of 2 in the product **2*i** is the **scale factor** resulting from the assumption that integer values occupy two bytes). Such a memory access, depending on the location of **i** and the architecture, might only need a single instruction. §

Nonlocal and static names in this environment cannot be accessed in the same way that local names are. Indeed, in the case we are considering here—languages with no local procedures—all nonlocals are global and hence static. Thus, in Figure 7.6, the external (global) C variable **x** has a fixed static location, and so can be accessed directly (or by offset from some base pointer other than the fp). The static local variable **x** from **f** is accessed in exactly the same fashion. Note that this mechanism implements static (or lexical) scope, as described in the previous chapter. If dynamic scope is desired, then a more complex accessing mechanism is required (described later in this section).

The Calling Sequence   The calling sequence now comprises approximately the following steps.[8] When a procedure is called,

1. Compute the arguments and store them in their correct positions in the new activation record of the procedure (pushing them in order onto the runtime stack will achieve this).
2. Store (push) the fp as the control link in the new activation record.
3. Change the fp so that it points to the beginning of the new activation record (if there is an sp, copying the sp into the fp at this point will achieve this).
4. Store the return address in the new activation record (if necessary).
5. Perform a jump to the code of the procedure to be called.

When a procedure exits,

1. Copy the fp to the sp.
2. Load the control link into the fp.
3. Perform a jump to the return address.
4. Change the sp to pop the arguments.

Example 7.5   Consider the situation just before the last call to **g** in Figure 7.6(b):

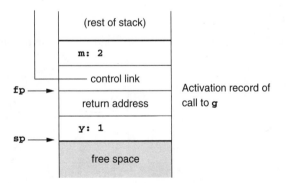

As the new call to **g** is made, first the value of parameter **m** is pushed onto the runtime stack:

---

8. This description ignores any saving of registers that must take place. It also ignores the need to place a return value into an available location.

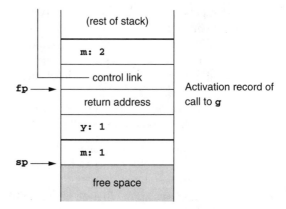

Then the fp is pushed onto the stack:

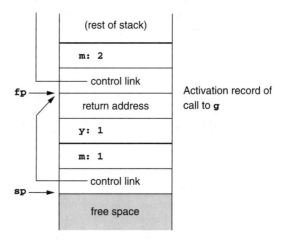

Now the sp is copied into the fp, the return address is pushed onto the stack, and the jump to the new call of **g** is made:

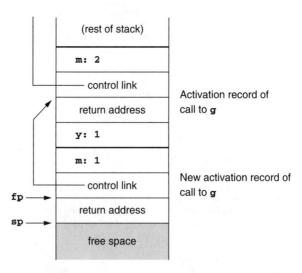

Finally, **g** allocates and initializes the new **y** on the stack to complete the construction of the new activation record:

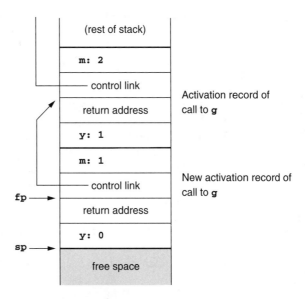

Dealing with Variable-Length Data   So far we have described a situation in which all data, whether local or global, can be found in a fixed place or at a fixed offset from the fp that can be computed by the compiler. Sometimes a compiler must deal with the possibility that data may vary, both in the number of data objects and in the size of each object. Two examples that occur in languages that support stack-based environments are (1) the number of arguments in a call may vary from call to call, and (2) the size of an array parameter or a local array variable may vary from call to call.

A typical example of situation 1 is the **printf** function in C, where the number of arguments is determined from the format string that is passed as the first argument. Thus,

```
printf("%d%s%c",n,prompt,ch);
```

has four arguments (including the format string **"%d%s%c"**), while

```
printf("Hello, world\n");
```

has only one argument. C compilers typically deal with this by pushing the arguments to a call **in reverse order** onto the runtime stack. Then, the first parameter (which tells the code for **printf** how many more parameters there are) is always located at a fixed offset from the fp in the implementation described above (indeed +4, using the assumptions of the previous example). Another option is to use a processor mechanism such as the ap (argument pointer) in VAX architectures. This and other possibilities are treated further in the exercises.

An example of situation 2 is the **unconstrained array** of Ada:

```
type Int_Vector is
        array(INTEGER range <>) of INTEGER;

procedure Sum (low,high: INTEGER;
                      A: Int_Vector) return INTEGER
is
    temp: Int_Array (low..high);
begin
    ...
end Sum;
```

(Note the local variable **temp** which also has unpredictable size.) A typical method for dealing with this situation is to use an extra level of indirection for the variable-length data, storing a pointer to the actual data in a location that can be predicted at compile time, while performing the actual allocation at the top of the runtime stack in a way that can be managed by the sp during execution.

Example 7.6   Given the Ada **Sum** procedure as defined above, and assuming the same organization for the environment as before,[9] we could implement an activation record for **Sum** as follows (this picture shows, for concreteness, a call to **Sum** with an array of size 10):

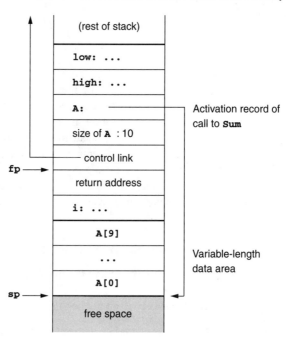

Now, for instance, access to **A[i]** can be achieved by computing

```
@6 (fp) +2*i
```

---

9. This is actually not sufficient for Ada, which allows nested procedures; see the discussion later in this section.

where the **@** means indirection, and where we are again assuming two bytes for integers and four bytes for addresses.   §

Note that in the implementation described in the previous example, the caller must know the size of any activation record of **Sum**. The size of the parameter part and the bookkeeping part is known to the compiler at the point of call (since the arguments sizes can be counted, and the bookkeeping part is the same for all procedures), but the size of the local variable part is not, in general, known at the point of call. Thus, this implementation requires that the compiler precompute a local-variable size attribute for each procedure and store it in the symbol table for this later use. Variable-length local variables can be dealt with in a similar way.

It is worth remarking that C arrays do not fall into the class of such variable-length data. Indeed, C arrays are pointers, so array parameters are passed by reference in C and not allocated locally (and they carry no size information).

Local Temporaries and Nested Declarations   There are two more complications to the basic stack-based runtime environment that deserve mention: local temporaries and nested declarations.

Local temporaries are partial results of computations that must be saved across procedure calls. Consider, for example, the C expression

```
x[i] = (i + j)*(i/k + f(j))
```

In a left-to-right evaluation of this expression, three partial results need to be saved across the call to **f**: the address of **x[i]** (for the pending assignment), the sum **i+j** (pending the multiplication), and the quotient **i/k** (pending the sum with the result of the call **f(j)**). These partial results could be computed into registers and saved and restored according to some register management mechanism, or they could be stored as temporaries on the runtime stack prior to the call to **f**. In this latter case, the runtime stack might appear as follows at the point just before the call to **f**:

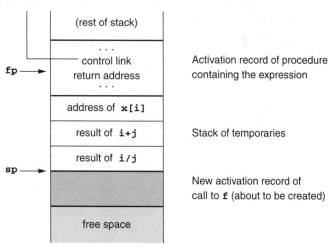

In this situation, the previously described calling sequence using the sp works without change. Alternatively, the compiler can also easily compute the position of the stack top from the fp (in the absence of variable-length data), since the number of required temporaries is a compile-time quantity.

Nested declarations present a similar problem. Consider the C code

```
void p( int x, double y)
{ char a;
  int i;
  ...
A:{ double x;
    int j;
    ...
  }
  ...
B:{ char * a;
    int k;
    ...
  }
  ...
}
```

In this code there are two blocks (also called *compound statements*), labeled **A** and **B**, nested inside the body of procedure **p**, each with two local declarations whose scope extends only over the block in which they are located (that is, up until the next closing bracket). The local declarations of each of these blocks do not need to be allocated until the block is entered, and the declarations of block **A** and block **B** do not need to be allocated simultaneously. A compiler *could* treat a block just like a procedure and create a new activation record each time a block is entered and discard it on exit. However, this would be inefficient, since such blocks are much simpler than procedures: such a block has no parameters and no return address and is always executed immediately, rather than called from elsewhere. A simpler method is to treat declarations in nested blocks in a similar way to temporary expressions, allocating them on the stack as the block is entered and deallocating them on exit.

For instance, just after entering block **A** in the sample C code just given, the runtime stack would appear as follows:

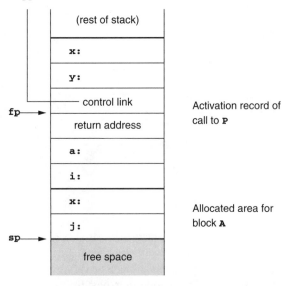

and just after entry to block **B** it would look as follows:

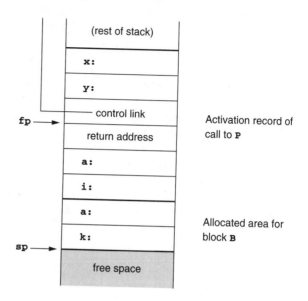

Such an implementation must be careful to allocate nested declarations in such a way that the offsets from the fp of the surrounding procedure block are computable at compile time. In particular, such data must be allocated before any variable-length data. For example, in the code just given, the variable **j** local to block **A** would have offset −17 from the fp of **p** (assuming again 2 bytes for integers, 4 bytes for addresses, 8 bytes for floating-point reals, and 1 byte for characters), while **k** in block **B** would have offset −13.

7.3.2 Stack-Based Environments with Local Procedures

If local procedure declarations are permitted in the language being compiled, then the runtime environment we have described so far is insufficient, since no provision has been made for nonlocal, nonglobal references.

Consider, for example, the Pascal code of Figure 7.8, page 366 (similar programs could be written in Ada). During the call to **q** the runtime environment would appear as in Figure 7.9. Using the standard static scoping rule, any mention of **n** inside **q** must refer to the local integer variable **n** of **p**. As we can see from Figure 7.9, this **n** cannot be found using any of the bookkeeping information that is kept in the runtime environment up to now.

It *would* be possible to find **n** using the control links, if we are willing to accept dynamic scoping. Looking at Figure 7.9, we see that the **n** in the activation record of **r** could be found by following the control link, and if **r** had no declaration of **n**, then the **n** of **p** could be found by following a second control link (this process is called **chaining**, a method we will see again shortly). Unfortunately, not only does this implement dynamic scope, but the offsets at which **n** can be found may vary with different calls (note that the **n** in **r** has a different offset from the **n** in **p**). Thus, in such an implementation, local symbol tables for each procedure must be kept during execution to allow an identifier to be looked up in each activation record, to see if it exists, and to determine its offset. This is a major additional complication to the runtime environment.

Figure 7.8

Pascal program showing nonlocal, nonglobal reference

```
program nonLocalRef;

procedure p;
var n: integer;

    procedure q;
    begin
      (* a reference to n is now
         non-local non-global *)
    end; (* q *)

    procedure r(n: integer);
    begin
      q;
    end; (* r *)

begin (* p *)
  n := 1;
  r(2);
end; (* p *)

begin (* main *)
  p;
end.
```

Figure 7.9

Runtime stack for the program of Figure 7.8

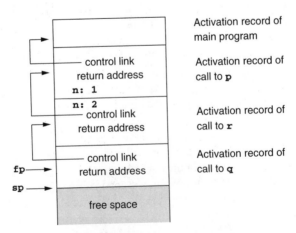

Activation record of main program

Activation record of call to p

Activation record of call to r

Activation record of call to q

The solution to this problem, which also implements static scoping, is to add an extra piece of bookkeeping information called the **access link** to each activation record. The access link is like the control link, except that it points to the activation record that represents the *defining environment* of the procedure instead of the calling environment. For this reason, the access link is sometimes also called the **static link**, even though it is not a compile-time quantity.[10]

Figure 7.10 shows the runtime stack of Figure 7.9 modified to include access links. In this new environment, the access links of the activation records of both **r** and **q** point to the activation record of **p**, since **r** and **q** are both declared within **p**. Now a nonlocal reference to **n** inside **q** will cause the access link to be followed, where **n** will be found at a fixed offset, since this will always be an activation record of **p**. Typically, this can be achieved in code by loading the access link into a register and then accessing **n** by offset from this register (which now functions as the fp). For instance, using the size conventions described earlier, if register r is used for the access link, then **n** inside **p** can be accessed as −6(r) after r has been loaded with the value 4(fp) (the access link has offset +4 from the fp in Figure 7.10).

Figure 7.10

Runtime stack for the program of Figure 7.8 with access links added

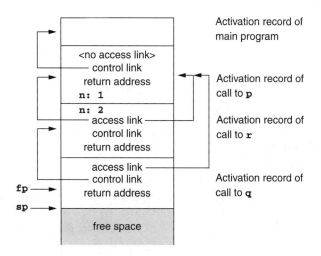

Note that the activation record of procedure **p** itself contains no access link, as indicated by the bracketed comment in the location where it would go. This is because **p** is a global procedure, so any nonlocal reference within **p** must be a global reference and is accessed via the global reference mechanism. Thus, there is no need for an access link. (In fact, a null or otherwise arbitrary access link may be inserted simply for consistency with the other procedures.)

The case we have been describing is actually the simplest situation, where the nonlocal reference is to a declaration in the next outermost scope. It is also possible that nonlocal references refer to declarations in more distant scopes. Consider, for example, the code in Figure 7.11.

---

10. The defining procedure is of course known, but not the exact location of its activation record.

Figure 7.11

Pascal code demonstrating
access chaining

```
program chain;

procedure p;
var x: integer;

   procedure q;
      procedure r;
      begin
        x := 2;
        ...
        if ... then p;
      end; (* r *)
   begin
     r;
   end; (* q *)

begin
  q;
end; (* p *)

begin (* main *)
  p;
end.
```

In this code, procedure **r** is declared in procedure **q**, which in turn is declared in procedure **p**. Thus, the assignment to **x** inside **r**, which refers to the **x** of **p**, must traverse two scope levels to find **x**. Figure 7.12 shows the runtime stack after the (first) call to **r** (there may be more than one call to **r**, since **r** may call **p** recursively). In this environment, **x** must be reached by following *two* access links, a process that is called **access chaining**. Access chaining is implemented by repeatedly fetching the access link, using the previously fetched link as if it were the fp. As a concrete example, **x** in Figure 7.12 can be accessed (using the previous size conventions) as follows:

Load 4(fp) into register r.

Load 4(r) into register r.

Now access **x** as −6(r).

For the method of access chaining to work, the compiler must be able to determine how many nesting levels to chain through before accessing the name locally. This requires the compiler to precompute a **nesting level** attribute for each declaration. Usually, the outermost scope (the main program level in Pascal or the external scope of C) is given nesting level 0, and each time a function or procedure is entered (during compilation), the nesting level is increased by 1, and decreased by the same amount on exit. For example, in the code of Figure 7.11, procedure **p** is given nesting level 0 since it is global; variable **x** is given nesting level 1, since the nesting level is increased when **p** is entered; procedure **q** is also given nesting level 1, since it is local to **p**; and procedure **r** is given nesting level 2, since the nesting level is again increased when **q** is entered. Finally, inside **r** the nesting level is again increased to 3.

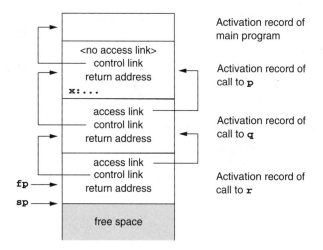

Figure 7.12

Runtime stack after the first call to **r** in the code of Figure 7.11

Now the amount of chaining necessary to access a nonlocal name can be determined by comparing the nesting level at the point of access with the nesting level of the declaration of the name; the number of access links to follow is the difference between these two nesting levels. For example, in the previous situation, the assignment to **x** occurs at nesting level 3, and **x** has nesting level 1, so two access links must be followed. In general, if the difference in nesting levels is *m*, then the code that must be generated for access chaining must have *m* loads to a register r, the first using the fp, and the remainder using r.

It may seem that access chaining is an inefficient method for variable access, since a lengthy sequence of instructions must be executed for each nonlocal reference with a large nesting difference. In practice, however, nesting levels are rarely more than two or three deep, and most nonlocal references are to global variables (nesting level 0), which can continue to be accessed by the direct methods previously discussed. There is a method of implementing access links in a lookup table indexed by nesting level that does not carry the execution overhead of chaining. The data structure used for this method is called the **display**. Its structure and use are treated in the exercises.

The Calling Sequence The changes to the calling sequence needed to implement access links are relatively straightforward. In the implementation shown, during a call, the access link must be pushed onto the runtime stack just before the fp, and after an exit, the sp must be adjusted by an extra amount to remove the access link as well as the arguments.

The only problem is that of finding the access link of a procedure during a call. This can be achieved by using the (compile-time) nesting level information attached to the declaration of the procedure being called. Indeed, all we need to do is to generate an access chain, just as if we were going to access a variable at the same nesting level as that of the procedure being called. The address so computed will be the appropriate access link. Of course, if the procedure is local (the difference in nesting levels is 0), then the access link and the control link are the same (and are equal to the fp at the point of the call).

Consider, for example the call to **q** from within **r** in Figure 7.8. Inside **r**, we are at nesting level 2, while the declaration of **q** carries a nesting level of 1 (since **q** is local to **p** and inside **p** the nesting level is 1). Thus, one access step is required to compute the access link of **q**, and indeed in Figure 7.10, the access link of **q** points to the activation record of **p** (and is the same as the access link of **r**).

Note that even in the presence of multiple activations of the defining environment, this process will compute the correct access link, since the computation is performed at runtime (using the compile-time nesting levels), not at compile time. For example, given the code of Figure 7.11, the runtime stack after the *second* call to **r** (assuming a recursive call to **p**) would look as in Figure 7.13. In this picture, **r** has two different activation records with two different access links, pointing at the different activation records of **q**, which represent different defining environments for **r**.

Figure 7.13

Runtime stack after the second call to **r** in the code of Figure 7.11

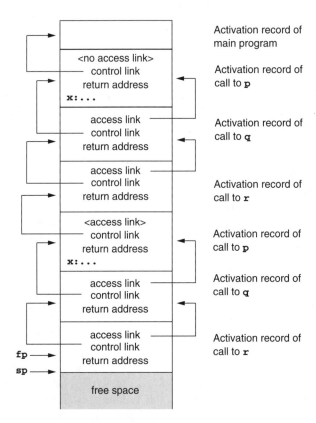

7.3.3   Stack-Based Environments with Procedure Parameters

In some languages, not only are local procedures allowed, but procedures may also be passed as parameters. In such a language, when a procedure that has been passed as a parameter is called, it is impossible for a compiler to generate code to compute the access link at the time of call, as described in the previous section. Instead, the access link for a procedure must be precomputed and passed along with a pointer to the code for the procedure when the procedure is passed as a parameter. Thus, a procedure parameter value can no longer be viewed as a simple code pointer, but must also include an access pointer that defines the environment in which nonlocal references are resolved. This pair of pointers—a code pointer and an access link or an **instruction pointer** and an **environment pointer**—together represent the value of a procedure or function parameter and are commonly called a **closure** (since the access link "closes" the "holes" caused by nonlocal references).[11] We will write closures as $<$ip, ep$>$, where ip refers to the instruction pointer (code pointer or entry point) of the procedure, and ep refers to the environment pointer (access link) of the procedure.

Example 7.7

Consider the Standard Pascal program of Figure 7.14, which has a procedure **p**, with a parameter **a** that is also a procedure. After the call to **p** in **q**, in which the local procedure **r** of **q** is passed to **p**, the call to **a** inside **p** actually calls **r**, and this call must still find the nonlocal variable **x** in the activation of **q**. When **p** is called, **a** is constructed as a closure $<$ip, ep$>$, where ip is a pointer to the code of **r** and ep is a copy of the fp at the point of call (that is, it points to the environment of the call to **q** in which **r** is defined). The value of the ep of **a** is indicated by the dashed line in Figure 7.15 (page 372), which represents the environment just after the call to **p** in **q**. Then, when **a** is called inside **p**, the ep of **a** is used as the static link in its activation record, as indicated in Figure 7.16.

§

Figure 7.14

Standard Pascal code with a procedure as parameter

```
program closureEx(output);

procedure p(procedure a);
begin
  a;
end;


procedure q;
var x:integer;

    procedure r;
    begin
      writeln(x);
    end;

begin
  x := 2;
  p(r);
end; (* q *)


begin (* main *)
  q;
end.
```

§

---

11. This term has its origin in lambda calculus and is not to be confused with the (Kleene) closure operation in regular expressions or the ε-closure of a set of NFA states.

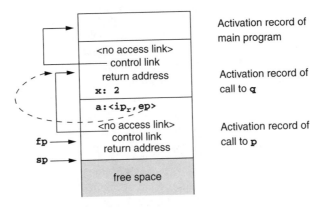

Figure 7.15

Runtime stack just after the call to **p** in the code of Figure 7.14

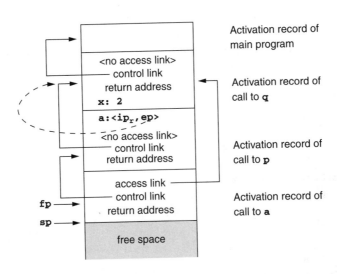

Figure 7.16

Runtime stack just after the call to **a** in the code of Figure 7.14

The calling sequence in an environment such as we have just described must now distinguish clearly between ordinary procedures and procedure parameters. An ordinary procedure is called, as before, by fetching the access link using the nesting level of the procedure and jumping directly to the code of the procedure (which is known at compile time). A procedure parameter, on the other hand, has its access link already available, stored in the local activation record, which must be fetched and inserted into the new activation record. The location of the code for the procedure, however, is not known directly to the compiler; instead, an indirect call must be performed to the ip stored in the current activation record.

A compiler writer may, for reasons of simplicity or uniformity, wish to avoid this distinction between ordinary procedures and procedure parameters and keep all procedures as closures in the environment. Indeed, the more general a language is in its treatment of procedures, the more reasonable such an approach becomes. For example, if procedure variables are allowed, or if procedure values can be dynamically computed, then the <ip, ep> representation of procedures becomes a requirement for all such situations. Figure 7.17 shows what the environment of Figure 7.16 would look like if all procedure values are stored in the environment as closures.

Figure 7.17

Runtime stack just after
the call to **a** in the code
of Figure 7.14 with all
procedures kept as closures
in the environment

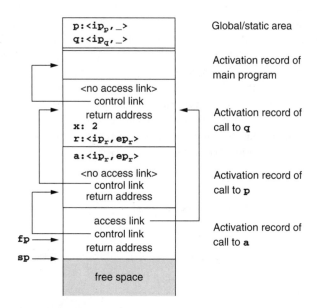

Finally, we note that C, Modula-2, and Ada all avoid the complications described in this subsection: C, because it has no local procedures (even though it has procedure parameters and variables); Modula-2, because of a special rule restricting procedure parameter and procedure variable values to global procedures; and Ada, because it has no procedure parameters or variables.

7.4 DYNAMIC MEMORY

7.4.1 Fully Dynamic Runtime Environments

The stack based runtime environments discussed in the previous section are the most common forms of environment among the standard imperative languages such as C, Pascal, and Ada. Such environments do have limitations, however. In particular, in a language where a reference to a local variable in a procedure can be returned to the caller, either implicitly or explicitly, a stack-based environment will result in a **dangling reference** when the procedure is exited, since the activation record of the procedure will be deallocated from the stack. The simplest example of this is when the address of a local variable is returned, as for instance in the C code:

```
int * dangle(void)
{ int x;
  return &x;}
```

An assignment **addr = dangle()** now causes **addr** to point to an unsafe location in the activation stack whose value can be arbitrarily changed by subsequent calls to any procedure. C gets around this problem by simply declaring such a program to be erroneous (although no compiler will give an error message). In other words, the semantics of C are built around the underlying stack-based environment.

A somewhat more complex instance of a dangling reference occurs if a local function can be returned by a call. For instance, if C were to allow local function definitions, the code of Figure 7.18 would result in an indirect dangling reference to the parameter **x** of **g**, which can be accessed by calling **f** after **g** has exited. C, of course, avoids this problem by prohibiting local procedures. Other languages, like Modula-2, which have local procedures as well as procedure variables, parameters, and returned values, must state a special rule that makes such programs erroneous. (In Modula-2 the rule is that only global procedures can be arguments or returned values—a major retreat even from Pascal-style procedure parameters.)

Figure 7.18

Pseudo-C code showing a dangling reference caused by the return of a local function

```
typedef int (* proc)(void);

proc g(int x)
{ int f(void) /* illegal local function */
   { return x;}
   return f; }

main()
{ proc c;
  c = g(2);
  printf("%d\n",c()); /* should print 2 */
  return 0;
}
```

There is a large class of languages, however, where such rules are unacceptable, that is, the functional programming languages, such as LISP and ML. An essential principle in the design of a functional language is that functions be as general as possible, and this means that functions must be able to be locally defined, passed as parameters, and returned as results. Thus, for this large class of languages, a stack-based runtime environment is inadequate, and a more general form of environment is required. We call such an environment **fully dynamic**, because it can deallocate activation records only when all references to them have disappeared, and this requires that activation records be dynamically freed at arbitrary times during execution. A fully dynamic runtime environment is significantly more complicated than a stack-based environment, since it involves the tracking of references during execution, and the ability to find and deallocate inaccessible areas of memory at arbitrary times during execution (this process is called **garbage collection**).

Despite the added complexity of this kind of environment, the basic structure of an activation record remains the same: space must be allocated for parameters and local variables, and there is still a need for the control and access links. Of course, now when control is returned to the caller (and the control link is used to restore the previous environment), the exited activation record remains in memory, to be deallocated at some later time. Thus, the entire additional complexity of this environment can be encapsulated in a memory manager that replaces the runtime stack operations with more general allocation and deallocation routines. We discuss some of the issues in the design of such a memory manager later in this section.

7.4.2 Dynamic Memory in Object-Oriented Languages

Object-oriented languages require special mechanisms in the runtime environment to implement their added features: objects, methods, inheritance, and dynamic binding. In this subsection we give a brief overview of the variety of implementation techniques for these features. We assume the reader is familiar with basic object-oriented terminology and concepts.[12]

Object-oriented languages vary greatly in their requirements for the runtime environment. Smalltalk and C++ are good representatives of the extremes: Smalltalk requires a fully dynamic environment similar to that of LISP, while much of the design effort in C++ has gone into retaining the stack-based environment of C, without the need for automatic dynamic memory management. In both these languages, an object in memory can be viewed as a cross between a traditional record structure and an activation record, with the instance variables (data members) as the fields of the record. This structure differs from a traditional record in how methods and inherited features are accessed.

One straightforward mechanism for implementing objects would be for initialization code to copy all the currently inherited features (and methods) directly into the record structure (with methods as code pointers). This is extremely wasteful of space, however. An alternative is to keep a complete description of the class structure in memory at each point during execution, with inheritance maintained by superclass pointers, and all method pointers kept as fields in the class structure (this is sometimes called an **inheritance graph**). Each object then keeps, along with fields for its instance variables, a pointer to its defining class, through which all methods (both local and inherited) are found. In this way, method pointers are recorded only once (in the class structure) and not copied in memory for each object. This mechanism also implements inheritance and dynamic binding, since methods are found by a search of the class hierarchy. The disadvantage is that, while instance variables may have predictable offsets (just as local variables in a standard environment), the methods do not, and they must be maintained by name in a symbol table structure with lookup capabilities. Nevertheless, this is a reasonable structure for a highly dynamic language like Smalltalk, where changes to the class structure can occur during execution.

An alternative to keeping the entire class structure within the environment is to compute the list of code pointers for available methods of each class, and store this in (static) memory as a **virtual function table** (in C++ terminology). This has the advantage that it can be arranged so that each method has a predictable offset, and a traversal of the class hierarchy with a series of table lookups is no longer necessary. Now each object contains a pointer to the appropriate virtual function table, rather than to the class structure. (Of course, the location of this pointer must also have predictable offset.) This simplification only works if the class structure itself is fixed prior to execution. It is the method of choice in C++.

---

12. The following discussion also assumes only single inheritance is available. Multiple inheritance is treated in some of the works cited in the Notes and References section.

Example 7.8   Consider the following C++ class declarations:

```
class A
{ public:
  double x,y;
  void f();
  virtual void g();
};

class B: public A
{ public:
  double z;
  void f();
  virtual void h();
};
```

an object of class **A** would appear in memory (with its virtual function table) as follows:

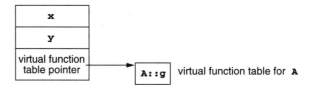

while an object of class **B** would appear as follows:

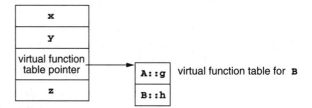

Note how the virtual function pointer, once added to the object structure, remains in a fixed location, so that its offset is known prior to execution. Note also that the function **f** does not obey dynamic binding in C++ (since it is not declared "virtual"), and so does not appear in the virtual function table (or anywhere else in the environment); a call to **f** is resolved at compile time.   §

7.4.3   Heap Management

In Section 7.4.1, we discussed the need for a runtime environment that is more dynamic than the stack-based environment used in most compiled languages, if general functions are to be fully supported. In most languages, however, even a stack-based environment needs some dynamic capabilities in order to handle pointer allocation and deallocation. The data structure that handles such allocation is called a *heap*, and the heap is usually allocated as a linear block of memory in such a way that it can grow, if necessary, while interfering as little as possible with the stack. (On page 347 we showed the heap sitting in a block of memory at the opposite end of the stack area.)

So far in this chapter, we have concentrated on the organization of activation records and the runtime stack. In this section, we want to describe how the heap can be managed, and how the heap operations might be extended to provide the kind of dynamic allocation required in languages with general function capabilities.

A heap provides two operations, *allocate* and *free*. The *allocate* operation takes a size parameter (either explicitly or implicitly), usually in bytes, and returns a pointer to a block of memory of the correct size, or a null pointer if none exists. The *free* operation takes a pointer to an allocated block of memory and marks it as being free again. (The *free* operation must also be able to discover the size of the block to be freed, either implicitly or by an explicit parameter.) These two operations exist under different names in many languages: they are called **new** and **dispose** in Pascal and **new** and **delete** in C++. The C language has several versions of these operations, but the basic ones are called **malloc** and **free** and are part of the standard library (**stdlib.h**), where they have essentially the following declarations:

```
void * malloc (unsigned nbytes);
void free (void * ap);
```

We will use these declarations as the basis for our description of heap management.

A standard method for maintaining the heap and implementing these functions is to use a circular linked list of free blocks, from which memory is taken by **malloc** and returned to by **free**. This has the advantage of simplicity, but it also has drawbacks. One is that the **free** operation cannot tell whether its pointer argument is really pointing at a legitimate block that was previously allocated by **malloc**. If the user should pass an invalid pointer, then the heap can become easily and quickly corrupted. A second, but much less serious, drawback is that care must be taken to **coalesce** blocks that are returned to the free list with blocks that are adjacent to it, so that a free block of maximal size will result. Without coalescing, the heap can quickly become **fragmented**, that is, divided into a large number of small-sized blocks, so that the allocation of a large block may fail, even though there is enough total space available to allocate it. (Fragmentation is of course possible even with coalescing.)

We offer here a slightly different implementation of **malloc** and **free** that uses a circular linked list data structure that keeps track of both allocated and free blocks (and thus is less susceptible to corruption) and that also has the advantage of providing self-coalescing blocks. The code is given in Figure 7.19 (page 379).

This code uses a statically allocated array of size **MEMSIZE** as the heap, but an operating system call could also be used to allocate the heap. We define a data type **Header** that will hold each memory block's bookkeeping information, and we define the heap array to have elements of type **Header** so that the bookkeeping information can be easily kept in the memory blocks themselves. The type **Header** contains three pieces of information: a pointer to the next block in the list, the size of the currently allocated space (which comes next in memory), and the size of any following free space (if there is any). Thus, each block in the list is of the form

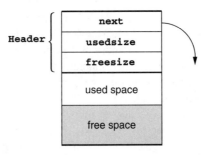

The definition of type **Header** in Figure 7.19 also uses a **union** declaration and an **Align** data type (which we have set to **double** in the code). This is to align the memory elements on a reasonable byte boundary and, depending on the system, may or may not be necessary. This complication can be safely ignored in the remainder of this description.

The one additional piece of data needed by the heap operations is a pointer to one of the blocks in the circular linked list. This pointer is called **memptr**, and it always points to a block that has some free space (usually the last space to be allocated or freed). It is initialized to **NULL**, but on the first call to **malloc**, initialization code is executed that sets **memptr** to the beginning of the heap array and initializes the header in the array, as follows:

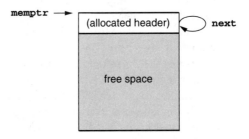

This initial header that is allocated on the first call to **malloc** will never be freed. There is now one block in the list, and the remainder of the code of **malloc** searches the list and returns a new block from the first block that has enough free space (this is a **first fit** algorithm). Thus, after, say, three calls to **malloc**, the list will look as follows:

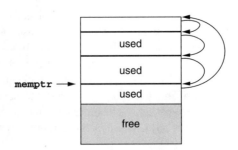

Figure 7.19

C code to maintain a heap
of contiguous memory using
a list of pointers to both
used and free blocks

```
#define NULL 0
#define MEMSIZE 8096 /* change for different sizes */

typedef double Align;
typedef union header
  { struct { union header *next;
                  unsigned usedsize;
                  unsigned freesize;
              } s;
    Align a;
  } Header;

static Header mem[MEMSIZE];
static Header *memptr = NULL;

void *malloc(unsigned nbytes)
{ Header *p, *newp;
  unsigned nunits;
  nunits = (nbytes+sizeof(Header)-1)/sizeof(Header) + 1;
  if (memptr == NULL)
  { memptr->s.next = memptr = mem;
    memptr->s.usedsize = 1;
    memptr->s.freesize = MEMSIZE-1;
  }
  for(p=memptr;
      (p->s.next!=memptr) && (p->s.freesize<nunits);
      p=p->s.next);
  if (p->s.freesize < nunits) return NULL;
  /* no block big enough */
  newp = p+p->s.usedsize;
  newp->s.usedsize = nunits;
  newp->s.freesize = p->s.freesize - nunits;
  newp->s.next = p->s.next;
  p->s.freesize = 0;
  p->s.next = newp;
  memptr = newp;
  return (void *) (newp+1);
}

void free(void *ap)
{ Header *bp, *p, *prev;
  bp = (Header *) ap - 1;
  for (prev=memptr,p=memptr->s.next;
       (p!=bp) && (p!=memptr); prev=p,p=p->s.next);
  if (p!=bp) return;
  /* corrupted list, do nothing */
  prev->s.freesize += p->s.usedsize + p->s.freesize;
  prev->s.next = p->s.next;
  memptr = prev;
}
```

Note that as the blocks are allocated in succession, a new block is created each time, and the free space left over from the previous block is carried with it (so that the free space of the block from which the allocation took place always has **freesize** set to 0). Also, **memptr** follows the construction of the new blocks, and so always points to a block with some free space. Note also that **malloc** always increments the pointer to the newly created block, so that the header is protected from being overwritten by the client program (as long as only positive offsets into the returned memory are used).

Now consider the code for the **free** procedure. It first decrements the pointer passed by the user to find the header of the block. It then searches the list for a pointer that is identical to this one, thus protecting the list from becoming corrupted, and also allowing the pointer to the previous block to be computed. When found, the block is removed from the list, and both its used and free space are added to the free space of the previous block, thus automatically coalescing the free space. Note that **memptr** is also set to point to the block containing the memory just freed.

As an example, suppose the middle block of the three used blocks in the previous picture is freed. Then the heap and its associated block list would look as follows:

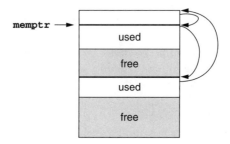

7.4.4 Automatic Management of the Heap

The use of **malloc** and **free** to perform dynamic allocation and deallocation of pointers is a **manual** method for the management of the heap, since the programmer must write explicit calls to allocate and free memory. By contrast, the runtime stack is managed **automatically** by the calling sequence. In a language that needs a fully dynamic runtime environment, the heap must similarly be managed automatically. Unfortunately, while calls to **malloc** can be easily scheduled at each procedure call, the calls to **free** cannot be similarly scheduled on exit, since activation records must persist until all references to them have disappeared. Thus, automatic memory management involves the reclamation of previously allocated but no longer used storage, possibly long after it was allocated, and without an explicit call to **free**. This process is called **garbage collection**.

Recognizing when a block of storage is no longer referenced, either directly or indirectly through pointers, is a much more difficult task than is the maintenance of a list of blocks of heap storage. The standard technique is to perform **mark and sweep** garbage collection.[13] In this method, no memory is freed until a call to **malloc** fails,

---

13. A simpler alternative called **reference counting** is also occasionally used. See the Notes and References section.

at which point a garbage collector is activated that looks for all storage that can be referenced and frees all unreferenced storage. It does this in two passes. The first pass follows all pointers recursively, starting with all currently accessible pointer values, and marks each block of storage reached. This process requires an extra bit of storage for the marking. A second pass then sweeps linearly through memory, returning unmarked blocks to free memory. While this process usually will find enough contiguous free memory to satisfy a series of new requests, it is possible that memory is still so fragmented that a large memory request will still fail, even after garbage collection has been performed. Hence, a garbage collection usually also performs **memory compaction** by moving all the allocated space to one end of the heap, leaving only one large block of contiguous free space at the other end. This process must also update all references to those areas in memory that were moved within the executing program.

Mark and sweep garbage collection has several drawbacks: it requires extra storage (for the marks), and the double pass through memory causes a significant delay in processing, sometimes as much as a few seconds, each time the garbage collector is invoked—which can be every few minutes. This is clearly unacceptable for many applications involving interactive or immediate response.

A bookkeeping improvement can be made to this process by splitting available memory into two halves and allocating storage only from one half at a time. Then during the marking pass, all reached blocks are immediately copied to the second half of storage not in use. This means that no extra mark bit is required in storage, and only one pass is required. It also performs compaction automatically. Once all reachable blocks in the used area have been copied, the used and unused halves of memory are interchanged, and processing continues. This method is called **stop-and-copy** or **two-space** garbage collection. Unfortunately, it does little to improve processing delays during storage reclamation.

Recently, a method has been invented that reduces this delay significantly. Called **generational garbage collection**, it adds a permanent storage area to the reclamation scheme of the previous paragraph. Allocated objects that survive long enough are simply copied into permanent space and are never deallocated during subsequent storage reclamations. This means that the garbage collector needs to search only a very small section of memory for newer storage allocations, and the time for such a search is reduced to a fraction of a second. Of course, it is possible for permanent memory still to become exhausted with unreachable storage, but this is a much less severe problem than before, since temporary storage tends to disappear quickly, while storage that stays allocated for some time tends to persist anyway. This process has been shown to work very well, especially with a virtual memory system.

We refer the reader to sources listed in the Notes and References section for details on this and other methods of garbage collection.

7.5   PARAMETER PASSING MECHANISMS

We have seen how, in a procedure call, parameters correspond to locations in the activation record, which are filled in with the arguments, or parameters values, by the caller, prior to jumping to the code of the called procedure. Thus, to the code of the called procedure, a parameter represents a purely formal value to which no code is attached, but which serves only to establish a location in the activation record, where the code can find its eventual value, which will only exist once a call has taken place.

The process of building these values is sometimes referred to as the **binding** of the parameters to the arguments. How the argument values are interpreted by the procedure code depends on the particular **parameter passing mechanism(s)** adopted by the source language. As we have already indicated, FORTRAN77 adopts a mechanism that binds parameters to locations rather than values, while C views all arguments as values. Other languages, like C++, Pascal, and Ada, offer a choice of parameter passing mechanisms.

In this section we will discuss the two most common parameter passing mechanisms—**pass by value** and **pass by reference** (sometimes also referred to as call by value and call by reference)—as well as two additional important methods, **pass by value-result** and **pass by name** (also called **delayed evaluation**). Some variations on these will be discussed in the exercises.

One issue not addressed by the parameter passing mechanism itself is the order in which arguments are evaluated. In most situations, this order is unimportant for the execution of a program, and any evaluation order will produce the same results. In that case, for efficiency or other reasons, a compiler may choose to vary the order of argument evaluation. Many languages, however, permit arguments to calls that cause side effects (changes to memory). For example, the C function call

```
f(++x,x);
```

causes a change in the value of **x**, so that different evaluation orders have different results. In such languages, a standard evaluation order such as left to right may be specified, or it may be left to the compiler writer, in which case the result of a call may vary from implementation to implementation. C compilers typically evaluate their arguments from right to left, rather than left to right. This allows for a variable number of arguments (such as in the **printf** function), as discussed in Section 7.3.1, page 361.

7.5.1 Pass by Value

In this mechanism, the arguments are expressions that are evaluated at the time of the call, and their values become the values of the parameters during the execution of the procedure. This is the only parameter passing mechanism available in C and is the default in Pascal and Ada (Ada also allows such parameters to be explicitly specified as **in** parameters).

In its simplest form, this means that value parameters behave as constant values during the execution of a procedure, and one can interpret pass by value as replacing all the parameters in the body of a procedure by the values of the arguments. This form of pass by value is used by Ada, where such parameters cannot be assigned to or otherwise used as local variables. A more relaxed view is taken by C and Pascal, where value parameters are viewed essentially as initialized local variables, which can be used as ordinary variables, but changes to them never cause any nonlocal changes to take place.

In a language like C that offers only pass by value, it is impossible to directly write a procedure that achieves its effect by making changes to its parameters. For example, the following **inc2** function written in C does not achieve its desired effect:

```
void inc2( int x)
/* incorrect! */
{ ++x;++x; }
```

While in theory it is possible, with suitable generality of functions, to perform all computations by returning appropriate values instead of changing parameter values, languages like C usually offer a method of using pass by value in such a way as to achieve nonlocal changes. In C, this takes the form of passing the address instead of the value (and thus changing the data type of the parameter):

```
void inc2( int* x)
/* now ok */
{ ++(*x);++(*x); }
```

Of course, now to increment a variable **y** this function must be called as **inc2(&y)**, since the address of **y** and not its value is required.

This method works especially well in C for arrays, since they are implicitly pointers, and so pass by value allows the individual array elements to be changed:

```
void init(int x[],int size)
/* this works fine when called
   as init(a), where a is an array */
{ int i;
    for(i=0;i<size;++i)  x[i]=0;
}
```

Pass by value requires no special effort on the part of the compiler. It is easily implemented by taking the most straightforward view of argument computation and activation record construction.

7.5.2   Pass by Reference

In pass by reference, the arguments must (at least in principle) be variables with allocated locations. Instead of passing the value of a variable, pass by reference passes the location of the variable, so that the parameter becomes an **alias** for the argument, and any changes made to the parameter occur to the argument as well. In FORTRAN77, pass by reference is the only parameter passing mechanism. In Pascal, pass by reference is achieved with the use of the **var** keyword and in C++ by the use of the special symbol **&** in the parameter declaration:

```
void inc2( int & x)
/* C++ reference parameter */
{ ++x;++x; }
```

This function can now be called without a special use of the address operator: **inc2(y)** works fine.

Pass by reference requires that the compiler compute the address of the argument (and it must have such an address), which is then stored in the local activation record.

The compiler must also turn local accesses to a reference parameter into indirect accesses, since the local "value" is actually the address elsewhere in the environment.

In languages like FORTRAN77, where only pass by reference is available, an accommodation is usually offered for arguments that are values without addresses. Rather than making a call like

```
p(2+3)
```

illegal in FORTRAN77, a compiler must instead "invent" an address for the expression **2+3**, compute the value into this address, and then pass the address to the call. Typically, this is done by creating a temporary location in the activation record of the caller (in FORTRAN77, this will be static). An example of this is in Example 7.1 (page 350), where the value 3 is passed as an argument by creating a memory location for it in the activation record of the main procedure.

One aspect of pass by reference is that it does not require a copy to be made of the passed value, unlike pass by value. This can sometimes be significant when the value to be copied is a large structure (or an array in a language other than C or C++). In that case, it may be important to be able to pass an argument by reference, but prohibit changes to be made to the argument's value, thus achieving pass by value without the overhead of copying the value. Such an option is provided by C++, in which one may write a call such as

```
void f( const MuchData & x )
```

where **MuchData** is a data type with a large structure. This is still pass by reference, but the compiler must also perform a static check that **x** never appears on the left of an assignment or may otherwise be changed.[14]

7.5.3   Pass by Value-Result

This mechanism achieves a similar result to pass by reference, except that no actual alias is established: the value of the argument is copied and used in the procedure, and then the final value of the parameter is copied back out to the location of the argument when the procedure exits. Thus, this method is sometimes known as copy-in, copy-out—or copy-restore. This is the mechanism of the Ada **in out** parameter. (Ada also has simply an **out** parameter, which has no initial value passed in; this could be called pass by result.)

Pass by value-result is only distinguishable from pass by reference in the presence of aliasing. For instance, in the following code (in C syntax),

```
void p(int x, int y)
{ ++x;
   ++y;
}
```

---

14. This cannot always be done in a completely secure way.

```
main()
{ int a = 1;
  p(a,a);
  return 0;
}
```

a has value 3 after p is called if pass by reference is used, while **a** has the value 2 if pass by value-result is used.

Issues left unspecified by this mechanism, and possibly differing in different languages or implementations, are the order in which results are copied back to the arguments and whether the locations of the arguments are calculated only on entry and stored or whether they are recalculated on exit.

Ada has a further quirk: its definition states that **in out** parameters may actually be implemented as pass by reference, and any computation that would be different under the two mechanisms (thus involving an alias) is an error.

From the point of view of the compiler writer, pass by value-result requires several modifications to the basic structure of the runtime stack and the calling sequence. First, the activation record cannot be freed by the callee, since the (local) values to be copied out must be still available to the caller. Second, the caller must either push the addresses of the arguments as temporaries onto the stack before beginning the construction of the new activation record, or it must recompute these addresses on return from the called procedure.

7.5.4 Pass by Name

This is the most complex of the parameter passing mechanisms. It is also called **delayed evaluation**, since the idea of pass by name is that the argument is not evaluated until its actual use (as a parameter) in the called program. Thus, the name of the argument, or its textual representation at the point of call, replaces the name of the parameter it corresponds to. As an example, in the code

```
void p(int x)
{ ++x; }
```

if a call such as **p(a[i])** is made, the effect is of evaluating **++(a[i])**. Thus, if **i** were to change before the use of **x** inside **p**, the result would be different from either pass by reference or pass by value-result. For instance, in the code (in C syntax),

```
int i;
int a[10];

void p(int x)
{ ++i;
  ++x;
}
```

```
main()
( i = 1;
  a[1] = 1;
  a[2] = 2;
  p(a[i]);
  return 0;
}
```

the result of the call to **p** is that **a[2]** is set to 3 and **a[1]** is left unchanged.

The interpretation of pass by name is as follows. The text of an argument at the point of call is viewed as a function in its own right, which is evaluated every time the corresponding parameter name is reached in the code of the called procedure. However, the argument will always be evaluated in the environment of the caller, while the procedure will be executed in its defining environment.

Pass by name was offered as a parameter passing mechanism (along with pass by value) in the language Algol60, but became unpopular for several reasons. First, it can give surprising and counterintuitive results in the presence of side effects (as the previous example shows). Second, it is difficult to implement, since each argument must be turned into what is essentially a procedure (sometimes called a **suspension** or **thunk**) that must be called whenever the argument is evaluated. Third, it is inefficient, since not only does it turn a simple argument evaluation into a procedure call, but it may also cause multiple evaluations to occur. A variation on this mechanism called **lazy evaluation** has recently become popular in purely functional languages, where reevaluation is prevented by **memoizing** the suspension with the computed value the first time it called. Lazy evaluation can actually result in a *more* efficient implementation, since an argument that is never used is also never evaluated. Languages that offer lazy evaluation as a parameter passing mechanism are **Miranda** and **Haskell**. We refer the reader to the Notes and References section for additional information.

7.6 A RUNTIME ENVIRONMENT FOR THE TINY LANGUAGE

In this final section of the chapter, we describe the structure of a runtime environment for the TINY language, our running example of a small, simple language for compilation. We do this in a machine-independent way here and refer the reader to the next chapter for an example of an implementation on a specific machine.

The environment needed by TINY is significantly simpler than any of the environments discussed in this chapter. Indeed, TINY has no procedures, and all of its variables are global, so that there is no need for a stack of activation records, and the only dynamic storage necessary is that for temporaries during expression evaluation (even this could be made static as in FORTRAN77—see the exercises).

One simple scheme for a TINY environment is to place the variables in absolute addresses at the bottom end of program memory, and allocate the temporary stack at the top end. Thus, given a program that used, say, four variables **x**, **y**, **z**, and **w**, these variables would get the absolute addresses 0 through 3 at the bottom of memory, and at a point during execution where three temporaries are being stored, the runtime environment would look as follows:

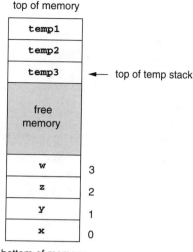

Depending on the architecture, we may need to set some bookkeeping registers to point to the bottom and/or top of memory, and then use the "absolute" addresses of the variables as offsets from the bottom pointer, and either use the top of memory pointer as the "top of temp stack" pointer or compute offsets for the temporaries from a fixed top pointer. It would, of course, also be possible to use the processor stack as the temporary stack, if it is available.

To implement this runtime environment, the symbol table in the TINY compiler must, as described in the last chapter, maintain the addresses of the variables in memory. It does this by providing a location parameter in the **st_insert** function and the inclusion of a **st_lookup** function that retrieves the location of a variable (Appendix B, lines 1166 and 1171):

```
void st_insert( char * name, int lineno, int loc );
int st_lookup ( char * name );
```

The semantic analyzer must, in its turn, assign addresses to variables as they are encountered the first time. It does this by maintaining a static memory location counter that is initialized to the first address (Appendix B, line 1413):

```
static int location = 0;
```

Then, whenever a variable is encountered (in a read statement, assignment statement, or identifier expression), the semantic analyzer executes the code (Appendix B, line 1454):

```
if (st_lookup(t->attr.name) == -1)
    st_insert(t->attr.name,t->lineno,location++);
else
    st_insert(t->attr.name,t->lineno,0);
```

When **st_lookup** returns −1, the variable is not yet in the table. In that case, a new location is recorded, and the location counter is incremented. Otherwise, the variable is already in the table, in which case the symbol table ignores the location parameter (and we write 0 as a dummy location).

This handles the allocation of the named variables in a TINY program; the allocation of the temporary variables at the top of memory, and the operations needed to maintain this allocation, will be the responsibility of the code generator, discussed in the next chapter.

EXERCISES

7.1 Draw a possible organization for the runtime environment of the following FORTRAN77 program, similar to that of Figure 7.2 (page 352). Be sure to include the memory pointers as they would exist during the call to **AVE**.

```
      REAL A(SIZE),AVE
      INTEGER N,I
   10 READ *, N
      IF (N.LE.0.OR.N.GT.SIZE) GOTO 99
      READ *,(A(I),I=1,N)
      PRINT *, 'AVE = ',AVE(A,N)
      GOTO 10
   99 CONTINUE
      END
      REAL FUNCTION AVE(B,N)
      INTEGER I,N
      REAL B(N),SUM
      SUM = 0.0
      DO 20 I=1,N
   20 SUM=SUM+B(I)
      AVE = SUM/N
      END
```

7.2 Draw a possible organization for the runtime environment of the following C program, similar to that of Figure 7.4 (page 354).
   a. After entry into block **A** in function **f**.
   b. After entry into block **B** in function **g**.

```
int a[10];
char * s = "hello";

int f(int i, int b[])
{ int j=i;
  A:{ int i=j;
       char c = b[i];
       ...
     }
  return 0;
}
```

```
void g(char * s)
{ char c = s[0];
   B:{ int a[5];

         ...

       }
}

main()
{ int x=1;
   x = f(x,a);
   g(s);
   return 0;
}
```

7.3 Draw a possible organization for the runtime environment of the C program of
Figure 4.1 (page 148) after the second call to **factor**, given the input string **(2)**.

7.4 Draw the stack of activation records for the following Pascal program, showing the control and access links, after the second call to procedure **c**. Describe how the variable **x** is
accessed from within **c**.

```
program env;

procedure a;
var x: integer;

   procedure b;
      procedure c;
      begin
         x := 2;
         b;
      end;
   begin (* b *)
         c;
      end;

begin (* a *)
   b;
end;

begin (* main *)
   a;
end.
```

7.5 Draw the stack of activation records for the following Pascal program
  a. After the call to **a** in the first call of **p**.

    b. After the call to **a** in the second call of **p**.

    c. What does the program print and why?

```
program closureEx(output);
var x: integer;

procedure one;
begin
  writeln(x);
end;

procedure p(procedure a);
begin
  a;
end;

procedure q;
var x:integer;
       procedure two;
       begin
          writeln(x);
       end;
begin
  x := 2;
  p(one);
  p(two);
end; (* q *)

begin (* main *)
  x := 1;
  q;
end.
```

7.6 Consider the following Pascal program. Assuming a user input consisting of the three numbers 1, 2, 0, draw the stack of activation records when the number 1 is printed the first time. Include all control and access links, as well as all parameters and global variables, and assume all procedures are stored in the environment as closures.

```
program procenv(input,output);

procedure dolist (procedure print);
var x: integer;
  procedure newprint;
  begin
    print;
    writeln(x);
  end;
```

```
begin (* dolist *)
  readln(x);
  if x = 0 then begin
    print;
    print;
  end
  else dolist(newprint);
end; (* dolist *)

procedure null;
begin
end;

begin (* main *)
  dolist(null);
end.
```

7.7 To perform completely static allocation, a FORTRAN77 compiler needs to form an estimate of the maximum number of temporaries required for any expression computation in a program. Devise a method for estimating the number of temporaries required to compute an expression by performing a traversal of the expression tree. Assume that expressions are evaluated from left to right and that every left subexpression must be saved in a temporary.

7.8 In languages that permit variable numbers of arguments in procedure calls, one way to find the first argument is to compute the arguments in reverse order, as described in Section 7.3.1, page 361.

    a. One alternative to computing the arguments in reverse would be to reorganize the activation record to make the first argument available even in the presence of variable arguments. Describe such an activation record organization and the calling sequence it would need.

    b. Another alternative to computing the arguments in reverse is to use a third pointer (besides the sp and fp), which is usually called the ap (argument pointer). Describe an activation record structure that uses an ap to find the first argument and the calling sequence it would need.

7.9 The text describes how to deal with variable-length parameters (such as open arrays) that are passed by value (see Example 7.6, page 362) and states that a similar solution works for variable length local variables. However, a problem exists when *both* variable-length parameters and local variables are present. Describe the problem and a solution, using the following Ada procedure as an example:

```
type IntAr is Array(Integer range <>) of Integer;
...
procedure f(x: IntAr; n:Integer) is
y: Array(1..n) of Integer;
i: Integer;
begin
  ...
end f;
```

7.10 An alternative to access chaining in a language with local procedures is to keep access links in an array outside the stack, indexed by nesting level. This array is called the **display**. For example, the runtime stack of Figure 7.12 (page 369) would look as follows with a display

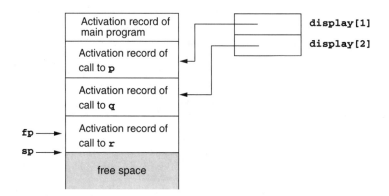

while the runtime stack of Figure 7.13 (page 370) would look as follows:

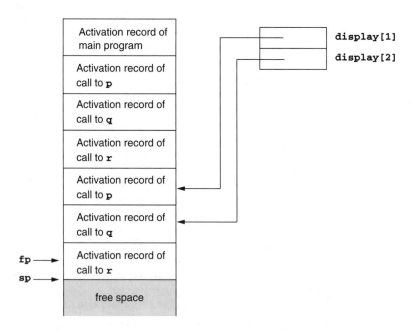

    a. Describe how a display can improve the efficiency of nonlocal references from deeply nested procedures.

    b. Redo Exercise 7.4 using a display.

    c. Describe the calling sequence necessary to implement a display.

    d. A problem exists in using a display in a language with procedure parameters. Describe the problem using Exercise 7.5.

7.11 Consider the following procedure in C syntax:

```
void f( char c, char s[10], double r )
{ int * x;
  int y[5];
  ...
}
```

    a. Using the standard C parameter passing conventions, and assuming the data sizes integer = 2 bytes, char = 1 byte, double = 8 bytes, address = 4 bytes, determine the offsets from the fp of the following, using the activation record structure described in this chapter: (1) **c**, (2) **s[7]**, (3) **y[2]**.

    b. Repeat (a) assuming all parameters are passed by value (including arrays).

    c. Repeat (a) assuming all parameters are passed by reference.

7.12 Execute the following C program and explain its output in terms of the runtime environment:

```
#include <stdio.h>

void g(void)
{ {int x;
   printf("%d\n",x);
   x = 3;}
  {int y;
   printf("%d\n",y);}
}

int* f(void)
{ int x;
  printf("%d\n",x);
  return &x;
}

void main()
{ int *p;
  p = f();
  *p = 1;
  f();
  g();
}
```

7.13 Draw the memory layout of objects of the following C++ classes, together with the virtual function tables as described in Section 7.4.2:

```
class A
{ public:
  int a;
  virtual void f();
  virtual void g();
};
```

```
class B : public A
{ public:
  int b;
  virtual void f();
  void h();
};
class C : public B
{ public:
  int c;
  virtual void g();
}
```

7.14 A virtual function table in an object-oriented language saves traversing the inheritance graph searching for a method, but at a cost. Explain what the cost is.

7.15 Give the output of the following program (written in C syntax) using the four parameter passing methods discussed in Section 7.5:

```
#include <stdio.h>
int i=0;

void p(int x, int y)
{ x += 1;
  i += 1;
  y += 1;
}

main()
{ int a[2]={1,1};
  p(a[i],a[i]);
  printf("%d %d\n",a[0],a[1]);
  return 0;
}
```

7.16 Give the output of the following program (in C syntax) using the four parameter passing methods of Section 7.5:

```
#include <stdio.h>
int i=0;

void swap(int x, int y)
{ x = x + y;
  y = x - y;
  x = x - y;
}
```

```
      main()
      { int a[3] = {1,2,0};
        swap(i,a[i]);
        printf("%d %d %d %d\n",i,a[0],a[1],a[2]);
        return 0;

      }
```

7.17 Suppose that the FORTRAN77 subroutine **P** is declared as follows

```
      SUBROUTINE P(A)
      INTEGER A
      PRINT *, A
      A = A + 1
      RETURN
      END
```

and is called from the main program as follows:

```
      CALL P(1)
```

In some FORTRAN77 systems, this will cause a runtime error. In others, no runtime error occurs, but if the subroutine is called again with 1 as its argument, it may print the value 2. Explain how both behaviors might occur in terms of the runtime environment.

7.18 A variation on pass by name is **pass by text**, in which the arguments are evaluated in delayed fashion, just as in pass by name, but each argument is evaluated in the environment of the called procedure rather than in the calling environment.

  a. Show that pass by text can have different results than pass by name.

  b. Describe a runtime environment organization and calling sequence that could be used to implement pass by text.

PROGRAMMING EXERCISES

7.19 As described in Section 7.5, pass by name, or delayed evaluation, can be viewed as packaging an argument in a function body (or suspension), which is called every time the parameter appears in the code. Rewrite the C code of Exercise 7.16 to implement the parameters of the **swap** function in this fashion, and verify that the result is indeed equivalent to pass by name.

7.20 a. As described in Section 7.5.4, an efficiency improvement in pass by name can be achieved by memoizing the value of an argument the first time it is evaluated. Rewrite your code of the previous exercise to implement such memoization, and compare the results to those of that exercise.

  b. Memoization can cause different results from pass by name. Explain how this can happen.

7.21 Compaction (Section 7.4.4) can be made into a separate step from garbage collection and can be performed by **malloc** if a memory request fails because of the lack of a sufficiently large block.

  a. Rewrite the **malloc** procedure of Section 7.4.3 to include a compaction step.

b. Compaction requires that the location of previously allocated space change, and this means that a program must find out about the change. Describe how to use a table of pointers to memory blocks to solve this problem, and rewrite your code of part (a) to include it.

NOTES AND REFERENCES

The fully static environment of FORTRAN77 (and earlier FORTRAN versions) represents a natural and straightforward approach to environment design and is similar to assembler environments. Stack-based environments became popular with the inclusion of recursion in languages such as Algol60 (Naur [1963]). Randell and Russell [1964] describe an early Algol60 stack-based environment in detail. The activation record organization and calling sequence for some C compilers is described in Johnson and Ritchie [1981]. The use of a display instead of access chains (Exercise 7.10) is described in detail in Fischer and LeBlanc [1991], including the problems with using it in a language with procedure parameters.

Dynamic memory management is discussed in many books on data structures, such as Aho, Hopcroft, and Ullman [1983]. A useful recent overview is given in Drozdek and Simon [1995]. Code for implementations of **malloc** and **free** that is similar to, but slightly less sophisticated than the code given in Section 7.4.3, appears in Kernighan and Ritchie [1988]. The design of a heap structure for use in compilation is discussed in Fraser and Hanson [1995].

An overview of garbage collection can be found in Wilson [1992] or Cohen [1981]. A generational garbage collector and runtime environment for the functional language ML is described in Appel [1992]. The Gofer functional language compiler (Jones [1984]) contains both a mark and sweep and a two-space garbage collector.

Budd [1987] describes a fully dynamic environment for a small Smalltalk system, including the use of the inheritance graph, and a garbage collector with reference counts. The use of a virtual function table in C++ is described in Ellis and Stroustrup [1990], together with extensions to handle multiple inheritance.

More examples of parameter passing techniques may be found in Louden [1993], where a description of lazy evaluation can also be found. Implementation techniques for lazy evaluation can be found in Peyton Jones [1987].

Chapter 8

Code Generation

In this chapter, we turn to the final task of a compiler, which is to generate executable code for a target machine that is a faithful representation of the semantics of the source code. Code generation is the most complex phase of a compiler, since it depends not only on the characteristics of the source language but also on detailed information about the target architecture, the structure of the runtime environment, and the operating system running on the target machine. Code generation usually also involves some attempt to **optimize**, or improve, the speed and/or size of the target code by collecting further information about the source program and by tailoring the generated code to take advantage of special features of the target machine, such as registers, addressing modes, pipelining, and cache memory.

Because of the complexity of code generation, a compiler typically breaks up this phase into several steps, involving various intermediate data structures, often including some form of abstract code called **intermediate code**. A compiler may also stop short of generating actual executable code but, instead, generate some form of assembly code that must be processed further by an assembler, a linker, and a loader, which may be provided by the operating system or bundled with the compiler. In this chapter, we will concentrate only on the basics of the generation of intermediate code and assembly code, which have many characteristics in common.

We ignore the question of further processing of assembly code into executable code, which can be more adequately handled by an assembly language or systems programming text.

In the first section of this chapter, we survey two popular forms of intermediate code, three-address code and P-code, and discuss some of their properties. In the second section, we describe the basic algorithms for generating intermediate or assembly code. In subsequent sections, code generation techniques for various language features are discussed, including expressions, assignment statements, control flow statements such as if-statements and while-statements, and procedure/function calls. These sections are followed by case studies of the code produced for these features by two commercial compilers: the Borland C compiler for the 80×86 architecture and the Sun C compiler for the Sparc RISC architecture.

In a subsequent section, we apply the techniques studied in previous sections to develop an assembly code generator for the TINY language. Since code generation at this level of detail requires an actual target machine, we first discuss a simple target architecture and machine simulator called TM, for which a source listing is provided in Appendix C. Then the complete code generator for TINY is described. Finally, we give a survey of standard code improvement, or optimization, techniques, and describe how a few of the simpler techniques can be incorporated into the TINY code generator.

8.1 INTERMEDIATE CODE AND DATA STRUCTURES FOR CODE GENERATION

A data structure that represents the source program during translation is called an **intermediate representation**, or **IR**, for short. In this text, we have up to now used an abstract syntax tree as the principal IR. In addition to the IR, the major data structure used during translation is the symbol table, which was studied in Chapter 6.

Although an abstract syntax tree is a pefectly adequate representation of the source code, even for code generation (as we shall see in a later section), it is not a representation that even remotely resembles target code, particularly in its representation of control flow constructs, where target code such as machine or assembly code employs jumps rather than high-level constructs such as if- and while-statements. Therefore, a compiler writer may wish to generate a new form of intermediate representation from the syntax tree that more closely resembles target code or replace the syntax tree altogether by such an intermediate representation, and then generate target code from this new representation. Such an intermediate representation that resembles target code is called **intermediate code**.

Intermediate code can take many forms—there are almost as many styles of intermediate code as there are compilers. All, however, represent some form of **linearization** of the syntax tree, that is, a representation of the syntax tree in sequential form. Intermediate code can be very high level, representing all operations almost as abstractly as a syntax tree, or it can closely resemble target code. It may or may not use detailed information about the target machine and runtime environment, such as the sizes of data types, the locations of variables, and the availability of registers. It may or may not incorporate all the information contained in the symbol table, such as scopes, nesting levels, and offsets of variables. If it does, then the generation of target code can be based purely on the intermediate code; if it does not, then the compiler must retain the symbol table for target code generation.

Intermediate code is particularly useful when the goal of the compiler is to produce extremely efficient code, since to do so requires a significant amount of analysis of the properties of the target code, and this is made easier by the use of intermediate code. In particular, additional data structures incorporating information from detailed postparse analysis can be easily generated from intermediate code, although it is not impossible to do this directly from the syntax tree.

Intermediate code can also be useful in making a compiler more easily retargetable: if the intermediate code is relatively target machine independent, then to generate code for a different target machine requires only that the translator from intermediate code to target code be rewritten, and this is usually easier than rewriting an entire code generator.

In this section we will study two popular forms of intermediate code: **three-address code** and **P-code**. Both of these occur in many different forms, and our study here will focus on general features only, rather than present a detailed description of a version of each. Such descriptions can be found in the literature described in the Notes and References section at the end of the chapter.

8.1.1   Three-Address Code

The most basic instruction of three address code is designed to represent the evaluation of arithmetic expressions and has the following general form:

```
x = y op z
```

This instruction expresses the application of the operator *op* to the values of **y** and **z** and the assignment of this value to be the new value of **x**. Here *op* may be an arithmetic operator such as + or − or some other operator that can operate on the values of **y** and **z**.

The name "three-address code" comes from this form of instruction, since in general each of the names **x**, **y**, and **z** represents an address in memory. Note, however, that the use of the address of **x** differs from the use of the addresses of **y** and **z** and that **y** and **z** (but not **x**) may represent constants or literal values with no runtime addresses.

To see how sequences of three-address code of this form can represent the computation of an expression, consider the arithmetic expression

```
2*a+(b-3)
```

with syntax tree

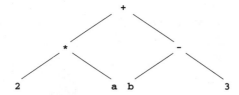

The corresponding three-address code is

```
t1 = 2 * a
t2 = b - 3
t3 = t1 + t2
```

Three-address code requires that the compiler generate names for temporaries, which we have called **t1**, **t2**, and **t3** in this example. These temporaries correspond to the interior nodes of the syntax tree and represent their computed values, with the final temporary (**t3**, in this example) representing the value of the root.[1] How these temporaries are eventually to be allocated in memory is left unspecified by this code; usually, they will be assigned to registers, but they may also be kept in activation records (see the discussion of the temporary stack in the previous chapter).

The three-address code just given represents a left-to-right linearization of the syntax tree, since the code corresponding to the evaluation of the left subtree of the root is listed first. It is possible that a compiler may wish to use a different order under certain circumstances. We simply note here that another order is possible for this three-address code, namely (with a different meaning for the temporaries),

```
t1 = b - 3
t2 = 2 * a
t3 = t2 + t1
```

Clearly, the one form of three-address code we have shown is insufficient to represent all the language features of even the smallest programming language. For instance, unary operators such as negation require a variation of three-address code that contains only two addresses, such as

```
t2 = - t1
```

To accommodate all the constructs of a standard programming language, it will be necessary to vary the form of three-address code for each construct. If a language contains unusual features, it may even be necessary to invent new forms of three-address code to express these features. This is one of the reasons that no standard form for three-address code exists (just as no standard form for syntax trees exists).

In the following sections of this chapter, we will treat some common programming language constructs individually and show how these constructs are typically translated as three-address code. However, to get a feel for what to expect, we present here a complete example using the TINY language introduced previously.

Consider the TINY sample program from Section 1.7 (Chapter 1) that computes the greatest common divisor of two integers, which we reprint in Figure 8.1. Sample three-address code for this program is given in Figure 8.2. This code contains a number of different forms of three-address code. First, the built-in input and output operations **read** and **write** have been translated directly into one-address instructions. Second,

---

1. The names **t1**, **t2**, and so on are only meant to be representative of the general style of such code. In fact, temporary names in three-address code must be distinct from any names that could be used in the actual source code, if source code names are to be mixed in, as they are here.

Figure 8.1
Sample TINY program

```
{ Sample program
  in TINY language--
  computes factorial
}
read x; { input an integer }
if 0 < x then { don't compute if x <= 0 }
  fact := 1;
  repeat
    fact := fact * x;
    x := x - 1
  until x = 0;
  write fact { output factorial of x }
end
```

Figure 8.2
Three-address code for the
TINY program of Figure 8.1

```
read x
t1 = x > 0
if_false t1 goto L1
fact = 1
label L2
t2 = fact * x
fact = t2
t3 = x - 1
x = t3
t4 = x == 0
if_false t4 goto L2
write fact
label L1
halt
```

there is a conditional jump instruction **if_false** that is used to translate both if-statements and repeat-statements and that contains two addresses: the conditional value to be tested and the code address to jump to. The positions of the jump addresses are also indicated by (one-address) **label** instructions. Depending on the data structures used to implement the three-address code, these **label** instructions may be unnecessary. Third, a **halt** instruction (with no addresses) serves to mark the end of the code.

Finally, we note that assignments in the source code result in the generation of **copy instructions** of the form

```
x = y
```

For example, the sample program statement

```
fact := fact * x;
```

translates into the two three-address code instructions

```
t2 = fact * x
fact = t2
```

even though one three-address instruction would suffice. This occurs for technical reasons to be explained in Section 8.2.

8.1.2   Data Structures for the Implementation of Three-Address Code

Three-address code is typically not implemented in textual form as we have written it (though this is possible). Instead, each three-address instruction is implemented as a record structure containing several fields, and the entire sequence of three-address instructions is implemented as an array or linked list, which may be kept in memory or written to and read from temporary files as needed.

The most common implementation is to implement three-address code essentially as shown, which means that four fields are necessary: one for the operation and three for the addresses. For those instructions that need fewer than three addresses, one or more of the address fields is given a null or "empty" value; the choice of which fields depends on the implementation. Because four fields are necessary, such a representation of three-address code is called a **quadruple**. A possible quadruple implementation of the three-address code of Figure 8.2 is given in Figure 8.3, where we have written the quadruples in mathematical "tuple" notation.

Possible C **typedef**'s to implement the quadruples shown in Figure 8.3 are given in Figure 8.4. In these definitions, we allow an address to be only an integer constant or a string (representing the name of a temporary or a variable). Also, since names are used, these names must be entered into a symbol table, and lookups will need to be performed during further processing. An alternative to keeping names in the quadruples is to keep pointers to symbol table entries. This avoids the need for additional lookups and is particularly advantageous in a language with nested scopes, where additional scope information beyond the name alone is necessary to perform a lookup. If constants are also entered into the symbol table, then there is no need for a union in the **Address** data type.

A different implementation of three-address code is to use the instructions themselves to represent the temporaries. This reduces the need for address fields from three to two, since in a three-address instruction containing all three addresses, the target address is always a temporary.[2] Such an implementation of three-address code is called a **triple**. It requires that each three-address instruction be referenceable, either as an index in an array or as a pointer in a linked list. For example, an abstract representation of an implementation of the three-address code of Figure 8.2 as triples is given in

---

2. This is not an inherent truth about three-address code, but can be ensured by the implementation. It is true, for example, of the code in Figure 8.2 (see also Figure 8.3).

Figure 8.3

Quadruple implementation for the three-address code of Figure 8.2

```
(rd,x,_,_)
(gt,x,0,t1)
(if_f,t1,L1,_)
(asn,1,fact,_)
(lab,L2,_,_)
(mul,fact,x,t2)
(asn,t2,fact,_)
(sub,x,1,t3)
(asn,t3,x,_)
(eq,x,0,t4)
(if_f,t4,L2,_)
(wri,fact,_,_)
(lab,L1,_,_)
(halt,_,_,_)
```

Figure 8.4

C code defining possible data structures for the quadruples of Figure 8.3

```
typedef enum {rd,gt,if_f,asn,lab,mul,
                    sub,eq,wri,halt,. . .} OpKind;
typedef enum {Empty,IntConst,String} AddrKind;
typedef struct
        { AddrKind kind;
          union
          { int val;
            char * name;
          } contents;
        } Address;
typedef struct
        { OpKind op;
          Address addr1,addr2,addr3;
        } Quad;
```

Figure 8.5 (page 404). In that figure we have used a numbering system that would correspond to array indices to represent the triples. Also, triple references are distinguished from constants by putting them in parentheses in the triples themselves. Further, in Figure 8.5 we have eliminated the **label** instructions and replaced them by references to the triple indices themselves.

Triples are an efficient way to represent three-address code, since the amount of space is reduced, and since the compiler does not need to generate names for temporaries. However, triples have one major drawback in that, if they are represented by array indices, then any movement of their positions becomes difficult. A linked list representation, on the other hand, does not suffer from this difficulty. Further questions involving triples, and appropriate C code for the definition of triples, are left to the exercises.

Figure 8.5

A representation of the three-address code of Figure 8.2 as triples

```
(0)      (rd,x,_)
(1)      (gt,x,0)
(2)      (if_f,(1),(11))
(3)      (asn,1,fact)
(4)      (mul,fact,x)
(5)      (asn,(4),fact)
(6)      (sub,x,1)
(7)      (asn,(6),x)
(8)      (eq,x,0)
(9)      (if_f,(8),(4))
(10)     (wri,fact,_)
(11)     (halt,_,_)
```

8.1.3   P-Code

P-code began as a standard target assembly code produced by a number of Pascal compilers of the 1970s and early 1980s. It was designed to be the actual code for a hypothetical stack machine, called the **P-machine**, for which an interpreter was written on various actual machines. The idea was to make Pascal compilers easily portable by requiring only that the P-machine interpreter be rewritten for a new platform. P-code has also proved useful as intermediate code, and various extensions and modifications of it have been used in a number of native-code compilers, mostly for Pascal-like languages.

Since P-code was designed to be directly executable, it contains an implicit description of a particular runtime environment, including data sizes, as well as a great deal of information specific to the P-machine, which must be known in order for a P-code program to be understandable. To avoid this detail, we will describe here a simplified and abstracted version of P-code that is suitable for exposition. Descriptions of various versions of actual P-code can be found in a number of references listed at the end of the chapter.

For our purposes, the P-machine consists of a code memory, an unspecified data memory for named variables, and a stack for temporary data, together with whatever registers are needed to maintain the stack and support execution.

As a first example of P-code, consider the expression

```
2*a+(b-3)
```

used in Section 8.1.1, whose syntax tree appears on page 399. Our version of P-code for this expression is as follows:

```
ldc 2        ; load constant 2
lod a        ; load value of variable a
mpi          ; integer multiplication
lod b        ; load value of variable b
ldc 3        ; load constant 3
sbi          ; integer subtraction
adi          ; integer addition
```

These instructions are to be viewed as representing the following P-machine operations. First, **ldc 2** pushes the value 2 onto the temporary stack. Then, **lod a** pushes the value of the variable **a** onto the stack. The instruction **mpi** pops these two values from the stack, multiplies them (in reverse order), and pushes the result onto the stack. The next two instructions (**lod b** and **ldc 3**) push the value of **b** and the constant 3 onto the stack (there are now three values on the stack). Then, the **sbi** instruction pops the top two values from the stack, subtracts the first from the second, and pushes the result. Finally, the **adi** instruction pops the remaining two values from the stack, adds them, and pushes the result. The code ends with a single value on the stack, representing the result of the computation.

As a second introductory example, consider the assignment statement

```
x := y + 1
```

This corresponds to the following P-code instructions:

```
lda x        ; load address of x
lod y        ; load value of y
ldc 1        ; load constant 1
adi          ; add
sto          ; store top to address
             ; below top & pop both
```

Note how this code computes the address of **x** first, then the value of the expression to be assigned to **x**, and finally executes an **sto** command, which requires that two values be on top of the temporary stack: the value to be stored and, below it, the address in variable memory to which it is to be stored. The **sto** instruction also pops both these values (leaving the stack empty in this example). P-code thus makes a distinction between loading addresses (**lda**) and ordinary values (**lod**), corresponding to the difference between the use of **x** on the left-hand side and the use of **y** on the right-hand side of the assignment **x:=y+1**.

As our last example of P-code in this section, we give a P-code translation in Figure 8.6 for the TINY program of Figure 8.1, together with comments describing each operation.

The P-code in Figure 8.6 (page 406) contains several new P-code instructions. First, the instructions **rdi** and **wri** (without parameters) implement the integer **read** and **write** statements built into TINY. The **rdi** P-code instruction requires that the address of the variable whose value is to be read be at the top of the stack, and this address is popped as part of the instruction. The **wri** instruction requires that the value to be written be at the top of the stack, and this value is popped as part of the instruction. Other P-code instructions that appear in Figure 8.6 that have not previously been discussed are the **lab** instruction, which defines the position of a label name; the **fjp** instruction ("false jump"), which requires a Boolean value at the top of the stack (which is popped); the **sbi** instruction (integer subtraction), whose operation is similar to the other arithmetic instructions; and the comparison operations **grt** ("greater than") and **equ** ("equal to"), which require two integer values at the top of the stack (which are popped), and which push their Boolean results. Finally, the **stp** instruction ("stop") corresponds to the **halt** instruction of the previous three-address code.

```
lda x        ; load address of x
rdi          ; read an integer, store to
             ; address on top of stack (& pop it)
lod x        ; load the value of x
ldc 0        ; load constant 0
grt          ; pop and compare top two values
             ; push Boolean result
fjp L1       ; pop Boolean value, jump to L1 if false
lda fact     ; load address of fact
ldc 1        ; load constant 1
sto          ; pop two values, storing first to
             ; address represented by second
lab L2       ; definition of label L2
lda fact     ; load address of fact
lod fact     ; load value of fact
lod x        ; load value of x
mpi          ; multiply
sto          ; store top to address of second & pop
lda x        ; load address of x
lod x        ; load value of x
ldc 1        ; load constant 1
sbi          ; subtract
sto          ; store (as before)
lod x        ; load value of x
ldc 0        ; load constant 0
equ          ; test for equality
fjp L2       ; jump to L2 if false
lod fact     ; load value of fact
wri          ; write top of stack & pop
lab L1       ; definition of label L1
stp
```

Comparison of P-Code to Three-Address Code   P-code is in many respects closer to actual machine code than three-address code. P-code instructions also require fewer addresses: all of the instructions we have seen are either "one-address" or "zero-address" instructions. On the other hand, P-code is less compact than three-address code in terms of numbers of instructions, and P-code is not "self-contained" in that the instructions operate implicitly on a stack (and the implicit stack locations are in fact the "missing" addresses). The advantage to the stack is that it contains all the temporary values needed at each point in the code, and the compiler need not assign names to any of them, as in three-address code.

Implementation of P-Code   Historically, P-code has largely been generated as a text file, but the previous descriptions of internal data structure implementations for three-address code (quadruples and triples) will also work with appropriate modification for P-code.

8.2   BASIC CODE GENERATION TECHNIQUES

In this section, we discuss basic approaches to code generation in general, while in subsequent sections, we treat code generation for individual language constructs individually.

8.2.1   Intermediate Code or Target Code as a Synthesized Attribute

Intermediate code generation (or direct target code generation without intermediate code) can be viewed as an attribute computation similar to many of the attribute problems studied in Chapter 6. Indeed, if the generated code is viewed as a string attribute (with instructions separated by newline characters), then this code becomes a synthesized attribute that can be defined using an attribute grammar and generated either directly during parsing or by a postorder traversal of the syntax tree.

To see how either three-address code or P-code can be defined as a synthesized attribute, consider the following grammar that represents a small subset of C expressions:

$$exp \rightarrow \textbf{\textit{id}} = exp \mid aexp$$
$$aexp \rightarrow aexp + factor \mid factor$$
$$factor \rightarrow (\ exp \ ) \mid \textbf{num} \mid \textbf{\textit{id}}$$

This grammar contains only two operations, assignment (with symbol **=**) and addition (with symbol **+**).[3] The token **_id_** stands for a simple identifier, and the token **num** stands for a simple sequence of digits representing an integer. Both these tokens are assumed to have a precomputed attribute *strval* that is the string value, or lexeme, of the token (e.g., "42" for a **num** or "xtemp" for an **_id_**).

P-Code   We consider the case of generating P-code first, since the attribute grammar is simpler, because there is no need to generate names for temporaries. However, the existence of embedded assignments is a complicating factor. In this situation, we wish to preserve the stored value as the resulting value of an assignment expression, yet the standard P-code instruction **sto** is destructive, in that the assigned value is lost. (Here P-code is showing its Pascal origins, in which embedded assignments do not exist.) We solve this problem by introducing a **nondestructive store** instruction **stn** into our P-code, which like the **sto** instruction, assumes a value at the top of the stack and an address below it; **stn** stores the value to the address but leaves the value at the top of the stack, while discarding the address. With this new instruction, an attribute grammar

---

3. Assignment in this example has the following semantics: **x** = **e** stores the value of **e** to **x** and has the same resulting value as **e**.

for a P-code string attribute is given in Table 8.1. In that figure, we have used the attribute name *pcode* for the P-code string. We have also used two different notations for string concatenation: ++ when instructions are to be concatenated with newlines inserted between them and ‖ when a single instruction is being built and a space is to be inserted.

We leave it to the reader to trace the computation of the *pcode* attribute in individual examples and to show that, for instance, the expression **(x=x+3)+4** has the *pcode* attribute

```
lda x
lod x
ldc 3
adi
stn
ldc 4
adi
```

Table 8.1

Attribute grammar of P-code as a synthesized string attribute

Grammar Rule	Semantic Rules
$exp_1 \rightarrow \textbf{\textit{id}} = exp_2$	$exp_1 .pcode =$ "**lda**" ‖ $\textbf{\textit{id}} .strval$ $++ \ exp_2 .pcode ++$ "**stn**"
$exp \rightarrow aexp$	$exp .pcode = aexp .pcode$
$aexp_1 \rightarrow aexp_2 \ \textbf{+} \ factor$	$aexp_1 .pcode = aexp_2 .pcode$ $++ \ factor .pcode ++$ "**adi**"
$aexp \rightarrow factor$	$aexp .pcode = factor .pcode$
$factor \rightarrow \textbf{(} \ exp \ \textbf{)}$	$factor .pcode = exp .pcode$
$factor \rightarrow \textbf{num}$	$factor .pcode =$ "**ldc**" ‖ $\textbf{num} .strval$
$factor \rightarrow \textbf{\textit{id}}$	$factor .pcode =$ "**lod**" ‖ $\textbf{\textit{id}} .strval$

Three-Address Code   An attribute grammar for three-address code for the previous simple expression grammar is given in Table 8.2. In that table, we have called the code attribute *tacode* (for three-address code), and, as in Table 8.1, we have used ++ for string concatenation with a newline and ‖ for string concatenation with a space. Unlike P code, three-address code requires that temporary names be generated for intermediate results in expressions, and this requires that the attribute grammar include a new *name* attribute for each node. This attribute is also synthesized, but for interior nodes to be assigned newly generated temporary names, we use a function *newtemp*( ) that is assumed to generate a sequence of temporary names **t1, t2, t3,** . . . (a new one is returned each time *newtemp*( ) is called). In this very simple example, only nodes corresponding to the **+** operator need new temporary names; the assignment operation simply uses the name of the expression on the right-hand side.

Note in Table 8.2 that, in the case of the unit productions $exp \rightarrow aexp$ and $aexp \rightarrow factor$, the *name* attribute as well as the *tacode* attribute is lifted from child to parent and that, in the case of the operator interior nodes, new *name* attributes are generated before the associated *tacode*. Note also that, in the leaf productions *factor* → **num** and *factor* → **id**, the string value of the token is used as *factor .name* and that (unlike P-

Table 8.2

Attribute grammar for three-address code as a synthesized string attribute

Grammar Rule	Semantic Rules
$exp_1 \to \mathbf{id} = exp_2$	$exp_1 .name = exp_2 .name$ $exp_1 .tacode = exp_2 .tacode\ ++$ $\qquad\qquad \mathbf{id} .strval \parallel \text{“=”} \parallel exp_2 .name$
$exp \to aexp$	$exp .name = aexp .name$ $exp .tacode = aexp .tacode$
$aexp_1 \to aexp_2 + factor$	$aexp_1 .name = newtemp(\,)$ $aexp_1 .tacode =$ $\qquad aexp_2 .tacode\ ++ factor .tacode$ $\qquad ++ aexp_1 .name \parallel \text{“=”} \parallel aexp_2 .name$ $\qquad\qquad \parallel \text{“+”} \parallel factor .name$
$aexp \to factor$	$aexp .name = factor .name$ $aexp .tacode = factor .tacode$
$factor \to (\ exp\ )$	$factor .name = exp .name$ $factor .tacode = exp .tacode$
$factor \to \mathbf{num}$	$factor .name = \mathbf{num} .strval$ $factor .tacode = \texttt{""}$
$factor \to \mathbf{id}$	$factor .name = \mathbf{id} .strval$ $factor .tacode = \texttt{""}$

code) no three-address code at all is generated at such nodes (we use `""` to represent the empty string).

Again, we leave it to the reader to show that, given the attribute equations of Table 8.2, the expression `(x=x+3)+4` has the *tacode* attribute

```
t1 = x + 3
x = t1
t2 = t1 + 4
```

(This assumes that *newtemp*( ) is called in postorder and generates temporary names starting with `t1`.) Note how the assignment `x=x+3` generates two three-address instructions using a temporary. This is a consequence of the fact that the attribute evaluation always creates a temporary for each subexpression, including right-hand sides of assignments.

Viewing code generation as the computation of a synthesized string attribute is useful to show clearly the relationships among the code sequences of different parts of the syntax tree and for comparing different code generation methods, but it is impractical as a technique for actual code generation, for several reasons. First, the use of string concatenation causes an inordinate amount of string copying and wasted memory (unless the concatenation operators are made very sophisticated). Second, it is usually much more desirable to generate small pieces of code as code generation proceeds and either write these pieces to a file or insert them in a data structure (such as an array of quadruples), and this requires semantic actions that do not adhere to standard postorder synthesis of attributes. Finally, even though it is useful to view code as purely synthesized, code generation in general depends heavily on inherited attributes, and this greatly complicates the attribute grammars. For this reason, we do not bother here to write any code (even pseudocode) to implement the attribute grammars of the previous examples (but see the exercises). Instead, in the next subsection, we turn to more direct code generation techniques.

8.2.2   Practical Code Generation

Standard code generation techniques involve modifications of the postorder traversals of the syntax tree implied by the attribute grammars of the preceding examples or equivalent actions during a parse if a syntax tree is not generated explicitly. The basic algorithm can be described as the following recursive procedure (for tree nodes with at most two children, but easily extendible to more):

```
procedure genCode ( T: treenode );
begin
    if T is not nil then
        generate code to prepare for code of left child of T ;
        genCode(left child of T ) ;
        generate code to prepare for code of right child of T ;
        genCode(right child of T ) ;
        generate code to implement the action of T ;
end;
```

Note that this recursive traversal procedure has not only a postorder component (generating code to implement the action of T) but also a preorder and an in-order component (generating the preparation code for the left and right children of T). In general, each action that T represents will require a slightly different version of the preorder and in-order preparation code.

To see in detail how the *genCode* procedure can be constructed in a specific example, consider the grammar for simple arithmetic expressions we have been using in this section (see the grammar on page 407). C definitions for an abstract syntax tree for this grammar can be given as follows (compare to those on page 111 of Chapter 3):

```
typedef enum {Plus,Assign} Optype;
typedef enum {OpKind,ConstKind,IdKind} NodeKind;
typedef struct streenode
    { NodeKind kind;
      Optype op; /* used with OpKind */
      struct streenode *lchild,*rchild;
      int val; /* used with ConstKind */
      char * strval;
        /* used for identifiers and numbers */
    } STreeNode;
typedef STreeNode *SyntaxTree;
```

With these definitions, a syntax tree for the expression **(x=x+3)+4** can be given as follows:

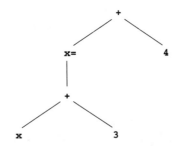

Note that the assignment node contains the identifier being assigned to (in the **strval** field), so that an assignment node has only a single child (the expression being assigned).[4]

Based on this structure for a syntax tree, we can write a *genCode* procedure to generate P-code as given in Figure 8.7. We make the following comments about the code in that figure. First, the code uses the standard C function **sprintf** to concatenate strings into the local temporary **codestr**. Second, the procedure **emitCode** is called to generate a single line of P-code, either in a data structure or an output file; its details are not shown. Finally, the two operator cases (**Plus** and **Assign**) require two different traversal orders: **Plus** needs only postorder processing, while **Assign** requires some preorder and some postorder processing. Thus, the recursive calls may not be written the same for all cases.

To show that code generation, even with the necessary variation in traversal order, can still be performed during a parse (without the generation of a syntax tree), we show a Yacc specification file in Figure 8.8 that corresponds directly to the code of Figure 8.7. (Note how the combined preorder and postorder processing of assignments translates into split action sections in the Yacc specification.)

We leave it to the reader to write a *genCode* procedure and Yacc specification for the generation of three-address code as specified in the attribute grammar of Table 8.2.

Figure 8.7

Implementation of a code generation procedure for P-code corresponding to the attribute grammar of Table 8.1

```
void genCode( SyntaxTree t)
{ char codestr[CODESIZE];
  /* CODESIZE = max length of 1 line of P-code */
  if (t != NULL)
  { switch (t->kind)
    { case OpKind:
        switch (t->op)
        { case Plus:
            genCode(t->lchild);
            genCode(t->rchild);
            emitCode("adi");
            break;
```

---

4. We also store numbers as strings in the **strval** field in this example.

Figure 8.7   *continued*

```
                          case Assign:
                            sprintf(codestr,"%s %s",
                                            "lda",t->strval);
                            emitCode(codestr);
                            genCode(t->lchild);
                            emitCode("stn");
                            break;
                          default:
                            emitCode("Error");
                            break;
                        }
                        break;
                    case ConstKind:
                        sprintf(codestr,"%s %s","ldc",t->strval);
                        emitCode(codestr);
                        break;
                    case IdKind:
                        sprintf(codestr,"%s %s","lod",t->strval);
                        emitCode(codestr);
                        break;
                    default:
                        emitCode("Error");
                        break;
                  }
               }
            }
```

Figure 8.8

Yacc specification for the generation P-code according to the attribute grammar of Table 8.1

```
%{
#define YYSTYPE char *
    /* make Yacc use strings as values */

/* other inclusion code ... */
%}

%token NUM ID

%%

exp     : ID
            { sprintf(codestr,"%s %s","lda",$1);
              emitCode(codestr); }
          '=' exp
            { emitCode("stn"); }
          | aexp
          ;
```

Figure 8.8 continued

```
aexp      : aexp '+' factor {emitCode("adi");}
          | factor
          ;

factor    : '(' exp ')'
          | NUM          { sprintf(codestr,"%s %s","ldc",$1);
                           emitCode(codestr); }
          | ID           { sprintf(codestr,"%s %s","lod",$1);
                           emitCode(codestr); }
          ;

%%
/* utility functions ... */
```

8.2.3 Generation of Target Code from Intermediate Code

If a compiler generates intermediate code, either directly during a parse or from a syntax tree, then a further pass over the intermediate code must be made to generate the final target code (usually after some further processing of the intermediate code). This step can itself be fairly complex, particularly if the intermediate code is highly symbolic and contains little or no information about the target machine or the runtime environment. In this case, the final code generation pass must supply all the actual locations of variables and temporaries, plus the code necessary to maintain the runtime environment. A particularly important issue is the proper allocation of registers and the maintenance of information on register use (i.e., which registers are available and which contain known values). We will delay a detailed discussion of such allocation issues until later in this chapter. For now, we will discuss only general techniques for this process.

Typically, code generation from intermediate code involves either or both of two standard techniques: macro expansion and static simulation. **Macro expansion** involves replacing each kind of intermediate code instruction with an equivalent sequence of target code instructions. This requires that the compiler keep track of decisions about locations and code idioms in separate data structures and that the macro procedures vary the code sequence as required by the particular kinds of data involved in the intermediate code instruction. Thus, this step can be significantly more complex than the simple forms of macro expansion available from the C preprocessor or macro assemblers. **Static simulation** involves a straight-line simulation of the effects of the intermediate code and generating target code to match these effects. This also requires extra data structures—and can vary from very simple forms of tracking used in conjunction with macro expansion to highly sophisticated **abstract interpretation** (keeping track of values algebraically as they are computed).

We can obtain some insight into the details of these techniques by considering the problem of translating from P-code to three-address code and vice versa. Consider the small expression grammar we have been using as a running example in this section, and consider the expression **(x=x+3)+4** whose translations into P-code and three-address code were given on pages 408 and 409, respectively. We consider first translating the P-code for this expression:

```
lda x
lod x
ldc 3
adi
stn
ldc 4
adi
```

into its corresponding three-address code:

```
t1 = x + 3
x = t1
t2 = t1 + 4
```

This requires that we perform a static simulation of the P-machine stack to find three-address equivalents for the given code. We do this with an actual stack data structure during translation. After the first three P-code instructions, no three-address instructions have yet been generated, but the P-machine stack has been modified to reflect the loads, and the stack appears as follows:

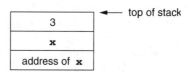

Now when the **adi** operation is processed, the three-address instruction

```
t1 = x + 3
```

is generated, and the stack is changed to

The **stn** instruction then causes the three-address instruction

```
x = t1
```

to be generated and the stack to be changed to

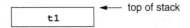

The next instruction pushes the constant 4 onto the stack:

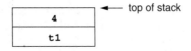

Finally, the **adi** instruction causes the three-address instruction

```
t2 = t1 + 4
```

to be generated, and the stack changes to

This completes the static simulation and the translation.

We now consider the case of translating from three-address code to P-code. This can be done by simple macro expansion, if we ignore the added complication of the temporary names. Thus, a three-address instruction

```
a = b + c
```

can always be translated into the P-code sequence

```
lda a
lod b ; or ldc b if b is a const
lod c ; or ldc c if c is a const
adi
sto
```

This results in the following (somewhat unsatisfactory) translation of the previous three-address code into P-code:

```
lda t1
lod x
ldc 3
adi
sto
lda x
lod t1
sto
lda t2     (continued)
```

```
lod t1
ldc 4
adi
sto
```

If we want to eliminate the extra temporaries, then a more sophisticated scheme than pure macro expansion must be used. One possibility is to generate a new tree from the three-address code, indicating the effect the code has by labeling the tree nodes with both the operator of each instruction and the name being assigned to. This can be viewed as a form of static simulation, and the resulting tree for the previous three-address code is

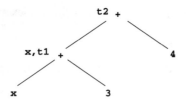

Note how the three-address instruction

```
x = t1
```

causes no extra nodes to be created in this tree, but causes the node with name **t1** to acquire the additional name **x**. This tree is similar, but not identical, to the syntax tree of the original expression (see page 411).[5] P-code can be generated from this tree in a very similar way to the generation of P-code from a syntax tree, as described earlier, but with temporaries eliminated by making assignments only to permanent names of interior nodes. Thus, in the sample tree, only **x** is assigned to, the names **t1** and **t2** are never used in the generated P-code, and the value corresponding to the root node (with name **t2**) is left on the P-machine stack. This results in precisely the same P-code generation as before, as long as we use **stn** instead of **sto** whenever a store is performed. We encourage the reader to write pseudocode or C code to carry out this process.

8.3 CODE GENERATION OF DATA STRUCTURE REFERENCES

8.3.1 Address Calculations

In the previous sections, we have seen how intermediate code can be generated for simple arithmetic expressions and assignments. In these examples, all the basic values were either constants or simple variables (either program variables such as **x**, or temporaries such as **t1**). Simple variables were identified by name only—translation to target code

---

5. This tree is a special case of a more general construction called the **DAG of a basic block**, which is described in Section 8.9.3.

requires that these names be replaced by actual addresses that could be registers, absolute memory addresses (for globals), or activation record offsets (for locals, possibly including a nesting level). These addresses can be inserted at the time intermediate code is generated or delayed until actual code generation (with the symbol table maintaining the addresses).

There are many situations, however, that require that address calculations be performed to locate the actual address in question, and these calculations must be expressed directly, even in intermediate code. Such calculations occur in array subscript, record field, and pointer references. We shall discuss each of these cases in turn. But, first, we must describe extensions to three-address code and P-code that allow us to express such address calculations.

Three-Address Code for Address Calculations   In three-address code, the need is not so much for new operations—the usual arithmetic operations can be used to compute addresses—but for ways to indicate the addressing modes "address of" and "indirect." In our version of three-address code, we will use the equivalent C notation "&" and "*" to indicate these addressing modes. For example, suppose we wished to store the constant value 2 at the address of the variable **x** plus 10 bytes. We would express this in three-address code as follows:

```
t1 = &x + 10
*t1 = 2
```

The implementation of these new addressing modes requires that the data structure for three-address code contain a new field or fields. For example, the quadruple data structure of Figure 8.4 (page 403) can be augmented by an enumerated **AddrMode** field with possible values **None**, **Address**, and **Indirect**.

P-Code for Address Calculations   In P-code, it is common to introduce new instructions to express new addressing modes (since there are fewer explicit addresses to which to assign addressing modes). The two instructions we will introduce for this purpose are as follows:

1. **ind** ("indirect load"), which takes an integer offset as parameter, assumes that an address is on the top of the stack, adds the offset to the address, and replaces the address on the stack with the value at the resulting location:

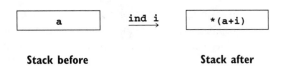

Stack before   Stack after

2. **ixa** ("indexed address"), which takes an integer scale factor as parameter, assumes an offset is at the top of the stack and a base address below it, multiplies the offset by the scale factor, adds the base address, pops both offset and base from the stack, and pushes the resulting address:

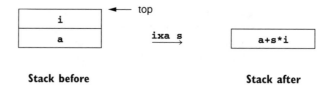

Stack before   **Stack after**

These two P-code instructions, together with the **lda** (load address) instruction introduced earlier, will allow us to perform the same address calculations and referencing as the addressing modes for three-address code.[6] For example, the previous sample problem (storing the constant value 2 at the address of the variable **x** plus 10 bytes) can now be solved in P-code as follows:

```
lda x
ldc 10
ixa 1
ldc 2
sto
```

We turn now to a discussion of arrays, records, and pointers, followed by a discussion of target code generation and an extended example.

8.3.2 Array References

An array reference involves the subscripting of an array variable by an expression to get a reference or value of a single array element, as in the C code

```
int a[SIZE]; int i,j;
...
a[i+1] = a[j*2] + 3;
```

In this assignment, the subscripting of **a** by the expression **i+1** produces an address (the target of the assignment), while the subscripting of **a** by the expression **j*2** produces the value at the computed address of the element type of **a** (namely, **int**). Since arrays are stored sequentially in memory, each address must be computed from the **base address** of **a** (its starting address in memory) and an offset that depends linearly on the value of the subscript. When the value rather than the address is desired, an extra indirection step must be generated to fetch the value at the computed address.

The offset is computed from the subscript value as follows. First, an adjustment must be made to the subscript value if the subscript range does not begin at 0 (this is possible in languages like Pascal and Ada, but not C). Second, the adjusted subscript value must be multiplied by a **scale factor** that is equal to the size of each array ele-

---

6. In fact, the **ixa** instruction could be simulated by arithmetic operations, except that in P-code, these operations are typed (**adi** = integer multiplication only) and thus cannot be applied to addresses. We do not emphasize the type constraints of P-code, since that involves extra parameters which, for simplicity, we have suppressed.

ment in memory. Finally, the resulting scaled subscript is added to the base address to get the final address of the array element.

For example, the address of the C array reference **a[i+1]** is[7]

```
a + (i + 1) * sizeof(int)
```

More generally, the address of an array element **a**[*t*] in any language is

$$base\_address(\mathbf{a}) + (t - lower\_bound(\mathbf{a})) * element\_size(\mathbf{a})$$

We now turn to ways of expressing this address calculation in three-address code and P-code. To do this in a target machine–independent notation, we assume that the "address" of an array variable is its base address. Thus, if **a** is an array variable, **&a** in three-address code is the same as *base_address*(**a**), and in P-code

```
lda a
```

loads the base address of **a** onto the P-machine stack. Also, since an array reference calculation depends on the size of the element data type on the target machine, we use the expression **elem_size(a)** for the element size of array **a** on the target machine.[8] Since this is a static quantity (assuming static typing), this expression will be replaced by a constant at compile time.

Three-Address Code for Array References   One possible way to express array references in three-address code is to introduce two new operations, one that fetches the value of an array element

```
t2 = a[t1]
```

and one that assigns to the address of an array element

```
a[t2] = t1
```

(these could be given the symbols **=[]** and **[]=**). Using this terminology, it is not necessary to express the actual address computation (and machine dependencies such as the element size disappear from this notation). For example, the source code statement

```
a[i+1] = a[j*2] + 3;
```

would translate into the three-address instructions

```
t1 = j * 2
t2 = a[t1]
t3 = t2 + 3
t4 = i + 1
a[t5] = t3
```

---

7. In C, the name of an array (such as **a** in this expression) stands for its own base address.
8. This could in fact be a function provided by the symbol table.

However, it is still necessary to introduce addressing modes as previously described when dealing with record field and pointer references, so it makes sense to treat all such address computations in a uniform way. Thus, we may also write out the address computations of an array element directly in three-address code. For instance, the assignment

```
t2 = a[t1]
```

can also be written as (using further temporaries **t3** and **t4**)

```
t3 = t1 * elem_size(a)
t4 = &a + t3
t2 = *t4
```

and the assignment

```
a[t2] = t1
```

can be written as

```
t3 = t2 * elem_size(a)
t4 = &a + t3
*t4 = t1
```

Finally, as a more complex example, the source code statement

```
a[i+1] = a[j*2] + 3;
```

translates to the three-address instructions

```
t1 = j * 2
t2 = t1 * elem_size(a)
t3 = &a + t2
t4 = *t3
t5 = t4 + 3
t6 = i + 1
t7 = t6 * elem_size(a)
t8 = &a + t7
*t8 = t5
```

P-Code for Array References   As described previously, we use the new address instructions **ind** and **ixa**. The **ixa** instruction was in fact constructed precisely with array address calculations in mind, and the **ind** instruction is used to load the value of a previously computed address (i.e., to implement an indirect load). The array reference

```
t2 = a[t1]
```

is written in P-code as

```
lda t2
lda a
lod t1
ixa elem_size(a)
ind 0
sto
```

and the array assignment

```
a[t2]  =  t1
```

is written in P-code as

```
lda a
lod t2
ixa elem_size(a)
lod t1
sto
```

Finally, the previous more complex example

```
a[i+1]  =  a[j*2]  +  3;
```

translates to the following P-code instructions:

```
lda a
lod i
ldc 1
adi
ixa elem_size(a)
lda a
lod j
ldc 2
mpi
ixa elem_size(a)
ind 0
ldc 3
adi
sto
```

A Code Generation Procedure with Array References   We show here how array references can be generated by a code generation procedure. We use the example of the subset of C expressions of the previous section (see the grammar on page 407), augmented by a subscript operation. The new grammar that we use is as follows:

$$exp \rightarrow subs \mathbf{=} exp \mid aexp$$
$$aexp \rightarrow aexp \mathbf{+} factor \mid factor$$
$$factor \rightarrow \mathbf{(}\ exp\ \mathbf{)} \mid \mathbf{num} \mid subs$$
$$subs \rightarrow \mathbf{id} \mid \mathbf{id\ [}\ exp\ \mathbf{]}$$

Note that the target of an assignment can now be either a simple variable or a subscripted variable (both included in the nonterminal *subs*). We use the same data structure for the syntax tree as before (see the declarations on page 410), except that there is an additional **Subs** operation for subscripting:

```
typedef enum {Plus,Assign,Subs} Optype;
/* other declarations as before */
```

Also, since a subscript expression can now be on the left of an assignment, it is not possible to store the name of the target variable in the assign node itself (since there may be no such name). Instead, assign nodes now have two children like plus nodes—the left child must be an identifier or a subscript expression. Subscripts themselves can only be applied to identifiers, so we do store the name of the array variable in subscript nodes. Thus, the syntax tree for the expression

(a[i+1]=2)+a[j]

is

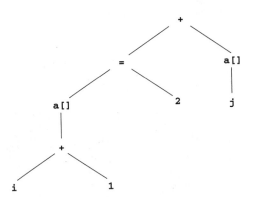

A code generation procedure that generates P-code for such syntax trees is given in Figure 8.9 (compare to Figure 8.7, page 411). The principal difference between this code and the code of Figure 8.7 is the need for an inherited attribute **isAddr** that distinguishes a subscripted expression or identifier on the left of an assignment from one on the right. If **isAddr** is set to **TRUE**, then the *address* of the expression must be returned; otherwise, the *value* is to be returned. We leave it to the reader to verify that this procedure generates the following P-code for the expression **(a[i+1]=2)+ a[j]**:

```
lda a
lod i
```

```
ldc 1
adi
ixa elem_size(a)
ldc 2
stn
lda a
lod j
ixa elem_size(a)
ind 0
adi
```

We also leave to the reader the construction of a code generator of three-address code
for this grammar (see the exercises).

Figure 8.9

Implementation of a code
generation procedure for
P-code corresponding to
the expression grammar
on page 422

```
void genCode( SyntaxTree t, int isAddr)
{ char codestr[CODESIZE];
  /* CODESIZE = max length of 1 line of P-code */
  if (t != NULL)
  { switch (t->kind)
    { case OpKind:
        switch (t->op)
        { case Plus:
            if (isAddr) emitCode("Error");
            else { genCode(t->lchild,FALSE);
                   genCode(t->rchild,FALSE);
                   emitCode("adi");}
          break;
        case Assign:
          genCode(t->lchild,TRUE);
          genCode(t->rchild,FALSE);
          emitCode("stn");
          break;
        case Subs:
          sprintf(codestr,"%s %s","lda",t->strval);
          emitCode(codestr);
          genCode(t->lchild,FALSE);
          sprintf(codestr,"%s%s%s",
              "ixa elem_size(",t->strval,")");
          emitCode(codestr);
          if (!isAddr) emitCode("ind 0");
          break;
        default:
          emitCode("Error");
          break;
        }
        break;
      case ConstKind:
```

Figure 8.9   *continued*

```
          if (isAddr) emitCode("Error");
          else
          { sprintf(codestr,"%s %s","ldc",t->strval);
            emitCode(codestr);
          }
          break;
        case IdKind:
          if (isAddr)
            sprintf(codestr,"%s %s","lda",t->strval);
          else
            sprintf(codestr,"%s %s","lod",t->strval);
          emitCode(codestr);
          break;
        default:
          emitCode("Error");
          break;
      }
    }
}
```

Multidimensional Arrays   A complicating factor in the computation of array addresses is the existence in most languages of arrays in several dimensions. For example, in C an array of two dimensions (with different index sizes) can be declared as

```
int a[15][10];
```

Such arrays can be partially subscripted, yielding an array of fewer dimensions, or fully subscripted, yielding a value of the element type of the array. For example, given the above declaration of **a** in C, the expression **a[i]** partially subscripts **a**, yielding a one-dimensional array of integers, while the expression **a[i][j]** fully subscripts **a** and yields a value of integer type. The address of a partially or fully subscripted array variable can be computed by the recursive application of the techniques just described for the one-dimensional case.

8.3.3   Record Structure and Pointer References

Computing the address of a record or structure field presents a similar problem to that of computing a subscripted array address. First, the base address of the structure variable is computed; then, the (usually fixed) offset of the named field is found, and the two are added to get the resulting address. Consider, for example, the C declarations

```
typedef struct rec
    { int i;
      char c;
      int j;
    } Rec;
...
Rec x;
```

Typically, the variable **x** is allocated in memory as the following picture shows, with each field (**i**, **c**, and **j**) having an offset from the base address of **x** (which may itself be an offset into an activation record):

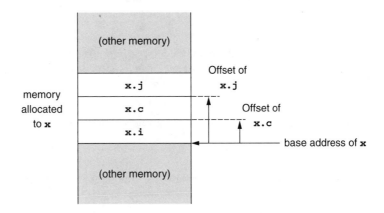

Note that the fields are allocated linearly (usually from low to high address), that the offset of each field is a constant, and that the first field (**x.i**) has offset 0. Note also that the offsets of the fields depend on the sizes of the various data types on the target machine, but that no scale factor as with arrays is involved.

To write target-independent intermediate code for record structure field address computations, we must introduce a new function that returns the offset of a field, given a structure variable and the field name. We call this function **field_offset**, and we write it with two parameters, the first being the variable name and the second the field name. Thus, **field_offset(x,j)** returns the offset of **x.j**. As with other, simi-lar functions, this function can be provided by the symbol table. In any case, this is a com-pile-time quantity, so the actual generated intermediate code will have instances of calls to **field_offset** replaced by constants.

Record structures are typically used together with pointers and dynamic memory allocation to implement dynamic data structures such as lists and trees. Thus, we also describe how pointers interact with field address computations. A pointer, for purposes of the discussion here, simply establishes an extra level of indirection; we ignore the allocation questions involved in the creation of pointer values (these were discussed in the previous chapter).

Three-Address Code for Structure and Pointer References   Consider, first, the three-address code for the computation of field addresses: to compute the address of **x.j** into a temporary **t1**, we use the three-address instruction

```
t1 = &x + field_offset(x,j)
```

A field assignment such as the C statement

```
x.j = x.i;
```

can be translated into the three-address code

```
t1 = &x + field_offset(x,j)
t2 = &x + field_offset(x,i)
*t1 = *t2
```

Now, consider pointers. Suppose, for example, that **x** is declared as a pointer to an integer, for example by the C declaration

```
int * x;
```

Suppose further that **i** is a normal integer variable. Then the C assignment

```
*x = i;
```

can be translated trivially into the three-address instruction

```
*x = i
```

and the assignment

```
i = *x;
```

into the three-address instruction

```
i = *x
```

To see how the indirection of pointers interacts with field address computations, consider the following example of a tree data structure and variable declaration in C:

```
typedef struct treeNode
  { int val;
    struct treeNode * lchild, * rchild;
  } TreeNode;
...
TreeNode *p;
```

Now, consider two typical assignments

```
p->lchild = p;
p = p->rchild;
```

These statements translate into the three-address code

```
t1 = p + field_offset(*p,lchild)
*t1 = p
t2 = p + field_offset(*p,rchild)
p = *t2
```

P-Code for Structure and Pointer References   Given the declaration of **x** at the beginning of this discussion (page 423), a straightforward computation of the address of **x.j** can be made into P-code as follows:

```
lda x
lod field_offset(x,j)
ixa 1
```

The assignment statement

```
x.j = x.i;
```

can be translated into the P-code

```
lda x
lod field_offset(x,j)
ixa 1
lda x
ind field_offset(x,i)
sto
```

Note how the **ind** instruction is used to fetch the value of **x.i** without first computing its complete address.

In the case of pointers (with **x** declared as an **int***), the assignment

```
*x = i;
```

translates into the P-code

```
lod x
lod i
sto
```

and the assignment

```
i = *x;
```

translates into the P-code

```
lda i
lod x
ind 0
sto
```

We conclude with the P-code for the assignments

```
p->lchild = p;
p = p->rchild;
```

(see the declaration of **p** on the previous page). These translate to the following P-code:

```
lod p
lod field_offset(*p,lchild)
ixa 1
lod p
sto
lda p
lod p
ind field_offset(*p,rchild)
sto
```

We leave the details of a code generation procedure that will generate these code sequences in either three-address code or P-code to the exercises.

8.4 CODE GENERATION OF CONTROL STATEMENTS AND LOGICAL EXPRESSIONS

In this section, we describe code generation for various forms of control statements. Chief among these are the structured if-statement and while-statement, which we cover in detail in the first part of this section. We also include in this description the use of the break-statement (as in C), but do not discuss low-level control such as the goto-statement, since such statements can be easily implemented directly in intermediate or target code. Other forms of structured control, like the repeat-statement (or do-while–statement), the for-statement, and the case-statement (or switch-statement), are left to the exercises. An additional implementation technique useful for the switch-statement, called a **jump table**, is also described in an exercise.

Intermediate code generation for control statements, both in three-address and P-code, involves the generation of **labels** in a manner similar to the generation of temporary names in three-address code, but which stand for addresses in the target code to which jumps are made. If labels are to be eliminated in the generation of target code, then a problem arises in that jumps to code locations that are not yet known must be **backpatched**, or retroactively rewritten, and we discuss this in the next part of this section.

Logical, or Boolean, expressions, which are used as control tests, and which may also be used independently as data, are discussed next, particularly with respect to **short-circuit evaluation**, in which they differ from arithmetic expressions.

Finally, in this section, we present a sample P-code code generation procedure for if- and while-statements.

8.4.1 Code Generation for If- and While-Statements

We consider the following two forms of the if- and while-statements, which are similar in many different languages (but which we give here in a C-like syntax):

if-stmt → **if** (*exp*) *stmt* | **if** (*exp*) *stmt* **else** *stmt*
while-stmt → **while** (*exp*) *stmt*

The chief problem in generating code for such statements is to translate the structured control features into an "unstructured" equivalent involving jumps, which can be directly implemented. Compilers arrange to generate code for such statements in a standard order that allows the efficient use of a subset of the possible jumps that a target architecture might permit. Typical code arrangements for each of these statements are shown in Figures 8.10 (below) and 8.11 (page 430). (Figure 8.10 shows an else-part (the FALSE case), but this is optional according to the grammar rule just given, and the arrangement shown is easy to modify for a missing else-part.) In each of these arrangements, there are only two kinds of jumps—unconditional jumps and jumps when the condition is false—the true case is always a "fall-through" case that needs no jump. This reduces the number of jumps that the compiler needs to generate. It also means that only two jump instructions are needed in the intermediate code. False jumps have already appeared in the three-address code of Figure 8.2 (as an **if_false..goto** instruction) and in the P-code of Figure 8.6 (as a **fjp** instruction). It remains to intro-

Figure 8.10

Typical code arrangement for an if-statement

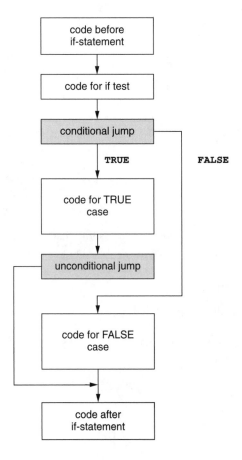

duce unconditional jumps, which we will will write simply as **goto** instructions in three-address code and as the **ujp** (unconditional jump) in P-code.

Figure 8.11

Typical code arrangement for a while-statement

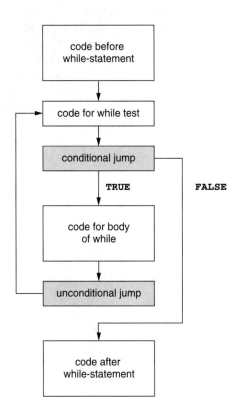

Three-Address Code for Control Statements   We assume that the code generator generates a sequence of labels with names such as **L1**, **L2**, and so on. For the statement

    if (*E*) *S1* **else** *S2*

the following code pattern is generated:

```
<code to evaluate E to t1>
if_false t1 goto L1
<code for S1>
goto L2
label L1
<code for S2>
label L2
```

Similarly, a while-statement of the form

```
while ( E ) S
```

would cause the following three-address code pattern to be generated:

```
label L1
<code to evaluate E to t1>
if_false t1 goto L2
<code for S>
goto L1
label L2
```

P-Code for Control Statements   For the statement

```
if ( E ) S1 else S2
```

the following P-code pattern is generated:

```
<code to evaluate E>
fjp L1
<code for S1>
ujp L2
lab L1
<code for S2>
lab L2
```

and for the statement

```
while ( E ) S
```

the following P-code pattern is generated:

```
lab L1
<code to evaluate E>
fjp L2
<code for S>
ujp L1
lab L2
```

Note that all these code sequences (both three-address code and P-code) end in a label declaration. We could call this label the **exit label** of the control statement. Many languages provide a language construct that allows loops to be exited from arbitrary locations within the loop body. C, for example, provides the **break** statement (which can also be used inside switch-statements). In these languages, the exit label must be made available to all code generation routines that may be called within the body of a loop, so that if an exit statement such as a break is encountered, a jump to the exit label can be generated. This makes the exit label into an inherited attribute during code generation, which must either be stored in a stack or passed as a parameter to appropriate code generation routines. More details about this, as well as examples of other situations where this may occur, will be given later in this section.

8.4.2 Generation of Labels and Backpatching

One feature of code generation for control statements that can cause problems during target code generation is the fact that, in some cases, jumps to a label must be generated prior to the definition of the label itself. During intermediate code generation, this presents few problems, since a code generation routine can simply call the label generation procedure when a label is needed to generate a forward jump and save the label name (locally or on a stack) until the label location is known. During target code generation, the labels can be simply passed on to an assembler if assembly code is generated, but if actual executable code is to be generated, these labels must be resolved into absolute or relative code locations.

A standard method for generating such forward jumps is either to leave a gap in the code where the jump is to occur or to generate a dummy jump instruction to a fake location. Then, when the actual jump location becomes known, this location is used to fix up, or **backpatch**, the missing code. This requires either that the generated code be kept in a buffer in memory, so that the backpatch can be made on the fly, or that the code be written to a temporary file and then reinput and backpatched as necessary. In either case, backpatches may need to be buffered on a stack or kept locally in recursive procedures.

During the backpatching process a further problem may arise in that many architectures have two varieties of jumps, a short jump or branch (within, say, 128 bytes of code) and a long jump that requires more code space. In that case, a code generator may need to insert **nop** instructions when shortening jumps, or make several passes to condense the code.

8.4.3 Code Generation of Logical Expressions

So far we have not said anything about generating code for the logical or Boolean expressions that are used as tests in control statements. If the intermediate code has a Boolean data type and logical operations such as **and** and **or**, then the value of a Boolean expression can be computed in intermediate code in exactly the same way as an arithmetic expression. This is the case for P-code, and intermediate code can be designed similarly. However, even if this is the case, the translation into target code usually requires that Boolean values be represented arithmetically, since most architectures do not have a built-in Boolean type. The standard way to do this is to represent the Boolean value **false** as 0 and **true** as 1. Then, standard bitwise **and** and **or** operators can be used to compute the value of a Boolean expression on most architectures. This does require that the result of comparison operations such as $<$ be normalized to 0 or 1. On some architectures, this requires that 0 or 1 be explicitly loaded, since the comparison operator itself only sets a condition code. In that case, conditional jumps need to be generated to load the appropriate value.

A further use of jumps is necessary if the logical operations are **short circuit**, as they are in C. A logical operation is short circuit if it may fail to evaluate its second argument. For example, if a is a Boolean expression that is computed to be false, then the Boolean expression a **and** b can be immediately determined to be false without evaluating b. Similarly, if a is known to be true, then a **or** b can be determined to be true without evaluating b. Short-circuit operations are extremely useful to the coder, in that the evaluation of the second expression would cause an error if an operator were not short circuit. For instance, it is common to write in C

```
if ((p!=NULL) && (p->val==0)) ...
```

where evaluation of `p->val` when `p` is null could cause a memory fault.

Short-circuit Boolean operators are similar to if-statements, except that they return values, and often they are defined using **if-expressions** as

a **and** $b \equiv$ **if** a **then** b **else false**

and

a **or** $b \equiv$ **if** a **then true else** b

To generate code that ensures that the second subexpression will be evaluated only when necessary, we must use jumps in exactly the same way as in the code for if-statements. For instance, short-circuit P-code for the C expression `(x!=0)&&(y==x)` is:

```
lod x
ldc 0
neq
fjp L1
lod y
lod x
equ
ujp L2
lab L1
lod FALSE
lab L2
```

8.4.4 A Sample Code Generation Procedure for If- and While-Statements

In this section, we exhibit a code generation procedure for control statements using the following simplified grammar:

$stmt \rightarrow if\text{-}stmt \mid while\text{-}stmt \mid$ **break** $\mid$ **other**
$if\text{-}stmt \rightarrow$ **if(** exp **)** $stmt \mid$ **if(** exp **)** $stmt$ **else** $stmt$
$while\text{-}stmt \rightarrow$ **while(** exp **)** $stmt$
$exp \rightarrow$ **true** $\mid$ **false**

For simplicity, this grammar uses the token **other** to represent statements not included in the grammar (like the assignment statement). It also includes only the constant Boolean expressions **true** and **false**. It includes a **break** statement to show how such a statement can be implemented using an inherited label passed as a parameter.

The following C declarations can be used to implement an abstract syntax tree for this grammar:

```
typedef enum {ExpKind,IfKind,
        WhileKind,BreakKind,OtherKind} NodeKind;
typedef struct streenode
        { NodeKind kind;
          struct streenode * child[3];
          int val; /* used with ExpKind */
        } STreeNode;
typedef STreeNode *SyntaxTree;
```

In this syntax tree structure, a node can have as many as three children (an if-node with an else-part), and expression nodes are constants with value true or false (stored in the **val** field as a 1 or 0). For example, the statement

```
if(true)while(true)if(false)break else other
```

has the syntax tree

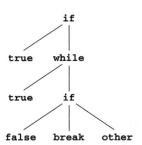

where we have only shown the non-null children of each node.[9]

Using the given **typedef**'s and the corresponding syntax tree structure, a code generation procedure that generates P-code is given in Figure 8.12. We make the following remarks about this code.

<hr />

9. The dangling else ambiguity in this grammar is solved by the standard "most closely nested" rule, as the syntax tree shows.

Figure 8.12

Code generation procedure
for control statements

```
void genCode( SyntaxTree t, char * label)
{ char codestr[CODESIZE];
  char * lab1, * lab2;
  if (t != NULL) switch (t->kind)
  { case ExpKind:
      if (t->val==0) emitCode("ldc false");
      else emitCode("ldc true");
      break;
    case IfKind:
      genCode(t->child[0],label);
      lab1 = genLabel();
      sprintf(codestr,"%s %s","fjp",lab1);
      emitCode(codestr);
      genCode(t->child[1],label);
      if (t->child[2] != NULL)
      { lab2 = genLabel();
        sprintf(codestr,"%s %s","ujp",lab2);
        emitCode(codestr);}
      sprintf(codestr,"%s %s","lab",lab1);
      emitCode(codestr);
      if (t->child[2] != NULL)
      { genCode(t->child[2],label);
        sprintf(codestr,"%s %s","lab",lab2);
        emitCode(codestr);}
      break;
    case WhileKind:
      lab1 = genLabel();
      sprintf(codestr,"%s %s","lab",lab1);
      emitCode(codestr);
      genCode(t->child[0],label);
      lab2 = genLabel();
      sprintf(codestr,"%s %s","fjp",lab2);
      emitCode(codestr);
      genCode(t->child[1],lab2);
      sprintf(codestr,"%s %s","ujp",lab1);
      emitCode(codestr);
      sprintf(codestr,"%s %s","lab",lab2);
      emitCode(codestr);
      break;
    case BreakKind:
      sprintf(codestr,"%s %s","ujp",label);
      emitCode(codestr);
      break;
    case OtherKind:
      emitCode("Other");
      break;
    default:
      emitCode("Error");
      break;
  }
}
```

First, the code assumes as before the existence of an **emitCode** procedure (this procedure could simply print the string passed to it). The code also assumes the existence of a parameterless **genLabel** procedure that returns label names in the sequence **L1**, **L2**, **L3**, and so on.

The **genCode** procedure here has an extra **label** parameter that is needed to generate an absolute jump for a break-statement. This parameter is only changed in the recursive call that processes the body of a while-statement. Thus, a break-statement will always cause a jump out of the most closely nested while-statement. (The initial call to **genCode** can use an empty string as the **label** parameter, and any break-statement encountered outside a while-statement will then generate a jump to an empty label, hence an error.)

Note also how the local variables **lab1** and **lab2** are used to save label names for which there are jumps and/or definitions still pending.

Finally, since an other-statement does not correspond to any actual code, this procedure simply generates the non-P-code instruction "**Other**" in this case.

We leave it to the reader to trace the operation of the procedure of Figure 8.12 and to show that for the statement

```
if(true)while(true)if(false)break else other
```

it generates the code sequence

```
ldc true
fjp L1
lab L2
ldc true
fjp L3
ldc false
fjp L4
ujp L3
ujp L5
lab L4
Other
lab L5
ujp L2
lab L3
lab L1
```

8.5 CODE GENERATION OF PROCEDURE AND FUNCTION CALLS

Procedure and function calls are the last language mechanism we will discuss in general terms in this chapter. The description of intermediate and target code for this mechanism is, even more than other language mechanisms, complicated by the fact that different target machines use considerably different mechanisms for performing calls and by the fact that calls depend heavily on the organization of the runtime environment.

Thus, it is difficult to achieve an intermediate code representation that is general enough to use for any target architecture or runtime environment.

8.5.1 Intermediate Code for Procedures and Functions

The requirements for intermediate code representations of function calls may be described in general terms as follows. First, there are actually *two* mechanisms that need description: function/procedure **definition** (also called **declaration**) and function/ procedure **call**.[10] A definition creates a function name, parameters, and code, but the function does not execute at that point. A call creates actual values for the parameters (or **arguments** to the call) and performs a jump to the code of the function, which then executes and returns. The runtime environment in which execution takes place is not known when the code for the function is created, except in its general structure. This runtime environment is partially built by the caller and partially by the code of the called function; this division of responsibility is part of the **calling sequence**, studied in the previous chapter.

Intermediate code for a definition must include an instruction marking the beginning, or **entry point**, of the code for the function, and an instruction marking the ending, or **return point**, of the function. Schematically, we can write this as follows:

Entry instruction

<code for the function body>

Return instruction

Similarly, a function call must have an instruction indicating the beginning of the computation of the arguments (in preparation for the call) and then an actual call instruction that indicates the point where the arguments have been constructed and the actual jump to the code of the function can take place:

Begin-argument-computation instruction

<code to compute the arguments>

Call instruction

Different versions of intermediate code have significantly different versions of these four bracketing instructions, particularly with regard to the amount of information about the environment, the parameters, and the function itself that is part of each instruction. Typical examples of such information include the number, size, and location of the parameters; the size of the stack frame; the size of the local variables and temporary space; and various indications of register usage by the called function. We will, as usual, present intermediate code that contains a minimal amount of information in the instructions themselves, with the idea that any necessary information can be kept separately in a symbol table entry for the procedure.

---

10. Throughout this text, we have taken the view that functions and procedures represent essentially the same mechanism, and, without further mention, we will consider them to be the same for purposes of this section. The difference is, of course, that a function must make a returned value available to the caller when it exits and the caller must know where to find it.

Three-Address Code for Procedures and Functions   In three-address code, the entry instruction needs to give a name to the procedure entry point, similar to the **label** instruction; thus, it is a one-address instruction, which we will call simply **entry**. Similarly, we will call the return instruction **return**. This instruction is also a one-address instruction: it must give the name of the returned value, if there is one.

For example, consider the C function definition

```
int f(int x, int y)
{ return x+y+1; }
```

This will translate into the following three-address code:

```
entry f
t1 = x + y
t2 = t1 + 1
return t2
```

In the case of a call, we need in fact three different three-address instructions: one to signal the start of argument computation, which we will call **begin_args** (and which is a zero-address instruction); an instruction that is used repeatedly to specify the names of argument values, which we will call **arg** (and which must include the address, or name, of the argument value); and, finally, the actual call instruction, which we will write simply as **call**, which also is a one-address instruction (the name or entry point of the function being called must be given).

For example, suppose the function **f** has been defined in C as in the previous example. Then, the call

```
f(2+3,4)
```

translates to the three-address code

```
begin_args
t1 = 2 + 3
arg t1
arg 4
call f
```

Here we have listed the arguments in left-to-right order. The order could, of course, be different. (See Section 7.3.1, page 361.)

P-Code for Procedures and Functions   The entry instruction in P-code is **ent**, and the return instruction is **ret**. Thus, the previous definition of the C function **f** translates into the P-code

```
ent f
lod x
```

```
lod y
adi
ldc 1
adi
ret
```

Note that the **ret** instruction does not need a parameter to indicate what the returned value is: the returned value is assumed to be at the top of the P-machine stack on return.

The P-code instructions for a call are the **mst** instruction and the **cup** instruction. The **mst** instruction stands for "mark stack" and corresponds to the **begin_args** three-address code instruction. The reason it is called "mark stack" is that the target code generated from such an instruction is concerned with setting up the activation record for the new call on the stack, that is, the first few steps in the calling sequence. This usually means, among other things, that space must be allocated or "marked" on the stack for such items as the arguments. The **cup** P-code instruction is the "call user procedure" instruction and corresponds directly to the **call** instruction of three-address code. The reason for this name is that P-code distinguishes two kinds of calls: **cup** and **csp**, or "call standard procedure." A standard procedure is a "built-in" procedure required by the language definition, such as the **sin** or **abs** procedures of Pascal (C has no built-in procedures to speak of). Calls to built-in procedures can use specific knowledge about their operation to improve the efficiency of the call (or even eliminate it). We will not consider the **csp** operation further.

Note that we do not introduce a P-code instruction equivalent to the three-address code **arg** instruction. Instead, all argument values are assumed to appear on the stack (in the appropriate order) when the **cup** instruction is encountered. This may result in a slightly different order for the calling sequence than that corresponding to the three-address code (see the exercises).

Our example of a call in C (the call **f(2+3,4)** to the function **f** described previously) now translates into the following P-code:

```
mst
ldc 2
ldc 3
adi
ldc 4
cup f
```

(Again, we have computed the arguments left to right.)

8.5.2 A Code Generation Procedure for Function Definition and Call

As in previous sections, we wish to exhibit a code generation procedure for a sample grammar with function definitions and calls. The grammar we will use is the following:

$$program \rightarrow decl\text{-}list\ exp$$
$$decl\text{-}list \rightarrow decl\text{-}list\ decl\ |\ \varepsilon$$
$$decl \rightarrow \textbf{fn}\ \textbf{\textit{id}}\ (\ param\text{-}list\ ) = exp$$
$$param\text{-}list \rightarrow param\text{-}list\ \textbf{,}\ \textbf{\textit{id}}\ |\ \textbf{\textit{id}}$$
$$exp \rightarrow exp\ \textbf{+}\ exp\ |\ call\ |\ \textbf{\textit{num}}\ |\ \textbf{\textit{id}}$$
$$call \rightarrow \textbf{\textit{id}}\ (\ arg\text{-}list\ )$$
$$arg\text{-}list \rightarrow arg\text{-}list\ \textbf{,}\ exp\ |\ exp$$

This grammar defines a program to be a sequence of function declarations, followed by a single expression. There are no variables or assignments in this grammar, only parameters, functions, and expressions, which may include function calls. All values are integers, all functions return integers, and all functions must have at least one parameter. There is only one numeric operation (aside from function call): integer addition. An example of a program as defined by this grammar is

```
fn f(x)=2+x
fn g(x,y)=f(x)+y
g(3,4)
```

This program contains two function definitions followed by an expression that is a call to **g**. There is also a call to **f** in the body of **g**.

We want to define a syntax tree structure for this grammar. We do so using the following C declarations:

```
typedef enum
  {PrgK,FnK,ParamK,PlusK,CallK,ConstK,IdK}
  NodeKind;
typedef struct streenode
        { NodeKind kind;
          struct streenode *lchild,*rchild,
                             *sibling;
          char * name; /* used with FnK,ParamK,
                          CallK,IdK */
          int val; /* used with ConstK */
        } STreeNode;
typedef STreeNode *SyntaxTree;
```

There are seven different kinds of nodes in this tree structure. Each syntax tree has a root that is a **PrgK** node. This node is used simply to bind the declarations and the expression of the program together. A syntax tree contains exactly one such node. The left child of this node is a sibling list of **FnK** nodes; the right child is the associated program expression. Each **FnK** node has a left child that is a sibling list of **ParamK** nodes. These nodes define the names of the parameters. The body of each function is the right child of its **FnK** node. Expression nodes are as usual, except that a **CallK** node contains the name of the called function and has a right child that is a sibling list of the argument expressions. For example, the previous sample program has the syntax tree given in Figure 8.13. For clarity we have included in that figure the node kind of each node, along with any name/value attributes. Children and siblings are distinguished by direction (siblings to the right, children below).

Figure 8.13

Abstract syntax tree for
the sample program on
page 440

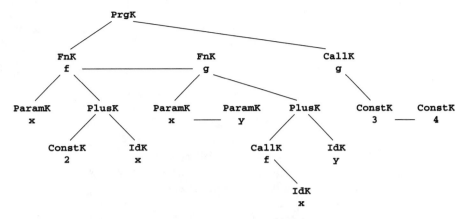

Given this syntax tree structure, a code generation procedure that produces P-code
is given in Figure 8.14. We make the following remarks about this code. First, the code
for a **PrgK** node simply recurses down the rest of the tree. The code for an **IdK**,
ConstK, or **PlusK** is virtually identical to that of previous examples.

Figure 8.14

Code generation procedure
for function definition
and call

```
void genCode( SyntaxTree t)
{ char codestr[CODESIZE];
  SyntaxTree p;
  if (t != NULL)
  switch (t->kind)
  { case PrgK:
      p = t->lchild;
      while (p != NULL)
      { genCode(p);
        p = p->sibling; }
      genCode(t->rchild);
      break;
    case FnK:
      sprintf(codestr,"%s %s","ent",t->name);
      emitCode(codestr);
      genCode(t->rchild);
      emitCode("ret");
      break;
    case ParamK: /* no actions */
      break;
    case ConstK:
      sprintf(codestr,"%s %d","ldc",t->val);
      emitCode(codestr);
      break;
    case PlusK:
      genCode(t->lchild);
      genCode(t->rchild);
      emitCode("adi");
      break;
```

Figure 8.14   *continued*

```
      case IdK:
        sprintf(codestr,"%s %s","lod",t->name);
        emitCode(codestr);
        break;
      case CallK:
        emitCode("mst");
        p = t->rchild;
        while (p!=NULL)
        { genCode(p);
          p = p->sibling; }
        sprintf(codestr,"%s %s","cup",t->name);
        emitCode(codestr);
        break;
      default:
        emitCode("Error");
        break;
    }
}
```

There remain the cases **FnK**, **ParamK**, and **CallK**. The code for a **FnK** node simply surrounds the code for the body of the function (the right child) with **ent** and **ret**; the parameters of the function are never visited. Indeed, parameter nodes never cause code to be generated—the arguments have already been computed by the caller.[11] This explains also why there are no actions at a **ParamK** node in Figure 8.14; indeed, because of the behavior of the **FnK** code, no **ParamK** nodes should even be reached in the tree traversal, so this case could actually be dropped.

The final case is the **CallK** case. The code for this case issues an **mst** instruction, then proceeds to generate code for each of the arguments, and finally issues a **cup** instruction.

We leave it to the reader to show that the code generation procedure of Figure 8.14 would produce the following P-code, given the program whose syntax tree is shown in Figure 8.13:

```
ent f
ldc 2
lod x
adi
ret
ent g
mst
```

---

11. Parameter nodes do, however, have an important bookkeeping role in that they determine the relative positions, or offsets, where the parameters may be found in the activation record. We assume this is handled elsewhere.

```
lod x
cup f
lod y
adi
ret
mst
ldc 3
ldc 4
cup g
```

8.6   CODE GENERATION IN COMMERCIAL COMPILERS: TWO CASE STUDIES

In this section, we examine the assembly code output produced by two different commercial compilers for different processors. The first is Borland's C compiler version 3.0 for Intel 80×86 processors. The second is Sun's C compiler version 2.0 for SparcStations. We will show the assembly output of these compilers for the same code examples that we have used to illustrate three-address code and P-code.[12] This should give further insight into code generation techniques, as well as the conversion from intermediate code to target code. It should also provide a useful comparison to the machine code produced by the TINY compiler, to be discussed in subsequent sections.

8.6.1   The Borland 3.0 C Compiler for the 80×86

We begin our examples of the output of this compiler with the assignment used in Section 8.2.1:

    (x=x+3)+4

We will assume that the variable **x** in this expression is stored locally in the stack frame.

The assembly code for this expression as produced by the Borland 3.0 compiler for the Intel 80×86 is as follows:

```
mov     ax,word ptr [bp-2]
add     ax,3
mov     word ptr [bp-2],ax
add     ax,4
```

In this code the accumulator register **ax** is used as the main temporary location for the computation. The location of the local variable **x** is **bp-2**, reflecting the use of the register **bp** (base pointer) as the frame pointer and the fact that integer variables occupy two bytes on this machine.

The first instruction moves the value of **x** to **ax** (the brackets in the address **[bp-2]** indicate an indirect rather than an immediate load). The second instruction

---

12. For purposes of this and most other examples, optimizations that these compilers perform are turned off.

adds the constant 3 to this register. The third instruction then moves this value to the location of **x**. Finally, the fourth instruction adds 4 to **ax**, so that the final value of the expression is left in this register, where it may be used for further computations.

Note that the address of **x** for the assignment in the third instruction is not precomputed (as an **lda** P-code instruction would suggest). A static simulation of the intermediate code, together with knowledge of available addressing modes, can delay the computation of the address of **x** until this point.

Array References   We use as our example the C expression

```
(a[i+1]=2)+a[j]
```

(see the example of intermediate code generation on page 422). We also assume that **i**, **j**, and **a** are local variables declared as

```
int i,j;
int a[10];
```

The Borland C compiler generates the following assembly code for the expression (for ease of reference, we have numbered the lines of code):

```
(1)    mov     bx,word ptr [bp-2]
(2)    shl     bx,1
(3)    lea     ax,word ptr [bp-22]
(4)    add     bx,ax
(5)    mov     ax,2
(6)    mov     word ptr [bx],ax
(7)    mov     bx,word ptr [bp-4]
(8)    shl     bx,1
(9)    lea     dx,word ptr [bp-24]
(10)   add     bx,dx
(11)   add     ax,word ptr [bx]
```

Since integers have size 2 in this architecture, **bp-2** is the location of **i** in the local activation record, **bp-4** is the location of **j**, and the base address of **a** is **bp-24** (24 = array index size 10 × integer size 2 bytes + 4 bytes space for **i** and **j**). Thus, instruction 1 loads the value of **i** into **bx**, and instruction 2 multiplies that value by 2 (a left shift of 1 bit). Instruction 3 loads the base address of **a** into **ax** (**lea** = load effective address), but already adjusted by adding 2 bytes for the constant 1 in the subscript expression **i+1**. In other words, the compiler has applied the algebraic fact that

$$address(\mathbf{a[i+1]}) = base\_address(\mathbf{a}) + (\mathbf{i}+1)*elem\_size(\mathbf{a})$$
$$= (base\_address(\mathbf{a}) + elem\_size(\mathbf{a})) + \mathbf{i}*elem\_size(\mathbf{a})$$

Instruction 4 then computes the resulting address of **a[i+1]** into **bx**. Instruction 5 moves the constant 2 into register **ax**, and instruction 6 stores this to the address of **a[i+1]**. Instruction 7 then loads the value of **j** into **bx**, instruction 8 multiplies this value by 2, instruction 9 loads the base address of **a** into register **dx**, instruction 10 computes the address of **a[j]** into **bx**, and instruction 11 adds the value stored at this address to the contents of **ax** (namely, 2). The resulting value of the expression is left in register **ax**.

Pointer and Field References   We assume the declarations of previous examples:

```
typedef struct rec
    { int i;
      char c;
      int j;
    } Rec;

typedef struct treeNode
    { int val;
      struct treeNode * lchild, * rchild;
    } TreeNode;
...
Rec x;
TreeNode *p;
```

We also assume that **x** and **p** are declared as local variables and that appropriate allocation of pointers has been done.

Consider, first, the sizes of the data types involved. In the 80×86 architecture, integer variables have size 2 bytes, character variables have size 1 byte, and pointers (unless otherwise declared) are so-called "near" pointers with size 2 bytes.[13] Thus, the variable **x** has size 5 bytes and the variable **p** 2 bytes. With these two variables declared locally as the only variables, **x** is allocated in the activation record at location **bp-6** (local variables are allocated only on even-byte boundaries—a typical restriction—so the extra byte goes unused), and **p** is allocated to register **si**. Further, in the **Rec** structure, **i** has offset 0, **c** has offset 2, and **j** has offset 3, while in the **TreeNode** structure, **val** has offset 0, **lchild** has offset 2, and **rchild** has offset 4.

The code generated for the statement

```
x.j = x.i;
```

is

```
mov     ax,word ptr [bp-6]
mov     word ptr [bp-3],ax
```

The first instruction loads **x.i** into **ax**, and the second stores this value to **x.j**. Note how the offset computation for **j** ($-6 + 3 = -3$) is performed statically by the compiler.

The code generated for the statement

```
p->lchild = p;
```

---

13. The 80×86 has a more general class of pointers called "far" pointers with size 4 bytes.

is

```
mov     word ptr [si+2],si
```

Note how the indirection and offset computation are combined into a single instruction. Finally, the code generated for the statement

```
p = p->rchild;
```

is

```
mov     si,word ptr [si+4]
```

If- and While-Statements   We show here code generated by the Borland C compiler for typical control statements. The statements we use are

```
if (x>y) y++;else x--;
```

and

```
while (x<y) y -= x;
```

In both cases, **x** and **y** are local integer variables.

The Borland compiler generates the following 80×86 code for the given if-statement, where **x** is located in register **bx** and **y** is located in register **dx**:

```
        cmp     bx,dx
        jle     short @1@86
        inc     dx
        jmp     short @1@114
@1@86:
        dec     bx
@1@114:
```

This code uses the same sequential organization as Figure 8.10, but note that this code does not compute the actual logical value of the expression **x<y** but simply uses the condition code directly.

The code generated by the Borland compiler for the while-statement is as follows:

```
        jmp     short @1@170
@1@142:
        sub     dx,bx
@1@170:
        cmp     bx,dx
        jl      short @1@142
```

This uses a different sequential organization from that of Figure 8.11, in that the test is placed at the end, and an initial unconditional jump is made to this test.

Function Definition and Call   The examples we will use are the C function definition

```
int f(int x, int y)
{ return x+y+1; }
```

and a corresponding call

```
f(2+3,4)
```

(these examples were used in Section 8.5.1).

Consider, first, the Borland compiler code for the call **f(2+3,4)**:

```
mov     ax,4
push    ax
mov     ax,5
push    ax
call    near ptr _f
pop     cx
pop     cx
```

Note how the arguments are pushed on the stack in reverse order: first 4, then 5. (The value $5 = 2 + 3$ is precomputed by the compiler, since it is a constant expression.) Note also that the caller is reponsible for removing the argments from the stack after the call; this is the reason for the two **pop** instructions after the call. (The target register **cx** is used as a "trash" receptacle: the popped values are never used.) The call itself should be relatively self-explanatory: the name **_f** has an underscore placed before the source name, which is a typical convention for C compilers, and the **near ptr** declaration means that the function is in the same segment (and thus needs only a two-byte address). We note finally that the **call** instruction on the 80×86 automatically pushes the return address onto the stack (and a corresponding **ret** instruction executed by the called function will pop it).

Now, consider the code generated by the Borland compiler for the definition of **f**:

```
_f      proc    near
        push    bp
        mov     bp,sp
        mov     ax,word ptr [bp+4]
        add     ax,word ptr [bp+6]
        inc     ax
        jmp     short @1@58
@1@58:
        pop     bp
        ret
_f      endp
```

Much of this code should be clear. Since the caller does no construction of the activation record except to compute and push the arguments, this code must finish its construction before the code of the body of the function is executed. This is the task of the second and third instructions, which save the control link (**bp**) on the stack and then set the **bp** to the current **sp** (which switches to the current activation). After these operations, the stack looks as follows:

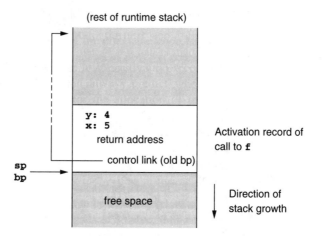

The return address is on the stack between the control link (the old **bp**) and the arguments as a result of the caller's execution of a **call** instruction. Thus, the old **bp** is at the top of the stack, the return address is at location **bp+2** (addresses are two bytes in this example), the parameter **x** is at location **bp+4**, and the parameter **y** is at location **bp+6**. The body of **f** then corresponds to the code that comes next

```
mov     ax,word ptr [bp+4]
add     ax,word ptr [bp+6]
inc     ax
```

which loads **x** into **ax**, adds **y** to it, and then increments it by one.

Finally, the code executes a jump (which is unnecessary here, but is generated anyway, since **return** statements embedded in the function code would need it), restores the old **bp** from the stack, and returns to the caller. The returned value is left in register **ax**, where it will be available to the caller.

8.6.2 The Sun 2.0 C Compiler for Sun Sparcstations

We repeat the code examples used in the previous sections to demonstrate the output of this compiler. As before, we begin with the assignment

(x=x+3)+4

and we assume that the variable **x** in this expression is stored locally in the stack frame.

The Sun C compiler produces assembly code that is very similar to the Borland code:

```
ld      [%fp+-0x4],%o1
add     %o1,0x3,%o1
st      %o1,[%fp+-0x4]
ld      [%fp+-0x4],%o2
add     %o2,0x4,%o3
```

In this code, register names begin with the percent symbol, and constants begin with the characters **0x** (**x** = hexadecimal), so that, for example, **0x4** is hexadecimal 4 (the same as decimal 4). The first instruction moves the value of **x** (in the location **fp-4**, since integers are four bytes long) to the register **o1**.[14] (Note that source locations are on the left and target locations on the right, opposite to the Intel 80×86 convention.) The second instruction adds the constant 3 to **o1**, and the third stores **o1** into the location of **x**. Finally, the value of **x** is again loaded, this time into register **o2**,[15] and 4 is added to it, with the result placed into register **o3**, where it is left as the final value of the expression.

Array References   The expression

```
(a[i+1]=2)+a[j]
```

with all variables local is translated to the following assembly code by the Sun compiler (with instructions numbered for ease of reference):

```
(1)     add     %fp,-0x2c,%o1
(2)     ld      [%fp+-0x4],%o2
(3)     sll     %o2,0x2,%o3
(4)     mov     0x2,%o4
(5)     st      %o4,[%o1+%o3]
(6)     add     %fp,-0x30,%o5
(7)     ld      [%fp+-0x8],%o7
(8)     sll     %o7,0x2,%10
(9)     ld      [%o5+%10],%11
(10)    mov     0x2,%12
(11)    add     %12,%11,%13
```

The computations performed by this code are affected by the fact that integers are 4 bytes in this architecture. Thus, the location of **i** is **fp-4** (written **%fp+-0x4** in this code), the location of **j** is **fp-8** (**%fp+-0x8**), and the base address of **a** is **fp-48** (written **%fp+-0x30**, since 48 decimal = 30 hex). Instruction 1 loads register

---

14. On the SparcStation, registers are indicated by a lowercase letter followed by a number. Different letters refer to different sections of a "register window" that may change with context and that correspond roughly to different uses of the registers. The distinctions among the different letters are immaterial for all the examples in this chapter except one involving function calls (see Section 8.5).

15. This step does not appear in the Borland code and is easily optimized away. See Section 8.9.

o1 with the base address of **a**, modified (as in the Borland code) to subtract 4 bytes for the constant 1 in the subscript **i+1** (2c hex = 44 = 48 − 4). Instruction 2 loads the value of **i** into register **o2**. Instruction 3 multiplies **o2** by 4 (a left shift of 2 bits) and puts the result into **o3**. Instruction 4 loads register **o4** with the constant 2, and instruction 5 stores it to the address of **a[i+1]**. Instruction 6 computes the base address of **a** into **o5**, instruction 7 loads the value of **j** into **o7**, and instruction 8 multiplies it by 4, placing the result into register **10**. Finally, instruction 9 loads the value of **a[j]** into **11**, instruction 10 reloads the constant 2 into **12**, and instruction 11 adds them, placing the result (and the final value of the expression) into register **13**.

Pointer and Field References   We consider the same example as previously (see page 445). On the Sun, the data type sizes are as follows: integer variables have size 4 bytes, character variables have size 1 byte, and pointers have size 4 bytes. However, all variables, including structure fields, are allocated only on 4-byte boundaries. Thus, the variable **x** has size 12 bytes, the variable **p** 4 bytes, and the offsets of **i**, **c**, and **j** are 0, 4, and 8, respectively, as are the offsets of **val**, **lchild**, and **rchild**. The compiler allocates both **x** and **p** in the activation record: **x** at location **fp-0xc** (hex c = 12) and **p** at location **fp-0x10** (hex 10 = 16).

The code generated for the assignment

```
x.j = x.i;
```

is

```
ld      [%fp+-0xc],%o1
st      %o1,[%fp+-0x4]
```

This code loads the value of **x.i** into register **o1** and stores it to **x.j** (again notice how the offset of **x.j** = −12 + 8 = −4 is statically computed).

The pointer assignment

```
p->lchild = p;
```

results in the target code

```
ld      [%fp+-0x10],%o2
ld      [%fp+-0x10],%o3
st      %o3,[%o2+0x4]
```

In this case the value of **p** is loaded into registers **o2** and **o3**. One of these copies (**o2**) is then used as the base address for storing the other copy to the location of **p->lchild**.

Finally, the assignment

```
p = p->rchild;
```

results in the target code

```
ld         [%fp+-0x10],%o4
ld         [%o4+0x8],%o5
st         %o5,[%fp+-0x10]
```

In this code the value of **p** is loaded into register **o4** and then used as the base address for loading the value of **p->rchild**. The final instruction stores this value to the location of **p**.

If- and While-Statements   We show the code generated by the Sun SparcStation C compiler for the same typical control statements as for the Borland compiler

```
if (x>y) y++;else x--;
```

and

```
while (x<y) y -= x;
```

with **x** and **y** local integer variables.

The Sun SparcStation compiler generates the following code for the if-statement, where **x** and **y** are located in the local activation record at offsets -4 and -8:

```
            ld         [%fp+-0x4],%o2
            ld         [%fp+-0x8],%o3
            cmp        %o2,%o3
            bg         L16
            nop
            b          L15
            nop
L16:
            ld         [%fp+-0x8],%o4
            add        %o4,0x1,%o4
            st         %o4,[%fp+-0x8]
            b          L17
            nop
L15:
            ld         [%fp+-0x4],%o5
            sub        %o5,0x1,%o5
            st         %o5,[%fp+-0x4]
L17:
```

Here **nop** instructions follow each branch instruction because the Sparc is pipelined (branches are delayed and the next instruction is always executed before the branch takes effect). Note that the sequential organization is the opposite of that in Figure 8.10: the true case is placed after the false case.

The code generated by the Sun compiler for the while-loop is

```
        ld      [%fp+-0x4],%o7
        ld      [%fp+-0x8],%10
        cmp     %o7,%10
        bl      L21
        nop
        b       L20
        nop
L21:
L18:
        ld      [%fp+-0x4],%11
        ld      [%fp+-0x8],%12
        sub     %12,%11,%12
        st      %12,[%fp+-0x8]
        ld      [%fp+-0x4],%13
        ld      [%fp+-0x8],%14
        cmp     %13,%14
        bl      L18
        nop
        b       L22
        nop
L22:
L20:
```

This code uses a similar arrangement to that of the Borland compiler, except that the test code is also duplicated at the beginning. Also, at the end of this code a "do-nothing" branch is made (to label **L22**) that can easily be eliminated by an optimization step.

Function Definition and Call   We use the same function definition as previously

```
int f(int x, int y)
{ return x+y+1; }
```

and the same call

```
f(2+3,4)
```

The code generated by the Sun compiler for the call is

```
mov     0x5,%o0
mov     0x4,%o1
call    _f,2
```

and the code generated for the definition of **f** is

```
_f:
        !#PROLOGUE#  0
        sethi    %hi(LF62),%g1
        add      %g1,%lo(LF62),%g1
        save     %sp,%g1,%sp
        !#PROLOGUE#  1
        st       %i0,[%fp+0x44]
        st       %i1,[%fp+0x48]
L64:
        .seg     "text"
        ld       [%fp+0x44],%o0
        ld       [%fp+0x48],%o1
        add      %o0,%o1,%o0
        add      %o0,0x1,%o0
        b        LE62
        nop
LE62:
        mov      %o0,%i0
        ret
        restore
```

We will not discuss this code in detail, but make the following comments. First, the call passes the arguments in registers **o0** and **o1**, rather than on the stack. The call indicates with the number **2** how many registers are used for this purpose. The call also performs several bookkeeping functions, which we do not describe further, except to say that the "o" registers (like **o0** and **o1**) become the "i" registers (e.g., **i0** and **i1**) after the call (and the "i" registers revert to being the "o" registers on return from the call).[16]

The code for the definition of **f** begins also with some bookkeeping instructions that finish the calling sequence (between the **!#PROLOGUE#** comments), which we also do not describe further. The code then stores the parameter values to the stack (from the "i" registers, which are the same as the "o" registers of the caller). After the return value is computed, it is placed in the register **i0** (where it will be available after the return as register **o0**).

8.7 TM: A SIMPLE TARGET MACHINE

In the section following this one we will present a code generator for the TINY language. To make this a meaningful task, we generate target code directly for a very simple machine that can be easily simulated. We call this machine TM (for Tiny Machine), and in Appendix C, we provide a C program listing of a complete TM simulator that can be used to execute the code produced by the TINY code generator. In the current section we describe the complete TM architecture and instruction set, as well as the use

---

16. Loosely speaking, "o" is for "output" and "i" is for "input." This switching of registers across calls is performed by a **register window** mechanism of the Sparc.architecture.

of the simulator of Appendix C. For ease of understanding, we will use C code fragments to aid this description, and the TM instructions themselves will always be given in assembly code format rather than as binary or hexadecimal codes. (The simulator reads only assembly code in any case.)

8.7.1   Basic Architecture of the Tiny Machine

TM consists of a read-only instruction memory, a data memory, and a set of eight general-purpose registers. These all use nonnegative integer addresses beginning at 0. Register 7 is the program counter and is the only special register, as described below. The C declarations

```
#define IADDR_SIZE ...
      /* size of instruction memory */
#define DADDR_SIZE ...
      /* size of data memory */
#define NO_REGS 8 /* number of registers */
#define PC_REG 7

Instruction iMem[IADDR_SIZE];
int dMem[DADDR_SIZE];
int reg[NO_REGS];
```

will be used in the descriptions that follow.

TM performs a conventional fetch-execute cycle:

```
do
  /* fetch */
  currentInstruction = iMem[reg[pcRegNo]++] ;
  /* execute current instruction */
  ...
while (!(halt||error)) ;
```

At start-up, the Tiny Machine sets all registers and data memory to 0, then loads the value of the highest legal address (namely **DADDR_SIZE** − 1) into **dMem[0]**. (This allows memory to be easily added to the TM, since programs can find out during execution how much memory is available.) The TM then starts to execute instructions beginning at **iMem[0]**. The machine stops when a **HALT** instruction is executed. The possible error conditions include **IMEM_ERR**, which occurs if **reg[PC_REG]** < 0 or **reg[PC_REG]** ≥ **IADDR_SIZE** in the fetch step above, and the two conditions **DMEM_ERR** and **ZERO_DIV**, which occur during instruction execution as described below.

The instruction set of the TM is given in Figure 8.15, together with a brief description of the effect of each instruction. There are two basic instruction formats: register-only, or RO instructions, and register-memory, or RM instructions. A register-only instruction has the format

opcode r,s,t

Figure 8.15

Complete instruction set
of the Tiny Machine

RO Instructions

| Format: | *opcode r,s,t* |

Opcode	Effect
HALT	stop execution (operands ignored)
IN	**reg[r]** ← integer value read from the standard input (*s* and *t* ignored)
OUT	**reg[r]** → the standard output (*s* and *t* ignored)
ADD	**reg[r] = reg[s] + reg[t]**
SUB	**reg[r] = reg[s] - reg[t]**
MUL	**reg[r] = reg[s] * reg[t]**
DIV	**reg[r] = reg[s] / reg[t]** (may generate **ZERO_DIV**)

RM Instructions

| Format: | *opcode r,d(s)* |

($a = d + $ **reg[s]**; any reference to **dMem[a]** generates **DMEM_ERR** if $a < 0$ or $a \geq$ DADDR_SIZE)

Opcode	Effect
LD	**reg[r] = dMem[a]** (load *r* with memory value at *a*)
LDA	**reg[r] = a** (load address *a* directly into *r*)
LDC	**reg[r] = d** (load constant *d* directly into *r*—*s* is ignored)
ST	**dMem[a] = reg[r]** (store value in *r* to memory location *a*)
JLT	**if (reg[r]<0) reg[PC_REG] = a** (jump to instruction *a* if *r* is negative, similarly for the following)
JLE	**if (reg[r]<=0) reg[PC_REG] = a**
JGE	**if (reg[r]>=0) reg[PC_REG] = a**
JGT	**if (reg[r]>0) reg[PC_REG] = a**
JEQ	**if (reg[r]==0) reg[PC_REG] = a**
JNE	**if (reg[r]!=0) reg[PC_REG] = a**

where the operands **r**, **s**, **t** are legal registers (checked at load time). Thus, such instructions are three address, and all three addresses must be registers. All arithmetic instructions are limited to this format, as are the two primitive input/output instructions.

A register-memory instruction has the format

opcode r,d(s)

In this code **r** and **s** must be legal registers (checked at load time), and **d** is a positive or negative integer representing an offset. This instruction is a two-address instruction, where the first address is always a register and the second address is a memory address **a** given by $a = d + $ **reg[r]**, where **a** must be a legal address ($0 \leq a <$ **DADDR_SIZE**). If **a** is out of the legal range, then **DMEM_ERR** is generated during execution.

RM instructions include three different load instructions corresponding to the three addressing modes "load constant" (**LDC**), "load address" (**LDA**), and "load memory" (**LD**). In addition, there is one store instruction and six conditional jump instructions.

In both RO and RM instructions, all three operands must be present, even though some of them may be ignored. This is due to the simple nature of the loader, which only distinguishes the two classes of instructions (RO and RM) and does not allow different instruction formats within each class.[17]

Figure 8.15 and the discussion of the TM up to this point represent the complete TM architecture. In particular, there is no hardware stack or other facilities of any kind. No register except for the pc is special in any way (there is no sp or fp). A compiler for the TM must, therefore, maintain any runtime environment organization entirely manually. While this may be somewhat unrealistic, it has the advantage that all operations must be generated explicitly as they are needed.

Since the instruction set is minimal, some comments are in order about how they can be used to achieve almost all standard programming language operations (indeed, this machine is an adequate if not comfortable target for even fairly sophisticated languages).

1. The target register in the arithmetic, **IN**, and load operations comes first, and the source register(s) come second, similar to the 80×86 and unlike the Sun SparcStation. There is no restriction on the use of registers for sources and target; in particular, the source and target registers may be the same.

2. All arithmetic operations are restricted to registers. No operations (except load and store operations) act directly on memory. In this, the TM resembles RISC machines such as the Sun SparcStation. On the other hand, the TM has only 8 registers, while most RISC processors have at least 32.[18]

3. There are no floating-point operations or floating-point registers. While it would not be too difficult to add a coprocessor to the TM with floating-point operations and registers, the translation of floating-point values to and from regular registers and memory would require some care. We refer the reader to the exercises.

4. There are no addressing modes specifiable in the operands as in some assembly code (such as **LD #1** for immediate mode, or **LD @a** for indirect). Instead, there are different instructions for each mode: **LD** is indirect, **LDA** is direct, and **LDC** is immediate. Indeed, the TM has very few addressing choices.

5. There is no restriction on the use of the pc in any of the instructions. Indeed, since there is no unconditional jump instruction, it must be simulated by using the pc as the target register in an **LDA** instruction:

```
LDA 7, d(s)
```

This instruction has the effect of jumping to location $a = d + \text{reg}[s]$.

---

17. It also makes the job of a code generator easier, since only two separate routines will be needed for the two classes of instructions.

18. While it would be easy to increase the number of TM registers, we do not do so here, since there is no need for them in basic code generation. See the exercises at the end of the chapter.

6. There is also no indirect jump instruction, but it too can be imitated, if necessary, by using an **LD** instruction. For example,

    LD 7,0(1)

    jumps to the instruction whose address is stored in memory at the location pointed to by register 1.
7. The conditional jump instructions (**JLT**, etc.) can be made relative to the current position in the program by using the pc as the second register. For example,

    JEQ 0,4(7)

    causes the TM to jump five instructions forward in the code if register 0 is 0. An unconditional jump can also be made relative to the pc by using the pc twice in an **LDA** instruction. Thus,

    LDA 7, -4(7)

    performs an unconditional jump three instructions backward.
8. There is no procedure call or **JSUB** instruction. Instead, we must write

    LD 7,d(s)

    which has the effect of jumping to the procedure whose entry address is **dMem[d+reg[s]]**. Of course, we should remember to save the return address first by executing something like

    LDA 0,1(7)

    which places the current pc value plus one into **reg[0]** (which is where we want to return to, assuming the next instruction is the actual jump to the procedure).

8.7.2 The TM Simulator

The machine simulator accepts text files containing TM instructions as described above, with the following conventions:

1. An entirely blank line is ignored.
2. A line beginning with an asterisk is considered a comment and is ignored.
3. Any other line must contain an integer instruction location followed by a colon followed by a legal instruction. Any text occurring after the instruction is considered a comment and is ignored.

The TM simulator contains no other features—in particular there are no symbolic labels and no macro facilities. A handwritten sample TM program corresponding to the TINY program of Figure 8.1 is given in Figure 8.16.

Strictly speaking, there is no need for the **HALT** instruction at the end of the code of Figure 8.16, since the TM simulator sets all instruction locations to **HALT** before loading the program. However, it is useful to keep it as a reminder—and as a target for jumps that wish to exit the program.

Figure 8.16

A TM program showing
format conventions

```
* This program inputs an integer, computes
* its factorial if it is positive,
* and prints the result

0:      IN    0,0,0       r0 = read
1:      JLE   0,6(7)      if 0 < r0 then
2:      LDC   1,1,0         r1 = 1
3:      LDC   2,1,0         r2 = 1
                         * repeat
4:      MUL  1,1,0           r1 = r1 * r0
5:      SUB  0,0,2           r0 = r0 - r2
6:      JNE   0,-3(7)        until r0 == 0
7:      OUT  1,0,0           write r1
8:      HALT 0,0,0       halt
* end of program
```

Also, there is no need for locations to appear in ascending sequence as they do in
Figure 8.16. Each input line is effectively a directive "store this instruction at this location": if a TM program were punched on cards, it would be perfectly all right to drop
them on the floor before reading them into the TM. This property of the TM simulator,
while possibly causing some confusion to the reader of a program, makes it easy to
backpatch jumps in the absence of symbolic labels, since code can be backpatched
without backing up in the code file. For example, a code generator is likely to generate
the code of Figure 8.16 in the following sequence:

```
0:      IN    0,0,0
2:      LDC   1,1,0
3:      LDC   2,1,0
4:      MUL   1,1,0
5:      SUB   0,0,2
6:      JNE   0,-3(7)
7:      OUT   1,0,0
1:      JLE   0,6(7)
8:      HALT 0,0,0
```

This is because the forward jump at instruction 1 cannot be generated until the location
after the body of the if-statement is known.

If the program of Figure 8.16 is in the file **fact.tm**, then this file can be loaded
and executed as in the following sample session (the TM simulator automatically
assumes a file extension **.tm** if one is not given):

```
tm fact
TM simulation (enter h for help) ...
Enter command: g
Enter value for IN instruction: 7
OUT instruction prints: 5040
```

```
HALT: 0,0,0
Halted
Enter command: q
Simulation done.
```

The **g** command stands for "go," meaning that the program is executed starting at the current contents of the pc (which is 0 just after loading), until a **HALT** instruction is seen. The complete list of simulator commands can be obtained by using the **h** command, which prints the following list:

```
Commands are:
    s(tep <n>      Execute n (default 1) TM instructions
    g(o            Execute TM instructions until HALT
    r(egs          Print the contents of the registers
    i(Mem <b <n>>  Print n iMem locations starting at b
    d(Mem <b <n>>  Print n dMem locations starting at b
    t(race         Toggle instruction trace
    p(rint         Toggle print of total instructions executed
                   ('go' only)
    c(lear         Reset simulator for new execution of program
    h(elp          Cause this list of commands to be printed
    q(uit          Terminate the simulation
```

The left parenthesis in each command indicates the mnemonic from which the letter command was derived (using more than one letter is also accepted, but the simulator only examines the first letter). The angle brackets **< >** indicate optional parameters.

8.8 A CODE GENERATOR FOR THE TINY LANGUAGE

We now wish to describe a code generator for the TINY language. We assume that the reader is familiar with the previous steps of the TINY compiler, particularly the syntax tree structure generated by the parser as described in Chapter 3, the symbol table construction as described in Chapter 6, and the runtime environment as described in Chapter 7.

In this section, we first describe the interface of the TINY code generator to the TM, together with the utility functions necessary for code generation. Then, we describe the steps of the code generator proper. Third, we describe the use of the TINY compiler in combination with the TM simulator. Finally, we discuss the target code file for the sample TINY program used throughout the book.

8.8.1 The TM Interface of the TINY Code Generator

We encapsulate some of the information the code generator needs to know about the TM in files **code.h** and **code.c**, which are listed in Appendix B, lines 1600–1685 and 1700–1796, respectively. We also put the code emitting functions in these files. Of course, the code generator will still need to know the TM instruction names, but these files do separate out the details of instruction formatting, the location of the target code file, and the use of particular registers in the runtime environment. Importantly, the **code.c** file completely encapsulates the sequencing of instructions into particular **iMem** locations, so that the code generator does not have to keep track of this detail. If the TM loader were to be improved, say, to allow symbolic labels and to remove the need for location numbers, then it would be easy to incorporate the label generation and format changes into the **code.c** file.

We review here some of the features of the constant and function definitions in the **code.h** file. First, consider the declarations of register values (lines 1612, 1617, 1623, 1626, and 1629). Clearly, the pc must be known to the code generator and code emitting utilities. Beyond this, the runtime environment for the TINY language, as described in the previous chapter, assigns locations at the top of data memory to temporaries (in a stack-based fashion) and locations at the bottom of data memory to variables. Since there are no activation records (and thus no fp) in TINY (because there are no scopes or procedure calls), the locations for variables and temporaries can be viewed as absolute addresses. However, the **LD** operation of the TM machine allows no absolute addressing mode, but must have a register base value in its computation of the address for a memory load. Thus, we assign two registers, which we call the mp (memory pointer) and gp (global pointer), to point to the top of memory and the bottom of memory, respectively. The mp will be used for memory access to temporaries and will always contain the highest legal memory location, while the gp will be used for all named variable memory accesses and will always contain 0, so that the absolute addresses computed by the symbol table can be used as offsets relative to the gp. For example, if a program has two variables **x** and **y**, and there are two temporary values currently stored in memory, then **dMem** would look as follows:

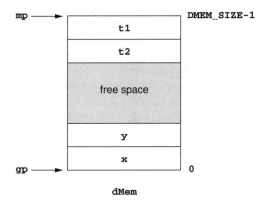

In this picture **t1** has address **0(mp)**, **t2** has address **-1(mp)**, **x** has address **0(gp)**, and **y** has address **1(gp)**. In this implementation, gp is register 5, and mp is register 6.

The other two registers that will be used by the code generator are registers 0 and 1, which are called "accumulators" and given the names ac and ac1. These will be used as scratch registers. In particular, the results of computations will always be left in the ac. Note that registers 2, 3, and 4 are not given names (and will never be used!).

We turn now to a discussion of the seven code emitting functions whose prototypes are given in the **code.h** file. The **emitComment** function prints its parameter string in the format of a comment on a separate line in the code file, if the **TraceCode** flag is set. The next two functions **emitRO** and **emitRM** are the standard code emitting functions that are used for the RO and RM classes of instructions, respectively. In addition to the instruction string and three operands, each function takes an additional string parameter, which is appended to the instruction as a comment (if the **TraceCode** flag is set).

The next three functions are used to generate and backpatch jumps. The **emitSkip** function is used to skip a number of locations that will later be backpatched, as well as to return the current instruction location, which is kept internally within **code.c**. Typically this is used only in the calls **emitSkip(1)**, which skips a single location that will be later filled with a jump instruction, and **emitSkip(0)**, which skips no locations, but is called simply to get the current instruction location to save for later reference in a backwards jump. The function **emitBackup** is used to set the current instruction location to a previous location for backpatching, and **emitRestore** is used to return the current instruction location to the value prior to a call to **emitBackup**. Typically, these instructions are used together as

```
emitBackup(savedLoc) ;
/* generate backpatched jump instruction here */
emitRestore() ;
```

The final code emitting function (**emitRM_Abs**) is needed to generate the code for such a backpatched jump or any jump to a code location returned by a call to **emitSkip**. It turns an absolute code address into a pc-relative address by subtracting the current instruction location plus 1 (which is what the pc will be during execution) from the passed location parameter, and by using the pc as the source register. Generally, this function will only be used with a conditional jump instruction such as **JEQ** or to generate an unconditional jump using **LDA** and the pc as target register, as described in the previous subsection.

This completes the description of the TINY code generation utilities, and we move on to a description of the TINY code generator itself.

8.8.2 The TINY Code Generator

The TINY code generator is contained in the file **cgen.c**, with its only interface to the TINY compiler the function **codeGen**, with prototype

```
void codeGen(void);
```

given as the only declaration in its interface file **cgen.h**. A complete listing of the **cgen.c** file is given in Appendix B, lines 1900–2111.

The **codeGen** function itself (lines 2095–2111) does very little: it generates a few comments and instructions (called the **standard prelude**) that set up the runtime environment on startup, then calls the **cGen** function on the syntax tree, and finally generates a **HALT** instruction to end the program. The standard prelude consists of two instructions: the first loads the mp register with the highest legal memory location (which the TM simulator has placed at location 0 on start-up), and the second clears location 0. (The gp does not need to be set to 0, since all registers are set to 0 on start-up.)

The **cGen** function (lines 2070–2084) is responsible for accomplishing the traversal of the TINY syntax tree that generates code in modified postorder, as described in previous sections. Recall that a TINY syntax tree has a form given by the declarations

```
typedef enum {StmtK,ExpK} NodeKind;
typedef enum {IfK,RepeatK,AssignK,ReadK,WriteK} StmtKind;
typedef enum {OpK,ConstK,IdK} ExpKind;

#define MAXCHILDREN 3
typedef struct treeNode
   { struct treeNode * child[MAXCHILDREN];
     struct treeNode * sibling;
     int lineno;
     NodeKind nodekind;
     union { StmtKind stmt; ExpKind exp;} kind;
     union { TokenType op;
             int val;
             char * name; } attr;
     ExpType type;
   } TreeNode;
```

There are two kinds of tree nodes: statement nodes and expression nodes. If a node is a statement node, then it represents one of the five different kinds of TINY statements (if, repeat, assign, read, or write), and if a node is an expression node, then it represents one of the three kinds of expressions (an identifier, an integer constant, or an operator). The **cGen** function tests only whether a node is a statement or expression node (or null), calling the appropriate function **genStmt** or **genExp**, and then calling itself recursively on siblings (so that sibling lists will have code generated in left to right order).

The **genStmt** function (lines 1924–1994) contains a large **switch** statement that distinguishes among the five kinds of statements, generating appropriate code and recursive calls to **cGen** in each case, and similarly for the **genExp** function (lines 1997–2065). In all cases, the code for a subexpression is assumed to leave a value in the ac, where it can be accessed by subsequent code. In cases where a variable access is needed (assignment and read statements and identifier expressions), the symbol table is accessed via the operation

```
loc = lookup(tree->attr.name);
```

The value of **loc** is the address of the variable in question and is used as the offset with the gp register to load or store its value.

The other case in which memory accesses are necessary is in the computation of the result of an operator expression, where the left-hand operand must be stored to a temporary before the right-hand operand is computed. Thus, the code for an operator expression includes the following code generation sequence before the operator can be applied (lines 2021–2027):

```
cGen(p1); /* p1 = left child */
emitRM("ST",ac,tmpOffset--,mp,"op: push left");
cGen(p2); /* p2 = right child */
emitRM("LD",ac1,++tmpOffset,mp,"op: load left");
```

Here **tmpOffset** is a static variable that is initialized to 0 and used as the offset of the next available temporary location from the top of memory (which is pointed to by the mp register). Note how **tmpOffset** is decremented after each store and incremented after each load. Thus, **tmpOffset** can be viewed as a pointer to the top of the "temporary stack," and the calls to the **emitRM** function correspond to a push and pop of this stack. This protects each temporary while it is held in memory. After the code generated by the above actions is executed, the left-hand operand will be in register 1 (ac1) and the right-hand operand in register 0 (ac). The appropriate RO operation can then be generated, in the case of the arithmetic operations.

The case of the comparison operators is slightly different. The semantics of the TINY language (as implemented by the semantic analyzer—see the previous chapter) allow comparison operators only in the test expressions of if-statements and while-statements. There are no Boolean variables or values other than in such tests, and comparison operators could be dealt with in the code generation of those statements. Nevertheless, we use a more general approach here, which is more widely applicable to languages with logical operations and/or Boolean values, and implement the result of a test as a 0 (for false) or 1 (for true), as in C. This requires that the constant 0 or 1 be explicitly loaded into the ac, and we accomplish this by using jumps to execute the correct load. For example, in the case of the less than operator, the following code is generated, once code has been generated to compute the left-hand operand into register 1 and the right-hand operand into register 0:

```
SUB   0,1,0
JLT   0,2(7)
LDC   0,0(0)
LDA   7,1(7)
LDC   0,1(0)
```

The first instruction subtracts the right operand from the left, leaving the result in register 0. If $<$ is true, this result will be negative, and the instruction **JLT 0,2(7)** will cause a jump over two instructions to the last instruction, which loads the value 1 into the ac. If $<$ is false, then the third and fourth instructions are executed, which load 0 into the ac and then jump over the last instruction (recall from the description of the TM that **LDA** using the pc as both registers causes an unconditional jump).

We finish the description of the TINY code generator with a discussion of the if-statement (lines 1930–1954). The remaining cases are left to the reader.

The first action of the code generator for an if-statement is to generate code for the test expression. The code for the test, as just described, leaves 0 in the ac in the false case and 1 in the true case. The code generator must next generate a **JEQ** to the code for the else-part of the if-statement. However, the location of this code is not yet known, since the code for then-part must still be generated. Hence, the code generator uses the **emitSkip** utility to skip the next statement and save its location for later back-patching:

```
savedLoc1 = emitSkip(1) ;
```

Code generation continues with the generation of code for the then-part of the if-statement. After that, an unconditional jump over the else-part code must be generated, but again that location is not known, so the location of this jump must also be skipped and its location saved:

```
savedLoc2 = emitSkip(1) ;
```

Now, however, the next step is to generate code for the else-part, so the current code location is the correct target for the false-case jump, which must now be backpatched to location **savedLoc1**, which the following code does:

```
currentLoc = emitSkip(0) ;
emitBackup(savedLoc1) ;
emitRM_Abs("JEQ",ac,currentLoc,"if: jmp to else");
emitRestore() ;
```

Note how the call **emitSkip(0)** is used to fetch the current instruction location, and how the **emitRM_Abs** procedure is used to convert the jump to this absolute location into a pc-relative jump, which is needed by the **JEQ** instruction. After this, code can be finally generated for the else-part, and then an absolute jump (**LDA**) backpatched to **savedLoc2** by a similar code sequence.

8.8.3 Generating and Using TM Code Files with the TINY Compiler

The TINY code generator is tuned to work seamlessly with the TM simulator. When the flags **NO_PARSE**, **NO_ANALYZE**, and **NO_CODE** are all set to false in the main program, the compiler creates a code file with the suffix **.tm** (assuming there are no errors in the source code) and writes the TM instructions to this file in the required TM simulator format. For example, to compile and execute the **sample.tny** program, one need only issue the following commands:

```
tiny sample
<listing produced on the standard output>
tm sample
<execution of the tm simulator>
```

For tracing purposes, there is a **TraceCode** flag declared in **globals.h** and defined in **main.c**. If it is set to **TRUE**, tracing information is generated by the code generator, which appears as comments in the code file, indicating where in the code generator each instruction or sequence of instructions was generated, and for what reason.

8.8.4 A Sample TM Code File Generated by the TINY Compiler

To show in greater detail how the code generator works, we present in Figure 8.17 the code file by the TINY code generator for the sample program of Figure 8.1, with **TraceCode = TRUE** so that code comments are also generated. This code file has 42 instructions, including the two instructions from the standard prelude. Comparing this to the nine instructions of the handwritten program of Figure 8.16, we can certainly see a number of inefficiencies. In particular, the program of Figure 8.16 uses the registers very efficiently—no memory at all is used other than the registers. The code of Figure 8.17 (pages 466–467), on the other hand, never uses more than two registers and performs many stores and loads that are unnecessary. Particularly stupid is the way it treats variable values, which are loaded, only to be stored again as temporaries, as in the code

```
16:    LD   0,1(5) load id value
17:    ST   0,0(6) op: push left
18:    LD   0,0(5) load id value
19:    LD   1,0(6) op: load left
```

which can be replaced by the two instructions

```
LD   1,1(5) load id value
LD   0,0(5) load id value
```

that have exactly the same effect.

Further substantial inefficiencies are incurred by the code generated for the tests and jumps. A particularly silly example is the instruction

```
40:    LDA 7,0(7) jmp to end
```

which is an elaborate **NOP** (a "no operation" instruction).

Nevertheless, the code of Figure 8.17 has one important property: it is correct. In the rush to improve the efficiency of generated code, compiler writers sometimes forget the need for this property and allow code to be generated that, while efficient, does not always execute correctly. Such behavior, if not well documented and predictable (and sometimes even then), can lead to disaster.

While it is beyond the scope of this text to study all the ways that the code produced by a compiler can be improved, in the final two sections of this chapter we will survey the major areas in which such improvements can be made, as well as the techniques that can be used to implement them, and briefly describe how some of them can be applied to the TINY code generator to improve the code it generates.

Figure 8.17
TM code output for the
TINY sample program of
Figure 8.1 (page 401)

```
* TINY Compilation to TM Code
* File: sample.tm
* Standard prelude:
  0:      LD 6,0(0)      load maxaddress from location 0
  1:      ST 0,0(0)      clear location 0
* End of standard prelude.
  2:      IN 0,0,0       read integer value
  3:      ST 0,0(5)      read: store value
* -> if
* -> Op
* -> Const
  4:      LDC 0,0(0)     load const
* <- Const
  5:      ST 0,0(6)      op: push left
* -> Id
  6:      LD 0,0(5)      load id value
* <- Id
  7:      LD 1,0(6)      op: load left
  8:      SUB 0,1,0      op <
  9:      JLT 0,2(7)     br if true
  10:     LDC 0,0(0)     false case
  11:     LDA 7,1(7)     unconditional jmp
  12:     LDC 0,1(0)     true case
* <- Op
* if: jump to else belongs here
* -> assign
* -> Const
  14:     LDC 0,1(0)     load const
* <- Const
  15:     ST 0,1(5)      assign: store value
* <- assign
* -> repeat
* repeat: jump after body comes back here
* -> assign
* -> Op
* -> Id
  16:     LD 0,1(5)      load id value
* <- Id
  17:     ST 0,0(6)      op: push left
* -> Id
  18:     LD 0,0(5)      load id value
* <- Id
  19:     LD 1,0(6)      op: load left
  20:     MUL 0,1,0      op *
```

Figure 8.17   continued

```
* <- Op
  21:         ST  0,1(5)      assign: store value
* <- assign
* -> assign
* -> Op
* -> Id
  22:         LD  0,0(5)      load id value
* <- Id
  23:         ST  0,0(6)      op: push left
* -> Const
  24:         LDC 0,1(0)      load const
* <- Const
  25:         LD  1,0(6)      op: load left
  26:         SUB 0,1,0       op -
* <- Op
  27:         ST  0,0(5)      assign: store value
* <- assign
* -> Op
* -> Id
  28:         LD  0,0(5)      load id value
* <- Id
  29:         ST  0,0(6)      op: push left
* -> Const
  30:         LDC 0,0(0)      load const
* <- Const
  31:         LD  1,0(6)      op: load left
  32:         SUB 0,1,0       op ==
  33:         JEQ 0,2(7)      br if true
  34:         LDC 0,0(0)      false case
  35:         LDA 7,1(7)      unconditional jmp
  36:         LDC 0,1(0)      true case
* <- Op
  37:         JEQ 0,-22(7)    repeat: jmp back to body
* <- repeat
* -> Id
  38:         LD  0,1(5)      load id value
* <- Id
  39:         OUT 0,0,0       write ac
* if: jump to end belongs here
  13:         JEQ 0,27(7)     if: jmp to else
  40:         LDA 7,0(7)      jmp to end
* <- if
* End of execution.
  41:         HALT 0,0,0
```

8.9 A SURVEY OF CODE OPTIMIZATION TECHNIQUES

Ever since the first compilers of the 1950s, the quality of the code generated by a compiler has been of major importance. This quality can be measured both by the speed and the size of the target code, although speed has generally been more important. Modern compilers address the problem of code quality by performing, at several points in the compilation process, a series of steps that include gathering information about the source code and then using this information to perform **code improving transformations** on the data structures representing the code. A great number and variety of techniques to improve code quality have been developed over the years, and these have come to be known as **code optimization techniques**. This terminology is misleading, however, since only in very special situations are any of these techniques capable of producing optimal code in the mathematical sense. Nevertheless, the name is so common that we will continue to use it.

Such a multitude and variety of code optimization techniques exist that we can only give a small glimpse here into the most important and most widely used of them, and even for these, we will not give the details of how to implement them. References are given at the end of the chapter to sources of more information about them. It is important to realize, however, that a compiler writer cannot hope to include every single optimization technique that has ever been developed, but must judge, for the language in question, which techniques are most likely to result in a significant code improvement with the smallest increase in the complexity of the compiler. Many papers have been written describing optimization techniques that require extremely complex implementations, while producing on average only relatively small improvements in the target code (say, a decrease in running time of a few percent). Experience has generally shown, however, that a few basic techniques, even when applied in what appears to be a very simple-minded way, can lead to the most significant improvements, sometimes even cutting execution time in half or more.

In judging whether the implementation of a particular optimization technique would be too complex relative to its payoff in actual code improvement, it is important to determine not only the complexity of the implementation in terms of data structures and extra compiler code, but also the effect the optimization step may have on the execution speed of the compiler itself. All the parsing and analysis techniques that we have studied have been aimed at a linear running time for the compiler—that is, the compilation speed is directly proportional to the size of the program being compiled. Many optimization techniques can increase the compilation time to a quadratic or cubic function of program size, so that the compilation of a sizable program can take minutes (or in worst cases hours) longer with full optimization. This can result in users avoiding the use of the optimizations (or avoiding the compiler altogether), and the time taken to implement the optimizations has been largely wasted.

In the following sections we will first describe the principal sources of optimizations and then describe various classifications of optimizations, followed by a brief survey of some of the important techniques together with the principal data structures used to implement them. Throughout, we will give simple examples of optimizations to illustrate the discussion. In the next section, we will give more detailed examples of how some of the discussed techniques can apply to the TINY code generator of the previous section, with suggestions for implementation methods.

8.9.1 Principal Sources of Code Optimizations

In the following, we list some of the areas in which a code generator may fail to produce good code, roughly in decreasing order of "payoff"—that is, how much code improvement can be achieved in each area.

Register Allocation   Good use of registers is the most important feature of efficient code. Historically, the number of available registers was severely limited—usually to 8 or 16 registers, including special-purpose registers like the pc, sp, and fp. This made good register allocation difficult, since competition for register space among variables and temporaries was intense. This situation still exists in some processors, particularly microprocessors. One approach to solving this problem has been to increase the number and speed of operations that can be performed directly in memory, so that a compiler, once it has exhausted the register space, can avoid the expense of having to reclaim registers by storing register values into temporary locations and loading new values (so-called **register spill** operations). Another approach (the so-called RISC approach) has been to *decrease* the number of operations that can be performed directly in memory (often to zero), but at the same time to increase the number of available registers to 32, 64, or 128. In such architectures proper register allocation becomes even more critical, since it should be possible to keep all, or almost all, simple variables in an entire program in registers. The penalty for failing to allocate registers properly in such architectures is increased by the need to constantly load and store values so that operations can be applied to them. At the same time, the job of allocating registers becomes easier, since so many are available. Thus, good register allocation must be the focus of any serious effort to improve code quality.

Unnecessary Operations   The second major source of code improvement is to avoid generating code for operations that are redundant or unnecessary. This kind of optimization can vary from a very simple search of localized code to complex analysis of the semantic properties of the entire program. The number of possibilities for identifying such operations is large, and there is a corresponding large number of techniques used for doing so. A typical example of such an optimization opportunity is an expression that appears repeatedly in the code, and whose value remains the same. Repeated evaluation can be eliminated by saving the first value for later use (so-called **common subexpression elimination**).[19] A second example is to avoid storing the value of a variable or temporary that is not subsequently used (this goes hand in hand with the previous optimization).

A whole class of optimization opportunities involves the identification of **unreachable** or **dead code**. A typical example of unreachable code is the use of a constant flag to turn debugging information on and off:

---

19. While a good programmer can avoid common expressions to a certain extent in the source code, the reader should not assume that this optimization exists only to help bad programmers. Many common subexpressions result from address calculations that are generated by the compiler itself and cannot be removed by writing better source code.

```
#define DEBUG 0
...
if (DEBUG)
{...}
```

If **DEBUG** is set to 0 (as in this code), then the bracketed code inside the if-statement is unreachable, and target code need not be generated for either it or the enclosing if-statement. Another example of unreachable code is a procedure that is never called (or is only called from code that is itself unreachable). The elimination of unreachable code does not usually affect execution speed significantly, but it can substantially reduce the size of the target code, and is worthwhile, particularly if only a small extra effort in analysis is used to identify the most obvious cases.

Sometimes in identifying unnecessary operations it is easier to proceed with code generation and then test the target code for redundancy. One case in which it is sometimes more difficult to test in advance for redundancy is in the generation of jumps to represent structured control statements. Such code can include jumps to the very next statement or jumps to jumps. A **jump optimization** step can remove these unnecessary jumps.

Costly Operations   A code generator should not only look for unnecessary operations, but should take advantage of opportunities to reduce the cost of operations that are necessary, but may be implemented in cheaper ways than the source code or a simple implementation might indicate. A typical example of this is the replacement of arithmetic operations by cheaper operations. For instance, multiplication by 2 can be implemented as a shift operation, and a small integer power, such as x^3, can be implemented as a multiplication, such as $x* x* x$. This optimization is called **reduction in strength**. This can be extended in various ways, such as replacing multiplications involving small integer constants by shifts and additions (e.g., replacing $5 * x$ by $2 * 2 * x + x$—two shifts and an addition).

A related optimization is to use information about constants to remove as many operations as possible or to precompute as many operations as possible. For example, the sum of two constants, such as $2 + 3$, can be computed by the compiler and replaced by the constant value 5 (this is called **constant folding**). Sometimes it is worthwhile trying to determine if a variable might also have a constant value for part or all of a program, and such transformations can then also apply to expressions involving that variable (this is called **constant propagation**).

One operation that can sometimes be relatively expensive is procedure call, where many calling sequence operations must be performed. Modern processors have reduced this cost substantially by offering hardware support for standard calling sequences, but the removal of frequent calls to small procedures can still produce measurable speedups. There are two standard ways to remove procedure calls. One is to replace the procedure call with the code for the procedure body (with suitable replacement of parameters by arguments). This is called **procedure inlining**, and sometimes is even a language option (as in C++). Another way to eliminate procedure call is to recognize **tail recursion**, that is, when the last operation of a procedure is to call itself. For example, the procedure

```
int gcd( int u, int v)
{ if (v==0) return u;
  else return gcd(v,u % v); }
```

is tail recursive, but the procedure

```
int fact( int n )
{ if (n==0) return 1;
  else return n * fact(n-1); }
```

is not. Tail recursion is equivalent to assigning the values of the new arguments to the parameters and performing a jump to the beginning of the body of the procedure. For example the tail-recursive procedure **gcd** can be rewritten by the compiler to the equivalent code

```
int gcd( int u, int v)
{ begin:
  if (v==0) return u;
  else
  { int t1 = v, t2 = u%v;
    u = t1; v = t2;
    goto begin;
  }
}
```

(Note the subtle need for temporaries in this code.) This process is called **tail recursion removal**.

One issue regarding procedure call relates to register allocation. Provision must be made at each procedure call to save and restore registers that remain in use across the call. If strong register allocation is provided, this can increase the cost of procedure calls, since proportionally more registers will need saving and restoring. Sometimes including call considerations into the register allocator can reduce this cost. Hardware support for calls with many registers in use can also reduce the cost.[20] But this is a case of a common phenomenon: sometimes optimizations can cause the reverse of the desired effect, and trade-offs must be made.

During final code generation, some last opportunities for reducing the cost of certain operations may be found by making use of special instructions available on the target machine. For example, many architectures include block move operations that are faster than copying individual elements of strings or arrays. Also, address calculations can sometimes be optimized when the architecture allows several addressing modes or offset computations to be combined into a single instruction. Similarly, there are sometimes autoincrement and autodecrement modes for use in indexing (the VAX architecture even has an increment-compare-and-branch instruction for loops). Such optimizations come under the heading **instruction selection** or **use of machine idioms**.

---

20. Register windows on the Sun SparcStation represent an example of hardware support for register allocation across procedure calls. See page 453.

Predicting Program Behavior   To perform some of the previously described optimizations, a compiler must collect information about the uses of variables, values, and procedures in programs: whether expressions are reused (and so become common subexpressions), whether or when variables change their values or remain constant, and whether procedures are called or not. A compiler must, within the reach of its computation techniques, make worst case assumptions about the information it collects or risk generating incorrect code: if a variable may or may not be constant at a particular point, the compiler must assume that it is not constant. This property is called **conservative estimation** of program information. It means that a compiler must make do with less than perfect, and often even crudely weak, information about program behavior. Naturally, the more sophisticated the analysis of the program becomes, the better the information that a code optimizer can use. Nevertheless, even in the most advanced compilers today, there may be provable properties of programs that are not discovered by the compiler.

A different approach is taken by some compilers in that statistical behavior about a program is gathered from actual executions and then used to predict which paths are most likely to be taken, which procedures are most likely to be called often, and which sections of code are likely to be executed the most frequently. This information can then be used to adjust jump structure, loops, and procedure code to minimize execution speed for the most commonly occurring executions. This process requires, of course, that such a **profiling compiler** have access to the appropriate data and that (at least some of) the executable code contain instrumentation code to generate this data.

8.9.2   Classification of Optimizations

Since there are so many optimization opportunities and techniques, it is worthwhile to reduce the complexity of their study by adopting various classification schemes to emphasize different qualities of the optimizations. Two useful classifications are the time during the compilation process when an optimization can be applied and the area of the program over which the optimization applies.

We consider, first, the time of application during compilation. Optimizations can be performed at practically every stage of compilation. For example, constant folding can be performed as early as during parsing (though it is usually delayed, so that the compiler can retain a representation of the source code exactly as it was written). On the other hand, some optimizations can be delayed until after target code has been generated—the target code is examined and rewritten to reflect the optimization. For example, jump optimizations could be performed in this way. (Sometimes optimizations performed on the target code are called **peephole optimizations**, since the compiler generally looks at small sections of target code to discover these optimizations.)

Typically, the majority of optimizations are performed either during intermediate code generation, just after intermediate code generation, or during target code generation. To the extent that an optimization does not depend on the characteristics of the target machine (called **source-level optimizations**), they can be performed earlier than those that do depend on the target architecture (**target-level optimizations**). Sometimes an optimization can have both a source-level component and a target-level component. For example, in register allocation, it is common to count the number of references to each variable and prefer those variables with higher reference counts for assignment to registers. This task can be divided into a source-level component, in which variables are selected to be allocated in registers without specific knowledge of how many registers are available. Then, a later **register assignment** step that is target machine dependent assigns actual registers to those variables tagged as register allocated, or to memory locations called **pseudoregisters**, if no registers are available.

In ordering the various optimizations, it is important to consider the effect that one optimization may have on another. For instance, it makes sense to propagate constants before performing unreachable code elimination, since some code may become unreachable based on the fact that test variables have been found to be constant. Occasionally, a **phase problem** may arise in that each of two optimizations may uncover further opportunities for the other. For example, consider the code

```
x = 1;
...
y = 0;
...
if (y) x = 0;
...
if (x) y = 1;
```

A first pass at constant propagation might result in the code

```
x = 1;
...
y = 0;
...
if (0) x = 0;
...
if (x) y = 1;
```

Now, the body of the first **if** is unreachable code; eliminating it yields

```
x = 1;
...
y = 0;
...
if (x) y = 1;
```

which now can benefit from a further constant propagation step and unreachable code elimination. For this reason, some compilers perform several iterations of a group of optimizations, to make sure that most opportunities for applying the optimizations have been found.

The second classification scheme for optimizations that we consider is by the area of the program over which the optimization applies. The categories for this classification are called **local**, **global**, and **interprocedural** optimizations. Local optimizations are defined to be those optimizations that are applied to **straight-line segments of**

code, that is, code sequences with no jumps into or out of the sequence.[21] A maximal sequence of straight-line code is called a **basic block**, and by definition the local optimizations are those that are restricted to basic blocks. Optimizations that extend beyond basic blocks, but are confined to an individual procedure, are called **global optimizations** (even though they are not truly "global," since they are confined to a procedure). Optimizations that extend beyond the boundaries of procedures to the entire program are called **interprocedural optimizations**.

Local optimizations are relatively easy to perform, since the straight-line nature of the code allows information to be propagated in simple ways down the code sequence. For example, a variable that was loaded into a register by a previous instruction in a basic block can be assumed to be still in that register at a later point in the block, provided the register was not the target of any intervening load. This conclusion would not be correct if a jump could be made into the intervening code, as the following diagram indicates:

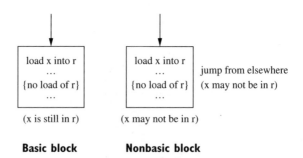

| Basic block | Nonbasic block |

Global optimizations, by contrast, are considerably more difficult to perform; they generally require a technique called **data flow analysis**, which attempts to collect information across jump boundaries. Interprocedural optimization is even more difficult, since it involves possibly several different parameter passing mechanisms, the possibility of nonlocal variable access, and the need to compute simultaneous information on all procedures that might call each other. An additional complication to interprocedural optimization is the possibility that many procedures may be compiled separately and only linked together at a later point. The compiler then cannot perform any interprocedural optimizations at all without the involvement of a specialized form of linker that carries out optimizations based on information that the compiler has gathered. For that reason, many compilers perform only the most basic interprocedural analysis, or none at all.

One special class of global optimizations is that applied to loops. Since loops are usually executed a large number of times, it is important to pay special attention to code inside loops, particularly with regard to reducing the complexity of the computations.

---

21. Procedure calls represent a special kind of jump, so normally they break straight-line code. However, since they always return to the immediate next instruction, they can often be included in straight-line code and treated later in the code generation process.

Typical loop optimization strategies focus on identifying variables that are incremented by fixed amounts with each iteration (so-called **induction variables**). These include loop control variables and other variables that depend on the loop control variables in fixed ways. Selected induction variables can be placed in registers, and their computation simplified. This code rewriting can include removing constant computations from the loop (so-called **code motion**). Indeed, rearranging code can also be helpful in improving the efficiency of code inside basic blocks.

Historically, an additional task in loop optimization has been the problem of actually identifying the loops in a program, so that they can be optimized. Such **loop discovery** was necessary because of the lack of structured control and the use of goto-statements to implement loops. Although loop discovery remains necessary in a few languages like FORTRAN, in most languages the syntax itself can be used to locate significant loop structures.

8.9.3 Data Structures and Implementation Techniques for Optimizations

Some optimizations can be made by transformations on the syntax tree itself. These can include constant folding and unreachable code elimination, where the appropriate subtrees are deleted or replaced by simpler ones. Information for use in later optimizations can also be gathered during the construction or traversal of the syntax tree, such as reference counts or other usage information, and kept either as attributes in the tree or entered into the symbol table.

For many of the optimizations mentioned earlier, however, the syntax tree is an unwieldy or unsuitable structure for collecting information and performing optimizations. Instead, an optimizer that performs global optimizations will construct from the intermediate code of each procedure a graphical representation of the code called a **flow graph**. The nodes of a flow graph are the basic blocks, and the edges are formed from the conditional and unconditional jumps (which must have as their targets the beginnings of other basic blocks). Each basic block node contains the sequence of intermediate code instructions of the block. As an example, the flow graph corresponding to the intermediate code of Figure 8.2 (page 401) is given in Figure 8.18 (page 476). (The basic blocks in this figure are labeled for future reference.)

A flow graph, together with each of its basic blocks, can be constructed by a single pass over the intermediate code. Each new basic block is identified as follows:[22]

1. The first instruction begins a new basic block.
2. Each label that is the target of a jump begins a new basic block.
3. Each instruction that follows a jump begins a new basic block.

For forward jumps to labels not yet reached, a new empty block node can be constructed and inserted into the symbol table under the label name, for later lookup when the label is reached.

---

22. These criteria allow procedure calls to be included inside basic blocks. Since calls do not contribute new paths to the flow graph, this is reasonable. Later, when basic blocks are processed individually, calls can be separated out for special processing if necessary.

Figure 8.18

The flow graph of the intermediate code of Figure 8.2

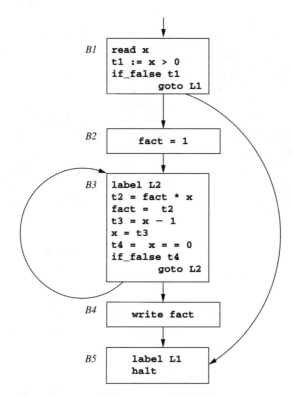

The flow graph is the major data structure needed by data flow analysis, which uses it to accumulate information to be used for optimizations. Different kinds of information may require different kinds of processing of the flow graph, and the information gathered can be quite varied, depending on the kinds of optimizations desired. While we do not have space in this brief overview to describe the technique of data flow analysis in detail (see the Notes and References section at the end of the chapter), it may be worthwhile to describe one example of the kind of data that can be accumulated by this process.

A standard data flow analysis problem is to compute, for each variable, the set of so-called **reaching definitions** of that variable at the beginning of each basic block. Here a **definition** is an intermediate code instruction that can set the value of the variable, such as an assignment or a read.[23] For example, the definitions of the variable **fact** in Figure 8.18 are the single instruction of basic block *B2* (**fact=1**) and the third instruction of block *B3* (**fact=t2**). Let us call these definitions *d1* and *d2*. A definition is said to **reach** a basic block if at the beginning of the block the variable can still have the value established by this definition. In the flow graph of Figure 8.18, it can be established that neither definition of **fact** reaches *B1* or *B2*, that both *d1* and *d2* reach *B3*, and that only *d2* reaches *B4* and *B5*. Reaching definitions can be used in a number of optimizations—in constant propagation, for example, if the only defini-

---

23. This is not to be confused with a C definition, which is a kind of declaration.

tions reaching a block represent a single constant value, then the variable can be replaced by this value (at least until another definition within the block is reached).

The flow graph is useful for representing global information about the code of each procedure, but the basic blocks are still represented as simple code sequences. Once data flow analysis is performed, and code for each basic block is to be generated, another data structure is frequently constructed for each block, called the **DAG of a basic block** (DAG = directed acyclic graph). (A DAG can be constructed for each basic block even without constructing the flow graph.)

A DAG data structure traces the computation and reassignment of values and variables in a basic block as follows. Values that are used in the block that come from elsewhere are represented as leaf nodes. Operations on those and other values are represented by interior nodes. Assignment of a new value is represented by attaching the name of the target variable or temporary to the node representing the value assigned. (A special case of this construction was described on page 416.)[24]

For example, the basic block *B3* in Figure 8.18 can be represented by the DAG of Figure 8.19. (Labels at the beginning of basic blocks and jumps at the end are usually not included in the DAG.) Note in this DAG that copy operations such as **fact=t2** and **x=t3** do not create new nodes, but simply add new labels to the nodes with labels **t2** and **t3**. Note, also, that the leaf node labeled **x** has two parents, resulting from the fact that the incoming value of **x** is used in two separate instructions. Thus, repeated use of the same value also is represented in the DAG structure. This property of a DAG allows it to represent repeated use of common subexpressions. For example, the C assignment

        x = (x+1)*(x+1)

translates into the three-address instructions

        t1 = x + 1
        t2 = x + 1
        t3 = t1 * t2
        x = t3

and the DAG for this sequence of instructions is given in Figure 8.20, showing the repeated use of the expression **x+1**.

Figure 8.19

The DAG of the basic block *B3* of Figure 8.18

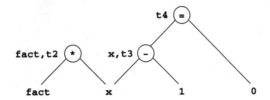

24. This description of the DAG structure is geared toward the use of three-address code as the intermediate code, but a similar DAG structure can be defined for P-code, or even for target assembly code.

Figure 8.20

The DAG of the three-address instructions corresponding to the C assignment

x = (x+1)*(x+1)

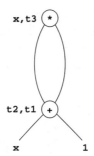

The DAG of a basic block can be constructed by maintaining two dictionaries. The first is a table containing variable names and constants, with a lookup operation that returns the DAG node to which a variable name is currently assigned (the symbol table could be used as this table). The second is a table of DAG nodes, with a lookup operation that, given an operation and child nodes, returns the node with that operation and children or nil if there is no such node. This operation allows the lookup of already existing values, without constructing a new node in the DAG. For example, once the **+** node in Figure 8.20 with children **x** and **1** is constructed and assigned the name **t1** (as a result of processing the three-address instruction **t1=x+1**), a lookup of (**+**, **x**, **1**) in the second table will return this already constructed node, and the three-address instruction **t2=x+1** simply causes **t2** to be also assigned to this node. The details of this construction can be found elsewhere (see the Notes and References section).

Target code, or a revised version of intermediate code, can be generated from a DAG by a traversal according to any of the possible topological sorts of the nonleaf nodes. (A **topological sort** of a DAG is a traversal such that the children of nodes are visited before all of their parents.) Since there are, in general, many topological sorts, it is possible to generate many different code sequences from a DAG. Which ones might be better than others depends on various factors, including details of the target machine architecture. For example, one of the legal traversal sequences of the three nonleaf nodes of Figure 8.19 would result in the following new sequence of three-address instructions, which could replace the original basic block:

```
t3 = x - 1
t2 = fact * x
x = t3
t4 = x == 0
fact = t2
```

Of course, we would probably wish to avoid the unnecessary use of temporaries, and so would want to generate the following equivalent three-address code, whose order must remain fixed:

```
fact = fact * x
x = x - 1
t4 = x == 0
```

A similar traversal of the DAG of Figure 8.20 results in the following revised three-address code:

```
t1 = x + 1
x = t1 * t1
```

Using a DAG to generate target code for a basic block, we automatically get local common subexpression elimination. The DAG representation also makes it possible to eliminate redundant stores (assignments) and tells us how many references to each value there are (the number of parents of a node is the number of references). This gives us information that permits good register allocation (e.g., if a value has many references, leave it in a register; if all references have been seen, the value is dead and need no longer be maintained; and so on).

A final method that is often used to assist register allocation as code generation proceeds involves the maintenance of data called **register descriptors** and **address descriptors**. Register descriptors associate with each register a list of the variable names whose value is currently in that register (of course, they must all have the same value at that point). Address descriptors associate with each variable name the locations in memory where its value is to be found. These could be registers (in which case, the variable is to be found in the corresponding register descriptor or descriptors) or memory or both (if the variable has just been loaded from memory into a register, but its value has not changed). Such descriptors allow the tracking of the movement of values between memory and registers and allow for the reuse of values already loaded into registers, as well as the reclamation of registers, either by discovering that they no longer contain the value of any variables with subsequent uses or by storing off of values to appropriate memory locations (spill operations).

Take, for example, the basic block DAG of Figure 8.19, and consider the generation of TM code according to a left-to-right traversal of the interior nodes, using the three registers 0, 1, and 2. Assume, also, that there are four address descriptors: **inReg(reg_no)**, **isGlobal(global_offset)**, **isTemp(temp_offset)**, and **isConst(value)** (this corresponds to the organization of the runtime environment of TINY on the TM machine, discussed in the previous section). Assume further that **x** is in global location 0, that **fact** is in global location 1, that global locations are accessed via the gp register, and that temporary locations are accessed via the mp register. Finally, assume also that none of the registers begin with any values in them. Then, before code generation for the basic block begins, the address descriptors for the variables and constants would be as follows:

Variable/Constant	Address Descriptors
fact	isGlobal(1)
x	isGlobal(0)
t2	-
t3	-
t4	-
1	isConst(1)
0	isConst(0)

The register descriptor table would be empty, and we do not print it.
Now assume that the following code is generated:

```
LD  0,1(gp)  load fact into reg 0
LD  1,0(gp)  load x into reg 1
MUL 0,0,1
```

The address descriptors would now be

Variable/Constant	Address Descriptors
fact	inReg(0)
x	isGlobal(0),inReg(1)
t2	inReg(0)
t3	-
t4	-
1	isConst(1)
0	isConst(0)

and the register descriptors would be

Register	Variables Contained
0	fact, t2
1	x
2	-

Now, given the subsequent code

```
LDC 2,1(0)  load constant 1 into reg 2
ADD 1,1,2
```

the address descriptors would become:

Variable/Constant	Address Descriptors
fact	inReg(0)
x	inReg(1)
t2	inReg(0)
t3	inReg(1)
t4	-
1	isConst(1),inReg(2)
0	isConst(0)

and the register descriptors would become:

Register	Variables/Constants
0	`fact, t2`
1	`x, t3`
2	`1`

We leave it to the reader to provide suitable code for the computation of the value at the remaining DAG node and describe the resulting address and register descriptors.

This concludes our brief tour of code optimization techniques.

8.10 SIMPLE OPTIMIZATIONS FOR THE TINY CODE GENERATOR

The code generator for the TINY language as given in Section 8.8 produces extremely inefficient code, as shown by a comparison of the 42 instructions of Figure 8.17 (page 466) to the nine hand-coded instructions of the equivalent program of Figure 8.16 (page 458). Primarily, the inefficiencies are due to two sources:

1. The TINY code generator makes very poor use of the registers of the TM machine (in fact, it never uses registers 2, 3, or 4 at all).
2. The TINY code generator unnecessarily generates logical values 0 and 1 for tests, when these tests only appear in if-statements and while-statements, where simpler code will do.

We wish to indicate in this section how even relatively crude techniques can substantially improve the code generated by the TINY compiler. Indeed, we do not generate either basic blocks or flow graphs, but continue to generate code directly from the syntax tree. The only machinery needed is an additional piece of attribute data and some slightly more complex compiler code. We do not give complete implementation details for the improvements described here, but leave them as exercises for the reader.

8.10.1 Keeping Temporaries in Registers

The first optimization we wish to describe is an easy method for keeping temporaries in registers rather than constantly storing and reloading them from memory. In the TINY code generator temporaries were always stored at the location

    `tmpOffset(mp)`

where **`tmpOffset`** is a static variable initialized to 0, decremented each time a temporary is stored, and incremented each time it is reloaded (see Appendix B, lines 2023 and 2027). A simple way to use registers as temporary locations is to interpret **`tmpOffset`** as initially referring to registers, and only after the available registers are exhausted, to use it as an actual offset into memory. For instance, if we want to use all the available registers as temporaries (after the pc, gp, and mp), then the **`tmpOffset`** values 0 through −4 may be interpreted as references to the registers 0 through 4, while values beginning with −5 are used as offsets (with 5 added to their values). This mechanism can be implemented directly in the code generator by appropriate tests or encapsulated into auxiliary procedures (which could be called **saveTmp** and **loadTmp**). Provision must also be made for the fact that the result of a subexpression calculation may be in a register other than 0 after recursive code generation.

With this improvement, the TINY code generator now generates the TM code sequence given in Figure 8.21 (compare with Figure 8.17). This code now is 20% shorter and contains no stores of temporaries (and no uses of register 5, the mp). Still, registers 2, 3, and 4 are never used. This is not unusual: expressions in programs are rarely complex enough to require more than two or three temporaries at one time.

8.10.2   Keeping Variables in Registers

A further improvement can be made to the use of the TM registers by reserving some of the registers for use as variable locations. This requires a little more work than the previous optimization, since the location of a variable must be determined prior to code generation and stored in the symbol table. A basic scheme is to simply pick a few registers and allocate these as the locations for the most used variables of the program. To determine which variables are the "most used," a count of references (uses and assignments) must be made. Variables that are references during loops (either in the body of the loop or the test expression) should be preferred, since the references are likely to be repeated as the loop executes. A simple approach that has been shown to work well in many existing compilers is to multiply the count of all references inside a loop by 10, inside a doubly nested loop by 100, and so on. This reference counting can be done during semantic analysis, and a separate variable allocation pass made after it is done. The location attribute that is stored in the symbol table must now account for those variables that are allocated to registers as opposed to memory. One simple scheme uses an enumerated type to indicate where a variable is located; in this case, there are only two possibilities: **inReg** and **inMem**. Additionally, the register number must be kept in the first case and the memory address in the second. (This is a simple example of address descriptors for variables; register descriptors are not needed because they remain fixed for the duration of code generation.)

With these modifications, the code of the sample program might now use register 3 for the variable **x** and register 4 for the variable **fact** (there are only two variables, so all of them can fit into registers), assuming that registers 0 through 2 are still reserved for temporaries. The modifications to the code of Figure 8.21 are given in Figure 8.22. This code is again considerably shorter than the previous code, but still much longer than the handwritten code.

8.10.3   Optimizing Test Expressions

The final optimization we discuss here is to simplify the code generated for tests in if-statements and while-statements. The code generated for these expressions is very general, implementing the Boolean values true and false as 0 and 1, even though TINY has no Boolean variables and does not need this level of generality. This also results in

Figure 8.21

TM code for the sample
TINY program with
temporaries kept
in registers

0:	LD	6,0(0)		17:	ST	0,1(5)
1:	ST	0,0(0)		18:	LD	0,0(5)
2:	IN	0,0,0		19:	LDC	1,1(0)
3:	ST	0,0(5)		20:	SUB	0,0,1
4:	LDC	0,0(0)		21:	ST	0,0(5)
5:	LD	1,0(5)		22:	LD	0,0(5)
6:	SUB	0,0,1		23:	LDC	1,0(0)
7:	JLT	0,2(7)		24:	SUB	0,0,1
8:	LDC	0,0(0)		25:	JEQ	0,2(7)
9:	LDA	7,1(7)		26:	LDC	0,0(0)
10:	LDC	0,1(0)		27:	LDA	7,1(7)
11:	JEQ	0,21(7)		28:	LDC	0,1(0)
12:	LDC	0,1(0)		29:	JEQ	0,-16(7)
13:	ST	0,1(5)		30:	LD	0,1(5)
14:	LD	0,1(5)		31:	OUT	0,0,0
15:	LD	1,0(5)		32:	LDA	7,0(7)
16:	MUL	0,0,1		33:	HALT	0,0,0

Figure 8.22

TM code for the sample
TINY program with
temporaries and variables
kept in registers

0:	LD	6,0(0)		13:	LDC	0,1(0)
1:	ST	0,0(0)		14:	SUB	0,3,0
2:	IN	3,0,0		15:	LDA	3,0(0)
3:	LDC	0,0(0)		16:	LDC	0,0(0)
4:	SUB	0,0,3		17:	SUB	0,3,0
5:	JLT	0,2(7)		18:	JEQ	0,2(7)
6:	LDC	0,0(0)		19:	LDC	0,0(0)
7:	LDA	7,1(7)		20:	LDA	7,1(7)
8:	LDC	0,1(0)		21:	LDC	0,1(0)
9:	JEQ	0,15(7)		22:	JEQ	0,-12(7)
10:	LDC	4,1(0)		23:	OUT	4,0,0
11:	MUL	0,4,3		24:	LDA	7,0(7)
12:	LDA	4,0(0)		25:	HALT	0,0,0

many extra loads of the constants 0 and 1, as well as extra tests that are generated separately by the **genStmt** code for the control statements.

The improvement we describe here depends on the fact that a comparison operator must appear as the root node of the test expression. The **genExp** code for this operator will simply generate code to subtract the value of the right-hand operand from the left-hand operand, leaving the result in register 0. The code for the if-statement or while-statement will then test for which comparison operator is applied and generate appropriate conditional jump code.

Thus, in the case of the code of Figure 8.22, the TINY code

```
if 0 < x then ...
```

that now corresponds to the TM code

```
4:      SUB   0,0,3
5:      JLT   0,2(7)
6:      LDC   0,0(0)
7:      LDA   7,1(7)
8:      LDC   0,1(0)
9:      JEQ   0,15(7)
```

will generate instead the simpler TM code

```
4:      SUB   0,0,3
5:      JGE   0,10(7)
```

(Notice how the false-case jump must be the complementary conditional **JGE** to the test operator <.)

With this optimization, the code generated for the test program becomes that given in Figure 8.23. (We have also included in this step the removal of the empty jump at the end of the code, corresponding to the empty else-part of the if-statement in the TINY code. This requires only the addition of a simple test to the **genStmt** code for the if-statement.)

The code of Figure 8.23 is now relatively close to that of the hand-generated code on page 458. Even so, there is still opportunity for a few more special-case optimizations, which we leave to the exercises.

Figure 8.23

TM code for the sample TINY program with temporaries and variables kept in registers, and with optimized jump tests

```
0:      LD    6,0(0)        9:      LDC   0,1(0)
1:      ST    0,0(0)       10:      SUB   0,3,0
2:      IN    3,0,0        11:      LDA   3,0(0)
3:      LDC   0,0(0)       12:      LDC   0,0(0)
4:      SUB   0,0,3        13:      SUB   0,3,0
5:      JGE   0,10(7)      14:      JNE   0,-8(7)
6:      LDC   4,1(0)       15:      OUT   4,0,0
7:      MUL   0,4,3        16:      HALT  0,0,0
8:      LDA   4,0(0)
```

8.1 Give the sequence of three-address code instructions corresponding to each of the following arithmetic expressions:

  a. 2+3+4+5

  b. 2+(3+(4+5))

  c. a*b+a*b*c

8.2 Give the sequence of P-code instructions corresponding to each of the arithmetic instructions of the previous exercise.

8.3 Give P-code instructions corresponding to the following C expressions:

  a. `(x = y = 2)+3*(x=4)`

  b. `a[a[i]]=b[i=2]`

  c. `p->next->next = p->next`

  (Assume an appropriate **struct** declaration.)

8.4 Give three-address code instructions for the expressions of the previous exercise.

8.5 Give the sequence of **(a)** three-address code or **(b)** P-code corresponding to the following TINY program:

```
{ Gcd program in TINY language }
read u;
read v; { input two integers }
if v = 0 then v := 0 { do nothing }
else
   repeat
     temp := v;
     v := u - u/v*v; { computes u mod v }
     u := temp
   until v = 0
end;
write u { output gcd of original u & v }
```

8.6 Give C data structure declarations appropriate for the triples of Figure 8.5 (Section 8.1.2), similar to those given for quadruples in Figure 8.4.

8.7 Extend the attribute grammar for P-code of Table 8.1 (Section 8.2.1, page 408) to **(a)** the subscript grammar of Section 8.3.2, page 422; **(b)** the control structure grammar of Section 8.4.4, page 433.

8.8 Repeat the previous exercise for the three-address code attribute grammar of Table 8.2, page 409.

8.9 Describe how the generic traversal procedure of Section 6.5.2 (page 337) might be adapted for code generation. Would this be worthwhile?

8.10 Add the unary address operators **&** and ***** (with C semantics) and the binary structure field selection operator **.** to

  a. the expression grammar of Section 8.2.1 (page 407);

  b. the syntax tree structure of Section 8.2.2 (page 410).

8.11 **a.** Add a repeat-until– or do-while–statement to the control grammar of Section 8.4.4 (page 433), and draw a suitable control diagram corresponding to that of Figure 8.11 (page 431).

  b. Rewrite the syntax tree structure declarations for the grammar (page 434) to include your new structure from part (a).

8.12 **a.** Describe how a for-statement can be systematically turned into a corresponding while-statement. Does it make sense to use this to generate code?

  b. Describe how a case- or switch-statement can be systematically turned into a sequence of nested if-statements. Does it make sense to use this to generate code?

8.13 **a.** Draw a control diagram corresponding to Figure 8.11, page 431, for the loop organization displayed by the Borland 80×86 C compiler in Section 8.6.1.

  b. Draw a control diagram corresponding to Figure 8.11 for the loop organization displayed by the Sun SparcStation C compiler in Section 8.6.2.

c. Suppose a conditional jump instruction takes three times as long to execute if the jump is followed than if the code "falls through" (i.e., the condition is false). Do the jump organizations of part (a) and (b) have any time advantage over that of Figure 8.11?

8.14 An alternative to implementing case- or switch-statements as a sequence of tests for each case is the so-called **jump table**, where the case index is used as an offset for an indexed jump into a table of absolute jumps.

a. This implementation method is advantageous only if there are many different cases that occur fairly densely over a fairly compact range of indices. Why?

b. Code generators tend to generate this kind of code only when there are more than about 10 cases. Determine whether your C compiler generates a jump table for a switch-statement and if there is a minimum number of cases for it to do so.

8.15 a. Develop a formula for the address computation of a multidimensional array element similar to that of Section 8.3.2 (page 419). State any assumptions you make.

b. Suppose an array variable **a** is defined by the C code

```
int a[12][100][5];
```

Assuming that an integer occupies two bytes in memory, use your formula of part (a) to determine the offset from the base address of **a** of the subscripted variable

```
a[5][42][2]
```

8.16 Given the following program written according to the function definition/call grammar on page 440:

```
fn f(x)=x+1
fn g(x,y)=x+y
g(f(3),4+5)
```

a. Write the sequence of P-code instructions that would be generated for this program by the **genCode** procedure of Figure 8.14, page 441.

b. Write a sequence of three-address instructions that would be generated for this program.

8.17 The text did not specify when the **arg** three-address instruction is to be issued during function calls: some versions of three-address code require that all **arg** statements come together immediately before the associated call, while others allow the computation of the arguments and the **arg** statements to be intermixed. (See page 438.) Discuss the pros and cons of these two approaches.

8.18 a. List all of the P-code instructions used in this chapter, together with a description of their meaning and use.

b. List all the three-address code instructions used in this chapter, together with a description of their meaning and use.

8.19 Write a TM program equivalent to the TINY gcd program of Exercise 8.5.

8.20 a. The TM has no register-to-register move instruction. Describe how this is done.

b. The TM has no call or return instruction. Describe how they can be imitated.

8.21 Design a floating-point coprocessor for the Tiny Machine that can be added without changing any of the existing register or memory declarations of Appendix C.

8.22 Write down the sequence of TM instructions generated by the TINY compiler for the following TINY expressions and assignments:

a. `2+3+4+5`

b. `2+(3+(4+5))`

c. `x:= x+(y+2*z)`, assuming **x**, **y**, and **z** have **dMem** locations 0, 1, and 2, respectively.

d. `v := u - u/v*v;`

(A line from the TINY gcd program of Exercise 8.5; assume the standard TINY runtime environment.)

8.23 Design a TM runtime environment for the function call grammar of Section 8.5.2.

8.24 The Borland 3.0 compiler generates the following 80×86 code to compute the logical result of a comparison **x<y**, assuming **x** and **y** are integers at offsets −2 and −4 in the local activation record:

```
           mov     ax,word ptr [bp-2]
           cmp     ax,word ptr [bp-4]
           jge     short @1@86
           mov     ax,1
           jmp     short @1@114
@1@86:
           xor     ax,ax
@1@114:
```

Compare this to the TM code produced by the TINY compiler for the same expression.

8.25 Examine how your C compiler implements short-circuit Boolean operations, and compare the implementation to the control structures of Section 8.4.

8.26 Draw a flow graph for the three-address code corresponding to the TINY gcd program of Exercise 8.5.

8.27 Draw a DAG for the basic block corresponding to the body of the repeat-statement of the TINY gcd program of Exercise 8.5.

8.28 Consider the DAG of Figure 8.19, page 477. Assuming that the equality operator of the rightmost node is imitated on the TM machine by subtraction, the TM code corresponding to this node might be as follows:

```
    LDC 2,0(0) load constant 0 into reg 2
    SUB 2,1,2
```

Write register and address descriptors (based on those on page 480) as they would become after the execution of the above code.

8.29 Determine the optimizations that your C compiler performs, and compare them to those described in Section 8.9.

8.30 Two additional optimizations that can be implemented in the TINY code generator are as follows:

1. If one of the operands of a test expression is the constant 0, then no subtraction need be performed before generating the conditional jump.

2. If the target of an assignment is already in a register, then the right-hand expression can be computed into this register, thus saving a register-to-register move.

Show the code for the sample TINY factorial program that would be generated if these two optimizations are added to the code generator that produces the code of Figure 8.23. How does this code compare to the hand-generated code of Figure 8.16 (page 458)?

8.31 Rewrite the code of Figure 8.7 (Section 8.2.2, page 412) to produce P-code as a synthe-sized string attribute according to the attribute grammar of Table 8.1 (page 408), and compare the complexity of the code to that of Figure 8.7.

8.32 Rewrite each of the following P-code generation procedures to produce three-address code instead:

  a. Figure 8.7, page 412 (simple C-like expressions).

  b. Figure 8.9, page 424 (expressions with arrays).

  c. Figure 8.12, page 435 (control statements).

  d. Figure 8.14, page 441 (functions).

8.33 Write a Yacc specification similar to that of Figure 8.8, page 413, corresponding to the code generation procedures of

  a. Figure 8.9, page 424 (expressions with arrays).

  b. Figure 8.12, page 435 (control statements).

  c. Figure 8.14, page 441 (functions).

8.34 Rewrite the Yacc specification of Figure 8.8 to produce three-address code instead of P-code.

8.35 Add the operators of Exercise 8.10 to the code generation procedure of Figure 8.7, page 412.

8.36 Rewrite the code generation procedure of Figure 8.12, page 435, to include the new con-trol structures of Exercise 8.11.

8.37 Rewrite the code of Figure 8.7, page 412, to produce TM code instead of P-code. (You may assume the code generation utilities in the **code.h** file of the TINY compiler.)

8.38 Rewrite the code of Figure 8.14 (page 441) to generate TM code, using your runtime environment design of Exercise 8.23.

8.39 **a.** Add simple arrays to the TINY language and compiler. This requires that array decla-rations be added before the statements themselves, as in

```
array a[10];
i := 1;
repeat
  read a[i];
  i := i + 1;
until 10 < i
```

  b. Add bounds checks to your code of part (a), so that out-of-bounds subscripting causes a halt of the TM machine.

8.40 **a.** Implement your TM floating-point coprocessor design of Exercise 8.21.

  b. Use your floating-point TM capability to replace integers by real numbers in the TINY language and compiler.

  c. Rewrite the TINY language and compiler to include both integer and floating-point values.

8.41 Write a P-code to three-address code translator.

8.42 Write a three-address code to P-code translator.

8.43 Rewrite the TINY code generator to generate P-code.

8.44 Write a P-code to TM machine code translator, assuming the P-code generator of the pre-vious exercise and the TINY runtime environment described in the text.

8.45 Rewrite the TINY code generator to generate three-address code.

8.46 Write a three-address code to TM machine code translator, assuming the three-address code generator of the previous exercise and the TINY runtime environment described in the text.

8.47 Implement the three optimizations of the TINY code generator described in Section 8.10:

a. Use the first three TM registers as temporary locations.

b. Use registers 3 and 4 as locations for the most used variables.

c. Optimize the code for test expressions so that it no longer generates the Boolean values 0 and 1.

8.48 Implement constant folding in the TINY compiler.

8.49 a. Implement optimization 1 of Exercise 8.30.

b. Implement optimization 2 of Exercise 8.30.

NOTES AND REFERENCES

There is a tremendous variety of code generation and optimization techniques; this chapter represents only an introduction. A good survey of such techniques (particularly data flow analysis), from a somewhat theoretical point of view, is contained in Aho, Sethi, and Ullman [1986]. A number of practical topics are treated in more detail in Fischer and LeBlanc [1991]. Jump tables for case/switch-statements (Exercise 8.14) are described in both. For examples of code generation on particular processors (MIPS, Sparc, and PC), see Fraser and Hanson [1995]. Code generation as attribute analysis is treated in Slonneger and Kurtz [1995].

The variability of intermediate code from compiler to compiler has been a source of portability problems since the first compilers were written. Originally, it was thought that a universal intermediate code could be developed that would serve for all compilers and solve the portability problem (Strong [1958], Steel [1961]). This has, unfortunately, not proved to be the case. Three-address code or quadruples is a traditional form of intermediate code and is used in many compiler texts. P-code is described in detail in Nori et al. [1981]. A somewhat more sophisticated form of P-code, called U-code, that permits better optimization of the target code, is described in Perkins and Sites [1977]. A similar version of P-code was used in a Modula-2 optimizing compiler (Powell [1984]). A specialized intermediate code for Ada compilers, called Diana, is described in Goos and Wulf [1981]. An intermediate code that uses LISP-like prefix expressions is called the register transfer language, or RTL, and is used in the Gnu compilers (Stallman [1994]); it is described in Davidson and Fraser [1984a,b]. For an example of a C-based intermediate code that can be compiled using a C compiler, see Holub [1990].

There is no comprehensive up-to-date reference for optimization techniques, although the standard references Aho, Sethi, and Ullman [1986] and Fischer and LeBlanc [1991] contain good summaries. Many powerful and useful techniques have been published in the *ACM Programming Languages Design and Implementation Conference Proceedings* (previously called the Compiler Construction Conference), which appears as part of the *ACM SIGPLAN Notices*. Additional sources for many optimization techniques are the *ACM Principles of Programming Languages Conference Proceedings* and the *ACM Transactions on Programming Languages and Systems*.

One aspect of code generation that we have not mentioned is the automatic generation of a code generator using a formal description of the machine architecture, in a manner similar to the way parsers and semantic analyzers can be automatically generated. Such methods vary from purely syntactic (Glanville and Graham [1978]) to attribute based (Ganapathi and Fischer [1985]) to intermediate code based (Davidson and Fraser [1984a]). A survey of these and other methods may be found in Fischer and LeBlanc [1991].

Appendix A

Compiler Project

We define here a programming language called **C-Minus** (or C—, for short), which is a suitable language for a compiler project, which is more complex than the TINY language in that it includes functions and arrays. It is essentially a subset of C, but is missing some important pieces, hence its name. This appendix consists of five sections. In the first, we list the lexical conventions of the language, including a description of the tokens of the language. In the second, we give a BNF description of each language construct, together with an English description of the associated semantics. In the third section, we give two sample programs in C—. In the fourth, we describe a Tiny Machine runtime environment for C—. The last section describes a number of programming projects using C— and TM, suitable for a compiler course.

A.1 LEXICAL CONVENTIONS OF C—

1. The keywords of the language are the following:

   else if int return void while

   All keywords are reserved, and must be written in lowercase.

2. **Special symbols are the following:**

   + - * / < <= > >= == != = ; , ( ) [ ] { } /* */

3. Other tokens are ***ID*** and ***NUM***, defined by the following regular expressions:

> ***ID = letter letter****
> ***NUM = digit digit****
> ***letter = a|..|z|A|..|z***
> ***digit = 0|..|9***

Lower- and uppercase letters are distinct.

4. White space consists of blanks, newlines, and tabs. White space is ignored except that it must separate ***ID***'s, ***NUM***'s, and keywords.

5. Comments are surrounded by the usual C notations **/*...*/**. Comments can be placed anywhere white space can appear (that is, comments cannot be placed within tokens) and may include more than one line. Comments may not be nested.

A.2   SYNTAX AND SEMANTICS OF C—

A BNF grammar for C— is as follows:

1. *program → declaration-list*
2. *declaration-list → declaration-list declaration | declaration*
3. *declaration → var-declaration | fun-declaration*
4. *var-declaration → type-specifier **ID** ; | type-specifier **ID** [**NUM**] ;*
5. *type-specifier → **int** | **void***
6. *fun-declaration → type-specifier **ID** (params) compound-stmt*
7. *params → param-list | **void***
8. *param-list → param-list , param | param*
9. *param → type-specifier **ID** | type-specifier **ID** [ ]*
10. *compound-stmt → { local-declarations statement-list }*
11. *local-declarations → local-declarations var-declaration | empty*
12. *statement-list → statement-list statement | empty*
13. *statement → expression-stmt | compound-stmt | selection-stmt*
                 | iteration-stmt | return-stmt
14. *expession-stmt → expression ; | ;*
15. *selection-stmt → **if** (expression) statement*
                *| **if** (expression) statement **else** statement*
16. *iteration-stmt → **while** (expression) statement*
17. *return-stmt → **return** ; | **return** expression ;*
18. *expression → var = expression | simple-expression*
19. *var → **ID** | **ID** [expression]*
20. *simple-expression → additive-expression relop additive-expression*
                   | additive-expression
21. *relop → **<=** | **<** | **>** | **>=** | **==** | **!=***
22. *additive-expression → additive-expression addop term | term*
23. *addop → **+** | **-***
24. *term → term mulop factor | factor*
25. *mulop → ***** | **/***
26. *factor → (expression) | var | call | **NUM***

27. *call* → **ID** (*args*)
28. *args* → *arg-list* | *empty*
29. *arg-list* → *arg-list* **,** *expression* | *expression*

For each of these grammar rules we give a short explanation of the associated semantics.

1. *program* → *declaration-list*
2. *declaration-list* → *declaration-list declaration* | *declaration*
3. *declaration* → *var-declaration* | *fun-declaration*

A program consists of a list (or sequence) of declarations, which may be function or variable declarations, in any order. There must be at least one declaration. Semantic restrictions are as follows (these do not occur in C). All variables and functions must be declared before they are used (this avoids backpatching references). The last declaration in a program must be a function declaration with the name **main**. Note that C— lacks prototypes, so that no distinction is made between declarations and definitions (as in C).

4. *var-declaration* → *type-specifier* **ID ;** | *type-specifier* **ID [NUM] ;**
5. *type-specifier* → **int** | **void**

A variable declaration declares either a simple variable of integer type or an array variable whose base type is integer, and whose indices range from 0 . . **NUM**−1. Note that in C— the only basic types are integer and void. In a variable declaration, only the type specifier **int** can be used. **Void** is for function declarations (see below). Note, also, that only one variable can be declared per declaration.

6. *fun-declaration* → *type-specifier* **ID** (*params*) *compound-stmt*
7. *params* → *param-list* | **void**
8. *param-list* → *param-list* **,** *param* | *param*
9. *param* → *type-specifier* **ID** | *type-specifier* **ID [ ]**

A function declaration consists of a return type specifier, an identifier, and a comma-separated list of parameters inside parentheses, followed by a compound statement with the code for the function. If the return type of the function is **void**, then the function returns no value (i.e., is a procedure). Parameters of a function are either **void** (i.e., there are no parameters) or a list representing the function's parameters. Parameters followed by brackets are array parameters whose size can vary. Simple integer parameters are passed by value. Array parameters are passed by reference (i.e., as pointers) and must be matched by an array variable during a call. Note that there are no parameters of type "function." The parameters of a function have scope equal to the compound statement of the function declaration, and each invocation of a function has a separate set of parameters. Functions may be recursive (to the extent that declaration before use allows).

10. *compound-stmt* → **{** *local-declarations statement-list* **}**

A compound statement consists of curly brackets surrounding a set of declarations and statements. A compound statement is executed by executing the statement sequence in the order given. The local declarations have scope equal to the statement list of the compound statement and supersede any global declarations.

11. *local-declarations → local-declarations var-declaration | empty*
12. *statement-list → statement-list statement | empty*

Note that both declarations and statement lists may be empty. (The nonterminal *empty* stands for the empty string, sometimes written as ε.)

13. *statement → expression-stmt*
        | compound-stmt
        | selection-stmt
        | iteration-stmt
        | return-stmt
14. *expession-stmt → expression **;** | **;***

An expression statement has an optional expression followed by a semicolon. Such expressions are usually evaluated for their side effects. Thus, this statement is used for assignments and function calls.

15. *selection-stmt → **if** (expression) statement*
           *| **if** (expression) statement **else** statement*

The if-statement has the usual semantics: the expression is evaluated; a nonzero value causes execution of the first statement; a zero value causes execution of the second statement, if it exists. This rule results in the classical dangling else ambiguity, which is resolved in the standard way: the else part is always parsed immediately as a substructure of the current if (the "most closely nested" disambiguating rule).

16. *iteration-stmt → **while** (expression) statement*

The while-statement is the only iteration statement in C−. It is executed by repeatedly evaluating the expression and then executing the statement if the expression evaluates to a nonzero value, ending when the expression evaluates to 0.

17. *return-stmt → **return** ; | **return** expression ;*

A return statement may either return a value or not. Functions not declared **void** must return values. Functions declared **void** must not return values. A return causes transfer of control back to the caller (or termination of the program if it is inside **main**).

18. *expression → var = expression | simple-expression*
19. *var → **ID** | **ID** [expression]*

An expression is a variable reference followed by an assignment symbol (equal sign) and an expression, or just a simple expression. The assignment has the usual storage semantics: the location of the variable represented by *var* is found, then the subexpression to the right of the assignment is evaluated, and the value of the subexpression is stored at the given location. This value is also returned as the value of the entire expression. A *var* is either a simple (integer) variable or a subscripted array variable. A negative subscript causes the program to halt (unlike C). However, upper bounds of subscripts are not checked.

Vars represent a further restriction of C— from C. In C the target of an assignment must be an **l-value**, and l-values are addresses that can be obtained by many operations. In C— the only l-values are those given by the *var* syntax, and so this category is checked syntactically, instead of during type checking as in C. Thus, pointer arithmetic is forbidden in C—.

20. *simple-expression* → *additive-expression relop additive-expression*
         | *additive-expression*
21. *relop* → `<=` | `<` | `>` | `>=` | `==` | `!=`

A simple expression consists of relational operators that do not associate (that is, an unparenthesized expression can only have one relational operator). The value of a simple expression is either the value of its additive expression if it contains no relational operators, or 1 if the relational operator evaluates to true, or 0 if it evaluates to false.

22. *additive-expression* → *additive-expression addop term* | *term*
23. *addop* → `+` | `-`
24. *term* → *term mulop factor* | *factor*
25. *mulop* → `*` | `/`

Additive expressions and terms represent the typical associativity and precedence of the arithmetic operators. The `/` symbol represents integer division; that is, any remainder is truncated.

26. *factor* → `(` *expression* `)` | *var* | *call* | **NUM**

A factor is an expression enclosed in parentheses, a variable, which evaluates to the value of its variable; a call of a function, which evaluates to the returned value of the function; or a NUM, whose value is computed by the scanner. An array variable must be subscripted, except in the case of an expression consisting of a single ID and used in a function call with an array parameter (see below).

27. *call* → **ID** `(` *args* `)`
28. *args* → *arg-list* | *empty*
29. *arg-list* → *arg-list* `,` *expression* | *expression*

A function call consists of an **ID** (the name of the function), followed by parentheses enclosing its arguments. Arguments are either empty or consist of a comma-separated list of expressions, representing the values to be assigned to parameters during a call. Functions must be declared before they are called, and the number of parameters in a declaration must equal the number of arguments in a call. An array parameter in a function declaration must be matched with an expression consisting of a single identifier representing an array variable.

Finally, the above rules give no input or output statement. We must include such functions in the definition of C—, since unlike C, C— has no separate compilation or linking facilities. We, therefore, consider two functions to be **predefined** in the global environment, as though they had the indicated declarations:

```
int input(void) { . . . }
void output(int x) { . . . }
```

The **input** function has no parameters and returns an integer value from the standard input device (usually the keyboard). The **output** function takes one integer parameter, whose value it prints to the standard output (usually the screen), together with a newline.

A.3 SAMPLE PROGRAMS IN C−

The following is a program that inputs two integers, computes their greatest common divisor, and prints it:

```
/* A program to perform Euclid's
   Algorithm to compute gcd. */

int gcd (int u, int v)
{ if (v == 0) return u ;
  else return gcd(v,u-u/v*v);
  /* u-u/v*v == u mod v */
}

void main(void)
{ int x; int y;
  x = input(); y = input();
  output(gcd(x,y));
}
```

The following is a program that inputs a list of 10 integers, sorts them by selection sort, and outputs them again:

```
/* A program to perform selection sort on a 10
   element array. */

int x[10];

int minloc ( int a[], int low, int high )
{ int i; int x; int k;
  k = low;
  x = a[low];
  i = low + 1;
  while (i < high)
    { if (a[i] < x)
        { x = a[i];
          k = i; }
      i = i + 1;
    }
  return k;
}
```

```
void sort( int a[], int low, int high)
{ int i; int k;
  i = low;
  while (i < high-1)
    { int t;
      k = minloc(a,i,high);
      t = a[k];
      a[k] = a[i];
      a[i] = t;
      i = i + 1;
    }
}

void main(void)
{ int i;
  i = 0;
  while (i < 10)
    { x[i] = input();
      i = i + 1; }
  sort(x,0,10);
  i = 0;
  while (i < 10)
    { output(x[i]);
      i = i + 1; }
}
```

A.4   A TINY MACHINE RUNTIME ENVIRONMENT FOR THE C— LANGUAGE

The following description assumes a knowledge of the Tiny Machine as given in Section 8.7 and an understanding of stack-based runtime environments from Chapter 7. Since C— (unlike TINY) has recursive procedures, the runtime environment must be stack based. The environment consists of a global area at the top of dMem, and the stack just below it, growing downward toward 0. Since C— contains no pointers or dynamic allocation, there is no need for a heap. The basic organization of each activation record (or stack frame) in C— is

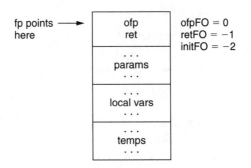

Here, fp is the **current frame pointer**, which is kept in a register for easy access. The ofp (old frame pointer) is the **control link** as discussed in Chapter 7 of the text. The constants to the right ending in FO (for frame offset) are the offsets at which each of the indicated quantities are stored. The value initFO is the offset at which the params and local vars begin their storage areas in an activation record. Since the Tiny Machine contains no stack pointer, all references to fields within an activation record will use the fp, with negative frame offsets.

For example, if we have the following C− function declaration,

```
int f(int x, int y)
{ int z;
  . . .
}
```

then **x**, **y**, and **z** must be allocated in the current frame, and the frame offset at the beginning of the generation of code for the body of **f** will be −5 (one location each for **x**, **y**, **z** and two locations for the bookkeeping information of the activation record). The offsets of **x**, **y**, and **z** are −2, −3, and −4, respectively.

Global references can be found at absolute locations in memory. Nevertheless, as with TINY, we prefer also to reference these variables by offset from a register. We do this by keeping a fixed register, which we call the gp, and which always points at the maximum address. Since the TM simulator stores this address into location 0 before execution begins, the gp can be loaded from location 0 on start-up, and the following standard prelude initializes the runtime environment:

```
0: LD  gp,   0(ac)  * load gp with maxaddress
1: LDA fp,   0(gp)  * copy gp to fp
2: ST  ac,   0(ac)  * clear location 0
```

Function calls also require that the beginning code location for their bodies be used in a calling sequence. We also prefer to call functions by performing a relative jump using the current value of the pc rather than an absolute jump. (This makes the code potentially relocatable.) The utility procedure **emitRAbs** in **code.h/code.c** can be used for this purpose. (It takes an absolute code location and relativizes it by using the current code generation location.)

For example, suppose we want to call a function f whose code begins at location 27, and we are currently at location 42. Then instead of generating the absolute jump

```
42: LDC pc, 27(*)
```

we would generate

```
42: LDA pc, -16(pc)
```

since $27 - (42 + 1) = -16$.

The Calling Sequence   A reasonable division of labor between caller and callee is to have the caller store the values of the arguments in the new frame and create the new frame, except for the storing of the return pointer in the retFO position. Instead of storing the return pointer itself, the caller leaves it in the ac register, and the callee stores it into the new frame. Thus, every function body must begin with code to store that value in the (now current) frame:

```
ST ac, retFO(fp)
```

This saves one instruction at each call site. On return, each function then loads the pc with this return address by executing the instruction

```
LD pc, retFO(fp)
```

Correspondingly, the caller computes the arguments one by one, and pushes each onto the stack in its appropriate position before pushing the new frame. The caller must also save the current fp into the frame at ofpFO before pushing the new frame. After a return from the callee, the caller then discards the new frame by loading the fp with the old fp. Thus, a call to a function of two parameters will cause the generation of the following code:

```
<code to compute first arg>
ST ac, frameoffset+initFO (fp)
<code to compute second arg>
ST ac, frameoffset+initFO-1 (fp)
ST fp, frameoffset+ofpFO (fp) * store current fp
LDA fp frameOffset(fp) * push new frame
LDA ac,1(pc) * save return in ac
LDA pc, ...(pc) * relative jump to function entry
LD fp, ofpFO(fp) * pop current frame
```

Address Computations Since both variables and subscripted arrays are allowed on the left-hand side of assignment, we must distinguish between addresses and values during compilation. For example, in the statement

```
a[i] := a[i+1];
```

the expression **a[i]** refers to the address of **a[i]**, while the expression **a[i+1]** refers to the value of **a** at the **i+1** location. This distinction can be achieved by using an **isAddress** parameter to the **cGen** procedure. When this parameter is true, **cGen** generates code to compute the address of a variable rather than its value. In the case of a simple variable, this means adding the offset to either the gp (in the case of a global variable) or the fp (in the case of a local variable) and loading the result into the ac:

```
LDA ac, offset(fp) ** put address of local var in ac
```

In the case of an array variable, this means adding the value of the index to the base address of the array and loading the result into the ac, as described below.

Arrays Arrays are allocated on the stack beginning at the current frame offset and extending downward in memory in order of increasing subscript, as follows:

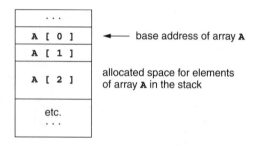

Note that array locations are computed by subtracting the index value from the base address.

When an array is passed to a function, only the base address is passed. The allocation of the area for the base elements is done only once and remains fixed for the life of the array. Function arguments do not include the actual elements of an array, only the address. Thus, array parameters become reference parameters. This causes an anomaly when array parameters are referenced inside a function, since they must be treated as having their base addresses rather than their values stored in memory. Thus, an array parameter has its base address computed using an LD operation instead of an LDA.

A.5 PROGRAMMING PROJECTS USING C— AND TM

It is not unreasonable for a one-semester compiler course to require as a project a complete compiler for the C− language, based on the TINY compiler discussed in this text (and whose listing can be found in Appendix B). This can be coordinated so that each phase of the compiler is implemented as the associated theory is studied. Alternatively, one or more parts of the C− compiler could be supplied by the instructor, and students required to complete the remaining parts. This is especially helpful when time is short (as in a quarter system) or if the students will be generating assembly code for a "real" machine, such as the Sparc or PC (which requires more detail in the code generation phase). It is less helpful to implement just one part of the C− compiler, since the interactions among the parts and the ability to test the code are then restricted. The following list of separate tasks are supplied as a convenience, with the caveat that each task may not be independent of the others and that it is probably best for all tasks to be completed in order to obtain a complete compiler-writing experience.

PROJECTS

A.1. Implement a symbol table utility suitable for the C− language. This will require a table structure that incorporates scope information, either as separate tables linked together or with a delete mechanism that operates in a stack-based fashion, as described in Chapter 6.

A.2. Implement a C− scanner, either by hand as a DFA or using Lex, as described in Chapter 2.

A.3. Design a syntax tree structure for C− suitable for generation by a parser.

A.4. Implement a C− parser (this requires a C− scanner), either by hand using recursive descent or using Yacc, as described in Chapter 4 or 5. The parser should generate a suitable syntax tree (see Project A.3).

A.5. Implement a semantic analyzer for C−. The major requirement of the analyzer, aside from gathering information in the symbol table, is to perform type checking on the use of variables and functions. Since there are no pointers or structures, and the only basic type is integer, the types that need to be treated by the type checker are void, integer, array, and function.

A.6. Implement a code generator for C−, according to the runtime environment described in the previous section.

Appendix B

TINY Compiler Listing

```
1  /*****************************************************/
2  /* File: main.c                                    */
3  /* Main program for TINY compiler                  */
4  /* Compiler Construction: Principles and Practice  */
5  /* Kenneth C. Louden                               */
6  /*****************************************************/
7
8  #include "globals.h"
9
10 /* set NO_PARSE to TRUE to get a scanner-only compiler */
11 #define NO_PARSE FALSE
12
13 /* set NO_ANALYZE to TRUE to get a parser-only compiler */
14 #define NO_ANALYZE FALSE
15
16 /* set NO_CODE to TRUE to get a compiler that does not
17  * generate code
18  */
19 #define NO_CODE FALSE
20
21 #include "util.h"
22 #if NO_PARSE
23 #include "scan.h"
24 #else
25 #include "parse.h"
26 #if !NO_ANALYZE
27 #include "analyze.h"
28 #if !NO_CODE
29 #include "cgen.h"
30 #endif
31 #endif
32 #endif
33
34 /* allocate global variables */
```

```
35  int lineno = 0;
36  FILE * source;
37  FILE * listing;
38  FILE * code;
39
40  /* allocate and set tracing flags */
41  int EchoSource = TRUE;
42  int TraceScan = TRUE;
43  int TraceParse = TRUE;
44  int TraceAnalyze = TRUE;
45  int TraceCode = TRUE;
46
47  int Error = FALSE;
48
49  main( int argc, char * argv[] )
50  { TreeNode * syntaxTree;
51    char pgm[20]; /* source code file name */
52    if (argc != 2)
53      { fprintf(stderr,"usage: %s <filename>\n",argv[0]);
54        exit(1);
55      }
56    strcpy(pgm,argv[1]) ;
57    if (strchr (pgm, '.') == NULL)
58        strcat(pgm,".tny");
59    source = fopen(pgm,"r");
60    if (source==NULL)
61    { fprintf(stderr,"File %s not found\n",pgm);
62      exit(1);
63    }
64    listing = stdout; /* send listing to screen */
65    fprintf(listing,"\nTINY COMPILATION: %s\n",pgm);
66  #if NO_PARSE
67    while (getToken()!=ENDFILE);
68  #else
69    syntaxTree = parse();
70    if (TraceParse) {
71      fprintf(listing,"\nSyntax tree:\n");
72      printTree(syntaxTree);
73    }
74  #if !NO_ANALYZE
75    if (! Error)
76    { fprintf(listing,"\nBuilding Symbol Table...\n");
77      buildSymtab(syntaxTree);
78      fprintf(listing,"\nChecking Types...\n");
79      typeCheck(syntaxTree);
80      fprintf(listing,"\nType Checking Finished\n");
```

```
81      }
82  #if !NO_CODE
83      if (! Error)
84      { char * codefile;
85        int fnlen = strcspn(pgm,".");
86        codefile = (char *) calloc(fnlen+4, sizeof(char));
87        strncpy(codefile,pgm,fnlen);
88        strcat(codefile,".tm");
89        code = fopen(codefile,"w");
90        if (code == NULL)
91        { printf("Unable to open %s\n",codefile);
92          exit(1);
93        }
94        codeGen(syntaxTree,codefile);
95        fclose(code);
96      }
97  #endif
98  #endif
99  #endif
100     return 0;
101 }


150 /****************************************************/
151 /* File: globals.h                                  */
152 /* Global types and vars for TINY compiler          */
153 /* must come before other include files             */
154 /* Compiler Construction: Principles and Practice   */
155 /* Kenneth C. Louden                                */
156 /****************************************************/
157
158 #ifndef _GLOBALS_H_
159 #define _GLOBALS_H_
160
161 #include <stdio.h>
162 #include <stdlib.h>
163 #include <ctype.h>
164 #include <string.h>
165
166 #ifndef FALSE
167 #define FALSE 0
168 #endif
169
170 #ifndef TRUE
171 #define TRUE 1
172 #endif
```

```
173
174   /* MAXRESERVED = the number of reserved words */
175   #define MAXRESERVED 8
176
177   typedef enum
178       /* book-keeping tokens */
179      {ENDFILE,ERROR,
180       /* reserved words */
181       IF,THEN,ELSE,END,REPEAT,UNTIL,READ,WRITE,
182       /* multicharacter tokens */
183       ID,NUM,
184       /* special symbols */
185       ASSIGN,EQ,LT,PLUS,MINUS,TIMES,OVER,LPAREN,RPAREN,SEMI
186      } TokenType;
187
188   extern FILE* source; /* source code text file */
189   extern FILE* listing; /* listing output text file */
190   extern FILE* code; /* code text file for TM simulator */
191
192   extern int lineno; /* source line number for listing */
193
194   /**************************************************/
195   /**********   Syntax tree for parsing   **********/
196   /**************************************************/
197
198   typedef enum {StmtK,ExpK} NodeKind;
199   typedef enum {IfK,RepeatK,AssignK,ReadK,WriteK} StmtKind;
200   typedef enum {OpK,ConstK,IdK} ExpKind;
201
202   /* ExpType is used for type checking */
203   typedef enum {Void,Integer,Boolean} ExpType;
204
205   #define MAXCHILDREN 3
206
207   typedef struct treeNode
208      { struct treeNode * child[MAXCHILDREN];
209        struct treeNode * sibling;
210        int lineno;
211        NodeKind nodekind;
212        union { StmtKind stmt; ExpKind exp;} kind;
213        union { TokenType op;
214                int val;
215                char * name; } attr;
216        ExpType type; /* for type checking of exps */
217      } TreeNode;
218
```

```
219  /****************************************************/
220  /**********     Flags for tracing     ***********/
221  /****************************************************/
222
223  /* EchoSource = TRUE causes the source program to
224   * be echoed to the listing file with line numbers
225   * during parsing
226   */
227  extern int EchoSource;
228
229  /* TraceScan = TRUE causes token information to be
230   * printed to the listing file as each token is
231   * recognized by the scanner
232   */
233  extern int TraceScan;
234
235  /* TraceParse = TRUE causes the syntax tree to be
236   * printed to the listing file in linearized form
237   * (using indents for children)
238   */
239  extern int TraceParse;
240
241  /* TraceAnalyze = TRUE causes symbol table inserts
242   * and lookups to be reported to the listing file
243   */
244  extern int TraceAnalyze;
245
246  /* TraceCode = TRUE causes comments to be written
247   * to the TM code file as code is generated
248   */
249  extern int TraceCode;
250
251  /* Error = TRUE prevents further passes if an error occurs */
252  extern int Error;
253  #endif


300  /****************************************************/
301  /* File: util.h                                     */
302  /* Utility functions for the TINY compiler          */
303  /* Compiler Construction: Principles and Practice   */
304  /* Kenneth C. Louden                                */
305  /****************************************************/
306
307  #ifndef _UTIL_H_
308  #define _UTIL_H_
309
```

```
310  /* Procedure printToken prints a token
311   * and its lexeme to the listing file
312   */
313  void printToken( TokenType, const char* );
314
315  /* Function newStmtNode creates a new statement
316   * node for syntax tree construction
317   */
318  TreeNode * newStmtNode(StmtKind);
319
320  /* Function newExpNode creates a new expression
321   * node for syntax tree construction
322   */
323  TreeNode * newExpNode(ExpKind);
324
325  /* Function copyString allocates and makes a new
326   * copy of an existing string
327   */
328  char * copyString( char * );
329
330  /* procedure printTree prints a syntax tree to the
331   * listing file using indentation to indicate subtrees
332   */
333  void printTree( TreeNode * );
334
335  #endif


350  /****************************************************/
351  /* File: util.c                                     */
352  /* Utility function implementation                  */
353  /* for the TINY compiler                            */
354  /* Compiler Construction: Principles and Practice   */
355  /* Kenneth C. Louden                                */
356  /****************************************************/
357
358  #include "globals.h"
359  #include "util.h"
360
361  /* Procedure printToken prints a token
362   * and its lexeme to the listing file
363   */
364  void printToken( TokenType token, const char* tokenString )
365  { switch (token)
366    { case IF:
367      case THEN:
368      case ELSE:
```

```
369        case END:
370        case REPEAT:
371        case UNTIL:
372        case READ:
373        case WRITE:
374          fprintf(listing,
375             "reserved word: %s\n",tokenString);
376          break;
377        case ASSIGN: fprintf(listing,":=\n"); break;
378        case LT: fprintf(listing,"<\n"); break;
379        case EQ: fprintf(listing,"=\n"); break;
380        case LPAREN: fprintf(listing,"(\n"); break;
381        case RPAREN: fprintf(listing,")\n"); break;
382        case SEMI: fprintf(listing,";\n"); break;
383        case PLUS: fprintf(listing,"+\n"); break;
384        case MINUS: fprintf(listing,"-\n"); break;
385        case TIMES: fprintf(listing,"*\n"); break;
386        case OVER: fprintf(listing,"/\n"); break;
387        case ENDFILE: fprintf(listing,"EOF\n"); break;
388        case NUM:
389          fprintf(listing,
390             "NUM, val= %s\n",tokenString);
391          break;
392        case ID:
393          fprintf(listing,
394             "ID, name= %s\n",tokenString);
395          break;
396        case ERROR:
397          fprintf(listing,
398             "ERROR: %s\n",tokenString);
399          break;
400        default: /* should never happen */
401          fprintf(listing,"Unknown token: %d\n",token);
402      }
403    }
404
405    /* Function newStmtNode creates a new statement
406     * node for syntax tree construction
407     */
408    TreeNode * newStmtNode(StmtKind kind)
409    { TreeNode * t = (TreeNode *) malloc(sizeof(TreeNode));
410      int i;
411      if (t==NULL)
412        fprintf(listing,"Out of memory error at line %d\n",lineno);
413      else {
414        for (i=0;i<MAXCHILDREN;i++) t->child[i] = NULL;
415        t->sibling = NULL;
```

```
416       t->nodekind = StmtK;
417       t->kind.stmt = kind;
418       t->lineno = lineno;
419     }
420     return t;
421  }
422
423  /* Function newExpNode creates a new expression
424   * node for syntax tree construction
425   */
426  TreeNode * newExpNode(ExpKind kind)
427  { TreeNode * t = (TreeNode *) malloc(sizeof(TreeNode));
428    int i;
429    if (t==NULL)
430      fprintf(listing,"Out of memory error at line %d\n",lineno);
431    else {
432      for (i=0;i<MAXCHILDREN;i++) t->child[i] = NULL;
433      t->sibling = NULL;
434      t->nodekind = ExpK;
435      t->kind.exp = kind;
436      t->lineno = lineno;
437      t->type = Void;
438    }
439    return t;
440  }
441
442  /* Function copyString allocates and makes a new
443   * copy of an existing string
444   */
445  char * copyString(char * s)
446  { int n;
447    char * t;
448    if (s==NULL) return NULL;
449    n = strlen(s)+1;
450    t = malloc(n);
451    if (t==NULL)
452      fprintf(listing,"Out of memory error at line %d\n",lineno);
453    else strcpy(t,s);
454    return t;
455  }
456
457  /* Variable indentno is used by printTree to
458   * store current number of spaces to indent
459   */
460  static indentno = 0;
461
462  /* macros to increase/decrease indentation */
```

```
463   #define INDENT indentno+=2
464   #define UNINDENT indentno-=2
465
466   /* printSpaces indents by printing spaces */
467   static void printSpaces(void)
468   { int i;
469     for (i=0;i<indentno;i++)
470       fprintf(listing," ");
471   }
472
473   /* procedure printTree prints a syntax tree to the
474    * listing file using indentation to indicate subtrees
475    */
476   void printTree( TreeNode * tree )
477   { int i;
478     INDENT;
479     while (tree != NULL) {
480       printSpaces();
481       if (tree->nodekind==StmtK)
482       { switch (tree->kind.stmt) {
483           case IfK:
484             fprintf(listing,"If\n");
485             break;
486           case RepeatK:
487             fprintf(listing,"Repeat\n");
488             break;
489           case AssignK:
490             fprintf(listing,"Assign to: %s\n",tree->attr.name);
491             break;
492           case ReadK:
493             fprintf(listing,"Read: %s\n",tree->attr.name);
494             break;
495           case WriteK:
496             fprintf(listing,"Write\n");
497             break;
498           default:
499             fprintf(listing,"Unknown ExpNode kind\n");
500             break;
501         }
502       }
503       else if (tree->nodekind==ExpK)
504       { switch (tree->kind.exp) {
505           case OpK:
506             fprintf(listing,"Op: ");
507             printToken(tree->attr.op,"\0");
508             break;
509           case ConstK:
```

```
510              fprintf(listing,"const: %d\n",tree->attr.val);
511              break;
512           case IdK:
513              fprintf(listing,"Id: %s\n",tree->attr.name);
514              break;
515           default:
516              fprintf(listing,"Unknown ExpNode kind\n");
517              break;
518        }
519      }
520      else fprintf(listing,"Unknown node kind\n");
521      for (i=0;i<MAXCHILDREN;i++)
522           printTree(tree->child[i]);
523      tree = tree->sibling;
524    }
525    UNINDENT;
526  }


550  /****************************************************/
551  /* File: scan.h                                     */
552  /* The scanner interface for the TINY compiler      */
553  /* Compiler Construction: Principles and Practice   */
554  /* Kenneth C. Louden                                */
555  /****************************************************/
556
557  #ifndef _SCAN_H_
558  #define _SCAN_H_
559
560  /* MAXTOKENLEN is the maximum size of a token */
561  #define MAXTOKENLEN 40
562
563  /* tokenString array stores the lexeme of each token */
564  extern char tokenString[MAXTOKENLEN+1];
565
566  /* function getToken returns the
567   * next token in source file
568   */
569  TokenType getToken(void);
570
571  #endif


600  /****************************************************/
601  /* File: scan.c                                     */
602  /* The scanner implementation for the TINY compiler */
603  /* Compiler Construction: Principles and Practice   */
```

```
604  /* Kenneth C. Louden                                    */
605  /*****************************************************/
606
607  #include "globals.h"
608  #include "util.h"
609  #include "scan.h"
610
611  /* states in scanner DFA */
612  typedef enum
613     { START,INASSIGN,INCOMMENT,INNUM,INID,DONE }
614     StateType;
615
616  /* lexeme of identifier or reserved word */
617  char tokenString[MAXTOKENLEN+1];
618
619  /* BUFLEN = length of the input buffer for
620     source code lines */
621  #define BUFLEN 256
622
623  static char lineBuf[BUFLEN]; /* holds the current line */
624  static int linepos = 0; /* current position in LineBuf */
625  static int bufsize = 0; /* current size of buffer string */
626
627  /* getNextChar fetches the next non-blank character
628     from lineBuf, reading in a new line if lineBuf is
629     exhausted */
630  static char getNextChar(void)
631  { if (!(linepos < bufsize))
632    { lineno++;
633      if (fgets(lineBuf,BUFLEN-1,source))
634      { if (EchoSource) fprintf(listing,"%4d: %s",lineno,lineBuf);
635        bufsize = strlen(lineBuf);
636        linepos = 0;
637        return lineBuf[linepos++];
638      }
639      else return EOF;
640    }
641    else return lineBuf[linepos++];
642  }
643
644  /* ungetNextChar backtracks one character
645     in lineBuf */
646  static void ungetNextChar(void)
647  { linepos-- ;}
648
649  /* lookup table of reserved words */
650  static struct
```

```
651        { char* str;
652          TokenType tok;
653        } reservedWords[MAXRESERVED]
654    =  {{"if",IF},{"then",THEN},{"else",ELSE},{"end",END},
655        {"repeat",REPEAT},{"until",UNTIL},{"read",READ},
656        {"write",WRITE}};
657
658 /* lookup an identifier to see if it is a reserved word */
659 /* uses linear search */
660 static TokenType reservedLookup (char * s)
661 { int i;
662    for (i=0;i<MAXRESERVED;i++)
663      if (!strcmp(s,reservedWords[i].str))
664        return reservedWords[i].tok;
665    return ID;
666 }
667
668 /******************************************/
669 /* the primary function of the scanner   */
670 /******************************************/
671 /* function getToken returns the
672  * next token in source file
673  */
674 TokenType getToken(void)
675 {  /* index for storing into tokenString */
676    int tokenStringIndex = 0;
677    /* holds current token to be returned */
678    TokenType currentToken;
679    /* current state - always begins at START */
680    StateType state = START;
681    /* flag to indicate save to tokenString */
682    int save;
683    while (state != DONE)
684    { char c = getNextChar();
685      save = TRUE;
686      switch (state)
687      { case START:
688          if (isdigit(c))
689            state = INNUM;
690          else if (isalpha(c))
691            state = INID;
692          else if (c == ':')
693            state = INASSIGN;
694          else if ((c == ' ') || (c == '\t') || (c == '\n'))
695            save = FALSE;
696          else if (c == '{')
697          { save = FALSE;
```

```
698                     state = INCOMMENT;
699                  }
700               else
701               { state = DONE;
702                 switch (c)
703                 { case EOF:
704                     save = FALSE;
705                     currentToken = ENDFILE;
706                     break;
707                   case '=':
708                     currentToken = EQ;
709                     break;
710                   case '<':
711                     currentToken = LT;
712                     break;
713                   case '+':
714                     currentToken = PLUS;
715                     break;
716                   case '-':
717                     currentToken = MINUS;
718                     break;
719                   case '*':
720                     currentToken = TIMES;
721                     break;
722                   case '/':
723                     currentToken = OVER;
724                     break;
725                   case '(':
726                     currentToken = LPAREN;
727                     break;
728                   case ')':
729                     currentToken = RPAREN;
730                     break;
731                   case ';':
732                     currentToken = SEMI;
733                     break;
734                   default:
735                     currentToken = ERROR;
736                     break;
737                 }
738               }
739             break;
740           case INCOMMENT:
741             save = FALSE;
742             if (c == '}') state = START;
743             break;
744           case INASSIGN:
```

```
745              state = DONE;
746              if (c == '=')
747                 currentToken = ASSIGN;
748              else
749              { /* backup in the input */
750                 ungetNextChar();
751                 save = FALSE;
752                 currentToken = ERROR;
753              }
754              break;
755           case INNUM:
756              if (!isdigit(c))
757              { /* backup in the input */
758                 ungetNextChar();
759                 save = FALSE;
760                 state = DONE;
761                 currentToken = NUM;
762              }
763              break;
764           case INID:
765              if (!isalpha(c))
766              { /* backup in the input */
767                 ungetNextChar();
768                 save = FALSE;
769                 state = DONE;
770                 currentToken = ID;
771              }
772              break;
773           case DONE:
774           default: /* should never happen */
775              fprintf(listing,"Scanner Bug: state= %d\n",state);
776              state = DONE;
777              currentToken = ERROR;
778              break;
779        }
780        if ((save) && (tokenStringIndex <= MAXTOKENLEN))
781           tokenString[tokenStringIndex++] = c;
782        if (state == DONE)
783        { tokenString[tokenStringIndex] = '\0';
784           if (currentToken == ID)
785              currentToken = reservedLookup(tokenString);
786        }
787     }
788     if (TraceScan) {
789        fprintf(listing,"\t%d: ",lineno);
790        printToken(currentToken,tokenString);
791     }
```

```
792      return currentToken;
793 } /* end getToken */


850 /****************************************************/
851 /* File: parse.h                                    */
852 /* The parser interface for the TINY compiler       */
853 /* Compiler Construction: Principles and Practice    */
854 /* Kenneth C. Louden                                 */
855 /****************************************************/
856
857 #ifndef _PARSE_H_
858 #define _PARSE_H_
859
860 /* Function parse returns the newly
861  * constructed syntax tree
862  */
863 TreeNode * parse(void);
864
865 #endif


900 /****************************************************/
901 /* File: parse.c                                    */
902 /* The parser implementation for the TINY compiler */
903 /* Compiler Construction: Principles and Practice    */
904 /* Kenneth C. Louden                                 */
905 /****************************************************/
906
907 #include "globals.h"
908 #include "util.h"
909 #include "scan.h"
910 #include "parse.h"
911
912 static TokenType token; /* holds current token */
913
914 /* function prototypes for recursive calls */
915 static TreeNode * stmt_sequence(void);
916 static TreeNode * statement(void);
917 static TreeNode * if_stmt(void);
918 static TreeNode * repeat_stmt(void);
919 static TreeNode * assign_stmt(void);
920 static TreeNode * read_stmt(void);
921 static TreeNode * write_stmt(void);
922 static TreeNode * exp(void);
923 static TreeNode * simple_exp(void);
924 static TreeNode * term(void);
925 static TreeNode * factor(void);
```

```
926
927  static void syntaxError(char * message)
928  { fprintf(listing,"\n>>> ");
929    fprintf(listing,"Syntax error at line %d: %s",lineno,message);
930    Error = TRUE;
931  }
932
933  static void match(TokenType expected)
934  { if (token == expected) token = getToken();
935    else {
936      syntaxError("unexpected token -> ");
937      printToken(token,tokenString);
938      fprintf(listing,"        ");
939    }
940  }
941
942  TreeNode * stmt_sequence(void)
943  { TreeNode * t = statement();
944    TreeNode * p = t;
945    while ((token!=ENDFILE) && (token!=END) &&
946            (token!=ELSE) && (token!=UNTIL))
947    { TreeNode * q;
948      match(SEMI);
949      q = statement();
950      if (q!=NULL) {
951        if (t==NULL) t = p = q;
952        else /* now p cannot be NULL either */
953        { p->sibling = q;
954          p = q;
955        }
956      }
957    }
958    return t;
959  }
960
961  TreeNode * statement(void)
962  { TreeNode * t = NULL;
963    switch (token) {
964      case IF : t = if_stmt(); break;
965      case REPEAT : t = repeat_stmt(); break;
966      case ID : t = assign_stmt(); break;
967      case READ : t = read_stmt(); break;
968      case WRITE : t = write_stmt(); break;
969      default : syntaxError("unexpected token -> ");
970                printToken(token,tokenString);
971                token = getToken();
972                break;
973    } /* end case */
```

```
974     return t;
975   }
976
977   TreeNode * if_stmt(void)
978   { TreeNode * t = newStmtNode(IfK);
979     match(IF);
980     if (t!=NULL) t->child[0] = exp();
981     match(THEN);
982     if (t!=NULL) t->child[1] = stmt_sequence();
983     if (token==ELSE) {
984       match(ELSE);
985       if (t!=NULL) t->child[2] = stmt_sequence();
986     }
987     match(END);
988     return t;
989   }
990
991   TreeNode * repeat_stmt(void)
992   { TreeNode * t = newStmtNode(RepeatK);
993     match(REPEAT);
994     if (t!=NULL) t->child[0] = stmt_sequence();
995     match(UNTIL);
996     if (t!=NULL) t->child[1] = exp();
997     return t;
998   }
999
1000  TreeNode * assign_stmt(void)
1001  { TreeNode * t = newStmtNode(AssignK);
1002    if ((t!=NULL) && (token==ID))
1003      t->attr.name = copyString(tokenString);
1004    match(ID);
1005    match(ASSIGN);
1006    if (t!=NULL) t->child[0] = exp();
1007    return t;
1008  }
1009
1010  TreeNode * read_stmt(void)
1011  { TreeNode * t = newStmtNode(ReadK);
1012    match(READ);
1013    if ((t!=NULL) && (token==ID))
1014      t->attr.name = copyString(tokenString);
1015    match(ID);
1016    return t;
1017  }
1018
1019  TreeNode * write_stmt(void)
1020  { TreeNode * t = newStmtNode(WriteK);
```

```
1021    match(WRITE);
1022    if (t!=NULL) t->child[0] = exp();
1023    return t;
1024 }
1025
1026 TreeNode * exp(void)
1027 { TreeNode * t = simple_exp();
1028    if ((token==LT)||(token==EQ)) {
1029       TreeNode * p = newExpNode(OpK);
1030       if (p!=NULL) {
1031          p->child[0] = t;
1032          p->attr.op = token;
1033          t = p;
1034       }
1035       match(token);
1036       if (t!=NULL)
1037          t->child[1] = simple_exp();
1038    }
1039    return t;
1040 }
1041
1042 TreeNode * simple_exp(void)
1043 { TreeNode * t = term();
1044    while ((token==PLUS)||(token==MINUS))
1045    { TreeNode * p = newExpNode(OpK);
1046       if (p!=NULL) {
1047          p->child[0] = t;
1048          p->attr.op = token;
1049          t = p;
1050          match(token);
1051          t->child[1] = term();
1052       }
1053    }
1054    return t;
1055 }
1056
1057 TreeNode * term(void)
1058 { TreeNode * t = factor();
1059    while ((token==TIMES)||(token==OVER))
1060    { TreeNode * p = newExpNode(OpK);
1061       if (p!=NULL) {
1062          p->child[0] = t;
1063          p->attr.op = token;
1064          t = p;
1065          match(token);
1066          p->child[1] = factor();
1067       }
```

```
1068      }
1069      return t;
1070  }
1071
1072  TreeNode * factor(void)
1073  { TreeNode * t = NULL;
1074    switch (token) {
1075      case NUM :
1076        t = newExpNode(ConstK);
1077        if ((t!=NULL) && (token==NUM))
1078          t->attr.val = atoi(tokenString);
1079        match(NUM);
1080        break;
1081      case ID :
1082        t = newExpNode(IdK);
1083        if ((t!=NULL) && (token==ID))
1084          t->attr.name = copyString(tokenString);
1085        match(ID);
1086        break;
1087      case LPAREN :
1088        match(LPAREN);
1089        t = exp();
1090        match(RPAREN);
1091        break;
1092      default:
1093        syntaxError("unexpected token -> ");
1094        printToken(token,tokenString);
1095        token = getToken();
1096        break;
1097      }
1098    return t;
1099  }
1100
1101  /***************************************/
1102  /* the primary function of the parser  */
1103  /***************************************/
1104  /* Function parse returns the newly
1105   * constructed syntax tree
1106   */
1107  TreeNode * parse(void)
1108  { TreeNode * t;
1109    token = getToken();
1110    t = stmt_sequence();
1111    if (token!=ENDFILE)
1112      syntaxError("Code ends before file\n");
```

```
1113     return t;
1114  }

1150  /*****************************************************/
1151  /* File: symtab.h                                    */
1152  /* Symbol table interface for the TINY compiler      */
1153  /* (allows only one symbol table)                    */
1154  /* Compiler Construction: Principles and Practice    */
1155  /* Kenneth C. Louden                                 */
1156  /*****************************************************/
1157
1158  #ifndef _SYMTAB_H_
1159  #define _SYMTAB_H_
1160
1161  /* Procedure st_insert inserts line numbers and
1162   * memory locations into the symbol table
1163   * loc = memory location is inserted only the
1164   * first time, otherwise ignored
1165   */
1166  void st_insert( char * name, int lineno, int loc );
1167
1168  /* Function st_lookup returns the memory
1169   * location of a variable or -1 if not found
1170   */
1171  int st_lookup ( char * name );
1172
1173  /* Procedure printSymTab prints a formatted
1174   * listing of the symbol table contents
1175   * to the listing file
1176   */
1177  void printSymTab(FILE * listing);
1178
1179  #endif

1200  /*****************************************************/
1201  /* File: symtab.c                                    */
1202  /* Symbol table implementation for the TINY compiler */
1203  /* (allows only one symbol table)                    */
1204  /* Symbol table is implemented as a chained          */
1205  /* hash table                                        */
1206  /* Compiler Construction: Principles and Practice    */
1207  /* Kenneth C. Louden                                 */
1208  /*****************************************************/
1209
1210  #include <stdio.h>
```

```
1211 #include <stdlib.h>
1212 #include <string.h>
1213 #include "symtab.h"
1214
1215 /* SIZE is the size of the hash table */
1216 #define SIZE 211
1217
1218 /* SHIFT is the power of two used as multiplier
1219    in hash function  */
1220 #define SHIFT 4
1221
1222 /* the hash function */
1223 static int hash ( char * key )
1224 { int temp = 0;
1225   int i = 0;
1226   while (key[i] != '\0')
1227   { temp = ((temp << SHIFT) + key[i]) % SIZE;
1228     ++i;
1229   }
1230   return temp;
1231 }
1232
1233 /* the list of line numbers of the source
1234  * code in which a variable is referenced
1235  */
1236 typedef struct LineListRec
1237    { int lineno;
1238      struct LineListRec * next;
1239    } * LineList;
1240
1241 /* The record in the bucket lists for
1242  * each variable, including name,
1243  * assigned memory location, and
1244  * the list of line numbers in which
1245  * it appears in the source code
1246  */
1247 typedef struct BucketListRec
1248    { char * name;
1249      LineList lines;
1250      int memloc ; /* memory location for variable */
1251      struct BucketListRec * next;
1252    } * BucketList;
1253
1254 /* the hash table */
1255 static BucketList hashTable[SIZE];
1256
1257 /* Procedure st_insert inserts line numbers and
```

```
1258    * memory locations into the symbol table
1259    * loc = memory location is inserted only the
1260    * first time, otherwise ignored
1261    */
1262   void st_insert( char * name, int lineno, int loc )
1263   { int h = hash(name);
1264     BucketList l =  hashTable[h];
1265     while ((l != NULL) && (strcmp(name,l->name) != 0))
1266       l = l->next;
1267     if (l == NULL) /* variable not yet in table */
1268     { l = (BucketList) malloc(sizeof(struct BucketListRec));
1269       l->name = name;
1270       l->lines = (LineList) malloc(sizeof(struct LineListRec));
1271       l->lines->lineno = lineno;
1272       l->memloc = loc;
1273       l->lines->next = NULL;
1274       l->next = hashTable[h];
1275       hashTable[h] = l; }
1276     else /* found in table, so just add line number */
1277     { LineList t = l->lines;
1278       while (t->next != NULL) t = t->next;
1279       t->next = (LineList) malloc(sizeof(struct LineListRec));
1280       t->next->lineno = lineno;
1281       t->next->next = NULL;
1282     }
1283   } /* st_insert */
1284
1285   /* Function st_lookup returns the memory
1286    * location of a variable or -1 if not found
1287    */
1288   int st_lookup ( char * name )
1289   { int h = hash(name);
1290     BucketList l =  hashTable[h];
1291     while ((l != NULL) && (strcmp(name,l->name) != 0))
1292       l = l->next;
1293     if (l == NULL) return -1;
1294     else return l->memloc;
1295   }
1296
1297   /* Procedure printSymTab prints a formatted
1298    * listing of the symbol table contents
1299    * to the listing file
1300    */
1301   void printSymTab(FILE * listing)
1302   { int i;
1303     fprintf(listing,"Variable Name  Location   Line Numbers\n");
1304     fprintf(listing,"-------------  -------    -----------\n");
```

```
1305    for (i=0;i<SIZE;++i)
1306    { if (hashTable[i] != NULL)
1307      { BucketList l = hashTable[i];
1308        while (l != NULL)
1309        { LineList t = l->lines;
1310          fprintf(listing,"%-14s ",l->name);
1311          fprintf(listing,"%-8d  ",l->memloc);
1312          while (t != NULL)
1313          { fprintf(listing,"%4d ",t->lineno);
1314            t = t->next;
1315          }
1316          fprintf(listing,"\n");
1317          l = l->next;
1318        }
1319      }
1320    }
1321 } /* printSymTab */


1350 /******************************************************/
1351 /* File: analyze.h                                    */
1352 /* Semantic analyzer interface for TINY compiler      */
1353 /* Compiler Construction: Principles and Practice     */
1354 /* Kenneth C. Louden                                  */
1355 /******************************************************/
1356
1357 #ifndef _ANALYZE_H_
1358 #define _ANALYZE_H_
1359
1360 /* Function buildSymtab constructs the symbol
1361  * table by preorder traversal of the syntax tree
1362  */
1363 void buildSymtab(TreeNode *);
1364
1365 /* Procedure typeCheck performs type checking
1366  * by a postorder syntax tree traversal
1367  */
1368 void typeCheck(TreeNode *);
1369
1370 #endif


1400 /******************************************************/
1401 /* File: analyze.c                                    */
1402 /* Semantic analyzer implementation                   */
1403 /* for the TINY compiler                              */
1404 /* Compiler Construction: Principles and Practice     */
```

```
1405  /* Kenneth C. Louden                                    */
1406  /***************************************************/
1407
1408  #include "globals.h"
1409  #include "symtab.h"
1410  #include "analyze.h"
1411
1412  /* counter for variable memory locations */
1413  static int location = 0;
1414
1415  /* Procedure traverse is a generic recursive
1416   * syntax tree traversal routine:
1417   * it applies preProc in preorder and postProc
1418   * in postorder to tree pointed to by t
1419   */
1420  static void traverse( TreeNode * t,
1421                  void (* preProc) (TreeNode *),
1422                  void (* postProc) (TreeNode *) )
1423  { if (t != NULL)
1424    { preProc(t);
1425      { int i;
1426        for (i=0; i < MAXCHILDREN; i++)
1427          traverse(t->child[i],preProc,postProc);
1428      }
1429      postProc(t);
1430      traverse(t->sibling,preProc,postProc);
1431    }
1432  }
1433
1434  /* nullProc is a do-nothing procedure to
1435   * generate preorder-only or postorder-only
1436   * traversals from traverse
1437   */
1438  static void nullProc(TreeNode * t)
1439  { if (t==NULL) return;
1440    else return;
1441  }
1442
1443  /* Procedure insertNode inserts
1444   * identifiers stored in t into
1445   * the symbol table
1446   */
1447  static void insertNode( TreeNode * t)
1448  { switch (t->nodekind)
1449    { case StmtK:
1450        switch (t->kind.stmt)
1451        { case AssignK:
```

```
1452            case ReadK:
1453              /* not yet in table, so treat as new definition */
1454              if (st_lookup(t->attr.name) == -1)
1455                st_insert(t->attr.name,t->lineno,location++);
1456              else
1457              /* already in table, so ignore location,
1458                 add line number of use only */
1459                st_insert(t->attr.name,t->lineno,0);
1460              break;
1461            default:
1462              break;
1463          }
1464          break;
1465        case ExpK:
1466          switch (t->kind.exp)
1467          { case IdK:
1468              /* not yet in table, so treat as new definition */
1469              if (st_lookup(t->attr.name) == -1)
1470                st_insert(t->attr.name,t->lineno,location++);
1471              else
1472              /* already in table, so ignore location,
1473                 add line number of use only */
1474                st_insert(t->attr.name,t->lineno,0);
1475              break;
1476            default:
1477              break;
1478          }
1479          break;
1480        default:
1481          break;
1482      }
1483 }
1484
1485 /* Function buildSymtab constructs the symbol
1486  * table by preorder traversal of the syntax tree
1487  */
1488 void buildSymtab(TreeNode * syntaxTree)
1489 { traverse(syntaxTree,insertNode,nullProc);
1490   if (TraceAnalyze)
1491   { fprintf(listing,"\nSymbol table:\n\n");
1492     printSymTab(listing);
1493   }
1494 }
1495
1496 static void typeError(TreeNode * t, char * message)
1497 { fprintf(listing,"Type error at line %d: %s\n",t->lineno,message);
1498   Error = TRUE;
```

```
1499  }
1500
1501  /* Procedure checkNode performs
1502   * type checking at a single tree node
1503   */
1504  static void checkNode(TreeNode * t)
1505  { switch (t->nodekind)
1506    { case ExpK:
1507        switch (t->kind.exp)
1508        { case OpK:
1509            if ((t->child[0]->type != Integer) ||
1510                (t->child[1]->type != Integer))
1511              typeError(t,"Op applied to non-integer");
1512            if ((t->attr.op == EQ) || (t->attr.op == LT))
1513              t->type = Boolean;
1514            else
1515              t->type = Integer;
1516            break;
1517          case ConstK:
1518          case IdK:
1519            t->type = Integer;
1520            break;
1521          default:
1522            break;
1523        }
1524        break;
1525      case StmtK:
1526        switch (t->kind.stmt)
1527        { case IfK:
1528            if (t->child[0]->type == Integer)
1529              typeError(t->child[0],"if test is not Boolean");
1530            break;
1531          case AssignK:
1532            if (t->child[0]->type != Integer)
1533              typeError(t->child[0],"assignment of non-integer value");
1534            break;
1535          case WriteK:
1536            if (t->child[0]->type != Integer)
1537              typeError(t->child[0],"write of non-integer value");
1538            break;
1539          case RepeatK:
1540            if (t->child[1]->type == Integer)
1541              typeError(t->child[1],"repeat test is not Boolean");
1542            break;
1543          default:
1544            break;
1545        }
```

```
1546          break;
1547       default:
1548          break;
1549
1550    }
1551 }
1552
1553 /* Procedure typeCheck performs type checking
1554  * by a postorder syntax tree traversal
1555  */
1556 void typeCheck(TreeNode * syntaxTree)
1557 { traverse(syntaxTree,nullProc,checkNode);
1558 }


1600 /****************************************************/
1601 /* File: code.h                                     */
1602 /* Code emitting utilities for the TINY compiler    */
1603 /* and interface to the TM machine                  */
1604 /* Compiler Construction: Principles and Practice   */
1605 /* Kenneth C. Louden                                */
1606 /****************************************************/
1607
1608 #ifndef _CODE_H_
1609 #define _CODE_H_
1610
1611 /* pc = program counter   */
1612 #define  pc 7
1613
1614 /* mp = "memory pointer" points
1615  * to top of memory (for temp storage)
1616  */
1617 #define  mp 6
1618
1619 /* gp = "global pointer" points
1620  * to bottom of memory for (global)
1621  * variable storage
1622  */
1623 #define gp 5
1624
1625 /* accumulator */
1626 #define  ac 0
1627
1628 /* 2nd accumulator */
1629 #define  ac1 1
1630
1631 /* code emitting utilities */
```

```
1632
1633  /* Procedure emitRO emits a register-only
1634   * TM instruction
1635   * op = the opcode
1636   * r = target register
1637   * s = 1st source register
1638   * t = 2nd source register
1639   * c = a comment to be printed if TraceCode is TRUE
1640   */
1641  void emitRO( char *op, int r, int s, int t, char *c);
1642
1643  /* Procedure emitRM emits a register-to-memory
1644   * TM instruction
1645   * op = the opcode
1646   * r = target register
1647   * d = the offset
1648   * s = the base register
1649   * c = a comment to be printed if TraceCode is TRUE
1650   */
1651  void emitRM( char * op, int r, int d, int s, char *c);
1652
1653  /* Function emitSkip skips "howMany" code
1654   * locations for later backpatch. It also
1655   * returns the current code position
1656   */
1657  int emitSkip( int howMany);
1658
1659  /* Procedure emitBackup backs up to
1660   * loc = a previously skipped location
1661   */
1662  void emitBackup( int loc);
1663
1664  /* Procedure emitRestore restores the current
1665   * code position to the highest previously
1666   * unemitted position
1667   */
1668  void emitRestore(void);
1669
1670  /* Procedure emitComment prints a comment line
1671   * with comment c in the code file
1672   */
1673  void emitComment( char * c );
1674
1675  /* Procedure emitRM_Abs converts an absolute reference
1676   * to a pc-relative reference when emitting a
1677   * register-to-memory TM instruction
1678   * op = the opcode
```

```
1679   * r = target register
1680   * a = the absolute location in memory
1681   * c = a comment to be printed if TraceCode is TRUE
1682   */
1683  void emitRM_Abs( char *op, int r, int a, char * c);
1684
1685  #endif


1700  /***********************************************/
1701  /* File: code.c                              */
1702  /* TM Code emitting utilities                */
1703  /* implementation for the TINY compiler      */
1704  /* Compiler Construction: Principles and Practice  */
1705  /* Kenneth C. Louden                         */
1706  /***********************************************/
1707
1708  #include "globals.h"
1709  #include "code.h"
1710
1711  /* TM location number for current instruction emission */
1712  static int emitLoc = 0 ;
1713
1714  /* Highest TM location emitted so far
1715     For use in conjunction with emitSkip,
1716     emitBackup, and emitRestore */
1717  static int highEmitLoc = 0;
1718
1719  /* Procedure emitComment prints a comment line
1720   * with comment c in the code file
1721   */
1722  void emitComment( char * c )
1723  { if (TraceCode) fprintf(code,"* %s\n",c);}
1724
1725  /* Procedure emitRO emits a register-only
1726   * TM instruction
1727   * op = the opcode
1728   * r = target register
1729   * s = 1st source register
1730   * t = 2nd source register
1731   * c = a comment to be printed if TraceCode is TRUE
1732   */
1733  void emitRO( char *op, int r, int s, int t, char *c)
1734  { fprintf(code,"%3d:  %5s  %d,%d,%d ",emitLoc++,op,r,s,t);
1735    if (TraceCode) fprintf(code,"\t%s",c) ;
1736    fprintf(code,"\n") ;
1737    if (highEmitLoc < emitLoc) highEmitLoc = emitLoc ;
```

```
1738  } /* emitRO */
1739
1740  /* Procedure emitRM emits a register-to-memory
1741   * TM instruction
1742   * op = the opcode
1743   * r = target register
1744   * d = the offset
1745   * s = the base register
1746   * c = a comment to be printed if TraceCode is TRUE
1747   */
1748  void emitRM( char * op, int r, int d, int s, char *c)
1749  { fprintf(code,"%3d:  %5s  %d,%d(%d) ",emitLoc++,op,r,d,s);
1750    if (TraceCode) fprintf(code,"\t%s",c) ;
1751    fprintf(code,"\n") ;
1752    if (highEmitLoc < emitLoc)  highEmitLoc = emitLoc ;
1753  } /* emitRM */
1754
1755  /* Function emitSkip skips "howMany" code
1756   * locations for later backpatch. It also
1757   * returns the current code position
1758   */
1759  int emitSkip( int howMany)
1760  {   int i = emitLoc;
1761      emitLoc += howMany ;
1762      if (highEmitLoc < emitLoc)  highEmitLoc = emitLoc ;
1763      return i;
1764  } /* emitSkip */
1765
1766  /* Procedure emitBackup backs up to
1767   * loc = a previously skipped location
1768   */
1769  void emitBackup( int loc)
1770  { if (loc > highEmitLoc) emitComment("BUG in emitBackup");
1771    emitLoc = loc ;
1772  } /* emitBackup */
1773
1774  /* Procedure emitRestore restores the current
1775   * code position to the highest previously
1776   * unemitted position
1777   */
1778  void emitRestore(void)
1779  { emitLoc = highEmitLoc;}
1780
1781  /* Procedure emitRM_Abs converts an absolute reference
1782   * to a pc-relative reference when emitting a
1783   * register-to-memory TM instruction
1784   * op = the opcode
```

```
1785   * r = target register
1786   * a = the absolute location in memory
1787   * c = a comment to be printed if TraceCode is TRUE
1788   */
1789 void emitRM_Abs( char *op, int r, int a, char * c)
1790 { fprintf(code,"%3d:   %5s   %d,%d(%d) ",
1791                  emitLoc,op,r,a-(emitLoc+1),pc);
1792   ++emitLoc ;
1793   if (TraceCode) fprintf(code,"\t%s",c) ;
1794   fprintf(code,"\n") ;
1795   if (highEmitLoc < emitLoc) highEmitLoc = emitLoc ;
1796 } /* emitRM_Abs */
```


```
1850 /****************************************************/
1851 /* File: cgen.h                                     */
1852 /* The code generator interface to the TINY compiler */
1853 /* Compiler Construction: Principles and Practice    */
1854 /* Kenneth C. Louden                                */
1855 /****************************************************/
1856
1857 #ifndef _CGEN_H_
1858 #define _CGEN_H_
1859
1860 /* Procedure codeGen generates code to a code
1861  * file by traversal of the syntax tree. The
1862  * second parameter (codefile) is the file name
1863  * of the code file, and is used to print the
1864  * file name as a comment in the code file
1865  */
1866 void codeGen(TreeNode * syntaxTree, char * codefile);
1867
1868 #endif
```


```
1900 /****************************************************/
1901 /* File: cgen.c                                     */
1902 /* The code generator implementation                */
1903 /* for the TINY compiler                            */
1904 /* (generates code for the TM machine)              */
1905 /* Compiler Construction: Principles and Practice    */
1906 /* Kenneth C. Louden                                */
1907 /****************************************************/
1908
1909 #include "globals.h"
1910 #include "symtab.h"
1911 #include "code.h"
```

```
1912  #include "cgen.h"
1913
1914  /* tmpOffset is the memory offset for temps
1915     It is decremented each time a temp is
1916     stored, and incremented when loaded again
1917  */
1918  static int tmpOffset = 0;
1919
1920  /* prototype for internal recursive code generator */
1921  static void cGen (TreeNode * tree);
1922
1923  /* Procedure genStmt generates code at a statement node */
1924  static void genStmt( TreeNode * tree)
1925  { TreeNode * p1, * p2, * p3;
1926    int savedLoc1,savedLoc2,currentLoc;
1927    int loc;
1928    switch (tree->kind.stmt) {
1929
1930        case IfK :
1931            if (TraceCode) emitComment("-> if") ;
1932            p1 = tree->child[0] ;
1933            p2 = tree->child[1] ;
1934            p3 = tree->child[2] ;
1935            /* generate code for test expression */
1936            cGen(p1);
1937            savedLoc1 = emitSkip(1) ;
1938            emitComment("if: jump to else belongs here");
1939            /* recurse on then part */
1940            cGen(p2);
1941            savedLoc2 = emitSkip(1) ;
1942            emitComment("if: jump to end belongs here");
1943            currentLoc = emitSkip(0) ;
1944            emitBackup(savedLoc1) ;
1945            emitRM_Abs("JEQ",ac,currentLoc,"if: jmp to else");
1946            emitRestore() ;
1947            /* recurse on else part */
1948            cGen(p3);
1949            currentLoc = emitSkip(0) ;
1950            emitBackup(savedLoc2) ;
1951            emitRM_Abs("LDA",pc,currentLoc,"jmp to end") ;
1952            emitRestore() ;
1953            if (TraceCode)  emitComment("<- if") ;
1954            break; /* if_k */
1955
1956        case RepeatK:
1957            if (TraceCode) emitComment("-> repeat") ;
1958            p1 = tree->child[0] ;
```

```
1959              p2 = tree->child[1] ;
1960              savedLoc1 = emitSkip(0);
1961              emitComment("repeat: jump after body comes back here");
1962              /* generate code for body */
1963              cGen(p1);
1964              /* generate code for test */
1965              cGen(p2);
1966              emitRM_Abs("JEQ",ac,savedLoc1,"repeat: jmp back to body");
1967              if (TraceCode)  emitComment("<- repeat") ;
1968              break; /* repeat */
1969
1970         case AssignK:
1971              if (TraceCode) emitComment("-> assign") ;
1972              /* generate code for rhs */
1973              cGen(tree->child[0]);
1974              /* now store value */
1975              loc = st_lookup(tree->attr.name);
1976              emitRM("ST",ac,loc,gp,"assign: store value");
1977              if (TraceCode)  emitComment("<- assign") ;
1978              break; /* assign_k */
1979
1980         case ReadK:
1981              emitRO("IN",ac,0,0,"read integer value");
1982              loc = st_lookup(tree->attr.name);
1983              emitRM("ST",ac,loc,gp,"read: store value");
1984              break;
1985         case WriteK:
1986              /* generate code for expression to write */
1987              cGen(tree->child[0]);
1988              /* now output it */
1989              emitRO("OUT",ac,0,0,"write ac");
1990              break;
1991         default:
1992              break;
1993      }
1994 } /* genStmt */
1995
1996 /* Procedure genExp generates code at an expression node */
1997 static void genExp( TreeNode * tree)
1998 { int loc;
1999    TreeNode * p1, * p2;
2000    switch (tree->kind.exp) {
2001
2002      case ConstK :
2003         if (TraceCode) emitComment("-> Const") ;
2004         /* gen code to load integer constant using LDC */
2005         emitRM("LDC",ac,tree->attr.val,0,"load const");
```

```
2006        if (TraceCode)  emitComment("<- Const") ;
2007        break; /* ConstK */
2008
2009    case IdK :
2010        if (TraceCode) emitComment("-> Id") ;
2011        loc = st_lookup(tree->attr.name);
2012        emitRM("LD",ac,loc,gp,"load id value");
2013        if (TraceCode)  emitComment("<- Id") ;
2014        break; /* IdK */
2015
2016    case OpK :
2017        if (TraceCode) emitComment("-> Op") ;
2018        p1 = tree->child[0];
2019        p2 = tree->child[1];
2020        /* gen code for ac = left arg */
2021        cGen(p1);
2022        /* gen code to push left operand */
2023        emitRM("ST",ac,tmpOffset--,mp,"op: push left");
2024        /* gen code for ac = right operand */
2025        cGen(p2);
2026        /* now load left operand */
2027        emitRM("LD",ac1,++tmpOffset,mp,"op: load left");
2028        switch (tree->attr.op) {
2029          case PLUS :
2030            emitRO("ADD",ac,ac1,ac,"op +");
2031            break;
2032          case MINUS :
2033            emitRO("SUB",ac,ac1,ac,"op -");
2034            break;
2035          case TIMES :
2036            emitRO("MUL",ac,ac1,ac,"op *");
2037            break;
2038          case OVER :
2039            emitRO("DIV",ac,ac1,ac,"op /");
2040            break;
2041          case LT :
2042            emitRO("SUB",ac,ac1,ac,"op <") ;
2043            emitRM("JLT",ac,2,pc,"br if true") ;
2044            emitRM("LDC",ac,0,ac,"false case") ;
2045            emitRM("LDA",pc,1,pc,"unconditional jmp") ;
2046            emitRM("LDC",ac,1,ac,"true case") ;
2047            break;
2048          case EQ :
2049            emitRO("SUB",ac,ac1,ac,"op ==") ;
2050            emitRM("JEQ",ac,2,pc,"br if true");
2051            emitRM("LDC",ac,0,ac,"false case") ;
2052            emitRM("LDA",pc,1,pc,"unconditional jmp") ;
```

```
2053                    emitRM("LDC",ac,1,ac,"true case") ;
2054                    break;
2055              default:
2056                    emitComment("BUG: Unknown operator");
2057                    break;
2058          } /* case op */
2059          if (TraceCode)  emitComment("<- Op") ;
2060          break; /* OpK */
2061
2062      default:
2063          break;
2064    }
2065 } /* genExp */
2066
2067 /* Procedure cGen recursively generates code by
2068  * tree traversal
2069  */
2070 static void cGen( TreeNode * tree)
2071 { if (tree != NULL)
2072    { switch (tree->nodekind) {
2073        case StmtK:
2074          genStmt(tree);
2075          break;
2076        case ExpK:
2077          genExp(tree);
2078          break;
2079        default:
2080          break;
2081    }
2082    cGen(tree->sibling);
2083    }
2084 }
2085
2086 /***************************************************/
2087 /* the primary function of the code generator   */
2088 /***************************************************/
2089 /* Procedure codeGen generates code to a code
2090  * file by traversal of the syntax tree. The
2091  * second parameter (codefile) is the file name
2092  * of the code file, and is used to print the
2093  * file name as a comment in the code file
2094  */
2095 void codeGen(TreeNode * syntaxTree, char * codefile)
2096 {   char * s = malloc(strlen(codefile)+7);
2097     strcpy(s,"File: ");
2098     strcat(s,codefile);
2099     emitComment("TINY Compilation to TM Code");
```

```
2100        emitComment(s);
2101        /* generate standard prelude */
2102        emitComment("Standard prelude:");
2103        emitRM("LD",mp,0,ac,"load maxaddress from location 0");
2104        emitRM("ST",ac,0,ac,"clear location 0");
2105        emitComment("End of standard prelude.");
2106        /* generate code for TINY program */
2107        cGen(syntaxTree);
2108        /* finish */
2109        emitComment("End of execution.");
2110        emitRO("HALT",0,0,0,"");
2111  }


3000  /****************************************************/
3001  /* File: tiny.l                                     */
3002  /* Lex specification for TINY                       */
3003  /* Compiler Construction: Principles and Practice   */
3004  /* Kenneth C. Louden                                */
3005  /****************************************************/
3006
3007  %{
3008  #include "globals.h"
3009  #include "util.h"
3010  #include "scan.h"
3011  /* lexeme of identifier or reserved word */
3012  char tokenString[MAXTOKENLEN+1];
3013  %}
3014
3015  digit          [0-9]
3016  number         {digit}+
3017  letter         [a-zA-Z]
3018  identifier     {letter}+
3019  newline        \n
3020  whitespace     [ \t]+
3021
3022  %%
3023
3024  "if"           {return IF;}
3025  "then"         {return THEN;}
3026  "else"         {return ELSE;}
3027  "end"          {return END;}
3028  "repeat"       {return REPEAT;}
3029  "until"        {return UNTIL;}
3030  "read"         {return READ;}
3031  "write"        {return WRITE;}
3032  ":="           {return ASSIGN;}
```

```
3033  "="              {return EQ;}
3034  "<"              {return LT;}
3035  "+"              {return PLUS;}
3036  "-"              {return MINUS;}
3037  "*"              {return TIMES;}
3038  "/"              {return OVER;}
3039  "("              {return LPAREN;}
3040  ")"              {return RPAREN;}
3041  ";"              {return SEMI;}
3042  {number}         {return NUM;}
3043  {identifier}     {return ID;}
3044  {newline}        {lineno++;}
3045  {whitespace}     {/* skip whitespace */}
3046  "{"              { char c;
3047                     do
3048                     { c = input();
3049                       if (c == '\n') lineno++;
3050                     } while (c != '}');
3051                   }
3052  .                {return ERROR;}
3053
3054  %%
3055
3056  TokenType getToken(void)
3057  { static int firstTime = TRUE;
3058    TokenType currentToken;
3059    if (firstTime)
3060    { firstTime = FALSE;
3061      lineno++;
3062      yyin = source;
3063      yyout = listing;
3064    }
3065    currentToken = yylex();
3066    strncpy(tokenString,yytext,MAXTOKENLEN);
3067    if (TraceScan) {
3068      fprintf(listing,"\t%d: ",lineno);
3069      printToken(currentToken,tokenString);
3070    }
3071    return currentToken;
3072  }


4000  /******************************************************/
4001  /* File: tiny.y                                       */
4002  /* The TINY Yacc/Bison specification file             */
4003  /* Compiler Construction: Principles and Practice     */
4004  /* Kenneth C. Louden                                  */
```

```
4005 /*****************************************************/
4006 %{
4007 #define YYPARSER /* distinguishes Yacc output from other code files */
4008
4009 #include "globals.h"
4010 #include "util.h"
4011 #include "scan.h"
4012 #include "parse.h"
4013
4014 #define YYSTYPE TreeNode *
4015 static char * savedName; /* for use in assignments */
4016 static int savedLineNo;  /* ditto */
4017 static TreeNode * savedTree; /* stores syntax tree for later return */
4018
4019 %}
4020
4021 %token IF THEN ELSE END REPEAT UNTIL READ WRITE
4022 %token ID NUM
4023 %token ASSIGN EQ LT PLUS MINUS TIMES OVER LPAREN RPAREN SEMI
4024 %token ERROR
4025
4026 %% /* Grammar for TINY */
4027
4028 program        : stmt_seq
4029                     { savedTree = $1;}
4030                ;
4031 stmt_seq       : stmt_seq SEMI stmt
4032                     { YYSTYPE t = $1;
4033                       if (t != NULL)
4034                       { while (t->sibling != NULL)
4035                            t = t->sibling;
4036                         t->sibling = $3;
4037                         $$ = $1; }
4038                       else $$ = $3;
4039                     }
4040                | stmt  { $$ = $1; }
4041                ;
4042 stmt           : if_stmt { $$ = $1; }
4043                | repeat_stmt { $$ = $1; }
4044                | assign_stmt { $$ = $1; }
4045                | read_stmt { $$ = $1; }
4046                | write_stmt { $$ = $1; }
4047                | error  { $$ = NULL; }
4048                ;
4049 if_stmt        : IF exp THEN stmt_seq END
4050                     { $$ = newStmtNode(IfK);
4051                       $$->child[0] = $2;
```

```
4052                          $$->child[1] = $4;
4053                      }
4054                  | IF exp THEN stmt_seq ELSE stmt_seq END
4055                      { $$ = newStmtNode(IfK);
4056                        $$->child[0] = $2;
4057                        $$->child[1] = $4;
4058                        $$->child[2] = $6;
4059                      }
4060              ;
4061  repeat_stmt  : REPEAT stmt_seq UNTIL exp
4062                      { $$ = newStmtNode(RepeatK);
4063                        $$->child[0] = $2;
4064                        $$->child[1] = $4;
4065                      }
4066              ;
4067  assign_stmt  : ID { savedName = copyString(tokenString);
4068                      savedLineNo = lineno; }
4069                  ASSIGN exp
4070                      { $$ = newStmtNode(AssignK);
4071                        $$->child[0] = $4;
4072                        $$->attr.name = savedName;
4073                        $$->lineno = savedLineNo;
4074                      }
4075              ;
4076  read_stmt    : READ ID
4077                      { $$ = newStmtNode(ReadK);
4078                        $$->attr.name =
4079                          copyString(tokenString);
4080                      }
4081              ;
4082  write_stmt   : WRITE exp
4083                      { $$ = newStmtNode(WriteK);
4084                        $$->child[0] = $2;
4085                      }
4086              ;
4087  exp          : simple_exp LT simple_exp
4088                      { $$ = newExpNode(OpK);
4089                        $$->child[0] = $1;
4090                        $$->child[1] = $3;
4091                        $$->attr.op = LT;
4092                      }
4093                  | simple_exp EQ simple_exp
4094                      { $$ = newExpNode(OpK);
4095                        $$->child[0] = $1;
4096                        $$->child[1] = $3;
4097                        $$->attr.op = EQ;
4098                      }
```

```
4099                      | simple_exp { $$ = $1; }
4100                      ;
4101   simple_exp         : simple_exp PLUS term
4102                          { $$ = newExpNode(OpK);
4103                            $$->child[0] = $1;
4104                            $$->child[1] = $3;
4105                            $$->attr.op = PLUS;
4106                          }
4107                      | simple_exp MINUS term
4108                          { $$ = newExpNode(OpK);
4109                            $$->child[0] = $1;
4110                            $$->child[1] = $3;
4111                            $$->attr.op = MINUS;
4112                          }
4113                      | term { $$ = $1; }
4114                      ;
4115   term               : term TIMES factor
4116                          { $$ = newExpNode(OpK);
4117                            $$->child[0] = $1;
4118                            $$->child[1] = $3;
4119                            $$->attr.op = TIMES;
4120                          }
4121                      | term OVER factor
4122                          { $$ = newExpNode(OpK);
4123                            $$->child[0] = $1;
4124                            $$->child[1] = $3;
4125                            $$->attr.op = OVER;
4126                          }
4127                      | factor { $$ = $1; }
4128                      ;
4129   factor             : LPAREN exp RPAREN
4130                          { $$ = $2; }
4131                      | NUM
4132                          { $$ = newExpNode(ConstK);
4133                            $$->attr.val = atoi(tokenString);
4134                          }
4135                      | ID { $$ = newExpNode(IdK);
4136                            $$->attr.name =
4137                                  copyString(tokenString);
4138                          }
4139                      | error { $$ = NULL; }
4140                      ;
4141
4142   %%
4143
4144   int yyerror(char * message)
4145   { fprintf(listing,"Syntax error at line %d: %s\n",lineno,message);
```

```
4146    fprintf(listing,"Current token: ");
4147    printToken(yychar,tokenString);
4148    Error = TRUE;
4149    return 0;
4150 }
4151
4152 /* yylex calls getToken to make Yacc/Bison output
4153  * compatible with earlier versions of
4154  * the TINY scanner
4155  */
4156 static int yylex(void)
4157 { return getToken(); }
4158
4159 TreeNode * parse(void)
4160 { yyparse();
4161    return savedTree;
4162 }


4200 /****************************************************/
4201 /* File: globals.h                                  */
4202 /* Yacc/Bison Version                               */
4203 /* Global types and vars for TINY compiler          */
4204 /* must come before other include files             */
4205 /* Compiler Construction: Principles and Practice   */
4206 /* Kenneth C. Louden                                */
4207 /****************************************************/
4208
4209 #ifndef _GLOBALS_H_
4210 #define _GLOBALS_H_
4211
4212 #include <stdio.h>
4213 #include <stdlib.h>
4214 #include <ctype.h>
4215 #include <string.h>
4216
4217 /* Yacc/Bison generates internally its own values
4218  * for the tokens. Other files can access these values
4219  * by including the tab.h file generated using the
4220  * Yacc/Bison option -d ("generate header")
4221  *
4222  * The YYPARSER flag prevents inclusion of the tab.h
4223  * into the Yacc/Bison output itself
4224  */
4225
4226 #ifndef YYPARSER
4227
```

```
4228  /* the name of the following file may change */
4229  #include "y.tab.h"
4230
4231  /* ENDFILE is implicitly defined by Yacc/Bison,
4232   * and not included in the tab.h file
4233   */
4234  #define ENDFILE 0
4235
4236  #endif
4237
4238  #ifndef FALSE
4239  #define FALSE 0
4240  #endif
4241
4242  #ifndef TRUE
4243  #define TRUE 1
4244  #endif
4245
4246  /* MAXRESERVED = the number of reserved words */
4247  #define MAXRESERVED 8
4248
4249  /* Yacc/Bison generates its own integer values
4250   * for tokens
4251   */
4252  typedef int TokenType;
4253
4254  extern FILE* source; /* source code text file */
4255  extern FILE* listing; /* listing output text file */
4256  extern FILE* code; /* code text file for TM simulator */
4257
4258  extern int lineno; /* source line number for listing */
4259
4260  /**************************************************/
4261  /**********   Syntax tree for parsing   ***********/
4262  /**************************************************/
4263
4264  typedef enum {StmtK,ExpK} NodeKind;
4265  typedef enum {IfK,RepeatK,AssignK,ReadK,WriteK} StmtKind;
4266  typedef enum {OpK,ConstK,IdK} ExpKind;
4267
4268  /* ExpType is used for type checking */
4269  typedef enum {Void,Integer,Boolean} ExpType;
4270
4271  #define MAXCHILDREN 3
4272
4273  typedef struct treeNode
4274     { struct treeNode * child[MAXCHILDREN];
```

```
4275        struct treeNode * sibling;
4276        int lineno;
4277        NodeKind nodekind;
4278        union { StmtKind stmt; ExpKind exp;} kind;
4279        union { TokenType op;
4280                int val;
4281                char * name; } attr;
4282        ExpType type; /* for type checking of exps */
4283    } TreeNode;
4284
4285 /***************************************************/
4286 /**********      Flags for tracing      **********/
4287 /***************************************************/
4288
4289 /* EchoSource = TRUE causes the source program to
4290  * be echoed to the listing file with line numbers
4291  * during parsing
4292  */
4293 extern int EchoSource;
4294
4295 /* TraceScan = TRUE causes token information to be
4296  * printed to the listing file as each token is
4297  * recognized by the scanner
4298  */
4299 extern int TraceScan;
4300
4301 /* TraceParse = TRUE causes the syntax tree to be
4302  * printed to the listing file in linearized form
4303  * (using indents for children)
4304  */
4305 extern int TraceParse;
4306
4307 /* TraceAnalyze = TRUE causes symbol table inserts
4308  * and lookups to be reported to the listing file
4309  */
4310 extern int TraceAnalyze;
4311
4312 /* TraceCode = TRUE causes comments to be written
4313  * to the TM code file as code is generated
4314  */
4315 extern int TraceCode;
4316
4317 /* Error = TRUE prevents further passes if an error occurs */
4318 extern int Error;
4319 #endif
4320
```

TINY Machine Simulator Listing

```
/******************************************************/
/* File: tm.c                                         */
/* The TM ("Tiny Machine") computer                   */
/* Compiler Construction: Principles and Practice     */
/* Kenneth C. Louden                                  */
/******************************************************/

#include <stdio.h>
#include <stdlib.h>
#include <string.h>
#include <ctype.h>

#ifndef TRUE
#define TRUE 1
#endif
#ifndef FALSE
#define FALSE 0
#endif

/******* const ******/
#define     IADDR_SIZE 1024 /* increase for large programs */
#define     DADDR_SIZE 1024 /* increase for large programs */
#define     NO_REGS 8
#define     PC_REG 7

#define     LINESIZE  121
#define     WORDSIZE  20

/******* type ******/

typedef enum {
   opclRR,        /* reg operands r,s,t */
   opclRM,        /* reg r, mem d+s */
   opclRA         /* reg r, int d+s */
   } OPCLASS;
```

```
typedef enum {
   /* RR instructions */
   opHALT,     /* RR      halt, operands must be zero */
   opIN,       /* RR      read into reg(r); s and t are ignored/
   opOUT,      /* RR      write from reg(r), s and t are ignored/
   opADD,      /* RR      reg(r) = reg(s)+reg(t) */
   opSUB,      /* RR      reg(r) = reg(s)-reg(t) */
   opMUL,      /* RR      reg(r) = reg(s)*reg(t) */
   opDIV,      /* RR      reg(r) = reg(s)/reg(t) */
   opRRLim,    /* limit of RR opcodes */

   /* RM instructions */
   opLD,       /* RM      reg(r) = mem(d+reg(s)) */
   opST,       /* RM      mem(d+reg(s)) = reg(r) */
   opRMLim,    /* Limit of RM opcodes */

   /* RA instructions */
   opLDA,      /* RA      reg(r) = d+reg(s) */
   opLDC,      /* RA      reg(r) = d ; reg(s) is ignored */
   opJLT,      /* RA      if reg(r)<0 then reg(7) = d+reg(s) */
   opJLE,      /* RA      if reg(r)<=0 then reg(7) = d+reg(s) */
   opJGT,      /* RA      if reg(r)>0 then reg(7) = d+reg(s) */
   opJGE,      /* RA      if reg(r)>=0 then reg(7) = d+reg(s) */
   opJEQ,      /* RA      if reg(r)==0 then reg(7) = d+reg(s) */
   opJNE,      /* RA      if reg(r)!=0 then reg(7) = d+reg(s) */
   opRALim     /* Limit of RA opcodes */
   } OPCODE;

typedef enum {
   srOKAY,
   srHALT,
   srIMEM_ERR,
   srDMEM_ERR,
   srZERODIVIDE
   } STEPRESULT;

typedef struct {
     int iop  ;
     int iarg1  ;
     int iarg2  ;
     int iarg3  ;
   } INSTRUCTION;
```

```
/******** vars ********/
int iloc = 0 ;
int dloc = 0 ;
int traceflag = FALSE;
int icountflag = FALSE;

INSTRUCTION iMem [IADDR_SIZE];
int dMem [DADDR_SIZE];
int reg [NO_REGS];

char * opCodeTab[]
      = {"HALT","IN","OUT","ADD","SUB","MUL","DIV","????",
          /* RR opcodes */
         "LD","ST","????", /* RM opcodes */
         "LDA","LDC","JLT","JLE","JGT","JGE","JEQ","JNE","????"
          /* RA opcodes */
        };

char * stepResultTab[]
      = {"OK","Halted","Instruction Memory Fault",
         "Data Memory Fault","Division by 0"
        };

char pgmName[20];
FILE *pgm ;

char in_Line[LINESIZE] ;
int lineLen ;
int inCol ;
int num ;
char word[WORDSIZE] ;
char ch ;
int done ;

/******************************************/
int opClass( int c )
{ if      ( c <= opRRLim) return ( opclRR );
  else if ( c <= opRMLim) return ( opclRM );
  else                    return ( opclRA );
} /* opClass */

/******************************************/
void writeInstruction ( int loc )
{ printf( "%5d: ", loc) ;
  if ( (loc >= 0) && (loc < IADDR_SIZE) )
  { printf("%6s%3d,", opCodeTab[iMem[loc].iop], iMem[loc].iarg1);
    switch ( opClass(iMem[loc].iop) )
```

```
      { case opclRR: printf("%1d,%1d", iMem[loc].iarg2, iMem[loc].iarg3);
                     break;
        case opclRM:
        case opclRA: printf("%3d(%1d)", iMem[loc].iarg2, iMem[loc].iarg3);
                     break;
      }
      printf ("\n") ;
   }
} /* writeInstruction */

/********************************************/
void getCh (void)
{ if (++inCol < lineLen)
    ch = in_Line[inCol] ;
    else ch = ' ' ;
} /* getCh */

/********************************************/
int nonBlank (void)
{ while ((inCol < lineLen)
          && (in_Line[inCol] == ' ') )
    inCol++ ;
  if (inCol < lineLen)
  { ch = in_Line[inCol] ;
    return TRUE ; }
  else
  { ch = ' ' ;
    return FALSE ; }
} /* nonBlank */

/********************************************/
int getNum (void)
{ int sign;
  int term;
  int temp = FALSE;
  num = 0 ;
  do
  { sign = 1;
    while ( nonBlank() && ((ch == '+') || (ch == '-')) )
    { temp = FALSE ;
      if (ch == '-') sign = - sign ;
      getCh();
    }
    term = 0 ;
    nonBlank();
    while (isdigit(ch))
```

```
      { temp = TRUE ;
        term = term * 10 + ( ch - '0' ) ;
        getCh();
      }
      num = num + (term * sign) ;
    } while ( (nonBlank()) && ((ch == '+') || (ch == '-')) ) ;
    return temp;
} /* getNum */


/*******************************************/
int getWord (void)
{ int temp = FALSE;
  int length = 0;
  if (nonBlank ())
  { while (isalnum(ch))
    { if (length < WORDSIZE-1) word [length++] = ch ;
      getCh() ;
    }
    word[length] = '\0';
    temp = (length != 0);
  }
  return temp;
} /* getWord */


/*******************************************/
int skipCh ( char c )
{ int temp = FALSE;
  if ( nonBlank() && (ch == c) )
  { getCh();
    temp = TRUE;
  }
  return temp;
} /* skipCh */


/*******************************************/
int atEOL(void)
{ return ( ! nonBlank ());
} /* atEOL */


/*******************************************/
int error( char * msg, int lineNo, int instNo)
{ printf("Line %d",lineNo);
  if (instNo >= 0) printf(" (Instruction %d)",instNo);
  printf("    %s\n",msg);
  return FALSE;
} /* error */
```

```
/*********************************************/
int readInstructions (void)
{ OPCODE op;
  int arg1, arg2, arg3;
  int loc, regNo, lineNo;
  for (regNo = 0 ; regNo < NO_REGS ; regNo++)
      reg[regNo] = 0 ;
  dMem[0] = DADDR_SIZE - 1 ;
  for (loc = 1 ; loc < DADDR_SIZE ; loc++)
      dMem[loc] = 0 ;
  for (loc = 0 ; loc < IADDR_SIZE ; loc++)
  { iMem[loc].iop = opHALT ;
    iMem[loc].iarg1 = 0 ;
    iMem[loc].iarg2 = 0 ;
    iMem[loc].iarg3 = 0 ;
  }
  lineNo = 0 ;
  while (! feof(pgm))
  { fgets( in_Line, LINESIZE-2, pgm ) ;
    inCol = 0 ;
    lineNo++;
    lineLen = strlen(in_Line)-1 ;
    if (in_Line[lineLen]=='\n') in_Line[lineLen] = '\0' ;
    else in_Line[++lineLen] = '\0';
    if ( (nonBlank()) && (in_Line[inCol] != '*') )
    { if (! getNum())
         return error("Bad location", lineNo,-1);
      loc = num;
      if (loc > IADDR_SIZE)
        return error("Location too large",lineNo,loc);
      if (! skipCh(':'))
        return error("Missing colon", lineNo,loc);
      if (! getWord ())
        return error("Missing opcode", lineNo,loc);
      op = opHALT ;
      while ((op < opRALim)
            && (strncmp(opCodeTab[op], word, 4) != 0) )
         op++ ;
      if (strncmp(opCodeTab[op], word, 4) != 0)
         return error("Illegal opcode", lineNo,loc);
      switch ( opClass(op) )
      { case opclRR :
        /*********************************/
         if ( (! getNum ()) || (num < 0) || (num >= NO_REGS) )
             return error("Bad first register", lineNo,loc);
         arg1 = num;
         if ( ! skipCh(','))
             return error("Missing comma", lineNo, loc);
```

```
            if ( (! getNum ()) || (num < 0) || (num >= NO_REGS) )
                return error("Bad second register", lineNo, loc);
            arg2 = num;
            if ( ! skipCh(','))
                return error("Missing comma", lineNo,loc);
            if ( (! getNum ()) || (num < 0) || (num >= NO_REGS) )
                return error("Bad third register", lineNo,loc);
            arg3 = num;
            break;

            case opclRM :
            case opclRA :
            /*********************************/
            if ( (! getNum ()) || (num < 0) || (num >= NO_REGS) )
                return error("Bad first register", lineNo,loc);
            arg1 = num;
            if ( ! skipCh(','))
                return error("Missing comma", lineNo,loc);
            if (! getNum ())
                return error("Bad displacement", lineNo,loc);
            arg2 = num;
            if ( ! skipCh('(') && ! skipCh(',') )
                return error("Missing LParen", lineNo,loc);
            if ( (! getNum ()) || (num < 0) || (num >= NO_REGS))
                return error("Bad second register", lineNo,loc);
            arg3 = num;
            break;
            }
        iMem[loc].iop = op;
        iMem[loc].iarg1 = arg1;
        iMem[loc].iarg2 = arg2;
        iMem[loc].iarg3 = arg3;
      }
  }
  return TRUE;
} /* readInstructions */



/********************************************/
STEPRESULT stepTM (void)
{ INSTRUCTION currentinstruction ;
  int pc  ;
  int r,s,t,m ;
  int ok ;
```

```
pc = reg[PC_REG] ;
if ( (pc < 0) || (pc > IADDR_SIZE) )
    return srIMEM_ERR ;
reg[PC_REG] = pc + 1 ;
currentinstruction = iMem[ pc ] ;
switch (opClass(currentinstruction.iop) )
{ case opclRR :
  /*********************************/
    r = currentinstruction.iarg1 ;
    s = currentinstruction.iarg2 ;
    t = currentinstruction.iarg3 ;
    break;

  case opclRM :
  /*********************************/
    r = currentinstruction.iarg1 ;
    s = currentinstruction.iarg3 ;
    m = currentinstruction.iarg2 + reg[s] ;
    if ( (m < 0) || (m > DADDR_SIZE) )
        return srDMEM_ERR ;
    break;

  case opclRA :
  /*********************************/
    r = currentinstruction.iarg1 ;
    s = currentinstruction.iarg3 ;
    m = currentinstruction.iarg2 + reg[s] ;
    break;
} /* case */

switch ( currentinstruction.iop)
{ /* RR instructions */
  case opHALT :
  /*********************************/
    printf("HALT: %1d,%1d,%1d\n",r,s,t);
    return srHALT ;
    /* break; */

  case opIN :
  /*********************************/
    do
    { printf("Enter value for IN instruction: ") ;
      fflush (stdin);
      gets(in_Line);
      inCol = 0;
      ok = getNum();
      if ( ! ok ) printf ("Illegal value\n");
      else reg[r] = num;
    }
```

```
      while (! ok);
      break;

    case opOUT :
      printf ("OUT instruction prints: %d\n", reg[r] ) ;
      break;
    case opADD :   reg[r] = reg[s] + reg[t] ;   break;
    case opSUB :   reg[r] = reg[s] - reg[t] ;   break;
    case opMUL :   reg[r] = reg[s] * reg[t] ;   break;

    case opDIV :
    /***********************************/
      if ( reg[t] != 0 ) reg[r] = reg[s] / reg[t];
      else return srZERODIVIDE ;
      break;

    /************** RM instructions *******************/
    case opLD :    reg[r] = dMem[m] ;  break;
    case opST :    dMem[m] = reg[r] ;  break;

    /************** RA instructions ******************/
    case opLDA :    reg[r] = m ; break;
    case opLDC :    reg[r] = currentinstruction.iarg2 ;  break;
    case opJLT :    if ( reg[r] < 0 ) reg[PC_REG] = m ; break;
    case opJLE :    if ( reg[r] <= 0 ) reg[PC_REG] = m ; break;
    case opJGT :    if ( reg[r] > 0 ) reg[PC_REG] = m ; break;
    case opJGE :    if ( reg[r] >= 0 ) reg[PC_REG] = m ; break;
    case opJEQ :    if ( reg[r] == 0 ) reg[PC_REG] = m ; break;
    case opJNE :    if ( reg[r] != 0 ) reg[PC_REG] = m ; break;

    /* end of legal instructions */
  } /* case */
  return srOKAY ;
} /* stepTM */

/*********************************************/
int doCommand (void)
{ char cmd;
  int stepcnt=0, i;
  int printcnt;
  int stepResult;
  int regNo, loc;
  do
  { printf ("Enter command: ");
    fflush (stdin);
    gets(in_Line);
    inCol = 0;
```

```
}
while (! getWord ());

cmd = word[0] ;
switch ( cmd )
{ case 't' :
  /**********************************/
    traceflag = ! traceflag ;
    printf("Tracing now ");
    if ( traceflag ) printf("on.\n"); else printf("off.\n");
    break;

  case 'h' :
  /**********************************/
    printf("Commands are:\n");
    printf("    s(tep <n>        "\
            "Execute n (default 1) TM instructions\n");
    printf("    g(o              "\
            "Execute TM instructions until HALT\n");
    printf("    r(egs            "\
            "Print the contents of the registers\n");
    printf("    i(Mem <b <n>>    "\
            "Print n iMem locations starting at b\n");
    printf("    d(Mem <b <n>>    "\
            "Print n dMem locations starting at b\n");
    printf("    t(race           "\
            "Toggle instruction trace\n");
    printf("    p(rint           "\
            "Toggle print of total instructions executed"\
            " ('go' only)\n");
    printf("    c(lear           "\
            "Reset simulator for new execution of program\n");
    printf("    h(elp            "\
            "Cause this list of commands to be printed\n");
    printf("    q(uit            "\
            "Terminate the simulation\n");
    break;

  case 'p' :
  /**********************************/
    icountflag = ! icountflag ;
    printf("Printing instruction count now ");
    if ( icountflag ) printf("on.\n"); else printf("off.\n");
    break;

  case 's' :
  /**********************************/
    if ( atEOL ())  stepcnt = 1;
```

```
      else if ( getNum ()) stepcnt = abs(num);
      else    printf("Step count?\n");
      break;

case 'g' :    stepcnt = 1 ;      break;

case 'r' :
/**********************************/
      for (i = 0; i < NO_REGS; i++)
      { printf("%1d: %4d      ", i,reg[i]);
        if ( (i % 4) == 3 ) printf ("\n");
      }
      break;


case 'i' :
/**********************************/
      printcnt = 1 ;
      if ( getNum ())
      { iloc = num ;
        if ( getNum ()) printcnt = num ;
      }
      if ( ! atEOL ())
        printf ("Instruction locations?\n");
      else
      { while ((iloc >= 0) && (iloc < IADDR_SIZE)
                 && (printcnt > 0) )
        { writeInstruction(iloc);
          iloc++ ;
          printcnt-- ;
        }
      }
      break;


case 'd' :
/**********************************/
      printcnt = 1 ;
      if ( getNum ())
      { dloc = num ;
        if ( getNum ()) printcnt = num ;
      }
      if ( ! atEOL ())
        printf("Data locations?\n");
      else
      { while ((dloc >= 0) && (dloc < DADDR_SIZE)
                 && (printcnt > 0))
        { printf("%5d: %5d\n",dloc,dMem[dloc]);
          dloc++;
```

```
            printcnt--;
          }
        }
        break;

    case 'c' :
    /********************************/
        iloc = 0;
        dloc = 0;
        stepcnt = 0;
        for (regNo = 0; regNo < NO_REGS ; regNo++)
              reg[regNo] = 0 ;
        dMem[0] = DADDR_SIZE - 1 ;
        for (loc = 1 ; loc < DADDR_SIZE ; loc++)
              dMem[loc] = 0 ;
        break;

    case 'q' : return FALSE; /* break; */

    default : printf("Command %c unknown.\n", cmd); break;
  }   /* case */
  stepResult = srOKAY;
  if ( stepcnt > 0 )
  { if ( cmd == 'g' )
    { stepcnt = 0;
      while (stepResult == srOKAY)
      { iloc = reg[PC_REG] ;
        if ( traceflag ) writeInstruction( iloc ) ;
        stepResult = stepTM ();
        stepcnt++;
      }
      if ( icountflag )
        printf("Number of instructions executed = %d\n", stepcnt);
    }
    else
    { while ((stepcnt > 0) && (stepResult == srOKAY))
      { iloc = reg[PC_REG] ;
        if ( traceflag ) writeInstruction( iloc ) ;
        stepResult = stepTM ();
        stepcnt-- ;
      }
    }
    printf( "%s\n",stepResultTab[stepResult] );
  }
  return TRUE;
} /* doCommand */
```

```
main( int argc, char * argv[] )
{ if (argc != 2)
  { printf("usage: %s <filename>\n" ,argv[0]);
    exit(1);
  }
  strcpy(pgmName,argv[1]) ;
  if (strchr (pgmName, '.') == NULL)
      strcat(pgmName,".tm");
  pgm = fopen(pgmName,"r");
  if (pgm == NULL)
  { printf("file '%s' not found\n",pgmName);
    exit(1);
  }

  /* read the program */
  if ( ! readInstructions ())
        exit(1) ;
  /* switch input file to terminal */
  /* reset( input ); */
  /* read-eval-print */
  printf("TM simulation (enter h for help)...\n");
  do
     done = ! doCommand ();
  while (! done );
  printf("Simulation done.\n");
  return 0;
}
```

Bibliography

Aho, A. V. 1979. Pattern matching in strings. *Proceedings of the Symposium on Formal Language Theory*, Santa Barbara, CA.

Aho, A. V., and J. D. Ullman. 1972. *The Theory of Parsing, Translation, and Compiling*, Vol. I: *Parsing*. Englewood Cliffs, NJ: Prentice Hall.

Aho, A. V., J. E. Hopcroft, and J. D. Ullman. 1983. *Data Structures and Algorithms*. Reading, MA: Addison-Wesley.

Aho, A. V., R. Sethi, and J. D. Ullman. 1986. *Compilers: Principles, Techniques and Tools*. Reading, MA: Addison-Wesley.

Amadio, R. M., and L. Cardelli. 1993. Subtyping recursive types. *ACM Trans. on Prog. Langs. and Systems* **15(4)**: 575–631.

Appel, A. W. 1992. *Compiling with Continuations*. Cambridge: Cambridge University Press.

Backus, J. W. 1981. The history of FORTRAN I, II, and III. In Wexelblat [1981], pp. 25–45.

Backus, J. W., et al. 1957. The FORTRAN automatic coding system. *Proceedings of the Western Joint Computing Conference*, pp. 188–198. Reprinted in Rosen [1967], pp. 29–47.

Barron, D. W. 1981. *Pascal—The Language and Its Implementation*. Chichester: J. Wiley.

Bratman, H. 1961. An alternative form of the UNCOL diagram. *Comm. ACM* **4(3)**: 142.

Budd, T. 1987. *A Little Smalltalk*. Reading, MA: Addison-Wesley.

Burke, M. G., and G. A. Fisher. 1987. A practical method for LR and LL syntactic error diagnosis. *ACM Trans. on Prog. Langs. and Systems* **9(2)**: 164–197.

Cardelli, L., and P. Wegner. 1985. On understanding types, data abstraction, and polymorphism. *ACM Computing Surveys* **17(4)**: 471–522.

Cichelli, R. J. 1980. Minimal perfect hash functions made simple. *Comm. ACM* **23(1)**: 17–19.

Cohen, J. 1981. Garbage collection of linked data structures. *Computing Surveys* **13(3)**: 341–367.

Cormen, T. H., C. E. Leiserson, and R. L. Rivest. 1990. *Introduction to Algorithms*. New York: McGraw-Hill.

Davidson, J. W., and C. W. Fraser. 1984a. Code selection through object code optimization. *ACM Trans. on Prog. Langs. and Systems* **6(4)**: 505–526.

Davidson, J. W., and C. W. Fraser. 1984b. Register allocation and exhaustive peephole optimization. *Software—Practice and Experience* **14(9)**: 857–866.

DeRemer, F. L. 1969. *Practical Translators for LR(k) Languages*, Ph.D. thesis, MIT, Cambridge, MA.

DeRemer, F. L. 1971. Simple LR(k) grammars. *Comm. ACM* **14(7)**: 453–460.

Drozdek, A., and D. L. Simon. 1995. *Data Structures in C*. Boston: PWS.

Ellis, M. A., and B. Stroustrup. 1990. *The Annotated C++ Reference Manual*. Reading, MA: Addison-Wesley.

Farrow, R. 1984. Generating a production compiler from an attribute grammar. *IEEE Software* **1(10)**: 77–93.

Fischer, C. N., and R. J. LeBlanc. 1991. *Crafting a Compiler with C*. Redwood City, CA: Benjamin-Cummings.

Fraser, C. W., and D. R. Hanson. 1995. *A Retargetable C Compiler: Design and Implementation*. Redwood City, CA: Benjamin-Cummings.

Ganapathi, M. J., and C. N. Fischer. 1985. Affix grammar driven code generation. *ACM Trans. on Prog. Lang. and Systems* **7(4)**: 560–599.

Ginsburg, S. 1966. *The Mathematical Theory of Context-Free Languages*. New York: McGraw-Hill.

Ginsburg, S. 1975. *Algebraic and Automata-Theoretic Properties of Formal Languages*. Amsterdam: North Holland.

Glanville, R. S., and S. L. Graham. 1978. A new method for compiler code generation. *Fifth Annual ACM Symposium on Principles of Programming Languages*, 231–240. New York: ACM Press.

Goos, G., and W. A. Wulf. 1981. Diana reference manual, CMU CS Report 81-101, Department of Computer Science, Carnegie-Mellon University, Pittsburgh.

Graham, S. L., C. B. Haley, and W. N. Joy. 1979. Practical LR error recovery. *SIGPLAN Notices* **14(8)**: 168–175.

Graham, S. L., M. A. Harrison, and W. L. Ruzzo. 1980. An improved context-free recognizer. *ACM Trans. on Prog. Langs. and Systems* **2(3)**: 415–462.

Hindley, J. R. 1969. The principal type-scheme of an object in combinatory logic. *Trans. Amer. Math. Soc.* **146 (Dec.)**: 29–60.

Hoare, C. A. R. 1962. Report on the Elliot Algol translator, *Computer J.* **5(2)**: 127–129.

Holub, A. I. 1990. *Compiler Design in C*. Englewood Cliffs, NJ: Prentice Hall.

Hopcroft, J. E., and J. D. Ullman. 1979. *Introduction to Automata Theory, Languages, and Computation*. Reading, MA: Addison-Wesley.

Horowitz, E. 1987. *Programming Languages: A Grand Tour*, 3rd ed. Rockville, MD: Computer Science Press.

Hutton, G. 1992. Higher-order functions for parsing. *J. Func. Prog.* **2(3)**: 323–343.

Jacobson, V. 1987. Tuning Unix Lex, or it's not true what they say about Lex. *Proceedings of the Winter Usenix Conference*, pp. 163–164.

James, L. R. 1972. A syntax-directed error recovery method, Technical Report CSRG-13, University of Toronto Computer Systems Research Group.

Jazayeri, M., W. F. Ogden, and W. C. Rounds. 1975. The intrinsic exponential complexity of the circularity problem for attribute grammars. *Comm. ACM* **18(12)**: 697–706.

Johnson, S. C. 1975. Yacc—Yet another compiler compiler. Computing Science Technical Report No. 32, AT&T Bell Laboratories, Murray Hill, NJ.

Johnson, S. C. 1978. A portable compiler: Theory and practice. *Fifth Annual ACM Symposium on Principles of Programming Languages*. New York: ACM Press, pp. 97–104.

Johnson, S. C., and D. M. Ritchie. 1981. The C language calling sequence. Computing Science Technical Report No. 102, AT&T Bell Laboratories, Murray Hill, NJ.

Jones, M. P. 1994. The implementation of the Gofer functional programming system. Yale University Department of Computer Science Research Report #1030, New Haven, CT.

Jones, N. D. 1980. *Semantics Directed Compiler Generation*. Springer Lecture Notes in Computer Science #94. New York: Springer-Verlag.

Kastens, U., B. Hutt, and E. Zimmermann. 1982. *GAG: A practical compiler generator*. Springer Lecture Notes in Computer Science #141. New York: Springer-Verlag.

Kernighan, B. W. 1975. Ratfor—A preprocessor for a rational FORTRAN. *Software—Practice and Experience* **5(4)**: 395–406.

Kernighan, B. W., and R. Pike. 1984. *The Unix Programming Environment*. Englewood Cliffs, NJ: Prentice Hall.

Kernighan, B. W., and D. M. Ritchie. 1988. *The C Programming Language* (ANSI Standard C), 2nd ed. Englewood Cliffs, NJ: Prentice Hall.

Knuth, D. E. 1965. On the translation of languages from left to right. *Information and Control* **8(6)**: 607–639.

Knuth, D. E. 1968. Semantics of context-free languages. *Math. Systems Theory* **2(2)**: 127–145. *Errata* **5(1)** (1971): 95–96.

Knuth, D. E. 1973. *The Art of Computer Programming*, Vol. 3, *Sorting and Searching*. Reading, MA: Addison-Wesley.

Koster, C. H. A. 1969. On infinite modes. *SIGPLAN Notices* **4(3)**: 109–112.

Landin, P. J. 1966. The next 700 programming languages. *Comm. ACM* **9(3)**: 157–165.

Lee, P. 1989. *Realistic Compiler Generation*. Cambridge, MA: MIT Press.

Lesk, M. E. 1975. Lex—A lexical analyzer generator. Computing Science Technical Report No. 39. AT&T Bell Laboratories, Murray Hill, NJ.

Lewis, P. M., and R. E. Stearns. 1968. Syntax-directed transduction. *J. ACM* **15(3)**: 465–488.

Lorho, B. 1984. *Methods and Tools for Compiler Construction*. Cambridge: Cambridge University Press.

Louden, K. 1993. *Programming Languages: Principles and Practice*. Boston: PWS.

Lyon, G. 1974. Syntax-directed least-error analysis for context-free languages. *Comm. ACM* **17(1)**: 3–14.

Mayoh, B. H. 1981. Attribute grammars and formal semantics. *SIAM J. on Computing* **10(3)**: 503–518.

Milner, R. 1978. A theory of type polymorphism in programming. *J. Computer and System Sciences* **17(3)**: 348–375.

Naur, P. 1963. Revised report on the algorithmic language Algol 60. *Comm. ACM* **6(1)**: 1–17. Reprinted in Horowitz [1987].

Nori, K. V., et al. 1981. Pascal P implementation notes. In Barron [1981].

Parr, T. J., H. G. Dietz, and W. E. Cohen. 1992. PCCTS reference manual. *ACM SIGPLAN Notices* **27(2)**: 88–165.

Paxson, V. 1990. Flex users manual (part of the Gnu ftp distribution). Cambridge, MA: Free Software Foundation.

Pennello, T. J., and F. L. DeRemer. 1978. A forward move algorithm of LR error recovery. *Fifth Annual Symposium on Principles of Programming Languages*. New York: ACM Press, pp. 241–254.

Perkins, D. R., and R. L. Sites. 1979. Machine independent Pascal code optimization. *ACM SIGPLAN Notices* **14(8)**: 201–207.

Peyton Jones, S. L. 1987. *The Implementation of Functional Programming Languages.* Englewood Cliffs, NJ: Prentice Hall.

Peyton Jones, S. L., and D. Lester. 1992. *Implementing Functional Languages.* Englewood Cliffs, NJ: Prentice Hall.

Powell, M. L. 1984. A portable optimizing compiler for Modula-2. *ACM SIGPLAN Notices* **19(6)**: 310–318.

Purdom, P., and C. A. Brown. 1980. Semantic routines and LR(k) parsers. *Acta Informatica* **14(4)**: 299–315.

Randell, B., and L. J. Russell. 1964. *Algol 60 Implementation.* New York: Academic Press.

Reade, C. 1989. *Elements of Functional Programming.* Reading, MA: Addison-Wesley.

Reps, T. W., and T. Teitelbaum. 1989. *The Synthesizer Generator: A System for Constructing Language-Based Editors.* New York: Springer-Verlag.

Rosen, S. (ed.). 1967. *Programming Systems and Languages.* New York: McGraw-Hill.

Sager, T. J. 1985. A polynomial time generator for minimal perfect hash functions. *Comm. ACM* **28(5)**: 523–532.

Schmidt, D. A. 1986. *Denotational Semantics: A Methodology for Language Development.* Dubuque, IA: Wm. C. Brown.

Schmidt, D. C. 1990. GPERF: A perfect hash function generator. *2nd USENIX C++ Conference Proceedings.* San Francisco, CA, pp. 87–102.

Schreiner, A. T., and H. G. Friedman, Jr. 1985. *Introduction to Compiler Construction with Unix.* Englewood Cliffs, NJ: Prentice Hall.

Sedgewick, R. 1990. *Algorithms in C.* Reading, MA: Addison-Wesley.

Sethi, R. 1996. *Programming Languages: Concepts and Constructs*, 2nd ed. Reading, MA: Addison-Wesley.

Slonneger, K., and B. L. Kurtz. 1995. *Formal Syntax and Semantics of Programming Languages.* Reading, MA: Addison-Wesley.

Stallman, R. 1994. Using and porting Gnu CC. Gnu ftp distribution (prep.ai.mit.edu). Cambridge, MA: Free Software Foundation.

Steel, T. B., Jr. 1961. A first version of UNCOL. *Proceedings of the Western Joint Computing Conference* **19**: 371–378.

Stirling, C. 1985. Follow set error recovery. *Software—Practice and Experience* **15(3)**: 239–257.

Strong, J., et al. 1958. The problem of programming communication with changing machines: A proposed solution. *Comm. ACM* **1(8)**: 12–18 and **1(9)**: 9–15.

Ungar, D. 1984. Generation scavenging: A non-disruptive high performance storage reclamation algorithm. Proceedings of the ACM SIGSOFT/SIGPLAN Symposium on Practical Software Development Environments. *ACM SIGPLAN Notices* **19(5)**: 157–167.

Wexelblat, R. L. (ed.). 1981. *History of Programming Languages.* New York: Academic Press.

Wilson, P. R. 1992. Uniprocessor garbage collection techniques. In Bekkers et al., eds., International Workshop on Memory Management, Springer Lecture. Notes in Computer Science 637, 1–42. New York: Springer-Verlag.

Wirth, N. 1971. The design of a Pascal compiler. *Software—Practice and Experience* **1(4)**: 309–333.

Index

Page references followed by *e* are to exercises; those followed by *n* are to footnotes; by *r* are to references and notes sections; by *t* are to tables; and by *illus.* to figures in the text.